AQA Science
Science A

Teacher's Book

New GCSE

Geoff Carr
Darren Forbes
Sam Holyman
Ruth Miller
Pauline Anning
Bev Cox
Niva Miles
Gavin Reeder
John Scottow
Series Editor
Lawrie Ryan

Nelson Thornes

Published in 2011 by:
Nelson Thornes Ltd
Delta Place
27 Bath Road
CHELTENHAM
GL53 7TH
United Kingdom

11 12 13 14 15 / 10 9 8 7 6 5 4 3 2 1

A catalogue record for this book is available from the British Library

ISBN 978 1 4085 0842 8

Cover photograph: Suzanne Laird/Getty Images (girls); Andrew Butterton/Alamy
(background)

Illustrations include artwork drawn by Tech-Set Ltd
Page make-up by Tech-Set Ltd

Printed and bound in Spain by GraphyCems

Science A — Contents

Welcome to AQA GCSE Science!

New AQA GCSE Science remains the only series to be endorsed and approved by AQA. This Teacher's Book is written and reviewed by experienced teachers who have worked closely with AQA on their specifications. This book is structured around the Student Book and offers guidance, advice, support for differentiation and lots of practical teaching ideas to give you what you need to teach the AQA specifications.

Learning objectives

These tell you what your students should know by the end of the lessons and relate to the learning objectives in the corresponding Student Book topic, although extra detail is provided for teachers.

Learning outcomes

These tell you what your students should be able to do to demonstrate that they have achieved against the learning objectives. These are differentiated where appropriate to provide suitable expectations for all your students. Higher Tier outcomes are labelled.

Specification link-up: Biology B1.1

These open every spread so you can see the AQA specification references covered in your lessons, at a glance.

Lesson structure

This provides you with guidance and ideas for tackling topics in your lessons. There are short and long starter and plenary activities so you can decide how you structure your lesson. Explicit **support** and **extension** guidance is given for some starters and plenaries.

Support

These help you to give extra support to students who need it during the main part of your lesson.

Extend

These provide ideas for how to extend the learning for students aiming for higher grades.

Further teaching suggestions

These provide you with ideas for how you might extend the lesson or offer alternative activities. These may also include extra activities or suggestions for homework.

Summary answers

All answers to questions within the Student Book are found in the Teacher's Book.

Practical support

For every practical in the Student Book you will find this corresponding feature which gives you a list of the equipment you will need to provide, safety references and additional teaching notes. There are also additional practicals given that are not found in the Student Book.

The following features are found in the Student Book, but you may find additional guidance to support them in the Teacher's Book:

 *Did you know ...?*

 *How Science Works*

 *Maths skills*

Activity

How Science Works

There is a chapter dedicated to 'How Science Works' in the Student Book as well as embedded throughout topics and end of chapter questions. The teacher notes within this book give you detailed guidance on how to integrate 'How Science Works' into your teaching.

End of chapter pages

And at the end of each chapter you will find Summary answers and AQA Examination-style answers. You will also find:

Kerboodle resources **k**

Kerboodle is our online service that holds all of the electronic resources for the series. All of the resources that support the chapter that are provided on Kerboodle are listed in these boxes.

Where you see **k** in the Student Book, you will know that there is an electronic resource on Kerboodle to support that aspect.

Just log on to www.kerboodle.com to find out more.

Practical support

These list the suggested practicals from AQA that you need to be aware of. Support for these practicals can be found on Kerboodle, or are covered within the practical support section of the Teacher Book. The **k** indicates that there is a practical in Kerboodle. The ⚙ indicates that there is a 'How Science Works' worksheet in Kerboodle. The 📖 indicates that the practical is covered in this Teacher's Book.

Bump up your grades

These are written by AQA examiners giving advice on how students can pick up additional marks to improve their grades.

Examiner's tip

These are written by AQA examiners giving advice on what students should remember for their exams and highlighting common errors.

H1

How does science work?

Students should learn:

- that observations are often the starting point for an investigation
- that a hypothesis is a proposal intended to explain certain facts or observations
- that a prediction is an intelligent guess, based on some knowledge
- that an experiment is a way of testing your prediction
- that a conclusion is when you decide whether or not your prediction was correct.

Learning outcomes

Students should be able to:

- make first-hand observations
- distinguish between a hypothesis and a prediction
- explain the purpose of an experiment
- show how results can help to decide if a prediction was correct.

AQA Specification link-up: How Science Works

'How Science Works' is treated here as a separate chapter. It offers the opportunity to teach the 'thinking behind the doing' as a discrete set of procedural skills. However, it is of course an integral part of the way students will learn about science and those skills should be nurtured throughout the course.

It is anticipated that sections of this chapter will be taught as the opportunity presents itself during the teaching programme. The chapter should also be referred back to at appropriate times when these skills are required and in preparation for the internally assessed ISAs.

The thinking behind the doing

Science attempts to explain the world in which we live. It provides technologies that have had a great impact on our society and the environment. Scientists try to explain phenomena and solve problems using evidence. The data to be used as evidence must be repeatable, reproducible and valid, as only then can appropriate conclusions be made.

A scientifically literate citizen should, among other things, be equipped to question, and engage in and debate on, the evidence used in decision-making.

The repeatability and the reproducibility of evidence refers to how much we trust the data. The validity of evidence depends on the reproducibility of the data as well as whether the research answers the question. If the data are not repeatable or reproducible, the research cannot be valid.

To ensure the repeatability, reproducibility and validity of evidence, scientists consider a range of ideas which relate to:

- how we observe the world
- designing investigations so that patterns and relationships between variables may be identified
- making measurements by selecting and using instruments effectively
- presenting and representing data
- identifying patterns, relationships and making suitable conclusions.

These ideas inform decisions and are central to science education. They constitute the 'thinking behind the doing' that is a necessary complement to the subject content of biology, chemistry and physics.

Lesson structure

Starters

Key words – Create a quiz looking at the meaning of key words used in this lesson: knowledge, observation, prediction and experiment. Support students by making this activity into a card sort. Extend students by asking them to put the key words into a context, i.e. the television remote control idea. *(5 minutes)*

Good science – Collect newspaper articles and news items from the television to illustrate good and poor uses of science. There are some excellent television programmes illustrating good and poor science. *(10 minutes)*

Main

- Students should begin to appreciate the 'thinking behind the doing' developed during KS3. It would be useful to illustrate this by a simple demonstration (e.g. *Elodea* bubbling oxygen) and posing questions that build into a flow diagram of the steps involved in a whole investigation, as shown in the Student Book. This could lead into recap questions to ascertain each individual student's progress. Emphasis should be placed on an understanding of the following terms: prediction, independent, dependent and control variables, repeatability and reproducibility.

- It is expected that students will be familiar with:
  - the need to work safely
  - making a prediction
  - controls
  - the need for repetition of some results
  - tabulating and analysing results
  - making appropriate conclusions
  - suggesting how they might improve methods.

- Revealing to the students that they use scientific thinking to solve problems during their everyday life can make their work in science more relevant. Use everyday situations to illustrate this and discuss in groups or as a class.

- When carrying out the fireworks activity, students could be given the headings in the form of a flow chart, with an 'either/or' option at each stage.

Extend

- Students could be allowed to use the internet to find out more about the ideal fuse-burning time for a firework.

For example:

'How can I clear the car windscreen when it "mists" up in the winter? It only seems to happen when we get into the car [observation]. The windscreen is probably cold, and I know we breathe out moist air [knowledge].'

'I can use observations and knowledge to make a prediction that switching on the hot air fan next to the windscreen will clear the "mist". I can test my prediction and see what the results are. I can check again the next day to see if I get the same results [repeatability].'

- Students should now be asked to complete the Investigating fireworks activity.

Plenaries

Misconceptions – Produce a list of statements about practical work (similar to the ones listed below), some of which are true and others are false. Support students by getting them to simply write 'true' or 'false' by each statement. Extend students by asking them to write down why the false statements are untrue. *(5 minutes)*

Poor science – Use the internet to organise a competition for who can bring in the poorest example of science used to sell products: shampoo adverts are very good examples! *(10 minutes)*

How Science Works

H1   How does science work? Ⓚ

Learning objectives
- What is meant by 'How Science Works'?
- What is a hypothesis?
- What is a 'prediction' and why should you make one?
- How can we investigate a problem scientifically?

👓 **links**
You can find out more about your ISA by looking at H10 The ISA at the end of this chapter.

This first chapter looks at 'How Science Works'. It is an important part of your GCSE because the ideas introduced here will crop up throughout your course. You will be expected to collect scientific **evidence** and to understand how we use evidence. These concepts will be assessed as the major part of your internal school assessment.

You will take one or more 45-minute tests. These tests are based on **data** you have collected previously plus data supplied for you in the test. They are called '**Investigative Skills Assignments' (ISA)**. The ideas in 'How Science Works' will also be assessed in your examinations.

How science works for us

Science works for us all day, every day. You do not need to know how a mobile phone works to enjoy sending text messages. But, think about how you started to use your mobile phone or your television remote control. Did you work through pages of instructions? Probably not!

You knew that pressing the buttons would change something on the screen (**knowledge**). You played around with the buttons, to see what would happen (**observation**). You had a guess based on your knowledge and observations at what you thought might be happening (**prediction**) and then tested your idea (**experiment**).

Perhaps 'How Science Works' should really be called 'How Scientists Work'.

Science moves forward by slow steady steps. When a genius, such as Einstein, comes along then it takes a giant leap. Those small steps build on knowledge and experience that we already have.

The steps don't always lead in a straight line, starting with an observation and ending with a conclusion. More often than not you find yourself going round in circles, but each time you go around the loop you gain more knowledge and so can make better predictions.

Figure 1 Albert Einstein was a genius, but he worked through scientific problems in the same way as you will in your GCSE

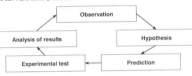

Observation → Hypothesis → Prediction → Experimental test → Analysis of results → Observation

Each small step is important in its own right. It builds on the body of knowledge that we have. In 1675 a German chemist tried to extract gold from urine. He must have thought that there was a connection between the two colours. He was wrong. But after a while, with a terrible stench coming from his laboratory, the urine began to glow.

He had discovered phosphorus. Phosphorus catches fire easily. A Swedish scientist worked out how to manufacture phosphorus without the smell of urine. That is why most matches these days are manufactured in Sweden.

Figure 2 Fireworks

Summary questions

1 Copy and complete the paragraph using the words below:

prediction knowledge experiment observation conclusion

You have learned before that a cup of tea loses heat if it is left standing. This is a piece of .... You make an .... that dark coloured cups will cool faster. So you make a .... that if you have a black cup, this will cool fastest of all. You carry out an .... to get some results, and from these you make a ....

Further teaching suggestions

Common misconceptions
Some common misconceptions that can be dealt with here and throughout the course are:
- The purpose of controls – some students believe that it is about making accurate measurements of the independent variable.
- The purpose of preliminary work – some believe that it is the first set of results.

Some students also think:
- 'That the table of results is constructed after the practical work' – students should be encouraged to produce the table before carrying out their work and complete it during their work.
- 'That anomalies are identified after the analysis' – they should preferably be identified during the practical work or at the latest before any calculation of a mean.
- 'They should automatically extrapolate the graph to its origin.'
- 'Lines of best fit must be straight lines.'
- 'You repeat readings to make sure your investigation is a fair test.'

Summary answers

1 knowledge, observation, prediction, experiment, conclusion

H2

Fundamental ideas about how science works

Learning objectives

Students should learn:

- to distinguish between opinions based on scientific evidence and non-scientific ideas
- the importance of continuous and categoric variables
- what it means to say that evidence is valid
- the difference between repeatability and reproducibility
- to look for links between the independent and dependent variables.

Learning outcomes

Students should be able to:

- identify when an opinion does not have the support of valid science
- recognise measurements as continuous, or categoric
- suggest how an investigation might demonstrate its reproducibility and validity
- distinguish between repeatability and reproducibility
- state whether variables are linked, and if so in what way.

Support

- When looking at the 'cress grown under different light conditions' practical, a list of possible variables could be made from which to select the most appropriate type of variable. This could be done as a card sort or as a table.

Extend

- Discussion could range into the ethics of drug provision and the increased importance of having scientifically based opinions. It might develop into an appreciation of the limits of science in terms of ethical delivery of drugs. Decisions of this nature are not always as clear-cut as scientists might want them to be. Some experts estimated the number of accidental deaths in the UK at 20 000 per year caused by prescribed medical drugs.

AQA Specification link-up: Controlled Assessment SA4.1

Plan practical ways to answer scientific questions, by:

- stating the purpose of an investigation *[SA4.1.1 a)]*
- recognise significant variables in an investigation *[SA4.1.1 b)]*
- recognising a control variable in an investigation *[SA4.1.1 c)]*
- understanding the purpose of a control group *[SA4.1.1 d)]*
- identifying intervals in measurements. *[SA4.1.1 e)]*

Lesson structure

Starters

Crazy science – Show a video clip of one of the science shows that are aimed at entertainment rather than education, or an advert that proclaims a scientific opinion. This should lead into a discussion of how important it is to form opinions based on sound scientific evidence. *(5 minutes)*

Types of variable – Produce a list of observable or measurable variables, e.g. colour, temperature, time, type of material. Ask students to sort them into two types: these can then be revealed as being either categoric or continuous. Support students by giving them a full definition of categoric and continuous variables. Extend students by asking them to add other examples of their own to the lists. *(10 minutes)*

Main

- Discuss some examples of adverts that make 'scientific' claims about products.
- Using the example of thalidomide, discuss how tragic situations can be created by forming opinions that are not supported by valid science. Search for video clips about thalidomide at www.britishpathe.com.
- Show some cress seedlings grown in different light levels. Review some of the terminology highlighted as key words in the Student Book. Discuss, in small groups, the different independent and dependent variables that could be investigated, identifying these as continuous or categoric variables.
- Discuss the usefulness in terms of forming opinions of each of the proposed measurements.
- Consider that this might be a commercial proposition and the students might be advising an investor in a company growing cress.
- Discuss how they could organise the investigation to demonstrate its validity and reproducibility to a potential investor.
- Discuss what sort of relationship there might be between the variables.

Plenaries

Evidence for opinions – Bring together the main features of scientific evidence that would allow sound scientific opinions to be formed from an investigation. *(5 minutes)*

Analyse conclusions – Use an example of a poorly structured investigation and allow the students to critically analyse any conclusions drawn, e.g. data from an investigation into different forms of insulation, using calorimeters and cooling curves. Support students by telling them the mistakes that had been made in the design and asking them to say why this would make the conclusion invalid. Extend students by allowing them to first identify the mistakes in the design. *(10 minutes)*

Practical support

Cress grown under different light conditions

Equipment and materials required
Petri dishes growing cress to show differences in height and colour. There should be enough for small group work.

Details
Students should look at the difference between cress grown under different light conditions and highlight the variables. There are different ways in which the independent and dependent variables could be judged, identifying these as continuous and categoric variables.

How Science Works

H2 | Fundamental ideas about how science works

Learning objectives
- How do you spot when an opinion is not based on good science?
- What is the importance of continuous and categoric variables?
- What does it mean to say that evidence is valid?
- What is the difference between a result being repeatable and a result being reproducible?
- How can two sets of data be linked?

AQA Examiner's tip

Read a newspaper article or watch the news on TV. Ask yourself if any research presented is valid. Ask yourself if you can trust that person's opinion and why.

Figure 1 Student recording a range of temperatures – an example of a continuous variable

Science is too important for us to get it wrong

Sometimes it is easy to spot when people try to use science poorly. Sometimes it can be funny. You might have seen adverts claiming to give your hair 'body' or sprays that give your feet 'lift'!

On the other hand, poor scientific practice can cost lives or have serious consequences.

Some years ago a company sold the drug thalidomide to people as a sleeping pill. Research was carried out on animals to see if it was safe. The research did not include work on pregnant animals. The opinion of the people in charge was that the animal research showed the drug could be used safely with humans.

Then the drug was also found to help ease morning sickness in pregnant women. Unfortunately, doctors prescribed it to many women, resulting in thousands of babies being born with deformed limbs. It was far from safe.

These are very difficult decisions to make. You need to be absolutely certain of what the science is telling you.

a Why was the opinion of the people in charge of developing thalidomide based on poor science?

Deciding on what to measure: variables

Variables are physical, chemical or biological quantities or characteristics.

In an investigation, you normally choose one thing to change or vary. This is called the independent variable.

When you change the independent variable, it may cause something else to change. This is called the dependent variable.

A control variable is one that is kept the same and is not changed during the investigation.

You need to know about two different types of these variables:
- A categoric variable is one that is best described by a label (usually a word). The 'colour of eyes' is a categoric variable, e.g. blue or brown eyes.
- A continuous variable is one that we measure, so its value could be any number. Temperature (as measured by a thermometer or temperature sensor) is a continuous variable, e.g. 37.6 °C, 45.2 °C. Continuous variables can have values (called a quantity) that can be found by making measurements (e.g. light intensity, flow rate, etc.).

b Imagine you were growing seedlings using different volumes of water. Would it be better to say that some were tall and some were short, or some were taller than others, or to measure the heights of all the seedlings?

Making your evidence repeatable, reproducible and valid

When you are designing an investigation you must make sure that other people can get the same results as you. This makes the evidence you collect reproducible. A repeatable measurement is one that consistently remains the same after several repeats.

A measurement is repeatable if the original experimenter repeats the investigation using the same method and equipment and obtains the same results.

A measurement is reproducible if the investigation is repeated by another person, or by using different equipment or techniques, and the same results are obtained.

You must also make sure you are measuring the actual thing you want to measure. If you don't, your data can't be used to answer your original question. This seems very obvious but it is not always quite so easy. You need to make sure that you have controlled as many other variables as you can, so that no one can say that your investigation is not valid. A measurement is valid if it measures what it is supposed to be measuring with an appropriate level of performance.

Figure 2 Cress seedlings growing in a Petri dish

c State one way in which you can show that your results are repeatable.

How might an independent variable be linked to a dependent variable?

Looking for a link between your independent and dependent variable is very important. The pattern in your graph or bar chart can often help you to see if there is a link.

But beware! There may not be a link! If your results seem to show that there is no link, don't be afraid to say so. Look at Figure 3.

The points on the top graph show a clear pattern, but the bottom graph shows random scatter.

AQA Examiner's tip

When designing your investigation you should always try to measure continuous data whenever you can. This is not always possible, so then you have to use a label (categoric variable). You might still be able to put the variables in an order so that you can spot a pattern. For example, you could describe flow rate as 'fast flowing', 'steady flow' or 'slow flowing'.

Figure 3 Which graph shows that there might be a link between x and y?

?? Did you know ...?

Aristotle, a brilliant Greek scientist, once proclaimed that men had more teeth than women! Do you think that his data collection was reproducible?

Summary questions

1 Copy and complete the paragraph using the words below:

categoric independent dependent continuous

Stefan wanted to find out which was the strongest supermarket plastic carrier bag. He tested five different bags by adding weight to them until they broke. The type of bag he used was the .... variable and the weight that it took to break it was the .... variable. The 'type of bag' is called a .... variable and the 'weight needed to break' it was a .... variable.

2 A researcher claimed that the metal tungsten 'alters the growth of leukaemia cells' in laboratory tests. A newspaper wrote that they would 'wait until other scientists had reviewed the research before giving their opinion.' Why is this a good idea?

Key points
- Be on the lookout for non-scientific opinions.
- Continuous data give more information than other types of data.
- Check that evidence is reproducible and valid.

Answers to in-text questions

a The original animal investigation did not include pregnant animals and was not carried out on human tissue; and so was not valid, when the opinion was formed that it could be given to pregnant women.

b Measure the heights of the seedlings. Continuous measurements (variables) are more powerful.

c If the experiment can be repeated to obtain the same results.

Summary answers

1 independent, dependent, categoric, continuous

2 The investigation can be shown to be reproducible if other scientists can repeat their investigations and get the same findings. Because it is reproducible, opinions formed from it are more useful.

H3

Starting an investigation

Learning objectives

Students should learn:

- how scientific knowledge can be used to observe the world around them
- how good observations can be used to make hypotheses
- how hypotheses can generate predictions that can be tested.

Learning outcomes

Students should be able to:

- state that observation can be the starting point for an investigation
- state that observations can generate hypotheses
- describe how hypotheses can generate predictions and investigations.

Specification link-up: Controlled Assessment SA4.1

Test scientific ideas, by:

- understanding the meaning of the term hypothesis *[SA4.1.2 a)]*
- being able to test a hypothesis. *[SA4.1.2 b)]*

Lesson structure

Starters

Demo observation – Begin the lesson with a demonstration, as simple as lighting a match or more involved such as a bell ringing in a vacuum, with air gradually being added. Students should, in silence and without further prompting, be asked to write down their observations. These should be collated and questions be derived from those observations. *(5 minutes)*

Linking observation to knowledge – Discuss with students any unusual events they saw on the way to school. If possible, take them into the school grounds to look and listen to events. Try to link their observations to their scientific knowledge. They are more likely to notice events that they can offer some scientific explanation for. Support students by prompting with some directed questions. Extend students by getting them to start to ask questions about those observations. *(10 minutes)*

Main

- If in a laboratory, allow students to participate in a 'scientific happening' of your choice, e.g. blowing large and small bubbles or dropping paper cups with different masses in. Preferably something that they have not met before, but which they will have some knowledge of. As an alternative, if possible take students onto the school field where there will be many opportunities to observe plants (ideally the school pond), or roof structure of buildings, or size of wires on electricity pylons compared to telephone wires, or siting of phone masts.
- If students need some help at this point, they should read through the section on observations in the Student Book. Then answer in-text questions **a** and **b**.
- Students should complete the 'making bubbles' practical. In groups they should discuss possible explanations for one agreed observation. Encourage a degree of lateral thinking. You might need to pose the questions for some groups, e.g. why were some bubbles larger than others?
- Ask the group to select which of their explanations is the most likely, based on their own knowledge of science.
- Work these explanations into a hypothesis.
- Students, working in groups, can now turn this into a prediction.
- They could suggest ways in which their prediction could be tested. Identify independent, dependent and control variables and the need to make sure that they are measuring what they actually intend to measure.
- Go over in-text question **c** as a class.

Plenaries

Poster – Ask students to design, but not make, a poster that links 'Observation + knowledge → hypothesis → prediction → investigation'. *(5 minutes)*

Discussion – Ask students to give examples of ideas of the past that have been later disproved. An idea might be to focus on the shape and position of the Earth in our galaxy. Support students by saying that at one time people believed that the Earth was flat. Discuss the observations that have led to the modern idea that the Earth is spherical (e.g. ships disappearing below the horizon, the shadow of the Earth on the Moon). Extend students by discussing the development of knowledge that the planets revolve around the Sun – it could be useful here to illustrate how scientists struggled with these ideas in the past. The story could be used at many points in this chapter but is particularly useful here.

Use secondary sources to look up the following scientists work. Aristarchus (third century BCE) proclaimed that the Earth revolved around the Sun. Copernicus (sixteenth century CE) reasserted the idea that all objects fall towards Earth. Tycho Brahe (late in the sixteenth century CE) was given immense sums of money to investigate the theory that the Earth orbits the Sun. Johannes Kepler (Brahe's assistant) predicted the position of the planets.

It is thought that these ideas about the Earth revolving around the Sun gave rise to the modern use of the term 'revolutionary'. *(10 minutes)*

Support

- Assist students in the 'making bubbles' activity by giving them a list of possible explanations and asking them to choose which is the most likely.

Extend

- Extend students in the 'making bubbles' activity by getting them to vary the amounts of detergent and glycerine added to the water and to make predictions regarding the effect this would have.

Practical support

Making bubbles

Equipment and materials required
Distilled water, 100 cm³ plastic beaker, paper towels, washing-up liquid, glycerine, different-sized loops, eye protection.

Details
Fill container three-quarters full with water add some detergent and glycerine.

Students should make a prediction linking the size of the bubble to the size of the loop, and then use different-sized loops to test their prediction.

Bell in a vacuum

Equipment and materials required
Vacuum pump, bell jar, electronic bell, safety screen, eye protection.

Details
Set the bell ringing in a bell jar. Remove the air using a vacuum pump, then turn off the pump. Slowly allow the air back into the jar. You should hear the bell becoming louder as the air returns.

Safety
Take care that the students are behind the safety screen as air is removed from the jar, as the jar could implode.

How Science Works

H3 Starting an investigation

Learning objectives
- How can you use your scientific knowledge to observe the world around you?
- How can you use your observations to make a hypothesis?
- How can you make predictions and start to design an investigation?

Figure 1 A plant showing positive phototropism

Did you know ...?
Some biologists think that we still have about one hundred millions species of insects to discover – plenty to go for then! Of course, observing one is the easy part – knowing that it is undiscovered is the difficult bit!

Observation
As humans we are sensitive to the world around us. We can use our senses to detect what is happening. As scientists we use observations to ask questions. We can only ask useful questions if we know something about the observed event. We will not have all of the answers, but we know enough to start asking relevant questions.

If we observe that the weather has been hot today, we would not ask if it was due to global warming. If the weather was hotter than normal for several years then we could ask that question. We know that global warming takes many years to show its effect.

When you are designing an investigation you have to observe carefully which variables are likely to have an effect.

a Would it be reasonable to ask if the plant in Figure 1 is 'growing towards the glass'? Explain your answer.

A farmer noticed that her corn was much smaller at the edge of the field than in the middle (observation). She noticed that the trees were quite large on that side of the field. She came up with the following ideas that might explain why this is happening:
1 The trees at the edge of the field were blocking out the light.
2 The trees were taking too many nutrients out of the soil.
3 The leaves from the tree had covered the young corn plants in the spring.
4 The trees had taken too much water out of the soil.
5 The seeds at the edge of the field were genetically small plants.
6 They had planted fewer seeds on that side of the field.
7 The fertiliser spray had not reached the side of the field.
8 The wind had been too strong over winter and had moved the roots of the plants.
9 The plants at the edge of the field had a disease.

b Discuss each of these ideas and use your knowledge of science to decide which four are the most likely to have caused the poor growth of the corn.

Observations, backed up by really creative thinking and good scientific knowledge can lead to a **hypothesis**.

Testing scientific ideas
Scientists always try to think of ways to explain how things work or why they behave in the way that they do.

After their observations, they use their understanding of science to come up with an idea that could explain what is going on. This idea is sometimes called a hypothesis. They use this idea to make a prediction. A prediction is like a guess, but it is not just a wild guess – it is based on previous understanding.

A scientist will say, 'If it works the way I think it does, I should be able to change **this** (the independent variable) and **that** will happen (the dependent variable).'

Predictions are what make science so powerful. They mean that we can work out rules that tell us what will happen in the future. For example, a weather forecaster can use knowledge and understanding to predict wind speeds. Knowing this, sailors and windsurfers can decide if it would be a good day to enjoy their sport. Knowledge of energy transfer could lead to an idea that the inside of chips cook by energy being conducted from the outside. You might predict that small, thinly sliced chips will cook faster than large, fat chips.

c Look at the photograph in Figure 2. How could you test your prediction about how fast chips cook?

Figure 2 Which cook faster? Small, thinly sliced chips or larger, fat chips?

Not all predictions are correct. If scientists find that the prediction doesn't work, then it's back to the drawing board! They either amend their original idea or think of a completely new one.

Starting to design a valid investigation

observation + knowledge ➡ hypothesis ➡ prediction ➡ investigation

We can test a prediction by carrying out an **investigation**. You, as the scientist, predict that there is a relationship between two variables.

The independent variable is one that is selected and changed by you, the investigator. The dependent variable is measured for each change in your independent variable. Then all other variables become control variables, kept constant so that your investigation is a fair test.

If your measurements are going to be accepted by other people then they must be valid. Part of this is making sure that you are really measuring the effect of changing your chosen variable. For example, if other variables aren't controlled properly, they might be affecting the data collected.

d Look at Figure 3. When investigating his heart rate before and after exercise, Darren got his girlfriend to measure his pulse. Would Darren's investigation be valid? Explain your answer.

Figure 3 Measuring a pulse

Summary questions
1 Copy and complete the paragraph using the words below:
controlled dependent independent knowledge prediction hypothesis
An observation linked with scientific .... can be used to make a .... A .... links an .... variable to a .... variable. All other variables need to be ....
2 What is the difference between a prediction and a guess?
3 Imagine you were testing the rate of a chemical reaction by using different concentrations of the reactants. The chemical reaction you are investigating might release energy which would alter the temperature of the solution.
   a How could you monitor the temperature?
   b What other control variables can you think of that might affect the results?

Key points
- Observation is often the starting point for an investigation.
- Testing predictions can lead to new scientific understanding.
- You must design investigations that produce valid results if you are to be believed.

6 | 7

Answers to in-text questions

a No, because we know that the glass is unlikely to be sensed by the plant, but light is.

b 1 The trees at the edge of the field were blocking out the light.
  2 The trees were taking too many nutrients out of the soil.
  4 The trees had taken too much water out of the soil.
  7 The fertiliser spray had not reached the side of the field.

c E.g. Prepare two portions of chips – one thin set and one thick set. Cook both sets and see which cooks faster. Control variables would include having the cooking oil at the same temperature for both sets, keeping the total mass of potato the same in each set.

d No, because his heart rate might increase because his hand is being held by his girlfriend and not just because of exercise. The results are not valid.

Summary answers

1 knowledge, hypothesis, prediction, independent, dependent, controlled

2 A prediction is based on knowledge or observation, a guess is not.

3 a By using a thermometer to check the temperature before and after the reaction.
  b Examples include the volume of the solutions, the degree of mixing or stirring, or the type of container.

H4

Planning an investigation

Learning objectives

Students should learn:

- how to design a fair test
- how to set up a survey
- how to set up a control group or control experiment
- how to reduce risks in hazardous situations.

Learning outcomes

Students should be able to:

- identify variables that need to be controlled in an investigation
- design a survey
- design a fair test and understand the use of control variables and control groups
- identify potential hazards and take action to minimise risk.

Support

- Show students an unfair test with some obvious errors, e.g. dropping two paper 'helicopters' with different wing sizes to see which takes longer to reach the ground, but drop them from different heights.

Extend

- Show students a complex experiment. An example might be using a bomb calorimeter. Give an example of one of the controlled variables. Ask them to list as many other variables as possible that should be controlled.

AQA Specification link-up: Controlled Assessment SA4.1 and SA4.2

Test scientific ideas (hypotheses), by:

- planning a fair test. *[SA4.1.2 c)]*.

Assess and manage risks when carrying out practical work, by:

- identifying some possible hazards in practical situations *[SA4.2.1 a)]*
- suggest ways of managing risks. *[SA4.2.1 b)]*

Lesson structure

Starters

Risk assessment – Give students a picture sheet illustrating a situation showing a number of hazards. Ask the students to spot the hazard and write down what could be done to minimise the risk. The situation illustrated could be one in the school laboratory, or it could be outside the school environment, e.g. in the road, in a factory or on a farm. *(5 minutes)*

Head start – Start, for example, with a video clip of a 100 m race. (Search for 'marathon' or 'race' at www.video.google.com or www.bbc.co.uk). This has to be a fair test. How is this achieved? Then show the mass start of the London marathon and ask if this is a fair test. Support students by asking why there is no official world record for a marathon. (Instead they have world best times.) This could lead to a discussion of how difficult it is to control all of the variables in the field. Extend students by going on to discuss why athletes can break the 100 m world record and for this not to be recognised because of a helping wind. *(10 minutes)*

Main

- Start with a group discussion about fair testing. Highlight any misconceptions about fair testing and stress that repeat readings do not make a test fair. Effectively controlling variables are what make a test fair.
- Challenge students with a test you set up in an 'unfair' way. You can differentiate by making some errors obvious and some more subtle. Students can observe then generate lists of mistakes in small groups. Ask each group to give one error from their list and record what should have been done to ensure fair testing until all suggestions have been considered.
- Group discussions on how and why we need to produce survey data. Use a topical issue here. It might be appropriate to see how it should *not* be done by using a vox pop clip from a news programme.
- Students will be familiar with the idea of a placebo, but possibly not with how it is used to set up a control group. This might need explanation.
- Consider the case of whether it is possible to tell the difference in taste if the milk is put in before or after the tea. R.A. Fisher tested this, using a double-blind taste test and went on to devise 'Statistical Methods for Research Workers'.
- Use the school or college laboratory rules to review safety procedures.
- Ask students to carry out a risk assessment on the burning alcohols experiment.

Plenaries

Key words – Using a card sort, ask students to match the definitions to the key words introduced in this lesson. *(5 minutes)*

Survey – Ask students to imagine they have been asked to conduct a survey to find out whether or not people prefer a particular brand of toothpaste. They should produce a questionnaire that lists the questions that you could ask people on the street. Support students by supplying them with a list of questions, some of which would be relevant, others irrelevant. Ask students to tick which questions would be the most appropriate. Extend students by asking them to suggest how many people should be chosen and on what basis they are selected. *(10 minutes)*

Practical support

Risk assessment on burning alcohols

Equipment and materials required

Boiling tube, thermometer, stopwatch, spirit burner and safety equipment, wooden splints, eye protection, tongs, retort stand, base clamp (to hold boiling tube at a fixed distance) from flame. 3 × alcohols suitable for burning. CLEAPSS Hazcard 40A Ethanol – harmful and highly flammable; Hazcard 84A Propan–1–01 – highly flammable and irritant; Hazcard 84B Butan–1–01 – harmful; Hazcard 84C Pentan–1–01, Hexan–1–01, Heptan–1–01 – harmful.

Details

Students could use a spirit burner to heat a small quantity of water in a boiling tube and measure the temperature rise. Before doing so, they should identify any possible hazards and then write down ways in which they would minimise any risk. After carrying out the experiment, they should discuss whether or not their plans for risk reduction were sufficient.

Safety

Look at the CLEAPSS Guide L195 'Safer chemicals, Safer reactions', which has a small section specifically on this experiment. Wear eye protection and keep room well-ventilated.

H4 Planning an investigation

Learning objectives

- How do you design a fair test?
- How do you set up a survey?
- How do you set up a control group or control experiment?
- How do you reduce risks in hazardous situations?

AQA Examiner's tip

If you are asked about why it is important to keep control variables constant, you need to give a detailed explanation. Don't just answer 'To make it a fair test'.

When you are asked to write a plan for your investigation, make sure that you give all the details. Ask yourself 'Would someone else be able to follow my written plan and use it to do the investigation?'

Fair testing

A **fair test** is one in which only the independent variable affects the dependent variable. All other variables called control variables should be kept the same. If the test is not fair, then the results of your investigation will not be valid.

Sometimes it is very difficult to keep control variables the same. However, at least you can **monitor** them, so that you know whether they have changed or not.

Surveys

Not all scientific investigations involve deliberately changing the independent variable.

If you were investigating the effect that using a mobile phone may have on health you wouldn't put a group of people in a room and make them use their mobile phones to see if they developed brain cancer!

Instead, you might conduct a **survey**. You might study the health of a large number of people who regularly use a mobile phone. You could then compare their health with those who never use a mobile phone.

You would have to choose people of the same age and same family history to test. The larger the sample size you test, the more valid your results will be.

Figure 1 Investigating the effect of using a mobile phone on health would involve using data from surveys as well as laboratory studies

Control group

Control groups are used in investigations to try to make sure that you are measuring the variable that you intend to measure. When investigating the effects of a new drug, the control group will be given a **placebo**. This is a 'pretend' drug that actually has no effect on the patient at all. The control group think they are taking a drug but the placebo does not contain the drug. This way you can control the variable of 'thinking that the drug is working' and separate out the effect of the actual drug.

Usually neither the patient nor the doctor knows until after the trials have been completed which of the patients were given the placebo. This is known as a **double-blind trial**.

Risks and hazards

One of the first things you must do is to think about any potential **hazards** and then assess the **risk**.

Everything you do in life presents a hazard. What you have to do is to identify the hazard and then decide the degree of risk that it gives. If the risk is very high, you must do something to reduce it.

For example, if you decide to go out in the pouring rain, lightning could be a possible hazard. However, you decide that the risk is so small that you decide to ignore it and go out anyway.

If you decide to cross a busy road, the cars travelling along it at high speed represent a hazard. You decide to reduce the risk by crossing at a pedestrian crossing.

Activity

Burning alcohols

Imagine you were testing alcohols to see how much energy they release when burned.

- Thermometer
- Glass beaker
- Water
- Spirit burner
- Alcohol
- Tripod

- What are the **hazards** that are present?
- What could you do to reduce the **risk** from these hazards?

Summary questions

1 Copy and complete the paragraph using the words below:
investigation hazards assessment risks
Before you carry out any practical ...., you need to carry out a risk .... You can do this by looking for any potential .... and making sure that the .... are as small as possible.

2 Explain the difference between a control group and a control variable.

3 Briefly describe how you would go about setting up a fair test in a laboratory investigation. Give your answer as general advice.

Figure 2 The hazard is the busy road. We reduce the risk by using a pedestrian crossing.

AQA Examiner's tip

Before you start your practical work you must make sure that it is safe. What are the likely hazards? How could you reduce the risk caused by these hazards? This is known as a **risk assessment**. You may well be asked questions like this on your ISA paper.

Key points

- Care must be taken to ensure fair testing – as far as is possible.
- Control variables must be kept the same during an investigation.
- Surveys are often used when it is impossible to carry out an experiment in which the independent variable is changed.
- Control groups allow you to make a comparison.
- A risk assessment must be made when planning a practical investigation.

Further teaching suggestions

Which?

Look at some recent *Which?* reports on consumer goods. Discuss issues such as:

- Was the size of the sample surveyed sufficient?
- Could the people who have been surveyed been biased?
- Could the people conducting the survey have been biased?

Summary answers

1 investigation, assessment, hazards, risks

2 In an experiment to determine the effect of changing a single variable, a **control variable** is often set up in which the independent variable is not changed, thus enabling a comparison to be made. If the investigation is of the survey type a **control group** is usually established to serve the same purpose.

3 Control all the variables that might affect the dependent variable, apart from the independent variable whose values you select.

H5 | Designing an investigation

Learning objectives

Students should learn:

- how to choose the best values for the variables
- how to decide on a suitable range
- how to decide on a suitable interval
- how to ensure accuracy and precision.

Learning outcomes

Students should be able to:

- use trial runs to establish the best values for the variables
- use trial runs to establish a suitable range for the independent variable
- use trial runs to establish a suitable interval for the independent variable
- design a fair test that will yield accurate and precise results.

Support

- In the spring experiment, students may find it easier to measure the total length of the spring rather than the extension.

Extend

- The spring experiment can be extended to investigate what happens beyond the elastic limit, and include a discussion as to why such data would not be valid.
- The resistance experiment (starter) can be extended to investigate length of resistance wire. The focus should be on producing a line graph that can give a better estimate of the true resistance of the wire.

AQA Specification link-up: Controlled Assessment SA4.1 and SA4.3

Devise appropriate methods for the collection of numerical and other data, by:

- carrying out preliminary work *[SA4.1.3 a)]*
- understanding sample size *[SA4.1.3 b)]*
- using appropriate technology *[SA4.1.3 c)]*.

Demonstrate an understanding of the need to acquire high quality data, by:

- appreciating that unless certain variables are controlled, the results may not be valid *[SA4.3.3 a)]*
- identifying when repeats are needed in order to improve reliability *[SA4.3.3 b)]*
- recognising the value of repeated readings to establish accuracy *[SA4.3.3 c)]*
- considering the resolution of the measuring device *[SA4.3.3 d)]*
- considering the precision of the measured data *[SA4.3.3 e)]*
- identifying the range of the measured data. *[SA4.3.3 f)]*

Lesson structure

Starters

Interval – Give students a graph of enzyme activity that shows a peak, but where the interval on the *x*-axis is very large so that it is difficult to judge the exact position of the peak. Ask students to suggest what other values should be tested in order to ascertain the peak more accurately. *(5 minutes)*

Preliminary work – Give students an expendable steel spring that reaches its elastic limit at about 10 N. Tell them that the main experiment would be to collect data to show how the extension of the spring varies with the force applied. Support students by giving them a number of 1.0 N weights and ask them to carry out a quick test to suggest a suitable range for the weights to be added. Extend students by giving them a selection of different weights (e.g. 0.1 N, 1.0 N, 10 N) and ask them to suggest a suitable interval for the weights to be added. *(10 minutes)*

Main

- Discuss the results of the preliminary work on springs.
- Carry out the main investigation on springs. Allow students to compare the results of different groups. Compile a table of pooled results and discuss the possible reasons for any differences.
- Discuss the benefits of repeating results.
- It is important that students appreciate the difference between accuracy and precision. Get students to plot their results on a large class graph, and then draw a line of best fit. Discuss the amount of scatter, and how far away the points are from the best-fit line (this is an indication of the **precision** of the individual measurements). Then discuss how far away from the 'true value' (the teacher's result?) the graph shows the extension to be for a weight somewhere in the middle of the range. Accurate readings will be taken by those that use their equipment most carefully.

Plenaries

Prize giving! – Award a prize to the group achieving a) the most accurate result and b) the most precise results. Let the groups try to explain their success. *(5 minutes)*

Out of range – Ask students to predict from the class graph what the extension would be for a weight of double the maximum tested. Support students by asking them what the value would be if the pattern showed by the graph continued in the same way, and then ask them why this might not happen. Extend students by asking them to discuss whether the precision is greater at the start of the range, greater near the end of the range or the same throughout the range. *(10 minutes)*

Practical support

Springs

Equipment and materials required

Expendable steel springs, stand, G-clamp, selection of slotted weights, ruler, plasticine or sticky-tac.

Details

Use a G-clamp to secure the stand. Hang weights from the spring using a weight hanger and measure the extension. Fix ruler vertically behind weight hanger and measure extension from the same point on the hanger. Run some preliminary tests using a range of weights. Suggest a suitable range of weights to test and a suitable interval for the weights.

Safety

Wear eye protection.

H5 — Designing an investigation

Learning objectives

- How do you make sure that you choose the best values for your variables?
- How do you decide on a suitable range?
- How do you decide on a suitable interval?
- How do you ensure accuracy and precision?

Choosing values of a variable

Trial runs will tell you a lot about how your early thoughts are going to work out.

Do you have the correct conditions?

A photosynthesis investigation that produces tiny amounts of oxygen might not have enough light, pondweed or carbon dioxide. Alternatively, the temperature might not be high enough.

Have you chosen a sensible range?

Range means the maximum and minimum values of the independent or dependent variables. It is important to choose a suitable range for the independent variable, otherwise you may not be able to see any change in the dependent variable.

For example, if results are all very similar, you might not have chosen a wide enough range of light intensities.

Have you got enough readings that are close together?

The gap between the readings is known as the interval.

For example, you might alter the light intensity by moving a lamp to different distances from the pondweed. A set of 11 readings equally spaced over a distance of 1 metre would give an interval of 10 centimetres.

If the results are very different from each other, you might not see a pattern if you have large gaps between readings over the important part of the range.

Figure 1 Measuring the extension of a spring

Practical

Springs

In this experiment you hang weights from the spring using a weight hanger and measure the extension of the spring. Once you have done some preliminary testing, suggest a suitable range of weights to test and a suitable interval for the weights.

Accuracy

Accurate measurements are very close to the **true value**.

Your investigation should provide data that are accurate enough to answer your original question.

However, it is not always possible to know what that true value is.

How do you get accurate data?

- You can repeat your measurements and your mean is more likely to be accurate.
- Try repeating your measurements with a different instrument and see if you get the same readings.
- Use high quality instruments that measure accurately.
- The more carefully you use the measuring instruments, the more accuracy you will get.

Precision, resolution, repeatability and reproducibility

A **precise** measurement is one in which there is very little spread about the mean value.

If your repeated measurements are closely grouped together then you have precision. Your measurements must be made with an instrument that has a suitable **resolution**. Resolution of a measuring instrument is the smallest change in the quantity being measured (input) that gives a perceptible change in the reading.

It's no use measuring the time for a fast reaction to finish using the seconds hand on a clock! If there are big differences within sets of repeat readings, you will not be able to make a valid conclusion. You won't be able to trust your data!

How do you get precise data?

- You have to use measuring instruments with sufficiently small scale divisions.
- You have to repeat your tests as often as necessary.
- You have to repeat your tests in exactly the same way each time.

If you repeat your investigation using the same method and equipment and obtain the same results, your results are said to be **repeatable**.

If someone else repeats your investigation in the same way, or if you repeat it by using different equipment or techniques, and the same results are obtained, it is said to be **reproducible**.

You may be asked to compare your results with those of others in your group, or with data from other scientists. Research like this is a good way of checking your results.

A word of caution!

Precision depends only on the extent of random errors – it gives no indication of how close results are to the true value. Just because your results show precision does not mean your results are accurate.

a Draw a thermometer scale reading 49.5°C, showing four results that are both accurate and precise.

Summary questions

1 Copy and complete the paragraph using the words below:
range   repeat   conditions   readings
Trial runs give you a good idea of whether you have the correct .... to collect any data, whether you have chosen the correct .... for the independent variable, whether you have enough ...., and if you need to do .... readings.

2 Use an example to explain how a set of repeat measurements could be accurate, but not precise.

3 Explain the difference between a set of results that are reproducible and a set of results that are repeatable.

You must know the difference between accurate and precise results.
Imagine measuring the temperature after a set time when a fuel is used to heat a fixed volume of water.
Two students repeated this experiment, four times each. Their results are marked on the thermometer scales below:

- A **precise** set of repeat readings will be grouped closely together.
- An **accurate** set of repeat readings will have a mean (average) close to the true value.

Precise (but not accurate)   Accurate (but not precise)

Key points

- You can use a trial run to make sure that you choose the best values for your variables.
- The range states the maximum and the minimum values of a variable.
- The interval is the gap between the values of a variable.
- Careful use of the correct equipment can improve accuracy and precision.
- You should try to reproduce your results carefully.

Further teaching suggestions

Reproducibility

- Using the data from the experiment, consider the range of their repeat measurements and judge reproducibility. Find the maximum range for the whole class – who got the highest reading/who got the lowest? Can we explain why?

Graphs and charts

- The spring experiment can be expanded to discuss whether the results should be plotted on a line graph or a bar chart.

Summary answers

1 conditions, range, readings, repeat

2 Any example that demonstrates understanding of the two terms, e.g. I measured the resistance of the wire as 3.5 ohms, 4.8 ohms, 2.2 ohms, 3.8 ohms, 3.2 ohms. The average of my results is 3.5 ohms and the manufacturer's results are 3.5 ohms. My results were accurate but not precise.

3 Results with the same values but obtained by different people or equipment are reproducible.
Results obtained using the same equipment, method and same values are repeatable.

Answers to in-text questions

a Diagram of thermometer showing the true value with four readings tightly grouped around it.

H6

Making measurements

Learning objectives

Students should learn:

- that they can expect results to vary
- that instruments vary in their accuracy
- that instruments vary in their resolution
- the difference between systematic errors and random errors
- that human error can affect results, and what to do with anomalies.

Learning outcomes

Students should be able to:

- distinguish between results that vary and anomalies
- explain that instruments vary in their accuracy and resolution
- explain that anomalies should be discarded or repeated before calculating a mean.

Support

- Students will need support when interpreting data on oil and identifying evidence for systematic and random errors. For systematic errors they should look to see if the measured values are always larger or smaller than the calculated values. For random errors, they should look to see if there is any scatter around the mean.

Extend

- Demonstrate a different experiment in which there is a built-in systematic error, e.g. measuring the effect of temperature on the rate of an exothermic reaction.

AQA Specification link-up: Controlled Assessment SA4.3 and SA4.5

Make observations, by:

- making simple observations from first-hand evidence of an object or an event [SA4.3.1 a)]
- carrying out practical work and research. [SA4.3.1 b)]

Demonstrate the correct use of equipment, by:

- choosing the most appropriate equipment or technique for the task [SA4.3.2 a)]
- understanding why a particular technique or piece of equipment is the most suitable for the task [SA4.3.2 b)]
- understanding the meaning of the term 'resolution' when applied to a measuring instrument. [SA4.3.2 d)]

Review methodology to assess fitness for purpose, by:

- identifying causes of variation in data [SA4.5.2 a)]
- recognising and identifying the cause of random errors [SA4.5.2 b)]
- recognising and identifying the cause of anomalous results [SA4.5.2 c)]
- recognising and identifying the cause of systematic errors. [SA4.5.2 d)]

Lesson structure

Starters

Demonstration – Demonstrate different ways of measuring the width of the laboratory. Use a 30 cm rule, a metre rule, a tape and a laser/sonic measure. Discuss the relative merits of using each of these devices for different purposes. Discuss the details of the measuring instrument – its percentage accuracy, its useful range and its resolution. *(5 minutes)*

Human reaction time – Allow students to test their reaction times using a computer program. (e.g. www.bbc.co.uk. Search for 'Sheep Dash'.) and then by dropping and catching a ruler, using a stopwatch. Discuss the advantages and disadvantages of each method. Support students by explaining that human reaction time is normally about 0.2 seconds. Extend students on the 'dropping the ruler' method by getting them to explain whether it would be better for the same person to drop the ruler and operate the watch, or whether it would be better to use two different people.

Main

- In small groups, plan the most accurate way to measure a person's height. They can have any equipment they need. Students will need to think about what a person's height includes, e.g. hair flat or not, shoes on or off. They might suggest a board placed horizontally on the head, using a spirit level, removing the person being measured and then using the laser/sonic measure placed on the ground.
- Stress that we do not have a true answer. We do not know the person's true height. We trust the instrument and the technique that is most likely to give us the most accurate result – the one nearest the true value.
- Demonstrate an experiment in which there is a built-in systematic error, e.g. weighing some chemicals using a filter paper without using the tare or measuring radioactivity without taking background radiation into account.
- Point out the difference between this type of systematic error and random errors. Also, how you might tell from results which type of error it is. You can still have a high degree of precision with systematic errors.
- Complete in-text questions **a** and **b** individually.
- Encourage students to identify anomalies whilst carrying out the investigation so that they have an opportunity to check and replace them.

Plenaries

Human v. computer – Class discussion of data logging compared to humans when collecting data. Stress the importance of data logging in gathering data over extended or very short periods of time. *(5 minutes)*

Check list – Ask students to draw up a check list for an investigation so that every possible source of error is considered. Support students by giving them a list of possible sources of error that includes a mixture of relevant and irrelevant suggestions. Ask them to tick the ones that they think are relevant. Extend students by asking them to suggest what they could do to minimise the effect of any errors. *(10 minutes)*

Further teaching suggestions

Data logging

- Data logging provides a good opportunity to exemplify changes in dependent variables.
- Use data logging to illustrate how detailed measurements taken frequently can show variation in results that would not have been seen by other methods.
- Data logging can increase the accuracy of readings that can be taken where other readings might not be possible to take accurately.

For example:

- Compare two students taking their hand temperatures – one with a thermometer, one with a logger.
- Set the logger to record room temperatures until next lesson.
- Compare measurements using a tape measure with those of a distance sensor linked to a computer. Draw attention to the ability to measure distances as you move the sensor.

How Science Works

H6   Making measurements

Learning objectives

- Why do results always vary?
- How do you choose instruments that will give you accurate results?
- What do we mean by the 'resolution' of an instrument?
- What is the difference between a systematic error and a random error?
- How does human error affect results and what do you do with anomalies?

Using instruments

Try measuring the temperature of a beaker of water using a digital thermometer. Do you always get the same result? Probably not. So can we say that any measurement is absolutely correct?

In any experiment there will be doubts about actual measurements.

When you choose an instrument you need to know that it will give you the accuracy that you want. You need to be confident that it is giving a true reading.

If you have used an electric water bath, would you trust the temperature on the dial? How do you know it is the true temperature? You could use a very expensive thermometer to calibrate your water bath. The expensive thermometer is more likely to show the true temperature. But can you really be sure it is accurate?

Instruments that measure the same thing can have different sensitivities. The **resolution** of an instrument refers to the smallest change in a value that can be detected. This is one factor that determines the precision of your measurements.

Errors

Even when an instrument is used correctly, the results can still show differences.

Results may differ because of **random error**. This is most likely to be due to a poor measurement being made. It could be due to not carrying out the method consistently.

If you repeat your measurements several times and then calculate a mean, you will reduce the effect of random errors.

The **error** might be a **systematic error**. This means that the method was carried out consistently but an error was being repeated. A systematic error will make your readings be spread about some value other than the true value. This is because your results will differ from the true value by a consistent amount each time a measurement is made.

No amount of repeats can do anything about systematic errors. If you think that you have a systematic error, you need to repeat using a different set of equipment or a different technique. Then compare your results and spot the difference!

A **zero error** is one kind of systematic error. Suppose that you were trying to measure the length of your desk with a metre rule, but you hadn't noticed that someone had sawn off half a centimetre from the end of the ruler. It wouldn't matter how many times you repeated the measurement, you would never get any nearer to the true value.

AQA Examiner's tip

If you are asked what may have caused an error, never answer simply 'human error' – you won't get any marks for this.

You need to say what the experimenter may have done to cause the error, or give more detail, e.g. 'Human reaction time might have caused an error in the timing when using a stopwatch'.

Check out these two sets of data that were taken from the investigation that Matt did. He tested five different oils. The bottom row is the time calculated from knowing the viscosity of the different oils:

Type of oil used	A	B	C	D	E
Time taken to flow down tile (seconds)	23.2	45.9	49.5	62.7	75.9
	24.1	36.4	48.7	61.5	76.1
Calculated time (seconds)	18.2	30.4	42.5	55.6	70.7

a   Discuss whether there is any evidence for random error in these results.

b   Discuss whether there is any evidence for systematic error in these results.

Anomalies

Anomalous results are clearly out of line. They are not those that are due to the natural variation you get from any measurement. These should be looked at carefully. There might be a very interesting reason why they are so different. You should always look for anomalous results and discard them before you calculate a mean, if necessary.

- If anomalies can be identified while you are doing an investigation, then it is best to repeat that part of the investigation.
- If you find anomalies after you have finished collecting data for an investigation, then they must be discarded.

??? Did you know ... ?

Sir Alexander Fleming had grown bacteria on agar plates. He noticed an anomaly. There was some mould growing on one of the plates and around it there were no bacteria. He decided to investigate further and grew more of the mould. Only because Fleming checked out his anomaly did it lead to the discovery of penicillin.

Summary questions

1 Copy and complete the paragraph using the words below:

   accurate discarded random resolution systematic
   use variation

   There will always be some .... in results. You should always choose the best instruments that you can in order to get the most .... results. You must know how to .... the instrument properly. The .... of an instrument refers to the smallest change that can be detected. There are two types of error: .... and .... Anomalies due to random error should be ....

2 What kind of error will most likely occur in the following situations?
   a   Asking everyone in the class to measure the length of the bench.
   b   Using a ruler that has a piece missing from the zero end.

Figure 1 Matt timing the flow of oil

links

B1 1.6 Using drugs to treat disease.

Key points

- Results will nearly always vary.
- Better quality instruments give more accurate results.
- The resolution of an instrument refers to the smallest change that it can detect.
- Human error can produce random and/or systematic errors.
- We examine anomalies as they might give us some interesting ideas. If they are due to a random error, we repeat the measurements. If there is no time to repeat them, we discard them.

Answers to in-text questions

a   First attempt for B is the random error.

b   Average results are close to individual results, which are consistently different to the calculated time, indicating systematic error.

Summary answers

1   variation, accurate, use, resolution, random, systematic, discarded

2   a   random,
     b   systematic.

H7

Presenting data

AQA Specification link-up: Controlled Assessment SA4.3 and SA4.4

Demonstrate an understanding of the need to acquire high quality data, by:
- identifying the range of the measured data. [SA4.3.3 f)]

Show an understanding of the value of means, by:
- appreciating when it is appropriate to calculate a mean [SA4.4.1 a)]
- calculating the mean of a set of at least three results. [SA4.4.1 b)]

Demonstrate an understanding of how data may be displayed, by:
- drawing tables [SA4.4.2 a)]
- drawing charts and graphs [SA4.4.2 b)]
- choosing the most appropriate form of presentation. [SA4.4.2 c)]

Lesson structure

Starters

Newspapers – Choose data from the press: particularly useful are market trends where they do not use (0, 0). This exaggerates changes. This could relate to the use of data logging, which can exaggerate normal variation into major trends. *(5 minutes)*

Excel – Prepare some data from a typical investigation that the students may have recently completed. Use all of the many ways of presenting the data in Excel to display it. Allow students to discuss and reach conclusions as to which is the best method. Support students by presenting data as either a line graph or a simple bar chart so that they can make the link between continuous data and line graphs and between categoric data and bar charts. Extend students by showing graphs and charts that have non-linear scales or false origins. *(10 minutes)*

Main

- Choose an appropriate topic to either demonstrate or allow small groups to gather data, e.g., the cooling of water against time; using food labels to determine saturated fat content of different foods; force applied and degree of bending in rules; investigating the period of a pendulum, i.e. any topic that will allow rapid gathering of data. Be aware at the outset that some data will lead to a bar chart, and that this might be more appropriate to groups struggling to draw line graphs.

- Students should be told what their task is and therefore know how to construct an appropriate table. This should be done individually prior to collecting the data. Refer to the first paragraph under 'Tables' in the Student Book.

- Run a group discussion on the best form of table.

- Carry out data gathering, putting data directly into table. Refer to the second paragraph under 'Tables' in the Student Book.

- Individuals produce their own graphs. Refer to the section 'Displaying your results' in the Student Book.

- Graphs could be exchanged and marked by others in the group, using the criteria in the section mentioned above.

Plenaries

Which type of graph? – Give students different headings from a variety of tables and ask them how best to show the results graphically. This could be done as a whole class with individuals showing answers as you reveal each table heading. Each student can draw a large letter 'L' (for line graph) on one side of a sheet of paper and 'B' (for bar chart) on the other, ready to show their answers. *(5 minutes)*

Key words – Students should be given key words to prepare posters for the lab. Key words should be taken from the summary questions in the first six spreads. Support students by giving them posters in two sections – one containing the key word, the other the definition. Students should then match the pairs together correctly. Extend students by getting them to write their own definitions. *(10 minutes)*

Further teaching suggestions

ICT link-up

- Students could use a set of data within spreadsheet software (e.g. Excel) to present the data as pie charts, line graphs, bar charts, etc. Allow them to decide on the most appropriate form. Care needs to be given to 'smoothing', which does not always produce a line of best fit.

How Science Works

H7 Presenting data

Learning objectives

- How do we calculate the mean from a set of data?
- How do you use tables of results?
- What is the range of the data?
- How do you display your data?

Figure 1 Petri dish with discs showing growth inhibition of bacteria

For this section you will be working with data from this investigation:

Mel spread some bacteria onto a dish containing nutrient jelly. She also placed some discs onto the jelly. The discs contained different concentrations of an antibiotic. The dish was taped and then left for a couple of days.

Then she measured the diameter of the clear part around each disc. The clear part is where the bacteria have not been able to grow. The bacteria grew all over the rest of the dish.

Tables 🅚

Tables are really good for getting your results down quickly and clearly. You should design your table **before** you start your investigation.

Your table should be constructed to fit in all the data to be collected. It should be fully labelled, including units.

You may want to have extra columns for repeats, calculations of means or calculated values.

Checking for anomalies

While filling in your table of results you should be constantly looking for anomalies.

- Check to see if any reading in a set of repeat readings is significantly different from others.
- Check to see if the pattern you are getting as you change the independent variable is what you expected.

Remember, a result that looks anomalous should be checked out to see if it really is a poor reading.

Planning your table

Mel had decided on the values for her independent variable. We always put these in the first column of a table. The dependent variable goes in the second column. Mel will find its values as she carries out the investigation.

So she could plan a table like this:

Concentration of antibiotic (µg/ml)	Size of clear zone (mm)
4	
8	
16	
32	
64	

Or like this:

Concentration of antibiotic (µg/ml)	4	8	16	32	64
Size of clear zone (mm)					

All she had to do in the investigation was to write the correct numbers in the second column to complete the top table.

Mel's results are shown in the alternative format in the table below.

Concentration of antibiotic (µg/ml)	4	8	16	32	64
Size of clear zone (mm)	4	16	22	26	28

The range of the data

Pick out the maximum and the minimum values and you have the range of a variable. You should always quote these two numbers when asked for a range. For example, 'the range of the dependent variables is between 4 mm (the lowest value) and 28 mm (the highest value)' – and don't forget to include the units!

a What is the range for the independent variable in Mel's set of data?

Maths skills

The mean of the data

Often you have to find the mean of each repeated set of measurements. The first thing you should do is to look for any anomalous results. If you find any, miss these out of the calculation. Then add together the remaining measurements and divide by how many there are.
For example:

- Mel takes four readings 15 mm, 18 mm, 29 mm, 15 mm
- 29 mm is an anomalous result and so is missed out. So
  15 + 18 + 15 = 48
- 48 divided by three (the number of valid results) = **16 mm**

The repeat values and mean can be recorded as shown below:

Concentration of antibiotic (µg/ml)	Size of clear zone (mm)			
	1st test	2nd test	3rd test	Mean
8	15	18	15	16

Displaying your results

Bar charts

If one of your variables is categoric then you should use a bar chart.

Line graphs

If you have a continuous independent and a continuous dependent variable then a line graph should be used. Plot the points as small 'plus' signs (+).

Summary questions

1 Copy and complete the paragraph using the words below:
   categoric continuous mean range

   The maximum and minimum values show the .... of the data. The sum of the values in a set of repeat readings divided by the total number of these repeat values gives the .... Bar charts are used when you have a .... independent variable and a continuous dependent variable. Line graphs are used when you have .... independent and .... dependent variables.

2 Draw a graph of Mel's results from the top of this page.

AQA Examiner's tip

When you make a table for your results remember to include:
- headings, including the units
- a title.

When you draw a line graph or bar chart remember to:
- use a sensible scale that is easy to work out
- use as much of the graph paper as possible; your data should occupy at least one-third of each axis
- label both axes
- draw a line of best fit if it is a line graph
- label each bar if it is a bar chart.

AQA Examiner's tip

Marks are often dropped in the ISA by candidates plotting points incorrectly. Also use **a line of best fit** where appropriate – don't just join the points 'dot-to-dot'!

Key points

- The **range** states the maximum and the minimum values.
- The **mean** is the sum of the values divided by how many values there are.
- Tables are best used during an investigation to record results.
- Bar charts are used when you have a **categoric** variable.
- Line graphs are used to display data that are **continuous**.

Answers to in-text questions

a 4–64 mm.

Summary answers

1 range, mean, categoric, continuous

2

Size of clear zone (mm) vs Concentration of antibiotic (µg/ml)

H8

Using data to draw conclusions

Learning objectives

Students should learn:

- how to use charts and graphs to identify patterns
- how to identify relationships within data
- how to draw valid conclusions from relationships
- how to evaluate the validity of an investigation.

Learning outcomes

Students should be able to:

- draw a line of best fit when appropriate
- identify different relationships between variables from graphs
- draw conclusions from data
- evaluate the validity of an investigation.

Support

- Provide students with a flow diagram of the procedure used to draw conclusions, so that students can see the process as they are going through it.

Extend

- Students could take the original investigation then design out some of the flaws, producing an investigation with improved validity and repeatability.
- Summary question 2 could be examined in some detail and the work researched on the internet.

AQA Specification link-up: Controlled Assessment SA4.5

Identify patterns in data, by:

- describing the relationship between two variables [SA4.5.3 a)].

Draw conclusions using scientific ideas and evidence, by:

- writing a conclusion, based on evidence that relates correctly to known facts [SA4.5.4 a)]
- using secondary sources [SA4.5.4 b)]
- identifying extra evidence that may be required for a conclusion to be made [SA4.5.4 c)]
- evaluating methods of data collection. [SA4.5.4 d)]

Lesson structure

Starters

Conclusions – Prepare a number of tables of results, some of which show that as *x* increases *y* increases, some that show as *x* increases *y* decreases, and some where there is no relationship between *x* and *y*. Ask students what conclusion they can draw from each set of results. *(5 minutes)*

Starter graphs – Prepare a series of graphs that illustrate the various types of relationship in the specification. Each graph should have fully labelled axes. Students should, in groups, agree statements that describe the patterns in the graphs. Support students by giving them graphs that illustrate simple linear relationships. Extend students by giving them more complex graphs with curved lines, and encourage them to use terms such as 'directly proportional' and 'inversely proportional'. Gather feedback from groups and discuss. *(10 minutes)*

Main

- Using the graphs from the previous lesson, students should be taught how to produce lines of best fit. Students could work individually with help from Figures 1 and 2 in the Student Book.
- They should identify the pattern in their graph.
- They now need to consider the repeatability and validity of their results. They may need their understanding of repeatability and validity reinforced. Questions can be posed to reinforce their understanding of both terms. If the investigation was not carefully controlled, then it is likely to be unrepeatable and invalid, thus posing many opportunities for discussion. There is also an opportunity to reinforce other ideas such as random and systematic errors.
- A brief demonstration of a test should be given. You can use a practical from this book or from Kerboodle. Make sure there are a number of variables you can control. Students should observe the teacher and make notes as the test is carried out. They should be as critical as they can be, and in small groups discuss their individual findings. One or two students could be recording the results and two more plotting the graph as the test is carried out. A spreadsheet could be used to immediately turn the results into graphs.
- Return to the original prediction. Look at the graph of the results. Ask how much confidence the group has in the results.
- Review the links that are possible between two sets of data. Ask them to decide which one their tests might support.
- Now the word 'conclusion' should be introduced and a conclusion made… if possible! It is sometimes useful to make a conclusion that is 'subject to … e.g. the repeatability being demonstrated'.

Plenaries

Flow diagram – When pulling the lesson together, it will be important to emphasise the process involved: graph → line of best fit → pattern → question the repeatability and validity → consider the links that are possible → make a conclusion → summarise evaluation. This could be illustrated with a flow diagram generated by a directed class discussion. *(5 minutes)*

Evaluating – Students could review the method used in the demonstration experiment of burning crisps. Support students by asking them to identify where errors could have been made. Extend students by asking them to suggest improvements that could be made to minimise these errors. *(10 minutes)*

Further teaching suggestions

Case studies

- Students should be able to transfer these skills to examine the work of scientists and to become critical of the work of others. Collecting scientific findings from the press and subjecting them to the same critical appraisal is an important exercise. They could be encouraged to collect these or be given photocopies of topical issues suitable for such appraisal.

H8 — Using data to draw conclusions

Learning objectives

- How do we best use charts and graphs to identify patterns?
- What are the possible relationships we can identify from charts and graphs?
- How do we draw conclusions from relationships?
- How can we decide if our results are good and our conclusions are valid?

Identifying patterns and relationships

Now that you have a bar chart or a line graph of your results you can begin to look for patterns. You must have an open mind at this point.

Firstly, there could still be some anomalous results. You might not have picked these out earlier. How do you spot an anomaly? It must be a significant distance away from the pattern, not just within normal variation. If you do have any anomalous results plotted on your graph, circle these and ignore them when drawing the **line of best fit**.

Now look at your graph. Is there a pattern that you can see? When you have decided, draw a line of best fit that shows this pattern.

A line of best fit is a kind of visual averaging process. You should draw the line so that it leaves as many points slightly above the line as there are points below. In other words it is a line that steers a middle course through the field of points.

The vast majority of results that you get from continuous data require a line of best fit.

Remember that a line of best fit can be a straight line or it can be a curve – you have to decide from your results.

You need to consider whether your graph shows a linear **relationship**. This simply means, can you be confident about drawing a straight line of best fit on your graph? If the answer is yes – then is this line positive or negative?

a Say whether graphs **i** and **ii** in Figure 1 show a positive or a negative linear relationship.

Look at the graph in Figure 2. It shows a positive linear relationship. It also goes through the origin (0, 0). We call this a **directly proportional** relationship.

Your results might also show a curved line of best fit. These can be predictable, complex or very complex! Look at Figure 3 below.

Figure 1 Graphs showing linear relationships

Figure 2 Graph showing a directly proportional relationship

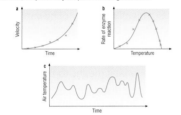

Figure 3 a Graph showing predictable results **b** Graph showing complex results **c** Graph showing very complex results

Drawing conclusions

If there is a pattern to be seen (for example, as one variable gets bigger the other also gets bigger), it may be that:

- changing one has caused the other to change
- the two are related, but one is not necessarily the cause of the other.

Your conclusion must go no further than the evidence that you have.

Activity

Looking at relationships

Some people think that watching too much television can cause an increase in violence.

The table shows the number of television sets in the UK for four different years, and the number of murders committed in those years.

Year	Number of televisions (millions)	Number of murders
1970	15	310
1980	25	500
1990	42	550
2000	60	750

Plot a graph to show the relationship. Do you think this proves that watching television causes violence? Explain your answer.

Poor science can often happen if a wrong decision is made here. Newspapers have said that living near electricity substations can cause cancer. All that scientists would say is that there is possibly an association.

Evaluation

You will often be asked to evaluate either the method of the investigation or the conclusion that has been reached. Ask yourself: Could the method have been improved? Is the conclusion that has been made a valid one?

Summary questions

1 Copy and complete the paragraph using the words below:

anomalous   complex   directly   negative   positive

Lines of best fit can be used to identify .... results. Linear relationships can be .... or .... If a straight line goes through the origin of a graph then the relationship is .... proportional. Often a line of best fit is a curve which can be predictable or ....

2 Nasma knew about the possible link between cancer and living near to electricity substations. She found a quote from a National Grid Company survey of substations:

Measurements of the magnetic field were taken at 0.5 metre above ground level within 1 metre of fences and revealed 1.9 microteslas. After 5 metres this dropped to the normal levels measured in any house.

Discuss the type of experiment and the data you would expect to see to support a conclusion that it is safe to build houses over 5 metres from an electricity substation.

AQA Examiner's tip

When you read scientific claims, think carefully about the evidence that should be there to back up the claim.

Key points

- Drawing lines of best fit help us to study the relationship between variables.
- The possible relationships are linear, positive and negative, directly proportional, predictable and complex curves.
- Conclusions must go no further than the data available.
- The repeatability and reproducibility of data can be checked by looking at other similar work done by others, perhaps on the internet. It can also be checked by using a different method or by others checking your method.

Answers to in-text questions

a Graph **i** – positive linear.

Graph **ii** – negative linear.

Summary answers

1 anomalous, positive, negative, directly, complex

2 Survey of substations – measure magnetic field drop – measure 'microteslas' – at different distances from sub-station – also in houses well away from substations – repeat all readings several times – fieldwork – check accuracy of measuring instruments.

H9

Scientific evidence and society

Learning objectives

Students should learn:

- that science must be presented in a way that takes into account the reproducibility and the validity of the evidence
- that science should be presented without bias from the experimenter
- that evidence must be checked to appreciate whether there is any political influence
- that the status of experimenter can influence the weight attached to a scientific report.

Learning outcomes

Students should be able to:

- make judgements about the reproducibility and the validity of scientific evidence
- identify when scientific evidence might have been influenced by bias or political influence
- judge scientific evidence on its merits, taking into account the weight given to it by the status of the experimenter.

Support

- Groups could prepare posters that use scientific data to present their case for or against any of the developments discussed.

Extend

- Arrange a class debate and nominate individuals to speak for or against any of the developments discussed.

AQA Specification link-up: Controlled Assessment SA4.5

Distinguish between a fact and an opinion, by:

- recognising that an opinion might be influenced by factors other than scientific fact [SA4.5.1 a)]
- identifying scientific evidence that supports an opinion. [SA4.5.1 b)]

Lesson structure

Starters

Ask a scientist – It is necessary at this point to make a seamless join between work that has mostly been derived from student investigations to work generated by scientists. Students must be able to use their critical skills derived in familiar contexts and apply them to second-hand data. One way to achieve this would be to bring in newspaper cuttings on a topic of current scientific interest. They should be aware that some newspaper reporters will 'cherry-pick' sections of reports to support sensational claims that will make good headlines. Students could be supported by highlighting key words in the article. To extend students ask them to produce a 'wish-list' of questions they would like to put to the scientists who conducted the research and to the newspaper reporter. *(5 minutes)*

Researching scientific evidence – With access to the internet, students could be given a topic to research. They should use a search engine and identify the sources of information from, for example, the first six web pages. They could then discuss the relative merits of these sources in terms of potential for bias. *(10 minutes)*

Main

- The following points are best made using topics that are of immediate importance to your students. The examples used are only illustrative. Some forward planning is required to ensure that there is a plentiful supply of newspaper articles, both local and national, to support the lesson. These could be displayed and/or retained in a portfolio for reference.

- Working in pairs, students should answer in-text question **a**. They should write a few sentences about the headline and what it means to them.

- It might be possible to expand on this discussion using secondary sources to find out what is unsafe about X-rays. It should lead to a balanced discussion of the possible benefits and hazards of having an X-ray.

- Use the next section to illustrate the possibility of bias in reporting science. Again use small group discussions followed by whole class plenary.

- If you have access to the internet for the whole class, then it is worth pursuing the issue of mobile phone masts in relation to their political significance. Pose the questions: 'What would happen to the economy of this country if it was discovered that mobile phone masts were dangerous?' 'Would different people come together to suppress that information? Should they be allowed to suppress scientific evidence?' Stress that there is no such evidence, yet people have that fear. Ask: 'Why do they have that fear? Should scientists have the task of reducing that fear to proper proportions?' There is much to discuss.

- Small groups can imagine that they are preparing a case against the siting of a cement works close to their village. They could be given data that relate to pollution levels from similar companies. Up-to-date data can be obtained from the internet, e.g. from the DEFRA website (www.defra.gov.uk). Students could be given the data as if they were information provided at a public enquiry for the cement works. They should be asked to prepare a case that questions, e.g., the reproducibility and the validity of the data. This links with work covered in C1 2.5 on limestone.

Plenaries

Contentious issues – Make a list of contentious issues to which scientists might be able to make a contribution to the debate. Examples might include the siting of wind farms or sewage works, the building of new motorways, the introduction of new drugs, etc. *(5 minutes)*

Group report – Groups should report their findings on the cement works case to the class. Support students by allowing them to present their findings by posters. Extend students by asking individuals to give a one-minute talk to the rest of the class. *(10 minutes)*

Further teaching suggestions

Role play
- Students could role-play a public enquiry. They could be given roles and asked to prepare a case for homework. The data should be available to them so that they all know the arguments before preparing their case. Possible link here with the English department. This activity could be allocated as a homework exercise.

Local visit
- Students might be able to attend a local public enquiry or even the local town council as it discusses local issues with a scientific context or consider the report of a local issue.

The limitations of science
Examples could be given of the following issues:
- We are still finding out about things and developing our scientific knowledge (e.g. the use of the Large Hadron Collider).
- There are some questions that we cannot yet answer, maybe because we do not have enough valid evidence (e.g. are mobile phones completely safe to use?).
- There are some questions that science cannot answer at all (e.g. Why was the universe created?).

How Science Works

H9 Scientific evidence and society

Scientific evidence and society

Learning objectives
- How can science encourage people to trust its research?
- How might bias affect people's judgement of science?
- Can politics influence judgements about science?
- Do you have to be a professor to be believed?

Now you have reached a conclusion about a piece of scientific research. So what is next? If it is pure research then your fellow scientists will want to look at it very carefully. If it affects the lives of ordinary people then society will also want to examine it closely.

You can help your cause by giving a balanced account of what you have found out. It is much the same as any argument you might have. If you make ridiculous claims then nobody will believe anything you have to say.

Be open and honest. If you only tell part of the story then someone will want to know why! Equally, if somebody is only telling you part of the truth, you cannot be confident with anything they say.

a 'X-rays are safe, but should be limited' is the headline in an American newspaper. What information is missing? Is it important?

You must be on the lookout for people who might be biased when representing scientific evidence. Some scientists are paid by companies to do research. When you are told that a certain product is harmless, just check out who is telling you.

b Suppose you wanted to know about safe levels of noise at work. Would you ask the scientist who helped to develop the machinery or a scientist working in the local university? What questions would you ask, so that you could make a valid judgement?

?? Did you know ...?
A scientist who rejected the idea of a causal link between smoking and lung cancer was later found to be being paid by a tobacco company.

AQA Examiner's tip
If you are asked about bias in scientific evidence, there are two types:
- The measuring instruments may have introduced a bias because they were not calibrated correctly.
- The scientists themselves may have a biased opinion (e.g. if they are paid by a company to promote their product).

We also have to be very careful in reaching judgements according to who is presenting scientific evidence to us. For example, if the evidence might provoke public or political problems, then it might be played down.

Equally others might want to exaggerate the findings. They might make more of the results than the evidence suggests. Take as an example the siting of mobile phone masts. Local people may well present the same data in a totally different way from those with a wider view of the need for mobile phones.

c Check out some websites on mobile phone masts. Get the opinions of people who think they are dangerous and those who believe they are safe. Try to identify any political bias there might be in their opinions.

Science can often lead to the development of new materials or techniques. Sometimes these cause a problem for society where hard choices have to be made.

Scientists can give us the answers to many questions, but not to every question. Scientists have a contribution to make to a debate, but so do others like environmentalists, economists, and politicians.

The limitations of science
Science can help us in many ways but it cannot supply all the answers. We are still finding out about things and developing our scientific knowledge. For example, the Hubble telescope has helped us to revise our ideas about the beginnings of the universe.

There are some questions that we cannot answer, maybe because we do not have enough reproducible, repeatable and valid evidence. For example, research into the causes of cancer still needs much work to be done to provide data.

There are some questions that science cannot answer at all. These tend to be questions where beliefs, opinions and ethics are important. For example, science can suggest what the universe was like when it was first formed, but cannot answer the question of why it was formed.

Figure 1 The Hubble space telescope can look deep into space and tell us things about the Universe's beginning from the formations of early galaxies

BIODIESEL
The Fuel of the Future?
The demand for palm oil has grown tremendously in the last few years. It is used in many food products like margarine and chocolate, in cosmetics, and increasingly for making biodiesel.

Some scientists say that it is the answer to the dwindling supplies of crude oil because palm oil is a renewable resource.

Other people say that planting millions of acres of palm trees is destroying natural habitats such as rainforests and peat bogs.

Summary questions
1 Copy and complete the paragraph using the words below:
   status   balanced   bias   political
   Evidence from scientific investigations should be given in a .... way. It must be checked for any .... from the experimenter. Evidence can be given too little or too much weight if it is of............ significance. The .... of the experimenter is likely to influence people in their judgement of the evidence.

2 Collect some newspaper articles to show how scientific evidence is used. Discuss in groups whether these articles are honest and fair representations of the science. Consider whether they carry any bias.

3 Extract from a newspaper report about Sizewell nuclear power station:
   A radioactive leak can have devastating results but one small pill could protect you. Our reporter reveals how for the first time these life-saving pills will be available to families living close to the Sizewell nuclear power station.
   Suppose you were living near Sizewell power station. Who would you trust to tell you whether these pills would protect you from radiation?

Key points
- Scientific evidence must be presented in a balanced way that points out clearly how valid the evidence is.
- The evidence must not contain any bias from the experimenter.
- The evidence must be checked to appreciate whether there has been any political influence.
- The status of the experimenter can influence the weight placed on the evidence.

Answers to in-text questions

a E.g. what level of X-rays is safe?; if they are safe why should they be limited?; what is meant by limited?; who did the research?

b Scientists in the local university; e.g. did she repeat her tests?; did she get someone else to repeat them?; what instruments were used?; what was the sensitivity of the instruments?; how were the readings of noise level taken?

c Identification of any political bias, this could be from companies and individuals as well as governments.

Summary answers

1 balanced, bias, political, status

2 Identification of any bias in reports.

3 The person should be independent, have the necessary skills as a scientist and not be capable of being influenced politically.

H10

The ISA

Learning objectives

Students should learn:
- how to write a plan
- how to make a risk assessment
- how to make a hypothesis
- how to make a conclusion.

Learning outcomes

Students should be able to:
- structure a plan for an investigation so as to include key points such as the range and interval of the independent variable
- identify potential hazards in practical work
- show how the results of an experiment can confirm or deny a hypothesis
- reach a valid conclusion from the results of an investigation.

AQA Specification link-up: Controlled Assessment SA4.5

Distinguish between a fact and an opinion, by:
- recognising that an opinion might be influenced by factors other than scientific fact [SA4.5.1 a)]
- identifying scientific evidence that supports an opinion. [SA4.5.1 b)]

Lesson structure

Starters

Structure of an investigation – Use an interactive whiteboard or sticky labels that show the different stages of an investigation and ask students to arrange them in the correct order. *(5 minutes)*

Predictions and hypotheses – Make a table containing one column of hypotheses and another column of predictions. Students should match the prediction to the correct hypothesis. *(10 minutes)*

Main

These activities may be spread over more than one lesson.
- Use a specimen ISA to guide students through the different stages that will be required.
- Start by outlining the problem that is to be investigated. Give the students a hypothesis and have a discussion as to the best way to test it.
- Research two possible methods that can be used to carry out an experiment to test the hypothesis.
- Review any possible hazards. Discuss how any risk associated with these hazards could be reduced.
- Discuss the control variables that should be kept constant in order to make it a fair test.
- Students should decide the range and interval of the values of the independent variable, and whether or not repeats will be needed.
- Allow the students to carry out a rough trial with the equipment in order to establish suitable values for these.
- Students should now be able to write a structured plan for the investigation.
- Ask students to design a blank table ready for the results. This should contain space to record all the measurements that will be taken during the experiment. Stress the need to include proper headings and units.
- Students carry out the investigation, recording their results.
- Draw a chart or graph of the results.
- Analyse the results and discuss any conclusion that could be reached. Make sure students refer back to the hypothesis when making their conclusion.

Plenaries

Graph or bar chart – Give students a list of titles of different investigations and ask them to decide whether the results should be plotted on a bar chart or on a line graph. *(5 minutes)*

Comparing results – Groups should report their findings to others and compare results. Support students by making a table of pooled results. Extend students by asking individuals to give a one-minute talk to the rest of the class explaining why they think their results are or are not repeatable and reproducible. *(10 minutes)*

Support

- Groups could prepare posters that show a flow diagram for the different stages of an ISA investigation.
- Students can be provided with a plan if their plan is unworkable, unsafe or unmanageable. An example plan will be provided by the AQA. Students should not lose any marks if their plan is unworkable for a good reason (i.e. lack of equipment), however, if their plan is dangerous or unworkable this must be reflected in their mark.

Extend

- Give students a hypothesis and ask them to make a prediction based on it.

Further teaching suggestions

Writing a plan

● Give students a plan of an investigation that contains a number of errors, e.g. control variables not kept constant or unsuitable range or interval of the independent variable and ask them to spot and explain the mistakes.

How Science Works

H10   The ISA

Learning objectives

● How do you write a plan?
● How do you make a risk assessment?
● What is a hypothesis?
● How do you make a conclusion?

There are several different stages to the ISA (Investigate Skills Assignment) that you will complete for your Controlled Assessment. This will make up 25% of your GCSE marks.

Stage 1

Your teacher will tell you the problem that you are going to investigate, and will give you a hypothesis. They will also set the problem in a context – in other words, where in real life your investigation could be useful. You should have a discussion about it, and talk about different ways that you might solve the problem. Your teacher should show you the equipment that you can use, and you should research one or two possible methods for carrying out an experiment to test the hypothesis. You should also research the context and do a risk assessment for your practical work. You will be allowed to make one side of notes on this research, which you can take into the written part of the ISA.

You should be allowed to handle the equipment and you may be allowed to carry out a preliminary experiment.

Make sure that you understand what you have to do – now is the time to ask questions if you are not sure.

Figure 1 Doing practical work allows you to develop the skills needed to do well in the ISA

  Examiner's tip

When you are making a blank table or drawing a graph or bar chart, make sure that you use full headings, e.g.

● 'the length of the leaf', **not** just 'length'
● 'the time taken for the reaction', **not** just 'time'
● 'the height from which the ball was dropped', **not** just 'height'
● and don't forget to include any units.

How Science Works

Section 1 of the ISA

At the end of this stage, you will answer Section 1 of the ISA. Among other things you will need to:

● identify one or more variables that you need to control
● describe how you would carry out the main experiment
● identify possible hazards and say what you would do to reduce any risk
● make a blank table ready for your results.

a What features should you include in your written plan?
b What should you include in your blank table?

Stage 2

This is where you carry out the experiment and get some results. Don't worry too much about spending a long time getting fantastically accurate results – it is more important to get some results that you can analyse. You will have to draw a graph or a bar chart.

c How do you decide whether you should draw a bar chart or a line graph?

Stage 3

This is where you answer Section 2 of the ISA. Section 2 of the ISA is all about your own results, so make sure that you look at your table and graph when you are answering this section. To get the best marks you will need to quote some data from your results.

How Science Works

Section 2 of the ISA

In this section you will need to:

● say what you were trying to find out
● analyse data that is given in the paper. This data will be in the same topic area as your investigation
● use ideas from your own investigation to answer questions about this data
● write a conclusion
● compare your conclusion with the hypothesis you have tested.

Summary questions

1 Copy and complete the sentences using the words below:
independent   dependent   control
When writing a plan, you need to state the variable that you are deliberately going to change, called the .... variable. You also need to say what you expect will change because of this; this is called the .... variable. You must also say what .... variables you will keep the same in order to make it a fair test.

AQA Examiner's tip

When you are comparing your conclusion with the hypothesis, make sure that you also talk about the **extent** to which your results support the hypothesis.

Which of these answers do you think would score the most marks?

● My results support the hypothesis.
● In my results, as *x* got bigger, *y* got bigger, the same as stated in the hypothesis.
● In my results, as *x* got bigger, *y* got bigger, the same as stated in the hypothesis, but unlike the hypothesis, *y* stopped increasing after a while.

Key points

● When you are writing the plan make sure that you include details about:
  – the range and interval of the independent variable
  – the control variables
  – the number of repeats.
● Try to put down at least two possible hazards, and say how you are going to minimise the risk from them.
● Look carefully at the hypothesis that you are given – this should give you a good clue about how to do the experiment.
● Always refer back to the hypothesis when you are writing your conclusion.

Answers to in-text questions

a Control variables, interval and range of the independent variable. Identify possible hazards and how to reduce any risk.

b Columns for quantities that are going to be measured, including complete headings and units.

c A bar chart if one of the variables is categoric, a line graph if both variables are continuous.

Summary answers

1 independent, dependent, control

Summary answers

1 a Could be some differences which would be fine, e.g. hypothesis; prediction; design; safety; controls; method; table; results; repeat; graph; conclusion; improve.

2 a Scientific opinion is based on reproducible and valid evidence, a prejudiced opinion might not be.

   b Continuous variable, because it is more powerful than an ordered or a categoric variable.

3 a A hypothesis is an idea that fits an observation and the scientific knowledge that is available. With the knowledge that sulfur dioxide in the air forms an acid, you can make a hypothesis and then a prediction.

   b Increasing the concentration of acid will increase the rate of attack.

   c Doing the rate of reaction marble chip and sulfuric acid experiment.

   d Run a survey (not suitable for this prediction).

4 a When all variables but the one being used as the independent variable are kept constant.

   b It would tell you what range of dilution to use; whether the technique used to measure pH was sensitive enough; whether repeat readings were necessary.

   c By repeating tests for each given dilution and seeing how closely grouped the results are.

   d The calculations would give you the true values so you could check your mean pH values against these to determine accuracy.

5 Was the clock started correctly? Was it stopped correctly? Was the oil measured out accurately? Was it put onto the correct spot? Was there a clear line at the bottom? Was the tile thoroughly washed and dried?

6 a Take the highest and the lowest.

   b The sum of all the readings divided by the number of readings.

   c When you have an ordered or categoric independent variable and a continuous dependent variable.

   d When you have a continuous independent variable and a continuous dependent variable.

7 a Examine to see if it is an error, if so, repeat it. If identified from the graph, it should be ignored.

   b Identify a pattern.

   c That it does not go further than the data, the reproducibility and the validity allow.

   d By carrying out the test again using the same method.

8 a The science is more likely to be accepted.

   b They are influenced by other factors, political bias, they are not impartial, or they are being funded by a party that have an agenda other than pure data collection and analysis.

9 a For many scientific developments there is a practical outcome which can be used – a technological development. Many technological developments allow further progress in science.

   b Society – all of us should have an opinion.

10 a Increasing the height of the turbine blades would increase the power output.

   b Height of the turbine blades.

   c Power output.

   d 32–85 m

   e Use the same turbine / in the same location / in the same weather condition.

Summary questions

1 a Put these words into order. They should be in the order that you might use them in an investigation.
design, prediction, conclusion, method, repeat, controls, graph, results, table, improve, safety, hypothesis

2 a How would you tell the difference between an opinion that was scientific and a biased or prejudiced opinion?

   b Suppose you were investigating the amount of gas produced in a reaction. Would you choose to investigate a categoric or a continuous variable? Explain why.

3 You might have seen that marble statues weather badly where there is air pollution. You want to find out why.

   a You know that sulfur dioxide in the air forms an acid. How could this knowledge help you to develop a hypothesis about the effect of sulfur dioxide on marble statues?

   b Develop a hypothesis about the effect of sulfur dioxide on marble statues.

   c What experiment could you do to test your hypothesis?

   d Suppose you are not able to carry out an experiment. How else could you test your hypothesis?

4 a What do you understand by a 'fair test'?

   b Suppose you were carrying out an investigation into what effect diluting acid had on its pH. You would need to carry out a trial. Describe what a trial would tell you about how to plan your method.

c How could you decide if your results were repe...

d It is possible to calculate the effect of dilution o... pH of an acid. How could you use this to check... accuracy of your results?

5 Suppose you were watching a friend carry out an investigation using the equipment shown on page... You have to mark your friend on how accurately he... making his measurements. Make a list of points th... would be looking for.

6 a How do you decide on the range of a set of dat...

   b How do you calculate the mean?

   c When should you use a bar chart?

   d When should you use a line graph?

7 a What should happen to anomalous results?

   b What does a line of best fit allow you to do?

   c When making a conclusion, what must you take... consideration?

   d How can you check on the repeatability and reproducibility of your results?

8 a Why is it important when reporting science to 'tell the truth, the whole truth and nothing but the truth'?

   b Why might some people be tempted not to be completely fair when reporting their opinions on scientific data?

9 a 'Science can advance technology and technolo... advance science.' What do you think is meant b... statement?

   b Who answers the questions that start with 'Sho... we .... '?

---

   f Ensured that the weather conditions did not alter as the investigation continued or bring several test rigs and use them all at the same time.

   g 139 kW is significantly lower than 162 kW and so could be considered an anomaly produced by random error.

   h Yes, there is a difference between all of the readings that is greater than the difference in the repeated readings (anomaly excepted).

   i Correct labelling; correct units; correct plotting; reasonable axes; height on *x*-axis, power output on *y*-axis.

   j Line of best fit that ignores the anomaly.

   k Positive linear relationship between the height of the wind turbine and the power generated. (Note if they think it is a curve they have probably plotted the 85 m reading as 90 m.)

   l Increasing the height has increased the power output. However, this was only in the weather conditions at that time, and there was some doubt over the 32 m reading, which should have been repeated.

   m E.g. the actual power output is small compared to the visual amenity lost. That the electricity company will want to build them as tall as they possibly can. That the increase in power output is greatest at 32 m so they could be smaller.

   n An independent expert.

d turbines are an increasingly popular way of
erating electricity. It is very important that they
sited in the best place to maximise energy output.
arly they need to be where there is plenty of wind.
rgy companies have to be confident that they get
ue for money. Therefore they must consider the most
nomic height to build them. Put them too high and
y might not get enough extra energy to justify the
a cost of the turbine. Before deciding finally on a site
y will carry out an investigation to decide the best
ght.

prediction is that increasing the height will increase
power output of the wind turbine. A test platform
s erected and the turbine placed on it. The lowest
ght that would allow the turbines to move was 32 m.
e correct weather conditions were waited for and
turbine began turning and the power output was
asured in kilowatts.

results are in the table.

eight of turbine (m)	Power output Test 1 (kW)	Power output Test 2 (kW)
32	162	139
40	192	195
50	223	219
60	248	245
70	278	270
80	302	304
85	315	312

a What was the prediction for this test?

b What was the independent variable?

c What was the dependent variable?

d What is the range of the heights for the turbine?

e Suggest a control variable that should have been used.

f This is a fieldwork investigation. Is it possible to control all of the variables? If not, say what you think the scientist should have done to produce more accurate results.

g Is there any evidence for an anomalous result in this investigation? Explain your answer.

h Was the resolution of the power output measurement satisfactory? Provide some evidence for your answer from the data in the table.

i Draw a graph of the results for the second test.

j Draw a line of best fit.

k Describe the pattern in these results.

l What conclusion can you make?

m How might these data be of use to people who might want to stop a wind farm being built?

n Who should carry out these tests for those who might object to a wind farm being built?

AQA Examiner's comments

Changes to How Science Works

Although HSW has remained largely unchanged, there have been some additions in this specification, particularly with regard to the Controlled Assessment Unit (ISA).

These include:

- a requirement for candidates to identify potential hazards and devise a plan to minimise risk
- understand the term 'hypothesis'
- test and/or make a prediction
- write a plan for an investigation, having been shown the basic technique to be used.

Candidates should be able to decide upon issues such as the range and interval of the independent variable, the control variables and the number of repeats.

B1 1.1

Diet and exercise

Learning objectives

Students should learn:

- that a healthy diet contains the right balance of the different foods you need and provides the right amount of energy
- that the metabolic rate is the rate at which the chemical reactions in the body are carried out
- that the less exercise you take, the less food you need; people who exercise regularly are usually fitter than those who take little exercise.

Learning outcomes

Most students should be able to:

- describe the constituents of a healthy diet
- define metabolic rate and explain how it can vary according to the amount of activity carried out and the proportion of muscle to fat in the body
- describe the relationships between food intake, exercise and fitness.

Some students should also be able to:

- explain all the interactions between food intake, exercise, fitness, metabolic rate, gender, genetic factors, etc., which affect body mass.

AQA Examiner's tip

Students need to be able to define metabolic rate. They often confuse it with breathing and heart rate.

Support

- Demonstrate how foods can contain the same amount of energy but have different masses. Choose three different foods, each with the same energy content but very different masses. Have the samples hidden and get the students to pick a substance, and then show how much of it would contain the specific amount of energy.

Extend

- Ask students to think of ways we could manufacture artificial extra-high energy foods in the future.

AQA Specification link-up: Biology B1.1

- A healthy diet contains the right balance of the different foods … *[B1.1.1 a)]*
- The rate at which all the chemical reactions in the cells … *[B1.1.1 c)]*
- Evaluate information about the effects of food on health. *[B1.1]*

Controlled Assessment: SA4.3 Collect primary and secondary data *[SA4.3.2 a) b) c)]* and *[SA4.3.3 a) b) c)]*; SA4.5 Analyse and interpret primary and secondary data. *[SA4.5.2 a) b) c) d)]*

Lesson structure

Starters

Do you have a healthy diet? – Ask each student to write out what they ate the previous day. Then assign the items to the correct food groups. Compare with the other students in small groups. Which food groups were eaten? Were any missing? Students could be supported by giving them the names of the seven food groups. Extend students by asking them to comment on whether their diet fulfilled the recommendations for a healthy diet. *(5 minutes)*

Sorting out food groups – Prepare six A4 sheets, each with the name of a major food group written in large letters on it and make a separate list of foods of all types. Give one A4 sheet to each of the first six students who come in through the door. As the other students enter, assign them a food from your list ('you are a tomato', 'you are a pint of milk,' etc.), making sure you have all food types covered. Ask the students to move to the food group that they feel they belong to, adding that they may well be able to fit into two groups. Go through a group at a time finding out which food groups are where and discussing any anomalies. *(10 minutes)*

Main

- **Measuring energy in foods** – This practical is based on a burning food experiment. It provides plenty of scope for the introduction of concepts covered in How science works. The accuracy of the measurements, the quantities of food used, the control of variables and evaluation of the results can all be discussed.

- **The 'How much energy do I use when …?'** Practical is based on the fact that 10 J of energy is required to raise a 1 kg mass a distance of 1 m. Ask students to raise a 100 g mass up into the air for 1 m and then tell them they have done 1 J of work. You can vary this with different masses depending on availability.

Plenaries

Matching diets to people – Write 'Energy intake (in kJ)' down on one side of the board, and different occupations, genders and ages down the other side. Students are asked to match the energy intake with age, gender and occupation. Students could be supported by using occupations and gender only. Students could be extended by including teenagers, a pregnant woman, a person training for a marathon, a senior citizen, etc. *(5 minutes)*

Role playing exercise – Ask students to take the roles of nutritional advisors and people with different energy needs, such as a pregnant woman, top athlete, body builder, etc. *(10 minutes)*

Answers to in-text questions

a For energy and to build new cells.

b Because a pregnant woman has to provide energy for a growing baby as well as herself.

c Athletes have a lot of muscle tissue and muscle tissue burns up a lot of energy.

Practical support

Measuring energy in food
Equipment and materials required
Each group will need: 25 cm³ measuring cylinder, boiling tubes/test tubes, mounted needles or 20 cm lengths of wire, a Bunsen burner, a test tube rack, a heatproof mat, a metal-jawed clamp, a thermometer, a range of foods cut into cubes or small pieces (exclude peanuts due to allergic reactions).

Details
A measured volume of cold water is put in each test tube and a thermometer used to record the initial temperature. A piece of food is chosen and placed on the end of a 20 cm length of wire, or a mounted needle, and ignited. As soon as it is alight, it is held as close as possible under the test tube of water. When it has finished burning, record the highest temperature reached in the water in the test tube. Suitable foods for testing are bite-sized shredded wheat, corn snacks such as 'Wotsits' and dry bread. If using sweets, beware of falling hot sugar, and fatty foods have a tendency to spit.

Students can work in groups or individually, and results pooled. It is advisable to avoid using nuts due to allergies.
Safety: See CLEAPSS Laboratory Handbook/CD-ROM section 9.4.2.

How much energy do I use when ...?
Equipment and materials required
A supply of weights ranging from 100 g to 1 kg would be useful, together with a metre rule. Access to a staircase, a measuring tape and scales to weigh the student volunteers are needed for the main experiment.

Details
This practical is based on the fact that 10 J of energy is required to raise a 1 kg mass a distance of 1 m. Ask students to raise a 100 g mass up into the air for 1 m and then tell them they have done 1 J of work. You can vary this with different masses depending on availability.

Safety: Care is needed with the handling of weights and when running up and down stairs. Do not encourage competition and be aware of student sensitivities.

B1 1.1 **Diet and exercise**

Learning objectives
- What does a healthy diet contain?
- Why can some people eat lots of food without getting fat?
- How does an athlete's diet differ from yours?

What makes a healthy diet? *k*
A balanced diet contains the correct amounts of:
- carbohydrates
- proteins
- fats
- vitamins
- minerals
- fibre
- water.

Your body uses carbohydrates, proteins and fats to release the energy you need to live and to build new cells. You need small amounts of vitamins and minerals for your body to work healthily. Without them you will suffer deficiency diseases. If you don't have a balanced diet then you will end up malnourished.

Figure 1 A balanced diet provides everything you need to survive, including plenty of energy

Fortunately, in countries like the UK, most of us take in all the minerals and vitamins we need from the food we eat. However, our diet can easily be unbalanced in terms of the amount of energy we take in. If we take in too much energy we put on weight. If we don't take in enough we become underweight.

It isn't always easy to get it right because different people need different amounts of energy. Even if you eat a lot, you can still lack vitamins and minerals if you don't eat the right food.

a Why do you need to eat food?

How much energy do you need?
The amount of energy you need to live depends on lots of different things. Some of these things you can change and some you can't.

Males need to take in more energy than a female of the same age – unless she is pregnant.

If you are a teenager, you will need more energy than if you are in your 70s.

b Why does a pregnant woman need more energy than a woman who isn't pregnant?

Your food supplies energy to your muscles as they work. So the amount of exercise you do affects the amount of energy you need. If you do very little exercise, then you don't need as much food. The more you exercise the more food you need to take in.

Figure 2 Athletes have a great deal of muscle tissue so they have to eat a lot of food to supply the energy they need

People who exercise regularly are usually much fitter than people who take little exercise. They make bigger muscles – up to 40% of their body mass. Muscle tissue transfers much more energy than fat. But exercise doesn't always mean time spent training or 'working out' in the gym. Walking to school, running around the house looking after small children or doing a physically active job all count as exercise too.

c Why do athletes need to eat more food than the average person?

The temperature where you live affects how much energy you need as well. In warmer countries you need to eat less food. This is because you use less energy keeping your body temperature at a steady level.

The metabolic rate
Think of a friend who is very similar in age, gender and size to you. Despite these similarities, you may need quite different amounts of energy in your diet. This is because the rate of chemical reactions in your cells (the metabolic rate) varies from person to person.

Men generally have a higher metabolic rate than women. The proportion of muscle to fat in your body affects your metabolic rate. Men often have a higher proportion of muscle to fat than women. You can change the proportion of muscle to fat in your body by exercising. This will build up more muscle.

Your metabolic rate is also affected by the amount of activity you do. Exercise increases your metabolic rate for a time even after you stop exercising.

Scientists think that your basic metabolic rate may be affected by genetic factors you inherit from your parents. This is an example of how inherited factors can affect our health.

Figure 3 If you work somewhere really cold your metabolic rate will go up to keep you warm. You will need lots of fat in your diet to supply the energy you need

Summary questions
1 What is 'a balanced diet'?
2 **a** Why do you need more energy in your diet when you are 18 than when you are 80?
   b Why does a top athlete need more energy in their diet than you do? Where does the energy in the diet come from?
3 **a** What is the 'metabolic rate'?
   b Explain why some people put on weight more easily than others.

Further teaching suggestions

Investigating fitness equipment
- Ask students to investigate the different types of fitness equipment available at their local gym, from articles in magazines or on the internet. Ask them to evaluate these against the exercise they get from PE periods in school and ordinary activities. Why do they think these machines have been devised and who benefits from them?

A sudden release of energy
- Carry out internet research on explosions in food factories.

Energy practical
- Extend the 'How much energy do I use when ...' practical by calculating the energy used/work done when carrying out activities such as climbing stairs or stepping up on to an object. The mass of the student should be measured and the height of the object or staircase determined. If several volunteers are used, the work done can be calculated and then this value can be used to work out the quantity of sugar they would need to eat to replace the energy. [100 g of sugar contains 1630 kJ of energy, so not much!]

Summary answers

1 A diet which contains the right amount of carbohydrates, proteins, fats, vitamins, minerals, fibre and water and the right amount of energy.

2 **a** Generally, teenagers use more energy than the very elderly because they are more active and to build new cells as they are still growing.

   b A top athlete probably has more muscle, which uses a lot of energy. The energy comes from proteins, fats and carbohydrates.

3 **a** The rate at which all the chemical reactions in the cells of the body are carried out.

   b Some people have a slower metabolic rate, some take less exercise, some eat more and do not use up all the energy they take in as food so they store the excess as fat.

B1 1.2

Weight problems

Learning objectives

Students should learn:

- that arthritis, diabetes, high blood pressure and heart disease are more common in overweight people than in thinner people
- exercise as part of a healthy lifestyle reduces the chance of developing serious health conditions.

Learning outcomes

Most students should be able to:

- describe the problems associated with excess food in the diet and how these may be overcome by modifying the diet
- describe how health problems can be reduced by regular exercise
- state some claims made by slimming programmes or products.

Some students should also be able to:

- evaluate, when supplied with relevant information, the claims made by different slimming programmes.

Support

- Students can be given a set of pictures and descriptions of fictitious characters and asked to match the characters with their correct BMI category.

Extend

- Speculate on societal factors that might correlate with body mass index. Students can look at the recommended exercise levels associated with various slimming regimes.
- The use of Wii Fit programs has increased. Students could discuss if they are a substitute for 'real' exercise?
- The 'comparison of foods' activity can be extended by making a more detailed comparison of the different types of fat (saturated and unsaturated), different types of carbohydrate, the use of different sweeteners, etc. It may also be of interest to consider some of these products in a diabetic diet.

AQA Specification link-up: Biology B1.1

- A healthy diet contains the right balance of the different foods ... *[B1.1.1 a)]*
- A person loses mass when the energy content of the food ... *[B1.1.1 b)]*
- People who exercise regularly are usually healthier than people who take little exercise. *[B1.1.1 e)]*
- Analyse and evaluate claims made by slimming programmes, and slimming products. *[B1.1]*

  Controlled Assessment: SA4.5 Analyse and interpret primary and secondary data. *[SA4.5.1 a) b)]*

Lesson structure

Starters

Punishment of luxury? – Imagine being invited to a fabulous party where there are unlimited quantities of excellent quality food. Ask students for all their favourites – they are all there, all free and in abundance! How will you know when you have had enough? What if the feast went on for weeks or months? Or a lifetime? How would you know when to stop? In pairs, discuss what makes people decide when they have had enough to eat. What advice would you give to someone at the big party? *(5 minutes)*

The food groups beetle game – This is a version of the traditional beetle game which can be used to recap the 'Diet and exercise' lesson. Students are supplied with an outline of a beetle with no legs but the letters C, P, F, V, M and Fi (C 5 carbohydrate, P 5 proteins, F 5 fats, V 5 vitamins, M 5 minerals, Fi 5 fibre) around the thorax. Call out names of different foods and ask the students to put them into the right group by labelling one of the 'legs' with the name of the food. To support students, give them images of food and restrict them to one food group per image. To extend students, try to use foods that fit into more than one group. The winning student is the one that completes their beetle first. *(10 minutes)*

Main

- Discuss with the students what is meant by the term 'obesity'. Distinguish between being overweight, moderately obese and clinically obese, introducing BMI values. Search the internet for 'obesity statistics' about various groups of people (different age groups, different ethnic groups, different countries). Students can discuss these statistics and consider the problems associated with the condition.
- A practical experiment on BMI can be suggested (optional – see 'Practical support').
- Remind students that some athletes with highly developed musculature have high BMIs and although very fit would fall into the obese category. This will encourage students to be aware of the limitations of formulae.
- This could lead into another practical investigation on 'Are "slimming", "low fat" or "diet" foods worth buying if you want to lose weight?' (see 'Practical support'). How Science Works concepts could be introduced here as this is a useful exercise in evaluation. Students should be encouraged to work out fat content per gram and energy content per gram, in order to make their investigation valid.

Plenaries

'What advice would you give Homer Simpson on how and why to lose weight?' – Search the internet for an image or cartoon clip of Homer Simpson, or Peter Griffin of *Family Guy*. Use either as a stimulus and award a doughnut as a prize for the best advice! *(5 minutes)*

The science behind the slimming diet – Compare different slimming programmes/ techniques, e.g. WeightWatchers, Atkins diet, glycaemic index. Support students by asking them to suggest what each diet is based on (e.g. GI is carbohydrate control, Atkins based on eating fat and protein, etc.). Students could be extended by being asked to explain/discuss and evaluate the scientific basis of each. *(10 minutes)*

Answers to in-text questions

a Arthritis, diabetes, high blood pressure, heart disease plus any other correct answers such as breathlessness.

b Reduce your food (energy) intake, increase your exercise (energy output) or both.

Practical support

Measurement of BMI

Equipment and materials required

Scales to measure mass in kilograms, measuring tapes to measure height in metres, or sheets of data for fictitious characters. The actual BMI formula is not difficult to use, but a BMI calculator can be found at www.bbc.co.uk. Search the internet for 'BMI calculators' to find graphs and normal ranges. There are also graphs for displaying the data and turning the BMI into a descriptor.

Details

Students can measure their own mass (kg) and height (m) and use the formula to calculate their own BMI.

Be aware that weight problems are widespread and this is a potentially sensitive topic. It might be wise to warn students in advance in order to prevent nasty comments. The actual activity should be optional.

Alternatively, a sheet of data for fictitious characters with heights and body masses could be supplied. If a set of fictitious characters is used, then you can ask the students to do the calculations and classify them into the correct categories. Those that come in the 'obese' and 'overweight' groups could then be recommended a slimming programme.

Are 'slimming', 'low fat' or 'diet' foods worth buying if you want to lose weight?

Equipment and materials required

A selection of foods – different brands of yogurt or cereal bars – make sure they have the information on fat and energy content etc. Include both normal and 'low fat' or 'diet' varieties of similar products.

Details

A comparison of such foods with 'normal' brands can be made by checking their fat and energy content and other constituents from their labels. This would work quite well with different brands of yogurt or cereal bars. Things to remember are differences in size, differences in mass and differences in contents as well as differences in price. Students could be encouraged to suggest/bring in their own yogurt/cereal bar for a general class comparison.

Students should be encouraged to work out fat content per gram and energy content per gram, in order to make their investigation reliable. Remind students that they are not allowed to eat in the laboratory.

B1 1.2 — Weight problems

Learning objectives

- What health problems are linked to being overweight?
- Why is it unhealthy to be too thin?
- Why are people who do exercise usually healthier than those who do not?

Figure 1 In spite of some of the media hype, most people are not obese – but the amount of weight people carry varies a great deal!

Obesity

If you take in more energy than you use, the excess is stored as fat. You need some body fat to cushion your internal organs. Your fat also acts as an energy store for when you don't feel like eating. But if someone eats a lot more food than they need, this is a form of malnourishment. Over time they could become overweight or even obese.

Carrying too much weight is often inconvenient and uncomfortable. Obesity can also lead to serious health problems such as arthritis, type 2 diabetes (high blood sugar levels which are hard to control), high blood pressure and heart disease. Obese people are more likely to die at an earlier age than non-obese people.

a What health problems are linked to obesity?

Losing weight

Many people want to be thinner. This might be for their health or just to look better. You gain fat by taking in more energy than you need. You lose mass when the energy content of your food is less than the energy you use in your daily life. There are three main ways you can lose mass.

- You can reduce the amount of energy you take in by cutting back the amount of food you eat. In particular, you can cut down on energy-rich foods like biscuits, crisps and chips.
- You can increase the amount of energy you use by doing more exercise.
- The best way to lose weight is to do both – reduce your energy intake and exercise more!

Scientists talk about 'mass', but most people talk about losing weight. Many people find it easier to lose weight by attending slimming groups. At these weekly meetings they get lots of advice and support from other slimmers. All slimming programmes involve eating fewer energy-rich foods and/or taking more exercise.

Exercise can make you healthier by helping to control your weight. It increases the amount of energy used by your body and increases the proportion of muscle to fat. It can make your heart healthier too. However, you need to take care. If you suddenly start taking vigorous exercise, you can cause other health problems.

Fitness instructors can measure the proportion of your body that is made up of fat. They can advise on the right food to eat and the exercise you need to become thinner, fitter, or both.

Different slimming programmes approach weight loss in different ways. Many simply give advice on healthy living. They advise lots of fruit and vegetables, avoiding too much fat or too many calories and plenty of exercise. Some are more extreme and suggest that you cut out almost all of the fat or the carbohydrates from your diet.

b What must you do to lose weight?

Figure 2 Fitness instructors can help with improving health and fitness

How Science Works

You can find lots of slimming products in the supermarket. Used in the right way, they can help you to lose weight. Some people claim that 'slimming teas' or 'herbal pills' will enable you to eat what you like and still lose weight.

- What sort of evidence would you look for to decide which approaches to losing weight work best?

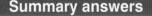

Figure 3 Slimming products can help you lose weight, but only if you control the total amount of energy you take in

Lack of food

In some parts of the world many people are underweight and malnourished because there is not enough food to eat. Civil wars, droughts and pests can all destroy local crops.

Deficiency diseases, due to lack of mineral ions and vitamins, are common in both children and adults when they never have enough food. Deficiency diseases can also occur if you do not have a balanced diet.

Did you know ...?

The number of obese and overweight people is growing. The WHO (World Health Organisation) says over 1 billion adults worldwide are now overweight or obese.

AQA Examiner's tip

The word 'malnourished' can be used to describe people who do not have a balanced diet. They may have too little food or too much food, or take in the wrong combination of foods.

Summary questions

1 Copy and complete using the words below:
energy   fat   less   more   obese
If you take in more _____ than you use, the excess is stored as _____ . If you eat too much over a long period of time, you will eventually become _____ . To lose weight you need to eat _____ and exercise _____ .

2 Why do people who are very thin, and some people who are obese, suffer from deficiency diseases?

3 One slimming programme controls your food intake. Another controls your food intake but also has an exercise programme. Which do you think would be the most effective? Explain your answer.

Key points

- If you take in more energy than you use, you will store the excess as fat.
- Obese people have more health problems than others.
- People who do not have enough to eat can develop serious health problems.
- Exercise helps reduce weight and maintain health.

Further teaching suggestions

Nutrition and dietary benefits

- Ask students how they could persuade their local doctor that they needed to employ a nutritionist or a dietician in their practice.

Weight discussion

- Start a discussion on role models and the pressure to be thin. Is the ideal body shape the same throughout the World? Some pictures of people of different shapes and sizes from around the world could help here. In order not to be sexist in a mixed school, include men and women, especially as men can suffer from weight problems as well.

Understanding obesity

- Write a letter of advice to a person who suffers from either obesity or anorexia, being supportive as well as helpful.

Summary answers

1 energy, fat, obese, less, more

2 People who are very thin do not take in enough food to get all the nutrients (vitamins, minerals, etc.) they need. Some people who are obese eat a lot of junk/fast food which is very low in minerals and vitamins, high in salt, fat, etc. So both can suffer from deficiency diseases.

3 The programme which combines controlled food intake and exercise. Taking in less energy and using up more energy will be most effective. It builds muscle which uses more energy.

B1 1.3   Inheritance, exercise and health

Learning objectives

Students should learn:

- that inherited factors, such as cholesterol level, can affect our health
- that there are two types of cholesterol
- that a diet high in saturated fats can upset the balance between good and bad forms of cholesterol in the blood and increase the risk of disease of the heart and blood vessels
- that people who exercise regularly are usually healthier than those who take little exercise.

Learning outcomes

Most students should be able to:

- explain what cholesterol is
- describe the effects of high levels of 'bad' cholesterol in the blood
- explain the benefits of regular exercise on health.

Some students should also be able to:

- evaluate information on the effects of exercise on our health
- explain the importance of the balance of the different types of cholesterol in the blood and how this is affected by diet.

Support

- Students could be given cards with the key words and their definitions and asked to match them correctly.
- Students could be given menus from different restaurants and asked to choose the healthy options, explaining their reasons.

Extend

- Students could research the structure of cholesterol and distinguish between 'good' and 'bad' cholesterol.
- Students could find out how much of different types of exercise may be needed to 'work off' items of fast food. For example, how much fast walking is needed for a blueberry muffin?

Specification link-up: Biology B1.1

- Inherited factors also affect our health; for example, cholesterol level. [B1.1.1 d)]
- People who exercise regularly are usually healthier than people who take little exercise. [B1.1.1 e)]
- Evaluate information about the effect of lifestyle on development of disease. [B1.1]
  Controlled Assessment: SA4.5 Analyse and interpret primary and secondary data. [SA4.5.4 b)]

Lesson structure

Starters

A diet of fast food for a month – Start a discussion of the film documentary *Super Size Me*, where a reporter, Morgan Spurlock, ate nothing but fast food for a month. *(5 minutes)*

Fast food as a way of life … – To support students you could bring in a fast food meal, such as pizza or burger and chips and show it to the class. Ask: 'What is in it? What problems might you get if you ate lots of these in the short term? What happens if it becomes a way of life (i.e. long term)?' To extend students, you could ask 'Why is fast food so popular?' Discuss and make a list of how and why eating habits have changed in the past 30 years. *(10 minutes)*

Main

- Practical on testing for fats in burger and chips or test any other fast foods, such as crisps, pizza, etc. The students could bring in some small samples of their own.
- An alternative to the emulsion test is to wipe pieces of fatty food on to greaseproof paper. A translucent mark is left if there is fat present. This might be quicker and less messy to do than the emulsion test if large numbers of food items are to be tested.
- As an extension, some 'low fat' alternatives, such as burgers made from Quorn, could be tested and compared with normal burgers. As these tests are not quantitative, only qualitative comparisons can be made.
- 'Good to eat Fred the Red' – This is an interactive food and nutrition programme to download from the Science Year CD website (www.sycd.co.uk), from Manchester United Football Club or on the Science Year CDs. If computers are available, the students can work through it themselves, or it can be projected, or accessed as homework.
- Look at the graph in the Student Book (Figure 3) to emphasise the effect of exercise on the risk of death and link with the benefits of exercise in keeping cholesterol levels low. This could lead to a discussion on different levels of exercise and the need to link diet and exercise in a healthy lifestyle. Students can draw conclusions from these data.

Plenaries

Explain the terms – Write or tack up key words from this topic on the board and pick/invite two students to come to the front and explain one each. They remove the word they have explained, if they are judged to have been successful in explaining it to the rest of the class. They can then choose the next pair and the key words to be explained. If stuck, a student can choose someone to help them. *(5 minutes)*

Why don't Inuits have high cholesterol levels? – Inuit tribesmen (show pictures) traditionally eat large amounts of fat in the form of seal and whale blubber. They do not have high average cholesterol readings. Support students by asking: 'Why might this be? What factors of their lifestyle, genetics and living conditions could account for this? Is it inherited?' Extend students by asking them to write down recommendations to an Inuit who is giving up the traditional lifestyle for a sedentary life. *(10 minutes)*

Practical support

Testing for fats in burger and chips

Equipment and materials required

Each group will need: a pestle and mortar, filter papers and filter funnels or greaseproof paper, test tubes and test tube rack, ethanol, fatty foods to test.

Details

Grind up portions of the foods to be tested with a little water in a pestle and mortar. Allow to settle, decant off some of the liquid and filter it into a small test tube. Add the filtrate to half a small test tube of ethanol and shake vigorously (caution with eyes and naked flames). If there is fat present, a creamy emulsion is obtained. Demonstrate what an emulsion looks like by shaking up some cooking oil in a gas jar three-quarters full of water (or, on a smaller scale in a test tube and then each group could do their own).

Safety: Wear eye protection and no naked flames. CLEAPSS Hazcard 40A Ethanol – highly flammable/harmful.

Keeping healthy

B1 1.3   Inheritance, exercise and health

Learning objectives

- How can inherited factors affect your health?
- Why does your cholesterol level matter?
- Does exercise make you healthier?

links

For information on metabolic rate, look back at B1 1.1 Diet and exercise.

Inheriting health

Inherited factors from your parents affect your appearance, such as the colour of your eyes. They also have a big effect on your health. They affect your metabolic rate, which affects how easily you lose and gain mass. Being overweight has a bad effect on your health. Inherited factors affect the proportion of muscle to fat in your body. They also affect your risk of heart disease, partly because they influence the levels of cholesterol in your blood.

Figure 1 Lots of things affect your health – your diet, how much exercise you take and what you inherit from your parents

Controlling cholesterol

The way your body balances cholesterol is an example of how an inherited factor can affect your health. You need cholesterol for your cell membranes and to make vital hormones. There are two forms of cholesterol carried around your body in your blood. One form is healthy but the other can cause health problems. If the balance of your cholesterol levels is wrong, your risk of getting heart disease increases.

a Why do you need cholesterol in your body?

The way your liver deals with the fat in your diet and makes the different types of cholesterol is inherited from your parents. For most people, eating a balanced diet means your liver can keep the balance of cholesterol right.

Eating lots of high-fat food means you are likely to have raised levels of harmful cholesterol and an increased risk of heart disease. But 1 in every 500 people inherit factors which mean they will have high levels of harmful cholesterol and an increased risk of heart disease whatever they eat. This is an example of how an inherited factor can affect your health.

Did you know ...?

The maximum healthy blood cholestrol is given as 6 mmol/l, 5 mmol/l and 4 mmol/l on different medical websites.

Scientists don't always agree!

Figure 2 Next time you eat a burger and fries, think about all the fat you are taking in. Will your body be able to deal with it, or are your blood cholesterol levels about to go up?

Exercise and health

Scientists have collected lots of evidence about exercise and health. It shows that people who exercise regularly are generally healthier than people who don't do much exercise. The graph in Figure 3 shows the results of an American study published in the journal *Circulation*. 6213 men were studied. The least active men were 4.5 times more likely to die early than the fittest, most active men.

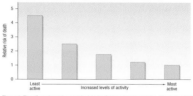

Figure 3 The effect of exercise on risk of death (Source: Jonathan Myers, *Circulation*, 2003)

These are some of the scientific explanations why exercise helps to keep you healthy.

- You are less likely to be overweight if you exercise regularly. This is partly because you will be using more energy.
- You will have more muscle tissue, which will increase your metabolic rate. If you can control your weight, you are less likely to be affected by problems such as arthritis, diabetes and high blood pressure.
- Your cholesterol levels are affected by exercise. Regular exercise lowers your blood cholesterol levels. It also helps the balance of the different types of cholesterol. When you exercise, your good cholesterol level goes up and the harmful cholesterol level goes down. This lowers your risk of heart disease and other health problems.

b How could you change your cholesterol levels?

Summary questions

1 Copy and complete using the words below:

heart metabolic inherited cholesterol balance

There are .... factors such as your .... rate that can affect your health. The way your liver makes .... is inherited and if the .... of cholesterol is wrong it can increase your risk of .... disease.

2 Why are people who exercise regularly usually healthier than people who take little exercise?

3 Using the data in Figure 3, which group of people do you think are most at risk of death? Why do you think this might be? What could they do to reduce the risk?

Key points

- Inherited factors affect our health. These include our metabolic rate and cholesterol level.
- People who exercise regularly are usually healthier than people who take little exercise.

28

29

Further teaching suggestions

Fat around the heart

- Search the internet for 'video heart surgery' to show the layers of fat around the heart.

Nutritional data on school meals

- Ask the school kitchen for nutritional data on the fat content of some sample school meals. This might need to be negotiated first! Alternatively, it could be useful to invite the person in charge of your school canteen in for a discussion about the nutritional guidelines they work to in producing school meals. Ask what they think about Jamie Oliver's suggestions for altering the school meals menus.

The structure of saturated and unsaturated fats

- Moly-models could be used to demonstrate the differences in the structure of saturated and unsaturated fats. Compare fats and oils from plant and animal sources and what they are used for.

Healthier fast food?

- Ask students to collect literature from fast-food restaurants explaining how they have made their food healthier and discuss whether this is true.

Answers to in-text questions

a To make the membranes of your body cells and maintain normal hormone production, e.g. your sex hormones.

b By exercising and reducing the amount of fat in your diet.

Summary answers

1 inherited, metabolic, cholesterol, balance, heart
2 They are less likely to be overweight and will have more muscle so will burn more energy. This controls their weight and means that they are less likely to get arthritis, diabetes and high blood pressure. It also reduces cholesterol levels which reduces the risk of heart disease.
3 People who are least active are most at risk of dying. Unfit people have the most health problems and so any careful improvement in activity levels will be of benefit and they will lose weight.

B1 1.4

Pathogens and disease

Learning objectives

Students should learn:

- what pathogens are
- how pathogens cause infectious diseases
- how Semmelweis tried to control the spread of infectious disease caused by microorganisms.

Learning outcomes

Most students should be able to:

- define the term 'pathogen'
- explain how pathogens cause disease
- describe the contribution made by Semmelweiss to the control of the spread of infection in hospitals.

Some students should also be able to:

- explain the process by which Semmelweiss came to his conclusions
- explain why Semmelweis' ideas were not immediately accepted.

Answers to in-text questions

a Pathogens/microorganisms/bacteria and viruses.

b Viruses are smaller than bacteria.

c Pathogens reproduce rapidly inside your body; they damage your cells; they produce toxins that make you feel ill. Your body reacts to pathogens and the damage they cause/toxins they make, which also makes you feel ill.

Support

- Use a 'pairs' cards activity with the key words from the spread which could be played like the game 'Fish', where a player holding one card of a group asks others if they have the matching cards. Players collect groups of cards that are linked.

Extend

- Students could research the life and times of Semmelweis. How did his work rank alongside the contributions made by Lister and Pasteur?
- Some Fungi and Protoctista are also pathogenic, causing diseases such as athlete's foot and ringworm (Fungi) and malaria (Protoctista); students could investigate how these diseases are spread. Are they infectious?

AQA Specification link-up: Biology B1.1

- Microorganisms that cause infectious disease are called pathogens. [B1.1.2 a)]
- Bacteria and viruses may reproduce rapidly inside the body and may produce poisons (toxins) that make us feel ill. Viruses damage the cells in which they reproduce. [B1.1.2 b)]
- Relate the contribution of Semmelweis in controlling infection to solving modern problems with the spread of infection in hospitals. [B1.1.2]
- Semmelweis recognised the importance of hand washing in the prevention of spreading some infectious diseases. By insisting that doctors washed their hands before examining patients, he greatly reduced the number of deaths from infectious diseases in his hospital. [B1.1.2 f)]

Controlled Assessment: SA4.1 Planning an investigation [SA4.1.1 b) c) d)]; SA4.3 Collect primary and secondary data. [SA4.3.3 b) c)]

Lesson structure

Starters

Bush tucker challenge – eat some bacteria! – Provide some small pieces of blue cheese, yogurt and 'helpful bacteria' culture drinks for the students to sample (under hygienic conditions in the food technology room and check for allergies). Alternatively, just allow students to inspect and smell the foods. Discuss the usefulness of bacteria, illustrating that not all bacteria are 'baddies'. (5 minutes)

Diseases we've had in our group – Give each small group of students a sheet of A3 paper and get them to write on the names of any diseases they have had. To support students, ask them to sort out which diseases were infectious and which were not. Which bench had the most? To extend students, ask 'What were they caused by? What medication, if any, did they take when they were ill?' [Note: some sensitivity is needed here about things students do not wish to discuss.] This could be extended to 'My family'. (10 minutes)

Main

- **Microorganisms and disease** – search image banks on the internet for 'bacteria and virus' and use them to show the differences between bacteria and viruses. There are some very good images of different bacteria and viruses (good electron microscope pictures available) and such a presentation could include references to size: what can be seen with the naked eye, with a microscope and with the electron microscope. Include some examples of other pathogenic microorganisms, such as fungi and protists.

- Experiment to show the benefits of washing hands (see 'Practical support'). Alternatively, this could be set up as a demonstration. Discuss the ideas of Semmelweis and why his recommendations were not immediately adopted by fellow doctors in hospitals. Discuss which aspects of 'How Science Works' can be applied to the work of Semmelweis.

- Experiment to demonstrate the presence of microorganisms in the air (see 'Practical support') – this experiment is similar to one carried out by Louis Pasteur. It can be done as a demonstration and set up a few days before the lesson. 'How Science Works' concepts can be introduced here. For example, the experiment illustrates the need for controls, replication of results for reliability and evaluation of the method used.

Plenaries

Do you know the key words? Wordsearch and crossword – To support students, give them a wordsearch using the key words in the spread. To extend students, ask the students to write definitions of the key words and use them as clues to construct a crossword. This could begin in the lesson and students could write more clues for homework. (5 minutes)

How can I make you understand? – Semmelweis was not the only person to struggle to get his ideas accepted. Discuss other examples, such as the theory of evolution or whether the Earth is round or flat, with students and get them to think about how people are persuaded to accept new theories. How do you convince other scientists? How do you convince the general public? Discuss how the acceptance of new theories has changed over time. (10 minutes)

Practical support

Was Semmelweis right?

Equipment and materials required
Sterile agar plates, adhesive tape, incubator at 25 °C.

Details
The benefits of washing hands can be demonstrated by touching the surface of a sterile agar plate with unwashed fingers, replacing the lid and securing the plate in the usual way. Wash hands thoroughly, dry them and then touch the surface of a similar sterile agar plate, replacing the lid and securing it as before. Label both plates. Incubate at 25 °C and observe what grows.

Safety: Sterile techniques should be used; agar plates should on no account be sealed all the way round the lid during incubation, incubated at a higher temperature or opened and should be disposed of safely following CLEAPSS advice. See CLEAPSS Handbook section 15.2.14.

Microorganisms in air demonstration

Equipment and materials required
Nutrient broth, three test tubes, distilled water, water bath, 250 cm³

glass beaker, tripod and gauze, Bunsen burner, heatproof mat, cotton wool, pressure cooker/autoclave, straight glass tube, S-shaped glass tube, test tube rack.

Details
Make up some nutrient broth in a test tube (using a broth tablet and 10 cm³ of distilled water). Boil the broth to sterilise it and then pour half of it into each of two test tubes. One test tube should then have a cotton wool plug through which a straight piece of glass tubing is inserted so that it does not reach the top of the liquid. The other test tube should also have a cotton wool plug, but the piece of glass tubing is longer, bent into an S-shape and inserted so that there is a straight piece going through the cotton wool and the S-shape arranged outside. Both test tubes should then be sterilised by heating them in a pressure cooker for 15 minutes and allowed to cool (or boiled in a water bath over a Bunsen burner for about a minute – care needed). Look at the tubes and their contents at intervals over the next few days. Ask: 'Which tube goes cloudy first? Why?' Discuss what is happening in both sets of apparatus.

Safety: Eye protection should be worn. Sterile techniques should be used; the contents of the tubes should be disposed of safely.

Keeping healthy

B1 1.4   Pathogens and disease

Learning objectives
- What are pathogens?
- How do pathogens cause disease?
- How did Ignaz Semmelweis change the way we look at disease?

Infectious diseases are found all over the world, in every country. Some diseases are fairly mild ones, such as the common cold and tonsillitis. Other diseases are known killers, such as tetanus, influenza and HIV/Aids.

An infectious disease is caused by a **microorganism** entering and attacking your body. People can pass these microorganisms from one person to another. This is what we mean by **infectious**.

Figure 1 Many bacteria are very useful but some, like these *E. coli*, can cause disease

Microorganisms which cause disease are called **pathogens**. Common pathogens are bacteria and viruses.

a What causes infectious diseases?

The differences between bacteria and viruses

Bacteria are single-celled living organisms that are much smaller than animal and plant cells.

Although some bacteria cause disease, many are harmless and some are really useful to us. We use them to make food like yoghurt and cheese, to treat sewage and to make medicines.

Viruses are even smaller than bacteria. They usually have regular shapes. Viruses cause diseases in every type of living organism from people to bacteria.

Figure 2 These tobacco mosaic viruses cause disease in plants

b How do viruses differ from bacteria?

How pathogens cause disease (k)

Once bacteria and viruses are inside your body they reproduce rapidly. This is how they make you ill. Bacteria simply split in two – they often produce toxins (poisons) which affect your body. Sometimes they directly damage your cells. Viruses take over the cells of your body as they reproduce, damaging and destroying the cells. They very rarely produce toxins.

Common disease symptoms are a high temperature, headaches and rashes. These are caused by the damage and toxins produced by the pathogens. The symptoms also appear as a result of the way your body responds to the damage and toxins.

You catch an infectious disease when you pick up a pathogen from someone else who is infected with the disease.

c How do pathogens make you feel ill?

∞ links
For more information on bacteria that are resistant to antibiotics, see B1 1.8 Changing pathogens.

🔬 How Science Works

The work of Ignaz Semmelweis
Ignaz Philipp Semmelweis was a doctor in the mid-1850s. At the time, many women in hospital died from childbed fever a few days after giving birth. However, no one knew what caused it.

Semmelweis noticed something about his medical students. They went straight from dissecting a dead body to delivering a baby without washing their hands. He wondered if they were carrying the cause of disease from the corpses to their patients.

Then another doctor cut himself while working on a body. He died from symptoms which were identical to childbed fever. Semmelweis was sure that the fever was caused by something that could be passed on – some kind of infectious agent.

He insisted that his medical students wash their hands before delivering babies. Immediately, fewer mothers died from the fever.

Getting his ideas accepted
Semmelweis talked to other doctors. He thought his evidence would prove to them that childbed fever was spread by doctors. But his ideas were mocked.

Many doctors thought that childbed fever was God's punishment to women. No one had ever seen bacteria or viruses. So it was hard to believe that disease was caused by something invisible passed from person to person. Doctors didn't like the idea that they might have been spreading disease. They were being told that their actions had killed patients instead of curing them.

In hospitals today, bacteria such as MRSA, which are resistant to antibiotics, are causing lots of problems. Getting doctors, nurses and visitors to wash their hands more often is part of the answer – just as it was in Semmelweis's time!

Summary questions
1 Copy and complete using the words below:
toxins viruses microorganisms reproduce pathogens damage symptoms bacteria
The _____ which cause infectious diseases are known as _____ . Once _____ and _____ get inside your body they _____ rapidly. They _____ your tissues and may produce _____ which cause the _____ of disease.

2 Give five examples of things we now know we can do to reduce the spread of pathogens to lower the risk of disease, e.g. hand-washing in hospitals.

3 Write a letter by Ignaz Semmelweis to a friend explaining how he formed his ideas and the struggle to get them accepted.

?? Did you know … ?

Semmelweis couldn't bear to think of the thousands of women who died because other doctors ignored his findings. By the 1860s he suffered a major breakdown and in 1865, aged only 47, he died – from an infection picked up from a patient during an operation.

Figure 3 Ignaz Semmelweis – his battle to get medical staff to wash their hands to prevent infections is still going on today

Key points
- Infectious diseases are caused by microorganisms called pathogens, such as bacteria and viruses.
- Bacteria and viruses reproduce rapidly inside your body. Bacteria can produce toxins which make you feel ill.
- Viruses damage your cells as they reproduce. This can also make you feel ill.
- Semmelweis recognised the importance of hand-washing in preventing the spread of infectious diseases in hospital.

Further teaching suggestions

Bacterial colonies
- Some sterile agar plates, which have previously been exposed to the air around the laboratory partially sealed, and incubated, can be fully sealed and examined for signs of bacterial colonies and compared with the results of the broth experiment.

The fate of microbes
- Watch a clip from *The Simpsons* episode 'Marge in chains' from the video 'Crime and Punishment', showing microbes getting into various characters and the immune system attacking them, followed by a discussion.

Biohazard warning symbol
- Introduce the biohazard warning symbol.

Summary answers

1 microorganisms, pathogens, viruses, bacteria, reproduce, damage, toxins, symptoms

2 Any sensible suggestions should be accepted, such as: wiping work surfaces, cleaning toilets, using tissues to blow nose, washing hands before handling food, etc.

3 Students should show in their letter the main points made in the relevant spread including an appreciation of why the new ideas met resistance.

B1 1.5 Defence mechanisms

Learning objectives

Students should learn:

- how pathogens get into the body and are spread from person to person
- that the body has different ways of preventing the entry of pathogens
- that white blood cells help to defend the body against pathogens that do gain entry.

Learning outcomes

Most students should be able to:

- explain the ways in which infectious diseases are spread
- describe the ways in which the body prevents the entry of pathogens
- describe the functions of the white blood cells within the body.

Some students should also be able to:

- explain in detail the role of the white blood cells.

Support

- Students could be provided with a series of pictures showing a bacterium being engulfed by a white blood cell and asked to put them in order.

Extend

- Students should be capable of extending the concept map, putting in further links and connections.

AQA Specification link-up: Biology B1.1

- The body has different ways of protecting itself against pathogens. [B1.1.2 c)]
- White blood cells help to defend against pathogens by:
  - ingesting pathogens
  - producing antibodies which destroy particular bacteria or viruses
  - producing antitoxins, which counteract the toxins released by the pathogens. [B1.1.2 d)]

Lesson structure

Starters

How does it get in? – Give the students a picture of four doors labelled 'Droplets', 'Direct contact', 'Food and drink' and 'Breaks in the skin' and a list of diseases underneath (flu, TB, impetigo, herpes, salmonellosis, Aids, hepatitis). Ask the students to join the disease with the way it enters the body, leaving undone any they do not know and completing these as the lesson proceeds. Check and discuss. (*5 minutes*)

Gaining entry – Show a picture of the human body and write up a list of the possible ways in which pathogens can get into the body. To support students give them red (not sure at all), green (entirely sure) and amber (partly sure) cards. Ask them to hold these up in response to questions about how certain organisms get into the body. Pick one student each time to explain their response. To extend students, use the same cards and questions but ask students to explain how the organisms are prevented from entering the body, i.e. what the defence strategy is. (*10 minutes*)

Main

The lesson suggestions here concentrate on students gaining an understanding of the ways in which the blood is involved in defending the body against pathogens. The activities vary in length; a shorter one could be paired with a longer one, e.g. show a video clip and play the dice game.

- Introduce a brief practical where students look at the two types of white blood cells (see 'Practical support').
- Search the internet for 'sneeze video' to show a clip of a sneeze in slow motion and/or video footage.
- Before the lesson, make a video to demonstrate clotting using a digital video camera. Show a finger being pricked with a sterile lancet, a drop of blood being forced out and then the tip of a needle being drawn through the blood until it starts to pick up threads of fibrin. These can very soon be drawn out from the blood. All materials used should be disposed of hygienically and safely. This should not be done during the lesson.
- Play a dice game in pairs. One student is allocated a bacterial disease. The student must state which way the disease is going to try to get into the body (the other student must check to see if this is appropriate). The first student must throw a six before entry can be gained. Once inside, they start to produce toxins, one for every point on the dice. They take turns with their opponent, who represents a defending white blood cell producing antitoxins. When the opponent throws the dice, the points represent antitoxins, which counteract the toxins produced by the bacterium. A running score should be kept until the white blood cell throws a six, which represents an antibody and kills the bacterium to win the game. If the running score of toxins reaches 10, the white cell dies and the bacterium wins.
- The game can be continued by playing against more partners. If, as a white cell, you have produced an antibody against a specific bacterium before, you can kill the bacterium with any even number, not just a six.

Plenaries

Fill in the missing concepts – Students to complete a preprepared concept map, which has the connections made and labelled already; they fill in the concepts. (*5 minutes*)

Overcrowded refugee camp – Pin up or project a picture of an overcrowded refugee camp. To support students, ask them to identify as many ways as they can in which the people shown are in danger from infectious diseases (e.g. lack of fresh water, contaminated food and drink, close proximity to people with diseases, raw sewage, etc.). Extend students by asking them to list the infectious diseases that could occur in such a situation and how they would spread in the crowded conditions. (*10 minutes*)

Practical support

Investigating white blood cells

Equipment and materials required

Microscopes and prepared slides of blood smears.

Details

Introduce students to the two types of white blood cells and their functions. Project images of these, including scanning electron microscope pictures. Set up microscopes and prepared slides of blood smears for students to look at. Get them to count the numbers of each type of white blood cell they can see in a field of view and compare with the numbers of red blood cells.

B1 1.5 Defence mechanisms

Learning objectives

- How does your body stop pathogens getting in?
- How do white blood cells protect us from disease?

There are a number of ways in which pathogens spread from one person to another. The more pathogens that get into your body, the more likely it is that you will get an infectious disease.

Figure 1 Droplets carrying millions of pathogens fly out of your mouth and nose at up to 100 miles an hour when you sneeze

Droplet infection: When you cough, sneeze or talk you expel tiny droplets full of pathogens from your breathing system. Other people breathe in the droplets, along with the pathogens they contain. So they pick up the infection, e.g. flu (influenza), tuberculosis or the common cold.

Direct contact: Some diseases are spread by direct contact of the skin, e.g. impetigo and some sexually transmitted diseases like genital herpes.

Contaminated food and drink: Eating raw or undercooked food, or drinking water containing sewage can spread disease, e.g. diarrhoea or salmonellosis. You get these by taking large numbers of microorganisms straight into your gut.

Through a break in your skin: Pathogens can enter your body through cuts, scratches and needle punctures, e.g. HIV/Aids or hepatitis.

When people live in crowded conditions, with no sewage treatment, infectious diseases can spread very rapidly.

a What are the four main ways in which infectious diseases are spread?

Preventing microbes getting into your body

Each day you come across millions of disease-causing microorganisms. Fortunately your body has several ways of stopping these pathogens getting inside.

Your skin covers your body and acts as a barrier. It prevents bacteria and viruses from reaching the tissues beneath that can be infected.

If you damage or cut your skin you bleed. Your blood quickly forms a clot which dries into a scab. The scab forms a seal over the cut, stopping pathogens getting in through the wound.

Your breathing system could be a weak link in your body defences. Every time you breathe you draw air full of pathogens inside your body. However, your breathing system produces sticky liquid, called mucus. This mucus covers the lining of your lungs and tubes. It traps the pathogens. The mucus is then moved out of your body or swallowed down into your gut. Then the acid in your stomach destroys the microorganisms. In the same way, the stomach acid destroys most of the pathogens you take in through your mouth.

Figure 2 When you get a cut, the platelets in your blood set up a chain of events to form a clot that dries to a scab. This stops pathogens from getting into your body. It also stops you bleeding to death!

b What are the three main ways in which your body prevents pathogens from getting in?

How white blood cells protect you from disease

In spite of your body's defence mechanisms, some pathogens still get inside your body. Once there, they will meet your second line of defence – the white blood cells of your immune system.

The white blood cells help to defend your body against pathogens in several ways.

Table 1 Ways in which your white blood cells destroy pathogens and protect you against disease

Role of white blood cell	How it protects you against disease
Ingesting microorganisms	Some white blood cells ingest (take in) pathogens, destroying them so they can't make you ill.
Producing antibodies Antibody — Antigen — Bacterium White blood cell — Antibody attached to antigen	Some white blood cells produce special chemicals called **antibodies**. These target particular bacteria or viruses and destroy them. You need a unique antibody for each type of pathogen. Once your white blood cells have produced antibodies once against a particular pathogen, they can be made very quickly if that pathogen gets into the body again.
Producing antitoxins	Some white blood cells produce antitoxins. These counteract (cancel out) the toxins (poisons) released by pathogens.

??? Did you know ... ?

Mucus produced from your nose turns green when you have a cold. This happens because some white blood cells contain green-coloured enzymes. These white blood cells destroy the cold viruses and any bacteria in the mucus of your nose when you have a cold. The dead white blood cells along with the dead bacteria and viruses are removed in the mucus, making it look green.

Summary questions

1 Explain how diseases are spread by:
  a droplet infection   c contaminated food and drink
  b direct contact   d through a cut in the skin.
2 Certain diseases mean you cannot fight infections very well. Explain why the following symptoms would make you less able to cope with pathogens.
  a Your blood won't clot properly.
  b The number of white cells in your blood falls.
3 Here are three common things we do. Explain carefully how each one helps to prevent the spread of disease.
  a Washing your hands before preparing a salad.
  b Throwing away tissues after you have blown your nose.
  c Making sure that sewage does not get into drinking water.
4 Explain in detail how the white blood cells in your body work.

Key points

- Your body has several methods of defending itself against the entry of pathogens using the skin, the mucus of the breathing system and the clotting of the blood.
- Your white blood cells help to defend you against pathogens by ingesting them, making antibodies and making antitoxins.

Further teaching suggestions

Blood clotting and haemophilia

- Link the blood-clotting video to haemophilia and discuss clotting times. This can be extended further with reference to the use of blood-thinning drugs such as warfarin.

Blood clotting and practical applications

- Also link blood clotting to the self-sealing fuel tanks on fighter aircraft and some racing cars.

Preservatives and bacteria

- Discuss the preservation of foods, such as onions, in vinegar and draw parallels with the destruction of bacteria by the stomach acids.

Investigating how infectious diseases enter the body

- 'How did you get in?' Put a list of diseases/infections on the board. Students are to break into small groups and come up with as many ways as possible for each particular infective agent to get into the body. Share with the rest of the class on completion.

White cell animation

- Stop motion animation of a model white cell engulfing a bacterium can be made using 'Digital Blue' or similar cameras in conjunction with Windows MovieMaker.

Answers to in-text questions

a Droplet infection; direct contact; contaminated food and drink; through a break in the skin.

b Skin acts as a barrier; breathing organs produce mucus to trap pathogens or acid in stomach kills pathogens; blood uses platelets to produce clots to seal wounds.

Summary answers

1 **a** When we cough, sneeze or talk, droplets full of pathogens pass into the air to be breathed in by someone else.
  b Pathogens on skin passed to someone else's skin on contact.
  c Pathogens taken in on food or in drink.
  d Pathogens can get through the barrier of the skin to the tissue underneath.

2 **a** Pathogens cannot be stopped from getting into cuts.
  b You have not got enough white blood cells to ingest pathogens or to produce antibodies/antitoxins, so pathogens are not destroyed.

3 **a** Prevents pathogens getting from your hands to the food.
  b Removes pathogens from where they might come into contact with other people or get on your hands.
  c Prevents pathogens from the gut being taken in with drinking water.

4 Explanation to include the ingestion of microorganisms, the production of antibodies and antitoxins.

B1 1.6

Using drugs to treat disease

Learning objectives

Students should learn:

- that medicines, such as painkillers, relieve symptoms but do not kill pathogens
- that antibiotics help to cure bacterial diseases by killing infective bacteria inside the body
- that antibiotics cannot kill viral pathogens which live and reproduce inside cells.

Learning outcomes

Most students should be able to:

- explain what is meant by the term 'medicine' and describe how some relieve symptoms but do not kill pathogens
- describe how antibiotics can be used to treat bacterial infections
- explain why antibiotics are not used to treat diseases caused by viruses.

Some students should also be able to:

- explain the difficulty of developing antiviral drugs.

AQA Examiner's tip

Remember: antibiotics are drugs that kill bacteria. Antibodies are produced by white blood cells to kill bacteria. Students often confuse antibodies, antitoxins and antibiotics so make sure that you know the differences.

Support

- Students could be shown pictures of people with various complaints and asked to decide which medicines they should be given.

Extend

- Encourage students to find out why we need new antibiotics to keep us ahead in the battle with pathogens. This should lead them to gain some knowledge of mutations in preparation for later topics.

AQA Specification link-up: Biology B1.1

- Some medicines, including painkillers, help to relieve ... [B1.1.2 g]]
- Antibiotics, including penicillin, are medicines that help ... [B1.1.2 h)]
- Explain how the treatment of disease has changed as ... [B1.1.2]

Controlled Assessment: SA4.1 Planning an investigation [SA4.1.2 b) c)] and [SA4.1.3 c)]; SA4.2 Assess and manage risks when carrying out practical work [SA4.2.1 a) b)]; SA4.3 Collect primary and secondary data [SA4.3.3 a) e) f)]; SA4.5 Analyse and interpret primary and secondary data. [SA4.5.4 a)]

Lesson structure

Starters

Horrible history! – Read a description of someone dying of an infection in the past, before the days of penicillin. For example, Lord Caernarvon dying from an infected mosquito bite following the discovery of Tutankhamen's tomb. Ask: 'Was the curse really an ancient biological hazard warning?' Discuss. *(5 minutes)*

What medicine do I need? – Either pretend to feel unwell yourself or pick someone from the class, wrap them up in a scarf and give them a hot water bottle. Produce a bottle of over-the-counter cough medicine, a box of aspirins or paracetamol, some throat sweets and a bottle of prescription antibiotics. To support students, discuss what should be given to the 'patient' and why. To extend students, allow them to question the 'patient' (as in a consultation at the doctor's), before making any decision as to what medicine should be given. They should offer an explanation to the 'patient'. *(10 minutes)*

Main

There are several important issues in this spread and some interesting ideas for practical work.

- If the first starter activity is not used, then ask the students what they understand by the term 'medicine' and compile a list of suggested medicines and their uses on the board. Distinguish between those that relieve symptoms, such as painkillers, and those that kill pathogens, such as antibiotics. Discuss the use of antibiotics and why they are effective in destroying bacteria but not effective against viruses.

- Search the internet to find pictures of Alexander Fleming, the discovery of penicillin and his work.

- Set up an experiment to show the sensitivity of bacteria to antibiotics (see 'Practical support'). It can be shown as a demonstration or carried out by the students in groups. Predictions can be made. This involves the introduction of many 'How Science Works' concepts. [Note: There are restrictions on the use of bacteria in schools, so guidelines would need to be consulted and all suitable precautions taken if this is to be used as a class experiment.]

Plenaries

Quick quiz – Support students by asking them to make a list of the key terms on the board and another list of the definitions and ask students to come up and match a key term with its definition. Extent students by getting them to use either the list of key terms or the list of definitions and, working in teams, ask them to supply the correct key term or definition. *(5 minutes)*

Should antibiotics be used for ... ? – Provide a list of statements about the use of antibiotics and ask students to say whether or not each is a good idea, with reasons to back up their decision. Statements could include:
'Chickens raised in barns are given antibiotics in their food.'
'If you have a cold you should go to the doctor for some antibiotics.'
'In some countries, antibiotics can be bought over the counter.'
'Milking cows may have tubes of antibiotics placed in their udders.'
'Some chopping boards have antibiotics/antibacterial substances built into them.'
(10 minutes)

Practical/demonstration support

Experiment to show the sensitivity of bacteria to antibiotics

Equipment and materials required

Agar plates, a suitable bacterium, such as *Bacillus subtilis* (several antibiotics; or different concentrations of one antibiotic could be used), Oxoid multodiscs (available from suppliers).

Details

This can be shown as a demonstration or carried out by the students in groups.

Agar plates are inoculated with a suitable bacterium, such as *Bacillus subtilis*, have antibiotic-impregnated discs placed on them and are incubated for 24 hours. The antibiotics diffuse from the discs into the agar and inhibit the growth of bacteria around them, resulting in clear zones in the agar. The diameter of these clear zones can be measured.

Safety: If this is to be carried out by the students, then all the usual precautions need to be taken. The agar plates could be set up for them and sealed after incubation, but if facilities allow it, it is more instructive if they do it themselves following all the safety measures involved with the handling of sterile equipment and bacteria. (Teacher should be trained in aseptic techniques.) More information available from the CLEAPSS Handbook Section 15.2.

Keeping healthy

B1 1.6 Using drugs to treat disease

Learning objectives
- What is a medicine?
- How do medicines work?
- Why can't we use antibiotics to treat diseases caused by viruses?

When you have an infectious disease, you generally take medicines which contain useful drugs. Often the medicine doesn't affect the pathogen that is causing the problems. It just eases the symptoms and makes you feel better.

Drugs like aspirin and paracetamol are very useful as painkillers. When you have a cold they will help relieve your headache and sore throat. On the other hand, they will have no effect on the viruses which have entered your tissues and made you feel ill.

Many of the medicines you can buy at a chemist's or supermarket are like this. They relieve your symptoms but do not kill the pathogens. They do not cure you any faster. You have to wait for your immune system to overcome the pathogens.

Figure 1 Taking paracetamol will make this child feel better, but she will not actually get well any faster as a result

a Why don't medicines like aspirin actually cure your illness?

Antibiotics

Drugs that make us feel better are useful but what we really need are drugs that can cure us. We use antiseptics and disinfectants to kill bacteria outside the body. But they are far too poisonous to use inside your body. They would kill you and your pathogens at the same time!

The drugs that have really changed the way we treat infectious diseases are **antibiotics**. These are medicines that can work inside your body to kill the bacteria that cause diseases.

b What is an antibiotic?

How antibiotics work

Antibiotics like penicillin work by killing the bacteria that cause disease while they are inside your body. They damage the bacterial cells without harming your own cells. They have had an enormous effect on our society. We can now cure bacterial diseases that killed millions of people in the past.

Unfortunately antibiotics are not the complete answer to the problem of infectious diseases. They have no effect on diseases caused by viruses.

The problem with viral pathogens is that they reproduce inside the cells of your body. It is extremely difficult to develop drugs that kill the viruses without damaging the cells and tissues of your body at the same time.

c How do antibiotics work?

Figure 2 Penicillin was the first antibiotic. Now we have many different ones which kill different types of bacterium. Scientists are always on the look out for new antibiotics to keep us ahead in the battle against pathogens.

How Science Works
Discovering penicillin

Alexander Fleming was a scientist who studied bacteria and wanted to find ways of killing them. In 1928, he was growing lots of bacteria on agar plates. Alexander was rather careless, and his lab was quite untidy. He often left the lids off his plates for a long time and forgot about experiments he had set up!

After one holiday, Fleming saw that lots of his culture plates had mould growing on them. He noticed a clear ring in the jelly around some of the spots of mould. Something had killed the bacteria covering the jelly.

Fleming saw how important this was. He called the mould 'penicillin'. He worked hard to extract a juice from the mould. But he couldn't get much penicillin and he couldn't make it survive, even in a fridge. So Fleming couldn't prove it would actually kill bacteria and make people better. By 1934 he gave up on penicillin and went on to do different work.

About 10 years after penicillin was first discovered, Ernst Chain and Howard Florey set about trying to use it on people. They gave some penicillin they extracted to Albert Alexander, who was dying of a blood infection. The effect was amazing and Albert recovered. But then the penicillin ran out. Florey and Chain even tried to collect unused penicillin from Albert's urine, but it was no good. The infection came back and sadly Albert died.

They kept working and eventually they managed to make penicillin on an industrial scale. The process was able to produce enough penicillin to supply the demands of the Second World War. We have used it as a medicine ever since.

Figure 3 Alexander Fleming was on the lookout for something that would kill bacteria. As a result of him noticing the effect of this mould on his cultures, millions of lives have been saved around the world.

d Who was the first person to discover penicillin?

Summary questions

1 What is the main difference between drugs such as paracetamol and drugs such as penicillin?

2 a How did Alexander Fleming discover penicillin?
   b Why was it so difficult to make a medicine out of penicillin?
   c Who developed the industrial process which made it possible to mass-produce penicillin?

3 Explain why it is so much more difficult to develop medicines against viruses than it has been to develop antibacterial drugs.

Remember:
- Antibiotics are drugs which kill bacteria.
- Antibodies are produced by white blood cells to kill bacteria.

Key points
- Some medicines relieve the symptoms of disease but do not kill the pathogens which cause it.
- Antibiotics cure bacterial diseases by killing the bacteria inside your body.
- Antibiotics do not destroy viruses because viruses reproduce inside the cells. It is difficult to develop drugs that can destroy viruses without damaging your body cells.

Further teaching suggestions

Aspirin – more than just a painkiller
- Remind students that aspirin has a role to play in the treatment of heart and other diseases as well as being a painkiller. It is also an anti-inflammatory which can be tolerated well by people with arthritis and other muscle conditions.

Old remedies, did they work?
- Ask: 'Is there any truth in old wives' tales and ancient remedies for healing?' Show a piece of mouldy bread in a sealed plastic bag, a jar of honey, a bottle of vinegar, a soldering iron (for cauterising), some wood ash and some cobwebs. Discuss the scientific background to these remedies and consider what was available to people before there were antibiotics.

Allergies to antibiotics
- 'What about people who are allergic to penicillin?' Introduce the idea that there are different antibiotics, perhaps mentioning narrow-spectrum and broad-spectrum antibiotics. Ask students if they have been prescribed antibiotics other than penicillin.

Answers to in-text questions

a Because they do not kill the pathogens that are making you ill.
b A drug that kills pathogenic bacteria in your body.
c They damage bacterial cells without damaging human cells.
d Alexander Fleming.

Summary answers

1 Paracetamol relieves symptoms/makes you feel better, whereas antibiotics kill the bacteria and actually make you better.

2 a He noticed a clear area around mould growing on bacterial plates.
   b It was difficult to get much penicillin out of the mould and it does not keep easily.
   c Florey and Chain.

3 Viral pathogens reproduce inside your cells, so it is very difficult to develop a drug that destroys them without destroying your cells as well.

B1 1.7

Growing and investigating bacteria

Learning objectives

Students should learn:

- to grow an uncontaminated culture of bacteria in the lab
- why we need uncontaminated cultures
- why we incubate bacteria at no more than 25 °C in schools.

Learning outcomes

Most students should be able to:

- successfully grow an uncontaminated culture of bacteria at below 25 °C
- explain why it is important to maintain sterile conditions
- describe the different conditions used to grow cultures in schools and industry.

Some students should also be able to:

- explain why cultures are incubated at a temperature below 25 °C in a school laboratory but industry uses higher temperatures.

Answers to in-text questions

a A nutrient-rich medium used to culture microorganisms such as fungi and bacteria.

b To prevent contamination by microbes already on the equipment.

Support

- Show a picture of a wound and an infected wound. Ask students what should be done with a wound to stop it from becoming infected. Draw out that there are bacteria all around us and that they will grow where conditions are right. Discuss the potential for blood poisoning and gangrene and the consequences.

Extend

- Show a photo of a child in an isolation tent. Get the students to give reasons why the child might be in there, what apparatus must be attached to the tent and why. What would happen if it were perforated, and how the necessities of living are catered for.

AQA

Specification link-up: Biology B1.1

- Uncontaminated cultures of microorganisms are required for … [B1.1.2 m)]
- In school and college laboratories, cultures should be incubated at … [B1.1.2 n)]
- In industrial conditions higher temperatures can produce more rapid growth. [B1.1.2 o)]

  Controlled Assessment: SA4.2 Assess and manage risks when carrying out practical work. [SA4.2.1 a) b)]

Lesson structure

Starters

Growing pure cultures – Show the students an agar plate that has been exposed to the air and then incubated. Ask them what this shows and what each colony represents. Draw out from them that we can only see the bacteria because there are such large numbers forming a colony. Ask for suggestions as to how they would set about obtaining a pure culture of one of the microorganisms on the plate. How could they stop other bacteria growing? Introduce the term 'aseptic' and discuss the techniques involved with growing pure cultures. *(5 minutes)*

What do we need to know in order to grow bacteria? – Support students by asking them what are the ideal growing conditions for living organisms and discuss whether these are the same for bacteria. Extend students by asking them for suggestions about where bacteria can be found (e.g. in air, on food, in soil, in hot springs, inside organisms) and then ask the students what would be the ideal growing conditions for the bacteria in each situation. This should draw out that the ideal conditions can vary according to the situation and introduce the idea that bacteria can be dormant until the conditions are right for them. *(10 minutes)*

Main

- The preparation of a pure (uncontaminated) culture of a microorganism is described in the Student Book and here (see 'Practical support'), with a series of steps to follow. This practical could be carried out by the students using a non-pathogenic bacterium such as *Bacillus subtilis*.

- As suggested in the Student Book, the cultures set up in the previous practical or pre-inoculated plates can be used to investigate the action of disinfectants and antibiotics on bacteria. The investigation of the sensitivity of bacteria to different antibiotics was described in the previous spread. A similar technique can be used to investigate the action of different antiseptics or different concentrations of the same antiseptic on bacteria. It would be helpful to the students for the techniques involved in inoculating an agar plate to be demonstrated to them before they carry out the activity for themselves. The need for sterile conditions and the use of aseptic techniques can be reinforced. Make sure that the students understand all the safety precautions and that they follow the instructions for the safe disposal of their agar plates.

- In addition to the experiment above, the action of antiseptics on bacteria could be investigated (see 'Practical support') and the results compared with those of the experiment described in the previous spread (B1.1.6).

Plenaries

The twit got it wrong! – Get students to imagine a scenario where improper techniques used in a lab led to unfortunate consequences. Have them write a 'tweet' of 140 characters or less on the subject and choose one or more students to read out their account. *(5 minutes)*

Summary time – To support students, prepare a series of cards with the steps of the procedure for growing a pure culture on them and ask students to place them in the correct order. Extend students by asking them to construct their own flow chart for the procedure. This will review the lesson and summarise the main points. For both groups, check the results and reinforce the points by use of questioning and getting students to vocalise their understanding. *(10 minutes)*

Practical support

Growing uncontaminated cultures

Equipment and materials required
Sterile Petri dishes, inoculating loops, Bunsen burners, cultures of suitable bacteria, adhesive tape.

Details
The Petri dishes must be sterilised before using them to grow microorganisms. The nutrient agar, which will provide their food, must also be sterilised. This kills off any unwanted microorganisms. Heat can be used to sterilise glass dishes. A special oven called an autoclave is often used. It sterilises by using steam at high pressure. Plastic Petri dishes are often bought already sterilised. UV light or gamma radiation is used to kill the bacteria. The next step is to inoculate the sterile agar with the microorganisms you want to grow.

Once the plates are inoculated, lids should be fixed with tape in three places. Do not seal all the way round. The sealed Petri dishes need to be incubated (kept warm) for several days so the microorganisms can grow. In school and college laboratories the maximum temperature at which cultures are incubated is 25 °C. Turning the dishes upside down during incubation stops condensation forming on the agar.

Investigating the action of disinfectants, antibiotics and antiseptics on bacteria

Equipment and materials required
Pre-inoculated agar plates; cork borers; discs impregnated with antibiotics, disinfectants or antiseptics as required; sterile forceps; Bunsen burners.

Details
Either use the cultures you set up yourself or use pre-inoculated agar. Agar plates are inoculated with a harmless bacterium and have wells cut into them by removing cylinders of agar with a cork borer. Solutions of the antimicrobial substances being tested could be placed in the wells and the plates incubated. Although it is common practice for plates to be inverted during incubation, these plates will contain liquid, so they should be incubated right-side-up. The relative effects can be judged by the diameter of the clear areas around the wells – an area of clear jelly indicates that the bacteria have been killed. (See CLEAPSS Handbook/CD ROM Section 15.2).

Safety: Precautions should be taken when handling and disposing of bacterial cultures and plates.

Keeping healthy

B1 1.7 — Growing and investigating bacteria

Learning objectives
- How can we grow an uncontaminated culture of bacteria in the lab?
- Why do we need uncontaminated cultures?
- Why do we incubate bacteria at no more than 25 °C in schools and colleges?

To find out more about microorganisms we need to culture them. This means we grow very large numbers of them so that we can see all of the bacteria (the colony) as a whole. Many microorganisms can be grown in the laboratory. This helps us to learn more about them. We can find out what nutrients they need to grow and investigate which chemicals are best at killing them. Bacteria are the most commonly cultured microorganisms.

Growing microorganisms in the lab
To culture (grow) microorganisms you must provide them with everything they need. This means giving them a liquid or gel containing nutrients – a culture medium. It contains carbohydrate as an energy source along with various minerals and sometimes other chemicals. Most microorganisms also need warmth and oxygen to grow.

You usually provide the nutrients in agar jelly. Hot agar containing all the nutrients your bacteria will need is poured into a Petri dish. It is then left to cool and set before you add the microorganisms.

You must take great care when you are culturing microorganisms. The bacteria you want to grow may be harmless. However, there is always the risk that a mutation (a change in the DNA) will take place and produce a new and dangerous pathogen.

You also want to keep the pure strains of bacteria you are culturing free from any other microorganisms. Such contamination might come from your skin, the air, the soil or the water around you. Investigations need uncontaminated cultures of microorganism. Whenever you are culturing microorganisms you must carry out strict health and safety procedures to protect yourself and others.

a What is agar jelly?

Figure 2 When working with the most dangerous pathogens, scientists need to be very careful. Sensible safety precautions are needed when working with microorganisms.

Figure 1 Culturing microorganisms like bacteria makes it possible for us to observe them and see how different chemicals affect them

Did you know ... ?
You are surrounded by disease-causing bacteria all the time. If you cultured bacteria at 37 °C – human body temperature – there would be a very high risk of growing some dangerous pathogens.

Growing useful organisms
You can prepare an uncontaminated culture of microorganisms in the laboratory by following a number of steps.

The Petri dishes on which you will grow your microorganisms must be sterilised before using them. The nutrient agar, which will provide their food, must also be sterilised. This kills off any unwanted microorganisms. You can use heat to sterilise glass dishes. A special oven called an autoclave is often used. It sterilises by using steam at high pressure. Plastic Petri dishes are often bought ready-sterilised. UV light or gamma radiation is used to kill the bacteria.

b Why must everything be sterilised before you start a culture?

The next step is to inoculate the sterile agar with the microorganisms you want to grow.

Sterilise the inoculating loop used to transfer micro-organisms to the agar by heating it until it is red hot in the flame of a Bunsen and then letting it cool. Do not put the loop down or blow on it as it cools.

Dip the sterilised loop in a suspension of the bacteria you want to grow and use it to make zigzag streaks across the surface of the agar. Replace the lid on the dish as quickly as possible to avoid contamination.

Seal the lid of the Petri dish with adhesive tape to prevent microorganisms from the air contaminating the culture – or microbes from the culture escaping. Do not seal all the way around the edge so oxygen can get into the dish and harmful anaerobic bacteria do not grow.

Figure 3 Culturing microorganisms safely in the laboratory

Once you have inoculated your plates, the sealed Petri dishes need to be incubated (kept warm) for several days so the microorganisms can grow. In school and college laboratories the maximum temperature at which cultures are incubated is 25 °C. This greatly reduces the likelihood that you will grow pathogens that might be harmful to people. In industrial conditions, bacterial cultures are often grown at higher temperatures, which allow the microorganisms to grow more rapidly.

Examiner's tip
Make sure you understand why we sterilise. We boil solutions and heat-treat apparatus in an autoclave to **kill bacteria** already in them. This is sterilising.

Practical

Investigating the action of disinfectants and antibiotics
You can use cultures you set up yourself or pre-inoculated agar to investigate the effect of disinfectants and antibiotics on the growth of bacteria. An area of clear jelly indicates that the bacteria have been killed or cannot grow.
- What are the safety issues in this investigation and how will you manage any risks?

Summary questions
1 Why do we culture microorganisms in the laboratory?
2 Why don't we culture bacteria at 37 °C in the school lab?
3 When you set up a culture of bacteria in a Petri dish (see Figure 3) you give the bacteria everything they need to grow as fast as possible. However these ideal conditions do not last forever. What might limit the growth of the bacteria in a culture on a Petri dish?

Key points
- An uncontaminated culture of microorganisms can be grown using sterilised Petri dishes and agar. You sterilise the inoculating loop before use and seal the lid of the Petri dish to prevent unwanted microorganisms getting in. The culture is left at about 25 °C for a few days.
- Uncontaminated cultures are needed so we can investigate the effect of chemicals such as disinfectants and antibiotics on microorganisms.
- Cultures should be incubated at a maximum temperature of 25 °C in schools and colleges to reduce the likelihood of harmful pathogens growing.

Further teaching suggestions

More practicals
- Once students are familiar with the techniques, they could try isolating bacteria from live yogurts. The usual precautions and safety regulations should be followed.

Using a culture broth
- Pure cultures of bacteria do not always have to be grown on agar plates. It could be useful to set up a broth culture as a demonstration. Students could compare the conditions, e.g. food sources, aeration, etc.

Useful commercial bacteria
- Ask students to compile a list of useful bacteria that might need to be produced as pure cultures for commercial use, e.g. in the food industry (yoghurt, cheese).

Keeping clean
- Give the students time to look at a more detailed coverage of aseptic techniques such as that found at www.biotopics.co.uk. Search for 'microbiological techniques – the basics'. Get them to make a note of key words from the text.

Summary answers
1 To find out more about them. To find out which nutrients they need to grow and to investigate what will affect them and stop them growing.

2 This is the human body temperature so any bacteria which grow at that temperature would be likely to be able to infect people and cause harm.

3 Using up the available food and oxygen, build up of waste products such as carbon dioxide and other toxins.

B1 1.8 — Changing pathogens

AQA Specification link-up: Biology B1.1

- Many strains of bacteria, including MRSA, have … [B1.1.2 i)]
- Mutations of pathogens produce new strains … [B1.1.2 j)]
- Antibiotics kill individual pathogens of the nonresistant strain … [B1.1.2 j)] [HT only]
- Explain how the treatment of disease has changed as a result of … [B1.1.2]
- Evaluate the consequences of mutations of bacteria … [B1.1.2]

Learning objectives

Students should learn:

- that bacteria and viruses can mutate causing new strains to appear
- that new strains of bacteria and viruses may be resistant to antibiotics
- that resistant strains of pathogens survive as a result of natural selection
- that overuse of antibiotics should be avoided in order to prevent more resistant strains of bacteria arising.

Learning outcomes

Most students should be able to:

- describe how mutations of bacteria and viruses can give rise to resistant strains
- describe how natural selection causes the populations of resistant strains to increase
- describe how new strains of pathogens can spread rapidly causing epidemics and pandemics.

Some students should also be able to:

- explain in detail how bacteria become increasingly resistant to antibiotics [HT only]
- evaluate the problems of preventing the spread of a new disease such as a mutated form of bird flu.

Support

- Students could make a poster with reasons why it is important to finish a course of antibiotics.
- Students could write a list of precautions that could be taken to avoid the spread of the flu virus during an epidemic.

Extend

- MRSA is not the only problem or cause of infection in hospitals. Students could research the incidence of other infections, such as *Clostridium difficile*, which can spread in a hospital environment.

Lesson structure

Starters

Let's get it clear! – This is a good opportunity to remind students of which diseases are caused by bacteria and which by viruses. To support students, ask them to draw up a list of ailments on the board and ask students to put a 'B' by those caused by bacteria and 'V' for those caused by a virus. To extend students, include some ailments such as athlete's foot, ringworm and malaria, which are caused by other organisms and, as well as asking students to identify the cause of the ailment, ask them to suggest which ones can be prevented by vaccination and why. *(5 minutes)*

Finish your medicine! – In discussion with the students, build up a flow chart of what happens when you are prescribed a course of antibiotics and how you should take them. What are the consequences of not finishing the course? What are the dangers of taking antibiotics too frequently? If appropriate, you could mention the effects that antibiotics have on the gut flora and the possible consequences. *(10 minutes)*

Main

It is important that students understand how antibiotic resistance arises and how mutations occur. It would be possible to combine two or more of these suggestions if time permits.

- What is a mutation and how does it occur? Prepare a PowerPoint presentation or a video on mutations and how they occur. Provide students with a worksheet which they can complete as the presentation proceeds. It could be worth pointing out that mutations occur under natural circumstances all the time, but that the mutation rate in microorganisms appears to be greater as they reproduce more rapidly than other organisms.
- A presentation on antibiotic resistance could follow the suggestion made above. Link in with the practical work suggested in the Main lesson notes in this book on spread B1 1.7 'Growing and investigating bacteria' on the sensitivity of bacteria to different antibiotics.
- Provide groups of students with reference material on the MRSA story, such as suitable websites, newspaper and magazine articles, and information given to hospitals, and suggest that they write a script for a radio or TV programme about MRSA. The emphasis is to be on the facts rather than on sensational reporting.
- Initiate a general discussion on the difference between the two terms 'pandemic' and 'epidemic' with examples. Using the information in the Student Book, students could draw up a list of how diseases spread from country to country. Alongside each method of spread, suggestions for a control could be made. Finally, the students could decide on how they personally would recommend precautions that they and their families could take to avoid exposure to the disease and thus survive.

Plenaries

Can you catch flu from …? – To support students, collect information from them about the different types of influenza virus they have heard of or read about. Discuss with them why it is rare for the strain of the virus that causes the disease in animals to cause the disease in humans. This reinforces the idea that a *change* or *mutation* is needed before humans are affected. Extend students by discussing why bird flu spreads so quickly in Asia and why Asia is a likely source of mutated viruses which might cause a pandemic. *(5 minutes)*

Get your flu jab! – Ask students why it is important that people aged 65 and over should be vaccinated against influenza every year. Who else qualifies for the flu jab? Why? Should it be given to everyone? If time permits, include a discussion about who was offered swine flu jabs and why there were different age restrictions. *(10 minutes)*

Further teaching suggestions

Survival poster
- Students could design a poster setting out how people can avoid/reduce their chances of catching flu or other infectious diseases. The poster could be displayed in schools, surgeries and public places.

Research previous flu pandemics
- Students may find it interesting to find out more about major outbreaks of influenza. Some of their grandparents might remember the outbreak in the 1950s. History websites could provide information on the rapidity with which the disease spread and how long it lasted. An interesting comparison could be made between the times involved previously, e.g. Spanish flu after the First World War, and the predicted timescales for any future outbreaks.

Swine flu – did you get it?
- This could be incorporated in the previous suggestion. Students could discuss whether they thought that the public were properly informed and that all the precautions taken were necessary.

Antiviral medicines and vaccines
- Initiate a class discussion on the use of antiviral medicines to bridge the gap between the outbreak of the disease and the development of a suitable vaccine. Why does it take so long for the vaccine to be developed? How do antiviral medicines work?

Keeping healthy

B1 1.8 — Changing pathogens

Learning objectives
- What is antibiotic resistance?
- How can we prevent antibiotic resistance developing? [H]
- Why is mutation in bacteria and viruses such a problem?

If you are given an antibiotic and use it properly, the bacteria that have made you ill are killed off. However some bacteria develop resistance to antibiotics. They have a natural mutation (change in the genetic material) that means they are not affected by the antibiotic. These mutations happen by chance and they produce new strains of bacteria by **natural selection**.

More types of bacteria are becoming resistant to more antibiotics. Diseases caused by bacteria are becoming more difficult to treat. Over the years antibiotics have been overused and used when they are not really needed. This increases the rate at which antibiotic resistant strains have developed.

Antibiotic-resistant bacteria

Normally an antibiotic kills the bacteria of a non-resistant strain. However individual resistant bacteria survive and reproduce, so the population of **resistant** bacteria increases.

Antibiotics are no longer used to treat non-serious infections such as mild throat infections, which are often caused by viruses. Hopefully this will slow down the rate of development of resistant strains.

Figure 1 Bacteria can develop resistance to many different antibiotics in a process of natural selection as this simple model shows

Antibiotic 1 → 95% of bacteria killed by antibiotic 5% survive – they have a mutation which makes them resistant to antibiotic 1

Colony of bacteria

Antibiotic 2 → 95% of bacteria killed by antibiotic 5% survive – they have a mutation which makes them resistant to antibiotic 2 as well

Colony of bacteria resistant to antibiotic 1

Antibiotic 3

Colony of bacteria resistant to antibiotic 1 and 2...

Higher

To prevent more resistant strains of bacteria appearing it is important not to overuse antibiotics. It's best to only use them when you really need them. Antibiotics don't affect viruses so people should not demand antibiotics to treat an illness which the doctor thinks is viral.

Some antibiotics treat very specific bacteria. Others treat many different types of bacteria. The right type of antibiotic must be used to treat each bacterial infection to prevent further antibiotic resistance developing. It is also important that people finish their course of medicine every time.

a Why is it important not to use antibiotics too frequently?

Examiner's tip
Washing hands removes the pathogens on them, but it may not kill the pathogens.

The MRSA story
Hospitals use a lot of antibiotics to treat infections. As a result of natural selection, some of the bacteria in hospitals are resistant to many antibiotics. This is what has happened with MRSA (the bacterium methicillin-resistant *Staphylococcus aureus*).

As doctors and nurses move from patient to patient, these antibiotic-resistant bacteria are spread easily. MRSA alone now contributes to around 1000 deaths every year in UK hospitals.

There are a number of simple steps which can reduce the spread of microorganisms such as MRSA. We have known some of them since the time of Semmelweis, but they sometimes get forgotten!
- Antibiotics should only be used when they are really needed.
- Specific bacteria should be treated with specific antibiotics.
- Medical staff should wash their hands with soap and water or alcohol gel between patients. They should wear disposable clothing or clothing that is regularly sterilised.
- Visitors should wash their hands as they enter and leave the hospital.
- Patients infected with antibiotic-resistant bacteria should be looked after in isolation from other patients.
- Hospitals should be kept clean – there should be high standards of hygiene.

b Is MRSA a bacterium or a virus?

Mutation and pandemics

Another problem caused by the mutation of pathogens is that new forms of diseases can appear. These new strains can spread quickly and cause widespread illness because no one is immune to them and there is no effective treatment. For example the flu virus mutates easily. Every year there are new strains of the virus that your immune system doesn't recognise. There is no effective treatment against viruses at all. The existing flu vaccine is not effective against new strains of the virus, and it takes time to develop a new vaccine.

There may be a flu **epidemic** (in one country) or even a **pandemic** (across several countries). In 1918–19, a new strain of flu virus killed over 40 million people around the world.

With modern international travel, a new strain of pathogen can spread very quickly. In 2009 there was a pandemic of a new strain of flu, known as swine flu, which spread very fast. Internationally, countries worked to stop it spreading and the death toll was kept relatively low.

Figure 2 Data that show how the number of deaths in which MRSA played a part from 1993 (Source: National Statistics Office)

links
For more information on the work of Semmelweis, look back at B1 1.4 Pathogens and disease.

Summary questions

1 Copy and complete using the words below:
antibiotics   bacterium (virus)   better   disease   mutation   mutate   resistant   virus (bacterium)

If bacteria change or .... they may become .... to .... This means the medicine no longer makes you .... A .... in a .... or .... can also lead to a new form of ....

2 Make a flow chart to show how bacteria develop resistance to antibiotics.

3 Use Figure 2 to help you answer these questions.
  a How could you explain the increase in deaths linked to MRSA?
  b How could you explain the fall in deaths linked to MRSA, which still continues?

Key points
- Many types of bacterium have developed antibiotic resistance as a result of natural selection. To prevent the problem getting worse we must not overuse antibiotics.
- If bacteria or viruses mutate, new strains of the pathogen can appear causing disease.
- New strains of disease which spread rapidly can cause epidemics and pandemics. Antibiotics and vaccinations may not be effective against the new strain.

AQA Examiner's tip

Washing hands removes the pathogens on them, it may not kill the pathogens.

It is worth reminding students that some resistant bacteria are not killed by the alcohol gels and hand washing is still needed.

Answers to in-text questions

a To prevent more antibiotic-resistant strains appearing.

b Bacterium.

Summary answers

1 mutate, resistant, antibiotics, better, mutation, virus (bacterium), bacterium (virus), disease

2 Students should show clear understanding of the different stages involved in the development of antibiotic resistance. Colony of bacteria treated with antibiotic 1 → 5% have mutation and survive → the surviving bacteria are treated with antibiotic 2 → 5% have a mutation and are resistant to antibiotic 1 and 2 → etc.

3 a Increased use of antibiotics leading to more resistant bacteria, lower hygiene standards in hospitals, people failing to wash their hands between patients, visitors, etc. Any other sensible point.

  b Could be an improvement in cleanliness in hospital, people being more careful about hand washing, introduction and use of alcohol gels for visitors and staff in hospitals, any sensible points.

B1 1.9 | Immunity

AQA
Specification link-up: Biology B1.1
- People can be immunised against a disease by ... *[B1.1.2 l)]*
- Explain how the treatment of disease has changed as ... *[B1.1.2]*
- The immune system of the body produces specific ... *[B1.1.2 e)]*

Controlled Assessment: SA4.5 Analyse and interpret primary and secondary data. *[SA4.5.1 a) b)]*

Learning objectives

Students should learn:

- how the immune system works
- how vaccination can protect you against bacterial and viral diseases.

Learning outcomes

Most students should be able to:

- describe how the immune system responds to pathogens in the body
- explain how vaccines work
- list some of the advantages and disadvantages of being vaccinated against a particular disease.

Some students should also be able to:

- evaluate the advantages and disadvantages of being vaccinated against a particular disease.

Lesson structure

Starters

Jabs: who has had them? – Discuss the vaccinations the students have had. Has anyone had special vaccinations in order to visit certain countries? Discuss what might be in the injections. *(5 minutes)*

The work of Edward Jenner – Get the students to locate a webpage about Edward Jenner and vaccination. After a short study of this, ask the students a series of questions to see how much information they have managed to discover. Support students by keeping the questions straightforward and factual (e.g. dates, places, names of people involved and procedure). Extend students by asking them why his work was so remarkable and if it would be allowed today. *(10 minutes)*

Main

- Introduce the key words connected to vaccination: antigen, immunity, immunisation and vaccination. Distinguish 'antigen' from similar words like 'antibody, antibiotic and antitoxin', by establishing clear definitions (use for revision cards). Draw out the links between the words, building up the connections in the context of defence against disease.

- Link with a presentation on what happens when you have your jabs and the importance of the second dose and the boosters. This can be illustrated by using a graph. Why do we need to keep up with tetanus jabs?

- Using the section in the Student Book, discuss the risks associated with vaccination and the controversies surrounding the vaccine debate. How Science Works concepts could be introduced here. Students should be able to distinguish between a fact and an opinion and drawing conclusions using scientific evidence.

- Using a computer, design a poster or a leaflet persuading parents to have their children vaccinated.

- Use graphs to show how many people used to die of infectious/contagious diseases in the past. Information can be obtained from the internet (try BBC, Wellcome Museum, etc. – either for statistics for individual diseases such as cholera and TB, or for more general information). As a practical exercise to emphasise and visualise the numbers involved, use grains of rice, one for each person who dies. By weighing and calculation, you can work out how many grains per gram and therefore how heavy the piles of rice for each year should be.

- It could be interesting to compare deaths from diseases such as TB in different countries, or to compare the decline in deaths from diseases such as smallpox with the increase in deaths from Aids, pointing out that there are always some infectious diseases about!

Plenaries

Why do we need booster doses of vaccines? – If not already done, show a graph of what happens after a single dose of vaccine, followed by a second dose. Discuss in relation to different diseases, such as polio, diphtheria and some of the less well-known ones, such as yellow fever and cholera. *(5 minutes)*

Key words challenge – Return to the key words on the board and support students by asking them to give definitions for each one. Extend students by asking them to make a sentence containing any two of the words. This can be a competition. *(10 minutes)*

Support

- Students can be given sheets with key words in one column with an empty box next to each one. Write the definitions in another column with a letter in a box next to each one. Students can match the words with the definitions and put the letter corresponding to the correct definition in the box next to each word.

Extend

- What are the consequences of totally eradicating infectious diseases such as smallpox? Discuss this in relation to a possible terrorist attack involving the release of diseases into highly populated areas.

- Students could be given more raw data to analyse, making predictions and extrapolating trend lines.

Further teaching suggestions

Making a display
- Extend the 'grains of rice' idea from the main section to make a display around the school highlighting how many people in the world die from preventable diseases now. This can be done for different countries, for deaths from specific diseases or as part of a wider campaign to draw attention to poverty in developing countries (campaigns such as 'Make Poverty History').

Investigating causes of death
- If students are interested in the past, there are websites that

give details of the causes of death in different parts of the country: data collected from records of death certificates. (See www.statistics.gov.uk.) They could also research parish registers. The history of the Great Plague of 1665, its spread to Eyam in Derbyshire and the consequences are well documented and accessible via the internet.

Lady Mary Wortley Montagu
- As a follow-up to the work of Edward Jenner, students could find out about the work of Lady Mary Wortley Montagu.

Keeping healthy

B1 1.9 Immunity

Immunity

Learning objectives
- How does your immune system work?
- How does vaccination protect you against disease?

Every cell has unique proteins on its surface called antigens. The antigens on the microorganisms that get into your body are different to the ones on your own cells. Your immune system recognises they are different.

Your white blood cells then make antibodies which join up with the antigens. This destroys the pathogens.

Your white blood cells 'remember' the right antibody needed to tackle a particular pathogen. If you meet that pathogen again, they can make the same antibody very quickly. So you become immune to that disease.

The first time you meet a new pathogen you get ill. That's because there is a delay while your body sorts out the right antibody needed. The next time, you completely destroy the invaders before they have time to make you feel unwell.

a What is an antigen?

Figure 1 No one likes having a vaccination very much – but they save millions of lives!

Vaccination

Some pathogens can make you seriously ill very quickly. In fact you can die before your body manages to make the right antibodies. Fortunately, you can be protected against many of these serious diseases by immunisation (also known as vaccination).

Immunisation involves giving you a vaccine. A vaccine is usually made of a dead or weakened form of the disease-causing microorganism. It works by triggering your body's natural immune response to invading pathogens.

A small amount of dead or inactive pathogen is introduced into your body. This gives your white blood cells the chance to develop the right antibodies against the pathogen without you getting ill.

Then, if you meet the live pathogens, your white blood cells can respond rapidly. They can make the right antibodies just as if you had already had the disease, so you are protected against it.

b What is an antibody?

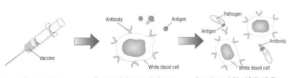

Small amounts of dead or inactive pathogen are put into your body, often by injection.

The antigens in the vaccine stimulate your white blood cells into making antibodies. The antibodies destroy the antigens without any risk of you getting the disease.

You are immune to future infections by the pathogen. That's because your body can respond rapidly and make the correct antibody as if you had already had the disease.

Figure 2 This is how vaccines protect you against dangerous infectious diseases

We use vaccines to protect us against both bacterial diseases (e.g. tetanus and diphtheria) and viral diseases (e.g. polio, measles and mumps). For example, the MMR vaccine protects against measles, mumps and rubella. Vaccines have saved millions of lives around the world. If a large proportion of the population is immune to a disease, the spread of the pathogen is very much reduced. One disease – smallpox – has been completely wiped out by vaccinations. Doctors hope polio will also disappear in the next few years.

c Give an example of one bacterial and one viral disease which you can be immunised against.

How Science Works

The vaccine debate

No medicine is completely risk free. Very rarely, a child will react badly to a vaccine with tragic results. Making the decision to have your baby immunised can be difficult.

Society needs as many people as possible to be immunised against as many diseases as possible. This keeps the pool of infection in the population very low. On the other hand, you know there is a remote chance that something may go wrong with a vaccination.

Because vaccines are so successful, we rarely see the terrible diseases they protect us against. A hundred years ago nearly 50% of all deaths of children and young people were caused by infectious diseases. The development of antibiotics and vaccines means that now only 0.5% of all deaths in the same age group are due to infectious disease. Many children were also left permanently damaged by serious infections. Parents today are often aware of the very small risks from vaccination – but sometimes forget about the terrible dangers of the diseases we vaccinate against.

If you are a parent it can be difficult to find unbiased advice to help you make a decision. The media highlight scare stories which make good headlines. The pharmaceutical companies want to sell vaccines. Doctors and health visitors can weigh up all the information, but they have vaccination targets set by the government.

Summary questions

1 Copy and complete using the words below:
   antibodies pathogen immunised dead immune inactive white
   People can be .... against a disease by introducing small quantities of .... or .... forms of a .... into your body. They stimulate the .... blood cells to produce .... to destroy the pathogen. This makes you .... to the disease in future.

2 Explain carefully, using diagrams if they help you:
   a how the immune system of your body works
   b how vaccines use your natural immune system to protect you against serious diseases.

3 Explain why vaccines can be used against both bacterial and viral diseases but antibiotics only work against bacteria.

AQA Examiner's tip

High levels of antibodies do not stay in your blood forever – immunity is the ability of your white blood cells to produce the right antibodies quickly if you are reinfected by a disease.

◯◯ links
For more information on antibiotics, look back at B1 1.8 Changing pathogens.

Key points
- Your white blood cells produce antibodies to destroy the pathogens. Then your body will respond rapidly to future infections by the same pathogen, by making the correct antibody. You become immune to the disease.
- You can be immunised against a disease by introducing small amounts of dead or inactive pathogens into your body.
- We can use vaccinations to protect against both bacterial and viral pathogens.

40

41

Answers to in-text questions

a A unique protein on the surface of a cell that identifies it.

b A chemical (protein) made by the white blood cells that target specific antigens.

c Bacterial: tetanus, diphtheria or any other sensible choice. Viral: measles, mumps, rubella, polio or any other sensible choice.

Summary answers

1 immunised, dead/inactive, inactive/dead, pathogen, white, antibodies, immune

2 **a** Every cell has unique proteins on its surface called 'antigens'. Your immune system recognises that the antigens on the microorganisms that get into your system are different from the ones on your own cells. Your white blood cells then make antibodies to destroy the antigens/pathogens. Once your white blood cells have learnt the right antibody needed to tackle a particular pathogen, they can make that antibody very quickly if the pathogen gets into your system again, and so you are immune to that disease.

   b A small quantity of dead or inactive pathogen is introduced into your body. This gives your white blood cells the chance to develop the right antibodies against the pathogen without you getting ill. Then if you meet the live pathogens, your body can respond rapidly, making the right antibodies just as if you had already had the disease.

3 Vaccines can be made using inactive viruses or bacteria so can stimulate antibody production against either type of pathogen thereby developing immunity. Viruses reproduce inside body cells so antibiotics cannot kill them without killing the cells of the body at the same time.

B1 1.10

How do we deal with disease?

Learning objectives

Students should learn:

- the advantages and disadvantages of being vaccinated
- how the treatment of disease has changed over time.

Learning outcomes

Most students should be able to:

- describe the advantages and disadvantages of being vaccinated against certain diseases
- understand that the treatment of disease has changed over time.

Some students should also be able to:

- describe how scientists are investigating the development of new medicines for the future.

Support

- Give the students a simple 'True' or 'False' exercise based on the content covered in the lesson.

Extend

- Students could research the difference between broad-spectrum and narrow-spectrum antibiotics.
- **Global Pertussis Initiative**. Students could be given the abstract from the paper *Prevention of pertussis: recommendations derived from the second Global Pertussis Initiative Roundtable meeting* (use a search engine to find this). Students could read this and summarise it in student-friendly language.

AQA

Specification link-up: Biology B1.1

- Evaluate the advantages and disadvantages of being vaccinated against a particular disease. [B1.1.2]
- Explain how the treatment of disease has changed as a result of increased understanding of the action of antibiotics and immunity. [B1.1.2]
- The development of antibiotic-resistant strains of bacteria necessitates the development of new antibiotics. [B1.1.2 k)]

Lesson structure

Starters

Plus and minus – Get the students to make a simple table with a plus sign heading above one column and a minus above the next. Show them a syringe and tell them that they have to think of themselves as parents and write down some reasons why they might have their children vaccinated against diseases, putting them in the plus column and some reasons why they might not want them to be vaccinated into the other column. To support students, provide a set of prompt cards. *(5 minutes)*

The bad old days – Split students into small groups and ask each group to imagine they were living in a time when there were no vaccinations. How might they have treated diseases? What was the effect on child mortality rates? After 5 minutes, pool the collective ideas. *(10 minutes)*

Main

- Exposition – Have the students read, either silently or out loud in sections, the text from the Student Book regarding whooping cough and the controversy surrounding it. Hold a discussion on the issue and then get the students to complete summary notes of the major points. Support students by providing a prompts sheet.
- Direct students to study Figure 1, which shows the effect of the whooping cough scare on both uptake of the vaccine and the number of cases of the disease. Ask them to break the graph into appropriate time segments and comment on what is happening in each one. Share these among the class once completed. Students could be supported by giving them guidance on the different time segments.
- Following some discussion with students, compile a list of questions that a parent might ask before they bring their child for a normal vaccination. Use these questions to design a webpage for parents, as suggested in the Student Book. Students can supply answers to the questions, combining scientific facts with reassurance.
- Show, or read out, an article on a scientific or medical topic (preferably one that glosses over the true facts or is scaremongering!) from a popular newspaper. Invite the students to comment on how accurate they think it is and whether it could have been improved. Working in groups, students could design a presentation making the case for responsible reporting of scientific and medical topics in the media. The whooping cough topic should be included, but the presentation could also include references to other topics, such as climate change or the side-effects of other medicines or treatments.

Plenaries

True or false? – Give the students a simple true or false exercise based on the content covered in the lesson. Alternatively have them devise one for themselves. *(5 minutes)*

Role play exercise – Direct students to read and discuss the whooping cough story in the Student Book. Then ask one student to play Dr John Wilson, one to play a worried parent seeking compensation, one to play someone from the medical authority insisting that the dangers of whooping cough outweigh any danger from the vaccine and one to play Lord Stuart-Smith. The rest of the class should offer their classmates their help. To support students, provide them with a script. To extend students, direct them to script their own. *(10 minutes)*

Further teaching suggestions

Making sure the drugs are safe
- Discuss the ways in which new drugs are tested. Why does it take so long? Is it right to use animals? Would you volunteer to be part of a drug trial?

Measles, mumps and rubella – what are the risks?
- Find out what the symptoms and effects are. Why can they be life-threatening? This activity can be extended to other infectious diseases for which we have vaccinations, such as diphtheria and polio.

Searching for new drugs
- Students could discuss other possible sources of new drugs. Are there more drugs to be extracted from plants? What effect do you think that rainforest destruction has had on the search for new drugs from plants? Research the development of new drugs and the problems of testing.

How much will it cost?
- The development of new antibiotics and other drugs costs money. Discuss the finances of the drugs industry and how the costs of development are recovered.

Writing a letter to a newspaper
- Ask the students to put themselves in the place of a parent who has lost a child to whooping cough and write a letter to a newspaper urging other parents to make use of the vaccination programme, providing clear reasons.

Creating an advert
- Having gone through the section on Medicines for the future in the Student Book, ask the students to make an advert for a future medicine derived from one of the sources mentioned. This could take the form of a drawing, a sound file, a PowerPoint slide, a song, etc.

Computer simulations
- With students, create computer simulations to model the effect of: balanced and unbalanced diets and exercise; the growth of bacterial colonies in varying conditions; action of the immune system and the effect of antibiotics and vaccines.

B1 1.10   How do we deal with disease?

Learning objectives
- What are the advantages and disadvantages of being vaccinated?
- How has the treatment of disease changed over time?

The whooping cough story

In the 1970s, Dr John Wilson, a UK specialist in treating children, published a report suggesting that the pertussis (whooping cough) vaccine might cause brain damage in some children. The report was based on his study of a small group of 36 patients.

The media publicised the story and parents began to panic. The number of children being vaccinated against whooping cough fell from over 80% to around 30%. This was too low to protect the population from the virus.

People were so worried about the vaccine that they forgot that whooping cough itself can cause brain damage and death. In Scotland about 100 000 children suffered from whooping cough between 1977 and 1991. About 75 of them died. A similar pattern was seen across the whole of the UK.

An investigation into the original research discovered that it had serious flaws. Identical twin girls who were included in the study, and later died of a rare genetic disorder, had never actually had the whooping cough vaccine. It was a small study and only 12 of the children investigated had shown any symptoms close to the time of their whooping cough vaccination. Their parents were involved in claims for compensation from the vaccine manufacturers.

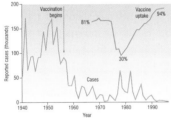

Figure 1 Graph showing the effect of the whooping cough scare on both uptake of the vaccine and the number of cases of the disease (Source: Open University)

Activity

Design a webpage for parents that answers the sort of questions they might ask about their child having the normal vaccines. Make it user-friendly, i.e. the sort of thing a health worker could use to help reassure worried parents.

OR

Produce a PowerPoint presentation on the importance of responsible media reporting of science and medicine, using the whooping cough case as one of your main examples.

No medical treatment (including vaccinations) is completely safe, but when the claims for compensation came to court, the whole study was questioned. After hearing all the evidence, the judge decided that the risks of whooping cough were far worse than any possible damage caused by the vaccine itself.

However, this judgement on the study got much less media coverage than the original scare story. Parents still felt there was 'no smoke without fire'. It was 20 years before vaccination levels, and the levels of whooping cough, returned to the levels before the scare. The number of people having vaccinations now is over 90%, and deaths from whooping cough are almost unknown in the UK.

Medicines for the future

Overuse of antibiotics has lead to spreading antibiotic resistance in many different bacteria. In recent years doctors have found strains of bacteria that are resistant to even the strongest antibiotics. When that happens, there is nothing more that antibiotics can do for a patient and he or she may well die.

The development of antibiotic resistant strains of bacteria means scientists are constantly looking for new antibiotics. It isn't easy to find chemicals which kill bacteria without damaging human cells.

Penicillin and several other antibiotics are made by moulds. Scientists are collecting soil samples from all over the world to try and find another mould to produce a new antibiotic that will kill antibiotic-resistant bacteria such as MRSA.

Crocodiles have teeth full of rotting meat. They live in dirty water and fight a lot. But scientists noticed that although crocodiles often give each other terrible bites, the bites do not become infected. They have extracted a chemical known as 'crocodillin' from crocodile blood and it seems to be a powerful antibiotic. Now the race is on to try and turn these amazing chemicals into antibiotics we can use.

Fish such as this plaice are covered with a slime which helps to protect them from damage and infection. Scientists have analysed this slime and found it contains proteins which have antibiotic properties. The proteins have been isolated from the slime and they still kill bacteria. So maybe fish will provide us with an antibiotic for the future.

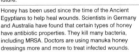

Honey has been used since the time of the Ancient Egyptians to help heal wounds. Scientists in Germany and Australia have found that certain types of honey have antibiotic properties. They kill many bacteria, including MRSA. Doctors are using manuka honey dressings more and more to treat infected wounds.

Figure 2 Where will the next antibiotic be found?

Activity

Produce a poster on antibiotic resistance in bacteria and the search for new antibiotics. Make sure you explain how antibiotic resistance has developed and why we need more antibiotics. Use the ideas given here and, if possible, look for more examples of possible sources of new antibiotics.

Key points
- Vaccination protects individuals and society from the effects of a disease.
- The treatment of disease has changed as our understanding of how antibiotics and immunity has increased.

Summary questions

1 Give one advantage and one disadvantage of being vaccinated.
2 List three examples of bad science from the story of the whooping cough vaccine and explain why the story should never have been published.

Summary answers

1 **Advantage:** protected against potentially serious disease.
Disadvantage: small chance of adverse reaction to the vaccine.

2 Bad science examples: Very small sample size, not all sample had actually had the vaccination, only a third of the group developed symptoms anywhere near the time of their vaccinations, financial gains were involved, no proper peer evaluation and repetition of findings.

The papers should not have published without checking the reproducibility and validity of the study. The potential impact of the study should have been considered first before publication to minimise both the drop in levels of vaccination below that needed to maintain herd immunity and illness and death among children who developed the disease.

Summary answers

1 a A diet that contains the right amount of carbohydrates, proteins, fats, vitamins, minerals, fibre and water, and energy.

b Lots of muscles so high metabolic rate. They use lots of energy which comes from food.

2 a Points to include: a realistic picture of healthy weight, sensible dieting to include a balanced diet, include exercise to increase metabolic rate and build up muscle, resist food like chocolate and eat fruit etc. instead.

b Sensible eating, plenty of protein to help build up muscle, complex carbohydrates such as pasta etc. to give stamina, balancing exercise with diet.

3 a Inherited factors, the way your liver makes cholesterol, the level of fat in your diet, the amount of exercise taken.

b Reduce the fat in your diet, take more exercise (take statins).

c Any sensible example e.g. the metabolic rate (which affects obesity, which in turn affects their likelihood of developing problems such as type 2 diabetes).

4 Once inside the body they reproduce rapidly. Bacteria simply split in two. They often produce toxins and sometimes directly damage cells. Viruses take over the cells to reproduce, damaging and destroying them and very rarely produce toxins. The diseases are caused by the cell damage and toxins produced by the pathogens, and also by the way your body responds to that.

5 Spread: droplet infection, direct, contaminated food and drink, through cuts. Ways of reducing spread of diseases – any sensible points, e.g. using tissues and throwing them away, washing hands, hand in front of mouth when coughing, etc.

6 a They have developed resistance to vancomycin through a process of natural selection. They are then spread from patient to patient by contact between patients, on the hands of doctors and nurses, or on the objects around in a hospital.

b Use antibiotics carefully – only when they are needed – and make sure people always finish the course.

7 a Use sterile Petri dish and agar.

Sterilise the inoculating loop by heating it to red hot in the flame of a Bunsen and then let it cool. Do not put the loop down as it cools.

Innoculate agar with zigzag streaks of bacteria using sterile loop. Replace the lid on the dish quickly to avoid contamination.

Secure the lid with adhesive tape but do not seal.

Label the culture and incubate at no warmer than 25 °C.

b Include points such as: Inoculate agar plates with bacteria – ideally from school floor.

Add circles of filter paper soaked with different strengths of the disinfectant and incubate at no higher than 25 °C. Look for areas of clear agar around the disinfectant soaked disk. Recommend lowest concentration that destroys the bacteria.

Summary questions

1 a Define the term 'balanced diet'.

b A top athlete needs to eat a lot of food each day. This includes protein and carbohydrate. Explain how they can eat so much without putting on weight.

2 Two young people have written to a lifestyle magazine problem page for advice about their diet and lifestyle. Produce an 'answer page' for the next edition of the magazine.

a Melanie: *I'm 16 and I worry about my weight a lot. I'm not really overweight but I want to be thinner. I've tried to diet but I just feel so tired when I do – and then I buy chocolate bars on the way home from school when my friends can't see me! What can I do?*

b Jaz: *I'm nearly 17 and I've grown so fast in the last year that I look like a stick! So my clothes look pretty silly. I'm also really good at football, but I don't seem as strong as I was and my legs get really tired by the end of a match. I want to build up a bit more muscle and stamina – but I don't just want to eat so much I end up getting really heavy. What can I do about it?*

3 a What factors affect the cholesterol levels in your blood?

b What can you do to help reduce your blood cholesterol levels?

c Cholesterol is one inherited factor which affects your health. Give one other example of an inherited factor which affects your health and explain how it does this.

4 How do tiny organisms like bacteria and viruses [make a] person ill?

5 There is going to be a campaign to try and stop the spread of colds in Year 7 of your school. There is [going] to be a poster and a simple PowerPoint presenta[tion]. Make a list of all the important things that the Year [7] children need to know about how diseases are s[pread]. Also cover how the spread of infectious diseases [from] one person to another can be reduced.

6 a Vancomycin is an antibiotic which doctors use [for] patients infected with MRSA and other antibio[tic] resistant bacteria. Now they are finding some infections are resistant to vancomycin. Explain [how] this may have happened.

b What can we do to prevent the problem of ant[ibiotic] resistance getting worse?

7 a How would you set up a culture of bacteria in a lab?

b Describe how you would test to find out the rig[ht] strength of disinfectant to use to wash the sch[ool] floors.

Kerboodle resources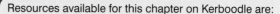

Resources available for this chapter on Kerboodle are:

- Chapter map: Keeping healthy
- Maths skills: BHI calculator (B1 1.1)
- Support: Health on the line (B1 1.1)
- Video: Pathogens (B1 1.4)
- Extension: Shape matters (B1 1.5)
- Bump up your grade: Doctor, doctor (B1 1.6)
- Support: What's what (B1 1.6)
- How Science Works: Does the concentration of a disinfectant change its effectiveness at killing bacteria? (B1 1.7)
- Practical: Growing microorganisms (B1 1.7)
- WebQuest: The chickenpox vaccination (B1 1.9)
- Animation: Immunity due to vaccination (B1 1.9)
- Interactive activity: Preventing disease
- Revision podcast: Healthy bodies
- Test yourself: Keeping healthy
- On your marks: Keeping healthy
- Examination-style questions: Keeping healthy
- Answers to examination-style questions: Keeping healthy

End of chapter questions

Examination-style questions 🄚

...s possible to grow microorganisms in the laboratory.
...t A shows some temperatures.
...t B shows situations for which these temperatures
...ght be suitable.
...tch each temperature to the correct situation.

List A	List B
...5°C	Used in industrial laboratories to grow microorganisms quickly
...5°C	Used in school laboratory to grow microorganisms safely
...0°C	Used to stop microorganisms growing without killing them
	Used to kill microorganisms

(3)

...his question you will be assessed on using good
...glish, organising information clearly and using
...ecialist terms where appropriate.

...need a balanced diet to keep us healthy. Explain the
...ys in which an unbalanced diet can affect the body. (6)

...erson's metabolic rate varies with the amount of
...ivity they do.
...Metabolic rate is ....
...Choose one answer.
...he breathing rate
...he rate of chemical reactions in cells
...he heart rate (1)
...Suggest **one** other factor which can change a
...person's metabolic rate. (1)

...io is a disease caused by a virus. In the UK, children
...given polio vaccine to protect them against the
...ease.

...Choose the correct words from each list to complete
...the sentences below.

i It is difficult to kill the polio virus inside the body
   because the virus .... (1)
   *is not affected by drugs   lives inside cells
   produces antitoxins*

ii The vaccine contains an .... form of the polio
   virus. (1)
   active   infective   inactive

iii The vaccine stimulates the white blood cells to
    produce .... which destroy the virus. (1)
    antibiotics   antibodies   drugs

b The graph shows the number of cases of polio in the
   UK between 1948 and 1968.

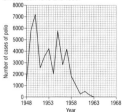

i In which year was the number of cases of polio
   highest? (1)

ii Polio vaccination was first used in the UK in 1955.
   How many years did it take for the number of cases
   of polio to fall to zero? (1)

iii There have been no cases of polio in the UK
    for many years. But children are still vaccinated
    against the disease.
    Suggest **one** reason for this. (1)
    AQA, 2006

5 Controlling infections in hospitals has become much
   more difficult in recent years.

a Suggest **two** reasons why MRSA is causing problems
   in many hospitals. (2)

b The pioneer in methods of treating infections in
   hospitals was Ignaz Semmelweis. He observed that
   women whose babies were delivered by doctors
   in hospital had a death rate of 18% from infections
   caught in the hospital. Women whose babies were
   delivered by midwives in the hospital had a death rate
   of 2%. He observed that doctors often came straight
   from examining dead bodies to the delivery ward.

   i In a controlled experiment, Semmelweis made
     doctors wash their hands in chloride of lime
     solution before delivering the babies. The death
     rate fell to about 2% – down to the same level
     as the death rate in mothers whose babies were
     delivered by midwives.
     Explain why the death rate fell. (1)

   ii Explain how Semmelweis's results could be
      used to reduce the spread of MRSA in a modern
      hospital. (2)
      AQA, 2005

45

Practical suggestions

Practicals	AQA	🄚	📖	⚙
Investigate the effectiveness of various antibiotic discs in killing bacteria.	✓	✓		
Growing microorganisms in Petri dishes to demonstrate sterile technique & growing pure cultures.	✓	✓	✓	
The use of pre-inoculated agar in Petri dishes to evaluate the effect of disinfectants & antibiotic	✓	✓	✓	✓
Computer simulations to model the effect of: balanced & unbalanced diets and exercise; the growth of bacterial colonies in varying conditions; action of the immune system and the effect of antibiotics and vaccines.	✓		✓	

Examination-style answers

1 25°C – Used in school laboratory to grow microorganisms
safely, 35°C – Used in industrial laboratories to grow
microorganisms quickly, 100°C – Used to kill microorganisms
(3 marks)

---

2 Marks awarded for this answer will be determined by the
Quality of Written Communication (QWC) as well as the
standard of the scientific response.

There is a clear, balanced and detailed description referring
to both overeating and deficiency. The answer shows almost
faultless spelling, punctuation and grammar. It is coherent
and in an organised, logical sequence. It contains a range of
appropriate or relevant specialist terms used accurately.
(5–6 marks)

There is some description of a range of the ways in which
the diet can be unbalanced and the effects. There are some
errors in spelling, punctuation and grammar. The answer has
some structure and organisation. The use of specialist terms
has been attempted, but not always accurately. *(3–4 marks)*

There is a brief description of at least two ways in which the
diet can be unbalanced, which has little clarity and detail.
The spelling, punctuation and grammar are very weak.
The answer is poorly organised with almost no specialist
terms and/or their use demonstrating a general lack of
understanding of their meaning. *(1–2 marks)*

No relevant content. *(0 marks)*

Examples of biology points made in the response:
- balanced diet contains all the correct nutrients in the
  correct amounts
- balanced diet has the correct amount of energy
- too much energy leads to mass/weight increase
- e.g. eating too much fat
- if activity increases use of energy increases
- too little energy leads to decrease in mass/weight
- can lead to anorexia/described symptom
- lack of vitamins/named vitamin can lead to deficiency
  disease/correctly named
- too much carbohydrate/sugar/overweight can lead to type
  2 diabetes
- lack of a mineral ion/named ion can lead to deficiency
  disease/correctly named
- obesity linked to, e.g. heart disease/arthritis/high blood
  pressure etc.

3 a the rate of chemical reactions in cells *(1 mark)*

b Any **one** from:
- the proportion of fat to muscle
- inherited factors
- other sensible suggestion, other than activity *(1 mark)*

4 a i lives inside cells *(1 mark)*
     ii inactive *(1 mark)*
     iii antibodies *(1 mark)*

b i 1950 *(1 mark)*
     ii 8 (years) *(1 mark)*
     iii Any **one** from: e.g.
       - disease could be reintroduced (from abroad)
       - disease would spread if it came back
       - protection on holiday abroad
       - high proportion of immune people needed to
         prevent epidemic *(1 mark)*

5 a Any **two** from:
- resistant to (most) antibiotics
- contagious or easily passed on or reference to open
  wounds
- patients ill therefore less able to combat disease
(2 marks)

b i Using chloride of lime to wash their hands killed
     any bacteria the doctors may have picked up from
     corpses. Allow diseases/germs/infection/disinfectants
     as alternative terms. *(1 mark)*
   ii people should wash hands after contact with patient
     so bacteria/pathogen/MRSA are not transferred to
     other patients *(2 marks)*

B1 2.1

Responding to change

Learning objectives

Students should learn:

- that the nervous system enables humans to react to their surroundings by means of cells called receptors
- that there are receptors that are sensitive to touch, light, sound, changes in position, chemicals, pressure, pain and temperature
- that information from these receptors passes along cells (neurons) in nerves to the brain, where the response is coordinated.

Learning outcomes

Most students should be able to:

- identify the sense organs involved in responding to light, sound, changes of position, chemicals, touch, pressure and temperature in humans
- describe how the nervous system works
- describe the difference between the functions of a sensory and a motor neuron.

Some students should also be able to:

- explain the importance of the coordination of impulses by the brain in our responses to changes in the environment.

Support

- Provide cards with the separate parts of a nervous pathway, such as 'receptor' and 'sensory neuron' etc. on them and ask students to place them in the correct order in the pathway.

Extend

- Show a picture of a poison arrow frog. Get the students to discuss the use of these in tropical hunting and ask them to speculate about the mechanisms which may be at work when the paralysing dart acts.

AQA Specification link-up: Biology B1.2

- The nervous system enables humans to react to their … *[B1.2.1 a)]*
- Cells called receptors detect stimuli (changes in the environment) … *[B1.2.1 b)]*
- Light receptor cells, like most animal cells, have a … *[B1.2.1 c)]*
- Information from receptors passes along cells … *[B1.2.1 d)]*

Controlled Assessment: SA4.1 Planning an investigation *[SA4.1.1 a) b) c)]*; SA4.3 Collect primary and secondary data *[SA4.3.3 a) b) c) d)]*; SA4.4 Select and process primary and secondary data *[SA4.4.1 a) b)]* and SA4.5 Analyse and interpret primary and secondary data. *[SA4.5.2 a) b) c) d)]*

Lesson structure

Starters

'Be aware!' – Get the class to sit in silence for 30 seconds exactly, asking them to focus on what sensations their skin is giving them. Discuss this. Spend another 30 seconds with eyes shut and silent, focusing on background sounds. How many can they identify? Spend another 30 seconds silently focusing on one spot or point in the room and keeping their eyes still. Discuss the experience. Round off by talking over how we are aware of our surroundings (via our senses). *(5 minutes)*

Circus of activities – Place 'feely' bags around the room involving senses and containing mystery objects, e.g. a sniff test with different essences in film containers, guess the sound on an MP3 player, mystery object photos or objects under a microscope, identifying mystery fruit (care with hygiene). Students could be supported by confining the mystery objects to one sense, e.g. smells, or by restricting the variety of objects for each test. Students could be extended by timing them and allocating points for correct answers. They could also be asked to comment on the amount of information needed to make a correct decision. *(10 minutes)*

Main

The main part of the lesson could be a practical session involving the testing of sensitivity using the following:

- Practical on identifying the density of nerve endings by investigating the sensitivity of different areas of the skin (see 'Practical support'). 'How Science Works' concepts can be introduced here, such as the accuracy of the measurements, the calculation of means, precision and the control of variables. If class results are collated, some indication of the variability can be discussed.

- Try an active learning exercise. Get five of the students to stand in a line, holding on to the cuffs of each others shirts or jumpers. Attach labels to each saying 'receptor', 'sensory neuron', 'coordinator', 'motor neuron', and 'effector'. Create a scenario, e.g. getting stung by a nettle. Get each volunteer to state what it is doing, e.g. the receptor is being stung and creating the impulse and passing it on to the sensory neuron (by tugging its cuff gently), the sensory neuron passes it on to the coordinator which passes it on to the motor neuron which passes it on to the effector. In this case, the effector is the muscles controlling the voice and says, 'Ow!' Repeat with other scenarios, e.g. smelling onions and crying, being cold and shivering, etc.

Plenaries

Does the colour smell right? – A variation of the 'feely' bags could involve the conflicting information from odd combinations of colour and smell, e.g. pink food smelling of peppermint, blue food smelling of strawberry. This could trigger a discussion of how senses are used and that information comes from more than one sense organ. *(5 minutes)*

What is the significance of the results? – What do the results of the experiments tell us? Is it touch, pressure or pain receptors that are being stimulated? Support students by discussing their results and encouraging them to write clear statements as conclusions. Extend students by asking them how this type of experiment could be modified for other receptors such as hot or cold receptors. Suggest that student's link up the density of the receptors to the areas tested. *(10 minutes)*

Practical support

Identifying of the density of nerve endings

Equipment and materials required

Small pieces of blunt wire (unbent paper clip, blunt tapestry needles) mounted in pieces of cork; if two wires are used they should be about 1 cm apart.

Details

Students could be asked to design an investigation to measure the sensitivity of the skin or can do the practical described here.

Working in pairs, one student is blindfolded or told to look in a different direction, while another student touches them on the back of the hand with either one or two pieces of blunt wire about 1 cm apart mounted in a cork. The blindfolded student has to say whether it was one point or two points that touched them. In addition to the back of the hand, other areas of the body, such as the upper arm or the back of the leg, could be investigated. In this way, a comparison could be made about the sensitivity of different areas of the body.

Safety: The wires should be blunt, not sharp, and students reminded not to exert pressure.

Coordination and control

B1 2.1   Responding to change

Learning objectives

- Why do you need a nervous system?
- What is a receptor?
- How do you respond to changes in your surroundings?

You need to know what is going on in the world around you. Your **nervous system** makes this possible. It enables you to react to your surroundings and coordinate your behaviour.

Your nervous system carries electrical signals (impulses) that travel fast – from 1 to 120 metres per second. This means you can react to changes in your surroundings very quickly.

a What is the main job of the nervous system?

The nervous system

Like all living things, you need to avoid danger, find food and, eventually, find a mate! This is where your nervous system comes into its own. Your body is particularly sensitive to changes in the world around you. Any changes (known as stimuli) are picked up by cells called receptors.

Receptor cells (e.g. the light receptor cells in your eyes) are like most animal cells. They have a nucleus, cytoplasm and a cell membrane. These receptors are usually found clustered together in special **sense organs**, such as your eyes and your skin. You have many different types of sensory receptor (see Figure 2).

b Where would you find receptors that respond to:
  i a loud noise
  ii touching a hot oven
  iii a strong perfume?

Figure 1 Your body is made up of millions of cells which have to work together. Whatever you do with your body – whether it's walking to school or playing on the computer – your movements need to be coordinated.

Did you know ... ?

Some male moths have receptors so sensitive they can detect the scent of a female several kilometres away and follow the scent trail to find her!

Figure 2 This cat relies on its sensory receptors to detect changes in the environment

Ears – receptors sensitive to sound

Ears – receptors sensitive to changes in position for balance

Eyes – receptors sensitive to light

Nose and tongue – receptors sensitive to chemicals for taste and smell

Skin – receptors sensitive to touch, pressure, pain and temperature changes

How your nervous system works

Once a sensory receptor detects a stimulus, the information (sent as an electrical impulse) passes along special cells called neurons. These are usually found in bundles of hundreds or even thousands of neurons known as nerves.

The impulse travels along the neuron until it reaches the central nervous system or CNS. The CNS is made up of the brain and the spinal cord. The cells which carry impulses from your sense organs to your central nervous system are called sensory neurons.

c What is the difference between a neuron and a nerve?

Your brain gets huge amounts of information from all the sensory receptors in your body. It coordinates the information and sends impulses out along special cells. These cells carry information from the CNS to the rest of your body. The cells are called motor neurons. They carry impulses to make the right bits of your body – the effector organs – respond.

Effector organs are muscles or glands. Your muscles respond to the arrival of impulses by contracting. Your glands respond by releasing (secreting) chemical substances.

The way your nervous system works can be summed up as:

receptor → sensory neuron → coordinator (CNS) → motor neuron → effector

d What is the difference between a sensory neuron and a motor neuron?

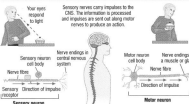

Your eyes respond to light

Sensory nerves carry impulses to the CNS. The information is processed and impulses are sent out along motor nerves to produce an action.

Sensory neuron cell body

Nerve fibre

Nerve endings in central nervous system

Sensory receptor   Direction of impulse

Sensory neuron

Motor neuron cell body

Nerve endings in a muscle or gland

Nerve fibre

Direction of impulse

Motor neuron

Figure 3 The rapid responses of our nervous system allow us to respond to our surroundings quickly – and in the right way!

Summary questions

1 Copy and complete using the words below:
  neurons receptors electrical CNS environment nervous
  Your .... system carries fast .... impulses. Changes in the .... are picked up by your .... and impulses travel along your .... to your ....

2 Make a table to show the different types of sense receptor. For each one, give an example of the sort of things it responds to, e.g. touch receptors respond to an insect crawling on your skin.

3 Explain what happens in your nervous system when you see a piece of chocolate, pick it up and eat it.

AQA Examiner's tip

Make sure you are clear that 'motor' means movement. 'Motor neurons' stimulate the muscles to contract.

AQA Examiner's tip

Be careful to use the terms neuron and nerve correctly.
Talk about **impulses** (*not* messages) travelling along a neuron.

Key points

- The nervous system uses electrical impulses to enable you to react quickly to your surroundings and coordinate what you do.
- Cells called receptors detect stimuli (changes in the environment).
- Like all animal cells, light receptor cells and other receptors have a nucleus, cytoplasm and cell membrane.
- Impulses from receptors pass along sensory neurons to the brain and spinal cord (CNS). Impulses are sent along motor neurons from the brain (CNS) to the effector organs.

Further teaching suggestions

How fast is a nerve impulse?

- If you stub your toe, there is a very short interval of time between the action of stubbing and the sensation of pain. Discuss this and suggest to students that they try to work out how the time interval between being touched on the toe and feeling the sensation of touch can be measured. Can this measurement be used to work out how fast the nerve impulse is transmitted? Hint: How might measuring the length of the leg help the calculation?

A receptors experiment

- Students could devise a simple experiment to investigate the density of hot and cold receptors in the skin. This exercise could be used to introduce HSW concept of planning a practical.

AQA Examiner's tip

Students do need to understand the difference between nerve and neuron. A clear definition of each could be made into a revision card. It could be helpful to students to have a good understanding of the different types of neuron and know that nerves can contain either sensory or motor neurons or a mixture of both.

Answers to in-text questions

a Coordination and control; awareness of surroundings.
b i Ears. ii Skin. iii Nose.
c A neuron is a single nerve cell; a nerve is a lot of neurons bundled together.
d A sensory neuron carries impulses from sensory receptors to the CNS; a motor neuron carries impulses from the CNS to the effector organs.

Summary answers

1 nervous, electrical, environment, receptors, neurons, CNS

2 Table showing receptors for light, sound, position, smell (could also have temperature, pain, pressure) with student example of a stimulus for each one.

3 Light from the chocolate is detected by the sensory receptors in the eyes, an impulse travels along the sensory neuron to the brain, information is processed in the brain and an impulse is sent along a motor neuron to the muscles of the arm and hand so you pick up the chocolate and put it in your mouth. Give credit if students add anything further, e.g. sensory impulses from mouth/nose to brain with information about taste, smell of chocolate, touch sensors send impulses about presence of chocolate, motor impulses to muscles for chewing, etc.

B1 2.2

Reflex actions

Learning objectives

Students should learn:

- that reflex actions are automatic and rapid responses to stimuli
- that simple reflex actions involve receptors, sensory neurons, motor neurons and relay neurons, together with synapses and effectors
- that reflex actions take care of basic functions, such as breathing, and help to avoid danger or harm to the body.

Learning outcomes

Most students should be able to:

- explain what is meant by the term 'reflex action'
- describe the roles of receptors; sensory, relay and motor neurons; synapses and effectors in a reflex action
- explain why reflex actions are so important.

Some students should also be able to:

- analyse a specific reflex action in terms of stimulus → receptor → coordinator → effector → response
- explain in detail how a synapse works.

Support

- Students could be given cards with the words needed to complete Question 1 of the Summary Questions on them and asked to place them in the correct places on a large copy of the passage.
- Alternatively, provide some volunteer students with A4 sheets on which the names of parts of the reflex pathway have been printed. The students should then arrange themselves in the correct order. They could be timed as a challenge. Using a lightning-shaped zap, ask the students to talk through their bit of the process as the impulse (zap) gets passed to them.

Extend

- Students could investigate the work of Pavlov and his dogs in the context of the reflex action.

AQA / Specification link-up: Biology B1.2

- Information from receptors passes along cells … [B1.2.1 d)]
- Candidates should understand the role of receptors … [B1.2.1 e)]

Controlled Assessment: SA4.3 Collect primary and secondary data [SA4.3.3 a) b) c) d)]; SA4.4 Select and process primary and secondary data [SA4.4.1 a) b)] and SA4.5 Analyse and interpret primary and secondary data. [SA4.5.2 a) b) c) d)]

Lesson structure

Starters

Bang goes the theory! – (Background music: 'The Reflex' by Duran Duran.) While the class are quietly settled on a task at the start of the lesson, such as writing the title and date into their books, make a sudden very loud noise. Slapping two dissection boards together will do, or turn the volume right up on a piece of loud music. Ask the students what happened to their bodies and then start to draw out their theories on why and how they responded. *(5 minutes)*

'Get a grip' – Show a photo of a baby gripping its mother's finger. Ask the class to write down what is happening, why and how it is happening. Support students by encouraging them to describe the function of the reflex, i.e. to hold on to the mother so as not to get lost. Extend students by encouraging them to speculate as to how this reflex has arisen and what the process might entail. *(10 minutes)*

Main

- Organise the stick-drop test for measuring reaction time (see 'Practical support'). This is a reaction, not a reflex, but most reflexes are too fast to measure in class. 'How Science Works' concepts can be introduced here: the accuracy of the measurements, the calculation of means, precision and the control of variables. If class results are collated, some indication of the variability can be discussed.
- Further work with the stick-drop test – Do reaction times alter with age, time of day or intake of caffeine? Results can be tabulated and class results compared. Boys can be compared with girls and distribution curves drawn.
- Try testing the knee jerk reflex (see 'Practical support'). Ask for a volunteer, or select a suitable student, from the class and demonstrate the knee jerk reflex on them. If appropriate, allow students to work in pairs and try it out on each other (caution needed here!). Discuss what is happening. NB The knee jerk reflex has to be so fast that it does not have a relay neuron.
- Can we alter reflex actions? – This activity can be included in a lesson if the Plenary 'The override button' is not used. Encourage students to think of situations where it is possible to alter the automatic response (not dropping a hot object, deliberately breathing more slowly, etc.). Are there some reflex actions over which we have no control? Discuss the situations and build up a list.

Plenaries

'The override button' – Can we learn to alter our reflex actions? Support students by showing them a photo of a strongman competition endurance event such as a truck pull. Ask them whether there is pain involved and ask what is going on inside the contestants to get them to keep going. *(5 minutes)*

Response timer exercise – There are many interactive response timer exercises on the internet, such as the BBC sheep tranquilising game at www.gamingdelight.com. (search under 'sheep reaction') which is great fun and can provide a motivating discussion piece for the end of a lesson as well as proving that you get better with practice. *(10 minutes)*

Practical support

The stick-drop test

Equipment and materials required
A metre rule, access to computers for the interactive reaction timers. It could be helpful to have preprinted sheets on which to record reaction times, so that it is easy for students to gather class results.

Details
Working in pairs, one student holds a metre rule vertically at the zero end, between the thumb and forefinger of another student, so that the 50 cm mark is level with the top of the forefinger. Without warning, the first student drops the rule and the second student attempts to catch it between the thumb and forefinger, noting the distance on the ruler just above the forefinger. Repeat several times, so that a mean can be calculated. Then change around so that everyone gets a turn. Write a report of the experiment.

Testing the knee jerk reflex (practical or demonstration)

Equipment and materials required
Ruler.

Details
Get students to work in pairs and try it out the knee jerk reaction on each other (caution needed here!). One student should sit on a chair with one leg loosely crossed over the other at the knee. The other student gives a gentle tap with the edge of a ruler just below the knee cap of the crossed leg. Discuss what is happening. N.B. The knee jerk reflex has to be so fast that it does not have a relay neuron.

Safety: The tap with the ruler does need to be gentle and not vigorous.

Coordination and control

B1 2.2   Reflex actions

Learning objectives
- What is a reflex?
- Why are reflexes so important?

Your nervous system lets you take in information from your surroundings and respond in the right way. However, some of your responses are so fast that they happen without giving you time to think.

When you touch something hot, or sharp, you pull your hand back before you feel the pain. If something comes near your face, you blink. Automatic responses like these are known as reflexes.

What are reflexes for?
Reflexes are very important both for human beings and for other animals. They help you to avoid danger or harm because they happen so fast. There are also lots of reflexes that take care of your basic body functions. These functions include breathing and moving food through your gut.

It would make life very difficult if you had to think consciously about those things all the time – and would be fatal if you forgot to breathe!

a Why are reflexes important?

How do reflexes work? *k*
Reflex actions involve just three types of neuron. These are:
- sensory neurons
- motor neurons
- relay neurons – these connect a sensory neuron and a motor neuron. Your relay neurons are in the CNS.

An electrical impulse passes from the sensory receptor along the sensory neuron to the CNS. It then passes along a relay neuron (usually in the spinal cord) and straight back along a motor neuron. From there the impulse arrives at the effector organ. The effector organ will be a muscle or a gland. We call this a reflex arc.

The key point in a reflex arc is that the impulse bypasses the conscious areas of your brain. The result is that the time between the stimulus and the reflex action is as short as possible.

b Why is it important that the impulses in a reflex arc do not go to the conscious brain?

How synapses work *k*
Your nerves are not joined up directly to each other. There are junctions between them called synapses. The electrical impulses travelling along your neurons have to cross these synapses. They cannot leap the gap. Look at Figure 1 to see what happens next.

The reflex arc in detail
Look at Figure 2. It shows what would happen if you touched a hot object.

When you touch it, a receptor in your skin is stimulated. An electrical impulse passes along a sensory neuron to the central nervous system – in this case the spinal cord.

Practical

The stick-drop test
You can investigate how quickly nerve impulses travel in your body using metre rules, and either stop clocks or ICT to measure how quickly you catch the ruler OR by standing in a circle holding hands with your eyes closed and measuring how long it takes a hand squeeze to pass around the circle.

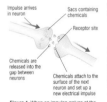

Figure 1 When an impulse arrives at the junction between two neurons, chemicals are released which cross the synapse and arrive at receptor sites on the next neuron. This starts up an electrical impulse in the next neuron.

When an impulse from the sensory neuron arrives in the synapse with a relay neuron, a chemical messenger is released. This chemical crosses the synapse to the relay neuron. There it sets off an electrical impulse that travels along the relay neuron.

When the impulse reaches the synapse between the relay neuron and a motor neuron returning to the arm, another chemical is released.

This chemical crosses the synapse and starts an electrical impulse travelling down the motor neuron. When the impulse reaches the effector organ, it is stimulated to respond.

In this example the impulses arrive in the muscles of the arm, causing them to contract. This action moves the hand rapidly away from the source of pain. If the effector organ is a gland, it will respond by releasing (secreting) chemicals.

Most reflex actions can be shown as follows:

stimulus → receptor → coordinator → effector → response

This is not very different from a normal conscious action. However, in a reflex action the coordinator is a relay neuron either in the spinal cord or in the unconscious areas of the brain. The whole reflex is very fast indeed.

An impulse also travels up the spinal cord to the conscious areas of your brain. You know about the reflex action, but only after it has happened.

Figure 2 The reflex action which moves your hand away from something hot can save you from being burned. Reflex actions are quick and automatic; you do not think about them.

AQA Examiner's tip
Make sure you know the correct sequence of links from the receptor to the effector.

Figure 3 Newborn babies have a number of special reflexes which disappear as they grow. This gripping reflex is one of them.

Summary questions

1 Copy and complete using the words below:
conscious motor reflex relay response sensory stimulus
In a .... arc the electrical impulse bypasses the .... areas of your brain. The time between the .... and the .... is as short as possible. Only .... neurons, ... neurons and .... neurons are involved.

2 Explain why some actions, such as breathing and swallowing, are reflex actions, while others such as speaking and eating are under your conscious control.

3 Draw a flow chart to explain what happens when you step on a pin. Make sure you include an explanation of how a synapse works.

Key points
- Some responses to stimuli are automatic and rapid and are called 'reflex actions'.
- Reflex actions run everyday bodily functions and help you to avoid danger.

Further teaching suggestions

Eye reflexes
- Working in pairs, the alteration in pupil size when the eyes are opened in bright light can be easily observed by students. Discuss the value of this reflex in protecting the eyes. The relay neuron for this reflex is on the surface of the brain.

Summary of the reflexes and activities of the lesson
- What do tests such as the stick-drop test tell us? Ask students to identify the parts of the body involved. What senses are being used? Can we train ourselves to react more quickly? Does practice make perfect? Can students relate the results to some of the computer games that depend on quick reactions?

Answers to in-text questions

a Reflexes protect the body by avoiding danger or damage, to control bodily functions without the need for conscious thought, e.g. breathing.

b They need to be very quick to avoid danger, so the shorter the distance they have to travel, the quicker you will react.

Summary answers

1 reflex, conscious, stimulus, response, sensory, relay, motor

2 Reflex actions that need to operate automatically, even when you are asleep, cannot rely on conscious thought processes, unlike speaking and eating, which we need to be able to choose when to do them.

3 Stimulus → receptor → sensory neuron → synapse → chemical message → relay neuron → synapse → chemical message → motor neuron → muscles in leg lift the foot.

B1 2.3
Hormones and the menstrual cycle

Learning objectives

Students should learn:

- that many processes within the body are coordinated by chemical substances called hormones
- that the menstrual cycle is controlled by several hormones secreted by the pituitary gland and the ovaries
- the function of FSH (follicle stimulating hormone).

Learning outcomes

Most students should be able to:

- state that hormones coordinate processes in the body
- name the hormones that control the menstrual cycle and state where each is produced
- describe the functions of each hormone and relate each hormone to the different phases of the cycle.

Some students should also be able to:

- explain the relationships between the different hormones and how they interact in the cycle.

Support

- Give students broken sentences to sequence, describing the role of the hormones in the menstrual cycle.

Extend

- Students could find out about the male hormones that are equivalent to FSH, LH and oestrogen. They could compare the production of eggs with the production of sperm.

AQA Specification link-up: Biology B1.2

- Many processes within the body are coordinated by ... [B1.2.2 b)]
- Hormones regulate the functions of many organs and cells ... [B1.2.2 c)]
- Several hormones are involved in the menstrual cycle of a woman ... [B1.2.2 d)]

Lesson structure

Starters

Jobs for the hormones – Get the students to make a list of the changes that bodies undergo during puberty. Discuss this and draw out any knowledge that they have on the sex hormones and the roles they perform. *(5 minutes)*

What I know so far – Divide the students into small groups. Give each group an A3 sheet of paper. Have them put the word 'period' in large letters in the centre then for three minutes write down anything they know about periods – what age girls are when they start, when they stop, what their function is, etc. Share the findings with the rest of the group. Support students by providing a prompt sheet of questions to think about if necessary. *(10 minutes)*

Main

This lesson does have to focus on the menstrual cycle, so the following suggestions describe some ways in which the information can be put across.

- Before explaining the menstrual cycle, it could be beneficial to discuss the properties of hormones, where they are produced and how they are transported around the body. Project a diagram of the human torso to illustrate the positions of the endocrine glands and the sites of actions of the hormones.
- You can show a PowerPoint presentation introducing the vocabulary and linking the actions of the hormones. A series of PowerPoint diagrams to illustrate the stages could be prepared. Firstly, show the pituitary gland and the female reproductive system; secondly, show secretion of FSH from the pituitary affecting the ovaries in two ways ('stimulation of oestrogen production' and 'stimulation of egg development'); thirdly, show oestrogen production linked to the uterus, labelled 'developing lining' and two links back to the pituitary gland, one labelled 'negative feedback – inhibits FSH production' and the other labelled 'stimulates LH production'; lastly, link from pituitary to ovaries labelled 'ovulation triggered'.
- The PowerPoint diagrams can be used in conjunction with a human torso model if available, so that the location of the pituitary gland and the female reproductive systems can be seen easily. This reinforces some of the properties of hormones, as the students could be asked to consider how the hormones get from one place to another.
- Show a video of ovulation if available. The series *The Human Body* (BBC) shows ovulation *in situ* in detail.
- Explaining Figure 2 in the Student Book using a series of PowerPoint diagrams could be helpful. Make a point of getting the students to understand when conception is likely to occur.

Plenaries

True or false? – Present the students with a series of statements about the hormones and the cycle, some of which are true and others not. Check answers at end. This offers an opportunity to make clear any points about the cycle that students do not understand. *(5 minutes)*

Crossword clues – Get the students to suggest some key words from the spread. Write them on the board and ask them to come up with crossword clues for each one. Collect the best ones and get a volunteer to take them home and produce a crossword as a starter for the next lesson (there are many free crossword compilers available on the internet). Extend students by suggesting they come up with cryptic or clever clues. Support students by providing prompts and examples if necessary. *(10 minutes)*

Further teaching suggestions

Mammalian ovaries

- Students could look at slides under the microscope, or projected slides, of mammalian ovaries to show follicles at various stages of development.

Preserved ovaries

- They could look at preserved specimens of ovaries if available (possibly from hens).

Class discussions

- Start a class discussion on mammals: 'Do other mammals have an equivalent of the menstrual cycle? Compare the monthly cycle of human females with the breeding seasons of other mammals.'
- Start a class discussion by asking 'Do males have hormones equivalent to FSH, LH and oestrogen?'

More information on ovulation and conception

- There are some very good pre-birth websites (some have a distinct pro-life angle) with information about ovulation and conception (try www.mumsnet.com).
- View and discuss 'Window on Life' (*Sunday Times* free CDs) for more general information and animations.

Coordination and control

B1 2.3   Hormones and the menstrual cycle

Learning objectives

- How is the menstrual cycle controlled?
- When is a woman most likely to conceive?

Hormones are chemical substances that coordinate many processes within your body. Special **glands** make and release (secrete) these hormones into your body. Then the hormones are carried around your body to their target organs in the bloodstream. Hormones regulate the functions of many organs and cells. They can act very quickly, but often their effects are quite slow and long lasting.

A woman's **menstrual cycle** is a good example of control by hormones. Hormones are made in a woman's pituitary gland and her ovaries control her menstrual cycle. The levels of the different hormones rise and fall in a regular pattern. This affects the way her body works.

What is the menstrual cycle?

The average length of the menstrual cycle is about 28 days. Each month the lining of the womb thickens ready to support a developing baby. At the same time an egg starts maturing in the ovary.

About 14 days after the egg starts maturing it is released from the ovary. This is known as ovulation. The lining of the womb stays thick for several days after the egg has been released.

If the egg is fertilised by a sperm, then pregnancy may take place. The lining of the womb provides protection and food for the developing embryo. If the egg is not fertilised, the lining of the womb and the dead egg are shed from the body. This is the monthly bleed or period.

All of these changes are brought about by hormones. These are made and released by the **pituitary gland** (a pea-sized gland in the brain) and the ovaries.

- **a** What controls the menstrual cycle?
- **b** Why does the lining of the womb build up each month?

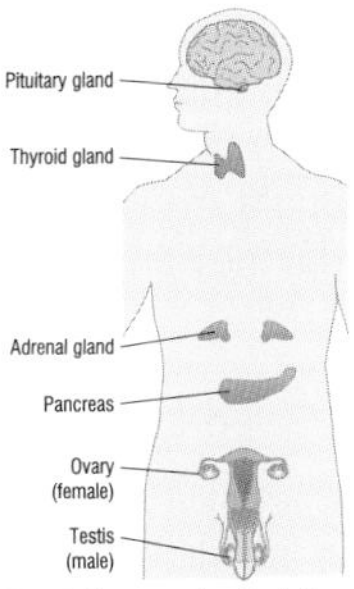

How the menstrual cycle works 🇰

Once a month, a surge of hormones from the pituitary gland in the brain starts eggs maturing in the ovaries. The hormones also stimulate the ovaries to produce the female sex hormone **oestrogen**.

- Follicle stimulating hormone (FSH) is secreted by the pituitary gland. It makes eggs mature in the ovaries. FSH also stimulates the ovaries to produce oestrogen.
- Oestrogen is made and secreted by the ovaries. It stimulates the lining of the womb to build up ready for pregnancy. It inhibits (slows down) the production of more FSH.
- Other hormones involved in the menstrual cycle are luteinising hormone (LH) and **progesterone**.

The hormones produced by the pituitary gland and the ovary act together to control what happens in the menstrual cycle. As the oestrogen levels rise they inhibit the production of FSH and encourage the production of LH by the pituitary gland. When LH levels reach a peak in the middle of the cycle, they stimulate the release of a mature egg.

Figure 1 Hormones act as chemical messages. They are made in glands in one part of the body but have an effect somewhere else.

Pituitary gland
Thyroid gland
Adrenal gland
Pancreas
Ovary (female)
Testis (male)

?? Did you know ...?

A baby girl is born with ovaries full of immature eggs, but they do nothing until she has gone through the changes of puberty.

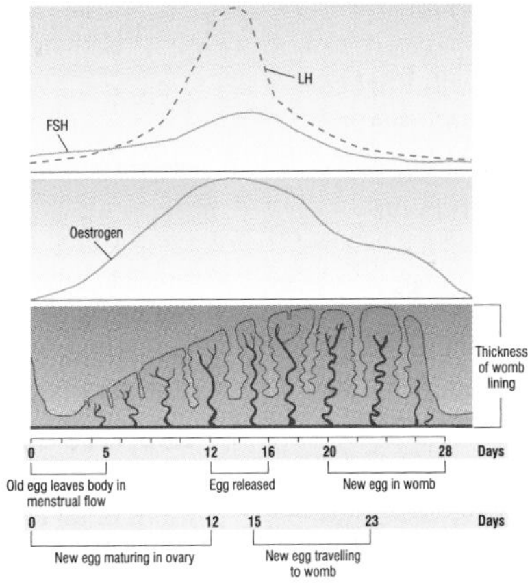

Figure 2 The changing levels of the female sex hormones control the different stages of the menstrual cycle

LH
FSH
Oestrogen

Thickness of womb lining

0   5   12   16   20   28   **Days**
Old egg leaves body in menstrual flow   Egg released   New egg in womb

0   12   15   23   **Days**
New egg maturing in ovary   New egg travelling to womb

AQA Examiner's tip

Be clear on the difference between FSH and oestrogen.

FSH
- causes eggs to mature
- stimulates the ovary to produce oestrogen.

Oestrogen
- causes the lining of the uterus to develop
- inhibits FSH production
- stimulates the release of a mature egg.

AQA Examiner's tip

Make sure you know the difference between eggs maturing and eggs being released.

Summary questions

1 Copy and complete using the words below:

    28   hormones   FSH   menstrual   oestrogen   ovary

    During the .... cycle a mature egg is released from the .... about every .... days. The cycle is controlled by several .... including .... and ....

2 Look at Figure 2 above:
    a Explain what happens to FSH.
    b On which days is the female having a menstrual period?
    c Which hormone controls the build-up of the lining of the womb?

3 Produce a poster to explain the events of the menstrual cycle to women who are hoping to start a family. You will need to explain the graphs at the top of this page and show when a woman is most likely to get pregnant. Remember sperm can live for up to three days inside the woman's body.

Key points

- Hormones control the release of an egg from the ovary and the build-up of the lining of the womb in the menstrual cycle.
- Some of the hormones involved are FSH from the pituitary gland and oestrogen from the ovary.

?? Did you know ...?

It might be interesting to get the students to calculate roughly how many of the eggs a baby girl is born with actually develop and are released between puberty and when ovulation ceases at the menopause.

Answers to in-text questions

- **a** Hormones made in the pituitary gland in the brain and in the ovary.
- **b** So that it would be ready to support the developing embryo if an egg was fertilised.

AQA Examiner's tip

Students can be confused by the development of an immature egg while it is in the ovary and the release of the egg. If the events are linked to the hormones involved, then it can become clearer.

Summary answers

1 menstrual, ovary, 28, hormones, FSH, oestrogen

2   **a** Levels rise in the first part of the cycle which stimulates the eggs to mature in the ovary and stimulates the ovary to produce more oestrogen.
    b Days 0–5.
    c Oestrogen.

3 Give credit for a clear poster, which contains good, accurate biology and demonstrates understanding of the relationship between ovulation, sexual intercourse and fertilisation of the ovum.

B1 2.4

The artificial control of fertility

Learning objectives

Students should learn:

- how oral contraceptives work
- how FSH can be used as a 'fertility drug'.

Learning outcomes

Most students should be able to:

- explain how oral contraceptives inhibit FSH production and prevent pregnancy
- describe how treatment with FSH can help a woman produce mature eggs if her own FSH production is too low
- describe how FSH is used in IVF treatments.

Some students should also be able to:

- evaluate the issues arising from the use of hormones to control fertility artificially.

Support

- The students could make a poster showing the stages of a course of IVF treatment.

Extend

- Mature eggs from a woman undergoing fertility treatment can be stored. Students could investigate the exact conditions needed for storage. Why are such conditions necessary? Is there any chance of deterioration if the eggs are kept in storage for long periods of time?
- In the early days of contraceptive pill manufacture, before careful air filtering, the male workers began to develop breasts as a result of being exposed to oestrogen. Students could research the effects of female hormones on males.

AQA Specification link-up: Biology B1.2

- The uses of hormones in controlling fertility include:
  Giving oral contraceptives that contain hormones to inhibit FSH production so that no eggs mature
  - oral contraceptives may contain oestrogen and ...
  - the first birth-control pills contained large amounts ...
  - progesterone-only pills lead to fewer side effects
  - birth-control pills now contain a much lower dose of ...
  Giving FSH and LH in a 'fertility drug' to a woman whose own level of FSH is too low to stimulate eggs to mature, for example in In Vitro Fertilisation (IVF) treatment
  - IVF involves giving a mother FSH and LH to ... [B1.2.2 e)]
- Evaluate the benefits of, and the problems that may arise from, the use of hormones to control fertility, including In Vitro Fertilisation (IVF). [B1.2]

Lesson structure

Starters

'To have or not to have ...' – Ask the students to imagine a young couple (get them to give them names) and to come up with a list of reasons why the couple might not want to start a family yet. Read out and share these. *(5 minutes)*

Babyless blues – Get the students to empathise with families that want to have children but for some reason cannot do so. They could write a letter to their unborn children telling them of all the lovely things they would like to do with them if only they had the chance. Differentiation – extension students should be able to empathise without aid. You may need to support other students by providing them with a list of things that they enjoy in life and dropping them into gaps in a preformed letter. *(10 minutes)*

Main

This lesson needs to focus on the two main issues: the use of oral contraceptives and the use of FSH as a 'fertility drug'. Both these issues will trigger discussions, so allow time for questions and for students to express their own opinions.

- Ask students to reflect on the question, 'What do I know about contraception and hormones in the menstrual cycle?' The students could be encouraged to write down a list of facts of what they think they know and remember about contraception and the hormones in the menstrual cycle.
- The students should be able to discuss exactly what the pill does and its effect on the secretion of other hormones involved in the cycle.
- The discussion could be extended to include the consequences of failing to take the pill regularly. What happens if the level of artificial hormones drops suddenly?
- Show a video of IVF treatment. You can use the free download IVF orientation video from the San Diego Fertility Center.
- Discuss the advantages and disadvantages of using hormones to control fertility. Ensure that students are encouraged to evaluate the relative importance of different points raised (See 'How Science Works' box in the Student Book).

Plenaries

Injections and patches – The hormones used in contraceptive pills can be given as injections or as patches that stick to the skin. Discuss the advantages and disadvantages of the use of these alternatives. *(5 minutes)*

Keep taking the tablets – Direct the students to write an advice label to go with packets of contraceptive pills, telling how they work and giving relevant instructions and warnings. You may need to support some students by providing a cloze passage label with a set of words to choose from. Students could be shown an advice label from a packet of prescription drugs or the warning labels on packets of painkillers. *(10 minutes)*

Further teaching suggestions

Alternatives to the contraceptive pill
- The contraceptive pill is not the only way to avoid pregnancy. It is not suitable for everyone and there may be medical reasons why it is not appropriate to prescribe it. Ask students to build up a list of other methods of contraception and discuss the advantages and disadvantages. This could lead to some discussion on sexually transmitted diseases and the incidence of HIV/Aids.

How would a contraceptive pill for males work?
- There has been some research on this, but students could be encouraged to work out what would need to happen and consider possible advantages and disadvantages compared with the female pill, e.g. Are men more likely to forget to take a pill?

What happens to the spare embryos?
- Students could carry out a web search for information on this topic. Use websites of newspapers, TV channels and the British Fertility Society (it is now the HFEA) to find stories and topics to discuss.

Louise Brown – the first 'test tube' baby
- Louise Brown was the first baby to be born as a result of IVF in 1978. Tell the students the story and ask them to write a short paragraph about how it might feel to be the first person to be born as the result of a new treatment. Select some students to read their accounts.

Coordination and control

The artificial control of fertility

B1 2.4 The artificial control of fertility

Learning objectives
- How can hormones be used to stop pregnancy?
- How can hormones help to solve the problems of infertility?

Contraceptive chemicals

In the 21st century it is possible to choose when to have children – and when not to have them. One of the most important and widely used ways of controlling fertility is to use oral contraceptives (the contraceptive pill).

The pill contains female hormones, particularly oestrogen. The hormones affect women's ovaries, preventing the release of any eggs. The pill inhibits the production of FSH so no eggs mature in the ovaries. Without mature eggs, women can't get pregnant.

Anyone who uses the pill as a contraceptive has to take it very regularly. If they forget to take it, the artificial hormone levels drop. Then their body's own hormones can take over very quickly. This can lead to the unexpected release of an egg – and an unexpected baby.

a What is a contraceptive?

The first birth control pills contained very large amounts of oestrogen. They caused serious side effects such as high blood pressure and headaches in some women. Modern contraceptive pills contain much lower doses of oestrogen along with some progesterone. They cause fewer side effects. Some contraceptive pills only contain progesterone. These cause even fewer side effects because they don't stop the eggs from maturing.

b What is the difference between the mixed pill and the progesterone-only pill?

Figure 1 The contraceptive pill contains a mixture of hormones which effectively trick the body into thinking it is already pregnant, so no more eggs are released

Fertility treatments

In the UK as many as one couple in six have problems having a family when they want one. There are many possible reasons for this infertility. It may be linked to a lack of female hormones. Some women want children but do not make enough FSH to stimulate the eggs in their ovaries. Fortunately, artificial FSH can be used as a fertility drug. It stimulates the eggs in the ovary to mature and also triggers oestrogen production.

AQA Examiner's tip

FSH and LH are used in IVF to stimulate the eggs to mature.

?? Did you know ... ?

In the early days of using fertility drugs there were big problems with the doses used. In 1971 an Italian doctor removed 15 four-month-old fetuses (ten girls and five boys) from the womb of a 35-year-old woman after treatment with fertility drugs. Not one of them survived.

Figure 2 Most people who take fertility drugs end up with one or two babies. But in 1983 the Walton family from Liverpool had six baby girls who all survived.

Fertility drugs are also used in IVF (in vitro fertilisation). Conception usually takes place in the fallopian tube. This is the tube between the ovary and the uterus that the egg travels along. If the fallopian tubes are damaged, the eggs cannot reach the uterus so women cannot get pregnant naturally.

Fortunately doctors can now help. They collect eggs from the ovary of the mother and fertilise them with sperm from the father outside the body. The fertilised eggs develop into tiny embryos. The embryos are inserted into the uterus (womb) of the mother. In this way they bypass the faulty tubes.

During IVF the woman is given FSH to make sure as many eggs as possible mature in her ovaries. LH is also given at the end of the cycle to make sure all the mature eggs are released. IVF is expensive and not always successful.

How Science Works

The advantages and disadvantages of fertility treatment

The use of hormones to control fertility has been a major scientific breakthrough. But like most things, there are advantages and disadvantages! Here are some points to think about:

In the developed world, using the pill has helped make families much smaller than they used to be. There is less poverty because with fewer children being born there are fewer mouths to feed and more money to go round.

The pill has also helped to control population growth in countries such as China, where they find it difficult to feed all their people. In many other countries of the developing world the pill is not available because of a lack of money, education and doctors.

The pill can cause health problems so a doctor always oversees its use.

The use of fertility drugs can also have some health risks for the mother and it can be expensive for society and parents. A large multiple birth can be tragic for the parents if some or all of the babies die. It also costs hospitals a lot of money to keep very small premature babies alive.

Controlling fertility artificially also raises many ethical issues for society and individuals. For example, some religious groups think that preventing conception is denying life and ban the use of the pill.

The mature eggs produced by a woman using fertility drugs may be collected and stored, or fertilised and stored, until she wants to get pregnant later. But what happens if the woman dies, or does not want the eggs or embryos any more?

- What, in your opinion, are the main advantages and disadvantages of using artificial hormones to control female fertility?

Summary questions

1 Explain the meaning of the following terms: oral contraceptive, fallopian tube, fertility drug, in vitro fertilisation.

2 Explain how artificial female hormones can be used to:
   a prevent unwanted pregnancies
   b help people overcome infertility.

Ovary
Ripe egg

1 Fertility drugs are used to make lots of eggs mature at the same time for collection.

2 The eggs are collected and placed in a special solution in a Petri dish.

3 A sample of semen is collected and the sperm and eggs are mixed in the Petri dish.

4 The eggs are checked to make sure they have been fertilised and the early embryos are developing properly.

5 When the fertilised eggs have formed tiny balls of cells, 1 or 2 of the tiny embryos are placed in the uterus of the mother. Then, if all goes well, at least one baby will grow and develop successfully.

Figure 3 New reproductive technology using hormones and IVF has helped thousands of infertile couples to have babies

Key points
- Hormones can be used to control fertility.
- Oral contraceptives contain hormones, which stop FSH production so no eggs mature.
- FSH can be used as a fertility drug for women, to stimulate eggs to mature in their ovaries. These eggs may be used in IVF treatments.

Answers to in-text questions

a Something that reduces the risk of you getting pregnant (conceiving).

b The mixed pill contains oestrogen and progesterone, which prevents ovulation, inhibits FSH secretion, stops the build up of lining of the uterus, etc. The progesterone-only pill doesn't stop ovulation, it is not quite as effective but it has fewer side effects.

Summary answers

1 Oral contraceptive: a pill taken by mouth that reduces the risk of pregnancy.

Fallopian tube: the tube between the ovary and the uterus that the egg travels along (where conception usually takes place).

Fertility drug: a drug which stimulates the ovaries to produce ripe eggs.

In vitro fertilisation: in humans this means combining the egg and sperm in a Petri dish, so fertilisation takes place outside the body.

2 **a** The hormones in contraceptive pills can be used to prevent the release of eggs, stop the build up of the lining of the uterus, etc., so that pregnancy cannot take place.

b Fertility drugs can be used to stimulate the production of eggs in the ovary so that infertile couples can become pregnant, either naturally, once the eggs have been produced or using IVF.

B1 2.5 | Controlling conditions

Learning objectives

Students should learn:

- that the nervous system and hormones help us to control conditions inside the body
- that internal conditions, such as temperature, blood sugar levels and the balance of water and ions, are controlled
- why it is important to control the internal environment.

Learning outcomes

Most students should be able to:

- describe how the temperature, blood sugar levels and balance of water and ions are controlled
- explain why it is important to control the internal environment.

Some students should also be able to:

- explain the effects of extremes of temperature on the human body.

Answers to in-text questions

a Homeostasis is important because cells of the body need a constant environment in which to work properly.
b The kidneys control the balance of water and mineral ions in the blood.
c 37 °C.
d It would go up.

Support

- Students could be given a preprinted copy of Summary question 1 and slips with the words on to fill in the gaps.
- Alternatively, put key terms from the Student Book spread on the board (suggest 'internal environment', 'homeostasis', 'ions', 'hormone', 'enzymes' and 'pancreas'). Read out definitions or descriptions of what the words mean. These words are wiped out when the students recognise them. This has the advantage of identifying difficult concepts and giving students the opportunity to get things right.

Extend

- Students could research hypothermia and heat stroke and produce a poster for each one.

AQA | Specification link-up: Biology B1.2

- Internal conditions which are controlled include:
  - the water content of the body – water leaves the body via the lungs when we breathe out and via the skin when we sweat, and excess water is lost via the kidneys in the urine
  - the ion content of the body – ions are lost via the skin when we sweat and excess ions are lost via the kidneys in the urine
  - temperature – to maintain the temperature at which the enzymes work best
  - blood sugar levels – to provide the cells with a constant supply of energy. [B1.2.2 a)]

Controlled Assessment: SA4.3 Collect primary and secondary data [SA4.3.3 a) b) c) d)]; SA4.4 Select and process primary and secondary data [SA4.4.1 a) b)] and SA4.5 Analyse and interpret primary and secondary data. [SA4.5.2 a) b) c) d)]

Lesson structure

Starters

What's in a word? – Put up the word 'homeostasis'. Break it into 'homeo' and 'stasis'. Ask what the words 'static' and 'stationary' mean. Explain that 'stasis' means 'standing still'. The 'homeo' means being 'like' or 'similar'. Link this to 'homeopathy', linking the '-pathy' part to 'pathology/pathogen/pathologist' – relating to diseases. 'Homeo' can then be linked with '-pathy' and explain the theory in homeopathy that very dilute substances which cause symptoms similar to a disease will cure it. *(5 minutes)*

Marathon man – Show a picture of a marathon runner. Show the students two test tubes filled with red liquid. Tell them it is a marathon runner's blood. Have one tube labelled 'start' and the other labelled 'finish'. Get them to write down a list of similarities and differences between the two tubes, based on thinking about what will change and what will stay the same in the runner's internal environment. Support students by providing them with a list to choose from. Extend students by encouraging them to research some numerical levels for norms of these substances. Discuss and share findings on completion of the exercise. *(10 minutes)*

Main

Each of the following suggestions could occupy the main part of the lesson, but the first two could be put together if time permitted. The control of blood sugar does highlight the differences between the nervous system and hormone action.

- Try measuring the body temperature of the class using forehead thermometers if available (see 'Practical support'). Some of the concepts in 'How Science Works' can be introduced into this activity: the accuracy of the measurements; the mean and range of a set of data; how the data can be displayed.
- Students could carry out a practical activity to investigate the change in body temperature (skin temperature) with an increase in exercise (see 'Practical support'). Again, class results could be collated: the differences are relevant here. A discussion about why the changes occur would be relevant.
- Finally you could look at the control of blood sugar levels. In this suggested activity, a comparison can be made between the action of hormones and the nervous system. Introduce with a discussion of the 'sugar rush' from eating several jelly babies (or other sweets) in a row.

Plenaries

Mix it! – Hold a competition with a small prize for students who can make the most words out of the word 'homeostasis'. It may be best to get any obvious words which may cause amusement out of the way as examples. *(5 minutes)*

Ins and outs – Support students by providing them with a table with three columns. Title the central column 'substance' and the outer two 'in' and 'out'. For each of water, ions and sugar, ask the students to fill in the relevant 'in' and 'out' boxes with information as to the processes involved. Extend students by getting them to make up their own table rather than being given one. Get them to add extra columns for 'consequences if the level gets too low' and 'consequences if the level gets too high.' *(10 minutes)*

Practical support

Measuring body temperature using forehead thermometers

Equipment and materials required
Forehead thermometers (or clinical thermometers if forehead thermometers not available).

Details
Follow the manufacturer's instructions given with the thermometers and standardise the time of exposure for each student. It is possible to obtain a mean value and also interesting to plot the variation, so that students understand that there is not a 'fixed' body temperature.

Safety: If clinical thermometers are used, they should be disinfected before and after use.

Measuring changes in body temperature during exercise using forehead thermometers

Equipment and materials required
Forehead thermometers.

Details
Students can record skin temperature before undergoing a period of exercise (such as running on the spot) for a set period of time (1–3 minutes). Skin temperature after the exercise should be recorded. The skin temperature should be measured in the same position each time.

Safety: Avoid competition between students.

Coordination and control

Controlling conditions

B1 2.5 Controlling conditions

Learning objectives
- How are conditions inside your body controlled?
- Why is it so important to control your internal environment?

Figure 1 Everything you do affects your internal environment

AQA Examiner's tip
Sweating causes the body to cool. Energy from the body is used to evaporate the water in sweat.

Figure 2 You can change your behaviour to help control your temperature, for example by adding extra clothing or turning up the heating when it's really cold

The conditions inside your body are known as its internal environment. Your organs cannot work properly if this keeps changing. Many of the processes which go on inside your body aim to keep everything as constant as possible. This balancing act is called homeostasis.

It involves your nervous system, your hormone systems and many of your body organs.

a Why is homeostasis important?

Controlling water and ions
Water can move in and out of your body cells. How much it moves depends on the concentration of mineral ions (such as salt) and the amount of water in your body. If too much water moves into or out of your cells, they can be damaged or destroyed.

You take water and minerals into your body as you eat and drink. You lose water as you breathe out, and also in your sweat. You lose salt in your sweat as well. You also lose water and salt in your urine, which is made in your kidneys.

Your kidneys can change the amount of salt and water lost in your urine, depending on your body conditions. They help to control the balance of water and mineral ions in your body. The concentration of the urine produced by your kidneys is controlled by both nerves and hormones.

So, for example, imagine drinking a lot of water all in one go. Your kidneys will remove the extra water from your blood and you will produce lots of very pale urine.

b What do your kidneys control?

Controlling temperature
It is vital that your deep core body temperature is kept at 37 °C. At this temperature your enzymes work best. At only a few degrees above or below normal body temperature the reactions in your cells stop and you will die.

Your body controls your temperature in several ways. For example, you can sweat to cool down and shiver to warm up. Your nervous system is very important in coordinating the way your body responds to changes in temperature.

Once your body temperature drops below 35 °C you are at risk of dying from hypothermia. Several hundred old people die from the effects of cold each year. So do a number of young people who get lost on mountains or try to walk home in the snow after a night out.

If your body temperature goes above about 40–42 °C your enzymes and cells don't work properly. This means that you may die of heat stroke or heat exhaustion.

c What is the ideal body temperature?

Controlling blood sugar
When you digest a meal, lots of sugar (glucose) passes into your blood. Left alone, your blood glucose levels would keep changing. The levels would be very high straight after a meal, but very low again a few hours later. This would cause chaos in your body.

However, the concentration of glucose in your blood is kept constant by hormones made in your pancreas. This means your body cells are provided with the constant supply of energy that they need.

d What would happen to your blood sugar level if you ate a packet of sweets?

Figure 3 Sweets like this are almost all sugar. When you eat them your body has to deal with the effect on your blood.

Summary questions
1 Copy and complete using the words below:
body constant homeostasis hormones internal nervous
Conditions in the .... environment of your .... must be kept .... This is called .... The control is given by both your .... and your .... system.

2 Why is it important to control:
   a water levels in the body
   b the body temperature
   c sugar (glucose) levels in the blood?

3 a Look at the marathon runners in Figure 1. List the ways in which the running is affecting their:
   i water balance
   ii ion balance
   iii temperature.
   b It is much harder to run a marathon in a costume than in running clothes. Explain why this is.

Key points
- Humans need to maintain a constant internal environment, controlling levels of water, ions and blood sugar, as well as temperature.
- Homeostasis is the result of the coordination of your nervous system, your hormones and your body organs.

Further teaching suggestions

Water balance
- Write on board 'hot day', 'running a marathon' and 'lazy day at home'. Ask students to suggest how their fluid intake and urine output would vary under these different circumstances and why.

More on blood sugar levels
- As a follow-up to the suggestion on the control of blood sugar levels activity, the process of what happens to the sugar can

be presented or volunteered by the students to build up a flow chart, so that the way in which the jelly babies affect the production of a hormone in the pancreas can be shown.

Measuring sweat
- Students could use lint or cotton wool to measure the amount of sweat produced during exercise. More 'How Science Works' concepts can be introduced here, e.g. the relationship between different variables.

Summary answers

1 internal, body, constant, homeostasis, nervous, hormones

2 a To stop too much water moving in or out of cells, damaging and destroying them.
   b Because the enzymes work best at 37 °C.
   c Because blood sugar that is too high or too low causes problems in the body.

3 a i Losing water through sweating.

   ii Losing salt through sweating.
   iii Temperature going up with exercising.

   b Sweating cools you down and helps to keep the body temperature down – a costume makes you sweat more (as you get hotter), which means you lose more water – but also makes it harder for sweat to evaporate (so you don't cool so effectively). Also, a costume is heavy so it's harder work to run.

B1 2.6

Hormones and the control of plant growth

Learning objectives

Students should learn that:

- that plants are sensitive to light, moisture and gravity
- that plants produce hormones to coordinate and control growth
- that plant growth hormones are used in agriculture and horticulture as weed killers and rooting hormones.

Learning outcomes

Most students should be able to:

- understand that plants respond to changes in their environment
- describe how plants respond to light, moisture and gravity
- describe how plant hormones can be used in agriculture and horticulture.

Some students should also be able to:

- explain how plant responses are due to uneven distribution of hormones causing unequal growth rates.

Answers to in-text questions

a Auxin.

Support

- Provide students with blank (unlabelled) diagrams of the bean seedlings from the Student Book and ask them to write captions in their own words to explain what is happening.

Extend

- Use the internet to research specific plant hormones such as gibberellins, cytokines, ethylene, abscisic acid, etc.

Specification link-up: Biology B1.2

- Plants are sensitive to light, moisture and gravity … *[B1.2.3 a)]*
- Plants produce hormones to coordinate and control … *[B1.2.3 b)]*
- The responses of plant roots and shoots to light … *[B1.2.3 c)]*

  Controlled Assessment: SA4.3 Collect primary and secondary data *[SA4.3.3 a) b)]*; SA4.4 Select and process primary and secondary data *[SA4.4.2 c)]*; SA4.5 Analyse and interpret primary and secondary data. *[SA4.5.4 a)]*

Lesson structure

Starters

Which way is up? – Take a dozen or so tennis balls. Place them in a deep tray. Gather the students around and say that the balls represent seeds. Mark each one on the top with a felt pen. State that the mark represents where the shoot comes out when it germinates. Ask the students whether, when seeds fall from the parent plant, they will all land on the soil the right way up. Mix up the tray of balls to imitate this. Get students to indicate all the different ways the felt pen marks are now pointing. Hand around some broad bean seeds (ensure they do not have toxic seed dressing on) and observe that this is the case in real life. Explain that during this lesson you will find out how come they all finish up growing in the same direction. *(5 minutes)*

Australian gardening – Support students by drawing a circle on the board. Tell them that this represents the Earth. Get volunteer students to come and draw some plants growing on it in a variety of places, including the poles, UK and Australia, including their roots. Establish that the roots grow towards gravity (towards the centre of the Earth) and the shoots grow away from gravity. Ask what else the roots might grow towards and what else the shoots might grow towards. Extend students by encouraging them to postulate mechanisms for how this can come about. *(10 minutes)*

Main

The following experiments need to be left for some time before the results can be recorded, so will need one lesson session to set up and some time in a later lesson to assess the results. Alternatively, they could be set up ahead of the lesson and shown as demonstrations.

- Practical experiment to investigate the effects of light on the growth of seedlings (see 'Practical support'). Get the students to discuss the results and draw conclusions about the effect of light on the seedlings. The results could be recorded by taking photographs of the pots.
- As an alternative, the experiment described in the Student Book can be set up. Cress seedlings growing on filter paper in a Petri dish can be placed under a lightproof box with a hole cut in one side, so that the seedlings are illuminated from one side only.

Plenaries

Day of the Triffids – Remind students of the book and the mini series featuring Eddie Izzard. Show a still from a search engine or a clip. Discuss what features the triffids would have to have to successfully hunt down humans. Discuss other plant movements such as daisies (their flowers close at night), Venus flytraps, sensitive mimosa, etc. *(5 minutes)*

Hormone uses – Support students by creating a jumbled sentence either on paper or using an internet tool such as Hot Potatoes. Students can unravel it and copy it down or link the sections with lines if printed. An example might be 'used Hormones be to help as can to grow can work roots and cuttings weedkillers' becomes 'Hormones can be used to help cuttings to grow roots and can work as weedkillers.' Extend students by getting them into groups to create their own jumbled sentences and then set them for other groups to sort out. *(10 minutes)*

Practical support

The effect of light on the growth of seedlings

Equipment and materials required (per group of students)

Three pots of young pea seedlings, 10–12 seedlings per pot; labels; suitable places for the pots to be placed, e.g. a cupboard etc.

Details

Working in groups, provide each with three pots of very young pea seedlings (the plumules should only just project above the surface of the compost). Get the students to label their pots, one should be placed in a position where it is exposed to light all around it, another should be placed in a cupboard with no light and the third should be placed in a box where it is exposed to light on one side only. The pots should be left for 7–10 days, but students should check to see that the pots do not dry out. When the seedlings have grown up, the pots should be inspected for differences (a movement sensor could be used) and the results recorded (perhaps by taking photographs of the pots). Get the students to discuss the results and draw conclusions about the effect of light on the seedlings.

Encourage the students to consider: What was the appearance of the seedlings in the different pots? Were there differences in colour?

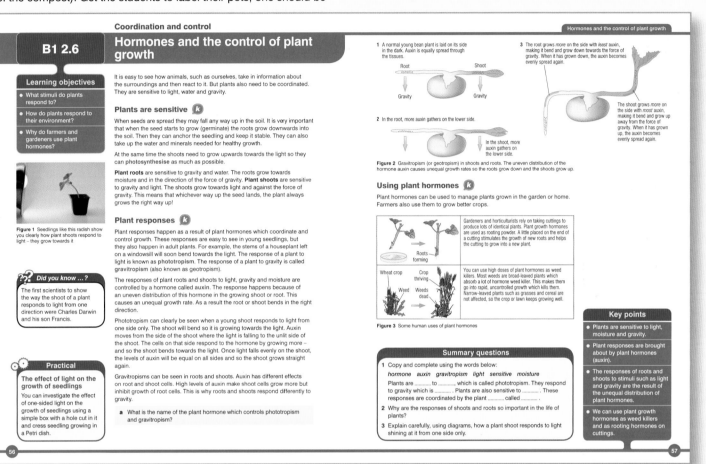

Further teaching suggestions

The effect of gravity on the growth of germinating seedlings

● Use a number of germinating broad bean seeds (5 to 6 with the seed just visible), a sheet of cork and some pins. Ask the students to fix the seeds to the cork in different positions using the pins. Place all the sheets of cork in a large tank with a little water at the bottom, cover with a dark cloth or cardboard to exclude the light and leave for about a week. Then get the students to record the positions of the roots and shoots of the beans and draw conclusions about the effect of gravity.

Demonstrate the effect of a selective weedkiller

● The use of plant hormones as weedkillers can be demonstrated by placing two sections of weedy turf into seed trays and watering one with a selective (hormone) weedkiller and the other with water. Students could record their observations using a movement sensors over a period of time, noting which plants were affected by the weedkiller and which were not.

Detecting the stimulus

● A demonstration could be set up, using maize or oat seedlings, to show where the light stimulus is detected and where the response occurs. Grow maize seedlings on moist filter paper in Petri dishes until they are 10 mm long then cover the tips of half of them with aluminium foil caps, leaving the rest uncovered. Place in a box with a slit in one side to allow light in. Leave for several days and record the differences between the two sets of seedlings.

Summary answers

1 sensitive, light, gravitropism, moisture, hormone, auxin

2 To make sure that whichever way up a seed lands, the roots grow down into the soil to anchor the plant and take water and minerals from the soil, and the shoots grow upwards towards the light so they can photosynthesise. This continues to make sure the plant grows to obtain the maximum light.

3 Suitable well-labelled diagram showing movement of auxin away from light and then faster growth on the side of the shoot away from the light until shoot is growing directly towards the light source. Plants responses are relatively slow, which indicates that they are brought about by hormones.

B1 2.7 — Using hormones

Learning objectives

Students should learn:

- that there are benefits and problems associated with the use of hormones to control human fertility
- that plant hormones are used to produce our food.

Learning outcomes

Most students should be able to:

- describe the benefits associated with the use of hormones to control human fertility
- describe the problems associated with the use of these hormones
- describe how plant hormones are involved in food production.

Some students should also be able to:

- evaluate the use of hormones in controlling fertility and in the production of food.

Answers to in-text questions

a FSH.

b A chemical based on plant hormones which strips the leaves off trees at high doses.

Support

- Students could produce a poster summarising the benefits of organic farming.

Extend

- Students could perform an internet search to find information on the herbicide Agent Orange. Produce a summary press report covering the Rainbow herbicides, Operation Ranch Hand and the birth deformities which have resulted from its use. Present this when time allows.

AQA — Specification link-up: Biology B1.2

- The uses of hormones in controlling fertility include … *[B1.2.2 e)]*
- Plant growth hormones are used in agriculture and horticulture as weed killers and as rooting hormones. *[B1.2.3 d)]*
- Evaluate the use of plant hormones in horticulture as weed killers and to encourage the rooting of plant cuttings. *[B1.2]*

  Controlled Assessment: SA4.3 Collect primary and secondary data *[SA4.3.3 a)]*; SA4.4 Select and process primary and secondary data *[SA4.4.2 c)]*; SA4.5 Analyse and interpret primary and secondary data. *[SA4.5.4 a)]*

Lesson structure

Starters

Dear old mum – Draw or project the numbers from 16 to 66 onto the board. Explain that these are ages from the age of consent to the oldest known mother. Ask the students to choose a range of ages they would consider to be acceptable for IVF treatment. If they rule out any age ranges they should be able to explain why they have done this. Be aware of any individuals for whom this may be a personal issue. *(5 minutes)*

Spray away! – Support students by showing them a photograph of an organic garden and the Soil Association sign. Ask what sort of activities organic gardeners could carry out to control weeds without the use of herbicides. Draw out some reasons why they might prefer not to use them in the first place. Extend students by giving them a set of cards with reasons for using herbicides and reasons for not doing so. Get them to place the cards in order of the ones they most agree with, or think are most important, to those they disagree with, or think are not important. They must be prepared to publicly justify their placements. *(10 minutes)*

Main

- Using the information in the Student Book and their own ideas, students could write a two–three-minute report for the school radio entitled 'Older mothers – should science help?' Students could work in groups, discuss the format of the report and make a presentation to the rest of the class.

- If the demonstration of the effects of a selective weedkiller described previously was not used, it would be appropriate here. The investigation could be set up by the students and extended by using different types of weedkiller or different concentrations of the same weedkiller.

- A rooting powder, containing a rooting hormone, can be used to encourage the formation of roots on cuttings from plants. This investigation requires one lesson session to set up and the cuttings need to be left for several weeks – longer if woody tissue is used. Set up some cuttings treated with the rooting powder and some without treatment as controls. The effects of the rooting powder can be assessed by measuring the root formation on the treated cuttings and on the controls.

- Ask students to prepare short speeches either in favour of or against the motion 'Synthetic plant hormones should be banned'. See the 'Is it worth it?' activity in the Student Book. Allow some time for research on the internet and combine it with the Plenary on Agent Orange. At a convenient time, arrange a debate.

Plenaries

Orphaned at 3 – Give the students a printed sheet of news coverage following the death in 2009 at the age of 69 of Maria Del Carmen Bousada de Lara who became the world's oldest mother at 66. Students are to give their views about the ethics of the situation. *(5 minutes)*

Orange hangover – Read the text section on Agent Orange. Support students by making a list of the animals that might be harmed if the jungle was stripped of its leaves and describe how this would harm them. Extend students by getting them to find more information from the internet about Agent Orange and discuss the general effect on wildlife and the surrounding communities. *(10 minutes)*

Practical support

The effect of weedkillers on the growth of plants
Equipment and materials required

Sections of weedy turf; seed trays; selective weedkiller made up according to manufacturer's instructions.

Details

The sections of weedy turf should be the same size and placed in the seed trays and then kept in the same conditions of light and temperature. They should be treated according to the instructions supplied with the weedkiller. Students can record changes in the plant species over a period of time. This can be set up as a demonstration or groups of students can set up their own investigation. The results can be recorded photographically or more quantitatively by estimating the numbers of weed species present in the treated and untreated sections.

Safety: Take care when handling weedkiller. Wash hands after experiment.

Using a rooting powder
Equipment and materials required

Cuttings of hardy perennials or small shrubs; rooting powder; compost; small plant pots.

Details

Cuttings of hardy perennials or small shrubs with soft stems and green leaves can be used. Sections of stem about 10 cm long, cut just below a leaf joint, and with the lower leaves removed, are dipped into rooting powder (follow the instructions provided) and then planted into damp compost. As a control, prepare some cuttings in the same way but do not dip into the rooting powder before planting in damp compost. All the pots should be kept moist.

Safety: Take care when handling rooting powder. Wash hands after experiment.

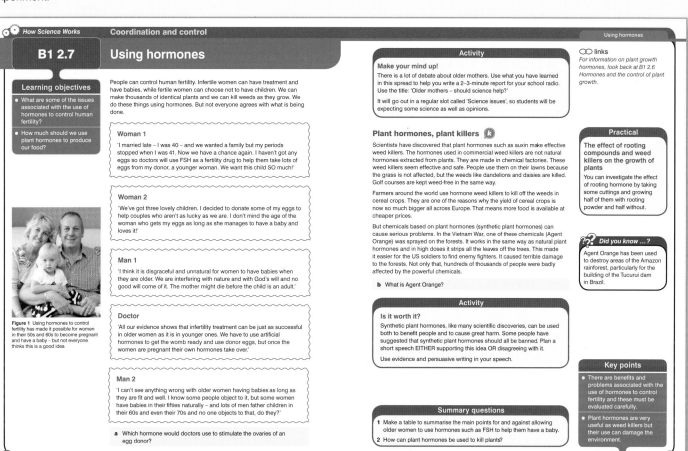

Further teaching suggestions

The use of plant hormones in micropropagation
- This topic could be researched and the practical investigation carried out.

The effect of the use of weedkillers on the production of cereal crops
- Students could research the increase in yield and discuss whether that increase means cheaper food at the price of environmental damage from the weedkillers.

Is organic food better for you?
- Continue the discussion begun in the Starter. This could form the basis of a debate – more research could be carried out. The debate could be extended to the use of hormones in the rearing of cattle and increased milk production.

Summary answers

1 Credit for any thoughtful points.

  For: allows people to become mothers if they find a partner late in life; people have a right to have a baby when they want one; if someone loses their child they might want to have another; the mother will be financially secure and have had a good career before she has a child; if you go to all that trouble, the baby will be very much wanted.

  Against: the mother will be old while the child is still young; the mother may die before the child is an adult; the mother is more likely to have serious illnesses than a younger mother; the mother may not be able to keep up with an energetic child.

2 They can be used to cause excessive growth that kills plants. They are absorbed more by broadleaved plants that are often weeds rather than by cereals. Hormones can also be used to cause leaf fall, which kills plants as well.

Summary answers

1 **a** F   **b** C   **c** D   **d** B   **e** A   **f** E

2 **a** It enables you to react to your surroundings and to coordinate your behaviour.

  b **i** Eye
    ii Ear
    iii Skin
    iv Skin

  c Diagram of reflex arc. The explanation needs to include the following points: reference to three types of neuron: a sensory neuron; a motor neuron; a relay neuron. The relay neuron is found in the CNS, often in the spinal cord. An electrical impulse passes from the sensory receptor, along the sensory neuron to the CNS. It then passes to a relay neuron and straight back along a motor neuron to the effector organ (usually a muscle in a reflex). This is known as the 'reflex arc'. The junction between one neuron and the next is known as a 'synapse'. The time between the stimulus and the reflex action is as short as is possible. It allows you to react to danger without thinking about it.

3 **a** It is the monthly cycle of fertility in women. The average length of the menstrual cycle is about 28 days. Each month the lining of the womb thickens ready to support a developing baby, and at the same time an egg starts maturing in the ovary. About 14 days after the egg starts maturing, it is released from the ovary. This is known as 'ovulation'. The lining of the womb stays thick for several days after the egg has been released before it is shed as the monthly 'period'.

  b **i** FSH is made by the pituitary gland; it stimulates the maturation of eggs in the ovaries and stimulates the ovaries to produce oestrogen.

    ii Oestrogen is made in the ovary and stimulates the lining of the womb to build up ready for pregnancy. It inhibits FSH production.

4 **a** Hormones are chemicals that control the processes of the body. Hormones are released from glands into the blood. Some hormones act quickly, but many act more slowly. All are slower than nervous control.
Nervous control can be very fast, especially reflexes. It involves the transmission of electrical impulses along neurons. Transmission from one neuron to the next involves chemical substances.

  b A synapse is the junction between two neurons. They are important because they are where neurons meet and the impulses pass from one neuron to another via a chemical (neurotransmitter).

  c Oral contraceptives (the contraceptive pill) contain hormones, including oestrogen, which act on the ovary preventing the release of any eggs. The production of FSH is inhibited so that no eggs mature in the ovaries. If there are no mature eggs, then you cannot get pregnant. If a woman does not make enough FSH to stimulate eggs to mature, she may be given FSH as a 'fertility' drug. As well as stimulating the development of eggs, FSH triggers oestrogen production.

5 **a** A = more, B = less, C = the same or less.

  b Sweating/evaporation.

  c From food (and respiration).

6 To begin with, the body would sweat to try to cool down. As the water shortage becomes apparent, the level of sweating would drop. The amount of water lost in urine would be reduced to maintain internal levels of water. You would feel thirsty and need to get a drink. Reduced sweating would allow body temperature to rise slightly.

Coordination and control: B1 2.1–B1 2.7

Summary questions

1 This question is about animal responses. Match up the following parts of sentences:

a Many processes in the body …		A … effector organs.	
b The nervous system allows you …		B … secreted by glands.	
c The cells which are sensitive to light …		C … to react to your surroundings and coordinate your behaviour.	
d Hormones are chemical substances …		D … are found in the eyes.	
e Muscles and glands are known as …		E … are known as nerves.	
f Bundles of neurons …		F … are controlled by hormones.	

2 **a** What is the job of your nervous system?

  b Where in your body would you find nervous receptors which respond to:
    i light
    ii sound
    iii heat
    iv touch?

  c Draw and label a simple diagram of a reflex arc. Explain carefully how a reflex arc works and why it allows you to respond quickly to danger.

3 **a** What is the menstrual cycle?

  b What is the role of the following hormones in the menstrual cycle:
    i FSH
    ii oestrogen?

4 **a** Explain carefully the difference between nervous and hormone control of your body.

  b What are synapses and why are they important in your nervous system?

  c How can hormones be used to control the fertility of a woman?

5 The table shows four ways in which water leaves y... body, and the amounts lost on a cool day:

Source of water loss	Cool day (water loss in cm³)	Hot day (lo... cm³)
Breath	400	The sam...
Skin	500	A
Urine	1500	B
Faeces	150	C

  a On a hot day, would the amount of water lost in ... and C be less, the same or more than the amou... water lost on a cool day?

  b Name the process by which we lose water from... skin.

  c On a cool day the body gained 2550 cm³ of wat... 1750 cm³ came directly from drinking. Where di... rest come from?

6 It is very important to keep the conditions inside t... body stable. Taking part in school sports on a hot... without a drink for the afternoon would be difficult... your body. Explain how your body would keep the... internal environment as stable as possible.

7 **a** What is gravitropism (geotropism)?

  b Explain carefully how the following respond to gravity, including the part played by plant horm... Diagrams may help in your explanations.
    i a root
    ii a shoot

8 You are provided with some very young single sho... Devise an experiment which would demonstrate th... shoots grow towards the light.

---

7 **a** The response of a plant root or shoot to gravity.

  b **i** A plant root responds positively to gravity, it grows down towards the force of the gravity. Auxin gathers on the side of the root nearest to the pull of gravity. The root grows more on the side with low auxin levels, this causes the root to bend and grow downwards towards gravity (a diagram will help with the explanation).

    ii Shoots respond by growing away from the force of gravity. For example if a shoot is horizontal, auxin accumulates at the lower surface of the shoot. The cells of the shoot grow rapidly in response to high levels of auxin. This means the lower side of the shoot grows faster than the upper side, so the shoot bends upwards away from the force of gravity.

8 Credit for well thought out investigation – needs to include unilateral light. Methods will vary – look for awareness of need for large sample of seedlings, controlling variables, etc.

AQA Practical suggestions

Practicals	AQA	k	📖	⚙
Investigation into candidates' reaction times – measuring reaction times using metre rules, stop clocks or ICT.	✓		✓	
Using forehead thermometers before and after exercise.		✓		✓

Examination-style questions

og responds to stimuli.

nk the receptor descriptions to the correct part of the
imal by choosing the correct letter (A, B, C or D).
- Contains receptors to detect chemicals (1)
- Contains receptors to detect light (1)
- Contains receptors to detect movement of the head and sound. (1)

he skin of a human contains receptors which are
ensitive to touch.
- Give **one** other stimulus which is detected by human skin. (1)
- Suggest why there are many touch receptors in a person's fingertips. (1)

Vhen a person touches a hot surface they move their
and away quickly.
- hoose the correct word to complete the sentence.
  his is called a .... action. (1)
  earned   reflex   thoughtful
- Vhat is the importance of this type of action? (1)

s picture shows a Venus flytrap.

he Venus flytrap catches flies for food. When a fly
nds on the leaf the trap closes.
- hoose the correct word to complete the sentence.
  he shutting of the trap is called a .... (1)
  etector   stimulus   response
- uggest **one** receptor the Venus flytrap has to detect
  e fly. (1)

4 Hormones are important chemicals which help to control
conditions inside living organisms.
- **a** List A shows three hormones

  List B shows where some hormones are produced.

  Match each hormone with where it is produced.

List A	List B
Hormone	**Where produced**
auxin	pituitary gland
oestrogen	kidney
FSH	plant stems and roots
	ovary

(3)

- **b** Choose the correct answer to complete each of the
  following sentences.
  - **i** The hormone which causes eggs to mature is
    .... (1)
    auxin   oestrogen   FSH
  - **ii** The hormone which causes growth of the
    uterus(womb) lining is .... (1)
    auxin   oestrogen   FSH

5 When light is shone in a person's eyes they blink. When
a plant is placed near a lamp the stem bends towards the
light.
- **a** Choose the correct answer to complete each of the
  following sentences.
  - **i** The response of the eye to bright light is called a
    .... action. (1)
    learned   reflex   stimulated
  - **ii** The response of the plant to light is called
    .... (1)
    gravitropism   hydrotropism   phototropism
- **b** *In this question you will be assessed on using good
  English, organising information clearly and using
  specialist terms where appropriate.*

  Plants respond to light and gravity. Describe how plant
  hormones control the growth of roots and shoots. (6)

61

Examination-style answers

1 a   **i** A   **ii** C   **iii** B   *(3 marks)*

  b   **i** temperature/pressure/pain   *(1 mark)*

       ii idea of increased sensitivity (for a particular task
e.g. to feel a pencil when writing)   *(1 mark)*

2 a reflex   *(1 mark)*

  b prevents damage/harm OR prevents skin burning   *(1 mark)*

3 a response   *(1 mark)*

  b any one of: touch/pressure/chemical   *(1 mark)*

4 a Auxin links to plant stems and roots, oestrogen links to
ovary, FSH links to pituitary gland.   *(3 marks)*

  b   **i** FSH   **ii** oestrogen   *(2 marks)*

5 a   **i** reflex   **ii** phototropism   *(2 marks)*

  b There is a clear and detailed scientific description of
phototropism and geotropism and how auxin controls
growth of both the root and shoot. The answer is
coherent and in a logical sequence. It contains a range of
appropriate or relevant specialist terms used accurately.
The answer shows very few errors in spelling, punctuation
and grammar.   *(5–6 marks)*

There is some description of how hormones cause the
root and shoot to bend. The answer has some structure
and the use of specialist terms has been attempted,
but not always accurately. There may be some errors in
spelling, punctuation and grammar.   *(3–4 marks)*

There is a brief description of how hormones control
growth in either the root or shoot which has little clarity
and detail. The answer is poorly constructed with an
absence of specialist terms or their use demonstrates
a lack of understanding of their meaning. The spelling,
punctuation and grammar are weak.   *(1–2 marks)*

No relevant content.   *(0 marks)*

Examples of biology points made in the response:
- Correct use of phototropism
- Correct use of gravitropism (allow geotropism)
- Auxin produced in root/shoot
- More hormone/auxin on lower side of root
- More hormone/auxin on lower/dark side of shoot
- Hormone inhibits growth of root cells
- Hormone stimulates growth of shoot/stem cells
- Longer cells on one side
- Causes root/shoot to bend
- Roots grow towards gravity
- Shoots grow towards light.

Kerboodle resources

Resources available for this chapter on Kerboodle are:
- Chapter map: Coordination and control
- Animation: Reflex action (B1 2.2)
- Bump up your grade: Reflexes in action (B1 2.2)
- Support: What's that for? (B1 2.3)
- WebQuest: Saviour siblings (B1 2.4)
- Bump up your grade: The artificial control of fertility (B1 2.4)
- Extension: The artificial control of fertility (B1 2.4)
- Support: The ups and downs of life (B1 2.6)
- How Science Works: Does light affect the germination of
  seedlings? (B1 2.6)
- Practical: Plant growth hormones (2.7)
- Interactive activity: Exploring reflex actions
- Revision podcast: Coordination and control
- Test yourself: Coordination and control
- On your marks: Coordination and control
- Examination-style questions: Coordination and control
- Answers to examination-style questions: Coordination and
  control

Practicals	AQA	k	📖	⚙
Demonstrating the speed of transmission along nerves by candidates standing in a semicircle and holding hands and squeezing with eyes closed.	✓		✓	
Design an investigation to measure the sensitivity of the skin.	✓		✓	
Demonstrating the knee jerk reaction.	✓		✓	
Investigation to measure the amount of sweat produced during exercise.	✓		✓	
Investigate: – the effect of light on the growth of seedlings – the effect of gravity on growth in germinating seedlings – the effect of water on the growth of seedlings – using a motion sensor to measure the growth of plants and seedlings – the effect of rooting compounds and weed killers on the growth of plants.	✓	✓	✓	✓

B1 3.1

Developing new medicines

Learning objectives

Students should learn:

- that new medical treatments and drugs need to be extensively tested and trialled before being used
- the possible consequences if drugs are not tested thoroughly.

Learning outcomes

Most students should be able to:

- describe and explain the reasons for testing new drugs
- explain the dangers of using drugs that have not been thoroughly tested.

Some students should also be able to:

- explain the main stages in testing drugs
- explain the flaws in the original development of thalidomide.

Support

- Make sets of cards, each with a sentence on regarding the process of drug testing. Students, working in small groups, are to put them into the correct order. This could be a competition to see which group can do it in the shortest time. (If you have the sets made up in different colours, then they are easier to sort out. Keep in separate bags.)
- Lead a session with students on 'Household safety in handling drugs and medicines.' Concentrate on things like: taking the whole prescribed course; keeping medicines away from children; taking care with the right dose and times at which medicines are taken; and discarding out-of-date drugs.

Extend

- Encourage students to explore the medical issues involved, such as the dilemma that doctors have in prescribing expensive treatments in the light of their budgets. Ask: 'Who gets them? Does it depend on age? Does it depend on your postcode?'

AQA
Specification link-up: Biology B1.3

- Scientists are continually developing new drugs. *[B1.3.1 a)]*
- When new medical drugs are devised, they have to be … *[B1.3.1 b)]*
- Thalidomide is a drug that was developed as … *[B1.3.1 d)]*

Controlled Assessment: SA4.1 Planning an investigation. *[SA4.1.1 d)]*

Lesson structure

Starters

A good medicine? – Discuss what would and, more importantly, would not make a good medicine. This provides an opportunity to examine what we expect implicitly from a medicine and make it explicit. *(5 minutes)*

'New drug, anybody?' – Show students a pill or medicine bottle and tell them it is a brand new medicine. Give the students a series of statements, adapted to their ability, that describe a sequence of events that would have to happen before a drug is put on the market. Get them to put the statements into a sensible order and then discuss them. This can be extended by asking students to write down, unsupported, what they think happens from the initial idea or discovery, up to the time it is obtainable from the chemist. Build up a sequence on the board from the ideas that the class come up with. *(10 minutes)*

Main

- Build up a more complete picture of the drug thalidomide by extending the information given in the Student Book. A video, or projected pictures, and a commentary could be used. More information about the development of the drug, the consequences of its use as a treatment for morning sickness during pregnancy, and the current possibilities of its use as a treatment for autoimmune diseases and Aids can be obtained from the internet. There are several websites providing information, e.g. www.britishpathe.com.

- Produce a PowerPoint presentation on good medicines and the stages of drug testing. Produce worksheets to accompany the presentation and allow opportunities for the students to discuss points and complete their sheets as you progress through the presentation. You might include consideration of the number of people involved in research and testing, the timescale and the sample size of any trials carried out, and the purpose of a control group using a placebo in double-blind trials, thereby including important elements of 'How Science Works'.

- Following the drug testing presentation, remind students that drugs are tested on healthy volunteers and point out that there are risks attached. Ask: 'Would you volunteer for drug testing?'; 'If so, under what circumstances?' If you would not, give your reasons and suggest other ways in which drugs should be trialled and tested'. This discussion can start in groups and then widen to include the whole class.

Plenaries

What do the words mean? – Write the words 'safe', 'effective', 'stable', 'incorporated' and 'excreted' on the board and discuss with the class how these words can be defined in terms of drugs. Students can be supported by giving them a list of meanings to choose from, or the activity can be extended by asking students to supply the definitions or be given an opportunity to extend the list for themselves. *(5 minutes)*

Should drugs be cheaper? – There has been a great deal of controversy about the cost of drugs and the availability of some new treatments for patients. The costs of development have to be recovered, but is it right that diseases for which there are drugs available are not treated because the costs are too high? Should the drugs to treat HIV and Aids be made available more cheaply in developing countries? Discuss. *(10 minutes)*

Answers to in-text questions

a Effective, safe, stable, successfully absorbed and excreted from our bodies.

b To help stop morning sickness.

Further teaching suggestions

Testing drugs on animals
- Discuss the problems associated with the testing of drugs on animals. Look at the activities of animal rights' supporters and try to get across the difference between antivivisectionist groups and those people concerned with animal welfare (often confused). Are people justified in making the protests they do? How would drugs be tested if animals were not used?

Who to target?
- Another aspect of the finances could be the basis of a class discussion. Who would you target if you wanted to maximise your profits? Are there any groups of the population who have lots of drug needs, but which there would be little point in targeting? What could be done to address this problem?

Feelings about thalidomide
- Provide each student with an A4 sheet divided into four sections: one section for the feelings of the doctor who prescribed thalidomide, one for the feelings of the person who was affected, one for the feelings of the parent and one for the feelings of the drug company. When completed, this could be discussed in class or used in a role play exercise.

Understanding placebos
- Find out what the term 'placebo' means and suggest why some people are given a placebo when new drugs are being trialled ('How Science Works').

Medicine and drugs

Developing new medicines

B1 3.1   Developing new medicines

Learning objectives
- What are the stages in testing and trialling a new drug?
- Why is testing new drugs so important?

Figure 1 The development of a new medicine takes millions of pounds, involves many people and lots of equipment

AQA Examiner's tip
Make sure you are clear that a medical drug is tested to establish:
- its effectiveness
- its toxicity
- the most appropriate dose.

We are developing new medicines all the time, as scientists and doctors try to find ways of curing more diseases. We test new medicines in the laboratory. Every new medical treatment has to be extensively tested and trialled before it is used. This process makes sure that it works well and is as safe as possible.

A good medicine is:
- **Effective** – it must prevent or cure a disease or at least make you feel better.
- **Safe** – the drug must not be too toxic (poisonous) or have unacceptable side effects for the patient.
- **Stable** – you must be able to use the medicine under normal conditions and store it for some time.
- **Successfully taken into and removed from your body** – it must reach its target and be cleared from your system once it has done its work.

Developing and testing a new drug
When scientists research a new medicine they have to make sure all these conditions are met. It can take up to 12 years to bring a new medicine into your doctor's surgery. It can also cost a lot of money; up to about £350 million!

Researchers target a disease and make lots of possible new drugs. These are tested in the laboratory to find out if they are toxic and if they seem to do their job. They are tested on cells, tissues and even whole organs. Many chemicals fail at this stage.

The small numbers of chemicals which pass the earlier tests are now tested on animals. This is done to find out how they work in a whole living organism. It also gives information about possible doses and side effects. The tissues and animals are used as models to predict how the drugs may behave in humans.

Drugs that pass animal testing will be tested on human volunteers in clinical trials. First very low doses are given to healthy people to check for side effects. Then it is tried on a small number of patients to see if it treats the disease. If it seems to be safe and effective, bigger clinical trials take place to find the optimum dose for the drug.

If the medicine passes all the legal tests it is licensed so your doctor can prescribe it. Its safety will be monitored for as long as it is used.

a What are the important properties of a good new medicine?

Double-blind trials
In human trials, scientists use a double-blind trial to see just how effective the new medicine is. Some patients with the target disease agree to take part in the trials. They are either given a placebo that does not contain the drug or the new medicine. Neither the doctor nor the patients know who has received the real drug and who has received the placebo until the trial is complete. The patients' health is monitored carefully.

Often the placebo will contain a different drug that is already used to treat the disease. That is so the patient is not deprived of treatment by taking part in the trial.

AQA Examiner's tip
Remember, the cells, tissues and animals act as models to predict how the drug may behave in humans.

Why do we test new medicines so thoroughly?
Thalidomide is a medicine which was developed in the 1950s as a sleeping pill. This was before there were agreed standards for testing new medicines. In particular, tests on pregnant animals, which we now know to be essential, were not carried out.

Then it was discovered that thalidomide stopped morning sickness during pregnancy. Because thalidomide seemed very safe for adults, it was assumed to be safe for unborn children. Doctors gave it to pregnant women to relieve their sickness.

Tragically, thalidomide was **not** safe for developing fetuses. It affected the fetuses of many women who took the drug in the early stages of pregnancy. They went on to give birth to babies with severe limb deformities.

The thalidomide tragedy led to a new law being passed. It set standards for the testing of all new medicines. Since the Medicines Act 1968, new medicines must be tested on animals to see if they have an effect on developing fetuses.

There is another twist in the thalidomide story. Doctors discovered it can treat leprosy. They started to use the drug against leprosy in the developing world but again children were born with abnormalities. Its use for leprosy has now been banned by the World Health Organisation (WHO).

However doctors are finding more uses for the drug. It can treat some autoimmune diseases (where the body attacks its own cells) and even some cancers. It is now used very carefully and never given to anyone who is or might become pregnant.

b Why was thalidomide prescribed to pregnant women?

Figure 2 This woman has limb deformities because her mother took thalidomide during her pregnancy. She was just one of thousands of people affected by the thalidomide tragedy, many of whom have gone on to live full and active lives.

Summary questions
1 Copy and complete using the words below:
   effective   trialled   safe   medicine   stable   tested
   Every new .... has to be extensively .... and .... before you can use it to make sure that it works well. A good medicine can be taken into and removed from your body, and it is ...., ... and ....
2 a Testing a new medicine costs a lot of money and can take up to 12 years. Make a flow chart to show the main stages in testing new drugs.
   b Why is an active drug often used as the control in a clinical trial instead of a sugar pill placebo which does nothing?
3 a What were the flaws in the original development of thalidomide?
   b Why do you think that the World Health Organisation has stopped the use of thalidomide to treat leprosy but the drug is still being used in the developed world to treat certain rare conditions?

Key points
- When we develop new medicines they have to be tested and trialled extensively before we can use them.
- Drugs are tested to see if they work well. We also make sure they are not too toxic and have no unacceptable side effects.
- Thalidomide was developed as a sleeping pill and was found to prevent morning sickness in early pregnancy. It had not been fully tested and it caused birth defects.

62   63

Summary answers

1 medicine, tested (trialled), trialled (tested), safe, effective, stable (last three in any order).

2 a Flow chart to show the main stages in the process.

   b If there is already a drug which works reasonably well against a disease, it would be unethical not to give that to a patient. It also allows us to compare how good the new drug is compared to existing drugs. It can only be done if there is already an active drug available.

3 a There was a lower standard of testing in those days. Extensive testing on pregnant animals was not carried out. It wasn't developed as a drug for morning sickness, but it turned out to have a beneficial effect and it was assumed that it would be safe.

   b When treating leprosy it was still causing complications for patients that were pregnant. Thalidomide is still used for rare diseases for which there is no other effective treatment. Its use in those countries is carefully controlled and it is never given to pregnant women.

B1 3.2

How effective are medicines?

AQA
Specification link-up: Biology B1.3

- Candidates should be aware of the use of statins in lowering the risk of heart and circulatory diseases. [B1.3.1 c)]
- Evaluate the effect of statins in cardiovascular disease. [B1.3]
- Evaluate claims made about the effect of prescribed and non-prescribed drugs on health. [B1.3]

Learning objectives

Students should learn:

- that statins are drugs that lower cholesterol levels in the blood
- that lower blood cholesterol levels reduce the risk of cardiovascular disease
- that the effectiveness of medicines can only be determined in proper double-blind trials.

Learning outcomes

Most students should be able to:

- describe the use of statins in lowering blood cholesterol levels
- evaluate the effect of statins in the treatment of cardiovascular disease
- evaluate the claims made about the effects of prescribed and non-prescribed medicines on health.

Some students should also be able to:

- explain in detail how and why double-blind tests are used.

Lesson structure

Starters

Good and bad cholesterol – Show a clip from *Futurama* season 3, episode 4 'Parasites Lost' where Dr Zoidberg, while in a miniaturised submarine inside the bloodstream, scraped cholesterol from a heart valve, spread it on a cracker and ate it. He comments, 'It's good cholesterol but it spreads like bad cholesterol.' Discuss the role of cholesterol in heart disease. *(5 minutes)*

The heart of the problem – Show the students a diagram of the heart, or an actual one. Draw out by questioning that it is mostly made of muscle. Ask what muscle must be supplied with in order to work? [Draw out oxygen and food (glucose).] Ask how this can be supplied? [Draw out through the blood and that there must be a good supply of oxygenated blood to the heart.] Show a picture of or the actual coronary artery. State that this is where the blood comes to the heart muscle. Ask what would happen if a lump of fat blocked the coronary artery? Link the outcome [heart attack] to cholesterol in the diet. Students could be supported by prompting but expect some students to be able to deduce much more by themselves. *(10 minutes)*

Main

- Students should look at the graph in the Student Book (Figure 1) and answer the following questions. The height of the bars shows the extent to which they were effective in reducing the levels of the 'bad' cholesterol. The different colours of the bars show the concentrations of the statins in the trial.

  Questions

  1 Which statin was trialled at four different concentrations? [Statin 1]

  2 Which two statins were only trialled at 20 and 40 mg doses? [Statin 3 and Statin 5]

  3 Which concentration was not tried for Statin 2? [80 mg]

  4 Which concentration was not tried for Statin 4? [10 mg]

  5 Which statin looks the most effective overall? [Statin 1]

  6 Which two concentrations would you compare in order to get a fair view of the performance of all the drugs? [20 and 40 mg]

  7 Compare Statin 1 and Statin 4. What notable difference do you spot in the effectiveness of different concentrations? [Increasing the concentration from 40 mg to 80 mg had a much more marked effect for Statin 4 as opposed to Statin 1.]

- The following activity helps the students understand double-blind trials. The idea is the patients don't know what they are getting and the doctors don't know what they are giving. That way neither can show any bias.

  Split the class into groups of three. One student acts as the Researcher, one as the Doctor and one as the Patient. The Researchers have to come to the teacher to collect crackers. One set (labelled A) have got butter on them, one set (labelled B) have a cheaper substitute spread on them. Check in advance that no one has a gluten or dairy allergy. As an alternative, one could have disposable cups of regular and diet cola. The Researchers have to make a note of which one is which and give them to the Doctors. The Doctors, without knowing which is which, give them to the Patients to consume and analyse. Students may have to go outside the laboratory to carry this out safely. They must decide on the basis of their experience whether they had butter or substitute (or regular/diet cola). The Doctors record this and report to the Researchers, who record this and draw conclusions. Researchers can collate their results on the board in a blank table. You should get an accurate picture of whether the class can tell these apart.

  Conclude by relating this to drugs trials. Get students to put into words the importance of neither those giving nor those receiving the treatment knowing which drug is which.

Support

- Ask students simple questions about the graph in Figure 1 – for example, which statin worked best? Which statin gave the poorest results or was least effective? etc. Alternatively, supply the answers which then have to be matched with the questions.

Extend

- Ask students to find out as much as they can about statins. What are they? Where are they found naturally?

Plenaries

The placebo effect – Get students to think of examples from their childhood of where they were convinced by their parents of something that would affect their feelings and give them relief from distress. *(5 minutes)*

Prescribed or not? – In groups, get the students to list some drugs you can buy over the counter and some you cannot. Students could be supported by supplying pre-prepared lists to choose from. Students could be extended by compiling their own lists. Compare each group's findings to compile a master list and create a summary definition. *(10 minutes)*

Further teaching suggestions

Prescribed drugs versus non-prescribed drugs
- Using the graph in the Student Book (Figure 2), discuss the findings and ask the students what they think are the advantages and disadvantages of using the non-prescribed drug.

Will it lower my blood cholesterol?
- Build up a list of food products that claim to lower cholesterol levels and get students to investigate the claims using secondary data and information from the internet. Working in groups, they could research one product each and then present a report to the rest of the class.

Alternative medicines
- Using suggestions from the class, build up a list of alternative, over-the-counter, medicines. Discuss their uses and their effectiveness compared to prescribed ones. Have ready – some suggestions – scan the shelves of the vitamins and supplements section of the local supermarket for ideas and examples.

Ethics
- Discuss the ethics of deliberately fooling people into believing they have taken an effective medicine if it is proved that this will be of assistance in helping them to feel better, even if the drug has no pharmaceutical efficacy itself.

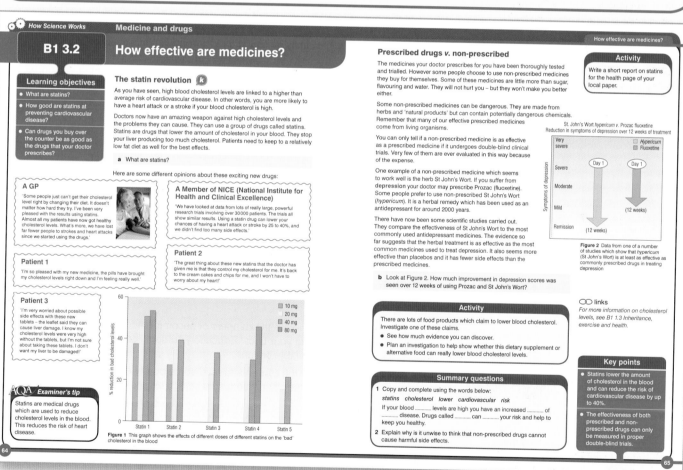

Answers to in-text questions

a Medical drugs that reduce the levels of cholesterol in the blood.

b St John's Wort was better than Prozac as it led to a remission whereas Prozac only reduced the symptoms of depression from 'severe' to 'mild'.

Summary answers

1 cholesterol, risk, cardiovascular, statins, lower

2 Because if natural remedies work, they contain chemicals that are drugs, and these can cause problems with side-effects like any other drug. Natural remedies that do not actually have any chemicals that can help you can still contain chemicals that can be harmful – natural does not mean harmless.

B1 3.3

Drugs

AQA
Specification link-up: Biology B1.3

- Candidates should be aware of the effects of misuse of the legal recreational drugs, alcohol and nicotine. Candidates should understand that the misuse of the illegal recreational drugs, ecstasy, cannabis and heroin may have adverse effects on the heart and circulatory system. *[B1.3.1 e)]*
- Drugs change the chemical processes in people's bodies so that they may become dependent or addicted to them and suffer withdrawal symptoms without them. Heroin and cocaine are very addictive. *[B1.3.1 h)]*
- Cannabis is an illegal drug. Cannabis smoke contains chemicals which may cause mental illness in some people. *[B1.3.1 f)]*

Learning objectives

Students should learn:
- that drugs are substances that affect the way in which the body works
- that drugs may cause harm by changing the chemical processes in the body
- that people using drugs may become dependent on them and unable to manage without them (addicted to drugs)
- that cannabis may cause psychological problems and the use of hard drugs such as cocaine and heroin can seriously damage health.

Learning outcomes

Most students should be able to:
- give a definition of the term 'drug'
- explain what is meant by addiction
- describe some of the problems caused by drug abuse.

Some students should also be able to:
- explain that the impact of drug use varies from individual to individual.

Lesson structure

Starters

Hooked? – Students are to describe what they understand addiction to mean. Students could be supported by being given a list of drugs and asked to tick those that they think are addictive. Students could be extended by being encouraged to come up with a list for themselves and to speculate about what would make some substances addictive and others not. *(5 minutes)*

Drugs in the house? – Write up a list of some of the places where there may be drugs in a house, such as alcohol, coffee and tea, tobacco products obviously, but also consider the First Aid kit or a typical family medicine cabinet (paracetamol, calamine, antihistamine cream, antiseptic or brands such as Calpol, Nurofen, Dettol) Use either examples or photographs. Ask the students to identify which they think are drugs, or contain drugs, and which are other substances. *(10 minutes)*

Main

- Get the students to either draw out or fill in a printed table with the following headings: 'Drugs', 'Other names', 'Legal?', 'Effects', 'Hazards'. They can gather the information for it from internet sites such as 'Talk to Frank.' (www.talktofrank.com).

- Discuss (or describe) the film *Trainspotting* with the students. Although it is an 18 certificate, quite a few could have seen it at home. Discuss what happens to the character Renton (played by Ewan McGregor) when he stops taking heroin (sweating, pain, craving and hallucinations that included a dead baby crawling over the ceiling). Explain about tolerance and the need for ever increasing dosages just to feel normal.

- Discuss the relative addictiveness of common drugs. Draw out that cannabis is not addictive although some users can become psychologically dependent on it and it can cause anxiety and paranoia and make latent psychological problems worse. Draw out that heroin and cocaine are very addictive and highly dangerous. Link to social problems.

- Show a suitable video covering the dangers of becoming addicted to drugs. Ask about drugs awareness videos at your Local Education Authority or Social Services – drugs teams will have these available on loan.

- Research and read or get the students to read some poetry about addiction, e.g. 'My name: Is Cocaine' by Desiree Kimbrue (use a search engine to locate).

Support

- Give students a list of important social problems associated with the use of drugs and ask them to place these in order of importance. This could be used as an alternative to the first Plenary.

Plenaries

Social problems linked with drug abuse – Ask students to compile a list of five important social problems associated with the use of drugs, including tobacco and alcohol. Compare lists and decide which ones top the list. *(5 minutes)*

Which one am I? – Bring a student to the front of the class. Get them to choose from a list (without telling anyone) a drug that they are to represent. The rest of the students can then ask questions of them to ascertain which drug they have chosen. Students could be supported by having a list of questions to choose from and a limited number of drugs to represent. Students could be extended by getting them to devise the activity themselves and possibly attach a list of taboo words to make it more demanding. *(10 minutes)*

Extend

- Ask students to investigate further the nature of drugs, how they affect nerve transmission and whether they act in the brain or on the nervous system generally.

Further teaching suggestions

Personal experience
- If students are willing, get them to share experiences of people they know who have been affected by drugs. This can be very powerful but must be carefully managed.

Local authority drugs specialist talk
- Ask the local authority to send in a drugs unit member to talk to the students. Ex-addicts can also have strong testimony but use great caution!

Answers to in-text questions

a People who have traditionally inhabited a region since ancient times.

b Any appropriate answers, such as alcohol and tobacco are legal, but cocaine and heroin are not.

c 'Addiction' means that you cannot function properly without a drug and suffer withdrawal symptoms if you are without it.

Medicine and drugs

B1 3.3 Drugs

Learning objectives
- What is a drug?
- What is addiction?
- Why are drugs such as cannabis, cocaine and heroin such a problem?

AQA *Examiner's tip*

Drugs are chemicals which alter the body's chemistry.

Many drugs are used as medicines to treat disease.

A **drug** is a substance that alters the way in which your body works. It can affect your mind, your body or both. In every society there are certain drugs which people use for medicine, and other drugs which they use for pleasure.

Many of the drugs that are used both for medicine and for recreation come originally from natural substances, often plants. Many of them have been known to and used by indigenous (long-term inhabitants of an area) peoples for many years. Usually some of the drugs that are used for pleasure are socially acceptable and legal, while others are illegal.

Figure 1 Millions of pounds worth of illegal drugs are brought into the UK every year. It is a constant battle for the police to find and destroy drugs like these.

a What do we mean by 'indigenous peoples'?

Drugs are everywhere in our society. People drink coffee and tea, smoke cigarettes and have a beer, an alcopop or a glass of wine. They think nothing of it. Yet all of these things contain drugs – caffeine, nicotine and alcohol (the chemical ethanol). These drugs are all legal.

Other drugs, such as cocaine, ecstasy and heroin are illegal. Which drugs are legal and which are not varies from country to country. Alcohol is legal in the UK as long as you are over 18, but it is illegal in many Arab states. Heroin is illegal almost everywhere.

b Give an example of one drug which is legal and one which is illegal in the UK.

Because drugs affect the chemistry of your body, they can cause great harm. This is even true of drugs we use as medicines. However, because medical drugs make you better, it is usually worth taking the risk.

But legal recreational drugs, such as alcohol and tobacco, and illegal substances, such as solvents, cannabis and cocaine, can cause terrible damage to your body. Yet they offer no long-term benefits to you at all.

links

For more information on the mental health problems that can be caused by cannabis, see B1 3.5 Does cannabis lead to hard drugs?

What is addiction?

Some drugs change the chemical processes in your body so that you may become addicted to them. You can become dependent on them. If you are addicted to a drug, you cannot manage properly without it. Some drugs, for example heroin and cocaine, are very addictive.

Once addicted, you generally need more and more of the drug to keep you feeling normal. When addicts try to stop using drugs they usually feel very unwell. They often have aches and pains, sweating, shaking, headaches and cravings for their drug. We call these **withdrawal symptoms**.

c What do we mean by 'addiction'?

The problems of drug abuse

People take drugs for a reason. Drugs can make you feel very good about yourself. They can make you feel happy and they can make you feel as if your problems no longer matter. Unfortunately, because most recreational drugs are addictive, they can soon become a problem themselves.

No drugs are without a risk. Cannabis is often thought of as a relatively 'soft' – and therefore safe – drug. But evidence is growing which shows that cannabis smoke contains chemicals which can cause mental illness to develop in some people.

Hard drugs, such as cocaine and heroin, are extremely addictive. Using them often leads to very severe health problems. Some of these come from the drugs themselves. Others come from the lifestyle that often goes with drugs.

Because these drugs are illegal, they are expensive. Young people often end up turning to crime to pay for their drug habit. They don't eat properly or look after themselves. They can also contract serious illnesses, such as hepatitis, STDs (sexually transmitted diseases) and HIV/Aids especially if drugs are taken intravenously (via a needle).

Boys arrested for drug offences by age group 2006/07 and 2007/08

Girls arrested for drug offences by age group 2006/07 and 2007/08

Figure 2 Illegal drugs are often linked with crime. In the UK more and more young people are being arrested for drug offences – using or selling illegal drugs.

Summary questions

1 Copy and complete using the words below:

mind   cocaine   ecstasy   legal   alcohol   drug   body

A .... alters the way in which your body works. It can affect the .... the .... or both. Some drugs are .... e.g. caffeine and .... Other drugs, such as ...., ... and heroin are illegal.

2 a Why do people often need more and more of a drug?
b What happens if you stop taking a drug when you are addicted to it?

3 a Why do people take drugs?
b Explain some of the problems linked with using cannabis, cocaine and heroin.
c Look at Figure 2. What does this tell you about the difference in drug use between boys and girls?
d What does Figure 2 tell you about the trend in drug use in young people?
e Why do you think young people continue to take these drugs when they are well aware of the dangers?

Key points
- Drugs change the chemical processes in your body, so you may become addicted to them.
- Addiction is when you become physically or mentally dependent on a drug.
- Smoking cannabis may cause mental health problems.
- Hard drugs, such as cocaine and heroin, are very addictive and can cause serious health problems.

66

67

Summary answers

1 drug, mind/body, body/mind, legal, alcohol, cocaine/ecstasy, ecstasy/cocaine

2 a They need more and more to get the same effect.
b You suffer withdrawal symptoms/feel ill.

3 a As medicines or for pleasure makes them feel good, feel they can cope with problems, fit in with the crowd.
b Addiction, health problems from drug or lifestyle needed to fund drug, risk of hepatitis and HIV/Aids from lifestyle, etc.
c Boys get arrested for drug offences much more than girls, which probably reflects that boys use drugs much more than girls, although it may also reflect more boys are arrested than girls.

d Both boys and girls would seem to be using drugs more from this limited evidence – although it could be that police are more effective at detecting and arresting people for drug crime.
e Any thoughtful points such as peer pressure, image, addiction.

B1 3.4

Legal and illegal drugs

Learning objectives

Students should learn:

- that many recreational drugs affect the nervous system, particularly the brain
- that drugs may be used recreationally and some are more harmful than others
- that some drugs are illegal and others legal; the overall impact of legal drugs on health is greater than that of illegal drugs.

Learning outcomes

Most students should be able to:

- list some common legal and illegal drugs
- explain why some people use illegal drugs for recreation and describe the effects of cannabis
- explain why the use of legal drugs has a greater impact on health than the use of illegal drugs.

Some students should also be able to:

- evaluate the impact of different types of drugs on society.

Answers to in-text questions

a Caffeine.

b Because many more people take (and abuse) legal drugs.

Support

- Give students the names of the different recreational drugs and ask them to place them in the correct categories under the headings 'Legal' and 'Illegal'.

Extend

- Ask students to design an experiment to investigate the effect of caffeine on memory.

AQA

Specification link-up: Biology B1.3

- The overall impact of legal drugs (prescribed and non-prescribed) on health is much greater than the impact of illegal drugs because far more people use them. *[B1.3.1 g)]*
- Evaluate different types of drugs and why some people use illegal drugs for recreation. *[B1.3]*

Controlled Assessment: SA4.1 Planning an investigation *[SA4.1.1 a) b) c) d)]*, *[SA4.1.2 a) b) c)]* and *[SA4.1.3 b]*; SA4.3 Collect primary and secondary data *[SA4.3.3 a) b) c)]* and SA4.5 Analyse and interpret primary and secondary data. *[SA4.5.2 a)]*, *[SA4.5.4 a) d)]*

Lesson structure

Starters

Which is which? – Put up charts of stick figures or dots onto the four walls: 90 000 on one, 9000 on another, 2000 on a third and 30 on the last. State that these are deaths in the UK due to drugs. Ask which chart might represent which drug? Following discussion, reveal that they refer to tobacco (nicotine) (90 000), alcohol (9000), all other illegal drugs (2000) and ecstasy (30). *(5 minutes)*

Quick quiz on different categories of drugs – Support students by handing out lists of different drugs as they enter the classroom and ask them to put two letters from M (medicinal), R (recreational) L (legal) or I (illegal) alongside each one. Check through the list. Students can be extended by suggesting the drugs themselves, filling in the categories and debating the nature of any overlaps. *(10 minutes)*

Main

- Give an exposition on which drugs are legal and which are not in the UK. Draw out an international perspective by overviewing differences, e.g. the approach of Muslim countries to alcohol.
- Review changes in UK drugs law over the years. Explain that commonly used legal drugs have physiological effects – lead on to practical on caffeine.
- You can ask students to investigate the effect of caffeine on reaction times. Caffeine has a mild stimulatory effect, increasing alertness. This experiment can be used to introduce 'How Science Works' concepts – predictions can be made, measurements repeated and controlled conditions are easy to ensure. However, generalising from data collected from one individual or a small group brings in the variety of factors that make humans different, and the need for large sample sizes in investigations where all variables cannot be controlled.
- 'How Science Works' concepts can be introduced. For example, they might focus on evaluating the reliability and validity of their investigation.

Plenaries

Drug symbols – Ask students to design an icon for each of a number of drugs to represent it on a website. Each icon should concisely sum up what the drug is about in a simple, visually effective way. This could be done individually or in groups and collectively producing a range. *(5 minutes)*

If I was in charge – Imagine you have been given the task of being in charge of drugs policy for the UK. What changes would you make? What would your desired outcomes be? What difficulties would you be likely to encounter when putting into effect your changes? Students can be supported by providing them with a list of suggestions and allowing them to discuss which they would implement. Extension level students should produce reasoned and cohesive strategies. *(10 minutes)*

Practical support

Investigation of the effect of caffeine on reaction times/heart rate

Equipment and materials required

Metre rulers, chocolate, cups of coffee (could have caffeinated and decaffeinated – but not to be consumed in the laboratory), data loggers and hand-held pulse meters (or a stop watch).

Details

Some students could look at the effect of caffeine on reaction times.

Using the stick-drop method of testing reaction times, the effect of caffeine can be measured. Students can volunteer to drink measured amounts of coffee, with a known/controlled caffeine content, and have their reaction times measured before and after drinking the coffee. A period of time (about 10 minutes) has to be allowed for the caffeine to be absorbed before the second test is

carried out. Remind the students that it is the difference between the two times that is significant.

This could also be an opportunity to teach about a double-blind test if technicians provide cups of coffee labelled as A and B (and only they know which is decaffeinated until after testing is complete).

Some students could look at the effect of caffeine on heart rate.

Changes in heart rate (measured by measuring the pulse rate) can be recorded before and after caffeine intake. This is best done using hand-held pulse meters attached to a data logger – the display can be projected to get a real time graph drawn of heart rate before and after consuming caffeine – a large lump of chocolate will do the trick!

● Is there any difference between before and after? Which variables need to be controlled?

Safety: Care needs to be taken with eating and drinking in a laboratory (should be done outside before the lesson or in a food technology room).

Medicine and drugs

B1 3.4 | Legal and illegal drugs

Learning objectives

● How do drugs like caffeine and heroin affect your nervous system?

● Which has the bigger overall impact on health – legal or illegal drugs?

What is the most widely used drug in the world? It is probably one that most of you will have used at least once today, yet no one really thinks about. The caffeine in your cup of tea, mug of coffee or can of cola is a drug.

Many people find it hard to get going in the morning without a mug of coffee. They are probably addicted to the drug caffeine. It stimulates your brain and increases your heart rate and blood pressure.

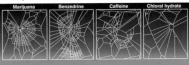

Marijuana | Benzedrine | Caffeine | Chloral hydrate

Normal web

Figure 1 NASA scientists have shown that common house spiders spin their webs very differently when given some commonly used legal and illegal drugs. The effect of caffeine on the nervous system of a spider is particularly dramatic!

a What drug is in a can of cola?

How do drugs affect you?

Many of the drugs used for medical treatments have little or no effect on your nervous system. However, all of the recreational drugs that people use for pleasure affect the way your nervous system works, particularly your brain. It is these changes that people enjoy when they use the drugs. The same changes can cause addiction. Once addicted, your body doesn't work properly without the drug.

Some drugs like caffeine, nicotine and cocaine speed up the activity of your brain. They make you feel more alert and energetic.

Others, like alcohol and cannabis, slow down the responses of your brain. They make you feel calm and better able to cope. Heroin actually stops impulses travelling in your nervous system. Therefore you don't feel any pain or discomfort. Cannabis produces vivid waking dreams. It can make you see or hear things that are not really there.

Why do people use drugs?

People use drugs for a variety of reasons. They feel that caffeine, nicotine and alcohol help them cope with everyday life. Few people who use these legal drugs would think of themselves as addicts. Yet the chemicals they take can have a big physical and psychological impact (see Figure 1).

As for the illegal recreational drugs – people who try them may be looking for excitement or escape. They might want to be part of the crowd or just want to see what happens. Yet many drugs are addictive and your body needs increasingly more to feel the effects.

AQA Examiner's tip

Drugs may be:
● legal or illegal
● addictive or non-addictive.
Learn examples of all of these.

Impact of drugs on health

Some recreational drugs are more harmful than others. Most media reports on the dangers of drugs focus on illegal drugs. But in fact the impact of legal drugs on health is much greater than the impact of illegal drugs. That's because far more people take them. Millions of people in the UK take medicines such as statins, or smoke or drink alcohol. Only a few thousand take heroin.

A recent case history shows you how emotions and politics can be more important than scientific evidence in the way society reacts to drugs. In 2010, several young people died after apparently taking a relatively new legal drug known as 'meow-meow'. The drug was made illegal even though at least one of the 'victims' had not taken meow-meow.

In fact, in the UK, there are around 2000 deaths linked to using illegal drugs each year.

But every year in the UK around 9000 people die as a result of alcohol-abuse. About 90000 people die from smoking-related diseases. Yet alcohol and nicotine remain completely legal.

Everyone can see the dangers to health of non-prescribed, illegal drugs. However, choosing which drugs to make illegal does not appear to be based on the scientific evidence of health damage alone.

DON'T LET DRUG DEALERS CHANGE THE FACE OF YOUR NEIGHBOURHOOD

Figure 2 Drugs can seem appealing, exciting and fun. Many people use them briefly and then leave them behind. But the risks of addiction are high, and no one can predict whom drugs will affect most.

b Why do legal drugs cause many more health problems than illegal drugs?

Figure 3 This graph shows how alcohol-related deaths almost doubled between 1990 and 2008 (Source: National Statistics Office)

Per 100 000 population — axis: 0, 2, 4, 6, 8, 10, 12, 14, 16, 18, 20
Year: 1992 1994 1996 1998 2000 2002 2004 2006 2008
— Males
— Females

Summary questions

1 Copy and complete using the words below:
brain   health   illegal   legal   recreation
Drugs which people use for .... all affect the nervous system, particularly the .... Some of these drugs are legal but some of them are .... More people suffer .... problems caused by .... drugs than illegal ones.

2 Use data from Figure 3 to help you answer these:
a How many men and women died of alcohol-related diseases per 100 000 of the population in 1992?
b How many men and women died of alcohol-related diseases per 100 000 of the population in 2008?
c Suggest reasons for this increase in alcohol-related deaths.
d Why do you think alcohol remains a legal drug when it causes so many deaths?

3 Compare the overall impact of legal and illegal drugs on the nation's health.

Key points

● Many recreational drugs affect the nervous system, particularly the brain. Some are more harmful than others.

● Some recreational drugs are legal and others are illegal.

● The overall impact of legal drugs on health is much greater than illegal drugs because more people use them.

68 | 69

Further teaching suggestions

Debate the issue

● Which are more dangerous – legal or illegal drugs? This question could be debated by the class. Each student could prepare a short case for and against and then the motion. Draw lots to decide which students speak.

The caffeine effect

● The experiment can compare the effect of caffeine on males and females. Is there a difference? If there is, can it be explained? Also, the effects of different quantities may differ between different sexes and age groups.

Summary answers

1 recreation, brain, illegal, health, legal

2 a 1992 men 9 per 100 000, women 5 per 100 000.
  b 2008 men 18–19 per 100 000, women 8–9 per 100 000.
  c More people drinking, younger people drinking, people drinking more at a time (binge drinking) and more people addicted to alcohol.
  d Very popular, part of culture, government revenue, enjoyed by many sensibly, hard to change legal status after so many years, many of the people who are in the government use alcohol themselves, prohibition already tried but unsuccessful and led to criminal activity. Any other

thoughtful points on the reasons some drugs are legal and others not, social standpoints, historical usage, etc.

3 Give credit for each valid point made. Look for understanding of the differences between legal and illegal drugs – the contact with criminal culture with illegal drugs, high costs, etc., compared with the ease of causing damage with legal drugs, the impact of drug abuse on individuals. Increased rates of accidents as a result of drug use and increased crime under influence of both legal and illegal drugs. Also look for the positive aspects of legal drugs as medicines – cure diseases, save lives, relieve symptoms, etc.

B1 3.5

Does cannabis lead to hard drugs?

Learning objectives

Students should learn:

- that some recreational drugs are more harmful than others
- that some people may progress from non-addictive recreational drugs to addiction to hard drugs
- that the use of cannabis can be harmful.

Learning outcomes

Most students should be able to:

- describe ways in which some recreational drugs are more harmful than others
- evaluate the facts about the recreational use of cannabis.

Some students should also be able to:

- compare the damage caused by the use of cannabis with that caused by other recreational drugs, such as alcohol and tobacco.

AQA Specification link-up: Biology B1.3

- Consider the possible progression from recreational drugs to hard drugs. [B1.3]
- Evaluate different types of drugs and why some people use illegal drugs for recreation. [B1.3]

Lesson structure

Starters

Cannabis information video – Use the internet to search for a suitable information video for the students to watch on cannabis. *(5 minutes)*

'I know this bloke!' – Initiate a discussion of anecdotal evidence on the effects of cannabis. Find out if anyone in the class has suitable stories to tell, either of no harmful effects from cannabis or of problems people have had. If possible, draw out a range of responses. You could support students by supplying a suitable newspaper article or personal account for them to read out and discuss. Students could be extended by getting them to discuss articles they have read or problems they have heard about. Differentiation can also be by outcome – supported students will hold a less wide-ranging and less deeply questioning discussion than extended students. *(10 minutes)*

Main

- Get the students to read through the text about facts on whether cannabis use is related to hard drugs. Consult the websites mentioned and/or any other relevant ones. *The Guardian* ran a series of articles promoting the lowering of cannabis classification from B to C. Refer to the changes in government policy with the B to C move and then its subsequent reversal.
- Group display work. Brainstorm the coverage of the topic and split the class into groups, giving each responsibility for a topic. Collect and collate these for a class display.
- Carry out the debate suggested in the Student Book activity box. It is suggested that the students prepare two short speeches, one in favour and one against the proposal. These speeches could be set as homework and then the debate held at a convenient time.
- Designate volunteers as 'concerned parent', 'teenage user', 'drug dealer', 'police officer', 'psychiatric doctor' and other such roles. Have each one in turn take to the 'empathy hotseat' at the front of the class and have the rest of the students ask them questions which they have to consider and answer in role. A list of prompt questions for each character may be beneficial.

Plenaries

Cause and effect? – Find some statistics which are potentially misleading. For example, the average human being has slightly less than one testicle, children with bigger feet are better at spelling than their smaller-footed peers, countries with higher divorce rates have lower death rates, etc. Give these to the students and see if they can untangle the reasons behind them. Students can be supported by giving some clue sheets for these. Students can be extended by suggesting they use the internet to find their own examples and try them out on each other. *(5 minutes)*

Who should we listen to? – Make a list of sources of information regarding cannabis and rate each one from 1 to 4, with 1 being 'wouldn't pay much attention' to 4 being 'would pay most attention'. Discuss and evaluate results as a class. *(10 minutes)*

Support

- Get students to design a poster on 'Keeping your children safe!' for the class display.

Extend

- Get students to consider the effects of the legalisation of cannabis. What effect could it have on the NHS, the Social Services and the police?

Further teaching suggestions

Drug facts
- The class display of drug facts could be used in an assembly or as a discussion focus during tutor times or PSHE lessons.

Cannabis on prescription?
- Students could find out more about the use of cannabis in treating the symptoms of multiple sclerosis, epilepsy and Alzheimer's disease. How does it work? What are the chemicals involved?

Guest speaker
- If it is felt appropriate, a guest speaker, such as a social worker or person trained in drug education, could be invited in to talk to students and answer questions. This could link with the plenary 'Who should we listen to?'

How Science Works   Medicine and drugs   Does cannabis lead to hard drugs?

B1 3.5   Does cannabis lead to hard drugs?

Learning objectives
- How do people move from using recreational drugs to hard drugs?
- Is cannabis harmful?

Cannabis – the facts?

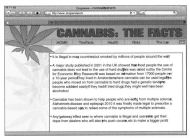

Figure 1 How can you find out the truth about cannabis and the effect it might have on you, your friend or – if you are a parent – your child?

a What diseases are helped by the chemicals in cannabis?

Cannabis – where do you stand?

A lot of scientific research has been done into the effects of cannabis on our health. The links between cannabis use and addiction to hard drugs has also been investigated.

Unfortunately many of the studies have been quite small. They have not used large sample sizes, so the evidence is not strong.

Figure 2 In the minds of many people – parents, teachers and politicians – cannabis is a 'gateway' drug. It opens the door to the use of other much harder drugs such as cocaine and heroin. Your health – and indeed your life itself – is at risk. How accurate is this picture?

The UK Government downgraded cannabis to a Class C drug in 2004. Then stronger negative evidence emerged. It found that cannabis use can trigger mental health problems in people who are vulnerable to such problems. In 2009 the decision to downgrade was reversed and cannabis is now a Class B drug again.

What the doctors say
- The evidence is clear that for some people cannabis use can trigger mental illness. This may be serious and permanent. It is particularly the case for people who have a genetic tendency to mental health problems.
- A study has been carried out on 1600 14- to 15-year-old students in Australia. It showed that the youngsters who use cannabis regularly have a significantly higher risk of depression. However it doesn't work the other way round. Children who are already suffering depression are no more likely than anyone else to use cannabis.
- All the evidence suggests that teenagers are particularly vulnerable to mental health problems triggered by cannabis. Consider a teenager who starts smoking cannabis before they are 15. They are four times more likely to develop schizophrenia or another psychotic illness by the time they are 26 than a non-user.

Figure 3 The doctors at the Royal College of Psychiatrists are the people who deal with mental health problems of all kinds. They have some real concerns about cannabis-use.

Untangling the evidence

The evidence shows that almost all heroin users were originally cannabis users. This is not necessarily a case of cannabis use causing heroin addiction. Almost all cannabis users are originally smokers – but we don't claim that smoking cigarettes leads to cannabis use! In fact the vast majority of smokers do not go on to use cannabis. Just as the vast majority of cannabis users do not move on to hard drugs like heroin. Most studies suggest that cannabis can act as a 'gateway' to other drugs. However, that is **not** because it makes people want a stronger drug but because it puts them in touch with illegal drug dealers.

b How much does using cannabis before you are 15 appear to increase your risk of developing serious mental illness?

Summary questions

1 **a** What is meant by a 'gateway' drug?
  b Why is cannabis considered a gateway drug?

2 Cannabis is linked to some mental health problems, but tobacco is known to cause hundreds of thousands of deaths each year through heart disease and lung cancer. Why do you think cannabis is illegal and tobacco is legal?

Activity

You are going to set up a classroom debate. The subject is:

'We believe that cannabis should be made a legal drug.'

You are going to prepare **two** short speeches – one **for** the idea of legalising cannabis and one **against**.

You can use the information on these pages and also look elsewhere for information. Try books and leaflets and on the internet.

In both of your speeches you must base your arguments on scientific evidence as well as considering the social, moral and ethical implications of any change in the law. You have to be prepared to argue your case (both for and against) and answer any questions – so do your research well!

Key points
- People can progress from using recreational drugs such as cannabis to addiction to hard drugs because cannabis is illegal and has to be obtained from a drug dealer.
- Cannabis smoke contains chemicals which may cause mental illness in some people. Teenagers are particularly vulnerable to this effect.

Answers to in-text questions

a Multiple sclerosis, Alzheimer's disease and epilepsy.

b Four times.

Summary answers

1 **a** A drug which makes it easier for an individual to begin taking 'harder' more damaging drugs through contact with people dealing with illegal drugs.

  b Because cannabis is seen as a soft drug (which is relatively harmless) and a lot of young people want to smoke it. Because it is illegal to buy cannabis, it puts them in contact with dealers who may well try to introduce them to more expensive, harder drugs which will make the dealer a bigger profit and that are more powerfully addictive.

2 Any thoughtful points on the reasons some drugs are legal and others not, social standpoints, historical usage, etc.

B1 3.6

Drugs in sport

Learning objectives

Students should learn:

- that some drugs can be used to enhance performance in sport
- that there are health risks and ethical issues associated with taking performance-enhancing drugs.

Learning outcomes

Most students should be able to:

- explain the nature of performance-enhancing drugs in different sports
- describe some of the health risks associated with taking performance-enhancing drugs
- evaluate the use of performance-enhancing drugs in sport
- consider the ethical implications of the use of drugs.

Some students should also be able to:

- explain how some performance-enhancing drugs affect an athlete's body.

Specification link-up: Biology B1.3

- There are several types of drug that an athlete can use to enhance performance. Some of these drugs are banned by law and some are legally available on prescription, but all are prohibited by sporting regulations ... [B1.3.1 i)]
- Evaluate the use of drugs to enhance performance in sport and to consider the ethical implications of their use. [B1.3]

Lesson structure

Starters

What we know already – Break the class into groups of about three. Give each group a piece of blank A3 paper and get them to write down collectively all that they know about drugs in sport. Have them share their responses with others. *(5 minutes)*

Drugs race 3000 – Imagine that you are living in the year 3000 and that the use of drugs in sport has been legal for nearly a thousand years. What sort of events would there be? What sort of records would be set? Might they have pharmaceutical manufacturer's prizes in the same way that they have constructor's prizes in Formula 1 motorsport? Write a 'back-in-time' blog based on the year 3000 Olympic Games. Students could be supported with prompts and scaffolded response sheets. Students could be extended by being encouraged to use open-ended thinking on this activity. *(10 minutes)*

Main

- Tell the students that using performance-enhancing drugs is not a new problem. The Ancient Greeks in 300 BCE had to ban some competitors because of eating certain mushrooms and animal protein.

- Prepare a PowerPoint presentation on the use of drugs in sport, to include drugs which build up muscle, ways of making the body produce more red blood cells, speeding up reactions and making competitors more alert. The presentation could include some case histories, frequency and details of testing for a range of different sports.

- The presentation could be accompanied by articles from newspapers relating to the illegal use of performance-enhancing drugs. Students could discuss the issues and express their opinions. What about the use of caffeine as a stimulant? Should everyone be tested rather than random tests?

- Produce a blank grid (see example below). Students can, from the text, from their own knowledge and from internet research fill in the grid with suitable sports, drugs and the attributes of the drug which help in the performance of the sport, along with problems.

Sport	Drug type	Why use them?	Problems
Bodybuilding	Painkillers	Compete when injured	Exacerbates injury
Archery	Beta blockers	Steady hands	Insomnia, depression
Cycling	Erythropoietin	More oxygen to legs	Kidney disease complications
Sprinting	Anabolic steroids	Muscle growth	Sexual characteristic changes

Plenaries

Getting away with it! – Is cheating okay if you don't get caught? Investigate the morality of the use of performance-enhancing drugs and try to get inside the mindset of the user. Discuss as a group. *(5 minutes)*

My threshold – Most of us would not consider using drugs as performance enhancers when we play sport. Given a large enough incentive though, most people will do most things. Ask the students to imagine they are in a competition that they can only win if they take an illegal drug. The consequences of being caught are severe (end of your career, loss of the respect of your colleagues and your possessions, adverse press coverage, prison, etc.) but it is by no means certain that you would be caught – say a 1 in 10 chance. Would you go for it, if the prize was big enough? What would your personal threshold be if you have one? What if the odds of getting caught were different? Discuss. (Differentiation will be by outcome). *(10 minutes)*

Support

- Provide students with lists of sports, drug types, effects on the body and problems so that they can match them up and fill in their blank grids.

Extend

- Ask students to find out about the drugs used for doping horses and dogs. Are they the same as those used by athletes?

Further teaching suggestions

Case studies
- Show case study videos or discuss examples of infamous drug scandals in sport, such as East Germany, Ben Johnson, Tour de France, Dwayne Chambers.

Random versus total testing
- Subtly take a few students to one side at the start of the lesson and tell them they have been taking performance enhancers. While explaining about random drug testing, get a volunteer who knows nothing of this to choose three people at random from the class and ask them if they have taken performance enhancers. Then get the ones you informed at the start to own up.

Drug tests in sport
- Find out from the internet what tests are used for the different drugs and how reliable they are. What are the permitted limits? What are the rules about testing and why is more than one sample taken?

B1 3.6 Drugs in sport

Learning objectives
- Can drugs make you better at sport?
- Is it ethical to use drugs to win?

The world of sport has a big problem with the illegal use of drugs. In theory, the only difference between competitors should be their natural ability and the amount they train. However, there are many performance-enhancing drugs that allow athletes to improve on their natural ability. The people who do this get labelled as cheats if they are caught.

Figure 1 Weightlifters need a lot of muscle so it can be tempting to cheat. Eleven Bulgarian weightlifters tested positive for anabolic steroids and were disqualified from the 2008 Olympics.

Performance-enhancing drugs

Different sports need different things from the competitors.

Anabolic steroids are drugs that help build up muscle mass. They are used by athletes who need to be very strong, such as weightlifters. Athletes who need lots of muscle to be very fast, such as sprinters, also sometimes use anabolic steroids. Taking anabolic steroids and careful training means you can make much more muscle and build it where you want it.

Strong painkilling drugs can allow an athlete to train and compete with an injury, causing further and perhaps permanent damage. These drugs are illegal for use by people involved in sport.

Different sports need great stamina – marathons and long distance cycling races are two examples. Some cyclists (and other athletes) use a drug to stimulate their body to make more red blood cells. This means they can carry more oxygen to their muscles. The drug is a compound found naturally in the body so drug-testers are looking for abnormally high levels of it.

Fast reactions are vital in many sports, and there are drugs that will make you very alert and on edge. On the other hand, in sports such as darts and shooting, you need very steady hands. Some athletes take drugs to slow down their heart and reduce any shaking in their hands to try and win medals.

a What are anabolic steroids and why do athletes use them?

Catching the cheats

Athletes found using illegal drugs are banned from competing. The sports authorities keep producing new tests for drugs and run random drugs tests to try and identify the cheats. But some competitors are always looking for new ways to cheat without being found out. So the illegal use of drugs in sport continues. Some medicines contain banned drugs which can enhance performance, so athletes need to be very careful so they don't end up 'cheating' by accident.

Figure 2 The Tour de France has had many drug problems. Cyclists have died after using illegal drugs to help them go faster. Floyd Landis, the winner in 2006, was disqualified for using steroids.

The ethics of using drugs in sport

There are lots of ways an athlete can improve their performance. Where does wanting to win end and cheating begin? Is the use of performance-enhancing substances ever acceptable in sport? These are questions scientists cannot answer – society has to decide.

For example, if an athlete lives and trains at high altitude for several weeks, their body makes a hormone which increases their red blood cell count. This is legal. But it is illegal to buy the hormone and inject it to make more red blood cells.

Here are some of the arguments that athletes use to justify the use of substances that are banned and could do them harm:
- They want to win.
- They feel that other athletes are using these substances, and unless they take them they will be left behind.
- They think the health risks are just scare stories.
- Some athletes claim that they did not know they were taking drugs – their coaches supply them hidden in 'supplements'.

There are a number of ethical points that society needs to consider. Top athletes compete for the satisfaction of winning and millions of people enjoy watching them. Most performance-enhancing drugs risk the health of the athlete at the high doses used in training. They can even cause death. Even if the individual is prepared to take the risk, is this ethically acceptable? At the moment most people say 'no'.

Often the substances used by cheats are so expensive, or new, that most competitors can't afford them. This gives the richest competitors an unfair advantage. For example, most athletes could afford anabolic steroids if they wanted to use them, but not the most recent versions that are not detected by the drug-testing process.

There are some people who think that athletes should be able to do what they like with their bodies. At the moment most of society does not agree with this view – what do you think?

b Why do athletes use drugs which could cause them harm?

Figure 3 Athletes can be asked to produce a urine sample for a drug test at any time, whether they are competing, training or resting

AQA Examiner's tip
Make sure you understand why athletes are banned from using some medical drugs.

Summary questions
1. Copy and complete using the words below:
   compete performance-enhancing muscles steroids athletes
   Some .... use .... drugs to help them .... more successfully. Many use anabolic .... which help them to develop bigger ....
2. Suggest the advantages and disadvantages to an athlete of using banned performance-enhancing drugs to help win a competition.
3. It has been suggested that athletes be allowed to use any drugs to improve their performance. Suggest arguments for and against this proposal.

Key points
- Anabolic steroids and other banned performance-enhancing drugs are used by some athletes.
- The use of performance-enhancing drugs is considered unethical by most people.

Answers to in-text questions

a Anabolic steroids are drugs which help athletes to build extra muscle mass – athletes use them to get extra strength and extra muscles for running, bodybuilding, etc.

b They are so keen to win at all costs that they feel the benefits outweigh the risks and they assume that the drugs will not affect them negatively etc.

Summary answers

1. athletes, performance-enhancing, compete, steroids, muscles

2. **Advantages**: the athlete will compete better (run faster and have more stamina), be able to lift heavier weights, etc., and build muscles more easily. They mean the athlete will have to do less work to perform well, which is likely to bring the financial benefits of success, e.g. sponsorship.

   Disadvantages: the health risks, the risk of being found out and disqualified, the possible loss of personal satisfaction in achievement.

3. **For**: For example, it removes the need to spend large amounts of time and money trying to catch people cheating; it puts all athletes on a level playing field because they can all use performance-enhancing drugs if they want to.

   Against: For example, the health risks to athletes, it means wealthy individual athletes or wealthy countries would be able to afford the latest developments and others wouldn't, questionable value of artificially-enhanced performance.

Summary answers

1 a To make sure that they are effective at treating the disease, that they are safe, that they are taken into the body effectively and can be removed from the body.

b Thousands of chemicals go through lab trials to result in a very small number which are put through animal testing and even fewer through human trials. All the stages are very expensive and the process can take up to 12 years.

c Any thoughtful point here – probably most likely response is yes, if a drug seems to be so good during trials that it would be unethical not to treat with it. This has happened on occasion – and there are also occasions when there is such a clear need for a drug in trial to be used on an individual patient as the only chance of avoiding death, that permission is granted there as well. However, equally valid to answer no because it is unethical to use drugs that have not been fully tested and to try and avoid problems such as thalidomide again.

2 a A drug which lowers cholesterol levels in the body.

b High cholesterol levels in the blood lead to an increased risk of cardiovascular disease. (Lowering the levels of cholesterol reduces risk of build up of fatty material in the arteries and so reduces the risk of CVD.)

c Statin 1.

d Some drugs might suit a patient better than others. The cost of the drug.

3 a The second group were asked to drink coffee without caffeine.

b Examples of control variables that could have been used include:
- drink the same amount of coffee
- wait for the same amount of time
- ensure that the students rest in the same conditions between drinking and pulse measurement.

c They could be expecting their pulse to rise and as a result it might have done.

d The students drinking decaffeinated coffee should not have an increase in pulse rate so there could be systematic error.

e The differences in the individual results are due to uncontrolled variables but the increase of 21 bpm in the 'with caffeine' group could be random error.

f The range for the increase in pulse rates without caffeine is 2 bpm to 7 bpm.

g i 14 beats per minute.
ii 5 beats per minute.

4 a Both data sets suggest males use drugs more than females.

b **Individuals**
Illegal drugs can be very addictive, damaging to health because of effect of drugs and effect of lifestyle, often illegal activities to get money, injecting drugs, etc., open to HIV and hepatitis, relatively small numbers of people affected.

Smoking and drinking – can have short-term impact but both generally longer-term health damage but on a massive scale in terms of heart disease, cancers, cirrhosis etc. Far bigger populations involved.

Society
Illegal – cost in terms of crime on population, financial cost of policing, hospital treatment, prisons, drug rehab, etc.
Legal drugs cost in terms of hospital treatment for thousands, lost working days, etc.

Summary questions 🔑

1 a Why do new medicines need to be tested and trialled before doctors can use them to treat their patients?

b Why is the development of a new medicine so expensive?

c Do you think it would ever be acceptable to use a new medicine before all the trials had been completed?

2 a What is a statin?

b How do statins help reduce the number of people who suffer from cardiovascular disease?

c Which of the statins in Figure 1, B1 3.2 is most effective?

d The most effective drug is not always the one used. Why do you think other statins might be prescribed?

3 Some students decided to test whether drinking coffee could affect heart rate. They asked the class to help them with their investigation. They divided the class into two groups. Both groups had their pulses taken. They gave one group a drink of coffee. They waited for 10 minutes and then took their pulses again. They then followed the same procedure with the second group.

a What do you think the second group were asked to drink?

b State a control variable that should have been used.

c Explain why it would have been a good idea not to tell the two groups exactly what they were drinking.

d Study this table of results that they produced.

Group	Increase in pulse rate (beats per minute)
With caffeine	12, 15, 13, 10, 15, 16, 10, 15, 16, 21, 14, 13, 16
Without caffeine	4, 3, 4, 5, 7, 5, 7, 4, 2, 6, 5, 4, 7

Can you detect any evidence for systematic error in these results? If so, describe this evidence.

e Is there any evidence for a random error in these results? If so, describe this evidence.

f What is the range for the increase in pulse rates without caffeine?

g What is the mean (or average) increase in pulse rate:
i with caffeine?
ii without caffeine?

4 Look at Figure 3, B1 3.4. Compare the data in that to Figure 2, B1 3.3. Both show impact of drug taki individuals in society.

a What are the similarities between the two data s

b Explain the relative impact of legal and illegal d individuals and on society.

5 a Why do some athletes use illegal drugs, such as anabolic steroids, when they are training or competing?

b What are the arguments for and against the use these performance-enhancing drugs?

c People sometimes use illegal performance-enh drugs on horses. They use pain killers, stimular and substances which make the skin on their le very sensitive. Sometimes they are given sedat they run slowly. Discuss the ethical aspects of performance-changing drugs to animals.

5 a To give them a competitive edge, to increase their physical development, to either reduce work needed or develop more than normal.

b **For**: build muscle, increased performance, make athletes capable of withstanding tougher training, etc.
Against: health risks, inequality of access, success/ records meaningless as result of drugs, not just ability.

c Any thoughtful points: the biggest ethical issue is consent – athletes usually choose to take substances which may harm them or allow them to compete with injuries which may be permanently damaging – animals cannot agree to that. Also, animals do not choose to compete and do not care if they win, so being put at risk through drug use for human satisfaction is not acceptable. It is also unfair to the public who have placed bets. However, many competitive animals appear to enjoy what they do – students could argue that they 'want' to compete. A possible good thing to reduce pain and teach them to pick up feet so they jump more safely, etc.

Examination-style questions k

...ple take drugs for many different reasons.

*...hol heroin penicillin statin steroid
...domide*

...se a word from above to match the following
...ences.

...n illegal drug which is highly addictive (1)

...drug used by athletes to make them perform better (1)

...medical drug which is used to reduce cholesterol
...vels (1)

...ug company wants to test a new painkiller called
...Go2. The company hope that the new drug will cure
...aches quicker than PainGo1.

...Go2 has to be tested in clinical trials. PainGo2 is
...e as strong as PainGo1.

...se 1 trial – a few healthy people will be given one or
...tablets of PainGo2.

...se 2 trial – a small group (200–300) of patients with
...aches will be given PainGo2.

...se 3 trial – 3 large groups (2000 in each group) of
...ents with headaches will be given either PainGo2 or
...Go1 or a placebo.

...hat is the purpose of the Phase 1 trial? (1)

...uggest why in Phase 2 the patients were asked to
...cord how they felt after taking the PainGo2.

...uggest why. (1)

...hat is a placebo? (1)

...hase 3 was done as a double-blind trial by doctors
...ho had patients with headaches.

...a double-blind trial who will know who is given the
...ew drug?

...hoose your answer from the choices below.

the patient only

the doctor only

both the doctor and the patient

neither the doctor nor the patient (1)

...hy is it important to use the placebo in the Phase 3
...al? (1)

...hy are some patients given PainGo1 in Phase 3? (1)

...ive **one** example of:

...a legal recreational drug (1)

...an illegal recreational drug. (1)

b Some recreational drugs are addictive.

  i Give **one** example of a recreational drug that is
very addictive. (1)

  ii Explain how the action of a drug makes a person
become addicted to it. (1)

c Some doctors think that smoking cannabis causes
depression. Doctors investigated the cannabis
smoking habits of 1500 young adults.

The table shows the percentage of cannabis smokers
in the investigation who became depressed.

How many times the men or women had smoked cannabis in the last 12 months	Percentage of men who became depressed	Percentage of women who became depressed
Less than 5 times	9	16
More than 5 times, but less than once per week	10	17
1–4 times per week	12	31
Every day	15	68

From the data, give **two** conclusions that can be
drawn about the relationship between cannabis and
depression. (2)

AQA, 2007

4 *In this question you will be assessed on using good
English, organising information clearly and using
specialist terms where appropriate.*

Read the description of an investigation into the link
between smoking cannabis and heroin addiction.

> Six 'teenage' rats were given a small dose of THC – the active
> chemical in cannabis – every three days between the ages of 28
> and 49 days. This is the equivalent of human ages 12 to 18.
>
> The amount of THC given was roughly equivalent to a human
> smoking one cannabis 'joint' every three days.
>
> A control group of six 'teenage' rats did not receive THC.
>
> After 56 days catheters (narrow tubes) were inserted in
> all twelve of the now adult rats and they were able to self-
> administer heroin by pushing a lever.
>
> All the rats began to self-administer heroin frequently. After a
> while, they stabilised their daily intake at a certain level.
>
> The ones that had been on THC as 'teenagers' stabilised their
> heroin intake at a much higher level than the others. They
> appeared to be less sensitive to the effects of heroin. This
> pattern continued throughout their lives.
>
> Reduced sensitivity to the heroin means that the rats take larger
> doses. This has been shown to increase the risk of addiction.

Evaluate this investigation with respect to establishing
a link between cannabis smoking and heroin addiction
in humans. Remember to include a conclusion to your
evaluation. (6)

AQA, 2007

75

AQA Examination-style answers

1 **a** heroin (1 mark)

  b steroid(s) (1 mark)

  c statin(s) (1 mark)

2 **a** To check for unexpected side effects with the higher dose/
stronger pain killer. (1 mark)

  b To see if the drug cured the headaches. (1 mark)

  c A tablet which does not contain a drug/contains a
harmless chemical/a 'blank'. (1 mark)

  d D Neither the doctor nor the patient. (1 mark)

  e To rule out psychological effects/description of this.
(1 mark)

  f To see if the PainGo2/the new drug is better
(at curing headaches) than PainGo1. (1 mark)

3 **a** **i** tobacco/nicotine/alcohol (*accept:* solvent/glue/
caffeine, *ignore:* cigarettes/coffee) (1 mark)

    ii cannabis/heroin/cocaine (*allow:* crack/weed/ecstasy/
LSD/amphetamine/speed/steroids/GHB). (1 mark)

  b **i** heroin/cocaine/tobacco/nicotine (*ignore:* alcohol/
cigarettes/cannabis/caffeine/coffee) (1 mark)

    ii alters body chemistry which causes the body to
become addicted to it (*ignore:* withdrawal symptoms/
craving/non-chemical effects on nervous system)
(1 mark)

  c Any **two** from:

- increase in cannabis smoking increases (%) depression
- greater effect in women/allow women become more
depressed
- depression linked with/not directly caused by
cannabis/ignore cannabis causes depression
- not all cannabis smokers get depression (2 marks)

4 There is a clear, balanced and detailed argument referring
to both pros and cons and a conclusion which matches the
pos and cons. The answer shows almost faultless spelling,
punctuation and grammar. It is coherent and in an organised,
logical sequence. It contains a range of appropriate or
relevant specialist terms used accurately. (5–6 marks)

The answer contains at least one pro and one con with a
conclusion. There are some errors in spelling, punctuation
and grammar. The answer has some structure and
organisation. The use of specialist terms has been attempted,
but not always accurately. (3–4 marks)

There is mention of either a pro or a con with an attempt at
a conclusion or a list of pros and cons without a conclusion,
has little clarity and detail. The spelling, punctuation and
grammar are very weak. The answer is poorly organised with
almost no specialist terms and/or their use demonstrating a
general lack of understanding of their meaning. (1–2 marks)

No relevant content. (0 marks)

Examples of biology points made in the response:
Pros, e.g.

- used 'teenage rats' as equivalent to human teenagers
- THC dose typical of human cannabis smoking habits
- used control group
- rats allowed to choose amount of heroin

Cons, e.g.

- sample size small/only used 12 rat
- heroin administration very different from human situation

Conclusions

- rats given THC/cannabis took more heroin
- (this) is evidence for a link between THC/cannabis and
heroin
- (but) rat behaviour/physiology not necessarily same as
human behaviour/physiology
- does not prove link in human/results not reliable for
humans.

Kerboodle resources k

Resources available for this chapter on Kerboodle are:

- Chapter map: Medicine and drugs
- How Science Works: Can we believe the claims? (B1 3.2)
- Support: What's the harm in that? (B1 3.3)
- Interactive activity: Drugs
- Revision podcast: Medicine and drugs
- Test yourself: Medicine and drugs
- On your marks: Medicine and drugs
- Examination-style questions: Medicine and drugs
- Answers to examination-style questions: Medicine and drugs

AQA Examiner's tip

When candidates are asked to evaluate information, they
should always give pros, cons and a conclusion. If they use
headings such as pros/advantages, cons/disadvantages,
conclusion, they will gain most of the marks. In a six-mark
answer, they should give at least two pros and two cons. The
conclusion should be backed up by their previous selections.

This type of question could also be used to assess the Quality
of Written Communication.

For full marks all the criteria are met, for the next band they may
miss a pro or a con or the conclusion, the lowest band might
include answers where only one side of the argument has been
given and the logic may be unclear.

This is a High Demand example but evaluation and QWC can
be tested at any level.

B1 4.1

Adapt and survive

Learning objectives

Students should learn:

- that organisms need a supply of materials from their surroundings and from other living organisms in order to survive and reproduce
- that organisms are adapted to the conditions in which they live
- how microorganisms have a wide range of adaptations enabling them to live in a wide range of conditions.

Learning outcomes

Most students should be able to:

- describe the materials that living organisms need in order to survive and reproduce
- explain that plants and animals are adapted to survive in their particular habitat
- explain that the adaptations of microorganisms enable them to survive in a wide range of conditions.

Some students should also be able to:

- explain how some microorganisms are able to survive in extreme conditions.

Specification link-up: Biology B1.4

- To survive and reproduce, organisms require a supply of materials from their surroundings and from the other living organisms there. *[B1.4.1 a)]*
- Organisms, including microorganisms have features (adaptations) that enable them to survive in the conditions in which they normally live. *[B1.4.1 d)]*
- Some organisms live in environments that are very extreme. Extremophiles may be tolerant to high levels of salt, high temperatures or high pressures. *[B1.4.1 e)]*
- Animals and plants may be adapted to cope with specific features of their environment, e.g. thorns, poisons and warning colours to deter predators. *[B1.4.1 g)]*

Lesson structures

Starters

Spaceship supplies – Suppose you were to take yourself, some animals, some plants and some microorganisms to start a colony on another planet. In order to keep them alive during the journey, what would you need to provide for the plants, the animals, and the microorganisms? Write down your own ideas, then share them with others. *(5 minutes)*

Can you tell where I live from what I look like? – Bring in some live or stuffed animals or alternatively project some good pictures on to a smart board. Then discuss their adaptations, drawing some conclusions about the conditions in the habitats in which they might be found. The points to get across are that the adaptations are physical features that you can touch or see, but that there are also behavioural adaptations, such as lizards basking in the sun, that are important. Students can be supported by giving them a list of adaptations to choose from. Students can be extended by asking them to explain how these adaptations may have arisen. *(10 minutes)*

Main

- Ask the students the question: 'What makes an animal an animal and a plant a plant?' Draw out the differences in nutrition. You may well have to point out that some animals don't move much, e.g. sea anemones and that plants do move, although generally slowly. Speeded up camera footage of plants moving would be useful here and you could remind students of the growth movements involved in phototropism.

- Use a PowerPoint slide show or short explanation to review the needs of animals and plants. Get the students to summarise their responses in a table.

- Draw out what microorganisms are. Explain the very large number of different types and the vast variety of environments that they survive in. Remind students about pathogens as well as useful microorganisms. One way could be to have a circus of cards around the room each with a microorganism type, its picture and nutritional details.

- Show some animals and plants with extreme adaptations. Examples could include animals and plants that live in situations such as very low temperatures, very high salt concentrations, etc. Discuss the adaptations shown.

Support

- Give the students a prepared table of adaptations and animals – they are to match one to another.
- Have a series of cards with the requirements for life, such as food, water, oxygen etc. and get the students to sort out what plants, animals and microorganisms need.

Extend

- Give students the term 'psychrophile' and ask them to find out what it means and give examples. The Natural History Museum website is a good starting point.
- Microbes on Mars? Students could investigate the possibility that some microbes could survive in the harsh weather conditions found on Mars. Try the Astrobiology magazine website.

Plenaries

Life on another planet – Discuss with students how, once your spaceship had landed on another planet, the animals, plants and microorganisms might have to adapt to live there. Would it be possible? Might you decide to take some extremophiles with you? *(5 minutes)*

What's in a name? – Following a discussion or presentation on animals, plants and microorganisms living in extreme conditions, get students to give you their ideas on the meaning of the following terms: thermophile, xerophile, osmophile, halophile, acidophile. You can support students by providing a list from which they can choose and by showing pictures of examples that might give them clues. Students can be extended by adding extra terms: alkalophile, thermoacidophile, etc. These students can be asked to give the meaning of the term, suggest a habitat and an example for each one. It could be helpful to tell students that the suffix '-phile' comes from the Greek word for 'love'. *(10 minutes)*

Further teaching suggestions

Extreme resources

● An internet search for animals and plants which survive in extreme conditions can produce some good results. There are a number of very good educational videos available on the topic of adaptations. If the library has a good selection of books with animal photos, the students could look through these and select suitable ones to talk about to their peers.

Adaptation for survival

B1 4.1   Adapt and survive

Learning objectives
● What do organisms need to live?
● How do organisms survive in many different conditions?

The variety of conditions on the surface of the Earth is huge. It ranges from hot, dry deserts to permanent ice and snow. There are deep, saltwater oceans and tiny freshwater pools. Whatever the conditions, almost everywhere on Earth you will find living organisms able to survive and reproduce.

Survive and reproduce

Living organisms need a supply of materials from their surroundings and from other living organisms so they can survive and reproduce successfully. What they need depends on the type of organism.

● Plants need light, carbon dioxide, water, oxygen and nutrients to produce glucose energy in order to survive.
● Animals need food from other living organisms, water and oxygen.
● Microorganisms need a range of things. Some are like plants, some are like animals and some don't need oxygen or light to survive.

Living organisms have special features known as **adaptations**. These features make it possible for them to survive in their particular habitat, even when the conditions are very extreme.

Plant adaptations

Plants need to photosynthesise to produce the glucose needed for energy and growth. They also need to have enough water to maintain their cells and tissues. They have adaptations that enable them to live in many different places. For example, most plants get water and nutrients from the soil through their roots. Epiphytes are found in rainforests. They have adaptations which allow them to live high above the ground attached to other plants. They collect water and nutrients from the air and in their specially adapted leaves.

Figure 1 Mangroves are trees that live in soil with very little oxygen, often with their roots covered by salty water. They have special adaptations to get rid of the salt through their leaves, and roots which grow in the air to get oxygen.

Some plant adaptations are all about reproduction. *Rafflesia arnoldii* produces flowers which are 1 m across, weigh about 11 kg and smell of a rotting corpse. The plants are rare so the dramatic and very smelly flower increases the chances of flies visiting and carrying pollen from one plant to another.

a Why do plants need to photosynthesise?

Animal adaptations

Animals cannot make their own food. They have to eat plants or other animals. Many of the adaptations of animals help them to get the food they need. So you can tell what a mammal eats by looking at its teeth. **Herbivores** have teeth for grinding up plant cells. **Carnivores** have teeth adapted for tearing flesh or crushing bones. Animals also often have adaptations to help them find and attract a mate.

links
For more information on plant adaptation, see B1 4.3 Adaptation in plants.

AQA Examiner's tip
Practise recognising plant and animal adaptations and try to work out where they might live from the adaptation. This will help in your examination where you may be asked to do the same.

links
For more information on animal adaptation, see B1 4.2 Adaptation in animals.

Adapting to the environment

Some of the adaptations seen in animals and plants help them to survive in a particular environment. Some sea birds get rid of all the extra salt they take in from the sea water by 'crying' very salty tears from a special salt gland. Animals that need to survive extreme winter temperatures often produce a chemical in their cells which acts as antifreeze. It stops the water in the cells from freezing and destroying the cell. Plants such as water lilies have lots of big air spaces in their leaves. This adaptation enables them to float on top of their watery environment and make food by photosynthesis.

Organisms that survive and reproduce in the most difficult conditions are known as **extremophiles**.

Living in extreme environments

Microorganisms are found in more places in the world than any other living thing. These places range from ice packs to hot springs and geysers. Microorganisms have a range of adaptations which make this possible. Many extremophiles are microorganisms.

Some extremophiles live at very high temperatures. Bacteria known as thermophiles can survive at temperatures of over 45 °C and often up to 80 °C or higher. In most organisms the enzymes stop working at around 40 °C. These extremophiles have specially adapted enzymes that do not denature and so work at these high temperatures. In fact, many of these organisms cannot survive and reproduce at lower temperatures.

Other bacteria have adaptations so they can grow and reproduce at very low temperatures, down to –15 °C. They are found in ice packs and glaciers around the world.

Most living organisms struggle to survive in a very salty environment because of the problems it causes with water balance. However, there are species of extremophile bacteria that can only live in extremely salty environments such as the Dead Sea and salt flats. They have adaptations to their cytoplasm so that water does not move out of their cells into their salty environment. But in ordinary sea water, they would swell up and burst!

b What is a thermophile?

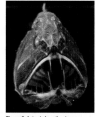

Figure 2 Animals from the deep oceans are adapted to cope with enormous pressure, no light and very cold, salty water. If these extremophiles are brought to the surface too quickly, they explode because of the rapid change in pressure.

Figure 3 Black smoker bacteria live in deep ocean vents, 2500 m down, at temperatures of well over 100 °C, with enormous pressure, no light and an acid pH of about 2.8. They have adaptations to cope with some of the most extreme conditions on Earth.

Summary questions

1 Copy and complete using the words below:
adaptations organisms materials survive extreme
To .... and reproduce, organisms need a supply of .... from their surroundings and the living .... in their habitat. They have .... that enable them to survive in their particular habitat, even when the conditions are very ....

2 Make a list of what plants and animals need from their surroundings to survive and reproduce.

3 a What is an extremophile?
   b Give two examples of adaptations found in different extremophiles.

Key points
● Organisms need a supply of materials from their surroundings and from other living organisms to survive and reproduce.
● Organisms have features (adaptations) that enable them to survive in the conditions in which they normally live.
● Extremophiles have adaptations enabling them to live in extreme conditions of salt, temperature or pressure.

Answers to in-text questions

a Plants need to photosynthesise to produce the glucose needed for energy and growth.

b A bacterium which can survive at temperatures of over 45 °C.

Summary answers

1 survive, materials, organisms, adaptations, extreme

2 **Plants:** carbon dioxide, water, light, minerals, oxygen
Animals: food from other living organisms, oxygen, water.

3 **a** An organism which can live in extremely difficult conditions where most other organisms cannot survive.

   b Enzymes which function in very high temperatures, enzymes which function at very low temperatures, ability to get rid of excesses of salt, ability to respire without oxygen, any other valid point.

B1 4.2

Adaptation in animals

Learning objectives

Students should learn:

- that animals are adapted for survival in their particular habitat
- that there is a relationship between body size and surface area : volume ratio
- that hair and body fat can provide insulation.

Learning outcomes

Most students should be able to:

- define the term 'adaptation'
- describe how animals are adapted to survive in cold climates
- describe how animals are adapted to life in a dry climate.

Some students should also be able to:

- explain in detail how organisms are adapted to the conditions in which they live, when provided with appropriate information.

Answers to in-text questions

a It keeps the surface area : volume ratio as small as possible and so helps them to reduce heat loss.

b Arctic animals have small ears, thick fur, and a layer of fat/blubber.

c Because sweating results in loss of water from the body. There is not much water in the desert, so they cannot rely on finding more to drink.

Support

- Have a floor dominoes session where students match animals and their adaptations. Include animals of all types and from different habitats. Played with cards in the form of dominoes, but make the cards large so that the game can be played on the floor.

Extend

- Ask students to design an experiment to investigate whether people who regularly swim in the sea have a different surface area to volume ratio than those who only swim in heated pools.

AQA Specification link-up: Biology B1.4

- Animals and plants may be adapted for survival in …. *[B1.4.1 f)]*

  Controlled Assessment: SA4.1 Planning an investigation *[SA4.1.1 a) b) c) d)]*, *[SA4.1.2 a) b) c)]*; SA4.3 Collect primary and secondary data *[SA4.3.3 a) b)]*; SA4.4 Select and process primary and secondary data *[SA4.4.2 b)]* and SA4.5 Analyse and interpret primary and secondary data. *[SA4.5.3 a)]*, *[SA4.5.4 a)]*

Lesson structure

Starters

Temperature regulation! – Get a student to dress up in a fur hat, scarf, thick coat and gloves (or dress up yourself). Contrast with pictures of Newcastle United football supporters taking their shirts off in the snow at matches. Discuss effects on temperature regulation. *(5 minutes)*

Life in the freezer – Search the internet for a video of Arctic animals (see the Discovery Channel at www.yourdiscovery.com) or project a series of images of arctic animals and get students to say what features the animals have which are adaptations to their environment. Students could be supported by being given a list of adaptations and matching the adaptation to the animal. Students could be extended by asking them to consider behavioural adaptations as well as physical ones. *(10 minutes)*

Main

- Surface area: volume ratio demonstrations with chocolate and building blocks. Show students a small chocolate bar. Ask if they think you could get it all in your mouth in one piece, without breaking it or biting it. Ask them to imagine if you did that, where would the saliva be able to touch? Draw out that is would be just the outside surface. Cut the bar into smaller and smaller bits, getting the students to see that the smaller the bits, the larger the surface area to volume ratio is. Make sure students do not eat in the laboratory.

- A further practical session could be used to introduce the concept of surface area : volume ratios having an effect on heat loss (see 'Practical support' for full details). 'How Science Works' concepts can also be introduced here.

- Set up a demonstration to show that the thickness of an insulating coat will affect the temperature loss (see 'Practical support'). This investigation is also useful for teaching and assessing investigative aspects of 'How Science Works', as it involves taking measurements, plotting graphs and drawing conclusions.

- Discuss the similarities between the adaptations in desert animals.

Plenaries

Mix and match adaptations and functions – Put a list of adaptations on the board alongside a list of functions. Ask students to come and link an adaptation to a function. *(5 minutes)*

Modify or die – Imagine that the climate has changed in the UK and is now very cold and icy for most of the year. Describe and/or draw how some of our familiar animals would eventually have to evolve or die. Do the same supposing that the UK became very hot and dry. Differentiation by outcome: some students will need to be supported by prompting and produce limited suggestions, whilst students can be extended by being encouraged to produce more detailed ones. *(10 minutes)*

??? Did you know …?

Polar bear hair is not white but colourless. It is hollow and transparent to allow the light to fall on to its skin, which is black to absorb the energy. It has been said that polar bears hide their noses with their paws when they are hunting to prevent their prey from spotting them.

Practical support

Surface area: volume ratios and energy loss
Equipment and materials required
Cups, saucers, digital thermometers, hot water (about 60 °C); a 1 litre beaker and ten 100 ml beakers; small conical flasks of different sizes.

Details
There are several ways of doing this. The simplest way is to give students cups and saucers and digital thermometers. Pour the same volume of hot (about 60 °C) water into each cup and measure the temperature drop. Alternatively, pour 1 litre of hot water into a litre beaker and divide another litre of water equally between ten 100 ml beakers. Monitor the temperature. Data loggers can be used here. It is also possible to use different sizes of flasks, allowing students to carry out their own temperature readings and plot their own graphs.

Predictions can be made, readings carried out and repeated, and conclusions drawn.

Safety: Care is needed with the handling of hot water.

The effect of insulation on energy loss
Equipment and materials required
For each group; two similar-sized flasks, thermometers, hot water, insulation.

Details
Two conical flasks of the same volume can be filled with hot water. One flask is left uncovered and the other surrounded by an insulating layer of cotton wool, or other material. The temperature drop can be recorded as before. This experiment could be done as a demonstration or by groups of students. It could be done at the same time as the previous experiment.

Safety: Care is needed with the handling of hot water.

Adaptation for survival

B1 4.2 — Adaptation in animals

Adaptation in animals

Learning objectives
- How can hair help animals survive in very cold climates?
- What are the advantages – and disadvantages – of lots of body fat?
- How do animals adapt to hot, dry climates?

AQA Examiner's tip

Remember, the *larger* the animal, the *smaller* the surface area : volume (SA : V) ratio.

Animals often have *increased* surface areas in *hot* climates, and *decreased* surface areas in *cold* climates.

Animals have adaptations that help them to get the food and mates they need to survive and reproduce. They also have adaptations for survival in the conditions where they normally live.

Animals in cold climates
To survive in a cold environment you must be able to keep yourself warm. Animals which live in very cold places, such as the Arctic, are adapted to reduce the energy they lose from their bodies. You lose body heat through your body surface (mainly your skin). The amount of energy you lose is closely linked to your surface area : volume (SA : V) ratio.

Maths skills
Surface area : volume ratio
The surface area : volume ratio is very important when you look at the adaptations of animals that live in cold climates. It explains why so many Arctic mammals, such as seals, walruses, whales and polar bears, are relatively large.

The ratio of surface area to volume falls as objects get bigger. You can see this clearly in the diagram. The larger the surface area : volume ratio, the larger the rate of energy loss. So mammals in a cold climate grow to a large size. This keeps their surface area : volume ratio as small as possible and so helps them hold on to their body heat.

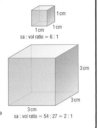

1 cm
1 cm
1 cm
sa : vol ratio = 6 : 1

3 cm
3 cm
3 cm
3 cm
sa : vol ratio = 54 : 27 = 2 : 1

a Why are so many Arctic animals large?

Animals in very cold climates often have other adaptations too. The surface area of the thinly skinned areas of their bodies, like their ears, is usually very small. This reduces their energy loss.

Many Arctic mammals have plenty of insulation, both inside and out. Inside they have blubber (a thick layer of fat that builds up under the skin). On the outside a thick fur coat will insulate an animal very effectively. These adaptations really reduce the amount of energy lost through their skin.

The fat layer also provides a food supply. Animals often build up their fat in the summer. Then they can live off their body fat through the winter when there is almost no food.

b List three ways in which Arctic animals keep warm in winter.

Figure 1 The Arctic is a cold and bleak environment. However, the animals that live there are well adapted for survival. Notice the large size, small ears, thick coat and white camouflage of this polar bear.

Camouflage
Camouflage is important both to predators (so their prey doesn't see them coming) and to prey (so they can't be seen). The colours that would camouflage an Arctic animal in summer against plants would stand out against the snow in winter. Many Arctic animals, including the Arctic fox, the Arctic hare and the stoat, have grey or brown summer coats that change to pure white in the winter. Polar bears don't change colour. They have no natural predators on the land. They hunt seals all year round in the sea, where their white colour makes them less visible among the ice.

The colour of the coat of a lioness is another example of effective camouflage. The sandy brown colour matches perfectly with the dried grasses of the African savannah. Her colour hides the lioness from the grazing animals which are her prey.

Surviving in dry climates
Dry climates are often also hot climates – like deserts. Deserts are very difficult places for animals to live. There is scorching heat during the day, followed by bitter cold at night. Water is also in short supply.

The biggest challenges if you live in a desert are:
- coping with the lack of water
- stopping body temperature from getting too high.

Many desert animals are adapted to need little or nothing to drink. They get the water they need from the food they eat.

Mammals keep their body temperature the same all the time. So as the environment gets hotter, they have to find ways of keeping cool. Sweating means they lose water, which is not easy to replace in the desert.

c Why do mammals try to cool down without sweating in hot, dry conditions?

Animals that live in hot conditions adapt their behaviour to keep cool. They are often most active in the early morning and late evening, when it is not so hot. During the cold nights and the heat of the day they rest in burrows where the temperature doesn't change much.

Many desert animals are quite small, so their surface area is large compared to their volume. This helps them to lose heat through their skin. They often have large, thin ears to increase their surface area for losing energy.

Another adaptation of many desert animals is to have thin fur. Any fur they do have is fine and silky. They also have relatively little body fat stored under the skin. These features make it easier for them to lose energy through the surface of the skin.

Figure 2 Jerboas are very small and elephants are very big. They both show clear adaptations that help them survive in the hot, dry places where they live.

Summary questions
1 **a** List the main problems that face animals living in cold conditions like the Arctic.
   b List the main problems that face animals living in the desert.
2 Animals that live in the Arctic are adapted to keep warm through the winter. Describe three of these adaptations and explain how they work.
3 **a** Using Figure 2, describe the visible adaptations of a jerboa and an elephant to keeping cool in hot conditions.
   b Suggest other ways in which animals might be adapted to survive in hot, dry conditions.

Key points
- All living things have adaptations that help them to survive in the conditions where they live.
- Animals that are adapted for cold environments are often large, with a small surface area : volume (SA : V) ratio. They have thick insulating layers of fat and fur.
- Changing coat colour in the different seasons gives animals year-round camouflage.
- Adaptations for hot, dry environments include a large SA : V ratio, thin fur, little body fat and behaviour patterns that avoid the heat of the day.

78

79

Further teaching suggestions

Sweating demonstration
- Demonstrate the cooling effect of sweating by wiping the backs of the hands of volunteer students with cotton wool soaked in ethanol and asking them how it feels. To show that it is the evaporation of alcohol that is doing the cooling, students could be given a test tube of ethanol in a rack with a digital thermometer in it. The temperature can be read and recorded. The thermometer should then be repeatedly dipped into the ethanol and waved in the air (gently and carefully) and the lowest temperature reached recorded. Ensure that there are no naked flames.

Comparing SA:V ratios
- Provide students with some data about the sizes of different animals and get them to work out the SA:V ratios. For example, comparing a mouse and an elephant. You can simplify the data by supplying them with the dimensions of a box into which the animal would fit.

Summary answers

1 **a** It is very cold, so there is a problem in keeping warm and finding enough food.
   b It is very hot, so the main problems are keeping the body cool and finding enough water.

2 Small ears (reduce SA (surface area) of thin skinned tissue to reduce heat loss), thick fur (insulating layer to help prevent heat loss), layer of fat/blubber (insulating layer), any other relevant adaptations, e.g. furry feet to insulate against contact with ice, large size reduces surface area:volume ratio so reduces heat loss, etc.

3 **a** E.g. **Jerboa** – big thin ears to increase SA (surface area) to lose heat, bare legs and tail to make it easier to lose heat, thin fine hair to increase heat loss. **Elephant** – big thin ears and large amount of wrinkled skin to increase SA and heat loss, little body hair to reduce insulation.
   b Animals living in hot dry conditions keep cool without sweating by avoiding the heat of the day and by having large ears, baggy skin, little fur, thin and silky fur and a large SA:V ratio to increase heat loss.

B1 4.3

Adaptation in plants

Learning objectives

Students should learn:

- how some plants are adapted to live in dry conditions
- that changes in the surface area of plants affect the rate at which water is lost
- how plants living in dry conditions may store water in their tissues.

Learning outcomes

Most students should be able to:

- describe the adaptations shown by plants that live in dry environments
- explain how these adaptations reduce the quantity of water lost by the plant.

Some students should also be able to:

- explain in detail the importance of water-storage tissues in desert plants.

Answers to in-text questions

a For photosynthesis and to keep the plant upright.

b By evaporation through the stomata.

c To prevent excessive water loss, e.g. in the desert. Water is lost through the surface of the leaf, so if the surface area is smaller, there will be less water lost.

d Leaves, stem and/or roots.

Support

- Ask students to measure the leaf areas of two contrasting plants by wax rubbing over large squared graph paper. Ask them to predict from this which plant will need more water.

Extend

- Ask students to try to work out a method for estimating the total leaf surface area on a tree.
- Ask students to consider how plants, such as cacti, are able to make enough food by photosynthesis if their leaves are reduced to spines?
- Look at flat-bladed cacti such as prickly pear (*Platyopuntia*). Shine a light on it and move the light around to model the apparent movement of the Sun during the day. Which orientation would be best for the cactus? Would the orientation change in different hemispheres?

AQA Specification link-up: Biology B1.4

- Animals and plants may be adapted for survival in …. *[B1.4.1 f)]*

  Controlled Assessment: SA4.1 Planning an investigation *[SA4.1.1 a) b) c)]*, *[SA4.1.2 a)]*; SA4.3 Collect primary and secondary data *[SA4.3.3 a) b)]*; SA4.4 Select and process primary and secondary data. *[SA4.4.1 a) b)]*, *[SA4.4.2 a) b)]*

Lesson structure

Starters

Saving water and storing water – Show the students a cactus plant and a potted geranium or similar plant. Ask the students which one could survive the longest in drought conditions and why? Draw out reduction in leaf surface area, possibility of storing water etc. Cut a slice of the cactus and show the water-storing tissue or project a slide of a section of the tissue. *(5 minutes)*

Losing water – Choose two identical soft-leaved plants (tomato plants or whatever is available) and two similar cactus plants. Leave one of each to dry out, so that the soft-leaved plant is wilted, but water the other two thoroughly. Present these to the students explaining how they have been treated. Students can be supported by asking what the differences are and getting them to describe what they see. Students can be extended by asking: 'Why are the differences not as great between the two cactus plants as they are between the two soft-leaved plants?' These students could be encouraged to speculate constructively as to the reasons and suggest further investigations to compare the two [e.g. weighing to calculate mass loss]. *(10 minutes)*

Main

- Search the internet to show pictures of adaptations of plants to arid conditions. Share with students the fact that the words 'stomach' and 'stoma' have the same origin from the Greek word for mouth. Show a picture of a stoma looking like a mouth. It would be useful to have a number of succulents and cactus plants available for students to be able to feel the texture and examine the structures in detail. Ask students to write a report on the adaptations.

- Set up a practical investigation into how variation in leaf size affects transpiration (see 'Practical support'). If preferred, this exercise can be set up as a demonstration where groups of students are given a 'leaf' of a different size, the measurements taken and then collected together and discussed. Many 'How Science Works' concepts, such as collecting and processing data and drawing conclusions, are introduced here.

- If you have a potometer (or a barometric pressure sensor) you can connect it to a leafy shoot. The rate of water uptake (equivalent to the rate of water loss) can be measured for the intact shoot. When several readings have been taken and a mean rate calculated, several leaves can be removed and the readings repeated. This can be done again removing more leaves. The effect will depend on the type of shoot chosen – one with soft leaves is better than laurel or rhododendron. Other conditions can be simulated using hair dryers and/or plastic bags.

- The surface area of the leaves can be measured as they are removed, by drawing around them on squared paper, cutting round the outlines and weighing them. If you know the mass of a known area of the squared paper, then it is possible to calculate the area of each leaf. (Dividing the mass of the leaf by the mass of 1 cm^2 will give the area of the leaf.)

Plenaries

Where do I come from? – Show a series of pictures of plants and ask students where they think the plants come from. Students can be supported by having a list of the different environments for them to select an appropriate one. Students can be extended by asking them to write down the name of an environment for each one. Compare answers and get them to suggest reasons for their choice of environment. *(5 minutes)*

Predictions

Ask students to make thumbnail sketches predicting what graphs would look like for the following:

- cuticle thickness v. habitat (rainforest/dry desert etc)
- surface area v. average humidity
- yearly rainfall v. water storage capacity.

These relate to 'How Science Works' – relationships between variables. This could be finished for homework. *(10 minutes)*.

Practical support

⚙ Investigation into how variation in leaf size affects transpiration

Equipment and materials required

Blotting paper, cotton string, drinking straws, boiling tube (or small measuring cylinder).

Details

Using pieces of blotting paper of known surface area, make up some 'leaves' of different sizes. Attach a piece of cotton string to one end of the blotting paper and pass the string down a drinking straw, so that the 'leaf' can be supported in a boiling tube (or small measuring cylinder). The blotting paper could have a thin card backing to give it strength. If a known volume of water is placed in each boiling tube (or the 'leaves' are placed in small measuring cylinders) the volume of water lost can be calculated in cm^3/hour against area in cm^2. The results can be shown graphically.

If preferred, this exercise can be set up as a demonstration where groups of students are given a 'leaf' of a different size, the measurements taken and then collected together and discussed.

B1 4.3 Adaptation in plants

Learning objectives

- How do plants lose water?
- How are plants adapted to live in dry conditions?

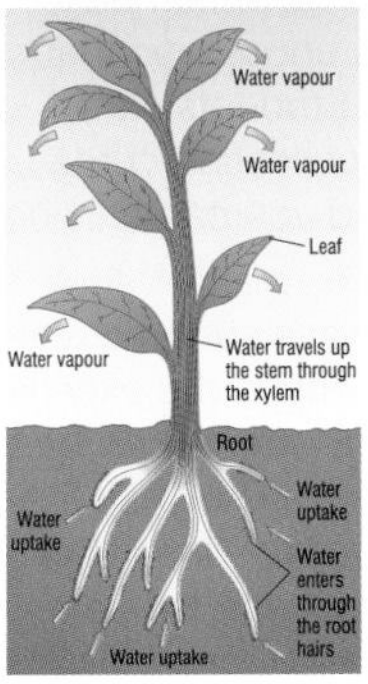

Plants need light, water, space and nutrients to survive. There are some places where plants cannot grow. In deep oceans no light penetrates and so plants cannot photosynthesise. In the icy wastes of the Antarctic it is simply too cold for plants to grow.

Almost everywhere else, including the hot, dry areas of the world, you find plants growing. Without them there would be no food for the animals. But plants need water for photosynthesis and to keep their tissues supported. If a plant does not get the water it needs, it wilts and eventually dies.

a Why do plants need water?

Plants take in water from the soil through their roots. It moves up through the plant and into the leaves. There are small openings called stomata in the leaves of a plant. These open to allow gases in and out for photosynthesis and respiration. At the same time water vapour is lost through the stomata by evaporation.

The rate at which a plant loses water is linked to the conditions it is growing in. When it is hot and dry, photosynthesis and respiration take place quickly. As a result, plants also lose water vapour very quickly. Plants that live in very hot, dry conditions need special adaptations to survive. Most of them either reduce their surface area so they lose less water or store water in their tissues. Some do both!

b How do plants lose water from their leaves?

Changing surface area

When it comes to stopping water loss through the leaves, the surface area:volume ratio is very important to plants. A few desert plants have broad leaves with a large surface area. These leaves collect the dew that forms in the cold evenings. They then funnel the water towards their shallow roots.

Some plants in dry environments have curled leaves. This reduces the surface area of the leaf. It also traps a layer of moist air around the leaf. This reduces the amount of water the plant loses by evaporation.

Most plants that live in dry conditions have leaves with a very small surface area. This adaptation cuts down the area from which water can be lost. Some desert plants have small fleshy leaves with a thick cuticle to keep water loss down. The cuticle is a waxy covering on the leaf that stops water evaporating.

The best-known desert plants are the cacti. Their leaves have been reduced to spines with a very small surface area indeed. This means the cactus only loses a tiny amount of water. Not only that, its sharp spines also put animals off eating the cactus.

c Why do plants often reduce the surface area of their leaves?

Figure 1 Plants lose water vapour from the surface of their leaves. When the conditions are hot and dry, they may lose water very quickly.

Labels on Figure 1: Water vapour; Water vapour; Leaf; Water vapour; Water travels up the stem through the xylem; Root; Water uptake; Water uptake; Water enters through the root hairs; Water uptake

⊂⊃ links

For information on surface area:volume ratio, look back at B1 4.2 Adaptation in animals.

Figure 2 Marram grass grows on sand dunes. It has tightly curled leaves to reduce the surface area for water loss so it can survive the dry conditions.

Collecting water

Many plants that live in very dry conditions have specially adapted and very big root systems. They may have extensive root systems that spread over a very wide area, roots that go down a very long way, or both. These adaptations allow the plant to take up as much water as possible from the soil. The mesquite tree has roots that grow as far as 50m down into the soil.

Storing water

Some plants cope with dry conditions by storing water in their tissues. When there is plenty of water after a period of rain, the plant stores it. Some plants use their fleshy leaves to store water. Others use their stems or roots.

For example, cacti don't just rely on their spiny leaves to help them survive in dry conditions. The fat green body of a cactus is its stem, which is full of water-storing tissue. These adaptations make cacti the most successful plants in a hot, dry climate.

Figure 3 A large saguaro cactus in the desert loses less than one glass of water a day. A UK apple tree can lose a whole bath of water in the same amount of time!

d In which parts can a plant store its water?

AQA Examiner's tip

Remember that plants need their stomata open for photosynthesis and respiration. This is why they lose water by evaporation from their leaves.

Summary questions

1 Copy and complete using the words below:
   adaptations desert plants spines stems water
   Cacti are .... that live in the .... They have two main .... to help them survive. Their leaves have become .... and they store .... in their ....

2 **a** Explain why plants lose water through their leaves all the time.
   b Why does this make living in a dry place such a problem?

3 Plants living in dry conditions have adaptations to reduce water loss from their leaves. Give three of these and explain how they work.

Key points

- Plants lose water vapour from the surface of their leaves.
- Plant adaptations for surviving in dry conditions include reducing the surface area of the leaves, having water-storage tissues and having extensive root systems.

Further teaching suggestions

Demonstration of expanding stem

- Fold a piece of green card into corrugations and sticky tape the ends together. Self-shading can be demonstrated and also, by pulling it wide and closing it up, the ability of barrel cacti to expand when water is plentiful.

Plants and water loss

- Not all plants showing adaptations to prevent loss of water live in hot, dry conditions. Ask students to consider other environments in which water may be unavailable to plants. Show them pictures of conifers and salt-marsh plants (many of which are succulent).
- Investigate the effect of phosphate on oxygen levels in water using jars with algae, water and varying numbers of drops of phosphate, then monitor using meter.

Summary answers

1 plants, desert, adaptations, spines, water, stems

2 **a** Water is lost by evaporation through the stomata. The stomata are open for gaseous exchange in photosynthesis and respiration and water is lost by evaporation at the same time.

   b Dry places are often hot, so photosynthesis and respiration occur at a faster rate. The stomata are open more, so there is more evaporation. If the air is dry, evaporation occurs at a faster rate.

3 Small leaves; curled leaves – reduce surface area; thick cuticle – also reduces rate of evaporation.

B1 4.4 Competition in animals

Learning objectives

Students should learn:

- how competition is essential for survival
- that animals compete with each other for food, territory and mates
- that a successful competitor is one which is better adapted.

Learning outcomes

Most students should be able to:

- explain how competition is necessary for survival
- describe those characteristics which make an animal a successful competitor
- suggest the factors for which an animal is competing in a given habitat.

Some students should also be able to:

- explain in detail why certain characteristics make an animal a successful competitor.

Answers to in-text questions

a There is only a limited amount of food, water and living space in an area.

b Any sensible choices here. For example, for a herbivore: eating a wide range of plants, sensitive hearing to hear predators. For a carnivore: ability to run fast; good eyesight; sharp teeth, etc.

Support

- Show students some plastic animals or pictures of animals and ask them to pick out an adaptation for each animal which makes it a good competitor.

Extend

- Introduce the concept of the 'ecological niche'. The students could research interesting or unusual examples of ecological niches.

AQA Specification link-up: Biology B1.4

- Animals often compete with each other for food, mates and territory. *[B1.4.1 c)]*
- Animals … may be adaped to cope with specific features … . *[B1.4.1 g)]*
- Suggest the factors for which organisms are competing in a given habitat. *[B1.4]*

Lesson structure

Starters

Competition for grass? – With the students working in pairs, ask them to list as many animals as they can that eat grass. Give them a time limit of 2 minutes. Students claiming to have the greatest number are asked to read out their list so that the rest of the class can agree or disagree. The winner gets a small prize. This leads to a discussion on competition. *(5 minutes)*

Survive! – Prepare small laminated cards with one of the following words written on it: 'food', 'shelter', 'water' or 'mate'. Place similar cards around the room, enough so that most, but not all, students can collect a complete set of all four cards. Students can be supported in this activity by telling them to move around the room collecting cards according to the rules: 'no swapping or taking from others by force and you can only hold one of each kind'.

Students who collect a full set can go to the front (or sit down) – they have survived. Those who do not manage to collect the set do not survive and at the end of the exercise have to share with their peers how they died (hunger, no mates, etc.). Students can be extended by allowing them to swap around the cards so that more can survive. Ask the students to speculate as to whether this sort of sharing-to-survive behaviour does take place in real life and what forms it may take. [To illustrate social effects or altruism, e.g. mothers feeding offspring but starving themselves.] *(10 minutes)*

Main

- Show the class courtship displays and mating behaviour. Find video or images of courtship displays (e.g. peacocks) or competition between males (e.g. sea lions) using the internet. References to the breeding plumage of different birds, behaviour of stags in the rutting season, etc. are other examples available. Search the Discovery Channel www.yourdiscovery.com.

- Introduce the ideas of 'interspecific' and 'intraspecific' competition: the words do not necessarily have to be used, only the idea that two types of animal eating the same food in the same habitat will be in competition with each other. There are some data available for the variation in numbers of two closely-related species of flour beetle (*Tribolium*) living in the same culture, and for two species of *Paramecium*: only one species will survive. You could also link this with the introduction of species, such as the grey squirrel, into this country and the rabbit (or more recently the camel) into Australia. For competition amongst members of the same species, there are data showing that when the density of limpets on a rocky shore increases, their length and biomass decrease.

- These examples can be presented to the students as OHPs or PowerPoint slides, and for each one discuss what they are competing for and why one wins and the other loses.

- Investigate a food web. Depending on the season, investigate a tree or a clump of plants in the school grounds to show the relationships between the different animals that feed on the plant. Using pooters and sweep nets, the small animals can be trapped and identified and a food web built up. There will be caterpillars and beetles eating the leaves; greenfly feeding directly on the plant sap; butterflies and moths feeding on the flowers; and other invertebrates feeding on the bark. Each group of animals can find plenty of food without being in competition with another species.

Plenaries

What makes a top competitor? – Discuss, for example, *Big Brother*, *The Weakest Link* or any other TV competition show. What parallels can be drawn between what goes on in such a show and competition in nature? *(5 minutes)*

Get off my patch! – Think of as many ways as you can by which animals mark out and defend territories. Write down a list of the animals and how each does this. Students can be supported by showing them pictures of some animals and asking them to suggest what territorial behaviour they may show. You can extend students by suggesting that they link territorial behaviour with survival and natural selection. Ask why changes in some DNA will result in survival and these changes are passed on to the next generation. *(10 minutes)*

Further teaching suggestions

Camouflage!
● Another exercise would be to get students to hunt the cocktail stick, using red and green cocktail sticks on a green background.

Camouflage effectiveness
● Find some good pictures of camouflaged animals and ask the students to time how long it takes them to identify the animals. There are some good examples, e.g. flatfish,

amphibians, snakes, etc. Does camouflage play a role in competition between animals?

Competition in birds
● Birds compete all the time for food, mates and territory. Ask students to research the different ways in which birds compete using colour, food preferences and song. Good examples to get the students started are robins and blackbirds.

Adaptation for survival

B1 4.4   Competition in animals

Learning objectives
● What is competition?
● What makes an animal a good competitor?

Figure 1 Some herbivores only feed on one particular plant. Pandas only eat bamboo, so they are open to competition from other animals or to diseases that damage bamboo.

Figure 2 The coral snake (top) is poisonous but the milk snake (bottom) is not. The milk snake is a mimic – it looks like the coral snake. As long as the two species live in the same area the milk snake is protected. Other animals and people leave it alone thinking it is a poisonous coral snake!

Animals and plants grow alongside lots of other living things. Some will be from the same species and others will be completely different. In any area there is only a limited amount of food, water and space, and a limited number of mates. As a result, living organisms have to compete for the things they need.

The best adapted organisms are most likely to win the **competition** for resources. They will be most likely to survive and produce healthy offspring.

a Why do living organisms compete?

What do animals compete for? 🄺

Animals compete for many things, including:
● food
● territory
● mates.

Competition for food

Competition for food is very common. Herbivores sometimes feed on many types of plant, and sometimes on only one or two different sorts. Many different species of herbivores will all eat the same plants. Just think how many types of animals eat grass!

The animals that eat a wide range of plants are most likely to be successful. If you are a picky eater, you risk dying out if anything happens to your only food source. An animal with wider tastes will just eat something else for a while!

Competition is common among carnivores. They compete for prey. Small mammals like mice are eaten by animals like foxes, owls, hawks and domestic cats. The different types of animals all hunt the same mice. So the animals which are best adapted to the area will be most successful.

Carnivores have to compete with their own species for their prey as well as with different species. Some successful predators are adapted to have long legs for running fast and sharp eyes to spot prey. These features will be passed on to their offspring.

Animals often avoid direct competition with members of other species when they can. It is the competition between members of the same species which is most intense.

Prey animals compete with each other too – to be the one that *isn't* caught! Their adaptations help prevent them becoming a meal for a predator. Some animals contain poisons which make anything that eats them sick or even kills them. Very often these animals also have bright warning colours so that predators quickly learn which animals to avoid. Poison arrow frogs are a good example.

b Give one useful adaptation for a herbivore and one for a carnivore.

Competition for territory

For many animals, setting up and defending a territory is vital. A territory may simply be a place to build a nest. It could be all the space needed for an animal to find food and reproduce. Most animals cannot reproduce successfully if they have no territory. So they will compete for the best spaces. This helps to make sure they will be able to find enough food for themselves and for their young.

Competition for a mate

Competition for mates can be fierce. In many species the male animals put a lot of effort into impressing the females. The males compete in different ways to win the privilege of mating with a female.

In some species – like deer and lions – the males fight between themselves. Then the winner gets the females.

Many male animals display to the females to get their attention. Some birds have spectacular adaptations to help them stand out. Male peacocks have the most amazing tail feathers. They use them for displaying to other males (to warn them off) and to females (to attract them).

What makes a successful competitor?

A successful competitor is an animal that is adapted to be better at finding food or a mate than the other members of its own species. It also needs to be better at finding food than the members of other local species. It must be able to breed successfully.

Many animals are successful because they avoid competition with other species as much as possible. They feed in a way that no other local animals do, or they eat a type of food that other animals avoid. For example, one plant can feed many animals without direct competition. While caterpillars eat the leaves, greenfly drink the sap, butterflies suck nectar from the flowers and beetles feed on pollen.

Figure 3 The territory of a gannet pair may be small but without a space they cannot build a nest and reproduce

Figure 4 The spectacular display of a male peacock attracts females. Unlike deer and lions he doesn't need to fight and risk injury.

Examiner's tip

Learn to look at an animal and spot the adaptations that make it a successful competitor.

Summary questions

1 **a** Give an example of animals competing with members of the same species for food.
   b Give an example of animals competing with members of other species for food.
   c Animals that rely on a single type of food can easily become extinct. Explain why.

2 **a** Give two ways in which animals compete for mates.
   b Suggest the advantages and disadvantages of the methods chosen in part **a**.

3 Explain the adaptations you would expect to find in:
   a an animal that hunts mice
   b an animal that eats grass
   c an animal that hunts and eats other animals
   d an animal that feeds on the tender leaves at the top of trees.

Key points
● Animals often compete with each other for food, territories and mates.
● Animals have adaptations that make them good competitors.

Summary answers

1 **a** Any suitable examples, such as lions, cheetahs and leopards etc.
   b Any suitable examples, such as rabbits, limpets on a sea shore.
   c If anything happens to their food supply, such as another animal eating it, fire or disease, then they will starve.

2 **a** Fighting: strength, antlers, teeth, etc.
   Displaying: spectacular appearance, colours, part of body to display (e.g. peacock's tail).
   b The answer to this will depend on the method selected for the first part of the answer.
   Fighting: advantages – possibility of winning lots of mates, becoming dominant, fathering lots of offspring, females don't usually have any choice, preventing others from mating. Disadvantages are that the animal could be hurt or killed, needs lots of body resources to grow antlers and to fight etc.
   Display: advantages – don't risk getting hurt, possibility of attracting several mates.
   Disadvantages – uses up lots of resources to grow feathers/ carry out displays, females usually choose and may not get noticed, vulnerable to disease or lack of food so don't produce good display, need to be seen. Any sensible points.

3 **a** Quite small, moves stealthily, so hard for mice to see and hear, sharp teeth to kill mice quickly, good eyesight to see small prey and judge distances when pouncing and hearing to pick up the sounds of mice in the undergrowth/grass; claws to help trap/hold mouse, hunts at time mice are active to increase chance of actually finding mice.
   b Special teeth to grind grass and break open cells, ability to run fast away from predators to avoid being caught, good all-round eyesight to detect predators creeping up, good hearing to detect predators, etc.
   c Fast to catch prey, good hearing and good eyesight to increase chances of seeing/hearing prey, eyes on front of head to give binocular vision to judge distance when pouncing on prey, sharp teeth and claws to catch, hold and kill prey, camouflage so prey doesn't notice predator creeping up.
   d Teeth and gut adapted to eating plants – crushing the cells to release the cell contents/breaking down cellulose cell walls, ability to reach the top of trees (long neck or good at climbing) to get to the tender leaves, ability to grip on to branches to get to the tender leaves/hold them to pull off the tree, possibly use tail for balance to get to the top of the tree.

B1 4.5

Competition in plants

Learning objectives

Students should learn:

- how plants compete with each other for water and nutrients from the soil
- how plants compete for light.

Learning outcomes

Most students should be able to:

- explain why plants need light
- explain why plants need nutrients (minerals)
- suggest the factors for which plants are competing in a given habitat.

Some students should also be able to:

- suggest why some plants are better competitors in a given habitat
- evaluate the strategies used by plants to make them successful competitors, e.g. seed dispersal mechanisms.

Support

- Supply students with a collection of seeds/fruits and ask them to match a dispersal/distribution method to each one. Sycamore, burdock, dandelion, strawberry, nuts and tomatoes are good examples.
- You could also give them some dandelion heads full of seeds and getting them to see how far the seeds will spread in different wind intensities. Use a small electric fan with a variable speed adjustment. Be aware of any hay fever or nut allergies.

Extend

- Students could be asked to find the best wing surface area to weight ratio for sycamore seeds by making small models from paper and paperclips. Provide them with a template for the wing, digital balances and litter pickers for dropping from a chosen height.
- Students could be provided with fruiting heads of dandelion and asked to design and carry out an experiment to investigate the rate of descent of the dandelion 'parachutes'.

AQA Specification link-up: Biology B1.4

- Plants often compete with each other for light and space, and for water and nutrients from the soil. *[B1.4.1 b)]*
- Suggest the factors for which organisms are competing in a given habitat. *[B1.4]*

  Controlled Assessment: SA4.1 Planning an investigation *[SA4.1.1 a) b) c) d)]*, *[SA4.1.2 b) c)]*; SA4.3 Collect primary and secondary data *[SA4.3.3 a)]*; SA4.4 Select and process primary and secondary data *[SA4.4.1 a)]*, *[SA4.4.2 b)]*; SA4.5 Analyse and interpret primary and secondary data. *[SA4.5.3 a)]*, *[SA4.5.4 a)]*

Lesson structure

Starters

How do coconut trees disperse their seeds? – Have a coconut complete with husk. Show the students the coconut, float it in a bucket of water and lead them into a discussion of seed distribution techniques. *(5 minutes)*

Seed dispersal – Have a range of seeds and fruits around the room, labelled with numbers. As the students enter the room, hand each one a list of numbers and get them to write the method of dispersal against each number using W (for wind), A (for animal) or E (for explosive). Students can be supported by providing them with a crib sheet for features of each type of seed distribution. Students can be extended by asking them to rate the relative efficiency of the various seed dispersal mechanisms. On completion of the exercise, ask the students to devise a plan for an experiment to investigate the relative efficiency of various seed dispersal mechanisms. *(10 minutes)*

Main

- There is an opportunity to investigate competition in plants. A spacing trial can be set up using radishes in late spring to early autumn. (See 'Practical support'.) 'How Science Works' concepts, such as experimental design, predicted outcomes, recording measurements and drawing conclusions can be reinforced here. Focus on one aspect you wish to develop.
- You might also wish to look at competition between weeds and crop plants (see 'Practical support'). Lead a discussion of the results prior to the students writing up a report. Experiments involving the growth of plants need time to yield results, so this should be planned ahead.
- Ask the question, 'Do plants shade out the competition?' Measure the surface area of nettle leaves growing in shady conditions and compare with the surface area of nettle leaves growing in brightly lit conditions. Squared paper can be used to measure leaf surface area or rubbings taken and light meters or data loggers used to record light intensity. This is a good opportunity to select 'How Science Works' concepts to teach. Predictions can be made and the results plotted as light intensity against surface area. Variable warning! There are some complex variables here: it is best to stick to the light intensity and pick leaves at the same height above the ground.

Plenaries

Competition! Competition! – Give the students a fixed time limit (the exact amount of time will vary with the ability level) and get them to fill in a missing words sentence '… competes with … for … .' Copy this line lots of times onto a sheet of paper. Give each student a copy. They have to fill in as many examples as they can in the given time. When time is up, the student with the most valid competition examples wins a small prize. *(5 minutes)*

What to do about weeds – What advice would you give gardeners who want to avoid weeds amongst their vegetables? Students can be supported by asking them to design a poster telling gardeners how to avoid problems with weeds. Give them a list of ideas, some desirable and some not so desirable, from which they choose the most sensible. Students can be extended by discussing their own ideas, giving reasons for their suggestions and designing a pamphlet to be displayed in garden centres. *(10 minutes)*

Practical support

Investigating competition in plants

Equipment and materials required

Balance for weighing seedlings; for each group or demonstration: radish seeds, potting compost, small trays.

Details

Plant seeds into small trays of moist potting compost at increasing distances apart on both *x*- and *y*-axes of the trays. The distances should be clearly marked along the sides of the trays, so that the experiment can be replicated. The trays should be watered regularly and kept in the same conditions of light and temperature. Using a 'watermoat' would help uneven watering. Weigh the seedlings, or plants, when grown to find the ideal spacing. This can be carried out on a larger scale with plants in a school garden or with rapid-cycling brassicas under a light bank at any time of year.

Investigating competition between weeds and crop plants

Equipment and materials required

Identical small pots, compost, radishes, a light box of the sort recommended by Science And Plants in Schools (SAPS) for their 'Rapid-cycling Brassicas'.

Details

Fill a number of identical small pots with compost and sow radishes and 'weed' (any other seeds such as marigolds etc.) seeds at different densities e.g. one radish to ten weeds, five radishes to five weeds, etc. Water the pots regularly and keep all other conditions (light, temperature) the same. A light box ensures even light distribution. Harvest the radishes at the appropriate time and compare the mass of radishes harvested at the different densities. The weeds could also be harvested and their wet mass determined, so that this can be compared with the mass of the radishes.

Adaptation for survival

B1 4.5 Competition in plants

Learning objectives

● What do plants compete for?
● How do plants compete?

Practical

Investigating competition in plants

Carry out an investigation to look at the effect of competition on plants. Set up two trays of seeds – one crowded and one spread out. Then monitor the plants' height and wet mass (mass after watering). Keep all of the conditions – light level, the amount of water and nutrients available and the temperature – exactly the same for both sets of plants. The differences in their growth will be the result of overcrowding and competition for resources in one of the groups. The data show growth of tree seedlings. You can get results in days rather than months by using cress seeds.

[Bar chart: Average height (cm) — Crowded plants (After 1 month, After 6 months) vs Spread out plants (After 1 month, After 6 months)]

[Bar chart: Total wet mass (g) — Crowded plants (After 1 month, After 6 months) vs Spread out plants (After 1 month, After 6 months)]

Plants compete fiercely with each other. They compete for:

● light for photosynthesis, to make food using energy from sunlight
● water for photosynthesis and to keep their tissues rigid and supported
● nutrients (minerals) so they can make all the chemicals they need in their cells
● space to grow, allowing their roots to take in water and nutrients, and their leaves to capture light.

a What do plants compete with each other for?

Why do plants compete?

Just like animals, plants are in competition both with other species of plants and with their own species. Big, tall plants such as trees take up a lot of water and nutrients from the soil. They also prevent light from reaching the plants beneath them. So the plants around them need adaptations to help them to survive.

When a plant sheds its seeds they might land nearby. Then the parent plant will be in direct competition with its own seedlings. Because the parent plant is large and settled, it will take most of the water, nutrients and light. So the plant will deprive its own offspring of everything they need to grow successfully. The roots of some desert plants even produce a chemical that stops seeds from germinating, killing the competition even before it begins to grow!

Sometimes the seeds from a plant will all land close together, a long way from their parent. They will then compete with each other as they grow.

b Why is it important that seeds are spread as far as possible from the parent plant?

Coping with competition

Plants that grow close to other species often have adaptations which help them to avoid competition.

Small plants found in woodlands often grow and flower very early in the year. This is when plenty of light gets through the bare branches of the trees. The dormant trees take very little water out of the soil. The leaves shed the previous autumn have rotted down to provide nutrients in the soil. Plants like snowdrops, anemones and bluebells are all adapted to take advantage of these things. They flower, set seeds and die back again before the trees are in full leaf.

Another way plants compete successfully is by having different types of roots. Some plants have shallow roots taking water and nutrients from near the surface of the soil. Others have long, deep roots, which go far underground. Both compete successfully for what they need without affecting the other.

If one plant is growing in the shade of another, it may grow taller to reach the light. It may also grow leaves with a bigger surface area to take advantage of all the light it does get.

Some plants are adapted to prevent animals from eating them. They may have thorns, like the African acacia or the blackberry. They may make poisons that mean they taste very bitter or make the animals that eat them ill. Either way they compete successfully because they are less likely to be eaten than other plants.

c How can short roots help a plant to compete successfully?

Spreading the seeds

To reproduce successfully, a plant has to avoid competition with its own seedlings. Many plants use the wind to help them spread their seeds as far as possible. They produce fruits or seeds with special adaptations for flight to carry their seeds away. Examples of this are the parachutes of the dandelion 'clock' and the winged seeds of the sycamore tree.

d How do the fluffy parachutes of dandelion seeds help the seeds to spread out?

Some plants use mini-explosions to spread their seeds. The pods dry out, twist and pop, flinging the seeds out and away.

Juicy berries, fruits and nuts are adaptations to tempt animals to eat them. The fruit is digested and the tough seeds are deposited well away from the parent plant in their own little pile of fertiliser!

Fruits that are sticky or covered in hooks get caught up in the fur or feathers of a passing animal. They are carried around until they fall off hours or even days later.

Sometimes the seeds of several different plants land on the soil and start to grow together. The plants that grow fastest will compete successfully against the slower-growing plants. For example:

● The plants that get their roots into the soil first will get most of the available water and nutrients.
● The plants that open their leaves fastest will be able to photosynthesise and grow faster still, depriving the competition of light.

Figure 1 Plants have different types of roots to compete for water and nutrients in the soil

Figure 2 The winged seeds of the sycamore tree

Figure 3 Coconuts will float for weeks or even months on ocean currents, which can carry them hundreds of miles from their parents – and any other coconuts!

Summary questions

1 **a** How can plants overcome the problems of growing in the shade of another plant?
   b How do bluebell plants grow and flower successfully in spite of living under large trees in a wood?

2 **a** Why is it so important that plants spread their seeds successfully?
   b Give three examples of successful adaptations for spreading seeds.

3 The dandelion is a successful weed. Carry out some research and evaluate the adaptations that make it a better competitor than other plants on a school field.

Key points

● Plants often compete with each other for light, for water and for nutrients (minerals) from the soil.
● Plants have many adaptations that make them good competitors.

Further teaching suggestions

Light intensity

● Use data loggers to investigate light intensity in different sites in the school garden or on school grounds. Correlate light intensity with the type of vegetation present.

Answers to in-text questions

a Light, water, minerals/nutrients and space.

b So that there is no competition between the parent and the offspring.

c The plant roots can take in water and minerals near the surface of the soil, while other plants with deeper roots take water from lower down in the soil so competition is reduced.

d The fluffy parachutes help the seeds to float in the air, so that they can be blown as far as possible from the parent plant.

Summary answers

1 **a** May grow taller, may have deeper/shallower roots, flower at a different time of year. May grow leaves with a bigger surface area to absorb more light.
   b They produce flowers before the oak tree's leaves have grown to full size, so they are not shaded.

2 **a** To avoid competition between the seedlings and the parent plants and to avoid competition between the seedlings, as far as possible.
   b Any three suitable adaptations – look for different ones, for example, fluffy seeds, winged seeds, seeds in berries/fruits which are eaten, explosive seeds, sticky seeds, hooked seeds, seeds that float on water. Any other sensible suggestion.

3 For example, deep taproot (difficult to remove, can regenerate well if severed); low rosette of leaves (avoids blades of lawnmowers and grazing animals) long flowering period, produces large numbers of seeds, very effective wind dispersal of seed over a large area.

B1 4.6

How do you survive?

Learning objectives

Students should learn:

- that organisms can survive in very unusual conditions
- that wherever they live, organisms are competing for the things they need to survive.

Learning outcomes

Most students should be able to:

- describe some adaptations of organisms to unusual conditions
- explain that adaptations are essential for survival.

Some students should also be able to:

- apply their knowledge to interpret the survival strategies of organisms.

AQA Specification link-up: Biology B1.4

- Organisms, including microorganisms have features (adaptations) that enable them to survive in the conditions in which they normally live. [B1.4.1 d)]
- Suggest how organisms are adapted to the conditions in which they live. [B1.4]
- Suggest the factors for which organisms are competing in a given habitat. [B1.4]
- Some organisms live in environments that are very extreme. Extremophiles may be tolerant to high levels of salt, high temperatures or high pressures. [B1.4.1 e)]
- Observe the adaptations, e.g. body shape, of a range of organisms from different habitats. [B1.4]
- Develop an understanding of the ways in which adaptations enable organisms to survive. [B1.4]

Lesson structure

Starters

Pick an organism – Have the names and pictures of a number of organisms on playing card size pieces of card, one per card. Hand out sets of these to groups. Students to take turns in picking a card and stating the survival strategy for the organism shown. *(5 minutes)*

That's pretty harsh! – Put a circus of information points up around the room, each with an example of an organism living in harsh conditions (ice fish, thermophilic bacteria in hot pools, *Helicobacter pylori* living in stomach acid, etc.) Students can be supported by being given a prepared sheet and ticking off the name of the organisms. Students can be extended by writing their own notes and explanations of the difficulties the environments would present. *(10 minutes)*

Main

- If available, watch sections from the 2009 BBC wildlife series *Life* episode 2 'Reptiles and amphibians' where Komodo dragons bite the heel of a water buffalo and wait for three weeks while the infected saliva they introduced causes septicaemia and weakens the buffalo to a point where they can kill it.
- Show video footage of life around black smoker thermal vents. Look especially at the giant tube worms, getting the students to realise that they are 2 metres plus in length. Explain about hydrogen sulphide gas acting as a nutrient for bacteria which line their insides (they have no mouth, anus or intestines).
- Watch video Nature 'The Queen of trees' 2005 if available. This covers the remarkable story of the African sycamore fig and the ecosystem it provides, especially the extraordinary fig wasp, so small it can fly through the eye of a needle.
- Use the internet to find images and video clips of Venus flytraps in action. Using a real one, investigate whether they can count the trigger hairs by touching. Use a flexicam or similar digital video camera to project the test.
- Explain the idea of polymorphism and describe how it works as a survival strategy. Mention the European banded snails and show examples or pictures of examples. If possible, carry out a search for banded snails in your area and discuss the different types found. How do they survive?

Support

- Get students to stick into their notebooks two coloured strips of paper cut to scale – one to show their reaction time and another to show that of the star nosed mole. Put them on a pair of axes and draw in the scale (some students may need a printed one).

Extend

- Give the students access to some neuroscience materials on myelination of neurons and the effect it has on speeding up the transmission of impulses.

Plenaries

Life on Europa? – Under a thick layer of ice, Europa, the sixth moon of Jupiter, has deep oceans of liquid water. It is speculated that life may exist around hydrothermal vents at the base of this ocean. Think about what the conditions there must be like. Students can be supported by giving them a list of the conditions and a list of adaptations to choose from. Students can be extended by getting them to write a list of the conditions and speculating as to what adaptations organisms might need to have to survive there. *(5 minutes)*

The fastest predator – From the internet, locate an interactive reflex timer programme. Time how fast the students can respond. Compare this with the reaction time of the Star nosed mole. If the timer used makes a sound, carry out the programme blindfolded as this more clearly imitates how the star-nosed mole catches its prey. *(10 minutes)*

Further teaching suggestions

Insectivorous plants
- There are a number of insectivorous plants with different mechanisms for trapping their prey. Some good sources of information are Kew Gardens, Darwin's book *Insectivorous Plants* and the internet.

The most amazing plants in the world?
- Find out more about amazing plants and the work of Dr Peter Scott on 'Resurrection plants' at the University of Sussex.

Crops for the future?
- Encourage students to think about the types of crops grown in areas prone to drought and the staple foods of the people who live in such regions. What adaptations might be needed?

Fact files
- Direct students to find out more about some of the plant species which have become problems because they are such good competitors' e.g. Japanese knotweed, water hyacinth and milfoil. An internet search of invasive plants could yield information on these examples.

Highly adapted animals
- More examples of highly adapted animals could be researched. Examples could include the vicuna (altitude), camels (arid conditions), springtails (low temperatures) and social insects.

How Science Works   Adaptation for survival

B1 4.6   How do you survive?

Learning objectives
- How do organisms survive in very unusual conditions?
- What factors are organisms competing for in a habitat?

So far in this chapter we have looked at lots of different ways in which living organisms are adapted. This helps them to survive and reproduce wherever they live. We have looked at why they need to compete successfully against their own species and others. Now we are going to consider three case studies of adaption in living organisms.

Figs and fig wasps

There are about 700 different species of fig trees. Each one has its own species of pollinating wasps, without which the trees will die. The fig flowers of the trees are specially adapted so that they attract the right species of wasp.

Female fig wasps have specially shaped heads for getting into fig flowers. They also have **ovipositors** that allow them to place their eggs deep in the flowers of the fig tree.

Male fig wasps vary. Some species can fly but others are adapted to live in a fig fruit all their life. If they are lucky, a female wasp will arrive in the flower and the male will fertilise her. After this he digs an escape tunnel for the female through the fruit and dies himself! The male wasp has special adaptations (such as the loss of his wings and very small eyes) which help him move around inside the fig fruit to find a female.

Figure 1 A fig tree

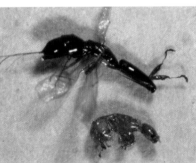

Figure 2 A female (top) and male (bottom) fig wasp

If a fig tree cannot attract the right species of wasp, it will never be able to reproduce. In fact in some areas the trees are in danger of extinction because the wasp populations are being wiped out.

The fastest predator in the world?

It takes you about 650 milliseconds to react to a crisis. But the star-nosed mole takes only 230 milliseconds from the moment it first touches its prey to gulping it down. That's faster than the human eye can see!

What makes this even more amazing is that star-nosed moles live underground and are almost totally blind. Their main sense organ is a crown of fleshy tendrils around the nose – incredibly sensitive to touch and smell but very odd to look at. The ultra-sensitive tendrils can try out 13 possible targets every second.

It seems likely that they have adapted to react so quickly because they can't see what is going on. They need to grab their prey as soon as possible after they touch it. If they don't it might move away or try to avoid them, and they wouldn't know where it had gone.

Figure 3 The star-nosed mole

A carnivorous plant

Venus flytraps are plants that grow on bogs. Bogs are wet and their peaty soil has very few nutrients in it. This makes it a difficult place for plants to live.

The Venus flytrap has special 'traps' that contain sweet smelling nectar. They sit wide open showing their red insides. Insects are attracted to the colour and the smell. Inside the trap are many small, sensitive hairs. As the insect moves about to find the nectar, it will brush against these hairs. Once the hairs have been touched, the trap is triggered. It snaps shut and traps the insect inside.

Special enzymes then digest the insect inside the trap. The Venus flytrap uses the nutrients from the digested bodies of its victims. This is in place of the nutrients that it cannot get from the poor bog soil. After the insect has been digested, the trap reopens ready to try again.

Figure 4 The Venus flytrap – an insect-eating plant

Activity

Case studies
- For each of these three case studies, list how the organisms are adapted for their habitat and how these adaptations help them to compete successfully against both their own species and other species.
- Choose three organisms that you know something about – or find out about three organisms which interest you. Make your own fact file on their adaptations and how these adaptations help them to compete successfully. Include at least one plant.

Summary questions

1. Explain how both of the animals featured compete successfully for food.
2. Why could any species of fig tree or fig wasp easily die out? Give a reason for each.
3. Carry out research to explain the adaptations of a giraffe and why they help it to compete successfully with other animals living in the same area.

Key points
- Organisms have adaptations which enable them to survive in the conditions in which they normally live.
- Plants often compete with each other for light, water and nutrients from the soil.
- Animals often compete with each other for food, mates and territory.

Summary answers

1. Fig wasps have exclusive relationship with species of fig tree which means they are always close to their source of food. Star-nosed moles have finger-like sensory tendrils. They are very sensitive to touch and smell and have very rapid reflex reactions.

2. Trees are vulnerable because they often have only one pollinator. So if anything happens to that species of fig wasp e.g. new disease or predator – the tree will not be pollinated and so the species of fig could die out.

   Wasps are vulnerable because one species of tree is their only food source. In some cases, the tree is the only place for meeting a mate – so any damage/disease/felling of trees could lead to extinction of wasps.

3. They are very tall and have a very long neck and tongue. This means they can reach leaves much higher from the ground than many other animals. They also have very long legs so they can cover the ground quickly and economically, moving from food source to food source. Their size means that they are unlikely to be attacked by predators. Any other sensible points – look to give extra credit to students who go beyond the long neck/tongue aspects of the animal.

B1 4.7 Measuring environmental change

Learning objectives

Students should learn:

- some factors that affect the distribution of living organisms
- that living and non-living factors can cause environmental changes
- that non-living indicators can be used to measure environmental changes
- how living organisms can be used as indicators of pollution.

Learning outcomes

Most students should be able to:

- list some factors that affect the distribution of living organisms
- describe some living and non-living factors that cause environmental changes
- measure some environmental changes using non-living indicators
- describe an example of a living organism that can be used as a pollution indicator.

Some students should also be able to:

- analyse data on changes in environmental conditions.

AQA Examiner's tip

Students often get confused when considering invertebrate indicators. They assume large numbers means more oxygen. They need to understand that some invertebrates, e.g. blood worms, survive well in low-oxygen concentrations.

Answers to in-text questions

a Temperature.
b Any suitable examples of each, for example: Living – new predator, new pathogen, food or competition; Non-living: temperature, amount of sunlight or rainfall.

Support

- Make a set of cards depicting non-living environmental factors and another set showing measuring equipment. Ask students to match the correct equipment to the factor.

Extend

- Get students to research the life cycles of lichens and their importance as colonisers of bare rock.

AQA Specification link-up: Biology B1.4

- … plants may be adapted to cope with specific features of their environment, e.g. thorns, poisons…. [B1.4.1 g)]
- Animals and plants are subjected to environmental changes. Such changes may be caused by living or non-living factors such as a change in a competitor, or in the average temperature or rainfall. [B1.4.2 b)]
- Living organisms can be used as indicators of pollution:
  - lichens can be used as air pollution indicators, particularly of the concentration of sulfur dioxide in the atmosphere
  - invertebrate animals can be used as water pollution indicators and are used as indicators of the concentration of dissolved oxygen in water. [B1.4.2 c)]
- Environmental changes can be measured using non-living indicators such as oxygen levels, temperature and rainfall. [B1.4.2 d)]

Lesson structure

Starters

What's it like outside? – Get the students to make a list of all the environmental parameters they can think of to describe their surroundings. Support students by having a display of measuring devices, such as measuring cylinders, rulers, maximum–minimum thermometers and perhaps an anemometer and a sundial. Extend students by asking them to suggest a measuring device for each parameter they come up with and give an estimate of the range of values they may find for each parameter. Read out and compare the lists. *(5 minutes)*

Link up – Ask the students to compete with each other to name pairs of organisms. Each pair of organisms should be linked through one affecting the other in some way, e.g. hawks and sparrows – the link is the hawks eat the sparrows. See if they can come up with a number of different types of interaction, not just feeding relationships. *(10 minutes)*

Main

- The use of equipment to measure non-living indicators of change can be demonstrated. Show the students maximum–minimum thermometers, rainfall gauges and oxygen meters and discuss with them how these can be used.
- There are two suggested activities here: one measuring oxygen levels and another measuring temperature and rainfall. Both activities involve fieldwork.
- Produce a PowerPoint presentation or exposition on lichens. Include some photographs of different forms and different places where lichens are found. Explain that lichens are sensitive to the levels of sulfur dioxide in the atmosphere and can therefore be used to indicate levels of pollution in an area. Provide the students with a worksheet which can be completed as the lesson proceeds.
- Consider the idea of lichens as pollution indicators by investigating the distribution of lichens on the trees in your neighbourhood. Provide the students with pictures of a couple of lichens, one that is fairly common and tolerant (the yellow *Xanthoria*) and a foliose or leafy type. Get the students to carry out a survey of lichens on the trees in the school grounds or a local park. You could do a preliminary survey and find out which species are likely to occur, so that the pictures and identification features are relevant to what they might find.
- Alternatively, a survey could be made of lichens on buildings and walls if it is more convenient. Discuss the results and consider the level of sulfur dioxide pollution in the area.
- As well as lichens, invertebrate species are indicators of pollution. Carry out a survey of the number of different species of invertebrates in the local pond or stream. The cleaner the water, the greater the number of species. Some species are only found in the cleanest, least polluted water and some are only found in the dirtiest, most polluted water.

Plenaries

Environmental charades – Write a list of the key words from the topic on the board. Select a student to stand up and using mime indicate which key word they have chosen. Wipe that parameter off the board when complete. Repeat for the rest of the key words until two are left then get two students to do these together; peers have to guess which one is which. *(5 minutes)*

Crossword – Use an internet-based crossword compiler (there are many free examples of these) to create a crossword based on the key words used in the lesson. Students can be supported by using easier clues and filling in the vowels. Students can be extended by using cryptic clues or asking the students to compile the clues themselves. *(10 minutes)*

Practical support

Indicators of pollution levels

Equipment and materials required
Pond nets (one per three students if possible, buckets, plastic containers, Petri dishes with lids, identification charts (laminated) and books, hand lenses, clipboards, pens and paper.

Details
Choose a suitable day regarding weather. It's a good idea to do a dipping exercise yourself in advance to find out what is there. If working with large groups it may be advisable to split the class in two.

Then, working with a colleague, do the practical pond dipping half a class at a time. Equipment needed should be gathered in advance. Run through behavioural expectations in advance, emphasising safety aspects of and due consideration for the creatures. Space the students around the pond. Collect organisms, observe them and identify, recording your findings. Ensure that you return the specimens to the pond before leaving and that they do not get too stressed.

Safety: Please check LA (Local Authorities) policy on school visits, with reference to safety and procedure. Students should be warned to wear suitable footwear and clothing. Wash hands after contact with pond water.

B1 4.7 Measuring environmental change

Learning objectives
- What affects the distribution of living things?
- What causes environmental changes?
- How can we measure environmental changes?

Have you noticed different types of animals and plants when you travel to different places? The distribution of living organisms depends on the environmental conditions and varies around the world.

Factors affecting the distribution of organisms

Non-living factors have a big effect on where organisms live. The average temperature or average rainfall will have a big impact on what can survive. You don't find polar bears in countries where the average temperature is over 20°C, for example! The amount of rainfall affects the distribution of both plants and animals. Light, pH and the local climate all influence where living organisms are found.

The distribution of different species of animals in water is closely linked to the oxygen levels. Salmon can only live in water with lots of dissolved oxygen, but bloodworms can survive in very low oxygen levels.

Living organisms also affect the distribution of other living organisms. So, for example, koala bears are only found where eucalyptus trees grow. Parasites only live where they can find a host.

One species of ant eats nectar produced by the flowers of the swollen-thorn acacia tree. The ants hollow out the vicious thorns and live in them. So any animal biting the tree not only gets the sharp thorns, they get a mouth full of angry ants as well. The distribution of the ants depends on the trees.

Figure 1 The distribution of bullhorn acacia ants depends on where the swollen-thorn acacia trees grow

a Which non-living environmental factor affects the distribution of polar bears?

Environmental changes

When the environment changes, it can cause a change in the distribution of living organisms in the area. Non-living factors often cause these changes in an environment.

The average temperature may rise or fall. The oxygen concentration in water may change. A change in the amount of sunlight, the strength of the wind or the average rainfall may affect an environment. Any of these factors can affect the distribution of living organisms.

Living factors can also cause a change in the environment where an organism lives, affecting distribution. A new type of predator may move into an area. A new disease-causing pathogen may appear and wipe out a species of animal or plant. Different plants may appear and provide food or a home for a whole range of different species.

b Give an example of a living and a non-living factor that can change an environment.

Measuring environmental change

When an environment changes, the living organisms in it are affected. If the change is big enough, the distribution of animals or plants in an area may change.

You can measure environmental change using non-living indicators. You can measure factors such as average rainfall, temperature, oxygen levels, pH and pollutant levels in water or the air, and much more. All sorts of different instruments are available to do these measurements. These range from simple rain gauges and thermometers to oxygen meters and dataloggers used in schools.

You can also use the changing distribution of living organisms as an indicator of environmental change. Living organisms are particularly good as indicators of pollution.

Lichens grow on places like rocks, roofs and the bark of trees. They are very sensitive to air pollution, particularly levels of sulfur dioxide in the atmosphere. When the air is clean, many different types of lichen grow. The more polluted the air, the fewer lichen species there will be. So a field survey on the numbers and types of lichen can be used to give an indication of air pollution. The data can be used to study local sites or to compare different areas of the country.

In the same way you can use invertebrate animals as water pollution indicators. The cleaner the water, the more species you will find. Some species of invertebrates are only found in the cleanest waters. Others can be found even in very polluted waters. Counting the different types of species gives a good indication of pollution levels, and can be used to monitor any changes.

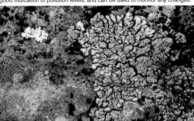

Practical

Indicators of pollution levels

Investigate both the variety of lichens in your local area and the number of invertebrate species in your local pond or stream. This will give you an idea of pollution levels in your area if you compare them to national figures.

Figure 2 Lichens grow well where the air is clean. In an area polluted with sulfur dioxide there would be fewer species. Lichens are good indicators of pollution.

Key points
- Animals and plants may be adapted to cope with specific features of their environment, e.g. thorns, poisons and warning colours.
- Environmental changes may be caused by living or non-living factors.
- Environmental changes can be measured using non-living indicators.
- Living organisms can be used as indicators of pollution.

Summary questions
1 Copy and complete these sentences using the words below:
   indicators   distribution   pollution   organisms
   Changes in the environment affect the .... of living .... This means living organisms can be used as .... of ....
2 Give three different methods you could use to collect environmental data. For each method, comment on its reliability and usefulness as a source of evidence of environmental change.

Further teaching suggestions

Further lichen surveys
- The lichen surveys could be extended by comparing a woodland with a suburban street, or a cemetery (look at the gravestones). A comparison of trees in woodland with trees in a suburban area could yield interesting results.

Discussion on how plants and animals cope with their environment
- Students should discuss how animals and plants cope with features of their environment, such as thorns, poisons and warning colours. Consider the examples in the student text and research other examples.

Internet investigation into symbiosis
- Get the students to carry out an internet investigation into organisms that have deeply involved relationships with other ones. Try using 'symbiosis' as a search term.

Investigation into the behaviour of woodlice
- Investigation of the behaviour of woodlice in choice chambers can show how organisms will move to the conditions to which they are best suited.

Summary answers

1 distribution, organisms, indicators, pollution

2 Methods along with evaluation of usefulness – should include at least one physical factor and one example of a bio indicator.
   Methods could include: measuring a non-living factor, e.g. rainfall, temperature, oxygen levels, levels of pollutants. For each method student must choose a suitable method of measuring changes in the factor they choose, e.g. rain gauge for rainfall, oxygen meter and datalogging for oxygen levels. They need to show that they realise that these measurements need to be taken over time, and using the same equipment to build up a record of data over time.
   Measuring the changing distribution of living organisms is another way. This can be done using quadrats, field surveys – again data collected over time in the same place in the same way examples could be lichens on trees, invertebrates in water. In that case students need to mention capture techniques, identification keys – again over time – measuring number of different species found and the types of different species is also indicative of the cleanliness of the water. Any other valid suggestions.

B1 4.8

The impact of change

Learning objectives

Students should learn:

- how changes in the environment can affect the distribution of living organisms.

Learning outcomes

Most students should be able to:

- explain that environmental changes can effect the distribution of living organisms
- describe some changes in both living and non-living factors that can affect distribution
- evaluate data concerned with environmental change on the distribution of living organisms.

Some students should also be able to:

- evaluate data concerned with the effect of environmental change on the behaviour of living organisms.

Specification link-up: Biology B1.4

- Changes in the environment affect the distribution of living organisms. *[B1.4.2 a)]*
- Animals and plants are subjected to environmental changes. Such changes may be caused by living or non-living factors such as a change in a competitor, or in the average temperature or rainfall. *[B1.4.2 b)]*
- Evaluate data concerned with the effect of environmental changes on the distribution and behaviour of living organisms. *[B1.4]*

Lesson structure

Starters

To bee or not to bee – Discuss with students the importance of bees both in making honey and as pollinators. Show some animation or video footage of bees pollinating flowers. Ensure that the students realise the importance of pollination. Ask them what would happen if there were no more bees? Get them to draw out a chain of consequences. Students can be supported by providing a list of consequences which they can put in the correct order. Students can be extended by considering which crops would disappear and what the alternatives might be. *(5 minutes)*

"When I were a lad..." – Ask the students to recount any stories their parents or grandparents may have told them about how things are different these days compared to the environment when they were young. Compile a collective list for the class. *(10 minutes)*

Main

- Provide exposition as to the changing environment and how it is affecting the distribution of species (the birds and the bees).
- Break the students into small groups. Give each an A3 sheet of paper with a large blank 5 × 5 squares frame in it. Ask them to devise a snakes and ladders style board game with snakes representing hazards for bees, such as diseases, chemicals and changing patterns of flowering. The ladders can be things that benefit the bees, such as disease-resistant strains, crop plants and successful swarming.
- Give the students data on the declining bee population in a table. They are to turn this into a graph, and extrapolate this to check the possible date for bee decline to be complete in the UK, i.e. no more bees by 2018.
- Changes in the concentrations of chemicals in the environment can cause changes in the populations of living organisms. The effect of changes in phosphate levels can alter the oxygen concentration in water. Set up containers of algae in water containing different levels of phosphate. Observe the effect on the growth of the algae. Monitor the oxygen levels using oxygen probes.
- Produce a poem to encourage young people to value our bee population.

Plenaries

Here today gone tomorrow – Show a photo of a mammoth tusk being brought up in fishing nets from the bottom of the North Sea. This can be linked with clips from the film *Ice Age*. Discuss how climate change is a normal part of the way the Earth works. *(5 minutes)*

What's the fuss? – Imagine you have a neighbour who doesn't care much about the environment. They are reading a newspaper headline about the decline of the bee population. They state that they 'don't see what all the fuss is about, bees are just a pest anyway'. How would you go about convincing them that they are wrong on this? Students can be supported by finding and reading out sections from the main text to get across the idea of bee preservation. Students can be extended by getting them to produce convincing and credible arguments in a friendly and persuasive manner. *(10 minutes)*

Support

- Show students pictures of dinosaurs and the type of vegetation which existed when they roamed the Earth. Ask them to suggest why there are no dinosaurs now. What has changed? Was it the climate or was it something else? Get them to express their ideas as to what does cause major changes.

Extend

- Ask 'What happened to the quagga?' An internet search will provide information about this animal, why it died out and attempts made to breed them again.

Further teaching suggestions

Linking data
- Look at some data regarding the increase in number of buzzards in the UK and link this to their making use of road kill as a change in feeding habits.

Changing patterns of migration
- Research the internet for evidence that climate change can affect the migration of birds and other animals.

ICT link-up
- Carry out computer simulations to model the effect on organisms from changes to the environment.

Compiling case histories
- Do changes in non-living and living factors in the environment affect the behaviour of living organisms? Students to research and compile case histories of such changes.

How Science Works   Adaptation for survival

B1 4.8   The impact of change

Learning objectives
- How do changes in the environment affect the distribution of living organisms?
- How reproducible are the data about the effect of environmental change on living organisms?

Figure 1 The Dartford warbler

Changing birds of Britain

Temperatures in the UK seem to be rising. Many people like the idea – summer barbeques and low heating bills. But rising temperatures will have a big impact on many living organisms. We could see changes in the distribution of many species. Food plants and animals might become more common, or die out, in different conditions.

The Dartford warbler is small brown bird that breeds mainly in southern Europe. A small population lived in Dorset and Hampshire. By 1963, two very cold winters left just 11 breeding pairs in the UK. But temperatures have increased steadily since. Dartford warblers are now found in Wales, the Midlands and East Anglia. If climate change continues, Dartford warblers could spread through most of England and Ireland. However, in Spain the numbers are dropping rapidly – 25% in the last 10 years – as it becomes too warm. Scientists can simulate the distribution of birds as the climate changes. They predict that by the end of the century Spain could lose most of its millions of Dartford warblers.

Scientists predict that by the end of this century, if climate change continues at its present rate, the range of the average bird species will move nearly 550 km north-east. About 75% of all the birds that nest in Europe are likely to have smaller ranges as a result and many species will be lost for good.

Key
- Species simulated as breeding
- Species simulated as absent

Simulated distribution in 1961–90   Potential late-21st-century distribution

Figure 2 The maps show how scientists think the distribution of these birds might change in the future

Table 1 Numbers of breeding pairs of Dartford warblers in the UK

Year	Number of breeding pairs
1961	450
1963	11
1974	560
1984	420
1994	1890
2010	3208

Activity
- Plot a bar graph to show the change in population of the Dartford warbler from 1961 to the present day. Draw an extra bar to show what you would expect the population to be in 2030 if climate change continues in the same way.
- Investigate the effect of climate change on the way birds migrate from one country to another and write a report for a wildlife programme or magazine.

Where are all the bees? 🄺

All around the world honey bees are disappearing. In the UK alone, around one in five bee hives has been lost in the last few years. In the United States, around 2 million colonies of bees were lost in 3 years. The bees had been struck down by a new, mystery disease called Colony Collapse Disorder or CCD. The bees either die, or simply fail to return to the hive. Without the mass of worker bees, those bees left in the hive quickly die.

Members of the British Beekeepers Association are alarmed. They say that if hives continue to be lost at the same rate there will be no honey bees left in Britain by 2018. You might think that having fewer bees doesn't really matter. It also means honey is more expensive to buy.

In fact, bees are vitally important in plant ecology. Honey bees pollinate flowers as they collect the nectar. Without them, flowers are not pollinated and fruit does not form. Without bees as pollinators we would have no apples, raspberries, cucumbers, strawberries, peaches … the list goes on and on. There would be cereal crops, because they are pollinated by the wind, but not much else.

No one yet fully understands what is happening to the bees and what is changing their distribution. Scientists think that viral diseases, possibly spread by a parasitic mite, are a major cause. So living factors – the agents of disease – are causing a major change in the environment of the honey bee. This in turn is affecting their distribution.

Other living and non-living factors affecting the environment have also been suggested. Flowering patterns are changing as temperatures vary with climate change. This may affect the food supply of the bees. Farmers spray chemicals that may build up in the bees. Some people have even suggested that mobile phones affect the navigation system of the bees.

Research is continuing all over the world. Disease-resistant strains of bees are being bred. Collecting the evidence to show exactly what environmental change is affecting the honey bee population is proving to be difficult. But until we can find out, the decline of the honey bee looks as if it will continue. There is a little good news – UK numbers have recovered slightly as more people have started keeping bees, probably as a result of all the publicity.

Figure 3 Honey bees are vital pollinators. Bee-pollinated fruits are worth about £50 billion of trade every year.

Activity
- List the main suggested causes for the decline of the honey bee. Use secondary sources to investigate the current state of the research findings for each cause.
- Produce a slide show to justify the investment of research funds into the loss of honey bees. Show what is happening to the bees, the main theories about what is causing the problem and how the problem is being tackled.

Summary questions
1 Using the information on this spread, what aspect of climate change seems to be linked to a change in the distribution of British birds?
2 a Why is the loss of honey bees so important?
  b Why is it important to find out whether the environmental cause of the problem is a living or non-living factor?

Key points
- Both living and non-living factors can cause changes in the environment that affect the distribution of living organisms.
- Reproducible data on the effect of environmental change are not always easy to collect or interpret.

Summary answers

1 Temperature changes.

2 a Because they act as pollinators to many different plants including many food crops, especially fruit. Also loss of honey and beeswax.

  b Because the way the problem is tackled will be very different – if it is a disease caused or carried by parasitic mites, then it becomes important to eradicate or control the mites or treat the disease. If it is a physical factor then we need to look at the environment and what, if anything, can be done to improve the situation for the bees.

Summary answers

1 a D **b** C **c** A **d** B

2 a The temperatures are too cold for reactions in the body to work and so for the organisms to survive.

b Problems: overheating in day, too cold at night and early morning to move much, water loss.
How they cope with problems: bask in the Sun in the morning to warm up, hide in burrows or shade of rocks to avoid heat of day and cold of night, reduce water loss by behaviour and don't sweat.

c Large surface area: volume ratio allows them to lose heat effectively.

3 a Lots of water loss through the leaves, not much water taken up by roots.

b Most water is lost through the leaves – less leaf surface area, less water loss.

c Spines, rolled leaves.

d Water storage in stems, roots or leaves, thick waxy cuticle, ability to withstand dehydration.

e They have several different adaptations to enable them to withstand water loss/little water available (spines, water storage in stem, etc).

4 a Makes sure there is plenty of food for the animals and their young, advertise their territory to reduce conflict with predators.

b Pandas feed almost exclusively on bamboo, so if it dies out they have no food and will die out as well. Other animals – bamboo only part of the diet so they simply eat other plants.

5 Because they are competing for exactly the same things.

6 Students use the bar charts in the practical activity on page 84 to answer these questions.

a First month: crowded seedlings taller than spread out seedlings. Crowded seedlings shade each other so each seedling grows taller to avoid the shade. Spread seedlings don't have that pressure. But over six months, the crowded seedlings do not get light as they shade each other. They photosynthesise less so they cannot grow as tall as the spread out seedlings which can make as much food as possible.

b i They relied mainly on the food stored in the seed – the crowded ones were taller but the spread ones had thicker stems and bigger leaves.

ii As before the spread out seedlings get the full effect of the light and grow as well as possible making lots of new plants (and so wet mass). The crowded plants each get less light therefore less photosynthesis and less wet mass.

c To eliminate as far as possible the effects of genetic variety in the seedlings – the bigger the sample, the more reproducable the results.

d i Any of: light level, amount of water and nutrients available, and temperature.

ii So that any differences would be the result of the crowding of the seedlings.

7 a New predator, new pathogen, introduction of different plants and more competition, the death of a competitor species from disease – any other sensible point.

b Change in temperature, change in oxygen level, change in pollution levels, addition of nitrates – any other sensible point.

Summary questions 🄚

1 Match the following words to their definitions:

a	competition	A	an animal that eats plants
b	carnivore	B	an area where an animal lives and feeds
c	herbivore	C	an animal that eats meat
d	territory	D	the way animals compete with each other for food, water, space and mates

2 Cold-blooded animals like reptiles and snakes absorb heat from their surroundings and cannot move until they are warm.

a Why do you think that there are no reptiles and snakes in the Arctic?

b What problems do you think reptiles face in desert conditions and what adaptations could they have to cope with them?

c Most desert animals are quite small. How does this help them survive in the heat?

3 a What are the main problems for plants living in a hot, dry climate?

b Why does reducing the surface area of their leaves help plants to reduce water loss?

c Describe **two** ways in which the surface area of the leaves of some desert plants is reduced.

d How else are some plants adapted to cope with hot, dry conditions?

e Why are cacti such perfect desert plants?

4 a How does marking out and defending a territory help an animal to compete successfully?

b Bamboo plants all tend to flower and die at the same time. Why is this such bad news for pandas, but doesn't affect most other animals?

5 Why is competition between animals of the same species so much more intense than the competition between different species?

6 Use the bar charts from the practical activity on B1 4.5 to answer these questions.

a Describe what happens to the height of both sets of seedlings over the first six months and explain why the changes take place.

b The total wet mass of the seedlings after one month was the same whether or not they were crowded. After six months there was a big difference.

i Why do you think both types of seedling ha[ve the] same mass after one month?

ii Explain why the seedlings that were more s[pread] out each had more wet mass after six mont[hs?]

c When scientists carry out experiments such as [the] one described, they try to use large sample si[zes.] Why?

d i Name a control variable mentioned in the p[assage]

ii Why were the other variables kept constant[?]

7 a Give **three** living factors that can change the environment and affect the distribution of living organisms.

b Give **three** non-living factors that can change t[he] environment and affect the distribution of living organisms.

8 Maize is a very important crop plant. It has many [uses:] it is made into cornflakes and it is also grown for [animal] feed. The most important part of the plant is the c[ob] which fetches the most money. In an experiment [to find] the best growing conditions, three plots of land w[ere] used. The young maize plants were grown in diffe[rent] densities in the three plots.

The results were as follows:

	Planting density (pla[nts per m²])	
	10	15
Dry mass of shoots (kg/m²)	9.7	11.6
Dry mass of cobs (kg/m²)	6.1	4.4

a What was the independent variable in this investigation?

b Draw a graph to show the effect of the planting [density] on the mass of the cobs grown.

c What is the pattern shown in your graph?

d This was a fieldwork investigation. What would[the] experimenter have taken into account when ch[oosing] the location of the three plots?

e Did the experimenter choose enough plots? Ex[plain] your answer.

f What is the relationship between the mass of c[obs] and the mass of shoots at different planting de[nsities?]

g The experimenter concluded that the best den[sity for] planting the maize is 10 plants per m². Do you [agree] with this as a conclusion? Explain your answer[?]

---

8 a The independent variable was planting density.

b Graph with correctly labelled axes and points plotted accurately. Density on the x-axis and dry mass on the y-axis.

c The pattern should show increasing density of planting reducing the dry mass of cobs.

d The three plots should have the same type of soil, the same amount of water and similar weather patterns.

e Three plots was too few to be certain of the pattern, five would have been better ideally with repeats.

f As the dry mass of cobs gets less per m², the dry mass of the shoots increases.

g It seems from this investigation to be correct, but does the pattern continue? If so, then planting fewer plants could give an even higher yield. The experimenter should investigate lower densities of planting.

AQA **Practical suggestions**

Practicals	AQA	🄚	📖	⚙
Investigations of environmental conditions and organisms in a habitat such as a pond.	✓		✓	
'Hunt the cocktail stick' using red and green cocktail sticks on a green background.	✓		✓	

Examination-style questions

The picture shows a solenodon.

Solenodons have lived on earth since the Age of the Dinosaurs. They are only found in forests in Haiti and are the only mammals which have a poisonous bite. They are rarely seen because they feed at night. They mainly eat insects and spiders.

The solenodon has adaptations which help it to survive.

Match the adaptation to the correct letter (A,B, C, D or E) for the following:
i This helps the solenodon to dig its burrow. (1)
ii This helps the solenodon to detect its food. (1)

The solenodon is at risk of dying out since new animals have been taken to the islands. Use the information and the picture to help answer the following questions.
i The solenodon is not adapted to flee from predators. Suggest why. (1)
ii If the solenodon is caught by a predator it can defend itself. Suggest how. (1)

Trees that live in the rainforests are very tall and often have broad leaves. This is a problem for young trees, which do not get much light.

Choose the correct answer to complete the sentence.
light   nutrients   space
Rainforest trees have broad leaves so they can compete for .... (1)

Choose the correct answer to complete the sentence.
larger trees   large seeds with stored food
Trees in the rainforest have adapted to lack of light near the ground by having .... (1)

3 The gemsbok is a large herbivore living in dry desert regions of South Africa. It feeds on grasses that are adapted to the dry conditions by obtaining moisture from the air as it cools at night. The table below shows the water content of these grasses and the feeding activity of the gemsbok over a 24-hour period.

Time of day	% water content of grasses	% of gemsboks feeding
03.00	18	40
06.00	23	60
09.00	25	20
12.00	08	17
15.00	06	16
18.00	05	19
21.00	07	30
24.00	14	50

a i Name the independent variable investigated. (1)
ii Is this a categoric, ordered, discrete or continuous variable? (1)
b How does the water content of the grasses change throughout the 24-hour period? (1)
c Between which recorded times are more than 30% of the gemsboks feeding? (1)
d Suggest **three** reasons why the gemsboks benefit from feeding at this time. (3)
AQA, 2008

Examination-style answers

1 a i D (1 mark)
   ii E (1 mark)

   b i any one of: poor eyesight, legs look awkward for running, no natural predators, other sensible suggestions. (1 mark)
   ii Poisonous bite, has poison, strong claws/description (1 mark)

2 a light (1 mark)

   b large seeds with stored food (1 mark)

3 a i Time of day (1 mark)
   ii Continuous (1 mark)

   b It rises during the night (some time after (1800) hours to a maximum of 25% at 0900 hours and then falls (more rapidly at first) to a minimum of 5% at 1800 hours (1 mark)
   Some accurate reference to actual figures in the table is necessary to obtain the mark.

   c Between 2400 hours and 0600 hours. (1 mark)
   The important words here are 'more than'. Candidates who ignore these words will include the figure of 30% and therefore give a response of 2100 hours to 0900 hours.

   d The water content of the grasses that it eats are high over this period.
   It is night and the gemsboks are therefore less easily seen by predators.
   It is cooler and therefore they are less likely to have to sweat and so this helps them conserve precious water.
   (1 mark for each point; 3 marks in total)

Practicals

Practicals	AQA	k	📖	⚙
Investigate the distribution of European banded snails.	✓		✓	
Investigate the behaviour of woodlice using choice chambers.	✓		✓	
Investigate the effect on plant growth of varying their environmental conditions, e.g. degrees of shade, density of sowing, supply of nutrients.	✓	✓		
Investigating particulate levels, e.g. with the use of sensors to measure environmental conditions.	✓		✓	
The use of maximum–minimum thermometers, rainfall gauges and oxygen meters.	✓		✓	
Investigating the effect of phosphate on oxygen levels in water using jars with algae, water and varying numbers of drops of phosphate, then monitor oxygen using a meter.	✓		✓	
Computer simulations to model the effect on organisms of changes to the environment.	✓		✓	

Kerboodle resources

Resources available for this chapter on Kerboodle are:
● Chapter map: Adaptation for survival
● Support: Making a living organism (B1 4.1)
● Data handling skills: Insulation (B1 4.2)
● How Science Works: Does changing the surface area to volume ratio affect water loss by evaporation? (B1 4.2)
● Bump up your grade: Survival rivals (B1 4.2)
● Practical: Density of sowing (B1 4.5)
● Practical: Measuring non-living factors in the environment (B1 4.7)
● Extension: Tied up in 'Knots' (B1 4.5)
● Extension WebQuest: Beeless Britain (B1 4.8)
● Interactive activity: Adaptation for survival
● Revision podcast: Adaptation
● Test yourself: Adaptation for survival
● On your marks: Adaptation for survival
● Examination-style questions: Adaptation for survival
● Answers to examination-style questions: Adaptation for survival

B1 5.1

Pyramids of biomass

Learning objectives

Students should learn:

- that solar radiation is the source of energy for all communities of living organisms
- that green plants and algae capture solar energy to build up energy stores in their cells
- that the biomass at each stage in a food chain is less than it was at the previous stage
- how to draw and interpret a pyramid of numbers.

Learning outcomes

Most students should be able to:

- explain where biomass comes from
- describe what a pyramid of biomass is and how it can be constructed
- interpret pyramids of biomass and construct them from appropriate information
- state that biomass is lost at each stage.

Some students should also be able to:

- explain in detail why all the biomass at one stage does not get passed on to the next stage.

Support

- Provide students with the components of a food chain written on cards, which they can put in the correct order.
- Similarly, students can build up pyramids of biomass if provided with the components.

Extend

- Ask students to consider whether or not pyramids of biomass tell the whole story. They could write a short paragraph on what the pyramid of biomass does tell us about the relationships between the organisms.

AQA Specification link-up: Biology B1.5

- Radiation from the Sun is the source of energy for most communities of living organisms. Green plants and algae absorb a small amount of the light that reaches them. The transfer from light energy to chemical energy occurs during photosynthesis. This energy is stored in the substances that make up the cells of the plants. [B1.5.1 a)]
- The mass of living material (biomass) at each stage in a food chain is less than it was at the previous stage. The biomass at each stage can be drawn to scale and shown as a pyramid of biomass. [B1.5.1 b)]
- Interpret pyramids of biomass and construct them from appropriate information. [B1.5]

Lesson structure

Starters

Food chains in the school canteen – Check out the menu for lunch and get students to discuss the food chains related to items on the menu. *(5 minutes)*

What am I? – Prepare a list of key words and phrases related to the topic, such as 'producer', 'primary consumer', 'secondary consumer, 'herbivore', 'carnivore', etc. and a list of their definitions. Students can be supported by writing up or projecting both lists on to the board and asking them to match the definitions to the key words and phrases. Students can be extended by giving them either the list of key words and asking them to write their own definitions or the definitions and getting them to supply the key word. *(10 minutes)*

Main

- Carry out the practical 'Investigation of leaf litter' (see 'Practical support'). Using a known mass or volume of leaf litter, allows students to sort through it by hand and separate out the soil organisms into containers. It is unwise to mix organisms in case they eat each other! This sorting should remove the larger organisms, but it might be necessary to use a Tullgren funnel to find the smaller invertebrates.
- The organisms should be identified as far as possible, counted and all those of one species weighed. It should be possible to classify most families of invertebrates into different feeding types (herbivore, carnivore or detritivore). It is then easy to add up the total numbers and the total masses for the different feeding types.
- A pyramid of biomass can be constructed. Students can construct these pyramids on squared paper, choosing suitable scales.
- Look at pyramids of biomass for different communities. Data can be obtained from different communities, such as a rocky shore, in woodland or open grassland.
- Investigate biomass in a pond or freshwater habitat. The method described in 'Practical support' can be modified to obtain a rough estimate of the biomass in a pond or stream. Sampling in water requires the use of a net and the technique needs to be standardised.
- In flowing water, kick sampling is carried out over a certain area (0.5 m²) and the disturbed organisms are allowed to flow into a net. The net can be emptied into sampling trays and the organisms identified, grouped and their wet mass determined.
- In still water, a sweeping technique is used. The net is swept through the water for a fixed period of time or over a fixed distance. The organisms caught are then tipped into a sampling tray and identified as before.
- Follow local guidelines on 'outside activities'.

Plenaries

Anagrams with a difference – Prepare anagrams of the key words. To support students leave in the vowels: students can be extended by leaving out the vowels. Write up or project the anagrams onto the board and ask the students to work out what they are. *(5 minutes)*

Numbers or biomass? – Students could compare a pyramid of numbers with a pyramid of biomass. They could discuss one that they have produced from their own investigations. Ask: 'Which shows the information more accurately? Are there advantages in using numbers?' *(10 minutes)*

Practical support

Investigation of leaf litter

Equipment and materials required
Quadrats, sweep nets, pooters, sorting trays and small beakers, identification keys, Tullgren funnel, balance for weighing organisms.

Details
The method is essentially the same for the different habitats and the results can be expressed as biomass per m².

Select an area and place a 1 m² or 0.5 m² square quadrat carefully onto the ground.

Collect the leaf litter within the quadrat or cut the plants at the base and place in a white tray.

Search carefully and remove all the animals present. Smaller animals can be removed using a pooter, larger ones with forceps.

Animals should be placed in suitable containers, such as plastic beakers.

Weigh the plant material.

Identify and sort the animals into groups.

Weigh the groups of animals separately.

Return the animals to their habitat.

Construct a pyramid of biomass.

Safety: Cover any open wounds on hands and wash hands after the investigation. Follow LA (Local Authorities) advice on outdoor activities.

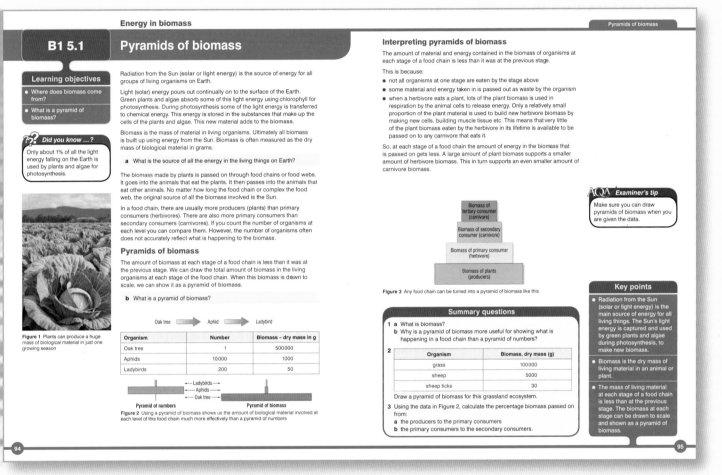

Energy in biomass

B1 5.1 — Pyramids of biomass

Learning objectives
- Where does biomass come from?
- What is a pyramid of biomass?

?? Did you know …?
Only about 1% of all the light energy falling on the Earth is used by plants and algae for photosynthesis.

Radiation from the Sun (solar or light energy) is the source of energy for all groups of living organisms on Earth.

Light (solar) energy pours out continually on to the surface of the Earth. Green plants and algae absorb some of this light energy using chlorophyll for photosynthesis. During photosynthesis some of the light energy is transferred to chemical energy. This energy is stored in the substances that make up the cells of the plants and algae. This new material adds to the biomass.

Biomass is the mass of material in living organisms. Ultimately all biomass is built up using energy from the Sun. Biomass is often measured as the dry mass of biological material in grams.

a What is the source of all the energy in the living things on Earth?

The biomass made by plants is passed on through food chains or food webs. It goes into the animals that eat the plants. It then passes into the animals that eat other animals. No matter how long the food chain or complex the food web, the original source of all the biomass involved is the Sun.

In a food chain, there are usually more producers (plants) than primary consumers (herbivores). There are also more primary consumers than secondary consumers (carnivores). If you count the number of organisms at each level you can compare them. However, the number of organisms often does not accurately reflect what is happening to the biomass.

Pyramids of biomass
The amount of biomass at each stage of a food chain is less than it was at the previous stage. We can draw the total amount of biomass in the living organisms at each stage of the food chain. When this biomass is drawn to scale, we can show it as a pyramid of biomass.

b What is a pyramid of biomass?

Figure 1 Plants can produce a huge mass of biological material in just one growing season

Oak tree → Aphid → Ladybird

Organism	Number	Biomass – dry mass in g
Oak tree	1	500000
Aphids	10000	1000
Ladybirds	200	50

Pyramid of numbers — Ladybirds / Aphids / Oak tree

Pyramid of biomass

Figure 2 Using a pyramid of biomass shows us the amount of biological material involved at each level of this food chain much more effectively than a pyramid of numbers

Interpreting pyramids of biomass
The amount of material and energy contained in the biomass of organisms at each stage of a food chain is less than it was at the previous stage.

This is because:
- not all organisms at one stage are eaten by the stage above
- some material and energy taken in is passed out as waste by the organism
- when a herbivore eats a plant, lots of the plant biomass is used in respiration by the animal cells to release energy. Only a relatively small proportion of the plant material is used to build new herbivore biomass by making new cells, building muscle tissue etc. This means that very little of the plant biomass eaten by the herbivore in its lifetime is available to be passed on to any carnivore that eats it.

So, at each stage of a food chain the amount of energy in the biomass that is passed on gets less. A large amount of plant biomass supports a smaller amount of herbivore biomass. This in turn supports an even smaller amount of carnivore biomass.

AQA Examiner's tip
Make sure you can draw pyramids of biomass when you are given the data.

Biomass of tertiary consumer (carnivore)

Biomass of secondary consumer (carnivore)

Biomass of primary consumer (herbivore)

Biomass of plants (producers)

Figure 3 Any food chain can be turned into a pyramid of biomass like this

Key points
- Radiation from the Sun (solar or light energy) is the main source of energy for all living things. The Sun's light energy is captured and used by green plants and algae during photosynthesis, to make new biomass.
- Biomass is the dry mass of living material in an animal or plant.
- The mass of living material at each stage of a food chain is less than at the previous stage. The biomass at each stage can be drawn to scale and shown as a pyramid of biomass.

Summary questions
1 **a** What is biomass?
   b Why is a pyramid of biomass more useful for showing what is happening in a food chain than a pyramid of numbers?

2

Organism	Biomass, dry mass (g)
grass	100000
sheep	5000
sheep ticks	30

Draw a pyramid of biomass for this grassland ecosystem.

3 Using the data in Figure 2, calculate the percentage biomass passed on from:
   a the producers to the primary consumers
   b the primary consumers to the secondary consumers.

Further teaching suggestions

Comparing leaf litter
- Leaf litter from two different areas could be compared.

Comparing pyramids
- Pyramids of biomass from the same area at different times of the year could be considered. For example, in the English Channel in January the biomass of animal plankton is greater than the biomass of the plant plankton (the producers). Discuss why pyramids could vary at different times of the year.

Answers to in-text questions
a The Sun.

b The biomass of organisms at each level of a food chain drawn as a pyramid.

Summary answers
1 **a** The mass of material in an animal or plant.
   b Because it shows the amount of biological material at each level more accurately.

2 Check students' answers for accuracy of pyramids.

3 **a** 5000/100 000 × 100 = 5%
   b 30/5000 × 100 = 0.6%

B1 5.2

Energy transfers

Learning objectives

Students should learn:

- that materials and energy are lost in an organism's waste materials
- that energy is used in movement
- that energy is transferred heating the surroundings.

Learning outcomes

Most students should be able to:

- state why biomass and energy are reduced at each successive stage of a food chain
- explain why energy is transferred in movement and heating the surroundings.

Some students should also be able to:

- explain in detail why energy transfers by heating are particularly large in warm-blooded organisms (mammals and birds).

Answers to in-text questions

a Because animals cannot digest everything they eat.

b The muscles use energy to contract, and the more an animal moves about the more energy (and biomass) it uses from its food. As the muscles contract they produce heat.

Support

- Supply the students with cards on which the components of a simple food chain and the processes which result in energy losses are written. Get the students to arrange these cards in the correct order so the energy losses at each level are clear.

Extend

- Ask students to look up specific heat capacity. Ask: 'How much more energy would a 10 kg animal have at 37 °C as opposed to 20 °C?' Assume flesh to have approximately the same specific heat capacity as water.

AQA

Specification link-up: Biology B1.5

- The amounts of material and energy contained in the biomass of organisms is reduced at each successive stage in a food chain because:
  - some materials and energy are always lost in the organisms' waste materials
  - respiration supplies all the energy needs for living processes, including movement. Much of this energy is eventually transferred to the surroundings. [B1.5.1 c)]

  Controlled Assessment: SA4.3 Collect primary and secondary data. [SA4.3.2 a) b) d)]

Lesson structure

Starters

Burning cowpats! – Show the students a picture of a pile of dried cowpats (try searching the internet for dung as fuel). Ask them what they think the picture shows. Draw out from them that there is energy in dung – energy that is lost and is not passed on to the next consumer – and that this is used in many countries as fuel. If time, discuss other uses for dung: elephant dung has been made into paper, dung used to generate ethanol and biogas. You could also mention that many insects and fungi can live on dung, making use of the food wastes of the consumer. *(5 minutes)*

Pass the energy – In groups, start off with a large sheet of paper labelled 'Energy'. Give the paper to a student who is designated to play the role of the Sun. The paper is passed to another student representing the Earth, some being torn off for reflection. The paper is then passed along a 'food chain' with a bit torn off at each level. Students can be supported by being given cues as to which order the stages in the food chain should come. Students can be extended by explaining the reasons in detail for energy being eventually lost to the surroundings at each level. *(10 minutes)*

Main

- Organise a 'great burger race'. This is a large scale outside practical activity for a sunny day. The idea is to show energy loss through trophic levels. Arrange a course with five posts in a line about 10 m apart: 1 At the first post have a picture of the Sun, two buckets with holes in and two large barrels (fruit barrels or similar) full of water; 2 At the second post have a large picture of the Earth and two similar buckets with holes in them; 3 At the third post have a large picture of a wheat plant and two more buckets with holes in; 4 At the fourth post, have on one side a large picture of a burger, on the other side a picture of a cow. On the side with the burger, have a collecting vessel large enough to contain several buckets of water. On the side with the cow have another bucket with holes in; 5 At the fifth post have a picture of a burger and a collecting vessel on the cow side (nothing on the other side).

- Water represents the energy and it is lost through the holes in the buckets at each stage. Stress the conservation of energy – just because the water is lost through the holes it has not disappeared. Pairs of students start the race, collecting water from the 'sun barrels' and passing it to the buckets of the next pair of students at the first post and so on up the course. The cow side has one more trophic level, so the student on that side should have less water in their bucket as measured with a dipstick when the time is up.

  Because this is hard to set up, it may be a good idea to video it for future reference!

- Investigate the energy released by respiration (see 'Practical support'). Set up the demonstration of energy production by germinating peas. Record the temperatures and plot a graph of temperature against time.

- Alternatively, the students, in groups, could set up their own experiments. They could plan the investigation, as suggested in the Student Book, making sure they understand the need for controls and explaining the reasons for the treatment of the peas. The 'How Science Works' skill of selecting measuring equipment appropriate for the task, and the concept of the resolution of a measuring instrument, can be reinforced here.

- Discuss the results of this experiment in terms of cellular respiration. Ask: 'Why include the dead peas? Why is so much respiration taking place in the peas?'

Plenaries

Fish v. fowl – Give the students a simple food chain involving a fish and another one involving a chicken [both just containing the producer, one primary consumer and one secondary consumer (humans)]. Ask them to compare the energy losses between the levels and suggest reasons for the differences. Differentiation by outcome. Support students by prompting, extend students by asking them to give appropriate details in their answers. *(5 minutes)*

Jumbled answers – Give the students Question 1 of the 'Summary questions' with the answers in the wrong places. Have a competition to see who can get the answers in the correct order the fastest. *(10 minutes)*

Practical support

Investigating the energy released by respiration

Equipment and materials required
Two vacuum flasks, thermometers or probes for data loggers, one batch of live germinating peas and one batch of boiled, dead peas that have been cooled, cotton wool. Both batches of peas should be rinsed in disinfectant to kill microorganisms.

Details
Into one flask, place some live germinating seeds and a thermometer. Close the mouth of the flask with cotton wool.

Into the second flask, place the same quantity of germinating peas that have been boiled to kill them and cooled.

Insert a thermometer and close the mouth of the flask with cotton wool.

Keep both flasks in similar conditions and monitor the temperature in both flasks at regular intervals.

Instead of thermometers, data loggers could be used to monitor the temperatures.

Energy in biomass

B1 5.2   Energy transfers

Learning objectives
- What happens to the material and energy in the biomass of organisms at each stage of a food chain?
- How is some energy transferred to the environment?

AQA Examiner's tip

Make sure you can explain the different ways in which energy is lost between the stages of a food chain.

The amounts of biomass and energy contained in living things get less as you progress up a food chain. Only a small amount of the biomass taken in gets turned into new animal material. What happens to the rest?

Figure 1 The amount of biomass in a lion is a lot less than the amount of biomass in the grass that feeds the zebra it preys on. But where does all the biomass go?

Energy loss in waste

The biomass that an animal eats is a source of energy, but not all of the energy can be used. Firstly, herbivores cannot digest all of the plant material they eat. The material they can't digest is passed out of the body in faeces.

The meat that carnivores eat is easier to digest than plants. This means that carnivores need to eat less often and produce less waste. But like herbivores, most carnivores cannot digest all of their prey, such as hooves, claws, bones and teeth. Therefore some of the biomass that they eat is lost in their faeces.

When an animal eats more protein than it needs, the excess is broken down. It gets passed out as urea in the urine. This is another way biomass – and energy – are transferred from the body to the surroundings.

Figure 2 Animals such as horses produce very large quantities of dung made up of all the biomass they can't digest

a Why is biomass lost in faeces?

Energy loss due to movement

Part of the biomass eaten by an animal is used for respiration in its cells. This supplies all the energy needs for the living processes taking place within the body, including movement.

Movement uses a great deal of energy. The muscles use energy to contract and also get hot. So the more an animal moves about the more energy (and biomass) it uses from its food.

Figure 3 These sea anemones don't move much so they don't need to eat much

b Why do animals that move around a lot use up more of the biomass they eat than animals that don't move much?

Keeping a constant body temperature

Much of the energy animals release from their food in cellular respiration is eventually transferred heating their surroundings. Some of this heat is produced by the muscles as the animals move.

Energy transfers to the surroundings are particularly large in mammals and birds. That is because they use energy to keep their bodies at a constant temperature. They use energy all the time, to keep warm when it's cold or to cool down when it's hot. So mammals and birds need to eat far more food than animals such as fish and amphibians to get the same increase in biomass.

Practical

Investigating the energy released by respiration

Even plants transfer energy by heating their surroundings in cellular respiration. You can investigate this using germinating peas in a vacuum flask.

- What would be the best way to monitor the temperature continuously?
- Plan the investigation.

Figure 4 Only between 2% and 10% of the biomass eaten by an animal such as this horse will get turned into new horse. The rest of the stored energy will be used for movement or transferred, heating the surroundings, or lost in waste materials.

Summary questions

1 Copy and complete using the words below:

biomass temperature energy chain growth movement producers respiration waste

The amounts of .... and .... contained in living things always get less at each stage of a food .... from .... onwards. Biomass is lost as .... products and used to release energy in .... This is used for .... and to control body .... Only a small amount is used for ....

2 Explain why so much of the energy from the Sun that lands on the surface of the Earth is not turned into biomass in animals.

Key points

- The amounts of biomass and energy get less at each successive stage in a food chain.

- This is because some material and energy are always lost in waste materials, and some are used for respiration to supply energy for living processes, including movement. Much of the energy is eventually transferred by heating to the surroundings.

Summary answers

1 biomass/energy, energy/biomass, chain, producers, waste, respiration, movement, temperature, growth

2 Most of the Sun's energy is not captured by plants. Plant biomass eaten by animals cannot all be digested. Some is broken down and used in respiration to release energy. Most energy is used for movement and control of body temperature. A small amount is used for growth to produce new biomass in animals.

B1 5.3

Decay processes

Learning objectives

Students should learn:

- that materials decay because they are broken down by microorganisms
- that the decay process releases substances which plants need to grow
- that the materials are constantly cycled.

Learning outcomes

Most students should be able to:

- explain the role of microorganisms in the process of decay
- explain why decay is important in the cycling of materials.

Some students should also be able to:

- explain the factors which affect the rate of decay.

Specification link-up: Biology B1.6

- Living things remove materials from the environment for growth and other processes. These materials are returned to the environment either in waste materials or when living things die and decay. *[B1.6.1 a)]*
- Materials decay because they are broken down (digested) by microorganisms. Microorganisms digest materials faster in warm, moist, aerobic conditions. *[B1.6.1 b)]*
- The decay process releases substances that plants need to grow. *[B1.6.1 c)]*
- In a stable community, the processes that remove materials are balanced by processes that return materials. The materials are constantly cycled. *[B1.6.1 d)]*

Controlled Assessment: SA4.1 Planning an investigation. *[SA4.1.1 a) b)]*, *[SA4.1.2 c)]*

Lesson structure

Starters

The magic pin mould – Show the students a piece of ordinary bread and a piece which you have left exposed to the air, and then cover with a clear plastic lunch box or Petri dish for a couple of days (it should either have a fluffy white growth on it or a mucky brown one depending on what spores are around.) The mould can then be seen via a stereomicroscope or digital microscope through the plastic. Do not open the box or dish. Show a picture of pin mould or *Rhizopus* – preferably much larger than life – with sporangia full of spores (use a search engine to find images on the internet). Ask the students to make the link and explain how the bread became mouldy. *(5 minutes)*

Rotless world – Get the students to imagine what would happen if decay didn't occur. What would the short term and long term consequences be? Differentiation is by outcome: students can be supported by verbal prompting, you can extend students by suggesting they explore a range of scenarios. Ask students to write down their ideas and then discuss. *(10 minutes)*

Main

- **Investigate decay.** Students could design and plan an investigation into the effect of temperature on the rate of decay. This can be done with cubes of bread exposed to the air and then placed in Petri dishes at different temperatures, such as in the refrigerator, classroom, etc. All other conditions, such as moisture levels, need to be kept the same. Observations will need to be made over a period of time, or allow a set time for the investigation, e.g. a week.

- This investigation introduces concepts of 'How Science Works' planning skills, involving the manipulation of variables. Predictions can also be made, measurements taken and conclusions drawn. The results can be assessed in a variety of ways: use digital cameras to record the appearance, assess the area of decay, etc. A time-lapse camera could be used.

- As an extension, the effect of different moisture levels could be investigated, but the temperature should be kept constant. Organise a potato decay competition using fresh potatoes. Students to decide on the conditions and set up an experiment to investigate the rate of decay of potatoes. The rate of decay over two weeks is judged.

Support

- Ask students to make a poster explaining how to make compost. They could be provided with pictures of vegetables, grass clippings and suitable words, etc., which can be pasted on to a sheet of A3.

Extend

- Students could find out about the human remains that have been found preserved in peat bogs. They could research: 'What are the conditions needed for peat formation? How can peat be used to provide us with information about what plants there were around thousands of years ago?'

Plenaries

Quickest rotter game – Provide the students with a piece of paper with six empty boxes connected in a line. Arrange pairs of boxes with 'warmth', 'air' and 'moisture' written above them. In pairs, students roll the dice: 1 and 2 lets them write in the letters 'R' and 'O' in the first two boxes; 3 and 4 lets them write in 'T' and 'T' into the middle two boxes and 5 and 6 lets them write 'E' and 'N' into the last boxes. Students race to see who gets rotten first. *(5 minutes)*

Stop the rot! – How do we stop things from decaying? Students can be supported by showing them vacuum-wrapped food, plastic wrapping from a pack of fruit, pasteurised milk, frozen food wrapper, tin of tomatoes, a jar of pickled onions, smoked fish, jam, etc. and asking them to say how decay has been prevented. Students can be extended by writing down five ways in which perishable foods can be treated to prevent decay. In each case, they need to explain why the treatment prevents the decay. Choose some to read out and compile a list on the board. *(10 minutes)*

Practical support

 ## Investigating decay
Equipment and materials required

Cubes of bread or other suitable material, Petri dishes with lids or small glass containers with lids, thermometers to register temperatures in the different locations, access to refrigerator, incubator (do not exceed 25 °C), etc. to provide different temperatures. Fix lids with tape but do not seal.

Details

The cubes of bread should be all the same size, exposed to the air but not allowed to dry out, placed in Petri dishes and the lids secured with tape. The temperatures at which the dishes are kept should be recorded. Leave the dishes for a week and then observe. The results could be recorded photographically.

Safety: The lids should not be opened and the contents disposed of safely.

Energy in biomass

Decay processes

B1 5.3   Decay processes

Learning objectives
- Why do things decay?
- Why are decay processes so important?
- How are materials cycled in a stable community?

AQA *Examiner's tip*

You need to know the type of organisms that cause decay, the conditions needed for decay and the importance of decay in recycling nutrients.

Figure 1 This tomato is slowly being broken down by the action of decomposers. You can see the fungi clearly but the bacteria are too small to be seen.

?? Did you know …?

The 'Body Farm' is a US research site where scientists have buried human bodies in many different conditions. They are studying every stage of human decay to help police forces all over the world work out when someone died and if they were murdered.

Plants take nutrients from the soil all the time. These nutrients are passed on into animals through food chains and food webs. If this was a one-way process the resources of the Earth would have been exhausted long ago.

Fortunately all these materials are recycled. Many trees shed their leaves each year, and most animals produce droppings at least once a day. Animals and plants eventually die as well. A group of organisms known as the **decomposers** then break down the waste and the dead animals and plants. In this process decomposers return the nutrients and other materials to the environment. The same material is recycled over and over again. This often leads to very stable communities of organisms.

a   Which group of organisms take materials out of the soil?

The decay process

Decomposers are a group of microorganisms that include bacteria and fungi. They feed on waste droppings and dead organisms.

Detritus feeders, such as maggots and some types of worms, often start the process of decay. They eat dead animals and produce waste material. The bacteria and fungi then digest everything – dead animals, plants and detritus feeders plus their waste. They use some of the nutrients to grow and reproduce. They also release waste products.

The waste products of decomposers are carbon dioxide, water, and nutrients that plants can use. When we say that things decay, they are actually being broken down and digested by microorganisms.

The recycling of materials through the process of decay makes sure that the soil contains the mineral ions that plants need to grow. The decomposers also 'clean up' the environment, removing the bodies of all the dead organisms.

b   What type of organisms are decomposers?

Conditions for decay

The speed at which things decay depends partly on the temperature. Chemical reactions in microorganisms, like those in most living things, work faster in **warm conditions**. They slow down and might even stop if conditions are too cold. Decay also stops if it gets too hot. The enzymes in the decomposers change shape and stop working.

Most microorganisms also grow better in **moist conditions**. The moisture makes it easier for them to dissolve their food and also prevents them from drying out. So the decay of dead plants and animals – as well as leaves and dung – takes place far more rapidly in warm, moist conditions than it does in cold, dry ones.

Although some microbes survive without oxygen, most decomposers respire like any other organism. This means they need oxygen to release energy, grow and reproduce. This is why decay takes place more rapidly when there is **plenty of oxygen** available.

c   Why are water, warmth and oxygen needed for the process of decay?

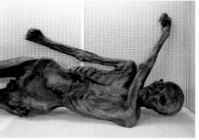

Figure 2 The decomposers cannot function at low temperatures so if an organism – such as this 4000-year-old man – is frozen as it dies, it will be preserved with very little decay

The importance of decay in recycling

Decomposers are vital for recycling resources in the natural world. What's more, we can take advantage of the process of decay to help us recycle our waste.

In sewage treatment plants we use microorganisms to break down the bodily waste we produce. This makes it safe to release into rivers or the sea. These sewage works have been designed to provide the bacteria and other microorganisms with the conditions they need. That includes a good supply of oxygen.

Another place where the decomposers are useful is in the garden. Many gardeners have a **compost heap**. Grass cuttings, vegetable peelings and weeds are put onto the compost heap. It is then left to allow decomposing microorganisms break all the plant material down. It forms a brown, crumbly substance known as compost which can be used as a fertiliser.

Practical

Investigating decay

Plan an investigation into the effect of temperature on how quickly things decay.
- Write a question that can be used as the title of this investigation.
- Identify the independent variable in the investigation.

Key points
- Living things remove materials from the environment as they grow. They return them when they die through the action of the decomposers.
- Materials decay because they are broken down (digested) by microorganisms. Microorganisms digest materials faster in warm, moist conditions. Many of them also need oxygen.
- The decay process releases substances that plants need to grow.
- In a stable community the processes that remove materials (particularly plant growth) are balanced by the processes that return materials.

Summary questions

1 Copy and complete using the words below:

bacteria carbon dead decomposers digest microorganisms nutrients waste water

.... are a group of .... that includes fungi and .... They feed on .... droppings and .... organisms. They .... them and use some of the .... They also release waste products which include .... dioxide and ...., which plants can use.

2 Explain why the processes of decay are so important in keeping the soil fertile.

98   99

Further teaching suggestions

Treatment of sewage
- Show a (simplified) diagram of a sewage treatment or photograph of the treatment of sewage (search for images using an internet search engine). The emphasis here is to be on the microorganisms involved in the breakdown of the waste. Students need to make notes or complete worksheets outlining the main points.

Visit a sewage treatment works
- If possible, arrange a visit to a treatment works.

A longer-term leaf experiment
- If leaf discs or leaf litter are put into nylon bags with different mesh sizes and then buried in soil, the contribution made by detritivores and decomposers can be assessed. If the mesh is small, then the detritivores will be unable to gain entry and the breakdown will be brought about by the decomposers. Mesh diameter of 6 mm allows the entry of earthworms, other detritivores and decomposers. Mesh sizes of about 0.5 mm will allow entry of other detritivores, but not earthworms. A mesh diameter of 0.003 mm will only allow decomposers through. The bags should contain a known mass of leaf material and be weighed every month. (This relates to 'How Science Works' – making measurements.)

Answers to in-text questions

a   Plants.

b   Bacteria, fungi, (maggots, worms).

c   Water is needed to prevent the microorganisms from drying out/to help them absorb their soluble food; warmth is needed for the enzymes to work efficiently; oxygen is needed for (aerobic) respiration.

Summary answers

1 decomposers, microorganisms, bacteria, waste, dead, digest, nutrients, carbon, water

2 Plants constantly take materials from the soil. These then pass into the animals which eat the plants. Animals produce droppings and animals and plants all die. The materials from the soil are held within those bodies. The decay process releases the minerals and nutrients back into the soil so they can be taken up again by plants.

B1 5.4

The carbon cycle

Learning objectives

Students should learn:

- that carbon dioxide is removed from the atmosphere by photosynthesis in green plants and used to make carbohydrates, fats and proteins
- that carbon dioxide is returned to the atmosphere when green plants, animals and decomposers respire
- that detritus feeders and microorganisms break down the waste products and dead bodies of organisms, returning materials to the ecosystem.

Learning outcomes

Most students should be able to:

- describe the processes in the carbon cycle
- explain the importance of the activities of the detritus feeders and microorganisms in the cycling of nutrients.

Some students should also be able to:

- explain in detail the changes that occur in the carbon cycle.

Support

- Ask students to write the word 'carbon' using a pencil. Then they can write it using a burned stick, a piece of burnt animal (a bone or a piece of burned beef jerky), a piece of coal and a charcoal briquette. These can be made into a poster for display along with a balloon of exhaled air.

Extend

- Students could speculate on whether there may be life on other planets that is not carbon-based. Ask: 'Do other elements have properties similar to carbon? What might non-carbon based life be like?'

$\mathcal{AQA}$ Specification link-up: Biology B1.6

- The constant cycling of carbon is called the carbon cycle. In the carbon cycle:
  - carbon dioxide is removed from the environment by green plants and algae for photosynthesis
  - the carbon from the carbon dioxide is used to make carbohydrates, fats and proteins, which make up the body of plants and algae
  - when green plants and algae respire, some of this carbon becomes carbon dioxide and is released into the atmosphere
  - when green plants and algae are eaten by animals and these animals are eaten by other animals, some of the carbon becomes part of the fats and proteins that make up their bodies
  - when animals respire some of this carbon becomes carbon dioxide and is released into the atmosphere
  - when plants, algae and animals die, some animals and microorganisms feed on their bodies
  - carbon is released into the atmosphere as carbon dioxide when these organisms respire
  - by the time the microorganisms and detritus feeders have broken down the waste products and dead bodies of organisms in ecosystems and cycled the materials as plant nutrients, all the energy originally absorbed by green plants and algae has been transferred
  - combustion of wood and fossil fuels releases carbon dioxide into the atmosphere. [B1.6.2 a)]

Lesson structure

Starters

Fossils in coal – Have some plant fossils in coal (real ones if possible but pictures if not). Ask students to write down how the carbon got there and what would happen to it if we burned the coal. *(5 minutes)*

Eggy tale – Show the students an egg. Ask them whether as it develops it gets heavier or lighter? Draw out both responses and encourage debate as to reasons for these beliefs. Clarify by showing diagrams of oxygen going into the egg and carbon dioxide coming out. Students could be supported by getting them to follow this up by measuring the weight of eggs as they develop in an incubator. Students can be extended by asking them to draw up a balanced equation, giving them the formula for glucose ($C_6H_{12}O_6$). *(10 minutes)*

Main

- If available, show students an animation of the carbon cycle. It is a good idea to provide the students with a worksheet and allow time for the explanation of points.
- Play a role-play game 'Pass the carbon'. In small groups, students to be labelled as parts of the carbon cycle, such as 'The atmosphere', 'Plants', 'Animals', 'Fossil fuels', etc. Have a soft ball labelled 'Carbon', which students are to pass around going from locations to other locations via the correct processes.
- Create a cartoon carbon cycle. Students to draw, or use, pictures to make a cartoon strip illustrating how a carbon atom goes from a lion's breath, into plants, into an impala, into a lion and out again through the lion's breath. This could be done in groups and the best displayed.

Plenaries

The carbon cycle – Label a diagram of the carbon cycle. *(5 minutes)*

Best of order, please! – Prepare sets of cards with stages of the carbon cycle on them. Also give the students sheets of paper with which to make connecting arrows. In pairs, students have to put them into a sensible arrangement, take a digital photograph of them as a record and then compare with another pair of students and feedback. Students can be supported by being given one-to-one assistance and labelled arrows. Students can be extended by asking them to annotate their arrows with details of the processes. *(10 minutes)*

Further teaching suggestions

Compost heap
- If the school has a compost heap, set up a data logger to take the temperature over a period of time. If there is no compost heap, students could investigate the possibility of setting one up in a suitable position. Investigate what types of material can be composted. Why is it best to use vegetable matter only? What kinds of organisms would you expect to find in a well-established compost heap? Why does the temperature change within the compost heap?

Measuring carbon dioxide
- Use a sensor to measure carbon dioxide levels.

Energy in decomposers
- Set fire to some dried mushrooms to show that there is energy in decomposers (risk assessment).

Carbon emissions
- There has been much discussion within the European Union and globally about the levels of carbon released into the atmosphere. Make a collection of newspaper and magazine articles about this topic. Find out how carbon emissions are controlled and what the targets are amongst the industrialised nations.

B1 5.4

The carbon cycle

Learning objectives
- What is the carbon cycle in nature?
- Which processes remove carbon dioxide from the atmosphere, and which processes return it?

Figure 1 Within the natural cycle of life and death in the living world, mineral nutrients are cycled between living organisms and the physical environment

?? Did you know …?
Every year about 166 gigatonnes of carbon are cycled through the living world. That's 166 000 000 000 tonnes – an awful lot of carbon!

Imagine a stable community of plants and animals. The processes that remove materials from the environment are balanced by processes that return materials. Materials are constantly cycled through the environment. One of the most important of these is carbon.

All of the main **molecules** that make up our bodies (carbohydrates, proteins, fats and DNA) are based on carbon atoms combined with other **elements**.

The amount of carbon on the Earth is fixed. Some of the carbon is 'locked up' in **fossil fuels** like coal, oil and gas. It is only released when we burn them.

Huge amounts of carbon are combined with other elements in carbonate rocks like limestone and chalk. There is a pool of carbon in the form of carbon dioxide in the air. It is also found dissolved in the water of rivers, lakes and oceans. All the time a relatively small amount of available carbon is cycled between living things and the environment. We call this the **carbon cycle**.

a What are the main sources of carbon on Earth?

Photosynthesis

Green plants and algae remove carbon dioxide from the atmosphere for photosynthesis. They use the carbon from carbon dioxide to make carbohydrates, proteins and fats. These make up biomass of the plants and algae. The carbon is passed on to animals that eat the plants. The carbon goes on to become part of the carbohydrates, proteins and fats in these animal bodies.

This is how carbon is taken out of the environment. But how is it returned?

b What effect does photosynthesis have on the distribution of carbon levels in the environment?

Respiration

Living organisms respire all the time. They use oxygen to break down glucose, providing energy for their cells. Carbon dioxide is produced as a waste product. This is how carbon is returned to the atmosphere.

When plants, algae and animals die their bodies are broken down by decomposers. These are animals and microorganisms such as blowflies, moulds and bacteria that feed on the dead bodies. The animals which feed on dead bodies and waste are called *detritus feeders*. They include animals such as worms, centipedes and many insects.

Carbon is released into the atmosphere as carbon dioxide when these organisms respire. All of the carbon (in the form of carbon dioxide) released by the various living organisms is then available again. It is ready to be taken up by plants and algae in photosynthesis.

Combustion

Fossil fuels contain carbon, which was locked away by photosynthesising organisms millions of years ago. When we burn fossil fuels, carbon dioxide is produced, so we release some of that carbon back into the atmosphere:

Photosynthesis: carbon dioxide + water (+ light energy) → glucose + oxygen

Respiration: glucose + oxygen → carbon dioxide + water (+ energy)

Combustion: fossil fuel or wood + oxygen → carbon dioxide + water (+ energy)

The constant cycling of carbon is summarised in Figure 2.

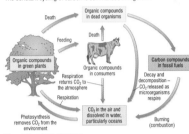

Figure 2 The carbon cycle in nature

Energy transfers

When plants and algae photosynthesise, they transfer light energy into chemical energy can be the food that they make. This chemical energy is transferred from one organism to another through the carbon cycle. Some of the energy can be used for movement or transferred as energy to the organisms and its surroundings at each stage. The decomposers break down all the waste and dead organisms and cycle the materials as plant nutrients. By this time all of the energy originally absorbed by green plants and algae during photosynthesis has been transferred elsewhere.

For millions of years the carbon cycle has regulated itself. However, as we burn more fossil fuels we are pouring increasing amounts of carbon dioxide into the atmosphere. Scientists fear that the carbon cycle may not cope. If the levels of carbon dioxide in our atmosphere increase it may lead to global warming.

AQA Examiner's tip
Make sure you can label the processes in a diagram of the carbon cycle.

Figure 3 Fossil fuels such as coal contain large amounts of carbon

Key points
- The constant cycling of carbon in nature is known as the carbon cycle.
- Carbon dioxide is removed from the atmosphere by photosynthesis. It is returned to the atmosphere through respiration and combustion.

Summary questions
1 a What is the carbon cycle?
  b What are the main processes involved in the carbon cycle?
  c Why is the carbon cycle so important for life on Earth?

2 a Where does the carbon come from that is used in photosynthesis?
  b Explain carefully how carbon is transferred through an ecosystem.

Answers to in-text questions

a Fossil fuels, carbonate rocks, the atmosphere, oceans and living things.

b It removes it from the atmosphere.

Summary answers

1 a The cycling of carbon between living organisms and the environment.

  b Photosynthesis, respiration and combustion.

  c Because it prevents all the carbon from getting used up; returns carbon dioxide to the atmosphere to be available for photosynthesis again.

2 a Carbon dioxide in the air.

  b Students can produce a written description of the carbon cycle or a diagram (See Figure 2, The carbon cycle in nature) to summarise the stages (must cover all points in the carbon cycle).

B1 5.5

Recycling organic waste

AQA

Specification link-up: Biology B1.6

- Evaluate the necessity and effectiveness of schemes for recycling organic kitchen or garden waste. [B1.6]

  Controlled Assessment: SA4.1 Planning an investigation [SA4.1.2 c)]; SA4.5 Analyse and interpret primary and secondary data. [SA4.5.4 a)]

Learning objectives

Students should learn:

- why we should recycle organic waste
- the most effective ways to recycle organic waste.

Learning outcomes

Most students should be able to:

- give reasons for the recycling of organic kitchen or garden waste
- describe ways in which organic waste is recycled
- evaluate the effectiveness of recycling schemes.

Some students should also be able to:

- explain the benefits of reducing the amount of waste that is put into landfill sites.

Answers to in-text questions

a Potato peelings, vegetable peelings, apple core, grass cuttings – any sensible suggestions that demonstrate an understanding of what goes into compost.

b Methane.

Support

- Ensure students understand that the household waste we produce consists of organic and non-organic materials. Help them make this distinction by providing them with a variety of materials that they can sort into containers labelled 'biodegradable' and 'non-biodegradable'.

Extend

- Ask students to research the nutrient contents of various types of waste and match this to the nutritional requirements of different types of plants.

Lesson structure

Starters

The core of the problem – Show the students a lunch box containing an apple core, an empty crisp packet, a half-eaten sandwich in its wrapper and an empty drinks can. Ask the students what would happen if the contents of the lunchbox were thrown out of the window. Ask what will happen to the apple core and the packaging? What would happen to the half-eaten sandwich and the can? Draw out the concept of biodegradability; get the students to use this word, to write it down and to give examples of biodegradable and non-biodegradable substances. *(5 minutes)*

Bin sort – Get litter-pickers, a plastic sheet, some large containers and some gloves. With the class, go out and find litter bins around school or bring in the contents of a bin. Empty the contents on to the sheet and using the litter-pickers and gloves sort the waste into recyclable, non-recyclable and compostable. Record results. Students can be supported by providing a writing frame. Students can be extended by getting them to weigh each portion, calculate the total, calculate percentages and draw up a pie chart. *(10 minutes)*

Main

- Investigate the factors that affect how quickly organic materials decay. This investigation could take two to three weeks. Each student, or group of students, will need a plant pot containing damp soil, a sealable plastic bag and a selection of objects, such as a leaf, a piece of fruit, an eggshell, some cardboard and a small piece of twig. (This links to 'How Science Works' – planning investigations.)

- When setting up the experiment, the students could discuss the nature of the objects and make predictions about what will happen and why. Ask, 'Why is it important not to let the soil dry out? Why use soil?' Students should also consider how the results are to be assessed. Is it possible to make measurements? How science works concepts can be introduced here. Ensure a range of factors are investigated across the whole class and draw together each set of results to draw a class conclusion about the ideal conditions for composting. Discuss the limitations of the conclusions you can draw.

- Alternatively, students can set up a practical activity on composting and investigate the rate at which grass clippings decompose under different conditions, including the use of a composting agent.

- Split the class into pairs. Each member of each pair is to prepare a short cloze passage for the other to complete. Put on the board a set of possible words which could be used in these. When they have both completed writing theirs, swap over and fill them in. Small prizes for the best sets of cloze questions.

Plenaries

Recycling building blocks – One team is to make a fish or other simple animal shape from construction toy bricks. Get a team of volunteers to dismantle it and use the parts to make it into another organism. Explain the link between this and recycling materials in nature. *(5 minutes)*

Compost corner – Design a label to go on a compost bin to be placed in the school food technology rooms. Students could be supported by providing a writing frame for the label. Or getting them to draw pictures of the items that should be placed in the bin. Students could be extended by getting them to include advice on composting materials and reasons why it is important. *(10 minutes)*

Practical support

Investigating the decay of organic matter
Equipment and materials required

Plant pots containing damp soil, plastic bags large enough to contain the plant pots, rubber bands, leaves, eggshells, twigs, small pieces of fruit, cardboard, labels and marker pens.

Details

Students should place selected objects on the surface of the damp soil, enclose the plant pot with the plastic bag and secure the top with a rubber band. The pots can be left in different conditions of light and temperature, labelled with the date and conditions and observations made at intervals.

How Science Works Energy in biomass Recycling organic waste

B1 5.5   Recycling organic waste ⓚ

Learning objectives

- Why should we recycle organic kitchen and garden waste?
- How can we investigate the most effective way to recycle this organic waste?

The problem of waste

People produce lots of waste – and getting rid of it is a big problem. Whenever we prepare food we produce organic waste to throw away, such as vegetable peelings. Gardening produces lots of organic waste too, including the grass cuttings when we mow the lawn. We put about 100 million tonnes of waste a year into landfill sites and about two thirds of that is organic matter. By recycling our organic waste we can reduce this mountain of waste material.

Figure 1 Some landfill sites now collect the methane that is produced as organic material decays and use it to generate electricity. But if everyone recycled their own organic waste, we would need far fewer landfill sites and there would be no problem.

Did you know …?

One tonne of organic kitchen and garden waste produces 200 to 400m³ of gas. Around 27% of the methane produced in the UK each year comes from landfill sites.

The kitchen and garden waste we put into landfill sites doesn't rot easily in the conditions there. It forms a smelly liquid which soaks into the ground and can pollute local rivers and streams. In these conditions the microorganisms that break down the plant and animal material produce mainly methane gas. This is a greenhouse gas that adds to the problem of global warming.

a   Give two examples of the organic waste you might put into a compost bin.

The simplest way to recycle kitchen and garden waste is to make compost. Natural decomposing organisms break down all the plant material to make a brown, crumbly substance. This compost is full of the nutrients that have been released by the decomposers. The process takes from a few months to over a year. The compost forms a really good, natural fertiliser. It also greatly reduces the amount of rubbish you need to send to the landfill site.

b   Which greenhouse gas, other than carbon dioxide, is given off as organic material decays in landfill sites?

Making compost

Composting can be done on a small scale or on a large scale. There are several different factors which are important in making successful compost:

- Compost can be made with or without oxygen – mixing your compost regularly helps air get in. If the microorganisms have oxygen they generate energy, which kills off weed seeds and speeds up the process. Without oxygen the process releases little energy and is slower.
- The warmer the compost mixture, the faster the compost will be made (up to about 70°C, at which point the microorganisms stop working properly).
- The decay process is faster in moist conditions than in dry ones. (In fact, decay does not take place at all in perfectly dry conditions.)

Activity

Plan an assembly to be used with students in Years 7–9 suggesting that the school introduces a scheme to recycle all the organic waste from the kitchens and the school grounds to make compost. The compost could then be sold to the local community for charity. Remember, you need to explain why and how this should be done as well as recruit volunteers to help run the compost bins.

Practical

Investigating the decay of organic matter

We have seen that the presence of oxygen and moisture, as well as the temperature, affect the rate of decay. Choose one of these factors to investigate. Carry out any tests on the sort of materials that might go into a garden compost bin.

- Plan to find out what effect your chosen factor has on the rate at which the material decays.
- Pool the conclusions of each group to decide on the ideal conditions for composting organic waste.
- Comment on the limitations of the conclusions you can draw.

A Compost heap: The simplest and cheapest method. Kitchen and garden waste is put in a pile, with new material added to the top, and left to rot down.

B Compost bin: Bins are often made of plastic and may be sold cheaply by local councils to encourage people to recycle their organic waste. Instructions include watering the bin in dry weather and mixing the contents from time to time.

C Council composting: Local councils may collect garden or kitchen waste and use large-scale bins to recycle the material to make compost. They may shred the material before adding it to the bins to increase the surface area. You can buy the compost from the schemes to put on your garden.

D Black bag composting: A black plastic bag is filled with kitchen and garden waste and sealed. The microorganisms work slowly as they have little or no oxygen, but in about a year the contents will have decomposed and formed compost.

Figure 2 Different methods of composting

Summary questions

1 Why is it important to recycle organic kitchen and garden waste?

2 Evaluate each of the four methods of making compost shown in Figure 2, giving advantages and disadvantages of each.

3 How does mixing the compost regularly, adding a variety of different types of organic waste and watering in dry weather improve the composting process?

Key points

- Recycling organic kitchen and garden waste is necessary to reduce landfill, reduce the production of methane and to recycle the minerals and nutrients in the organic material.
- Composting organic waste can be done in a variety of different ways.

Further teaching suggestions

Compost heap

- If the school has a compost heap, set up a data logger to take the temperature over a period of time. If there is no compost heap, students could investigate the possibility of setting one up in a suitable position. Investigate what types of material can be composted. Why is it best to use vegetable matter only? What kinds of organisms would you expect to find in a well-established compost heap? Why does the temperature change within the compost?

Set up a wormery

- A wormery is a fun, easy and efficient way of converting organic kitchen or garden waste into compost.

Summary answers

1 It is important to recycle organic material to prevent it going into landfill sites, to reduce levels of methane.

2 **Compost heap:** Advantages are it is simple, cheap, and anyone can do it.
Disadvantages are it can be smelly, it can be slow and inefficient at decomposing, it can get big, and can attract vermin.

Compost bin: Advantages are it is neat, tidy, efficient, not expensive, and reduces risk of vermin.
Disadvantages are that it needs water in hot dry weather and may need forking over. Probably need two compost bins working together.

Council composting: Advantages are economy of scale, any smell and inconvenience out of your garden, can be used to make money for local council.

Disadvantages are it may be limited to how much will be collected, and you don't have your own compost to use.

Black bag composting: Advantages are it is neat, there is no smell, and it is easy to use.
Disadvantages are it is slow, limited quantity.

3 Mixing compost adds oxygen – aerobic digestion is faster, so compost is made quicker and hotter (so kills more weed seeds). Variety of material makes compost better – more varied nutrients. Adding water in dry weather – microbes that bring about decay work better in a damp environment, so adding water allows them to work as fast as possible.

Summary answers

1 a i 10% **ii** 8% **iii** 12.5%

b The mass of the producers has to support the whole pyramid, relatively little energy is transferred from producers to primary consumers (difficult to digest).

c Relatively little energy is passed up the chain, so not enough to support many carnivores.

d Less energy passed on as warm blooded animals use energy to generate warmth. This is transferred to the environment and so that energy is no longer available to pass on up the chain.

2 The amount of biomass transferred along food chain gets less. Biomass is needed for energy. So by eating plants, the maximum amount of biomass is passed on to people. Eating meat – plant biomass transferred to animals, animal biomass to people – biomass lost at both stages. Draw pyramid of biomass to show plant/person and plant/cow or sheep/person.

3 a Graph plotting, correct scale, labelled axes, axes correct way round, accurate points.

b Chickens use little energy maintaining their body temperature, so have more energy for growth.

c To reduce movement. So reduce energy used in movement, so more energy for growth.

d So they grow fast to a weight when they can be eaten and another set of chickens started up – economic reasons.

4 a Low temperatures prevent growth of decay – causing microorganisms.

b Cooking destroys the microorganisms, denatures enzymes so no decay.

c Most decomposers need oxygen to respire – no air, no oxygen, so microbes cannot grow.

d Heat kills microorganisms, no oxygen so no decay.

5 a Photosynthesis.

b Respiration, burning (decay and decomposition).

c Oceans, air (carbonate rocks).

d CO_2 is important for photosynthesis and keeping surface of Earth warm. Excess CO_2 surface gets warmer; affects sea levels, living organisms. Less CO_2 means surface cools, affects life.

6 a Higher-temperature means faster reactions. Warm compost means microorganisms digest, grow and reproduce faster. More decomposers = faster decomposition.

b Makes sure all the decomposing microorganisms have enough oxygen to respire as fast as possible.

Kerboodle resources

Resources available for this chapter on Kerboodle are:
- Chapter map: Energy in biomass
- Practical: Composting (B1 5.2)
- Simulation: Microorganisms and decay (B1 5.3)
- How Science Works: What can speed up the decay of bread? (B1 5.3)
- Bump up your grade: What a load of rubbish! (B1 5.5)
- Interactive activity: Exploring energy in biomass
- Revision podcast: Energy flows
- Test yourself: Energy in biomass
- On your marks: Energy in biomass
- Examination-style questions: Energy in biomass
- Answers to examination-style questions: Energy in biomass

Summary questions

1

a From this diagram, calculate the percentage biomass passed on:
  i from producers to primary consumers
  ii from primary to secondary consumers
  iii from secondary consumers to top carnivores.

b In any food chain or food web the biomass of the producers is much larger than that of any other level of the pyramid. Why is this?

c In any food chain or food web there are only small numbers of top carnivores. Use your calculations to help you explain why.

d All of the animals in the pyramid of biomass shown here are cold blooded. What difference would it have made to the average percentage of biomass passed on between the levels if mammals and birds had been involved? Explain the difference.

2 The world population is increasing and there are food shortages in many parts of the world. Explain, using pyramids of biomass to help you, why it would make a better use of resources if people everywhere ate much less meat and more plant material.

3 Chickens for us to eat are often farmed intensively to provide meat as cheaply as possible. The birds arrive in the broiler house as 1-day-old chicks. They are slaughtered at 42 days of age when they weigh about 2 kg. The temperature, amount of food and water and light levels are carefully controlled. About 20 000 chickens are reared together in one house. The table below shows their weight gain.

Age (days)	1	7	14	21	28	35	42
Mass (g)	36	141	404	795	1180	1657	1998

a Plot a graph to show the growth rate of one of these chickens.

b Explain why the temperature is so carefully controlled in the broiler house.

c Explain why so many birds are reared together in a relatively small area.

d Why are birds for eating reared like this?

4 Microorganisms decompose organic waste and d bodies. We preserve food to stop this decompos taking place. Use your knowledge of decomposit explain how each method stops the food going b

a Food may be frozen.

b Food may be cooked – cooked food keeps lon than fresh food.

c Food may be stored in a vacuum pack – with a sucked out.

d Food may be tinned – it is heated and sealed ir airtight container.

5

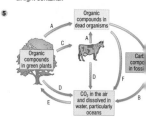

a How is carbon dioxide removed from the atmos in the carbon cycle?

b How does carbon dioxide get into the atmosph

c Where is most of the carbon stored?

d Why is the carbon cycle so important and what happen if the balance of the reactions was distu

6 a The temperature in the middle of a compost he be quite warm. Heat is produced as microbes r How does this help the compost to be broken d more quickly?

b In sewage works oxygen is bubbled through the containing sewage and microorganisms. How c this help make sure the human waste is broken completely?

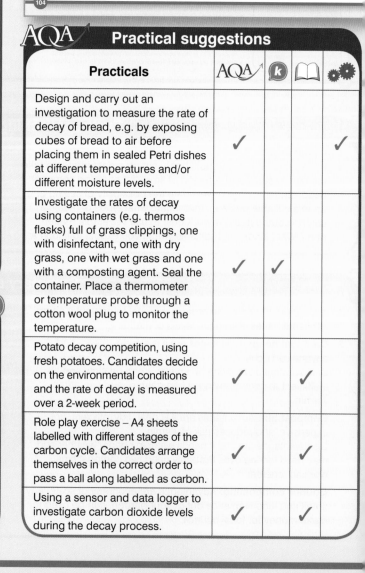

AQA **Practical suggestions**

Practicals	AQA	(k)	📖	⚙️
Design and carry out an investigation to measure the rate of decay of bread, e.g. by exposing cubes of bread to air before placing them in sealed Petri dishes at different temperatures and/or different moisture levels.	✓			✓
Investigate the rates of decay using containers (e.g. thermos flasks) full of grass clippings, one with disinfectant, one with dry grass, one with wet grass and one with a composting agent. Seal the container. Place a thermometer or temperature probe through a cotton wool plug to monitor the temperature.	✓	✓		
Potato decay competition, using fresh potatoes. Candidates decide on the environmental conditions and the rate of decay is measured over a 2-week period.	✓		✓	
Role play exercise – A4 sheets labelled with different stages of the carbon cycle. Candidates arrange themselves in the correct order to pass a ball along labelled as carbon.	✓		✓	
Using a sensor and data logger to investigate carbon dioxide levels during the decay process.	✓		✓	

Examination-style questions

...its eat very large amounts of grass. A single hawk
...a few rabbits.

...aw a pyramid of biomass for the rabbits, grass and
...e hawk. (2)

...uch of the energy from the grass is not transferred to
...e hawk.

...ggest **two** reasons why. (2)

...ose words from below to complete each sentence.

on dioxide   cool   dry   insects   microorganisms
t   nitrogen   oxygen   rats   warm

...ant waste in a compost heap is decayed by .... (1)

...e plant waste decays faster in conditions which are
.... and .... (2)

...e plant waste will also decay faster when the air
...ntains plenty of .... (1)

...diagram shows what happens to the energy in the
...a calf eats.

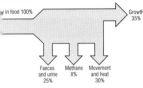

...e calculations show clearly how you work out your
...ver.

...lculate the percentage of energy lost in
...ethane (X). (2)

...e energy in the food the calf eats in one day is
... megajoules.
...alculate the amount of this energy that would be lost
... faeces and urine. (2)

...ame the process which transfers the energy from the
...od into movement. (1)

...e farmer decides to move his calf indoors so that it
...ll grow quicker.
...ggest **two** reasons why. (2)

4 In this question you will be assessed on using good
English, organising information clearly and using
specialist terms where appropriate.

The constant cycling of carbon in nature is called 'The
carbon cycle'.

Each autumn, trees lose their leaves.

Describe how the carbon in the leaves is recycled so that
the trees can use it again. (6)

5 The diagram shows a pyramid of biomass drawn to
scale.

> Trout
> Frogs
> Insects
> Water plants

a What is the source of energy for the water plants? (1)

b The ratio of the biomass of water plants to the biomass
of insects is 5 : 1.
Calculate the ratio of the biomass of insects to the
biomass of frogs.
Show clearly how you work out your answer. (2)

c Give **two** reasons why the biomass of the frog
population is smaller than the biomass of the insect
population. (2)

d Some insects die.
Describe how the carbon in the dead insect bodies
may be recycled. (4)

AQA, 2006

Examination-style answers

1 a Pyramid drawn with three layers
widest to narrowest either way up but correctly labelled
(2 marks)

b Any **two** from:
- not all the grass eaten is used to make rabbit grow/
waste in urea faeces/roots not eaten
- energy is lost due to movement by rabbits/rabbits run
around
- energy used to keep rabbits warm
- hawks do not eat the whole rabbit *(2 marks)*

2 a microorganisms *(1 mark)*

b moist and warm (either order) *(2 marks)*

c oxygen *(1 mark)*

3 a 10 (%) = 2 marks. If wrong answer allow 25+35+30 for
1 mark. *(2 marks)*

b 2.5 = 2 marks, if incorrect answer allow 1 mark for correct
working. *(2 marks)*

c respiration *(1 mark)*

d It reduces the calf's movement because it won't walk
about, therefore it will use that energy for growth. It also
reduces the energy the calf will need to use to keep warm
and that energy can be used for growth.
reduces movement/walking about
reduces energy/transferred by heating/keeps (calf)warm
(2 marks)

4 There is a clear and detailed description of the sequence of
events in the carbon cycle. The answer is coherent and in a
logical sequence. It contains a range of appropriate or relevant
specialist terms used accurately. The answer shows very few
errors in spelling, punctuation and grammar. *(5–6 marks)*

There is some description of the sequence of events in the
carbon cycle but there is a lack of clarity and detail. The
answer has some structure and the use of specialist terms
has been attempted, but not always accurately. There may be
some errors in spelling, punctuation and grammar.
(3–4 marks)

There is a brief description of the carbon cycle, which has
little clarity and detail. The answer is poorly constructed with
an absence of specialist terms or their use demonstrates
a lack of understanding of their meaning. The spelling,
punctuation and grammar are weak. *(1–2 marks)*

No relevant content. *(0 marks)*

Examples of biology points made in the response:
- microorganisms – only allow once if no mention of
bacteria or fungi
- bacteria
- fungi
- digest/break down organic matter/leaves/decompose/
reference decomposers/decay/rot
- respiration
- combustion
- release of carbon dioxide
- into the air
- CO_2 can be used (by trees) in photosynthesis
- Reference to faster in warmer weather/slower during the
winter/cold weather.

5 a the sun/light/sunshine/solar
allow radiation from the sun
ignore photosynthesis/respiration
apply list principle
*do **not** allow water/minerals/heat* *(1 mark)*

b 2.5 (:1)
correct answer with or without working
ignore rounding with correct working
*do **not** allow other equivalent ratios for both marks*
*evidence of selection of 10(insects) **and** 4(frogs) **or** 50*
***and** 20 **or** 1 **and** 0.4 for **1** mark*

*if no other working allow **1** mark for (1):0.4 on answer line*
(2 marks)

c Any **two** from:
*allow for insects **or** frogs*
allow energy for biomass
- some parts indigestible/faeces
- waste/examples of waste eg urea/nitrogenous
compounds/urine/excretion
- movement/eg of movement
allow keeping warm
- heat
- not all eaten/eg of not all eaten
- respiration
do not accept energy for respiration *(2 marks)*

d Any **four** from:
- (bodies) consumed by animals/named/scavengers/
detritus feeders
- microorganisms/bacteria/fungi/decomposers
- reference to enzymes
- decay/breakdown/decompose/rot
ignore digest(ion)
- respiration
- carbon dioxide produced
- photosynthesis
- sugar/glucose produced
accept other organic molecules
- fossilisation/fossil fuels/named
- combustion/burning
must be linked with fossilisation/fossil fuels
- (burning) produces carbon dioxide
allow carbon dioxide produced once only *(4 marks)*

B1 6.1

Inheritance

Learning objectives

Students should learn:

- that genetic information is passed from parent to offspring in the gametes from which the offspring develop
- that the genetic information is located on the chromosomes in the nucleus of a cell.

Learning outcomes

Most students should be able to:

- state that genetic information is present in the gametes from each parent
- describe the relationship between chromosomes and genes
- identify where the chromosomes are located in the cells
- state that each gene affects a different characteristic.

Some students should also be able to:

- recognise that genes are found in pairs on paired chromosomes.

Answers to in-text questions

a Because you have inherited genetic information from them, which determines what you will look like.

b In the nucleus of your cells.

c On your chromosomes in the nucleus of your cell.

Support

- Provide students with pictures of stages in mitosis which they can be asked to place in order.

Extend

- Ask students to find out how many pairs of chromosomes there are in a list of common plants and animals (cat, dog, mouse, chicken, fruit fly, garden pea, bean, etc.).

AQA Specification link-up: Biology B1.7

- The information that results in plants and animals having similar characteristics to their parents is carried by genes, which are passed on in the sex cells (gametes) from which the offspring develop. [B1.7.1 a)]
- The nucleus of a cell contains chromosomes. Chromosomes carry genes that control the characteristics of the body. [B1.7.1 b)]
- Different genes control the development of different characteristics of an organism. [B1.7.1 c)]

Lesson structure

Starters

Where are my genes? – Remind students of the structure of cells by projecting, or drawing, a generalised cell and getting them to name the parts: cytoplasm, cell membrane, and nucleus. Project an image of a sperm and an egg cell and ask students where they think the genetic material is. Search the internet for and show a picture of a 'Drosophila' chromosome. (5 minutes)

Offspring naming race – Show the students a list or a series of pictures of ten types of animal and ask them to name their offspring. Students can be supported by providing them with a list of the names of the offspring from which to choose. Students can be extended by including some difficult ones in the list. In a discussion at the end, show photographs and talk over why they resemble each other to establish current knowledge. (10 minutes)

Main

- Following on from the 'Where are my genes?' starter, show the students a series of pictures or a video clip of cells undergoing mitotic cell division. Ask: 'What are the rods that can be seen? What would we see if we could look closer?'
- This leads into a discussion of how the genetic material is organised and how it is being shared out equally between the daughter cells. Show a picture of a 'giant' plastic chromosome from a Drosophila salivary gland and then build up a picture of a chromosome, so that the relationship between chromosomes and genes is clear.
- Show the students a photograph of a human karyotype (the human chromosome complement), emphasising that there are 23 pairs of chromosomes. One of each pair comes from the father and the other from the mother. If the karyotypes are large enough, photocopy examples and get the students to work in groups and do a cut and stick pairing exercise. In order to help students, some of the more difficult ones could be done for them and they finish it off with a small number of obviously different chromosomes.
- It would be interesting to give the students a mixture of male and female karyotypes and see if they can discover which they have been given, by identifying the 'odd' male chromosome. In a karyotype of a Down's syndrome person, it should be possible to identify trisomy 22 when compared with the karyotype of a normal person. There are other examples of differences in number and structure of the chromosomes causing abnormalities (search the internet for examples) and it could be pointed out to the students that these conditions can be detected in a karyotype. Search the internet for pictures of different karyotypes.
- Show pictures of horse chestnut trees with red and white flowers. Hand round some conkers and ask the students what will decide whether the conkers will produce plants with red flowers or white flowers. Discuss the concept of a gene for flower colour. For a long-term investigation, students could plant the conkers and label them for future groups to find the answer. A time capsule description of the experiment (the best selected by the class) should be placed in a plastic bag, put inside a cigar tube and glued shut. Instructions could be written on a laminated tag and attached to the trees. (Before considering whether or not to do this exercise, think about whether you want the students to carry out one of the cloning exercises, which also involves growing plants – you may run out of pots or growing space!)

Plenaries

Clues for key words – Give the students the key words: 'cell, nucleus, chromosome, gene'. Ask students to identify and then place them in order of size. Students can be supported by giving them the key words on cards and asked to place them in order of size. Students can be extended by writing cryptic clues for the words. These can be used later to compile a crossword. *(5 minutes)*

Karyotypes – If the human karyotype exercise was used above, discuss the value of such karyotypes. Ask: 'Who would use them? What conditions could they show?' This could lead into a discussion about the value of amniocentesis and other diagnostic tests for the inheritance of chromosome abnormalities. *(10 minutes)*

Variation, reproduction and new technology

B1 6.1 Inheritance

Learning objectives
- How do parents pass on genetic information to their offspring?
- In which part of a cell is the genetic information found?

Young animals and plants resemble their parents. Horses have foals and people have babies. Chestnut trees produce conkers that grow into little chestnut trees. Many of the smallest organisms that live in the world around us are actually identical to their parents. So what makes us the way we are?

Figure 1 This mother cat and her kittens are not identical, but they are obviously related

AQA Examiner's tip
Make sure you know the difference between chromosomes, genes and DNA.

Why do we resemble our parents?

Most families have characteristics that we can see clearly from generation to generation. People like to comment when one member of a family looks very much like another. Characteristics like nose shape, eye colour and dimples are inherited. They are passed on to you from your parents.

Your resemblance to your parents is the result of information carried by genes. These are passed on to you in the sex cells (gametes) from which you developed. This genetic information determines what you will be like.

a Why do you look like your parents?

Chromosomes and genes

The genetic information is carried in the nucleus of your cells. It is passed from generation to generation during reproduction. The nucleus contains all the plans for making and organising a new cell. What's more, the nucleus contains the plans for a whole new you!

b In which part of a cell is the genetic information found?

Inside the nucleus of all your cells there are thread-like structures called **chromosomes**. The chromosomes are made up of a special chemical called **DNA** (deoxyribonucleic acid). This is where the genetic information is actually stored.

DNA is a long molecule made up of two strands that are twisted together to make a spiral. This is known as a double helix – imagine a ladder that has been twisted round.

Figure 2 The nucleus of each of your cells contains your chromosomes. The chromosomes carry the genes, which control the characteristics of your whole body.

Each different type of organism has a different number of chromosomes in their body cells. Humans have 46 chromosomes while turkeys have 82. You inherit half your chromosomes from your mother and half from your father, so chromosomes come in pairs. You have 23 pairs of chromosomes in all your normal body cells.

Each of your chromosomes contains thousands of genes joined together. These are the units of inheritance.

Each gene is a small section of the long DNA molecule. Genes control what an organism is like. They determine its size, its shape and its colour. Genes work at the level of the molecules in your body to control the development of all the different characteristics you can see. They do this by controlling all the different enzymes and other proteins made in your body.

Your chromosomes are organised so that both of the chromosomes in a pair carry genes controlling the same things. This means your genes also come in pairs – one from your father and one from your mother.

c Where would you find your genes?

Some of your characteristics are decided by a single pair of genes. For example, there is one pair of genes which decides whether or not you will have dimples when you smile. However, most of your characteristics are the result of several different genes working together. For example, your hair and eye colour are both the result of several different genes.

Did you know that scientists are still not sure exactly how many genes we have? At the moment they think it is between 20 000 to 25 000.

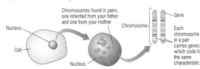

Figure 3 The nucleus of your cell contains the chromosomes that carry the genes which control the characteristics of your whole body

Summary questions

1 Copy and complete using the words below:
chromosomes genes genetic gametes nucleus
Offspring look like their parents because of .... information passed on to them in the .... (sex cells) from which they developed. The information is contained in the ...., which are found in the .... of the cell. The information is carried by the ....

2 a What is the basic unit of inheritance?
b Offspring inherit information from their parents, but do not look exactly like them. Why not?

3 a Why do chromosomes come in pairs?
b Why do genes come in pairs?
c How many genes do scientists think humans have?

Key points
- Parents pass on genetic information to their offspring in the sex cells (gametes).
- The genetic information is found in the nucleus of your cells. The nucleus contains chromosomes, and chromosomes carry the genes that control the characteristics of your body.
- Different genes control the development of different characteristics.

Further teaching suggestions

Your own inherited characteristics
- An interesting homework exercise would be to ask students to research their own families for inherited characteristics. There are some obvious ones, such as tongue rolling, straight thumbs *v.* bendy thumbs, dimples *v.* no dimples, ear lobes *v.* no ear lobes. They might be able to produce a family tree or pedigree. This exercise could produce material for discussion in preparation for the next spread.

'Window on Life'
- Show the visual summary *Window on Life (Sunday Times CD)*.

Mendel
- Either tell the story of Mendel and his peas or get students to research the topic for themselves.

Did you know ...?

We do know that we share more than 95% of our DNA with chimpanzees, so we obviously have some genes in common with them!

Summary answers

1 genetic, gametes, chromosomes, nucleus, genes

2 a The gene.
   b Offspring inherit information from both parents and so end up with a combination of characteristics, some from father and some from mother.

3 a You inherit one set from each parent.
   b Genes are carried on the chromosomes, so because chromosomes come in pairs, so do the genes – one from each parent.
   c 20 000–25 000.

B1 6.2

Types of reproduction

Specification link-up: Biology B1.7

- There are two forms of reproduction:
  - Sexual reproduction – the joining (fusion) of male and female gametes. The mixture of the genetic information from two parents leads to variety in the offspring
  - Asexual reproduction – no fusion of gametes and only one individual is needed as the parent. There is no mixing of genetic information and so no variation in the offspring. These genetically identical individuals are known as clones. [B1.7.2 a)]

Learning objectives

Students should learn:

- the differences between sexual and asexual reproduction
- that the offspring produced by asexual reproduction are genetically identical to their parents and show no variation
- why the offspring produced by sexual reproduction differ slightly from each other and from their parents.

Learning outcomes

Most students should be able to:

- state the meaning of the term 'clone'
- describe why asexual reproduction produces identical offspring
- describe how variety is achieved in individuals produced by sexual reproduction.

Some students should also be able to:

- explain the genetic differences between sexually and asexually produced offspring.

Answers to in-text questions

a Offspring only have one parent; there is no joining or fusion of sex cells from two parents; so identical genetic information is passed on.

b There is genetic information from both parents, so there is a mixture of characteristics from both.

c There is a great advantage in making sure that the species survives. The more variety there is in a group of individuals, the more likely it is that at least a few of them will have the ability to survive difficult conditions.

Support

- Supply students with pictures to represent the different possibilities in the inheritance of dimples presentation.

Extend

- Ask students to research and explain the types of nuclear division involved in both types of reproduction.

Lesson structure

Starters

Recognising variation – Write up on the board the list of human characteristics controlled by a single pair of genes. Ask students to look at each other and decide which version of each characteristic they have. Add up the numbers for each one. Ask the students if there appears to be a pattern. Is one of the pair of characteristics more common than the other? *(5 minutes)*

Fruit or vegetable? – Have a range of fruit and vegetables available, to include onions, potatoes, yams, root ginger, peas in a pod, runner beans, and tomatoes. Students can be supported by asking them which are fruits and which are vegetables and then discussing with them the differences between a fruit and a vegetable. Students can be extended by getting them to say whether they are produced as the result of sexual or asexual reproduction. For the examples that are produced by asexual reproduction, students should name the organs involved. *(10 minutes)*

Main

- Create an OHP presentation of variety in sexual reproduction. Use the example in the Student Book for the inheritance of dimples. Explain again that this characteristic is controlled by a single pair of genes and that one gene for the characteristic is inherited from each parent. One form of the gene enables the formation of dimples and the other form of the gene does not. If a person has dimples, then they have inherited the 'dimples' form of the gene, but if they do not have dimples then they have not inherited this form of the gene. In order for a person to have dimples, they only have to inherit the 'dimples' form of the gene from one parent. Ask the students: Is it possible for two parents without dimples to produce a child with dimples? Can two parents with dimples have a child without dimples? What happens if one parent has dimples and the other does not?

- Provide worksheets for the students and explain about the relationship between chromosomes and genes. Remind them that dimples dominate over no dimples. After showing the different possibilities and asking the questions, get them to decide whether or not the offspring will have dimples. They have to justify their answers. After they have had time to decide and write their answers, discuss in class, or proceed to the next activity to back up the theoretical predictions.

- Set up a practical to demonstrate how sexual reproduction produces variety (see 'Practical support').

Plenaries

Why do some plants do both? – This is a brainstorming session on why a number of plants have both strategies. Ask: 'Has it got something to do with the differences between plants and animals?' *(5 minutes)*

What are the advantages and disadvantages of asexual v. sexual reproduction? – This question produces a quick balance sheet of ideas with suggestions from the students. Students can be supported by providing them with statements about each type of reproduction and getting them to decide which are advantages and which are disadvantages. Students can be extended by making their own lists and building up a balance sheet of ideas. *(10 minutes)*

Practical support

Investigation into how sexual reproduction produces variety

Equipment and materials required

For this experiment, you will need two sets (about 50 in each set) of different-coloured beads for each group of students. If beads are difficult, it is possible to use haricot beans dyed different colours. Each group of students will need two beakers into which 50 beads can be mixed.

Details

It is suggested that one set of coloured beads represents the 'dimples' form of the gene and the other set represents the 'non-dimples' form of the gene. The idea is to get the students to appreciate how the variations arise, so set them the task of investigating the different possibilities.

Tell the students to set up the possibilities using sets of beads to represent the parental genes: all one colour for the 'dimples' form, all the second colour for the 'non-dimples' form and a mixture of half of each colour for a parent with both forms of the gene. They can set up the situations described above and work out what happens if beans are chosen randomly from the beakers. With closed eyes, the students should take one bead from each beaker and record what colours they have selected. Beads should continue to be chosen and recorded until all the beads in the beakers have been used up. Simple arithmetic will show what the ratios/numbers of the offspring having a particular characteristic are.

Variation, reproduction and new technology

Types of reproduction

B1 6.2 Types of reproduction

Learning objectives

- What is a clone?
- Why does asexual reproduction result in offspring that are identical to their parents?
- How does sexual reproduction produce variety?

Reproduction is very important to living things. It is during reproduction that genetic information is passed on from parents to their offspring. There are two very different ways of reproducing – **asexual reproduction** and **sexual reproduction**.

Asexual reproduction

Asexual reproduction only involves one parent. There is no joining of special sex cells and there is no variety in the offspring.

Asexual reproduction gives rise to identical offspring known as **clones**. Their genetic material is identical both to the parent and to each other.

a Why is there no variety in offspring from asexual reproduction?

Asexual reproduction is very common in the smallest animals and plants and in bacteria. However, many bigger plants like daffodils, strawberries and brambles do it too. The cells of your body reproduce asexually all the time. They divide into two identical cells for growth and to replace worn-out tissues.

Figure 1 A mass of daffodils like this can contain hundreds of identical flowers. This is because they come from bulbs that reproduce asexually. They also reproduce sexually using their flowers.

Sexual reproduction

Sexual reproduction involves a male sex cell and a female sex cell from two parents. These two special sex cells (gametes) join together to form a new individual.

The offspring that result from sexual reproduction inherit genetic information from both parents. This means you will have some characteristics from both of your parents, but won't be exactly like either of them. This introduces variety. The offspring of sexual reproduction show much more variation than the offspring from asexual reproduction. In plants the gametes involved in sexual reproduction are found within ovules and pollen. In animals they are called ova (eggs) and sperm.

Sexual reproduction is risky because it relies on the sex cells from two individuals meeting but it also introduces variety. That's why we find sexual reproduction in organisms ranging from bacteria to people.

b How does sexual reproduction cause variety in the offspring?

AQA Examiner's tip

- asexual reproduction – one parent → clones
- sexual reproduction – two parents → variety

Variation

Why is sexual reproduction so important? The variety it produces is a great advantage in making sure a species survives. Variety makes it more likely that at least a few of the offspring will have the ability to survive difficult conditions.

If you take a closer look at how sexual reproduction works, you can see how variation appears in the offspring.

Different genes control the development of different characteristics about you. Most things about you, such as your hair and eye colour, are controlled by several different pairs of genes. A few of your characteristics are controlled by one single pair of genes. For example, there are genes that decide whether:

- your earlobes are attached closely to the side of your head or hang freely
- your thumb is straight or curved
- you have dimples when you smile
- you have hair on the second segment of your ring finger.

We can use these genes to help us understand how inheritance works.

c Why is variety important?

Figure 2 Although these young people have some family likenesses, the variety caused by the mixing of their parents' genetic information is clear

Curved thumb

Straight thumb

Attached ear lobe

Unattached ear lobe

Dimples

No dimples

Figure 3 These are all human characteristics that are controlled by a single pair of genes. They can help us to understand how sexual reproduction introduces variety and how inheritance works.

You will get a random mixture of genetic information from your parents, which is why you don't look exactly like either of them!

Summary questions

1 Define the following words:
  a asexual reproduction   **c** gamete
  b sexual reproduction   **d** variation.

2 Compare the advantages and disadvantages of sexual reproduction with asexual reproduction.

3 A daffodil reproduces asexually using bulbs and sexually using flowers.
  a How does this help to make them very successful plants?
  b Explain the genetic differences between a daffodil's sexually and asexually produced offspring.

Key points

- In asexual reproduction there is no joining of gametes and only one parent. There is no genetic variety in the offspring.
- The genetically identical offspring of asexual reproduction are known as clones.
- In sexual reproduction male and female gametes join. The mixture of genetic information from two parents leads to genetic variety in the offspring.

Further teaching suggestions

Interactive programs on inherited genes
- There are some interactive programmes on the inheritance of different genes and how variation is achieved.

Family similarities and differences
- Suggest to students that they investigate family photographs and family members for similarities and differences. Sometimes it is possible that a characteristic 'skips' a generation, e.g. 'he has his grandfather's nose'. Students could write a short paragraph about any inherited tendencies in their family. If this is a sensitive issue, then supply pictures of the Hapsburgs or other dynasties where there are obvious family characteristics.

Characteristics of your pets!
- Those students who keep pets, such as budgerigars or mice, could investigate some of their characteristics. Coat colour in mice is a good example.

More than one gene involved?
- The human characteristics described in the student book are examples of variation due to a single gene, but these are the exceptions rather than the rule. Ask: 'What other characteristics are inherited? How are hair colour and height affected by inheritance?'

Summary answers

1 **a** No fusion of gametes, only one parent, no variety.
  b Two parents, fusion of gametes, variety.
  c Sex cell.
  d The differences between individuals as a result of their genetic material.

2 **Advantages:** mixes genes, leads to variation, allows process of evolution, increases chances of a species surviving if environment changes.
  Disadvantages: need to find a partner which uses resources, more waste in producing gametes, generally slower.

3 **a** They have the best of both worlds – safe reproduction through bulbs and variety from seeds.
  b There will be genetic variety in the sexually produced offspring as they inherit characteristics from both parents whereas there is no genetic variety resulting from asexual reproduction as this only involves one parent plant.

Variation, reproduction and new technology

B1 6.3

Genetic and environmental differences

Learning objectives

Students should learn that:

- that differences between individuals of the same species may be due to the genes they have inherited
- how differences may be due to environmental causes
- how differences may be due to a combination of both genetic and environmental causes.

Learning outcomes

Most students should be able to:

- explain what makes them different to the rest of their family
- explain why identical twins are not exactly the same in every way.

Some students should also be able to:

- evaluate evidence for the different characteristics caused by genetic and environmental effects.

Answers to in-text questions

a Your parents.

b Because any differences in the adult plants are the result of environmental differences as they are genetically identical.

Support

- Provide students with a list of environmental factors that could affect the growth of the beans and get them to decide the most favourable factors. Tell them that this would reduce variation due to the environment, so that they could then deduce any variation that would be genetic.

Extend

- Get students to investigate the link between IQ and environment and consider whether nutrition affects IQ?

AQA Specification link-up: Biology B1.7

- Differences in the characteristics of different individuals of the same kind may be due to differences in:
  - the genes they have inherited (genetic causes)
  - the conditions in which they have developed (environmental causes)

  Or a combination of both. [B1.7.1 d)]

  Controlled Assessment: SA4.1 Planning an investigation [SA4.1.1 a) b) c) d) e)], [SA4.1.2 b)]; SA4.3 Collect primary and secondary data. [SA4.3.2 a) b) c)], [SA4.3.3 a) f)]

Lesson structure

Starters

Scars and birth marks – Project two torso outlines onto a whiteboard. Ask students to draw onto one any scars they have and onto the other any moles or birthmarks they have (be sensitive about using this activity where students have obvious distinctive birthmarks). Point at individual ones and ask who drew them and how they got them. Draw out that some differences are caused by the environment, such as scars, but some are not, such as birthmarks. *(5 minutes)*

Hairy moments – show the students pictures of a range of heads of hair. Encourage them to look at each other's hair and see how it varies. Some in the class may have coloured hair or extensions. Some may have been to sunny places on holiday. Discuss how hair colour changes during the year and over time. Relate this to genetic and environmental causes. Students can be supported by flagging up on the board in advance the common differences and causes, so students can refer to them when answering questions. Students can be extended by getting them to speculate as to the causes of the colour changes in terms of biochemical events, interaction with light, how DNA can bring about colour change etc. *(10 minutes)*

Main

- Split the class into small groups. Give each group a beaker containing some dry runner bean seeds without fungicide coating (cheaply bought by the half pint from garden centres) and an electronic balance. Get them to weigh the individual beans and record their mass as marks in a tally chart of categories. A range from 0.8 g through to 1.5 g should do. Get the students to make a bar chart of the results. Line the beans up, lightest to heaviest. Ask the students to write down reasons why the smaller beans were smallest and why the largest one grew largest. Ask them to speculate as to whether if you planted the smallest bean it would produce small seeds – what might complicate things? Ask how you could investigate this practically.

- Compare the bar chart of bean size with bell-shaped curves of normal distribution and draw out that there is a range of values of physical parameters within organisms and that this variation may have genetic or environmental causes. Lead into a discussion of causes of variation and draw out examples of inherited, environmental and combined variation.

- Try to find two beans which are as alike as possible. Ask how you could try to produce different sized beans or bean plants from each. Use this to link to a discussion of identical twins and twin studies to investigate the percentage hereditability of characteristics.

- There is some interesting information on twin studies in an article entitled 'Seeing doubles' (The Human Genome at the Wellcome Trust website). Summarise the project and some of the findings. Discuss with the students the work being done on the genetic basis of diseases of ageing.

Plenaries

G, E or B? – Give the students mini-whiteboards and dry-wipe markers. Project a series of photographs from the internet showing features which may show genetic variability, environmental variability or both. Get them on the command 'show me' to raise their boards. Have discussions where there is disagreement. *(5 minutes)*

110

Cloze passage – Draw out a cloze passage summarising the learning objectives suitable for your class's abilities. Students could be supported by making the passage simple and giving the missing words in a list at the end. Students can be extended by asking them to devise the cloze passage themselves and to use some more challenging omissions. Get the students to complete the passage and peer mark it. *(10 minutes)*

B1 6.3

Genetic and environmental differences

Learning objectives

- What makes you different from the rest of your family?
- Why aren't identical twins exactly the same in every way?

Figure 1 However much this Falabella eats, it will never be as tall as the Shire. It just isn't in the genes.

Have a look at the ends of your fingers and notice the pattern of your fingerprints. No one else in the world will have exactly the same fingerprints as you. Even identical twins have different fingerprints. What factors make you so different from other people?

Nature – genetic variety

The genes you inherit determine a lot about you. An apple tree seed will never grow into an oak tree. Environmental factors, such as the weather or soil conditions do not matter. The basic characteristics of every species are determined by the genes they inherit.

Certain human characteristics are clearly inherited. Features such as eye colour, the shape of your nose and earlobes, your sex and dimples are the result of genetic information inherited from your parents. But your genes are only part of the story.

a Where do the genes you inherit come from?

Nurture – environmental variety

Some differences between you and other people are completely due to the environment you live in. For example, if a woman drinks heavily when she is pregnant, her baby may be very small when it is born and have learning difficulties. These characteristics are a direct result of the alcohol the fetus has to deal with as it develops. You may have a scar as a result of an accident or an operation. These characteristics are all environmental, not genetic.

Genes certainly play a major part in deciding how an organism will look. However, the conditions in which it develops are important too. Genetically identical plants can be grown under different conditions of light or soil nutrients. The resulting plants do not look identical. Plants deprived of light, carbon dioxide or nutrients do not make as much food as plants with plenty of everything. The deprived plants will be smaller and weaker. They have not been able to fulfil their 'genetic potential'.

b Why are genetically identical plants so useful for showing the effect of the environment on appearance?

Combined causes of variety

Many of the differences between individuals of the same species are the result of both their genes and the environment. For example, you inherit your hair colour and skin colour from your parents. However, whatever your inherited skin colour, it will be darker if you live in a sunny environment. If your hair is brown or blonde, it will be lighter if you live in a sunny country.

Your height and weight are also affected by both your genes and the conditions in which you grow up. You may have a genetic tendency to be overweight. However, if you never have enough to eat you will be underweight.

Figure 2 The differences in these cows are partly genetic and partly down to their environment, from the milk they drank as calves to the quality of the grass they eat each day

Investigating variety

It is quite easy to produce genetically identical plants to investigate variety. You can then put them in different situations to see how the environment affects their appearance. Scientists also use groups of animals that are genetically very similar to investigate variety. You cannot easily do this in a school laboratory.

The only genetically identical humans are identical twins who come from the same fertilised egg. Scientists are very interested in identical twins, to find out how similar they are as adults.

It would be unethical to take identical twins away from their parents and have them brought up differently just to investigate environmental effect. But there are cases of identical twins who have been adopted by different families. Some scientists have researched these separated identical twins.

Often identical twins look and act in a remarkably similar way. Scientists measure features such as height, weight and IQ (a measure of intelligence). The evidence shows that human beings are just like other organisms. Some of the differences between us are mainly due to genetics and some are largely due to our environment.

In one study, scientists compared four groups of adults:
- separated identical twins
- identical twins brought up together
- non-identical, same sex twins brought up together
- same sex, non-twin siblings brought up together.

The differences between the pairs were measured. A small difference means the individuals in a pair are very alike. If there was a big difference between the identical twins the scientists could see that their environment had more effect than their genes.

Table 1 Differences in pairs of adults

Measured difference in:	Identical twins brought up together	Identical twins brought up apart	Non-identical twins	Non-twin siblings
height (cm)	1.7	1.8	4.4	4.5
mass (kg)	1.9	4.5	4.6	4.7
IQ	5.9	8.2	9.9	9.8

links

For more information on producing genetically identical plants, see B1 6.4 Cloning.

Figure 3 Whether identical twins are brought up together or apart, they are often very similar as adults

Summary questions

1 Copy and complete using the words below.

combination identical developed genes

Everybody is different, even .... twins. Some of the differences are caused by our .... Some differences are caused by the conditions in which we have .... Many differences are caused by a .... of both.

2 **a** Using the data from Table 1, explain which human characteristic appears to be mostly controlled by genes and which appears to be most affected by the environment.

b Why do you think non-twin siblings reared together were included in the study as well as twins reared together and apart?

3 You are given 20 pots containing identical cloned seedlings, all the same height and colour. Explain how you would investigate the effect of temperature on the growth of these seedlings compared to the impact of their genes.

AQA Examiner's tip

- Genes control the development of characteristics.
- Characteristics may be changed by the environment.

Key points

- The different characteristics between individuals of a family or species may be due to genetic causes, environmental causes or a combination of both.

Further teaching suggestions

Dr Josef Mengele
- Research the crimes committed in the name of studies on twins by the Nazi Dr Josef Mengele.

Is variation due to nature or nurture?
- Discuss the table of differences in height, mass and IQ given in the text. Is it possible to say whether the variation is due more to nature rather than nurture?

Investigations
- Provide the students with a tray of identical small geranium plants (available from garden centres). Ask them to design and carry out an investigation into the effect of light on their growth and colour.
- A similar investigation could be done to find out what effect differences in nutrition have on the growth of the seedlings. Use a proprietary plant food.

Summary answers

1 identical, genes, developed, combination

2 **a** Height seems to be most closely controlled by genetics as there is least difference between the identical twins regardless of whether they are brought up together or apart. Mass seems to be most affected by the environment as identical twins brought up apart are no more identical than ordinary siblings.

b For comparison with the normal population: Identical twins reared together and twins reared apart mean you can compare the impact of different environments on genetically identical humans. Even twins brought up in the same household will not have identical environments – and there are small differences between them for all features. But when twins are reared apart, if they remain very similar, then that is largely controlled by genetics whilst if there are big differences then environment is having a big effect. Non-twin siblings show the level of similarity you would expect from two siblings (not genetically identical) reared in the same environment.

3 Credit for any sensible suggestions along with recognition of the need to control variables, how to get the most reliable and valid data from the investigation etc.

B1 6.4

Cloning

AQA

Specification link-up: Biology B1.7

- New plants can be produced quickly and cheaply by taking cuttings from older plants. These new plants are genetically identical to the parent plant. *[B1.7.2 b)]*
- Modern cloning techniques include:
  - tissue culture – using small groups of cells from part of a plant
  - embryo transplants – splitting apart cells from a developing animal embryo before they become specialised, then transplanting the identical embryos into host mothers
  - adult cell cloning … *[B1.7.2 c)]*
- Interpret information about cloning techniques and genetic engineering techniques. *[B1.7]*
- Make informed judgements about economic, social and ethical issues concerning cloning and genetic engineering, including genetically modified (GM) crops. *[B1.7]*

  Conrolled Assessment: SA4.1 Planning an investigation *[SA4.1.1 a) b) c) d)]*, *[SA4.1.2 c)]*; SA4.3 Collect primary and secondary data *[SA4.3.3 a)]*; SA4.4 Select and process primary and secondary data. *[SA4.4.2 b)]*

Learning objectives

Students should learn:
- that a clone is genetically identical to its parent
- taking cuttings is a rapid and cheap method of obtaining new plants
- modern cloning techniques, such as tissue culture and embryo transplants, use small groups of cells to produce many identical offspring.

Learning outcomes

Most students should be able to:
- define a clone
- explain the importance to gardeners and plant growers of cloning plants
- describe cloning by tissue culture in plants
- describe the process of embryo transplanting in animals
- discuss issues involving embryo cloning.

Some students should also be able to:
- interpret information about the advantages and disadvantages of different cloning techniques
- make informed judgements on the economic and ethical issues concerning embryo cloning.

Lesson structure

Starters

Photographs of 'Mini-Me' and Dolly – Show the photograph from the Austin Powers films. Ask: 'How was he made?' Show a photograph of Dolly the sheep for a real-life version and ask: 'How was she made?' *(5 minutes)*

Identical twins – Search the internet for a photograph of identical twins (or from within the school, if possible, with permission). Ask: 'How did they get to be identical?' Students can be supported by giving them a series of statements which they are asked to put in the correct order. Students can be extended by writing down the stages as bullet points. *(10 minutes)*

Main

This topic lends itself to practical work on cloning plants. The ideal time to do this is spring or early summer, but provided cuttings are kept in suitable conditions, it can be done at any time of year. With both practical experiments, students could be given a sheet of instructions to help them.

- Set up a practical on growing potatoes – this is best carried out during April–May, when pots can be left outside or in glasshouses (see 'Practical support'). Students should note the developments (digital photos can help here), until harvesting when the flowers have died off. A small prize can be awarded to the student whose pot yields the greatest mass at harvest. All students can take their potatoes home at the end of the experiment.

- If this is run as a competition, then the pots need to be kept in the same place, given the same quantities of water and nutrients and harvested at the same time. These conditions introduce the students to the idea of controlling variables, so that the test can be made as fair as possible. Be prepared to allow some time for checking progress and measuring during the course of the investigation. This activity can be used to teach aspects of 'How Science Works'.

- This practical exercise is similar, but can be done at any time of year using geraniums or zonal pelargoniums, growing them in a propagator (see 'Practical support'). Students can take a series of digital photographs for a PowerPoint presentation of their plant's development.

Answers to in-text questions

a A cutting looks the same as its parent plant because it is genetically identical. It has been grown from a small piece of the parent plant.

b Tissue culture allows you to make thousands of new plants from a tiny piece of plant tissue.

Support

- Give students definitions from Question 1 of the Summary questions and ask them to fill in the correct terms.

Extend

- Ask students to research tissue culture as practised in horticultural research and development establishments. They could investigate the different mixtures of hormones and conditions needed to form new plants.

Plenaries

Thanks for the memories – Imagine it was possible to produce a clone of yourself. This could take place when you were old and had lived a full and happy life. Suppose you could transfer these memories to a young clone of yourself. Would it still be you? Discuss. *(5 minutes)*

Cloning cattle – Give students an empty flow diagram for cloning cattle and the associated labels, but in the wrong order. Students can be supported by asking them to sort them out and complete the diagram. Students could be extended by getting them to put in additional links or information boxes. *(10 minutes)*

Practical support

Growing potatoes
Equipment and materials required
Large potatoes with obvious 'eyes', and preferably the beginnings of shoots (chits), knives, 10 cm pots, compost, plant food.

Details
You will need large potatoes that have obvious 'eyes', and preferably the beginnings of shoots (chits). Give each group of student's one potato; tell them to cut it into sections, each with at least one 'eye'. The sections should be allowed to dry off and then placed in pots of compost. The pots should be stored in a frost-free area, kept watered and supplied with nutrients. They can be repotted as necessary, noting developments (digital photos can help here), until harvesting when the flowers have died off.

Safety: Care taken when using cutting instruments.

Cloning plants: Growing geraniums
Equipment and materials required
Propagator, geraniums or zonal pelargoniums, 10 cm pots, cutting compost, dibber, hormone rooting compound (if applicable).

Details
Take cuttings from geraniums, or zonal pelargoniums, by using 10 cm growing tips cut straight across just beneath a node. Remove most of the leaves, leaving only the top two or three, which can be reduced in size to cut down on water loss. Fill 10 cm pots to the brim with cutting compost and use a dibber to make a hole. Place the cutting in the hole so that the base of the stem is about halfway down the depth of the compost. Firm in, water and label. Pots can be placed in a propagator or covered with a polythene bag over the top, secured round the pot with an elastic band and left on a windowsill.

Safety: Care taken when using cutting instruments.

Variation, reproduction and new technology

B1 6.4 — Cloning

Learning objectives
- How do we clone plants?
- How do we clone animals?
- Why do we want to create clones?

A clone is an individual that has been produced asexually and is genetically identical to the parent. Many plants reproduce naturally by cloning and this has been used by farmers and gardeners for many years.

Cloning plants

Gardeners can produce new plants by taking cuttings from older plants. How do you take a cutting? First you remove a small piece of a plant. This is often part of the stem or sometimes just part of the leaf. If you keep it in the right conditions, new roots and shoots will form. It will grow to give you a small, complete new plant.

Using this method you can produce new plants quickly and cheaply from old plants. The cuttings will be genetically identical to the parent plants.

Many growers now use hormone rooting powders to encourage cuttings to grow. Cuttings are most likely to develop successfully if you keep them in a moist atmosphere until their roots develop. We produce plants such as orchids and many conifer trees commercially by cloning in this way.

a Why does a cutting look the same as its parent plant?

Cloning tissue

Taking cuttings is a form of artificial asexual reproduction. It has been carried out for hundreds of years. In recent years scientists have come up with a more modern way of cloning plants called **tissue culture**. It is more expensive but it allows you to make thousands of new plants from one tiny piece of plant tissue.

The first step is to use a mixture of plant hormones to make a small group of cells from the plant you want to clone produce a big mass of identical plant cells.

Then, using a different mixture of hormones and conditions, you can stimulate each of these cells to form a tiny new plant. This type of cloning guarantees that you can produce thousands of offspring with the characteristics you want from one individual plant.

b What is the advantage of tissue culture over taking cuttings?

Figure 1 Simple cloning by taking cuttings is a technique used by gardeners and nurserymen all around the world.

Cloning animals

In recent years cloning animals has become quite common in farming, particularly transplanting cloned cattle embryos. Cows normally produce only one or two calves at a time. If you use embryo cloning, your best cows can produce many more top-quality calves each year.

How does embryo cloning work? You give a top-quality cow fertility hormones so that it produces a lot of eggs. You fertilise these eggs with sperm from a really good bull. Often this is done inside the cow and the embryos that are produced are then gently washed out of her womb. Sometimes the eggs are collected and you add sperm in a laboratory to produce the embryos.

Figure 2 Tissue culture makes it possible to produce thousands of identical plants quickly and easily

links
For information on taking plant cuttings, look back at B1 2.6 Hormones and the control of plant growth.

At this very early stage of development every cell of the embryo can still form all of the cells needed for a new cow. They have not become specialised.

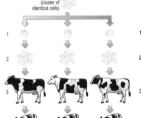

1 Divide each embryo into several individual cells.

2 Each cell grows into an identical embryo in the lab.

3 Transfer embryos into their host mothers, which have been given hormones to get them ready for pregnancy.

4 Identical cloned calves are born. They are not biologically related to their mothers.

Figure 3 Cloning cattle embryos

Cloning cattle embryos and transferring them to host cattle is skilled and expensive work. It is worth it because using normal reproduction, a top cow might produce 8–10 calves during her working life. Using embryo cloning she can produce more calves than that in a single year.

Cloning embryos means we can transport high-quality embryos all around the world. They can be carried to places where cattle with a high milk yield or lots of meat are badly needed for breeding with poor local stock. Embryo cloning is also used to make lots of identical copies of embryos that have been **genetically modified** to produce medically useful compounds.

AQA Examiner's tip
- Remember clones have identical genetic information.
- Make sure you are clear about the difference between a tissue and an embryo.

links
For more information on cloning embryos, see B1 6.5 Adult cell cloning.

Key points
- New plant clones can be produced quickly and cheaply by taking cuttings from mature plants. The new plants are genetically identical to the older ones.
- A modern technique for cloning plants is tissue culture using cells from a small part of the original plant.
- Transplanting cloned embryos is one way in which animals are cloned.

Summary questions

1 Define the following words:
   a cuttings
   b tissue cloning
   c asexual reproduction
   d embryo cloning.

2 Make a table to compare the similarities and differences between tissue cloning and taking cuttings.

3 a Cloning cattle embryos is very useful. Why?
   b Draw a flow chart to show the stages in the embryo cloning of cattle.
   c Suggest some of the economic and ethical issues raised by embryo cloning in cattle.

Summary answers

1 a **Cuttings**: Taking a small piece of a stem or leaf and growing it on in the right conditions to produce a new plant.

b **Tissue cloning**: Getting a few cells from a desirable plant to make a big mass of identical cells each of which can produce a tiny identical plant.

c **Asexual reproduction:** Reproduction which involves only one parent, there is no joining of gametes and the offspring are genetically identical to the parent.

d **Embryo cloning**: Splitting cells apart from a developing embryo before they become specialised to produce several identical embryos.

2 **Cuttings:** Put a small piece of plant into the right conditions and it grows into a new plant genetically identical to the parent plant.

Tissue cloning: Take a few cells from the plant; provide the right conditions to produce a mass of cells; separate individual cells and provide the right conditions; can form thousands of tiny plants identical to the parent.

3 a It allows the production of far more calves from the best cows; can carry good breeding stock to poor areas of the world; as frozen embryos; can replicate genetically engineered animals quickly.

b **Either** cow given hormones to produce large numbers of eggs → then cow inseminated with sperm → embryos collected and taken to the lab → embryos split to make more identical embryos → cells grown on again to make more identical embryos → embryos transferred to host mothers. **Or** cow given hormones to produce large numbers of eggs → eggs collected and taken to lab → eggs and sperm mixed → embryos grown → embryos split up to make more identical embryos → cells grown on to make bigger embryos → embryos transferred to host mothers.

c Student shows understanding of issues involved in embryo cloning. For example, economic issues – only wealthy farmers/wealthy countries can afford the technology, is it acceptable to produce large numbers of identical cattle, etc.

B1 6.5   Adult cell cloning

Learning objectives

Students should learn:

- that the steps in the techniques of adult cell cloning
- how scientists were able to clone a sheep
- that the potential benefits and risks of cloning animals.

Learning outcomes

Most students should be able to:

- explain the processes of adult cell cloning
- describe how Dolly the sheep was cloned
- list some of the benefits and disadvantages of cloning animals.

Some students should also be able to:

- evaluate the advantages and disadvantages of cloning
- discuss the ethical issues raised by adult cell cloning techniques.

Support

- Give students pictures of Dolly the sheep and ask them to make a scrapbook or poster as suggested in the 'Main' section.

Extend

- Ask students to research ways in which animals, such as cows and sheep, can be genetically engineered and then cloned to produce useful substances in their milk. Has it been done? What substances have been produced? What substances would it be beneficial to produce?

AQA Specification link-up: Biology B1.7

- Modern cloning techniques include:
  - tissue culture – using small groups of cells from part of a plant
  - embryo transplants – splitting apart cells from a developing animal embryo before they become specialised, then transplanting the identical embryos into host mothers.
  - Adult cell cloning – the nucleus is removed from an unfertilised egg cell. The nucleus from an adult body cell, e.g. a skin cell, is then inserted into the egg cell. An electric shock then causes the egg cell to begin to divide to form embryo cells. These embryo cells contain the same genetic information as the adult skin cell. When the embryo has developed into a ball of cells, it is inserted into the womb of an adult female to continue its development. [B1.7.2 c)]
- Interpret information about cloning techniques and genetic engineering techniques. [B1.7]
- Make informed judgements about the economic, social and ethical issues concerning cloning and genetic engineering, including genetically modified (GM) crops. [B1.7]

Lesson structure

Starters

Fill in the vowels – Write a list of key words and phrases used in this chapter on the board, but leave out the vowels (e.g. CLNNG, NCLS). Students can be supported by indicating where the vowels should go by writing the words with dashes for the missing letters. Ask students to fill in the missing vowels. Students can be extended by completing the words and writing a definition for each word or phrase. *(5 minutes)*

Would you like to be a twin? – If there are twins in the class, get them to describe what it is like to be a twin. Open up the discussion and then ask the students to write down a list of advantages and disadvantages of being an identical twin. Build up a general list on the board. *(10 minutes)*

Main

The main purpose of this lesson is to ensure that the students have a sound understanding of the basic technique of adult cell cloning and how it can be used to clone animals.

- Prepare a PowerPoint presentation illustrating the steps of adult cell cloning. Give students worksheets so that they can follow the sequence and write about the stages in their own words. Allow time for questions and further explanations.
- The story of Dolly is well-documented and it would be possible to show some of the material from websites such as the Science Museum Antenna (http://antenna.sciencemuseum.org.uk), the BBC (www.bbc.co.uk) or the Roslin Institute, Edinburgh (www.roslin.co.uk) (where the cloning was carried out). Alternatively, if there is good access to computers, the students could be given a list of suitable sites and then carry out their own search in groups. Each group of students could then be asked to produce a poster about Dolly and her life, for display in the laboratory.
- The Science Museum Antenna link is a particularly good one and covers the story of Dolly well in a sequence of topics. It combines details of the techniques involved, with details of Dolly's life and demise.
- Give students, working in groups, large A3 sheets of paper on which they can write their ideas about the advantages and disadvantages of this type of cloning. Ask one group to present their ideas and then discuss generally adding ideas from the other groups. At the end of the discussion, ask students to list the advantages and disadvantages in order of importance and compile a class list.

Plenaries

Why is it ...? – Why is it easier to clone plants than it is to clone animals? Students can be supported by providing them with a list of reasons from which they can choose. Students can be extended by asking them to make a list of the differences between plants and animals that might affect the outcome of cloning. *(5 minutes)*

The quagga ... is cloning the answer? – Tell the story of the quagga, a type of zebra that became extinct in the 1880s and the attempts by the Quagga Project Committee to revive it. Is this a case for the use of a cloning technique or selective breeding? Discuss cloning as an alternative to selective breeding. *(10 minutes)*

Further teaching suggestions

Designer babies or cloned babies
● Research Bionet website (www.bionetonline.org) for the topic 'Design-a-baby'? Print out or project the information. Ask students to discuss whether it would be more desirable to design a baby or clone one. What are the pros and cons of each technique if it were possible to do it?

How much does it all cost?
● One factor which has so far not been considered is the cost of developing these new methods for cloning animals. The initial research has to be funded and then the cost of producing cloned animals could be quite high. Humans have been producing new varieties of animals through the techniques of selective breeding for centuries, so why should money be spent on cloning? Will it make food more expensive?

Answers to in-text questions
a Adult cell cloning.
b It could be used to help infertile couples have their own genetic child.

B1 6.5 Adult cell cloning

Learning objectives
● How did scientists clone a sheep?
● What are the steps in the techniques of adult cell cloning?

True cloning of animals, without sexual reproduction involved at all, has been a major scientific breakthrough. It is the most complicated form of asexual reproduction you can find.

Adult cell cloning

To clone a cell from an adult animal is easy. The cells of your body reproduce asexually all the time to produce millions of identical cells. However, to take a cell from an adult animal and make an embryo or even a complete identical animal is a very different thing.

When a new whole animal is produced from the cell of another adult animal, it is known as **adult cell cloning**. This is still relatively rare. You place the nucleus of one cell into the empty egg cell of another animal of the same species. Then you place the resulting embryo into the uterus of another adult female where it develops until it is born.

Here are the steps involved:
● The nucleus is removed from an unfertilised egg cell.
● At the same time the nucleus is taken from an adult body cell, e.g. a skin cell of another animal of the same species.
● The nucleus from the adult cell is inserted (placed) in the empty egg cell.
● The new cell is given a tiny electric shock that makes it start dividing to form embryo cells. These contain the same genetic information as the original adult cell and the original adult animal.
● When the embryo has developed into a ball of cells it is inserted into the womb of an adult female to continue its development.

Adult cell cloning has been used to produce a number of whole animal clones. The first large mammal ever to be cloned from the cell of another adult animal was Dolly the sheep, born in 1997.

Figure 1 Dolly the sheep was the first large mammal to be cloned from another adult mammal. She went on to have lambs of her own in the normal way.

a What is the name of the technique that produced Dolly the sheep?

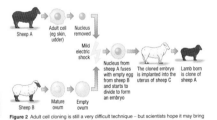

Figure 2 Adult cell cloning is still a very difficult technique – but scientists hope it may bring benefits in the future

AQA Examiner's tip
Animals can be cloned by using embryo transplants or by adult cell cloning.

When Dolly was produced she was the only success from hundreds of attempts. The technique is still difficult and unreliable, but scientists hope that it will become easier in future.

How Science Works

The benefits and disadvantages of adult cell cloning

One big hope for adult cell cloning is that animals that have been genetically engineered to produce useful proteins in their milk can be cloned. This would give us a good way of producing large numbers of cloned, medically useful animals.

This technique could also be used to help save animals from extinction, or even bring back species of animals that died out years ago. The technique could be used to clone pets or prized animals so that they continue even after the original has died. However, some people are not happy about this idea.

There are some disadvantages to this exciting science as well. Many people fear that the technique could lead to the cloning of human babies. This could be used to help infertile couples, but it could also be abused. At the moment this is not possible, but who knows what might be possible in the future?

Another problem is that modern cloning techniques produce lots of plants or animals with identical genes. In other words, cloning reduces variety in a population. This means the population is less able to survive any changes in the environment that might happen in the future. That's because if one of them does not contain a useful characteristic, none of them will.

In a more natural population, at least one or two individuals can usually survive change. They go on to reproduce and restock. This could be a problem in the future for cloned crop plants or for cloned farm animals.

b How might adult cell cloning be used to help people?

Summary questions

1 Copy and complete using the words below:
mammal adult technique genetic Dolly
In .... cell cloning an animal is produced that is an exact .... copy of another adult animal. .... the sheep was the first large .... to be produced using this modern cloning ....

2 Produce a flow chart to show how adult cell cloning works.

3 What are the main advantages and disadvantages of the development of adult cell cloning techniques?

links
For more information on adult cell cloning, see B1 6.7 Making choices about technology.

Did you know ...?
The only human clones alive at the moment are natural ones known as identical twins! But the ability to clone mammals such as Dolly the sheep has led to fears that some people may want to have a clone of themselves produced – whatever the cost.

Key points
● Scientists cloned Dolly the sheep using adult cell cloning.
● In adult cell cloning the nucleus of a cell from an adult animal is transferred to an empty egg cell from another animal. A small electric shock causes the egg cell to begin to divide and starts embryo development. The embryo is placed in the womb of a third animal to develop. The animal that is born is genetically identical to the animal that donated the original adult cell.

Summary answers

1 adult, genetic, Dolly, mammal, technique

2 The nucleus is removed from an unfertilised egg cell → the nucleus is taken from an adult body cell → the nucleus from the adult cell is inserted (placed) in the empty egg cell → new cell is given a tiny electric shock → new cell fuses together → begins to divide to form embryo cells → ball of cells inserted into womb to continue its development.

3 **Advantages:** enabled us to clone adult animals so we can clone genetically engineered organisms, making it possible to clone new tissues and organs for people with diseases or needing transplants, could help infertile couples, could help conserve very endangered species. Any valid points.

Disadvantages: people are concerned about human cloning, reduces variety in a population, objections to the formation of embryos which are then used to harvest tissues, people object to the cloning of endangered or extinct animals. Any other valid points.

B1 6.6

Genetic engineering

Learning objectives

Students should learn:

- that genetic engineering involves artificially changing the genetic material of an organism
- that genes can be transferred from one organism to another
- that genes can be transferred into plants and animals so that they develop desired characteristics.

Learning outcomes

Most students should be able to:

- explain the term 'genetic engineering'
- describe how genes from one organism can be transferred into another organism
- list some advantages and disadvantages of genetic engineering
- interpret information about cloning techniques and genetic engineering techniques.

Some students should also be able to:

- explain the process of genetic engineering, and the difference between genetically modified organisms which produce useful proteins and organisms which are improved themselves
- evaluate the advantages and disadvantages of genetic engineering.

Support

- Provide students with cards for the stages in genetic engineering and getting them to put them in the correct order.

Extend

- Students could be introduced to some of the terms used in genetic engineering such as the correct names of the enzymes, plasmids, vectors, marker genes, recombinant DNA.

AQA Specification link-up: Biology B1.7

- In genetic engineering, genes from the chromosomes of humans and other organisms can be 'cut out' using enzymes and transferred to cells of other organisms. [B1.7.2 d)]
- Genes can also be transferred to the cells of animals, plants or microorganisms at an early stage in their development so that they develop with desired characteristics.
  - new genes can be transferred to crop plants
  - crops that have had their genes modified in this way are called genetically modified crops (GM crops)
  - examples of genetically modified crops include ones that are resistant to insect attack or to herbicides
  - genetically modified crops generally show increased yields. [B1.7.2 e)]
- Concerns about GM crops include the effect on populations of wild flowers and insects, and uncertainty about the effects of eating GM crops on human health. [B1.7.2 f)]
- Make informed judgements about the economic, social and ethical issues concerning cloning and genetic engineering, including genetically modified (GM) crops. [B1.7]

Lesson structure

Starters

'Glow in the dark mouse' – Search online news stories about genetic engineering such as 'glow in the dark' mice. For example, try www.bbc.co.uk. Discuss how this might come about. *(5 minutes)*

Genetic engineering – good or bad? – Ask students to think about the advantages and disadvantages of genetically modified (GM) crops. Students can be supported by writing up six statements on the board, three positive points about GM crops and three negative points. Ask the students to sort out the positive points from the negative ones. Students can be extended by asking them to suggest points of their own. Give them two minutes to do this and then build up a list on the board. Students can also be extended by asking them to think of an ethical framework for their decision-making, so that it will work independent of content. *(10 minutes)*

Main

- What is genetic engineering? Take students through the sequence of selecting a gene, cutting it out, putting it into a bacterium; mention the different enzymes (not necessarily by name but according to what they are doing). A good example to choose as an illustration is the human growth hormone. The production of the hormone is under the control of one gene, so the sequence is clear. As this is a difficult concept, a worksheet for the students to fill in during the presentation will help them.

- Make your own genetically modified bacterium. Use a digital camera and a stop motion animation program, provide the students with the materials to make a plasticine model of a genetically modified bacterium. They will need to remove the required gene from a chromosome model and insert it into a plasmid in a bacterium. Use a knife labelled 'enzymes'.

- To explain genetic engineering, type a random DNA sequence into a word processor and copy/paste a part of this into a drawing of a bacterium. Now copy the two and paste as many copies of the new bacterium as quickly as you can.

- Provide material from pro-GM organisations, such as Monsanto, and anti-GM organisations, such as Greenpeace and the Soil Association, together with articles from the general media coverage. Ask students to gather information from the sources during class time, and then for homework design a case for or against.

Plenaries

Designer kids quandary – Imagine how you would feel if your parents had chosen all sorts of features about you – your hair, eyes, gender etc. How would that affect the way you feel about your own identity? Discuss as a class. *(5 minutes)*

Review genetic engineering – good or bad? – Review the list of pros and cons made at the beginning. Have any ideas changed? Students can be supported by asking them which they think are the most important and giving each a rank. Students could be extended by getting them to add extra points about the pros and cons of human engineering. *(10 minutes)*

Further teaching suggestions

Genetic diseases

- There are references on the internet to specific genetic diseases. There is a good account of the story of Sammi Sparke, who suffered from cystic fibrosis and had a successful lung transplant, at www.organdonation.nhs.uk.

GM videos

- There are videos on GM crops giving a negative slant. These can be obtained free of charge from the organisation 'Compassion in World Farming' (Charles House, 5a Charles Street, Petersfield, Hants GU32 3EH, Tel. (01730 264 208). However, students will be expected to present a balanced view of this topic.

Answers to in-text questions

a It is cut out using enzymes.

b There is a limit to the types of protein bacteria can make.

c A genetic disease is a disease or problem caused by a mistake in the genetic material in your cells.

B1 6.6

Genetic engineering

- What is genetic engineering?
- How are genes transferred from one organism to another?
- What are the issues involved in genetic engineering?

What is genetic engineering? K

Genetic engineering involves changing the genetic material of an organism. You take a gene from one organism and transfer it to the genetic material of a completely different organism. So, for example, genes from the chromosomes of a human cell can be 'cut out' using enzymes and transferred to the cell of a bacterium. The gene carries on making a human protein, even though it is now in a bacterium.

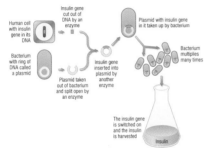

Figure 1 The principles of genetic engineering. A bacterial cell receives a gene from a human being so it makes the human hormone insulin.

a How is a gene taken out of one organism to be put into another?

If genetically engineered bacteria are cultured on a large scale they will make huge quantities of protein from other organisms. We now use them to make a number of drugs and hormones used as medicines.

Transferring genes to animal and plant cells

There is a limit to the types of proteins that bacteria are capable of making. As a result, genetic engineering has moved on. Scientists have found that genes from one organism can be transferred to the cells of another type of animal or plant at an early stage of their development. As the animal or plant grows it develops with the new desired characteristics from the other organism. For example, glowing genes from jellyfish have been used to produce crop plants which give off a blue light when they are attacked by insects. Then the farmer knows when they need spraying.

b Why are genes inserted into animals and plants as well as into bacteria?

The benefits of genetic engineering

Genetically engineered bacteria can make exactly the proteins we need, in exactly the amounts needed and in a very pure form. For example, people with diabetes need supplies of the hormone insulin. In the past people used animal insulin extracted from the pancreases of pigs and cattle. Now they can use pure human insulin produced by genetically engineered bacteria (see Figure 1).

We can use engineered genes to improve the growth rates of plants and animals. They can be used to improve the food value of crops as genetically modified (GM) crops usually have much bigger yields than ordinary crops. They can also be designed to grow well in dry, hot or cold parts of the world so could help to solve the problems of world hunger. Crops can be engineered to produce plants which make their own pesticide or are resistant to herbicides used to control weeds.

Human engineering

If there is a mistake in your genetic material, you may have a genetic disease. These can be very serious. Many people hope that genetic engineering can solve the problem.

It might become possible to put 'healthy' genes into the affected cells by genetic engineering, so they work properly. Perhaps the cells of an early embryo can be engineered so that the individual develops into a healthy person. If these treatments become possible, many people would have new hope of a normal life for themselves or their children.

c What do we mean by a 'genetic disease'?

The disadvantages of genetic engineering

Genetic engineering is still a very new science. No one knows what all of the long-term effects might be. For example, insects may become pesticide-resistant if they eat a constant diet of pesticide-forming plants.

Some people are concerned about the effect of eating GM food on human health. Genes from genetically modified plants and animals might spread into the wildlife of the countryside. GM crops are often made infertile, which means farmers in poor countries have to buy new seed each year.

People might want to manipulate the genes of their future children. This may be to make sure they are born healthy, but there are concerns that people might want to use it to have 'designer' children with particular characteristics such as high intelligence. Genetic engineering raises issues for us all to think about.

Figure 2 You can't tell that food is genetically modified just by looking at it! In the UK, few GM foods are sold and they have to be clearly labelled. Many other countries, including the USA, are less worried and use GM food widely.

Key points

- Genes can be transferred to the cells of animals and plants at an early stage of their development so they develop desired characteristics. This is genetic engineering.

- In genetic engineering, genes from the chromosomes of humans and other organisms can be 'cut out' using enzymes and transferred to the cells of bacteria and other organisms.

- There are advantages and disadvantages associated with genetic engineering.

Summary questions

1 Copy and complete using the words below:

   cell   engineering   enzymes   gene   genetic   transfer

   Genetic .... involves changing the .... material of an organism. You cut a .... from one organism using .... and .... it to the .... of a completely different organism.

2 **a** Make a flow chart that explains the stages of genetic engineering.
   b Make two lists, one to show the possible advantages of genetic engineering and the other to show the possible disadvantages.

Summary answers

1 engineering, genetic, gene, enzymes, transfer, cell

2 **a** Suitable flow diagram based on B1 6.6 Figure 1 in the Student Book.

   b **Advantages** – any suitable points such as:
   - Bacteria can make human medicines and hormones.
   - Improve the growth rates of plants and animals.
   - Improve the food value of crops.
   - Reduce the fat levels in meat.
   - Produce plants that make their own pesticide chemicals.
   - Crop plants can give off a blue light when attacked by insects, so that the farmer knows when they need to be sprayed.
   - Possible cures for genetic diseases.
   - Fruit does not go bad so quickly.

Disadvantages – any suitable points such as:
   - Insects may become pesticide-resistant if they eat a constant diet of pesticide-forming plants.
   - Effect on human health of eating genetically modified food.
   - Genes from genetically modified plants and animals might spread into the wildlife.
   - Genetically modified crops are often infertile, so farmers in poor countries have to buy new seed each year.
   - People may want to manipulate the genes of their future children.

B1 6.7

Making choices about technology

Learning objectives

Students should learn:

- that there are economic, social and ethical issues concerning new techniques such as cloning and genetic engineering.

Learning outcomes

Most students should be able to:

- interpret information about cloning and genetic engineering techniques
- describe some of the ethical problems associated with these techniques
- make informed judgements about the issues.

Some students should also be able to:

- make balanced judgements, explaining their reasoning clearly, about the issues involved.

AQA Specification link-up: Biology B1.7

- Interpret information about cloning techniques and genetic engineering techniques. *[B1.7]*
- Make informed judgments about the economic, social and ethical issues concerning cloning and genetic engineering, including genetically modified (GM) crops. *[B1.7]*
- Concerns about GM crops include the effect on populations of wild flowers and insects, and uncertainty about the effects of eating GM crops on human health. *[B1.7.2 f)]*

Lesson structure

Starters

Who's bothered? – Show a photograph of a GM protester (Greenpeace or similar). Ask the students to write down any ideas they have as to why the protester might be angry? What might they be trying to change? *(5 minutes)*

Opinions on the line – Draw a series of long, parallel horizontal lines on the board. Get students to draw them either on rough paper or on mini-whiteboards. Put the word 'agree' on one side and the word 'disagree' on the other. Read out a series of statements based on the content of the student text (adjust the language level to suit the class). Get each student to put crosses on their lines according to where their opinion lies. Get some volunteers to come to the front of the class and show where they have placed their crosses and explain their reasoning. Students can be supported by making the statements very simple and unambiguous. They will also need some guidance. Students can be extended by giving them more challenging and/or ambiguous statements and the activity should generate discussion. *(10 minutes)*

Main

- Hold a discussion of the issues raised during the 'opinions on the line' starter. If not used, discuss the Student Book directly after having given the students an opportunity of reading it.

- Explain that it took 188 attempts to bring Copycat, the cloned cat, into existence. Debate as to whether it is worth doing this kind of research when it is so expensive in embryos.

- The Canadian Museum of Nature (http://nature.ca) has an excellent online game involving cloning cats. Search for 'geee in genome – copycat'.

- Discuss the film *The Boys from Brazil* about clones of Hitler. Get the students to come up with a list of situations in which it would be OK to carry out cloning and a list where it would not be approved. Discuss who should be in charge of this. Carry out internet research to find out who the controlling bodies are in the UK and internationally.

- There is an opportunity here for introducing the concept of the formal debate with a motion, proposer and seconder, opposer and their second, questions from the floor and a vote to see if it is carried. This can tie in with the coverage of debates in PSHE or citizenship.

- Show some rice and show some children with vitamin A deficiency symptoms. Discuss the issue of biofortification and draw out opinions with reasons.

Plenaries

£100 000 pet – Imagine you are going to write a short email addressed to the people in the USA who spent £100 000 cloning their Labrador. What would you say? Read out some when the exercise is completed. *(5 minutes)*

Speech bubble summaries – Give the students cut out speech bubbles. Get them to put their opinions on the topics covered during the discussions within the lesson onto their speech bubble and then tack them to the walls around the room. Allow the students to circulate and read each other's opinions. Students can be supported by giving them speech bubble summaries to choose from. Students can be extended by getting them to pick one speech bubble summary (not their own) and to critically evaluate it. The class must be trustworthy in order to carry out this without silliness. *(10 minutes)*

Support

- Get students to design a poster to summarise how Copycat was cloned

Extend

- Get students to research the current situation on the growing of GM crops in the UK.

Further teaching suggestions

Local farmers opinions on GM
- If possible, ask local farmers for their opinions on GM either via email or see if you can get some visiting speakers who have personal involvement.

GM trials
- Research information on the trialling of GM crops.

Designing an advertisement
- Design an advertisement for a company who will clone your pet for you.

Researching cheese
- More than 30% of cheese is made using fungal enzymes from genetically modified yeast. This topic could be researched and students could find out whether or not this information is included on the wrappers of cheese.

B1 6.7   Making choices about technology

Learning objectives
- What sort of economic, social and ethical issues are there about new techniques such as cloning and genetic engineering?

Cloning pets

Cc, or Copycat, was the first cloned cat to be produced. Most of the research into cloning had been focused on farm and research animals – but cats are thought of first and foremost as pets.

Much of the funding for cat cloning in the US comes from companies who are hoping to be able to clone people's dying or dead pets for them. It has already been shown that a successful clone can be produced from a dead animal. Cells from beef from a slaughter house were used to create a live cloned calf.

It took one hundred and eighty-eight attempts to make Cc, producing 87 cloned embryos, only one of which resulted in a kitten. Cloning your pet won't be easy or cheap. The issue is, should people be cloning their dead cats, or would it be better to give a home to one of the thousands of unwanted cats already in existence? Even if a favourite pet cat is cloned, it may look nothing like the original because the coat colour of many cats is the result of genes switching on and off at random in the skin cells. The clone will develop and grow in a different environment to the original cat as well. This means other characteristics that are affected by the environment will probably be different too.

?? Did you know ...?
Dogs have also been cloned. In 2009, an American couple paid more than £100 000 to have a clone of their much-loved pet Labrador. The new dog is called Lancelot encore (encore means 'again').

Figure 1 The cat on the left is Rainbow. The cat on the right is Cc, Rainbow's clone. Rainbow and Cc share the same DNA – but they don't look the same.

To some people these are exciting events. To others they are a waste of time, money and the lives of all the embryos that don't make it. What do you think?

Figure 2 Lancelot encore, a clone of a much-loved pet, and a portrait of the original dog

Activity
In B1 6.4 and B1 6.5 there is information about cloning animals and plants for farming. Here you have two different stories about cloning animals for money (Cc and Lancelot encore).

There is talk of a local company setting up a laboratory to clone cats, dogs and horses for anyone in the country who wants to do this.

Write a letter or post a blog either *for* the application or *against* it. Make sure you use clear, sensible arguments and put the science of the situation across clearly.

The debate about GM foods

Ever since genetically modified foods were first introduced there has been controversy and discussion about them. For example, varieties of GM rice known as 'golden rice' and 'golden rice 2' have been developed. These varieties of rice produce large amounts of vitamin A. Up to 500 000 children go blind each year as a result of lack of vitamin A in their diets. In theory golden rice offers a solution to this problem. In fact, many people objected to the way trials of the rice were run and the cost of the product. No golden rice is yet being grown in countries affected by vitamin A blindness.

There is a lot of discussion about genetically modified crops. Here are some commonly expressed opinions.

Figure 3 The amount of beta carotene in golden rice and golden rice 2 is reflected in the depth of colour of the rice

John, 49, plumber, UK
'I'm very concerned about GM foods. Who knows what we're all eating nowadays. I don't want strange genes inside me, thank you very much. We've got plenty of fruit and vegetables as it is – why do we need more?'

Ali, 26, shop assistant, UK
'I think GM food is such a good idea. If the scientists can modify crops so they don't go off so quickly, food should get cheaper, and there will be more to go around. And what about these plants that produce pesticides? That'll stop a lot of crop spraying, so that should make our food cleaner and cheaper. It's typical of us in the UK that we moan and panic about it all.'

Tilahun, 35, farmer, Ethiopia
'I have some real worries about the GM crops that don't form fertile seeds. In the past, farmers in poorer countries just kept seeds from the previous year's crops, so it was cheap and easy. With the GM crops we have to buy new seeds every year – although I hear that won't be the case with golden rice. On the other hand, these GM crops don't need spraying very much. They grow well in our dry conditions, they give a much bigger crop yield and keep well too – so there are some advantages.'

Summary questions
1. People get very concerned about cloning. Do you think these fears are justified? Explain your answer.
2. Summarise the main advantages and disadvantages of genetic engineering expressed here.

Activity
You are going to produce a 5-minute slot for a daytime television show on '**Genetic engineering – a good thing or not?**' Using the information here and on B1 6.6 Genetic engineering (and extra research if you have time), plan out a script for your time on air, remembering that you have to inform the public about genetic engineering, entertain them and make them think about the issues involved.

Key points
- There are a number of economic, social and ethical issues concerning cloning and genetic engineering which need to be considered when making judgements about the use of this science.

Summary answers

1 Credit for relevant comments backed by science

No: e.g. cloning has many potential benefits such as reproducing genetically engineered organisms, saving organisms from extinction, producing cheap plants. Some forms of cloning have been going on for centuries (cuttings) and these have been/may be used to produce medical treatments, etc.

Yes: e.g. most animals produced by adult cell cloning have problems, wasteful process, risk of human cloning for the wrong reasons, etc.

2 Advantages: Food won't go off so fast: less pesticide use; food cheaper and cleaner; plants can be developed to grow well in particular environments, e.g. dry conditions of some areas of developing World.

Disadvantages: People are concerned about eating engineered DNA; infertile crops which is a problem for farmers in the developing world; cost.

Summary answers

1 a From a runner – a special stem from the parent plant with small new identical plant on the end.

b Asexual.

c By sexual reproduction (flowers, pollination, etc.).

d The new plants from the packet will be similar to, but not identical to their parents – each one will be genetically different. The plants produced by asexual reproduction will be identical to their parents.

2 a A unit of inheritance – a small piece of DNA.

b On the chromosomes in the nucleus of a cell.

c A sex cell.

3 a Traditional cuttings used parts of whole stems and roots, but tissue culture uses minute collections of cells as the starting point. Cuttings result in up to hundreds of identical plants, tissue culture can give thousands.

b Embryo cloning – flushing out early embryos and dividing them before replacing in surrogate mother cows.

c Both allow large numbers of genetically identical individuals to be produced from good parent stock much faster and more reliably than would be possible using traditional techniques.

d Cloning plants uses bits of the adult plant as the raw material for the cloning. Animal embryo cloning, as it is used at the moment, involves using embryos as the raw material for the cloning, although this may change in the future.

e There are more and more people in the world needing to be fed, so techniques for reproducing high yielding plants and animals are always helpful and are financially beneficial for farmers. Also in developed countries people demand high quality but cheap food – so techniques which reproduce valuable animals and plants more quickly are valued.

4 a Clear description of adult cell cloning, e.g. The nucleus is removed from an unfertilised egg cell.
At the same time the nucleus is taken from an adult body cell, e.g. a skin cell of another animal of the same species. The nucleus from the adult cell is inserted (placed) in the empty egg cell. The new cell is given a tiny electric shock which fuses the new cells together, and causes it to begin to divide to form embryo cells. These contain the same genetic information as the original adult cell and the original adult animal. When the embryo has developed into a ball of cells, it is inserted into the womb of an adult female to continue its development.

b Plant cloning has been accepted for a long time and doesn't threaten people – only advantages seen in general. Cloning animals is seen as worrying in itself but also raises concerns of human cloning. Cloning pets etc., is seen as frivolous.

5 a See Figure 1, 6.6 Genetic engineering – it should look similar but with growth hormone instead of insulin.

b It is pure – free from any contamination. It is the human version of a hormone. It can be produced in large amounts relatively easily and cheaply as and when it is needed.

6 a They have been raised and trained on different establishments so it is environmental factors which are influencing their racing ability.

b As a control – to see how the animal turns out if not trained up as a racing mule.

Summary questions

1

a How has the small plant shown in diagram A been produced?

b What sort of reproduction is this?

c How were the seeds in B produced?

d How are the new plants that you would grow from the packet of seeds shown in B different from the new plants shown in A?

2 a What is a gene?

b Where do you find genes?

c What is a gamete?

3 Tissue culture techniques mean that 50 000 new raspberry plants can be grown from one old one instead of two or three by taking cuttings. Cloning embryos from the best bred cows means that they can be genetically responsible for 30 or more calves each year instead of two or three.

a How does tissue culture differ from taking cuttings?

b How can one cow produce 30 or more calves in a year?

c What are the similarities between cloning plants and cloning animals in this way?

d What are the differences in the techniques for cloning animals and plants?

e Why do you think there is so much interest in finding different ways to make the breeding of farm animals and plants increasingly efficient?

4 a Describe the process of adult cell cloning.

b There has been a great deal of media interest and concern about cloning animals but very little about cloning plants. Why do you think there is such a difference in the way people react to these two different technologies?

5 Human growth is usually controlled by growth ho produced by the pituitary gland in your brain. If yo don't make enough hormones, you don't grow pr and remain very small. This condition affects 1 in 5000 children. Until recently the only way to get g hormone was from the pituitary glands of dead bo Genetically engineered bacteria can now make p pure growth hormone.

a Draw and label a diagram to explain how a hea human gene for making growth hormone can b from a human chromosome and put into a wor bacterial cell.

b What are the advantages of producing substan growth hormone using genetic engineering?

6 In 2003 two mules called Idaho Gem and Idaho S were born in America. They were clones of a famo racing mule. They both seem very healthy. They w separated and sent to different stables to be reare trained for racing. So far Idaho Gem has been mo successful than his cloned brother, winning sever against ordinary racing mules. There is a third clo Utah Pioneer, which has not been raced.

a The mules are genetically identical. How do yo explain the fact that Idaho Gem has beaten Ida in several races?

b Why do you think one of the clones is not being raced?

c Their progress is being carefully monitored by scientists. What type of data do you think will b available from these animals?

7 One concern people have about GM crops is that might cross pollinate with wild plants. Scientists n find out how far pollen from a GM crop can travel able to answer these concerns.

Describe how a trial to investigate this might be se

---

c Data on effect of diet, handling, intensity of training etc. on the temperament, running speed, stamina, etc., of the mules.

7 Plant a GM crop. After pollination, collect samples of plants at increasing distances, in all directions. Inspect the pollen collected; analyse for GM cells; plot distribution.

Kerboodle resources

Resources available for this chapter on Kerboodle are:

- Chapter map: Variation, reproduction and new technology
- Practical: Stem and leaf cuttings (B1 6.2)
- Practical: New plants from tissue culture (B1 6.2)
- How Science Works: Twin studies (B1 6.3)
- Support: You're never alone with a clone (B1 6.4)
- Viewpoint: Designer babies (B1 6.5)
- Animation: Genetic modification (B1 6.6)
- Viewpoint: Genetically modified crops (B1 6.6)
- Extension: Genetic history (B1 6.6)
- Interactive activity: Variation, reproduction and new technology
- Revision podcast: Variation, reproduction and new technology
- Test yourself: Variation, reproduction and new technology
- On your marks: Variation, reproduction and new technology
- Examination-style questions: Variation, reproduction and new technology
- Answers to examination-style questions: Variation, reproduction and new technology

Examination-style questions (k)

...wberries are able to reproduce many plants from one
...nt plant.

...ose the correct answer to complete each sentence.
...oducing new plants with one parent is called ....
(1)

...sexual reproduction   genetic engineering
...xual reproduction

...ne advantage of this is that all the strawberry fruits
...ll ....
(1)

...e bigger   all taste better   all taste the same

...disadvantage of this to the strawberry plants
...that ....
(1)

...ere is more variation   they are genetically identical
...ey cannot mate

...d the passage. Use the information and your own
...wledge to answer the questions.

...one time, the boll weevil destroyed cotton crops. Farmers
...ayed the crops with a pesticide.

...e weevil died out but another insect, the bollworm moth,
...ame resistant to this pesticide.

...he 1990s large crops of the cotton plant were destroyed by
...bollworm moth. The pesticides then used to kill the moth
...e expensive and very poisonous, resulting in deaths to
...mans.

...entists investigated alternative ways to control the bollworm
...h. They found out that a type of bacterium produced a
...son which killed bollworm larvae (grubs).

...M cotton crop plant was developed which produced the
...son to kill bollworms. This proved to be very effective and
...ners were able to stop using pesticide sprays.

...w farmers have another problem. Large numbers of other
...cts have multiplied because they were not killed when the
...ners stopped using pesticides. Some of these insects have
...ted to destroy the GM cotton and farmers are beginning to
...pesticides again!

...Give **one** advantage of spraying crops with
pesticides.
(1)

...Give **two** disadvantages of spraying crops with
pesticides.
(2)

...Give **one** economic advantage of using GM cotton.
(1)

...Some people object to using GM crops. Suggest
one reason why.
(1)

...*this question you will be assessed on using good
...nglish, organising information clearly and using
...pecialist terms where appropriate.*

...he GM cotton was genetically engineered to produce
...e same poison as the bacterium.
...escribe fully how this is done.
(6)

3 The use of cloned animals in food production is
controversial.

> It is now possible to clone 'champion' cows.
>
> Champion cows produce large quantities of milk.

a Describe how adult cell cloning could be used to
produce a clone of a 'champion' cow.
(4)

b Read the passage about cloning cattle.

> The Government has been accused of 'inexcusable behaviour'
> because a calf of a cloned American 'champion' cow has been
> born on a British farm. Campaigners say it will undermine trust
> in British food because the cloned cow's milk could enter the
> human food chain.
>
> But supporters of cloning say that milk from clones and their
> offspring is as safe as the milk we drink every day.
>
> Those in favour of cloning say that an animal clone is a genetic
> copy. It is not the same as a genetically engineered animal.
> Opponents of cloning say that consumers will be uneasy about
> drinking milk from cloned animals.

Use the information in the passage and your own
knowledge and understanding to evaluate whether the
government should allow the production of milk from
cloned 'champion' cows.

Remember to give a conclusion to your evaluation.   (5)
AQA, 2006

121

Practical suggestions

Practicals	AQA	(k)	📖	⚙️
Investigate the optimum conditions for the growth of cuttings of, e.g. Mexican hat plants, spider plants, African violets.	✓	✓	✓	
Investigate the best technique for growing new plants from tissue cultures (e.g. cauliflower).	✓	✓		

AQA Examination-style answers

**Note to teachers – DNA is strictly introduced in Unit BLY2. If
candidates give an answer where DNA would be appropriate
they will gain credit in BLY1 but it is not essential knowledge.**

1 a asexual reproduction   (1 mark)

b all taste the same   (1 mark)

c they are genetically identical   (1 mark)

2 a i Kills insects (which eat crop) **or** increases yield
(1 mark)

ii Any **two** from:
- kills insects which may not be pests
- poisonous to humans
- expensive
- pollutes the environment
- other relevant suggestions e.g. is not organic
(2 marks)

---

iii Increases crop yield **or** reduces cost of pesticide use
(1 mark)

iv Any **one** from:
- May lead to increased use of pesticides in the long run/description /ref to last paragraph
- ethical considerations e.g. alters genes of crop
- Do not allow 'not natural' 'against genes may get into wildlife idea, religion' or similar, not organic.
(1 mark)

b There is a clear and detailed scientific description of the
sequence of events in genetic engineering. The answer is
coherent and in a logical sequence. It contains a range of
appropriate or relevant specialist terms used accurately.
The answer shows very few errors in spelling, punctuation
and grammar.   (5–6 marks)

There is some description of the sequence of events in
genetic engineering but there is a lack of clarity and detail.
The answer has some structure and the use of specialist
terms has been attempted, but not always accurately.
There may be some errors in spelling, punctuation and
grammar.   (3–4 marks)

There is a brief description of the genetic engineering,
which has little clarity and detail. The answer is poorly
constructed with an absence of specialist terms or
their use demonstrates a lack of understanding of their
meaning. The spelling, punctuation and grammar are
weak.   (1–2 marks)

No relevant content.   (0 marks)

Examples of biology points made in the response:
- gene from the bacterium
- is cut from the chromosome
- using enzymes
- gene transferred to the cotton
- (cotton) chromosome – allow cell
- (the gene) controls characteristics
- causes the cotton (cells) to produce the poison.

3 a Any **four** from:
- nucleus/DNA/chromosomes/genetic material removed (from egg)
- from (unfertilised) egg/ovum
linked to second point
*allow 'empty egg cell' for first **two** marks*
*do **not** allow fertilised egg*
allow egg from champion cow
- nucleus from body cell of champion (cow)
- inserted into egg/ovum
- electric shock
- to make cell divide **or** develop into embryo
- (embryo) inserted into womb/host/another cow
allow this point if wrong method eg embryo splitting
(4 marks)

b Any **four** from:
Pros: Max 2 marks
- economic benefit eg increased yield/more profit
- clone calf not genetically engineered
- genetic material not altered
- milk safe to drink/same as ordinary milk
Cons: Max 2 marks
- consumer resistance
- caused by misunderstanding process
- not proved that milk is safe
*ignore 'God would not like it' **or** 'it's not natural'*
- ethical/religious argument
- reduce gene pool/eg
Conclusion: Max 1 mark
    sensible conclusion for or against, substantiated by
    information from the passage and/or own knowledge
conclusion at end
(5 marks)

B1 7.1 Theories of evolution

Learning objectives

Students should learn:

- the theory of evolution
- that there is evidence that evolution has taken place.

Learning outcomes

Most students should be able to:

- state Darwin's theory of evolution
- describe some of the evidence that evolution has taken place
- identify the differences between Darwin's theory of evolution and conflicting theories, e.g. Lamarck's.

Some students should also be able to:

- suggest reasons for the different theories explaining life on Earth.

Support

- Ask students to complete simple sentences summarising natural selection in a simple way.
- Present students with pictures of three or four animals with fairly obvious different characteristics (e.g. horn length in antelope, speed of response in rabbits they can run at about 30 mph, etc.). Ask them to choose which one would survive to have offspring.

Extend

- Suggest that the students do some more research on the attitude of all religions to evolutionary theory, in Darwin's time and also at the present time. Try The Richard Dawkins Foundation for information.

AQA Specification link-up: Biology B1.8

- Darwin's theory of evolution by natural selection states … . [B1.8.1 a)]
- The theory of evolution by natural selection was only … . [B1.8.1 b)]
- Other theories, including that of Lamarck, are based … . [B1.8.1 c)]
- Interpret evidence relating to evolutionary theory. [B1.8]
- Identify the differences between Darwin's theory of evolution and conflicting theories, such as that of Lamarck. [B1.8]

Lesson structure

Starters

Sorted! – Give a number of students a card or sheet with the picture of a different organism on it. These organisms should represent a spread over the timescale from life first emerging to human development. Students are to arrange themselves in order according to when they think the organism they are holding evolved. Match this with the real order and see who came in approximately the correct place. Students can be supported by giving them simple animal examples. Students can be extended by giving them a range of plants and animals. *(5 minutes)*

How much do we already know? – This is formative assessment task on the words 'Darwin', 'Natural selection', 'Origin of Species' and 'Evolution'. Write these words on a large sheet of quartered A2 paper. Allow the sheet to be circulated around the room with students adding comments. *(10 minutes)*

Main

- Gather together some details of as many different theories of evolution as you can: Darwin, Lamarck, the Creation, spontaneous generation, etc. and give a brief summary of each. This would be a good introduction to some of the following suggestions. Discuss the merits of each one.

- The life and times of Charles Darwin – Show a video (one is produced by Hawkhill Associates, Madison, WI) of Darwin's journey and discoveries, together with some details of his life (when he published his work etc.). Alternatively, search the internet for 'Charles Darwin video'. Discuss how his trip led to his point of view. As an alternative, show some excerpts from the film *Creation* about the life of Charles Darwin. The showing of the video could be followed by building up a cartoon summary of Darwin's voyage. Decide on the frames and get the students to complete it.

- Find out more about the life and times of Lamarck. There are some interesting videos (particularly from Cornell University) comparing and explaining the theories of Darwin and Lamarck. Try researching 'Jean-Baptiste Lamarck video' online.

Plenaries

Which ones shall we have? L, D or LD? – Give students individual cards or whiteboards on which they can respond to various statements and key words from both theories. For example: parents pass on acquired characteristics (L), survival of the fittest (D), law of use and disuse (L), natural selection (D), species do not stay the same (LD). L for Lamarck only, D for Darwin only and LD if applicable to both. *(5 minutes)*

Faking the evidence – How easy would it be to fake a fossil and so provide some evidence in support of evolution? Show some pictures or models of real fossils and discuss how fakes could be made and how you could prove that they were fakes. Students could be supported by prompting and suggestions. Students could be extended by getting them to research fakes (go to the BBC Nature and Science website, www.bbc.co.uk/sn). You could include a couple of 'fakes' in the examples you show to the students. *(10 minutes)*

Further teaching suggestions

Summarising the issues
- There are some good summaries of the issues in *A Short History of Nearly Everything* by Bill Bryson.

What makes the Galapagos so special?
- Students could find out why the Galapagos Islands are so special and research: 'Are there any other locations where similar conditions might have existed?' If available, show some footage from the film *Master and Commander: The Far Side of the World* (2003), where one of the characters has the chance to explore the Galapagos Islands.

Find out more about Darwin
- Although Darwin is probably best known for his work on the theory of evolution, he did work in other areas of biology. Use some of the information from the film and from other sources, such as libraries and the internet, to build up an account of all his scientific work.

Answers to in-text questions
a Useful changes or characteristics that organisms developed during their lives to help them survive are passed on to their offspring.

b *HMS Beagle*.

c Galapagos Islands.

Evolution

B1 7.1 Theories of evolution

Learning objectives
- What is the theory of evolution?
- What is the evidence that evolution has taken place?

We are surrounded by an amazing variety of life on planet Earth. Questions such as 'Where has it all come from?' and 'When did life on Earth begin?' have puzzled people for many generations.

The theory of evolution tells us that all the species of living things alive today have evolved from the first simple life forms. Scientists think these early forms of life developed on Earth more than 3 billion years ago. Most of us take these ideas for granted – but they are really quite new.

Up to the 18th century most people in Europe believed that the world had been created by God. They thought it was made, as described in the Christian Bible, a few thousand years ago. However, by the beginning of the 19th century scientists were beginning to come up with new ideas.

Lamarck's theory of evolution
Jean-Baptiste Lamarck was a French biologist. He thought that all organisms were linked by what he called a 'fountain of life'. He made the great step forward of suggesting that individual animals adapted and evolved to suit their environment. His idea was that every type of animal evolved from primitive worms. The change from worms to other organisms was caused by the inheritance of acquired characteristics.

Lamarck's theory was that the way organisms behaved affected the features of their body – a case of 'use it or lose it'. If animals used something a lot over a lifetime he thought it would grow and develop. Any useful changes that took place in an organism during its lifetime would be passed from a parent to its offspring. The neck of the giraffe is a good example. If a feature wasn't used, Lamarck thought it would shrink and be lost.

Lamarck's theory influenced the way **Charles Darwin** thought. However, there were several problems with Lamarck's ideas. There was no evidence for his 'fountain of life' and people didn't like the idea of being descended from worms. People could also see quite clearly that changes in their bodies – such as big muscles, for example – were not passed on to their children.

We now know that in the great majority of cases Lamarck's idea of inheritance cannot happen. However, scientists have discovered that in a few cases the way an animal behaves actually changes its genes. This results in the next generation behaving in the same way.

Figure 1 In Lamarck's model of evolution, giraffes have long necks because each generation stretched up to reach the highest leaves. So each new generation had a slightly longer neck.

a What do you think is meant by the phrase 'inheritance of acquired characteristics'?

Charles Darwin and the origin of species
Our modern ideas about evolution began with the work of one of the most famous scientists of all time – Charles Darwin. Darwin set out in 1831 as the ship's naturalist on *HMS Beagle*. He was only 22 years old at the start of the voyage to South America and the South Sea Islands.

Darwin planned to study geology on the trip. But as the voyage went on he became as excited by his collection of animals and plants as by his rock samples.

b What was the name of the ship that Darwin sailed on?

AQA Examiner's tip
Remember the basic key stages in natural selection:
survive → breed → pass on genes

In South America, Darwin discovered a new form of the common rhea, an ostrich-like bird. Two different types of the same bird living in slightly different areas set Darwin thinking.

On the Galapagos Islands he was amazed by the variety of species. He noticed that they differed from island to island. Darwin found strong similarities between types of finches, iguanas and tortoises on the different islands. Yet each was different and adapted to make the most of local conditions.

Darwin collected huge numbers of specimens of animals and plants during the voyage. He also made detailed drawings and kept written observations. The long journey home gave him plenty of time to think about what he had seen. Charles Darwin returned home after five years with some new and different ideas forming in his mind.

Figure 2 Darwin was very impressed by the giant tortoises he found on the Galapagos Islands. The tortoises on each island had different-shaped shells and a slightly different way of life. Darwin made detailed drawings of them all.

c What is the name of the famous islands where Darwin found so many interesting species?

After returning to England, Darwin spent the next 20 years working on his ideas. Darwin's theory of evolution by natural selection is that all living organisms have evolved from simpler life forms. This evolution has come about by a process of natural selection.

Reproduction always gives more offspring than the environment can support. Only those that have inherited features most suited to their environment – the 'fittest' – will survive. When they breed, they pass on the genes for those useful inherited characteristics to their offspring. This is natural selection.

When Darwin suggested how evolution took place, no one knew about genes. He simply observed that useful inherited characteristics were passed on. Today, we know it is useful genes which are passed from parents to their offspring in natural selection.

Figure 3 Darwin worked here in his study for around 20 years, carrying out experiments and organising his ideas on evolution by natural selection

AQA Examiner's tip
Avoid confusion between:
- the *theory of evolution* and
- the *process of natural selection*.

Summary questions
1 Explain what is meant by the following terms:
  a evolution
  b natural selection
2 What was the importance of the following in the development of Darwin's ideas?
  a South American rheas
  b Galapagos tortoises, iguanas and finches
  c the long voyage of *HMS Beagle*
  d the 20 years from his return to the publication of his book *The Origin of Species*.

Key points
- The theory of evolution states that all the species which are alive today – and many more which are now extinct – evolved from simple life forms that first developed more than 3 billion years ago.
- Darwin's theory is that evolution takes place through natural selection.

Summary answers

1 a All the species of living organisms which are alive today (and many more which are now extinct) have evolved from simple life forms, which first developed more than 3 billion years ago.

  b Only the animals and plants most suited to their environment – the 'fittest' – will survive to breed and so pass on their characteristics.

2 a South American rheas – Darwin found a new species – two types of the bird living in slightly different areas made Darwin start to think about how they came about.

  b Galapagos tortoises, iguanas and finches – these were some of the animals in the Galapagos Islands that varied from island to island, and made Darwin wonder what had brought about the differences.

  c The long voyage of *HMS Beagle* – this gave Darwin lots of opportunities to collect specimens and time to think about his theories and ideas.

  d The twenty years from his return to the publication of the book *The Origin of Species* in the development of Darwin's ideas gave Darwin time to work out his ideas very carefully and to collect a lot of evidence to support them.

B1 7.2

Accepting Darwin's ideas

Learning objectives

Students should learn:

- how Darwin's ideas were only gradually accepted
- how his ideas conflicted with religious beliefs
- that he could not explain how variety and inheritance happened.

Learning outcomes

Most students should be able to:

- explain why Darwin's ideas were only gradually accepted
- explain why there was conflict with religious beliefs
- describe some of the evidence that was lacking.

Some students should also be able to:

- explain why knowledge of genetics is necessary to understand how inheritance works.

Support

- Provide students with a synopsis of the events of Genesis.

Extend

- Introduce students to Darwin's *The Descent of Man* and get them to find out about more recent work on the origins of humans. Guide them to the work of Professor Chris Stringer at the Natural History Museum.

AQA Specification link-up: Biology B1.8

- Suggest reasons for the different theories. *[B1.8]*
- Suggest reasons why Darwin's theory of natural selection was only gradually accepted. *[B1.8]*
- Interpret evidence relating to evolutionary theory. *[B1.8]*

Lesson structure

Starters

Seeing is believing – Introduce this activity as a 'true or false' game to see who will believe unusual suggestions. Tell the students that everything they see is upside down. The ceiling is really on the floor and the floor is really on the ceiling. Get a 'hands-up' show of who believes that this is the case. Use a diagram of the eye, an overhead projector and a lens to project an upside-down image of a student onto an A3 sheet of paper. Refer to an experiment in 1896 where scientist George Stratton wore inverting glasses for a week. At first he couldn't walk or function at all but by the end of the week, everything appeared normal. He then took off the inverting glasses and everything looked upside down! Discuss and link to Darwin's views seeming unbelievable at the time but now widely accepted to be true. *(5 minutes)*

Darwin's life and times – a potted biography – Get the students to put the events of Darwin's life in chronological order. Students could be supported by providing a list of the major events (voyage on HMS Beagle, publication of books, etc.). Students could be extended by getting them to do a timeline emphasising the length of time it took him to publish his findings. *(10 minutes)*

Main

- Use the images in the text or search the internet for 'Darwin's finches', which will clearly show the beaks, and try to match them with their function. Show a map of the Galapagos Islands with the location of the different finches and also a picture of the original type of finch which colonised the Galapagos Islands. Why were these islands interesting?

- Find other examples of Darwin's collection from the Galapagos Islands and the voyage of *HMS Beagle* (the turtles are quite a good starting point). Discuss how he collected his evidence. What was he looking for?

- Produce a students PowerPoint presentation or exposition on the objections. During the exposition, give an opportunity to express their views and to discuss the objections.

- Get the students to imagine that they were one of Darwin's fellow scientists and had just heard about his ideas on evolution. Ask them to suggest what further evidence they would have needed to be convinced that he was right. Would they be convinced by fossils? (It might be worth pointing out that although fossils were collected as curiosities, people just thought they were preserved skeletons of creatures they had not seen yet.) Would they think of other ways in which his theories could be tested? Ask students what they consider is the most compelling piece of evidence to support the theories. What convinces them today that Darwin was right?

Plenaries

Let's make sure! – Darwin did not publish his theory for many years after he first thought of it. Imagine you are Darwin and write a diary entry giving reasons why he delayed the publication – what might he have been afraid of? What negative consequences could there be for him, for his family, for society? Discuss and then summarise. *(5 minutes)*

Assume the position – Darwin's work was so controversial because it went against the assumptions and collective world view of the time. What assumptions and collective world view do we have today on his theories? List things we take as given in current Western society. Support students by giving some examples, e.g. scientists will always find the correct answers to problems, many people assume that there is no reality beyond the physical etc. How do we react to people who challenge these assumptions? What lessons from the past can we draw from the ridicule Darwin experienced and the eventual acceptance of his views and his veneration? More able students will succeed in empathising with Darwin and gaining an awareness of the blinding effect of scepticism. They will probably be able to provide some more examples of theories that have been ridiculed. *(10 minutes)*

Further teaching suggestions

Challenging society
- List ideas which would appear provocative to the assumptions of our current society. Try to evaluate which may have merit and how you might go about finding if they have merit in a non-presumptive fashion.

If only Darwin had known about…
- Get students to think about how much easier it would have been for Darwin if he had known about genetics and inheritance.

Darwin and Mendel
- Imagine a meeting between Darwin and Mendel. Darwin could have talked about his observations on pigeons and domestic birds and Mendel could have talked about his peas.

How Science Works | Evolution

B1 7.2 Accepting Darwin's ideas

Learning Objectives
- Why was Darwin's theory of evolution only gradually accepted?

Charles Darwin came back from his trip on *HMS Beagle* with new ideas about the variety of life on Earth. He read many books and thought about the ideas of many other people such as Lamarck, Lovell and Malthus. He gradually built up his theory of evolution by natural selection.

He knew his ideas would be controversial. He expected a lot of opposition both from fellow scientists and from religious leaders.

Building up the evidence

Darwin realised he would need lots of evidence to support his theories. This is one of the reasons why it took him so long to publish his ideas. He spent years trying to put his evidence together in order to convince other scientists.

He used the amazing animals and plants he had seen on his journeys as part of that evidence. They showed that organisms on different islands had adapted to their environments by natural selection. So they had evolved to be different from each other.

Darwin carried out breeding experiments with pigeons at his home. He wanted to show how features could be artificially selected. Darwin also studied different types of barnacles (small invertebrates found on seashore rocks) and where they lived. This gave him more evidence of organisms adapting and forming different species.

Darwin built up a network of friends, fellow scientists and pigeon breeders. He didn't travel far from home (he was often unwell) but he spent a lot of time discussing his ideas with this group of friends. They helped him get together the evidence he needed and he trusted them as he talked about his ideas.

Figure 1 The finches found on the different Galapagos islands look very different but all evolved from the same original type of finch by natural selection

Why did people object?

In 1859, Darwin published his famous book *On the Origin of Species by means of Natural Selection* (often known as *The Origin of Species*). The book caused a sensation. Many people were very excited by his ideas and defended them enthusiastically. Others were deeply offended, or simply did not accept them.

There were many different reasons why it took some scientists a long time to accept Darwin's theory of natural selection. They include:
- The theory of evolution by natural selection challenged the belief that God made all of the animals and plants that live on Earth. This religious view was the generally accepted belief among most people in early Victorian England.
- In spite of all Darwin's efforts, many scientists felt there was not enough evidence to convince them of his theory.
- There was no way to explain how variety and inheritance happened. The mechanism of how inheritance happens – by genes and genetics – was not known until 50 years *after* Darwin published his ideas. Because there was no mechanism to explain how characteristics could be inherited, it was much harder for people to accept and understand.

The arguments raged and it took some time before the majority of scientists accepted Darwin's ideas. However, by the time of his death in 1882 he was widely regarded as one of the world's great scientists. He is buried in Westminster Abbey along with other great people like Sir Isaac Newton.

Figure 3 It wasn't just scientists who were interested in Darwin's ideas. Cartoonists loved the idea of evolution too.

Figure 2 Darwin's famous book – it sold out on the first day of publication!

?? Did you know …?

Darwin let his children use the back of his original manuscript of *The Origin of Species* as drawing paper. Not many of these original pages exist. Darwin kept the ones that remain because of his children's drawings rather than his own writing!

Key points
- Darwin's theory of evolution by natural selection was only gradually accepted for a number of reasons. These include:
  – a conflict with the widely held belief that God made all the animals and plants on the Earth
  – insufficient evidence
  – no mechanism for explaining variety and inheritance – genetics were not understood for another 50 years.

Summary questions

1 a Darwin set out in *HMS Beagle* in 1831. How many years later did he publish *The Origin of Species*?
  b What was Darwin's big idea?

2 What type of evidence did Darwin put together to convince other scientists his ideas were right?

3 Why did it take some time before most people accepted Darwin's ideas?

Summary answers

1 a *On the Origin of Species* published in 1859, so 28 years.

b All the species which are alive today, and many more that are now extinct, evolved from simple life forms which first developed more than three billion years ago through a process of natural selection. The organism most suited to its environment is most likely to survive and breed and so pass on the useful characteristic.

2 He used evidence from the voyage of *HMS Beagle* to show different organisms on different islands which were very similar but had adapted to fill different niches etc., breeding experiments with pigeons, and evidence of different species of barnacles, discussion with and use of observations from fellow scientists.

3 There was a clash between the establishment which was based on the Church and the idea that everything had its place and was created by God. A lot of inertia and strong belief to overcome. Also, it was just the status quo.

Although Darwin had put together a lot of evidence, it wasn't enough for some scientists, particularly the links higher up the evolutionary tree thinking about human evolution. He was missing the fossil records that would fill in some of the gaps.

No obvious mechanism until genes and genetics were discovered, so it was a process without an obvious model of how it came about.

B1 7.3

Natural selection

Specification link-up: Biology B1.8

Learning objectives

Students should learn:

- how individuals best suited to their environment survive to breed successfully
- that these individuals pass their genes on to the next generation
- that a mutation is a change in an existing gene.

Learning outcomes

Most students should be able to:

- explain what is meant by natural selection
- describe how mutation results in changes to genes.

Some students should also be able to:

- explain how mutation can affect the evolution of an organism.

- Evolution occurs via natural selection:
  - individual organisms within a particular species may show a wide range of variation because of differences in their genes
  - individuals with characteristics most suited to the environment are more likely to survive to breed successfully
  - the genes which have enabled these individuals to survive are then passed on to the next generation. *[B1.8.1 e)]*
- Where new forms of a gene result from mutation, there may be relatively rapid change in a species if the environment changes. *[B1.8.1 f)]*

Lesson structure

Starters

Six fingers better than five? – Show a picture of a person with six fingers on each hand. Ask what are the advantages and disadvantages. Students can be supported by providing a list of suggestions and getting them to select which they think are the most important and why. Students can be extended by getting them to make their own lists, followed by a discussion. They could also be asked to think of mutations in other animals which could affect survival, e.g. albinism. *(5 minutes)*

Blinky, the three-eyed mutant fish – Search the internet for images of 'Blinky the fish' from *The Simpsons* or show sections from season 2, episode 4, 'Two Cars in Every Garage and Three Eyes on Every Fish'. Discuss how this mutant could have arisen and whether three eyes would be an advantage. *(10 minutes)*

Main

- There are a number of interactive natural selection games available on the internet. These can be recommended to students or used in class if there is appropriate computer access. Try PBS Teacher Source at www.pbs.org or www.echalk.co.uk.
- Consider the peppered moth. This moth (*Biston betularia*) with its black mutant is well-documented. Prepare a PowerPoint presentation about the distribution of the two forms of the moth, together with some statistics on how populations have changed since the decline of industry in some areas. Students can be asked to compile a single A4 sheet summary of the evidence. This case provides support for the mechanism of survival of the fittest, natural selection and evolution.
- The activity above can be linked to another example of natural selection at work: the banded snail. Students may find evidence of this in their own gardens or in the school grounds. There are pictures of the different forms of the snail available; look for references to polymorphism. Essentially, there are more variations in the banded snail which provide camouflage in different situations. The snails best camouflaged survive, the rest do not.
- The fruit fly (*Drosophila*) is used in genetics experiments to investigate the inheritance of characteristics. Show some fruit flies and photographs of some of the mutations that have been studied. Discuss how these mutations might have arisen or been induced. In order to gain an understanding of how rapidly a mutation could spread, calculate how long it would take a pair of fruit flies to produce a billion offspring if each female produces 200 offspring every two weeks.

Answers to in-text questions

a Charles Darwin.

b Because it would be more likely to hear the approach of a predator and also to hear warning signs from other animals.

c A change in the genes/DNA.

d A disease of oysters where they do not grow properly; they are small, flabby and they develop pus-filled blisters and die.

Support

- Provide students with pictures of backgrounds and different banded snails and get them to match the snails with the most favourable background.

Extend

- Students could be asked to draw analogies between the evolution of animals and plants and the development of communications equipment over the last century.

Plenaries

The 'mutant schoolchild' – Imagine that Dr Who has returned to Earth in the Tardis many thousands of years in the future to find that schoolchildren have mutated to suit their environment. Build up a picture of a 'mutant schoolchild', who has adapted to an extreme extent. Suggestions from the students can be used to build up a picture on the board. Alternatively, each student could be given a sheet of paper and asked to draw or describe their mutant. Results to be displayed. *(5 minutes)*

Favourable adaptations? – Project or display photographs of a number of adaptations shown by plants and animals and discuss and explain how each could have arisen by natural selection. Some fairly obvious ones are thorns on stems, brightly coloured flowers, prehensile tails, eyes that swivel in chameleons, etc. Students could be supported by using very obvious examples and if necessary linking these with clue or prompt sheets. Students could be extended by getting them to imagine a very useful adaptation for an animal or a plant. Get the students to draw out a sequence chart of what must happen and over what timescale in order for this to take place. *(10 minutes)*

Further teaching suggestions

Linking animal evolution to plant evolution
- How far is the evolution of animals linked to the evolution of plants or vice versa? A possible example of parallel evolution is that of insects and insect-pollinated plants, i.e. the evolution of flowers. This could be the basis of a discussion on links between plants and animals.

Evolution in action
- Studies of the occurrence of heavy metal tolerant plants on spoil heaps can provide some evidence for evolution in

action. Students need to be provided with some background information and then asked to summarise the process. Link to the peppered moth story.

The mutant schoolchild
- The plenary can be extended by encouraging students to describe and explain the selective advantages of the features of their mutant. Would it survive?

Evolution

B1 7.3 Natural selection ⓚ

Learning objectives
- How does natural selection work?
- What is mutation?

Scientists explain the variety of life today as the result of a process called natural selection. The idea was first suggested about 150 years ago by Charles Darwin.

Animals and plants are always in competition with each other. Sometimes an animal or plant gains an advantage in the competition. This might be against other species or against other members of its own species. That individual is more likely to survive and breed. This is known as natural selection.

a Who first suggested the idea of natural selection?

Survival of the fittest ⓚ

Charles Darwin was the first person to describe natural selection as the 'survival of the fittest'. Reproduction is a very wasteful process. Animals and plants always produce more offspring than the environment can support.

The individual organisms in any species show lots of variation. This is because of differences in the genes they inherit. Only the offspring with the genes best suited to their habitat manage to stay alive and breed successfully. This is natural selection at work.

Think about rabbits. The rabbits with the best all-round eyesight, the sharpest hearing and the longest legs will be the ones that are most likely to escape being eaten by a fox. They will be the ones most likely to live long enough to breed. What's more, they will pass those useful genes on to their babies. The slower, less alert rabbits will get eaten and their genes are less likely to be passed on.

b Why would a rabbit with good hearing be more likely to survive than one with less keen hearing?

The part played by mutation

New forms of genes result from changes in existing genes. These changes are known as mutations. They are tiny changes in the long strands of DNA.

Mutations occur quite naturally through mistakes made in copying DNA when the cells divide. Mutations introduce more variety into the genes of a species. In terms of survival, this is very important.

c What is a mutation?

Many mutations have no effect on the characteristics of an organism, and some mutations are harmful. However, just occasionally a mutation has a good effect. It produces an adaptation that makes an organism better suited to its environment. This makes it more likely to survive and breed.

Whatever the adaptation, if it helps an organism survive and reproduce it will get passed on to the next generation. The mutant gene will gradually become more common in the population. It will cause the species to evolve.

When new forms of a gene arise from mutation, there may be a relatively more rapid change in a species. This is particularly true if the environment changes. If the mutation gives the organism an advantage in the changed environment, it will soon become common.

◯◯ links
For more information on the competition between plants and animals in the natural world, look back at B1 4.4 Competition in animals and B1 4.5 Competition in plants.

Figure 1 The natural world is often brutal. Only the best adapted predators capture prey – and only the best adapted prey animals escape.

⁇ Did you know ...?
Fruit flies can produce 200 offspring every two weeks. The yellow star thistle, an American weed, produces around 150000 seeds per plant per year. If all those offspring survived we'd be overrun with fruit flies and yellow star thistles!

◯◯ links
For information on genes, see B1 6.1 Inheritance.

Natural selection in action

Malpeque Bay in Canada has some very large oyster beds. In 1915, the oyster fishermen noticed a few small, flabby oysters with pus-filled blisters among their healthy catch.

By 1922 the oyster beds were almost empty. The oysters had been wiped out by a destructive new disease (soon known as Malpeque disease).

Fortunately a few of the oysters had a mutation which made them resistant to the disease. These were the only ones to survive and breed. The oyster beds filled up again and by 1940 they were producing more oysters than ever.

A new population of oysters had evolved. As a result of natural selection, almost every oyster in Malpeque Bay now carries a gene that makes them resistant to Malpeque disease. So the disease is no longer a problem.

Figure 2 The tiny number of dandelion seeds that survive and grow into plants have a combination of genes that gives them an edge over all the others

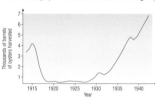

Figure 3 Oyster yields from Malpeque Bay 1915–40. As you can see, disease devastated the oyster beds. However, thanks to the process of natural selection, a healthy population of oysters managed to survive and reproduce again.

d What is Malpeque disease?

Summary questions

1 Copy and complete using the words below:

adaptation breed environment generation mutation selection organism survive

When a _____ has a good effect it produces an _____ that makes an _____ better suited to it's _____ . This makes it more likely to _____ and _____ . The mutation then gets passed on to the next _____ . This is natural _____ .

2 Many features that help animals and plants survive are the result of natural selection. Give three examples, e.g. all-round eyesight in rabbits.

3 Explain how the following characteristics of animals and plants have come about in terms of natural selection.
   a Male red deer have large sets of antlers.
   b Cacti have spines instead of leaves.
   c Camels can tolerate their body temperature rising far higher than most other mammals.

Key points
- Natural selection works by selecting the organisms best adapted to a particular habitat.
- Different organisms in a species show a wide range of variation because of differences in their genes.
- The individuals with the characteristics most suited to their environment are most likely to survive and breed successfully.
- The genes that have produced these successful characteristics are then passed on to the next generation.
- Mutation is a change in the genetic material (DNA) which results in a new form of a gene.

126   127

Summary answers

1 mutation, adaptation, organism, environment, survive, breed, generation, selection

2 [Any suitable examples from the spread]

3 **a** Mutation gave some deer antlers to make them more successful in battles with other stags and more attractive to females. This means that they are more likely to mate and pass on their genes. This process continues until antlers become normal in the population. The stags with the biggest or most effective antlers are the ones which mate most successfully.

b Mutation produced spines instead of leaves. Cactus loses very little water and so survives well and reproduces, passing on advantageous genes until normal in population.

c Mutation gives increased temperature tolerance. These camels have an advantage, so more likely to survive and breed, passing on the mutation until it is normal in the population.

B1 7.4

Classification and evolution

AQA
Specification link-up: Biology B1.8

- Studying the similarities and differences between organisms allows us to classify living organisms into animals, plants and microorganisms, and helps us to understand evolutionary and ecological relationships. Models allow us to suggest relationships between organisms. *[B1.8.1 d)]*

Learning objectives

Students should learn:

- that studying the similarities and differences between organisms allows us to classify living organisms
- that living organisms are classified into animals, plants and microorganisms
- that systems of classification help us to understand evolutionary and ecological relationships.

Learning outcomes

Most students should be able to:

- define classification
- describe some of the criteria used in the classification of organisms
- explain how evolutionary trees are used to show relationships between organisms.

Some students should also be able to:

- describe how DNA evidence can be used to work out evolutionary relationships.

Lesson structure

Starters

Tree of life – Find a 'Tree of life with genome size' illustration on the internet and explain what is being displayed. Discuss and record student observations on who we are and where we fit in to the larger picture of life on Earth. *(5 minutes)*

Types of living things – Get the students to think of as many different kinds of living things as they can within one minute. Have a small prize for the person with the largest list. Explain that there are at least 1.75 million known species alive at the moment and there may be many more as yet undiscovered (so there may be 3–10 million species). A board with a million dots on can bring this into perspective. Link this to a need for a classification system.

Support students by showing them a range of toy animals and getting them to place them into groups with reasons for their decisions. Extend students by showing them pictures of organisms which although similar in form have a very different evolutionary ancestry (e.g. marsupial and eutherian placental relatives such as rats and dogs). Get them to speculate as to reasons why this situation should arise. *(10 minutes)*

Main

- Break into groups and give the students a list of organisms for them to classify in whatever way they decide. Emphasise that there is no right or wrong way for this exercise. Photographs or models will help but a list will suffice. To get them started, you could suggest a group called 'water organisms' or 'organisms of the air'. To conclude, get the students to state how they went about the exercise, comparing the ways in which different groups approached the problem. Draw out that it would be a good idea if everyone used the same agreed system and that many of the names we use for groups describe some of an organism's features (e.g. mammal).

- Define species using lions and tigers as examples – they can mate but their offspring are infertile so they are separate species. Photographs of ligers and tigrons would help here. The students do not need to memorise the system, just to know about what a species is and that an international system of classification exists.

- Show examples of printed evolutionary tree diagrams, from early ones to the most recent. Get students to comment of these.

- Review any recent case from the news where DNA fingerprinting has been instrumental in securing a conviction. Explain the basic principles behind DNA profiling. Link this to phylogenic tracing of ancestry and get the students to copy down some phylogenic ancestry diagrams projected from the internet.

Plenaries

Thumbs up – Review the flow chart in Figure 3 of the Student Book and trace the evolution of the thumb in both red pandas and giant pandas. *(5 minutes)*

Classified data – Use a phylogenic key from the internet to follow the ancestry of humans back through time. Get the students to make a list of human forefathers until they get back to the single ancestor from which all beings have evolved. Bear in mind that some of the genetic information from many millions of years ago is still present in us. Reflect on this. Students could be supported by giving them a phylogenic key with certain stages in the evolution of humans highlighted. Students could be extended by allowing them to speculate on where this phylogenic tree could extend to in the future. Get the students to appreciate that in evolutionary terms the human race has only just begun! *(10 minutes)*

Support

- Provide students with cards on which the names of the taxonomic groups (Kingdom, Phylum etc.) are printed and sets of the names of the groups to which selected animals belong (Animalia, Mammalia etc.). Give them some examples such as frog, snake etc. and adapt the number of groups to the student ability. The students have to match the name with the correct taxonomic group.

Extend

- Get students to examine data from embryonic studies showing evidence of our evolutionary ancestry.

- Ask students to find out about Linnaeus and his binomial system of classification on which the system we use today is based.

Further teaching suggestions

Variation in a species

- Get the students to suggest as many different types of dog as they can and tell them that all these are different varieties of the same species. Therefore, they can potentially interbreed. Get the students to think of differences between some of these breeds and discuss how different a breed has to be before it can be considered a new species. How different are some of these breeds from their ancestors? Reinforce the criteria that determine a species and the variation within it. There are other examples of large numbers of breeds amongst domesticated animals. It might be useful to speculate why the different breeds of domesticated animals have been developed.

Trying to classify objects

- Giving the students groups or collections of objects which they have to sort out and classify. Examples could be: coins, buttons and beads, pins, needles and safety pins.

Evolution

B1 7.4 Classification and evolution

Learning objectives

- What is classification?
- How does classification help us understand evolution?

?? Did you know ... ?

The most widely accepted kingdoms of microorganisms are Monera, Protista and Fungi. However, there is still a lot of argument between scientists as to exactly which organisms fit into each kingdom.

How are organisms classified?

Classification is the organisation of living things into groups according to their similarities.

There are millions of different types of living organisms. Biologists classify living things to make it easier to study them. Classification allows us to make sense of the living world. It also helps us to understand how life began and how the different groups of living things are related to each other.

Living things are classified by studying their similarities and differences. By looking at similarities and differences between organisms we can decide which should be grouped together.

The system we use for classifying living things is known as the natural classification system. The biggest groups are the kingdoms, and the best known are the animal kingdom and the plant kingdom. The microorganisms are then split between three different kingdoms.

Kingdoms contain lots of organisms with many differences but a few important similarities. For example, all animals move their whole bodies about during at least part of their life cycle, and their cells do not have cell walls. Plants on the other hand do not move their whole bodies about, and their cells have cell walls. Also some plant cells contain chloroplasts full of chlorophyll for photosynthesis.

The smallest group is a species. Members of the same species are very similar. Any differences are small variations of the same feature. A species is a group of organisms that can breed together and produce fertile offspring. Orang-utans, dandelions and brown trout are all examples of species of living organisms.

a What is classification?

Classification and evolutionary relationships

In the past, we relied on careful observation of organisms to decide which group they belonged to. Out in the field, this is still the main way we identify an organism. However, scientists develop models to suggest relationships between living organisms.

Since Darwin's time, scientists have used classification to show the evolutionary links between different organisms. These models are called **evolutionary trees**. They are built up by looking at the similarities and differences between different groups of organisms. One of the most famous evolutionary trees was produced by Darwin himself. It was found in one of the notebooks that he used to plan his book *The Origin of Species*. It starts off with the words 'I think'. Then it shows how Darwin was beginning to see relationships between different groups of living organisms (see Figure 2).

However, observation may not tell you the whole story. Some organisms look very different but are closely related. Others look very similar but come from very different groups. Now scientists are increasingly using DNA evidence to decide what species an animal belongs to. They look for differences as well as similarities in the DNA. This allows them to work out the **evolutionary relationships** between organisms. It also means they can see how long ago different organisms had a common ancestor.

b What is an evolutionary tree?

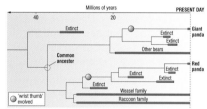

Figure 1 Animals, plants and microorganisms are identified by the differences between them rather than the similarities

Evolutionary and ecological relationships 🄺

Classifying organisms helps us to understand how they evolved. It can also help us understand how species have evolved together in an environment. We call this their ecological relationships and it is another way of modelling relationships between organisms.

For example, pandas have a thumb which they use to grip bamboo. However it is not like a human thumb – it has evolved from specialised wrist bones. The only other animals to have a similar 'wrist thumb' are the red pandas. Both red pandas and giant pandas eat bamboo. Based on their modern ecological feeding relationships, it looks as if they are closely related. However, based on their anatomy and DNA, giant pandas are closely related to other species of bears. Red pandas are much more closely related to racoons.

Recently scientists found a fossil ancestor of red pandas which also had a 'wrist thumb'. There is also evidence from the ecological relationships of this fossil animal. This suggests the thumb evolved as an adaptation for a quick escape into trees carrying prey stolen from sabre-toothed tigers. This is rather different from the giant panda evolving to feed on bamboo.

Now the ecological models and the evolutionary models match – the two species had a common ancestor a very long time ago, but the special 'wrist thumb' evolved separately as adaptations to solve two different ecological problems.

Figure 2 This evolutionary tree was found in one of the notebooks that Darwin used to plan his book *The Origin of Species*

Figure 3 Evolutionary trees like this show us the best model of the evolutionary relationships between organisms

Figure 4 Both the giant panda and the red panda use the 'wrist thumb' to eat bamboo

Summary questions

1 Copy and complete using the words below:

kingdoms animals organisms species classify microorganisms similarities

Scientists .... living .... by studying .... and differences between them. The big groups are called .... and the smallest are called .... All living organisms are either ...., plants or ....

2 What observations can be made to compare living organisms?

3 How are evolutionary trees useful to us?

Key points

- Studying the similarities and differences between organisms allows us to classify them into animals, plants and microorganisms.
- Classification also helps us to understand evolutionary and ecological relationships.

Answers to in-text questions

a Putting organisms into groups based on similarities and differences between them.

b A model suggesting the evolutionary relationships between different groups of organisms.

Summary answers

1 classify, organisms, similarities, kingdoms, species, animals/microorganisms, microorganisms/animals

2 External appearance, internal structures, DNA evidence.
Any other valid points (there are other observations which are not covered within the scope of this specification but if students know them they should get credit).

3 Evolutionary trees look at the relationships between different groups of animals and how long ago they divided away from a common ancestor. They are very useful for helping to understand evolutionary pathways and relationships between species. DNA evidence has become very important in the development of evolutionary trees and changed some of the ideas based on observation alone.

Summary answers

1 Lamarck thought that animals adapted and evolved to suit their environment and that they had all evolved from primitive worms by the inheritance of acquired characteristics. Lamarck's theory was that an organism's behaviour affected their structures, so if an animal used something a lot over several generations it would grow and develop and this improved feature would be passed from parents to offspring. If a structure wasn't used, Lamarck thought it would shrink and be lost.

2 a He started with his work on barnacles but it was the observations he made on the voyage on the *Beagle* that really made him recognise the great variety of life and start to consider how it had come about.

b Darwin's theory is that all organisms produce more offspring than can survive. Some of these are better fitted to the environment than others, and these are the ones that are most likely to survive, breed and pass on those beneficial characteristics. This process of natural selection is most noticeable if there is a change in the environment.

3 a Similarities: They both suggest evolution of living things from simpler organisms, both suggest it took a long time; both suggest changes passed from parents to offspring. **Differences:** Lamarck suggests primitive worms as a starting point, suggests it is acquired characteristics which are passed on; Darwin suggests it is inherited features which are passed on, and the process of natural selection ('survival of the fittest') to decide which organisms survive and breed.

b Any thoughtful point, e.g. It helped to pave the way for Darwin's ideas, people had already come to terms with a theory other than the Bible, debate was opened up, the idea of organisms evolving and changing was already there, Darwin's ideas of natural selection then made more sense – (people could see it happening with their own livestock) – than the idea of acquired characteristics which people could see didn't happen in their own experience.

4 Credit careful explanations which include an understanding of the basic concepts. E.g. a pair of founder finches on one island with a high insect population has mutation which results in birds with a slightly different shape beak. This makes it easier (for example) to poke its beak into cracks to find insects. These birds can get food that others can't reach which gives them an advantage. They get more food therefore more likely to survive, breed and pass on the genes for the thinner beak shape. Eventually a whole group of birds evolve with thinner beaks which feed on insects. As they are separate from the other birds – a new species has been formed. A similar process occurs on another island where there are a lot of fruit bushes – these birds evolve beaks suited to eating fruit and buds etc. The birds evolve to take advantage of the available food on the islands.

5 a That species exist in different forms and the species which are not well adapted to conditions are most likely to die out.

b Both relatively isolated islands with lots of organisms which are found only there and are well adapted to the conditions. These different organisms would have helped Wallace as the differences were clear and obviously related to the conditions in Borneo just as Darwin observed the very specialised organisms on the Galapagos islands.

Summary questions 🄺

1 What was Jean-Baptiste Lamarck's theory of evolution?

2 a What started Charles Darwin thinking about the variety of life and how it has come about?

b Explain Darwin's theory of evolution.

3 a Summarise the similarities and differences between Darwin's and Lamarck's theories of evolution.

b Why do you think Lamarck's theory was so important to the way Darwin's theory was subsequently received?

4

Figure 1 Darwin's finches – more evidence for evolution

Look at the birds in Figure 1. They are known as Darwin's finches. They live on the Galapagos Islands. Each one has a slightly different beak and eats a different type of food.

Explain carefully how natural selection can result in so many different beak shapes from one original type of founder finch.

5 Alfred Russel Wallace came from a poor family but he was a gifted naturalist. He went on a collecting expedition to Borneo, an island in South East Asia that has a rich variety of unique animal and plant life. While he was there, Wallace became ill with a fever and while he was unwell he developed his theory. He had the idea that if species exist in various forms, the organisms that are not well adapted to change are likely to die out. This would leave only the better-adapted forms to survive and breed. Wallace put his ideas down in a paper and sent it to Charles Darwin for advice. Darwin and Wallace both published papers together on their ideas in London at the same time. It was Wallace's work that shocked Darwin into finally writing *The Origin of Species*.

Wallace's ideas were not as well thought out as D[arwin's] and he did not have the evidence to back them u[p, which] is why it is largely Darwin who is remembered fo[r the] theory of evolution by natural selection.

a What was Wallace's theory?

b What are the similarities between Borneo and [the] Galapagos and how would this have helped W[allace] develop his theory?

c Why do you think the arrival of Wallace's letter [and] paper was such a shock to Darwin?

d Wallace's theories were not strongly supporte[d by] evidence. What sort of evidence did Darwin br[ing] forward to support his ideas in *The Origin of S[pecies]*?

6 a What is classification?

b Explain two alternative ways of deciding how t[o] classify an organism.

c What are the differences and similarities betwe[en] an evolutionary relationship and an ecological relationship between organisms?

7 It is difficult to gather data that illustrate evolution[. It is] possible to gather data to show natural selection [but] this usually takes a long time. Simulations are us[eful] because, while they are not factually correct, the[y can] show how natural selection might work.

A class decided to simulate natural selection, usi[ng] different tools to pick up seeds.

Four students each chose a particular tool to pic[k up] seeds. The teacher then scattered hundreds of s[eeds] onto a patch of grass outside the lab. The four st[udents] were given 5 minutes to pick up as many seeds a[s they] could.

James, who was using a spoon, picked up 23 se[eds] whilst Farzana, using a fork, could only pick up t[?] Claire managed seven seeds with the spatula, b[ut] Jenny struggled to pick up her two seeds with a [pair of] scissors.

a Put the essential data into a table.

b How would the data be best presented? Expla[in your] choice.

c Was this a fair test? Explain your answer.

d What conclusion can you draw from this simu[lation]?

e How does this simulation model the situation [with the] finches on the Galapagos Islands, which evolv[ed into] many different species?

---

c Darwin was still working on his ideas and building up evidence – he was not expecting someone else to come up with basically the same idea on the strength of a short period of work.

d Darwin had many different species which were closely related showing adaptations from Galapagos. He had years of breeding experiments with pigeons; both his own and from others, huge collections of drawings and classification of barnacles with adaptations to different environments etc.

6 a The organisation of living organisms into groups based on the similarities and differences between them.

b Simple observation of external physical characteristics, habitat, etc.

Analysis of the DNA to show the genetic links between the organisms.

c Both show the ways in which organisms are related and may have evolved from a common ancestor.

An evolutionary relationship shows how closely linked different organisms are genetically and so shows when the different species evolved away from each other.

An ecological relationship shows how different organisms have developed together within their environment, and how this has affected their evolution.

Examination-style questions

This diagram shows a timeline for the evolution of some dinosaurs. The mass of each dinosaur is shown in the brackets by its name.

Choose the correct answer to complete each sentence.

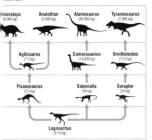

Dinosaur evolution timeline

A dinosaur which lived between 100 and 150 million years ago is .... (1)

Agilisaurus   Saturnalia   Tyrannosaurus

Camarasaurus evolved from .... (1)

Agilisaurus   Alamosaurus   Saturnalia

The difference in mass between Agilisaurus and the smallest dinosaur is .... kg. (1)

1.82   5.5   7.32

The earliest life forms developed on Earth more than 3 .... years ago. (1)

billion   million   thousand

The earliest life forms can be described as .... (1)

bony   complex   simple

Darwin suggested a theory of evolution. His theory is described as evolution by .... (1)

required characteristics   a god   natural selection

2 Giraffes have developed their long necks over millions of years.

Two scientists tried to explain why the giraffes have long necks. They are called Darwin and Lamarck.

Match the name in List A to the correct statement in List B.

List A	List B
Name	**Statement**
Darwin only	Noticed that the neck of the giraffe changed over time
Lamark only	Had enough evidence to prove why the giraffe's neck got longer
Both Lamark and Darwin	Thought that natural selection worked on variations in neck length present at birth
	Thought the giraffe stretched its neck while eating leaves in trees. Then its young inherited the longer neck

(3)

3 The photograph shows a snake eating a toad.

Cane toads were first introduced into Australia in 1935. The toads contain toxins and most species of Australian snake die after eating the toad. The cane toad toxin does not affect all snakes the same way. Longer snakes are less affected by toad toxin. Scientists investigated how red-bellied black snakes had changed in the 70 years since cane toads were introduced into their area. They found that red-bellied black snakes had become longer by around 3–5%.

Suggest an explanation for the change in the body length of the red-bellied black snakes since the introduction of the cane toads.

(4)
AQA, 2005

131

AQA Examination-style answers

1	**a**	**i**	Agilisaurus	*(1 mark)*
		ii	Saturnalia	*(1 mark)*
		iii	7.32	*(1 mark)*
	b	**i**	billion	*(1 mark)*
		ii	simple	*(1 mark)*
	c		Natural selection	*(1 mark)*

2 Darwin only – Thought that natural selection worked on variations in neck length present at birth.

Lamark only – Thought the giraffe stretched its neck while eating leaves in trees. Then its young inherited the longer neck.

Both Lamark and Darwin – Noticed that the neck of the giraffe changed over time. *(3 marks)*

3 Accept any **four** from:

- mutation (*do **not** accept 'had to mutate/decided to mutate'*)
- produces longer snake **or** there is variation in snake length (*do **not** accept 'had to adapt and became longer'*)
- longer snake less susceptible to toxin **or** longer snake survives
- survivors reproduce
- gene passed to next generation (*allow characteristic passed to next generation*) *(4 marks)*

7 a

Tool used	spoon	fork	spatula	scissors
Number of seeds	23	2	7	2

b Data would best be presented in a bar chart, because the independent variable is categoric.

c No, this was not a fair test. The different people could have performed differently, so it was not a test of the tools used. The results are not valid.

d That different people using different tools can pick up different numbers of seeds. Possibly the spoon was the best tool.

e The spoon is like the finch's beak, which is most successful at picking up seeds. The other beaks (fork, spatula and scissors) were less successful and so less likely to be carried into the next generation.

Kerboodle resources

Resources available for this chapter on Kerboodle are:

- Chapter map: Evolution
- How Science Works: How the peppered moth changed colour (B1 7.3)
- Bump up your grade: Natural selection (B1 7.3)
- Extension: Evolutionary trees (B1 7.3)
- Interactive activity: Evolution
- Revision podcast: Evolution
- Test yourself: Evolution
- On your marks: Evolution
- Examination-style questions: Evolution
- Answers to examination-style questions: Evolution

AQA Examination-style answers

1 a i C *(1 mark)*
ii A *(1 mark)*
iii D *(1 mark)*

b (Sun) light – not sun alone *(1 mark)*

c Any **two** from:
- the snails/bluetits use some of the energy
- some of the food energy is not eaten or digested/idea e.g. bones cannot be digested
- (energy used) for movement (by snails or bluetits)
- (energy used) to keep (bluetits) warm *(2 marks)*

2 a Extremophiles *(1 mark)*

b Enzymes *(1 mark)*

c 3 billion years *(1 mark)*

d Genes *(1 mark)*

3 a Any **two** from:
- live inside/infect body cells
- difficult for drugs to enter (body) cells/drug would kill (body) cell
- antibiotics ineffective against viruses
- viruses mutate **frequently** *(2 marks)*

b i 420
*correct answer with **or** without working*
if answer incorrect evidence of 'number of deaths' × 7
or *60 seen gains **1** mark*
ignore 6 000 000 *(2 marks)*

ii Any **three** from:
- virus/flu mutates
- people no longer/not immune
ignore resistance
- white blood cells/memory cells/immune system do not recognise virus
- relevant reference to antibodies/antigens
- current vaccine ineffective **or** no vaccine available then
or takes time to develop new vaccine
allow no tamiflu/anti-viral drugs
- conditions less hygienic/lack of hygiene
- people in poor health (following world wars)
allow people had 'weak' immune system *(3 marks)*

4 There is a clear, balanced and detailed argument referring to both pros and cons and a conclusion which matches the pros and cons. The answer shows almost faultless spelling, punctuation and grammar. It is coherent and in an organised, logical sequence. It contains a range of appropriate or relevant specialist terms used accurately. *(5–6 marks)*

The answer contains at least one pro and one con with a conclusion. There are some errors in spelling, punctuation and grammar. The answer has some structure and organisation. The use of specialist terms has been attempted, but not always accurately. *(3–4 marks)*

There is mention of either a pro or a con with an attempt at a conclusion or a list of pros and cons without a conclusion, has little clarity and detail. The spelling, punctuation and grammar are very weak. The answer is poorly organised with almost no specialist terms and/or their use demonstrating a general lack of understanding of their meaning. *(1–2 marks)*

No relevant content. *(0 marks)*

1 The diagrams show some biological processes.

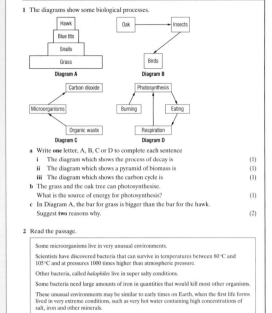

Diagram A · **Diagram B** · **Diagram C** · **Diagram D**

a Write **one** letter, A, B, C or D to complete each sentence
i The diagram which shows the process of decay is (1)
ii The diagram which shows a pyramid of biomass is (1)
iii The diagram which shows the carbon cycle is (1)
b The grass and the oak tree can photosynthesise.
What is the source of energy for photosynthesis? (1)
c In Diagram A, the bar for grass is bigger than the bar for the hawk.
Suggest **two** reasons why. (2)

2 Read the passage.

> Some microorganisms live in very unusual environments.
>
> Scientists have discovered bacteria that can survive in temperatures between 80 °C and 105 °C and at pressures 1000 times higher than atmospheric pressure.
>
> Other bacteria, called *halophiles* live in super salty conditions.
>
> Some bacteria need large amounts of iron in quantities that would kill most other organisms.
>
> These unusual environments may be similar to early times on Earth, when the first life forms lived in very extreme conditions, such as very hot water containing high concentrations of salt, iron and other minerals.

a What is the name given to all the bacteria which live in these unusual environments? (1)
b Which chemical in human cells would not work at temperatures between 80 °C and 105 °C? (1)
c How long ago did early life forms appear on Earth? (1)
d Halophiles breed in very salty conditions. The offspring of halophiles can also live in very salty conditions.
Choose the correct answer to complete the sentence.
The offspring can live in salty conditions because the parents pass on their ....
genes   iron   salt (1)

132

Examples of biology points made in the response:
Pros
- large scale trial gave better results
- chose uneducated women so that if these women could use it correctly, women elsewhere would be able to.

Cons
- used pill with high dose of hormone – *either* so results not valid for general use of hormone *or* dangerous
- side effects ignored
- women not told pill was experimental/pill might have side effects
- no placebo
- should have tried a range of doses
- should have done pre-trial to check for side effects

Conclusion 1 mark, e.g.
- trials flawed therefore cons outweigh pros
- *accept reverse* e.g. trials flawed but pros outweigh cons.

fluenza is a disease caused by a virus.

Suggest **two** reasons why it is difficult to treat diseases caused by viruses. (2)

In some years there are influenza epidemics.

The graph shows the death rate in Liverpool during three influenza epidemics.

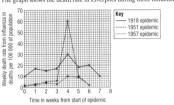

Key
— 1918 epidemic
- - - 1951 epidemic
····· 1957 epidemic

i   The population of Liverpool in 1951 was approximately 700 000.
    Calculate the approximate number of deaths from influenza in week 4 of the
    1951 epidemic.
    Show clearly how you work out your answer. (2)

ii In most years, the number of deaths from influenza in Liverpool is very low.
    Suggest, in terms of the influenza virus and the body's immune system, **three**
    reasons why there were large numbers of deaths in years such as 1918 and 1951. (3)

this question you will be assessed on using good English, organising information clearly
d using specialist terms where appropriate.

ormones are used in contraceptive pills.

ead the information about the trialling of the first contraceptive pill.

> The Pill was developed by a team of scientists led by Gregory Pincus. The team needed to
> carry out large-scale trials on humans.
>
> In the summer of 1955, Pincus visited the island of Puerto Rico. Puerto Rico is one of the
> most densely populated areas in the world. Officials supported birth control as a form of
> population control. Pincus knew that if he could demonstrate that the poor, uneducated
> women of Puerto Rico could use the Pill correctly then so could women anywhere in the
> world.
>
> The scientists selected a pill with a high dose of hormones to ensure that no pregnancies
> would occur while test subjects were taking the drug. The Pill was found to be 100%
> effective when taken properly. But 17% of the women in the study complained of side
> effects. Pincus ignored these side effects.
>
> The women in the trial had been told only that they were taking a drug that prevented
> pregnancy. They had not been told that the Pill was experimental or that there was a
> chance of dangerous side effects.

valuate the methods used by Pincus in trialling the contraceptive pill. (6)

AQA Examiner's tip

Before answering a graph question be sure to read all the information before the graph and then read the axis labels. When a graph has several lines, as in 3b, check the key before you take any readings.

Next, read the question instructions. Why has the examiner told you the population is 700 000? You need this information because the numbers of deaths is given per 100 000.

Before doing the calculation, check again that you are reading the point on the correct graph line.

AQA Examiner's tip

When you see the following instruction

In this question you will be assessed on using good English, organising information clearly and using specialist terms where appropriate.

Be aware that you will lose marks if you do not:
● write in a logical order
● use the correct scientific terms and spell them correctly
● PLAN before you WRITE.

AQA Examiner's comments

Proportion seems to baffle many Foundation candidates. They do not appear to relate what they learn in Maths to Biology questions. Examiners sometimes accept answers which are not strictly proportion if they have been derived from the correct figures, e.g. a percentage is given – but students should not bank on this!

AQA Examiner's comments

It may be worth having a 'Maths for biology' lesson so that the average and Foundation Tier students are supported to improve their maths skills. Several marks can be lost by carelessness and they should be encouraged to think whether the answer looks unrealistic, e.g. it is over 100% or is in millions instead of tens – these mistakes are often made when using a calculator.

AQA Examiner's comments

Examiners are always looking for novel ways for data to be presented to avoid predictability – make a collection of some of these from past papers, e.g. pie charts, overlapping circles, scattergrams – small posters/flash cards of these can make them look familiar and less daunting.

Bump up your grades

Questions on examination papers sometimes include the comment: 'To gain full marks in the question you should write your ideas in good English. Put them in a sensible order and use the correct scientific words' or words to that effect. It should be impressed on students that this is not just a request to write clearly so that the examiner finds their papers easier to mark. It is an instruction that, if not followed, will cost marks.

Ensuring that a candidate gets full marks is less about having a wide vocabulary and more about expressing themselves in a **logical** and **scientific** manner. To help those students who have difficulty with this aspect of examinations, they could attempt any one of the questions in the Student Book that carry an allowance of 4 or more marks or that use the term 'explain'. These almost invariably involve the need to organise facts and express ideas. Better still, take some of the answer schemes in this book and firstly, rewrite them in bad English and with imprecise scientific terms, then mix up the order of the points. Get the students to rewrite the answers in clear, logical, scientific English.

C1 1.1

Atoms, elements and compounds

Learning objectives

Students should learn:

- that elements are made of only one type of atom
- that symbols are used to represent atoms of a certain element
- the basic structure of the atom.

Learning outcomes

Most students should be able to:

- define an element
- recognise names, symbols, formulae and diagrams of elements or compounds
- label the nucleus and electrons in an atom, when the key words are given
- find symbols for elements in the periodic table.
- give examples and draw diagrams to explain the difference between elements and compounds
- draw and label an atom with the nucleus and electrons.

Support

- Make sure that you start by showing students the elements that have a symbol which is the same as the first letter of its name. Carbon, Nitrogen and Oxygen are a good start. Stress to students that this letter is capitalised.

Extend

- Students could undertake research, using the internet, to find the origin of some symbols of elements that are unrelated to their names in English, such as Pb.
- Students could look at different representations of the periodic table, such as those which show abundance, only the naturally occurring elements, 3-D models, etc.

AQA Specification link-up: Chemistry C1.1

- All substances are made of atoms. A substance that is made of only one sort of atom is called an element. There are about 100 different elements. Elements are shown in the periodic table. The groups contain elements with similar properties. *[C1.1.1 a)]*
- Atoms of each element are represented by a chemical symbol, e.g. O represents an atom of oxygen, and Na represents an atom of sodium. *[C1.1.1 b)]*
- Atoms have a small central nucleus, … around which there are electrons. *[C1.1.1 c)]*

Lesson structure

Starters

Anagrams – Students could try to create as many 'scientific' words as they can, using the letters from the term 'periodic table'. *(5 minutes)*

5,4,3,2,1 – Ask students to list five solid elements, four metal elements, three non-metal elements, two gaseous elements at room temperature, and one liquid element at room temperature. This task draws on the idea that most elements are solids at room temperature and most are metals. Students could be supported by being given a list of common elements or a copy of the periodic table. Students could be extended by being asked to give the symbols of the elements chosen as well as their names. *(10 minutes)*

Main

- Some students may not have had the opportunity to handle elements, apart from metals that they use in everyday life. Separate the class into groups of about five students. Give each group of students sealed samples of different elements. The students should then be instructed to sort them into different sets. Each group can feed back to the class how they classified the elements (possible sets might include: state, colour, metal/non-metal, hazard). Draw out from the students, using questions and answers, that there are a finite number of elements – about 100. Challenge the students to think about how we get the immense variety of materials in the world. This should lead on to a discussion of compounds and bonding.

- Play the elements song (this also has a flash animation): Search for 'flash animation' and 'elements' under www.privatehand.com

- Some students struggle with defining atoms, molecules, elements and compounds. A kinaesthetic, cut-and-stick activity could be used. The student should create a four-column (atom, molecule, element, compound) table in their exercise book. Different images representing atoms, molecules, elements and compounds, and the definitions of these four words, can then be given to the student to put into their table.

Plenaries

Code breaker – Ask the students to use the periodic table to decode this hidden message:

Carbon, radon, carbon, potassium, thorium, einsteinium, yttrium, M, boron, oxygen, L, sulfur. [CRaCKThEsYMBOLS]. Students could be supported by having the appropriate elements already highlighted on the periodic table, so they can find them more easily. This activity could be extended by getting the students to write their own secret message. *(5 minutes)*

Favourite – Ask students to think about their favourite element, giving reasons for their choice [e.g. copper, because it makes spiders' blood blue]. Students should then share their idea with a partner. The teacher could then ask a few pairs what their favourite elements are and why. *(10 minutes)*

Answers to in-text questions

a about 100
b Because you can combine them together in millions of different ways.
c Because an element may have different names in different languages.
d metals – barium (Ba), vanadium (V), mercury (Hg)
   non-metals – phosphorus (P), krypton (Kr)

Further teaching suggestions

Display work

● Each student can be assigned a different element. They are then given a piece of card to draw its chemical symbol and write five facts about the element found from secondary sources. In the following lesson, an electron diagram of one of its atoms, with the subatomic particles labelled, could be added. These cards can then be used to make a display in the classroom.

Spider diagram

● Begin to make a spider diagram using the key points on this spread. Then at the end of each lesson during this unit, or as a homework activity, the other key points from the topic can be added. By the end of the topic, a powerful revision resource will have been created.

?? Did you know … ?

Most of the f-block elements were only discovered when nuclear reactors were invented. Under these conditions, these heavy elements have been synthesised. However, a number decay with very short half-lives and they are difficult to study.

For example, the element lawrencium (Lr, atomic number 103) was first discovered in 1961 in California. Lawrencium-260 has a half-life of three minutes.

Fundamental ideas

C1 1.1   Atoms, elements and compounds

Learning objectives

● What are elements made of?
● How do we represent atoms and elements?
● What is the basic structure of an atom?

Look at the things around you and the substances that they are made from. You will find wood, metal, plastic, glass … the list is almost endless. Look further and the number of different substances is mind-boggling.

All substances are made of **atoms**. There are about 100 different types of atom found naturally on Earth. These can combine in a huge variety of ways. This gives us all those different substances.

Some substances are made up of only one type of atom. We call these substances elements. As there are only about 100 different types of atom, there are only about 100 different elements.

a How many different types of atom are there?
b Why can you make millions of different substances from these different types of atom?

Elements can have very different properties. Elements such as silver, copper and gold are shiny **solids**. Other elements such as oxygen, nitrogen and chlorine are **gases**.

Atoms have their own symbols 🄺

The name we use for an element depends on the language being spoken. For example, sulfur is called *schwefel* in German and *azufre* in Spanish! However, a lot of scientific work is international. So it is important that we have symbols for elements that everyone can understand. You can see these symbols in the **periodic table**.

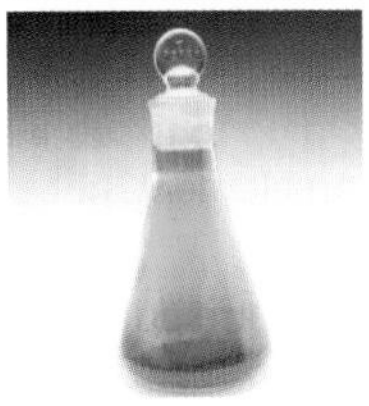

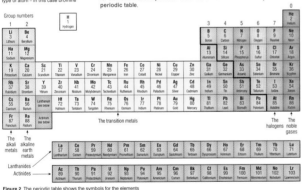

Figure 1 An element contains only **one** type of atom – in this case bromine

Figure 2 The periodic table shows the symbols for the elements

The symbols in the periodic table represent atoms. For example, O represents an atom of oxygen; Na represents an atom of sodium. The elements in the table are arranged in columns, called **groups**. Each group contains elements with similar chemical properties. The 'staircase' drawn in bold is the dividing line between metals and non-metals. The elements to the left of the line are metals. Those on the right of the line are non-metals.

c Why is it useful to have symbols for atoms of different elements?
d Sort these elements into metals and non-metals: phosphorus (P), barium (Ba), vanadium (V), mercury (Hg) and krypton (Kr).

Atoms, elements and compounds

Most of the substances we come across are not pure elements. They are made up of different types of atom joined together. These are called **compounds**. Chemical bonds hold the atoms tightly together in compounds. Some compounds are made from just two types of atom (e.g. water, made from hydrogen and oxygen). Other compounds consist of more different types of atom.

An atom is made up of a tiny central **nucleus** with **electrons** around it.

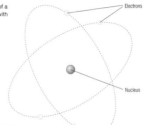

Figure 3 Each atom consists of a small nucleus surrounded by electrons

?? Did you know … ?

Only 92 elements occur naturally on Earth. The other heavier elements in the periodic table have to be made artificially and might only exist for fractions of a second before they decay into other, lighter elements.

⃝ links

For more information on what is inside an atom, see C1 1.2 Atomic structure and 1.3 The arrangement of electrons in atoms.

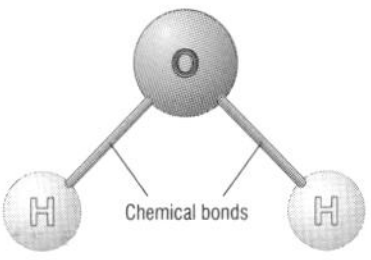

Figure 4 A grouping of two or more atoms bonded together is called a molecule. Chemical bonds hold the hydrogen and oxygen atoms together in the water molecule. Water is an example of a compound.

Summary questions

1 Copy and complete using the words below:
   atoms bonds molecule compounds
   All elements are made up of ………… . When two or more atoms join together a ………… is formed. The atoms in elements and ………… are held tightly to each other by chemical ………… .

2 Explain why when we mix two elements together we can often separate them again quite easily. However, when two elements are chemically combined in a compound, they can be very difficult to separate.

3 Draw diagrams to explain the difference between an element and a compound. Use a hydrogen molecule (H_2) and a hydrogen chloride molecule (HCl) to help explain.

4 Draw a labelled diagram to show the basic structure of an atom.

Key points

● All substances are made up of atoms.
● Elements contain only one type of atom.
● Compounds contain more than one type of atom.
● An atom has a tiny nucleus in its centre, surrounded by electrons.

Summary answers

1 atoms, molecule, compounds, bonds

2 In a mixture, the different substances are not joined to each other by chemical bonds, but in a compound the atoms are held together tightly by chemical bonds – this makes them difficult to separate.

3

Element
e.g. hydrogen

Compound
e.g. hydrogen chloride

4
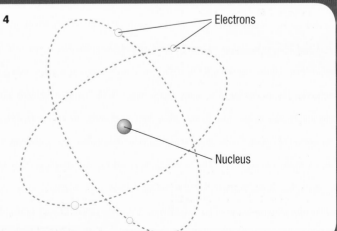
Electrons

Nucleus

C1 1.2 Atomic structure

Learning objectives

Students should learn:

- the relative charges on subatomic particles
- that the number of protons equals the number of electrons in an atom
- that the number of protons in each atom of an element is its atomic number and the number of protons plus neutrons is the mass number
- that atoms are arranged in order of their atomic number in the periodic table.

Learning outcomes

Most students should be able to:

- label the subatomic particles in an atom
- state the charge of the subatomic particles in an atom
- define atomic number and mass number
- describe how the elements are ordered in the periodic table.

Some students should also be able to:

- explain why atoms are electrically neutral.

Support

- Ask students to fill in a table for a selection of elements, where they find the symbol, its atomic (proton) number from the periodic table and use this to determine the number of protons and electrons. Students often forget that the number of protons equals the number of electrons in a neutral atom.

Extend

- Ask students to write a timeline to show when, who and how the subatomic particles were discovered. Students should use secondary sources like the internet to help them. This links well to the How Science Works chapter.
- Students could research and list the general physical and chemical properties of the first 20 elements in the periodic table.

AQA Specification link-up: Chemistry C1.1

- Atoms have a small central nucleus, which is made up of protons and neutrons and around which there are electrons. *[C1.1.1 c)]*
- The relative electrical charges are as shown. *[C1.1.1 d)]*

Name of particle	Charge
Proton	+1
Neutron	0
Electron	−1

- In an atom, the number of electrons is equal to the number of protons in the nucleus. Atoms have no overall electrical charge. *[C1.1.1 e)]*
- All atoms of a particular element have the same number of protons. Atoms of different elements have different numbers of protons. *[C1.1.1 f)]*
- The number of protons in an atom of an element is its atomic number. The sum of the protons and neutrons in an atom is its mass number. *[C1.1.1 g)]*

Lesson structure

Starters

Spot the mistake – 'When different compounds join together, atoms of the same element are made.' [Compounds do not join together; different types of atom join up to make compounds. Also, if all the atoms are the same in a material, then it is an element, not a compound.] *(5 minutes)*

Create the question – Give students three answers [atom, element, and compound]. They should create three questions that have these three answers. For example, what is the name of the smallest particle that can exist on its own? [Answer: atom.] Students can be supported by being asked to work in small groups. Students can be extended by being asked to come up with other correct answers to the same question. *(10 minutes)*

Main

- Ask students to define a proton, an electron and a neutron. You could support students by asking them to match the key word with the definition. Students could be extended by also being asked to label a diagram of an atom with the key words. You may wish to give students a partially filled table from the specification which contrasts the subatomic particles. They could then fill in the information for each of the subatomic particles using the definitions to help them.
- Give each student an element from the first 20 in the periodic table. Encourage them to research their element, define the term atomic number and represent its structure in as many different ways that they can find.
- Students could compile their diagrams into a poster, with the subatomic particles labelled. The posters could be displayed in the classroom.
- Atoms were discovered and grouped in many different ways. Supply students with cards for the first 20 elements in the periodic table. On one side of the card there should be the element's name, symbol, numbers of protons, neutrons (most common isotope) and electrons. On the reverse, its general physical and chemical properties should be listed. Students should then work in small teams to order the elements in different ways [alphabetically, number of protons, number of neutrons, physical properties, etc.]. You should tour the other teams, asking them about their grouping structure and encourage them to find new ways to group the elements.
- Then ask the students to sort their cards into the order of the periodic table. Ask the students what they notice [that the elements are in order of atomic number]. Then ask the students to summarise in one sentence how the atoms are arranged in the periodic table.
- Ensure students are familiar with 'atomic number' and 'mass number' and can use them to list the subatomic particles in atoms.

Plenary

Label – On the board draw a diagram of a helium atom. Students should copy the diagram and label the subatomic particles with their name and their charge. *(5 minutes)*

Further teaching suggestions

Elements cards
- Instead of organising cards with the elements' details on them, the elements themselves could be provided in sealed gas jars and Petri dishes. The relevant information could then be stuck onto the container with tape.

Representing the atom
- Give students lots of different examples of representing an atom, e.g. 2-D drawing, 3-D computer model, artist's impression, electron microscope. Students could look at the different ways of representing the atom and evaluate them. Students should discuss their thoughts and decide which they think is the most useful way of representing the atom and explain why.

Building mobiles
- Mobiles of atoms can be created. A 5 cm diameter circle and a ring are drawn onto a piece of card. The rings need to be drawn so that the circle fits inside and a gap is left between them [e.g. inner diameter of the ring is 13 cm and outer diameter of the ring is 15 cm]. The student cuts out the template and draws subatomic particles using colours to highlight the charges. The circle represents the nucleus and the ring the shell of electrons. They could be encouraged to find out an interesting fact and write it on another piece of card (10 cm × 5 cm). String and tape is then used to join the fact to the ring (electron shell), the ring to the circle (nucleus) and that in turn to the top part of the ring. Excess string should be available at the top to suspend the mobile. Note that to be chemically correct the students can only complete a mobile of H or He at this stage; to complete large atoms, additional rings need to be added.

Fundamental ideas

C1 1.2 — Atomic structure

Learning objectives
- What is the charge on a proton, a neutron and an electron?
- What can we say about the number of protons in an atom compared with its number of electrons?
- What is the 'atomic number' and 'mass number' of an atom?
- How are atoms arranged in the periodic table?

In the middle of an atom there is a very small nucleus. This contains two types of particles, which we call protons and neutrons. A third type of particle orbits the nucleus. We call these really tiny particles electrons.

Any atom has the same number of electrons orbiting its nucleus as it has protons in its nucleus.

Protons have a positive charge. Neutrons have no charge – they are neutral. So the nucleus itself has an overall positive charge.

The electrons orbiting the nucleus are negatively charged. The relative charge on a proton is +1 and the relative charge on an electron is −1.

Because any atom contains equal numbers of protons and electrons, the positive and negative charges cancel out. So there is no overall charge on any atom. Its charge is zero. For example, a carbon atom is neutral. It has 6 protons, so we know it must have 6 electrons.

a What are the names of the three particles that make up an atom?

b An oxygen atom has 8 protons – how many electrons does it have?

Figure 1 Understanding the structure of an atom gives us important clues to the way chemicals react together

Type of subatomic particle	Relative charge
Proton	+1
Neutron	0
Electron	−1

To help you remember the charge on the subatomic particles:
- **P**rotons are **P**ositive;
- **Neut**rons are **Neut**ral;
- so that means Electrons must be Negative!

Atomic number and the periodic table

All the atoms of a particular element have the same number of protons. For example, hydrogen has 1 proton in its nucleus, carbon has 6 protons in its nucleus and sodium has 11 protons in its nucleus.

We call the **number of protons** in each atom of an element its **atomic number**.

Did you know ...?
In 1808, a chemist called John Dalton published a theory of atoms. It explained how atoms joined together to form new substances (compounds). Not everyone liked his theory though – one person wrote 'Atoms are round bits of wood invented by Mr Dalton!'

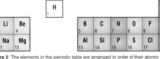

Figure 2 The elements in the periodic table are arranged in order of their atomic number. (As atoms are neutral, this is also the same order as their number of electrons.)

The elements in the periodic table are arranged in order of their atomic number (number of protons). If you are told that the atomic number of an element is 8, you can identify it using the periodic table. It will be the 8th element listed. In this case it is oxygen.

c What is the 14th element in the periodic table?

You read the periodic table from left to right, and from the top down – just like reading a page of writing.

d Look at the elements in the last group of the abbreviated periodic table in Figure 2. What pattern do you notice about the number of protons going from helium to neon to argon?

Mass number

The **number of protons plus neutrons** in the nucleus of an atom is called its **mass number**.

- So, if an atom has 4 protons and 5 neutrons, its mass number will be $4 + 5 = 9$.
- Given the atomic number and mass number, we can work out how many protons, electrons and neutrons are in an atom. For example, an argon atom has an atomic number of 18 and a mass number of 40.

Its atomic number is 18 so it has **18 protons**. Remember that atoms have an equal number of protons and electrons. So argon also has **18 electrons**. The mass number is 40, so we know that:

18 (the number of protons) + the number of neutrons = 40

Therefore argon must have **22 neutrons** (as $18 + 22 = 40$).

We can summarise the last part of the calculation as:

number of neutrons = mass number − atomic number

Summary questions

1 Copy and complete using the words below:
   electrons   atomic   negative   neutrons
   In the nucleus of atoms there are protons and .... Around the nucleus there are .... which have a .... charge. In the periodic table, atoms are arranged in order of their .... number.

2 Atoms are always neutral. Explain why.

3 How many protons, electrons and neutrons do the following atoms contain?
   a A nitrogen atom whose atomic number is 7 and its mass number is 14.
   b A chlorine atom whose atomic number is 17 and its mass number is 35.

AQA Examiner's tip
In an atom, the number of protons is always equal to the number of electrons. You can find out the number of protons and electrons in an atom by looking up its atomic number in the periodic table.

links
For more information on the patterns in the periodic table, see C1 1.3 The arrangement of electrons in atoms.

Key points
- Atoms are made of protons, neutrons and electrons.
- Protons and electrons have equal and opposite electric charges. Protons are positively charged, and electrons are negatively charged.
- Neutrons have no electric charge. They are neutral.
- Atomic number = number of protons (= number of electrons) Mass number = number of protons + neutrons
- Atoms are arranged in the periodic table in order of their atomic number.

Did you know ...?
Atoms are very small. Ask students to guess how small this would be. [About 0.000 000 000 1 m in diameter.]

Answers to in-text questions
a protons, neutrons, electrons
b 8 electrons
c silicon
d They increase by 8 between each element.

Summary answers
1 neutrons, electrons, negative, atomic

2 Because protons and electrons have the same amount of charge but with opposite signs, the charge on a proton is exactly cancelled out by the charge on an electron.

3 a 7 protons, 7 electrons and 7 neutrons.
   b 17 protons, 17 electrons and 18 neutrons.

C1 1.3

The arrangement of electrons in atoms

Learning objectives

Students should learn that:

- Limestone is used to make a variety of building materials.
- Limestone will undergo thermal decomposition.

Learning outcomes

Most students should be able to:

- Recall the composition of limestone and list some uses.
- Complete a word equation for the thermal decomposition of limestone.
- Write the formula of calcium carbonate.

Some students should also be able to:

- Explain the process of thermal decomposition of limestone.

Support

- Students could be supported by being shown diagrams of only the outer shell electrons. They could then focus on the relationship between the outer electrons and position in the periodic table.

Extend

- Extend students by asking them to reflect further on the electronic structure of the atom and the periodic table. Students should find out that the period number and the number of electron shells is the same for the first three periods.
- You could also extend students by asking them to find out about instances when noble gases do react, which noble gases they are and under what conditions they react.

AQA Specification link-up: Chemistry C1.1

- Electrons occupy particular energy levels. Each electron in an atom is at a particular energy level (in a particular shell). The electrons in an atom occupy the lowest available energy levels (innermost available shells). Candidates may answer questions in terms of either energy levels or shells. *[C1.1.1 h)]*
- Elements in the same group in the periodic table have the same number of electrons in the highest energy levels (outer electrons) and this gives them similar chemical properties. *[C1.1.2 a)]*
- The elements in Group 0 of the periodic table are called the noble gases. They are unreactive because their atoms have stable arrangements of electrons. *[C1.1.2 b)]*

Lesson structure

Starters

Revision card sort – Give the students nine cards, each with different labels: proton, electron, neutron, nucleus (there should be two of these), shell, +1, 0, −1. Students should also be given a table on a piece of laminated card, consisting of three columns, labelled subatomic particle, charge, position, and three rows. They then sort the cards, putting them in the appropriate positions on the table. *(5 minutes)*

List – Ask students to list all the information they can remember about electrons. Then ask students to share their ideas in small groups and each group takes it in turn to write a piece of information on the board. You should address any misconceptions revealed in this activity. You could support students by giving them some key points, e.g. −1, which they have to use as a prompt to come up with pieces of information. Students could be extended by asking them to do the same for the other subatomic particles. *(10 minutes)*

Main

- Give students a diagram of an argon atom, which includes the electronic structure and the number of protons and neutrons in the nucleus. Use this diagram to explain why atoms have no charge, the positioning of electrons in shells, or energy levels. Discuss the energy levels further and the number of electrons that the shell can hold. State that the maximum number of electrons in the first three shells is 2,8,8, as shown in the argon atom. Encourage students to annotate their diagram to explain the terms 'energy level' and 'electron shell', and why an atom is neutral.
- Students should already be familiar with the periodic table from KS3. Refresh students' memories by reminding them that the columns are called 'groups' and rows are called 'periods'.
- Give students cards with the electronic structure of the first 20 elements with their names. Ask students to use the periodic table to order the cards. Students should be encouraged to reflect on the relationship between the outer electrons and the group that the element belongs in.
- Demonstrate the reactions of Group 1 metals with water and their reactions with oxygen (see 'Demonstration support'). Ensure that you relate the chemistry to the number of outer shell electrons.
- Encourage students to write word equations for each of these reactions. Students could be extended by being asked to write a general equation for the reaction.

Plenaries

Reflection – Ask students to consider a fact that they have revisited from KS3 in the lesson and a new fact that they have learned in the lesson. As they leave the classroom, ask them for their facts. You should challenge any misconceptions during the reflection plenary of the following lesson. *(5 minutes)*

Which atom? – Create flash cards to show the electronic structure of the first 20 elements in a random order. Ask the students to look at the images and work out which atom is being displayed. Students can be supported by being encouraged to use their notes and the Student Book, etc. Students could be extended by only being given the atomic number of an element and then using the periodic table to determine the number of electrons in its outer shell. *(10 minutes)*

Demonstration support

Reactions of Group 1 metals with water

Equipment and materials required

Lithium, sodium, potassium (all stored under oil), white tile, filter paper, spatula, tweezers, water trough, water, safety screen, eye protection (chemical splashproof).

Details

Half-fill the trough with water. Cut a small piece of lithium (no more than 3 mm). Wipe off the excess oil and put into the water. Repeat with the other metals.

Safety: You should wear chemical splashproof safety goggles or face visor and students should also wear safety goggles. There should be a safety screen between the water trough and the students. Be sure not to get the metal on the skin – if this does happen remove with paper or tweezers and only then wash the affected area well under cold water. CLEAPSS Hazcard 58, 88, 76 – highly flammable and corrosive. Leave equipment safe for technicians.

Reactions of Group 1 metals with oxygen

Equipment and materials required

Lithium, sodium, potassium (all stored under oil), 3 × deflagrating spoon, 3 × gas jar (with lid) of oxygen, Bunsen burner and safety equipment, safety screen, eye protection (chemical splashproof).

Details

Cut a small piece of lithium (no more than 3 mm), wipe off the excess oil and put on the deflagrating spoon. Heat the metal in the Bunsen flame until it ignites. Ask students to note the colour and quickly remove the gas jar lid and plunge the deflagrating spoon into the gas jar. Repeat with the other metals.

Safety: You should wear safety goggles or face visor and students should also wear safety goggles. There should be a safety screen between the water trough and the students. Be sure not to get the metal on the skin – if this does happen remove with paper or tweezers and only then wash the affected area well under cold water. CLEAPSS Hazcard 58, 88, 76 – highly flammable and corrosive. CLEAPSS Hazcard 69 Oxygen – oxidising. Leave equipment safe for technician.

Fundamental ideas
The arrangement of electrons in atoms

C1 1.3
The arrangement of electrons in atoms (k)

Learning objectives

- How are the electrons arranged inside an atom?
- How is the number of electrons in the highest energy level of an atom related to its group in the periodic table?
- How is the number of electrons in the highest energy level of an atom related to its chemical properties?
- Why are the atoms of Group 0 elements so unreactive?

One model of the atom which we use has electrons arranged around the nucleus in **shells**, rather like the layers of an onion. Each shell represents a different **energy level**. The lowest energy level is shown by the shell which is nearest to the nucleus. The electrons in an atom occupy the lowest available energy level (the shell closest to the nucleus).

a Where are the electrons in an atom?
b Which shell represents the lowest energy level in an atom?

Electron shell diagrams (k)

We can draw diagrams to show the arrangement of electrons in an atom. A carbon atom has 6 protons, which means it has 6 electrons. Figure 1 shows how we represent an atom of carbon.

An energy level (or shell) can only hold a certain number of electrons.

- The first, and lowest, energy level holds 2 electrons.
- The second energy level can hold up to 8 electrons.
- Once there are 8 electrons in the third energy level, the fourth begins to fill up, and so on.

To save drawing atoms all the time, we can write down the numbers of electrons in each energy level. This is called the **electronic structure**. For example, the carbon atom in Figure 1 has an electronic structure of 2,4.

A silicon atom with 14 electrons has the electronic structure 2,8,4. This represents 2 electrons in the first, and lowest, energy level, then 8 in the next energy level. There are 4 in the highest energy level (its outermost shell).

The best way to understand these arrangements is to look at some examples.

Figure 1 A simple way of representing the arrangement of electrons in the energy levels (shells) of a carbon atom

AQA Examiner's tip

Make sure that you can draw the electronic structure of the atoms for all of the first 20 elements. You will always be given their atomic number or their position in the periodic table (which tells you the number of electrons) – so you don't have to memorise these numbers.

Figure 2 Once you know the pattern, you should be able to draw the energy levels (shells) and electrons in any of the first 20 atoms (given their atomic number)

c How many electrons can the first energy level hold?
d What is the electronic structure of sulfur (whose atoms contain 16 electrons)?

Electrons and the periodic table

Look at the elements in any one of the main groups of the periodic table. Their atoms will all have the same number of electrons in their highest energy level. These electrons are often called the outer electrons because they are in the outermost shell. Therefore, all the elements in Group 1 have one electron in their highest energy level.

Demonstration

Properties of the Group 1 elements

Your teacher will show you the Group 1 elements lithium, sodium and potassium. The elements in this group are called the alkali metals. Make sure you wear eye protection for all the demonstrations.

- In what ways are the elements similar?
- Watch their reactions with water and comment on the similarities.
- You might also be shown their reactions with oxygen.

Figure 3 The Group 1 metals are all reactive metals, stored under oil

The chemical properties of an element depend on how many electrons it has. The way an element reacts is determined by the number of electrons in its highest energy level (or outermost shell). So as the elements in a particular group all have the same number of electrons in their highest energy level, they all react in a similar way.

For example:

lithium + water → lithium hydroxide + hydrogen
sodium + water → sodium hydroxide + hydrogen
potassium + water → potassium hydroxide + hydrogen

The elements in Group 0 of the periodic table are called the noble gases because they are unreactive. Their atoms have a very stable arrangement of electrons. They all have 8 electrons in their outermost shell, except for helium, which has only 2 electrons.

Summary questions

1 Copy and complete using the words below:
   electrons   energy   group   nucleus   shells
   The electrons in an atom are arranged around the .... in .... (energy levels). The electrons further away from the nucleus have more .... than those close to the nucleus. All elements in the same .... of the periodic table have the same number of .... in their outermost shell.

2 Using the periodic table, draw the arrangement of electrons in the following atoms and label each one with its electronic structure.
   a Li   b B   c P   d Ar

3 What is special about the electronic structure of neon and argon?

Key points

- The electrons in an atom are arranged in energy levels or shells.
- Atoms with the same number of electrons in their outermost shell belong to the same group of the periodic table.
- The number of electrons in the outermost shell of an element's atoms determines the way that element reacts.
- The atoms of the unreactive noble gases (in Group 0) all have very stable arrangements of electrons.

Further teaching suggestions

Periodic table

- Give students an A3 or A2 enlarged copy of the periodic table and ask them to draw the electronic structure of the first 20 directly onto the table. To extend students, ask them to find out about reactivity trends and add trend arrows on to the groups to show how reactivity changes going down/up the group.

Group 1 video

- You many wish to show videos of how all the Group 1 metals except for francium react with water. You can find suitable videos on www.teachers.tv by searching for 'Ferocious elements'.

Answers to in-text questions

a Arranged around the nucleus in shells.
b The energy level closest to the nucleus.
c 2   d 2,8,6

Summary answers

1 nucleus, shells, energy, group, electrons

2 a
     Li   2, 1

  b   B   2, 3

  c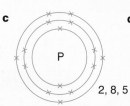
     P   2, 8, 5

  d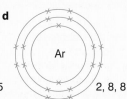
     Ar   2, 8, 8

3 They both have full outer shells or energy levels of electrons/very stable arrangements of electrons.

C1 1.4

Forming bonds

Learning objectives

Students should learn:

- that metals and non-metals form ions when they react to make compounds
- that non-metals can bond to each other by sharing electrons, forming covalent bonds
- that a compound can be represented by its chemical formula.

Learning outcomes

Most students should be able to:

- name the two types of bonding possible in compounds
- interpret formula in terms of number and type of atoms that have joined.

Some students should also be able to:

- explain how the two types of bonding happen.

$\mathcal{AQA}$ ### Specification link-up: Chemistry C1.1

- When elements react, their atoms join with other atoms to form compounds. This involves giving, taking or sharing electrons to form ions or molecules. Compounds formed from metals and non-metals consist of ions. Compounds formed from non-metals consist of molecules. In molecules the atoms are held together by covalent bonds. [C1.1.3 a)]
- Chemical reactions can be represented by word equations or by symbol equations. [C1.1.3 b)]

Lesson structure

Starters

Fume cupboard demonstration – The formation of sodium chloride from its elements is an exciting and impressive reaction. The elements can be shown to the students in sealed containers. You could then demonstrate the formation of sodium chloride in a fume cupboard. *(5 minutes)*

Charge revision – Ask students to draw a table (similar to the one that appears in C1 1.2 Atomic structure) contrasting the charges of the subatomic particles in an atom. Students could be supported by being given the information so that they could cut and stick it into the table. Students could be extended by being asked to display this data in a labelled diagram of an atom. *(10 minutes)*

Main

- Use the step-by-step example of LiF in the Student Book to show how ionic bonds are formed.
- Students could describe the properties of these elements and their electronic structure and write it in their exercise books.
- Following this, ask students to note down the formula of the new compound and state the number of each type of atom. Using electronic structure diagrams of the outer shell electrons for lithium and fluorine, explain how the outer shell electron from lithium has been donated to fluorine. This has formed a positive lithium ion and a negative fluoride ion. Students should classify the bonding as ionic.
- Introduce the idea of covalent bonding and overlapping shells. Use H_2S, H_2O and CH_4 to illustrate covalent bonding.
- Students can form water from its elements, by completing the hydrogen pop! test (see 'Demonstration support').
- Gas jars of oxygen, boiling tubes of hydrogen and beakers of water can be used to allow the students to contrast the properties of the elements with the compound. Students should visually inspect the samples. They should be encouraged to note down the formula of water and classify the bonding as covalent.

Support

- Students could be supported by being given a 'cut-and-stick' activity to contrast covalent and ionic bonding. Students should be able to sort the definitions and examples to form a table of information.

Extend

- Students could be extended by being asked to find out about compound ions, such as sulfate and nitrate ions, and how we write the formulae of their compounds. Students could also be extended by writing the formula of a compound from its name and vice versa.

Plenaries

Reflection – Ask the students to note down:

- What I have seen ...
- What I have heard ...
- What I have done ...

These can be collected in from the class to be used to see what the students have remembered. *(5 minutes)*

Chemical equations – Ask students to write a word equation for the reaction to make sodium chloride from its elements. Support students by giving them the chemical names and a missing word equation to complete. Extend students by asking them to write a balanced symbol equation (which could be used to introduce some of them to state symbols). *(10 minutes)*

Demonstration support

Sodium with chlorine gas

Equipment and materials required

Sodium stored under oil, gas jar of chlorine, deflagrating spoon, Bunsen burner with safety equipment, safety goggles, fume cupboard.

Details

Cut a small piece of sodium (no more than 3 mm), wipe off the excess oil and put on the deflagrating spoon. Heat the metal in the Bunsen flame until it burns, and quickly put into the gas jar. You may wish to record the demonstration using a webcam. The film can then be played back, annotated and paused on an interactive whiteboard during a discussion about the reaction.

Safety: You should wear safety goggles and the reaction should be undertaken in a fume cupboard. Be sure not to get the metal on the skin – if this does happen remove with paper or tweezers and wash the affected area well under cold water. CLEAPSS Hazcard 22 Chlorine – toxic. Warn asthmatics. CLEAPSS Hazcard 88 Sodium – highly flammable and corrosive.

Hydrogen pop! test

Equipment and materials required

Borosilicate test tube of hydrogen, splint, Bunsen burner and safety equipment, chemical splashproof safety goggles.

Details

Light the splint and remove the bung from the test tube. Quickly waft the lighted splint over the neck of the boiling tube.

More details on gas preparations in the CLEAPSS Handbook 13.2.2.

Safety: You should wear safety goggles. CLEAPSS Hazcard 48 Hydrogen – extremely flammable.

To avoid the brown fumes, a 'purer' version is suggested in CLEAPSS guide L195 'safer chemicals, safer reactions', 9.3.

Fundamental ideas

Forming bonds

C1 1.4 — Forming bonds

Learning objectives

- How do metals and non-metals bond to each other?
- How do non-metals bond to each other?
- How do we write the formula of a compound?

AQA Examiner's tip

When counting atoms, think of each symbol as a single atom and the formula of each ion as a single ion. Small numbers in a chemical formula only multiply the symbol they follow. Brackets are needed when there is more than one atom in the ion being multiplied. For example, a hydroxide ion has the formula OH^-. So calcium hydroxide, in which Ca^{2+} and OH^- combine, has the formula $Ca(OH)_2$.

Figure 2 The positive and negative charge on the ions in a compound balance each other, making the total charge zero

It is useful for us to know how atoms bond to each other in different substances. It helps us to predict and explain their properties.

How Science Works

Predicting what material to use

A team of research chemists and material scientists are working to make a new compound for the latest surfboard. Knowing about chemical bonding will make the process of designing a new compound a lot quicker.

Figure 1 Surfboards have to be very strong and have a relatively low density

The substances used to make a surfboard have to be very strong (to withstand large forces) and have a relatively low density (to float on water). Chemists help design materials with suitable properties. They will know before they start which combinations of atoms might prove useful to investigate.

Sometimes atoms react together by **transferring** electrons to form chemical bonds. This happens when metals react with non-metals. If the reacting atoms are all non-metals, then the atoms **share** electrons to form chemical bonds.

Forming ions

When a metal bonds with a non-metal, the metal atom gives one or more electrons to the non-metal atom. Both atoms become charged particles called **ions**.

- Metal atoms form positively charged ions (+).
- Non-metal atoms form negatively charged ions (–).

Opposite charges attract each other. There are strong attractions between the positive and negative ions in a compound of a metal and non-metal. These strong forces of attraction are the chemical bonds that form. They are called **ionic bonds**.

To see how ions are formed we can look at an example. Lithium metal will react with the non-metal fluorine. They make the compound lithium fluoride. Lithium atoms have 3 electrons, each negatively charged. As all atoms are neutral, we know it also has 3 positive protons in its nucleus. The charges on the negative electrons are balanced by the positive protons.

When lithium reacts with fluorine it loses 1 electron. This leaves it with only 2 electrons. However, there are still 3 protons in the nucleus. Therefore the lithium ion carries a 1+ charge. 3 protons = 3+ 2 electrons = 2– Charge on ion = 1+ We show the formula of a lithium ion as Li^+.	The electron lost from lithium is accepted by a fluorine atom. A fluorine atom has 9 electrons and 9 protons, making the atom neutral. However, with the extra electron from lithium, it has an extra 1– charge: 9 protons = 9+ 10 electrons = 10– Charge on ion = 1– We show the formula of a fluoride ion as F^-. Notice the spelling – we have a fluor**ine** atom which turns into a negatively charged fluor**ide** ion.

In compounds between metals and non-metal, the charges on the ions always cancel each other out. This means that their compounds have no overall charge. So the formula of lithium fluoride is written as **LiF**.

a Potassium (K) is a metal. It loses one electron when it forms an ion. What is the formula of a potassium ion?

Forming molecules

Non-metal atoms bond to each other in a different way. The outermost shells of their atoms overlap and they share electrons. Each pair of shared electrons forms a chemical bond between the atoms. These are called **covalent bonds**. No ions are formed. They form molecules, such as hydrogen sulfide, H_2S, and methane, CH_4 (see Figure 3).

b What do we call the bonds between nitrogen and hydrogen atoms in an ammonia molecule, NH_3?

Chemical formulae

The chemical formula of an ionic compound tells us the ratio of each type of ion in the compound. We use a ratio because when ions bond together they form structures made of many millions of ions. The ratio depends on the charge on each ion. The charges must cancel each other out.

An example is magnesium chloride. Magnesium forms Mg^{2+} ions and chlorine forms Cl^- ions. So the formula of magnesium chloride is $MgCl_2$. We have 2 chloride ions for every one magnesium ion in the compound (see Figure 4).

In covalent molecules we can just count the number of each type of atom in a molecule to get its formula. Figure 3 shows two examples.

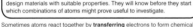

Hydrogen sulfide   Methane

Figure 3 There are strong covalent bonds between the non-metal atoms in each of these molecules. These are shown as lines between each atom or between the symbols of each atom in the molecule (H_2S and CH_4).

Figure 4 The 2+ positive charge on the magnesium ion balances the two 1– negative charges on the chloride ions in magnesium chloride ($MgCl_2$).

Key points

- When atoms from different elements react together they make compounds. The formula of a compound shows the number and type of atoms that have bonded together to make that compound.
- When metals react with non-metals, charged particles called ions are formed.
- Metal atoms form positively charged ions. Non-metal atoms form negatively charged ions. These oppositely charged ions attract each other in ionic bonding.
- Atoms of non-metals bond to each other by sharing electrons. This is called covalent bonding.

Summary questions

1 Copy and complete using the words below:
   covalent   lose   ionic   negative   attract   share   positive
   Metal atoms form .... ions because they .... one or more electrons when they combine with non-metals. Non-metal atoms .... electrons in the reaction, forming .... ions. The oppositely charged ions .... each other. This is called .... bonding.
   When non-metals combine with each other, they form .... bonds. Their atoms .... electrons.

2 Sodium (Na) atoms lose one electron when they combine with fluorine (F). Each fluorine atom gains one electron in the reaction.
   a What is the name of the compound formed when sodium reacts with fluorine?
   b Write down the formula of a sodium ion and a fluoride ion.
   c What is the formula of the compound made when sodium reacts with fluorine.

140

141

Further teaching suggestions

Salt research

- Sodium chloride is an important compound in our diet. Ask students to research why humans need to eat salt, and what can happen if we consume too much salt.

Summary

- Students can be given secondary sources of information about ionic and covalent bonding. They should use this information and the Student Book to summarise in no more than 50 words the differences and similarities between these types of bonding. Students should be encouraged to illustrate their answer with at least one example, not yet seen in the lesson, of each type of bonding.

Answers to in-text questions

a K^+

b covalent bonds

Summary answers

1 positive, lose, gain, negative, attract, ionic, covalent, share

2 **a** Sodium fluoride
  b Na^+ and F^-
  c NaF

C1 1.5

Chemical equations

AQA
Specification link-up: Chemistry C1.1

- No atoms are lost or made during a chemical reaction so the mass of the products equals the mass of the reactants. *[C1.1.3 c)]*

  Controlled Assessment: SA4.1 Planning an investigation. *[SA4.1.1 a) b) c) d) e)]*

Learning objectives

Students should learn:

- how a chemical reaction can be represented
- what happens to the atoms in a chemical reaction
- that mass is conserved in a chemical reaction
- how to balance a chemical equation. **[HT only]**

Learning outcomes

Most students should be able to:

- state a definition of a chemical reaction in terms of reactants and products
- describe how atoms cannot be created or destroyed in a chemical reaction
- state that mass is conserved in a chemical reaction.

Some students should also be able to:

- explain why mass is conserved in a chemical reaction
- balance symbol equations. **[HT only]**

Lesson structure

Starters

Sorting – Write the following word equations on the board and ask students to determine the reactants and the products of the reaction.

$$sodium + chlorine \rightarrow sodium\ chloride$$

$$hydrogen + oxygen \rightarrow water$$

Students could be supported by being given the definitions of reactants and products. Students could be extended by being given a passage describing a reaction from which they need to make the word equation. *(5 minutes)*

Card sort – Give the students separate cards with images (just use coloured circles) and others with the word 'compound', 'element', 'molecule', or 'mixture' written on them. Students should then try to match the image with the key term. *(10 minutes)*

Main

- Ask students to define the term 'chemical reaction' [a change where a new substance is made]. You may wish to encourage students to give some everyday examples of chemical reactions, e.g. rusting, burning.

- Explain to students that atoms are neither created nor destroyed in a chemical reaction, they are just rearranged. Using molecular model kits demonstrate how sulfur reacts with oxygen to make sulfur dioxide [$S + O_2 \rightarrow SO_2$]. Show students that there are the same number and type of atoms on the reactant side as on the product side, but they are rearranged. Ask them to predict how mass would therefore change in a reaction. [It remains the same.]

- Then lead students through combustion of methane using the molymod [$CH_4 + 2O_2 \rightarrow 2H_2O + CO_2$]. Give students the word equation and, through question and answer, try and get the students to give you the formulae of the chemicals. Then ask the students to use the molecular model to make one of each molecule.

- You may wish to allow students to demonstrate the conservation of mass using precipitation reactions (see 'Practical support'). Encourage students to consider how to record their results in a scientific manner. You may need to support students by giving them an appropriate results table to complete.

- Ask students to reflect on how many atoms they have on each side, and explain that you can't add just extra odd atoms, you have to add whole molecules. Students then make one extra oxygen molecule and an extra water molecule and they should see that it balances. Finally they should then write the complete symbol equation. **[HT only]**

Plenaries

Demonstration – Ignite a hydrogen balloon to get the attention of the class and generate excitement. The hydrogen will explode, as it reacts with the oxygen in the air to make water (steam). Encourage the students to write word and balanced symbol equations for this reaction. *(5 minutes)*

Balancing equations – Give the students word equations, which they then convert into balanced symbol equations.

$$magnesium + oxygen \rightarrow magnesium\ oxide\ [2Mg + O_2 \rightarrow 2MgO]$$

$$ethanol + oxygen \rightarrow carbon\ dioxide + water\ [C_2H_5OH + 3O_2 \rightarrow 2CO_2 + 3H_2O]$$

Students can be supported by being given the symbol equation and so they only need to balance it. Students could be extended by being given a prose description of the reaction, which they then have to use to derive the symbol equation. *(10 minutes)* **[HT only]**

Support

- Some students will struggle with balancing equations. Encourage students to write out the number and type of atom in each formula under the symbol equation to complete 'atom accounting'. You may wish to relate to maths and remind students that $a + a$ is written $2a$, and this is the same in science where $2O_2$, means $2 \times O_2$.

Extend

- Extend students by introducing the idea of state symbols and getting them to use them in balanced symbol equations. You can extend students by giving them symbol equations to balance that contain compounds with several compound ions (formulae in brackets).

Practical support

Investigating the mass of reactants and products

Equipment and materials required

0.1 mol/dm³ lead nitrate, 0.1 mol/dm³ potassium iodide, 0.1 mol/dm³ barium chloride, 0.1 mol/dm³ sodium sulfate, top-pan balance, 2 × 25 cm³ measuring cylinder, eye protection (chemical splashproof).

Details

Measure the mass of each empty measuring cylinder. In the first measuring cylinder, measure 10 cm³ of lead nitrate and record its mass. Into a second measuring cylinder, measure 10 cm³ of

potassium iodide and record its mass. Carefully pour the lead nitrate into the potassium iodide and observe [bright yellow precipitate]. Record the new mass. Calculate the mass of the reactants and the mass of the products. Repeat the experiment using barium chloride and sodium sulfate [white precipitate].

Safety: Lead compounds are foetal toxins and toxic. Barium chloride is toxic. Ensure that safety googles are worn and students wash their hands after completing the experiment. CLEAPSS Hazcard 10A Barium chloride; 57A Lead nitrate; 57A Lead iodide – toxic.

Dispose of waste following CLEAPSS advice.

CLEAPSS also suggests you could conduct this experiment at 0·01 mol/dm³ lead nitrate. At this strength the lead solution is only low hazard.

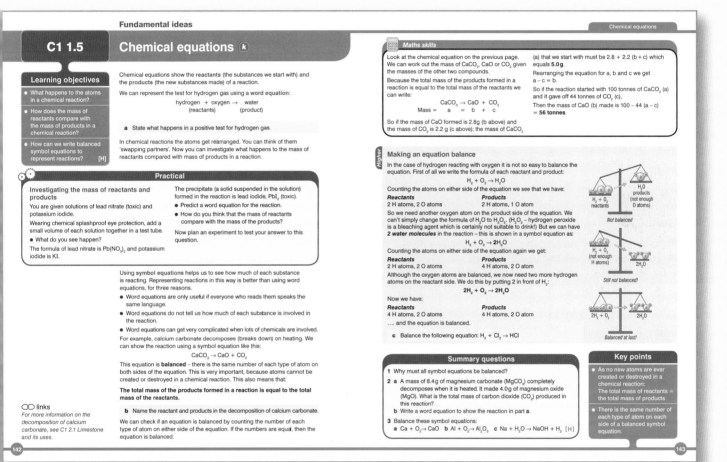

Further teaching suggestions

Lots of balancing equations

- Students could be given a selection of the same symbol equation but balanced, unbalanced and 'balanced' by altering the formula. Ask students to select the correctly balanced symbol equation and comment on why the others are not correct.
- Give students a list of symbol equations to balance, starting off with simple equations and working up to equations which need bigger numbers.

Answers to in-text questions

a A lighted splint burns with a squeaky 'pop'.

b Reactant: calcium carbonate. Products: calcium oxide and carbon dioxide.

c $H_2 + Cl_2 \rightarrow 2HCl$

Summary answers

1. As no new atoms can be created or destroyed in a chemical reaction, the number and type of atoms in the reactants must equal the number and type of atoms in the products.

2. **a** 4.4 g
   b magnesium carbonate → magnesium oxide + carbon dioxide

3. **a** $2Ca + O_2 \rightarrow 2CaO$
   b $4Al + 3O_2 \rightarrow 2Al_2O_3$
   c $2Na + 2H_2O \rightarrow 2NaOH + H_2$

Summary answers

1 a Elements contain only one type of atom, whereas compounds contain more than one type of atom.

b **i** 6 atoms of hydrogen
ii 3 elements
iii 9 atoms in total

2 a

Subatomic particle	Relative charge
proton	+1
neutron	0
electron	−1

b **i** in the nucleus
ii in the nucleus
iii In energy level or shells around the nucleus.

c **i** zero/no charge/neutral
ii 7 electrons

3 a **i** a non-metal
ii more metals
iii 18 protons
iv Group 0, the noble gases
v 8 electrons

b **i** 56 protons
ii 2 electrons, as it is in Group 2
iii metal

4 a 19 protons

b potassium, K

c **i** a charged particle
ii Metal ions are positively charged whereas non-metal ions are negatively charged.
iii The atom loses one electron/number of electrons decreases by one.
iv K^+
v ionic bonding

d **i** potassium chloride
ii KCl

5 a $Na + Cl_2 \rightarrow 2NaCl$
b $2Zn + O_2 \rightarrow 2ZnO$
c $4Cr + 3O_2 \rightarrow 2Cr_2O_3$
d $C_3H_8 + 5O_2 \rightarrow 3CO_2 + 4H_2O$

6 a $H_2 + Br_2 \rightarrow 2HBr$
b $2Mg + O_2 \rightarrow 2MgO$
c $2H_2O_2 \rightarrow 2H_2O + O_2$
d $2Li + 2H_2O \rightarrow 2LiOH + H_2$
e $2NaNO_3 \rightarrow 2NaNO_2 + O_2$
f $4Fe + 3O_2 \rightarrow 2Fe_2O_3$

7 a 1.6 g.

b The mass of the reactants must equal the mass of the product, so we subtract the mass of iron from the mass of iron sulfide. This will give us the mass of sulfur that reacted with the 2.8 g of iron.

AQA Examiner's tip

Bonding is covered more fully in Unit 2. In this unit, students only need to be aware of ionic and covalent bonding. They should know that compounds of metals and non-metals contain ions. They should also know that molecules are held together by covalent bonds.

Summary questions 🄺

1 a What is the difference in the definitions of an element and a compound?

b The chemical formula of ethanol is written as C_2H_5OH.
i How many atoms of hydrogen are there in an ethanol molecule?
ii How many different elements are there in ethanol?
iii What is the total number of atoms in an ethanol molecule?

2 a Draw a table to show the relative charge on protons, neutrons and electrons.

b In which part of an atom do we find:
i protons
ii neutrons
iii electrons.

c **i** What is the overall charge on any atom?
ii A nitrogen atom has 7 protons. How many electrons does it have?

3 This question is about the periodic table of elements. You will need to use the periodic table at the back of this book to help you answer some parts of the question.

a Argon (Ar) is the 18th element in the periodic table.
i Is argon a metal or a non-metal?
ii Are there more metals or non-metals in the periodic table?
iii How many protons does an argon atom contain?
iv State the name and number of the group to which argon belongs.
v How many electrons does argon have in its highest energy level (outermost shell)?

b The element barium (Ba) has 56 electrons.
i How many protons are in the nucleus of each barium atom?
ii How many electrons does a barium atom have in its highest energy level (outermost shell)? How did you decide on your answer?
iii Is barium a metal or a non-metal?

4 The diagram below shows the arrangement of electrons in an atom.

a How many protons are in the nucleus of this atom?

b Use the periodic table at the back of this book to give the name and symbol of the element whose atom is shown here.

c This element forms ions with a 1+ charge.
i What is an ion?
ii How does the charge on the ion tell us whet[...] element above is a metal or non-metal?
iii Describe what happens to the number of ele[...] when the atom forms a 1+ ion.
iv Write the chemical formula of the ion.
v This ion can form compounds with negative[...] charged ions. What type of bonding will we[...] these compounds?

d A compound is formed when this element reac[...] chlorine gas.
i What is the name of the compound formed?
ii Chloride ions carry a 1− charge. Write the c[...] formula of the compound formed.

5 What is the missing number needed to balance th[...] following symbol equations?

a $2Na + Cl_2 \rightarrow .... NaCl$
b $2Zn + O_2 \rightarrow .... ZnO$
c $.... Cr + 3O_2 \rightarrow 2Cr_2O_3$
d $C_3H_8 + ... O_2 \rightarrow 3CO_2 + 4H_2O$

6 Balance the following symbol equations:

a $H_2 + Br_2 \rightarrow HBr$
b $Mg + O_2 \rightarrow MgO$
c $H_2O_2 \rightarrow H_2O + O_2$
d $Li + H_2O \rightarrow LiOH + H_2$
e $NaNO_3 \rightarrow NaNO_2 + O_2$
f $Fe + O_2 \rightarrow Fe_2O_3$

7 When a mixture of iron and sulfur is heated, a com[...] called iron sulfide is made.
In an experiment 2.8 g of iron made 4.4 g of iron s[...]
a What mass of sulfur reacted with the 2.8 g of iro[...]
b Explain how you worked out your answer to pa[...]

144

AQA Examiner's tip

Students are expected to be familiar with the formulae of the substances named in the specification. A data sheet will be provided in the examinations for all Chemistry units, including Unit 1. The data sheet has a periodic table, the reactivity series for metals and a table of common ions, but students are not expected to work out the formulae of ionic compounds in this unit. All formulae will be given if students are asked to balance symbol equations.

Kerboodle resources 🄺

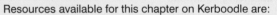

Resources available for this chapter on Kerboodle are:
- Chapter map: Fundamental ideas
- Bump up your grade: Arranging the elements (C1 1.1)
- Support: Arranging the elements (C1 1.1)
- Extension: In orbit (C1 1.3)
- Interactive activity: Atoms and the periodic table (C1 1.4)
- Maths skills: Balancing equations (C1 1.5)
- Practical: Conservation of mass (C1 1.5)
- Revision podcast: Atom anatomy
- Test yourself: Fundamental ideas
- On your marks: Electronic structure and reactivity in groups
- Examination-style questions: Fundamental ideas
- Answers to examination-style questions: Fundamental ideas

Examination-style questions k

numbers from the list to complete the table to show
harge on each subatomic particle.

+1 0 −1 −2

Subatomic particle	Charge
...tron	
...tron	
...on	

(3)

the periodic table at the back of your book to help
o answer this question.

ow many protons are in an atom of fluorine? (1)

ow many electrons are in an atom of carbon? (1)

omplete the electronic structure of aluminium:
8, ... (1)

hat is the electronic structure of potassium? (1)

a is a noble gas.
hat does this tell you about its electronic structure? (1)

aw a diagram to show the electronic structure of
on. (2)

agnesium has the electronic structure 2,8,2. Explain,
terms of its electronic structure, why magnesium is
Group 2 of the periodic table. (1)

ve **one** way in which the electronic structures of the
oms of Group 2 elements are:
 the same (1)
 different. (1)

hen magnesium is heated in air it burns with a bright
me and produces magnesium oxide.

alcium is also in Group 2. Describe what you expect
 happen and what would be produced when calcium
heated in air. (2)

5 Sodium reacts with water to produce sodium hydroxide
and hydrogen.

The word equation for this reaction is:

sodium + water → sodium hydroxide + hydrogen

a Name one substance in this equation that is:
  i an element (1)
  ii a compound (1)
  iii has ionic bonds (1)
  iv has covalent bonds (1)

b If 2.3 g of sodium reacted with 1.8 g of water, what
would be the total mass of sodium hydroxide and
hydrogen produced?
Explain your answer. (2)

c Balance the symbol equation for this reaction.
.... Na + ... H_2O → .... NaOH + H_2 [H] (1)

d Lithium is in the same group of the periodic table as
sodium.
  i Write a word equation for the reaction of lithium
with water. (1)
  ii What is the formula of lithium hydroxide? (1)
  iii How many atoms are shown in the formula of
lithium hydroxide you have written? (1)

AQA Examination-style answers

1

Subatomic particle	Charge
electron	−1
neutron	0
proton	+1

(3 marks)

2 a 9 (1 mark)

b 6 (1 mark)

c 2,8,3 (1 mark)

d 2,8,8,1 (1 mark)

3 a It is stable or it has 8 electrons in its outer energy
level/shell (not it has a full shell). (1 mark)

b Two electrons (dots or crosses) on inner circle,
8 electrons on outer circle. (2 marks)

4 a Two electrons in its highest energy level/outer shell.
(1 mark)

b **i** Same number of electrons or 2 electrons in
highest energy level/outer shell.
(accept same number of electrons in first energy
level/shell) (1 mark)
  ii Different number of energy levels/shells. (1 mark)

c burns (with a bright flame)
(produces) calcium oxide (2 marks)

5 a **i** sodium or hydrogen (1 mark)
  ii water or sodium hydroxide (1 mark)
  iii sodium hydroxide (1 mark)
  iv water or hydrogen (1 mark)

b 4.1 g
mass is conserved in reactions or mass of reactants
= mass of products (2 marks)

c $2Na + 2H_2O → 2NaOH + H_2$ (1 mark)

d **i** lithium + water → lithium hydroxide + hydrogen
(1 mark)
  ii LiOH (1 mark)
  iii 3 or error carried forward from answer to (**ii**) (1 mark)

AQA Practical suggestions

Practicals	AQA	k	📖	⚙
Modelling of atoms (using physical models or computer simulations) to illustrate chemical reactions at the atomic level.	✓		✓	
Precipitation reactions, such as lead nitrate with potassium iodide, to show conservation of mass.	✓	✓	✓	

C1 2.1

Limestone and its uses

Learning objectives

Students should learn:

- that limestone is used to make a variety of building materials
- that calcium carbonate in limestone will undergo thermal decomposition.

Learning outcomes

Most students should be able to:

- list some uses of limestone
- write the formula of calcium carbonate
- complete a word equation for the thermal decomposition of calcium carbonate.

Some students should also be able to:

- explain the process of thermal decomposition of calcium carbonate, including the balanced symbol equation.

Support

- Students often get confused about the formula of a compound. You may wish to support students by using formula jigsaws to kinaesthetically show students how the formula is made up.

Extend

- Give students the formulae of different metal carbonates. Ask them to write out the numbers and type of each atom that they contain from the formula. You could further extend students by asking them to write the formulae of carbonates of their choice. You may wish to encourage students to use the table of common ions that are listed on their data sheet, which they would have access to in the examination.
- Students could be asked to find out why spotlights caused so many explosions in early theatres.

AQA Specification link-up: Chemistry C1.2

- Limestone, mainly composed of the compound calcium carbonate ($CaCO_3$), is quarried and can be used as a building material. *[C1.2.1 a)]*
- Calcium carbonate can be decomposed by heating (thermal decomposition) to make calcium oxide and carbon dioxide. *[C1.2.1 b)]*

Lesson structure

Starters

Characteristics – Ask the students to consider what the following materials have in common: limestone, marble and chalk [they are all made up mainly of the same compound – calcium carbonate]. This task could be expanded to think about other groupings of these substances, e.g. chalk and limestone are sedimentary rocks, whereas marble is metamorphic. *(5 minutes)*

Classify – Students could read through the pages in this topic and classify the chemicals that are named as elements [calcium, oxygen, and carbon], compounds [calcium carbonate, calcium oxide, carbon dioxide, water] and mixtures [limestone, chalk]. Students may need to be supported by being given a reminder of the definitions of elements, compounds and mixtures. Ask them to find the symbols or the formulae of the elements and compounds. *(10 minutes)*

Main

- Using the Student Book for information, students could create a fully labelled diagram of a lime kiln. Students should include information about the raw material [limestone] and reactant [calcium carbonate], the products [carbon dioxide and calcium oxide]. Foundation Tier students should include a word equation and Higher Tier students should include a balanced symbol equation.

- Students could then create a flow chart to explain the process that occurs in a rotary lime kiln. Again students should include word and/or balanced symbol equations to detail the reactions that take place.

- Students can decompose calcium carbonate in the practical 'Thermal decomposition' in the Student Book. This reaction will be revisited later in the chapter and students should just concentrate on observing the reaction safely here and discussing the equation. Students should be encouraged to notice how brightly the calcium carbonate shines. Explain that in old theatres, acetylene and oxygen were combusted to heat limestone to produce this bright light. It was then focused using a lens and made into a spotlight.

- Often it is clear that students are confused about the scientific language, what it means and how it can be used. Students could write the key words (highlighted in the text) in their exercise book. They then need to summarise the meaning of each word in just one sentence. Note that the common names 'quicklime' and 'slaked lime' are no longer required knowledge in the current specification.

Plenaries

Fact finder – Ask students to think about one fact that they already knew before the lesson that had been reviewed and one fact that was completely new to them. *(5 minutes)*

Key-word bingo – The students should choose three of the following key words: limestone, calcium carbonate, cement, concrete, calcium oxide, thermal decomposition, calcium oxide. These can be written in the back of their exercise books, or on a pre-made bingo card that has spaces for the students to write in. Explain the word, and the student crosses it off (if they chose it). The first student to cross off all of the words could be given a reward! Students could be supported by being given the key words and a definition to refer to. Students could be extended by using the symbols, formulae or balanced symbol equations rather than the key words themselves on their bingo cards. *(10 minutes)*

Practical support

Thermal decomposition

Equipment and materials required

Gauze, tripod, Bunsen burner and safety equipment, eye protection, tongs, calcium carbonate chip.

Details

Place a piece of calcium carbonate onto a gauze mounted on a tripod. Turn the Bunsen burner to a blue flame, and direct the tip of the blue cone onto a corner of the calcium carbonate. As the Bunsen burner will need to be directed at the calcium carbonate, it will need to be picked up off the bench so extra care should to be taken. Hold the base and ensure the rubber tube is tightly secured to the gas tap and the Bunsen burner before starting the experiment. Do not allow students to overstretch the tubing. Firstly calcium carbonate will glow red/orange, then a whiter orange. Once part of the material glows white for a few minutes, turn off the Bunsen burner. Leave sufficient time for the heated product to cool down. Dispose of with tongs; do not touch the calcium oxide.

Alternatively, the calcium carbonate chip is placed on the woven steel corner of a gauze, and the tip of a roaring Bunsen flame is positioned on the chip from below, another method uses a sling/holder for the chip fashioned from thick nichrome wire, which is then clamped at the other end using a boss and clamp, and the tip of a roaring Bunsen flame is positioned on the chip from below.

Safety: CLEAPSS Hazcard 19B Calcium carbonate. CLEAPSS Hazcard 18 Calcium oxide – corrosive.

Ensure the rubber tube is tightly secured to the gas tap and the Bunsen burner before starting the experiment. Do not allow students to overstretch the tubing. Leave sufficient time for the heated product to cool down. Dispose of with tongs; do not touch the calcium oxide.

C1 2.1 Limestone and its uses

Learning objectives

- What are the uses of limestone?
- What happens when we heat limestone?

Uses of limestone (k)

Limestone is a rock that is made mainly of **calcium carbonate**. Some types of limestone were formed from the remains of tiny animals and plants that lived in the sea millions of years ago. We dig limestone out of the ground in quarries all around the world. It has many uses, including its use as a building material.

Many important buildings around the world are made of limestone. We can cut and shape the stone taken from the ground into blocks. These can be placed one on top of the other, like bricks in a wall. We have used limestone in this way to make buildings for hundreds of years.

Powdered limestone can also be heated with powdered clay to make **cement**. When we mix cement powder with water, sand and crushed rock, a slow chemical reaction takes place. The reaction produces a hard, stone-like building material called **concrete**.

Figure 1 St Paul's Cathedral in London is built from limestone blocks

Figure 2 These white cliffs are made of chalk. This is one type of limestone, formed from the shells of tiny sea plants.

Figure 3 This building contains plenty of concrete which is made from limestone

a What is the main compound found in limestone?
b How do we use limestone to make buildings?

Heating limestone

The chemical formula for calcium carbonate is **CaCO₃**. It is made up of calcium ions, Ca^{2+}, and carbonate ions, CO_3^{2-}. The 2+ and 2− charges tell us that there are the same number of calcium ions and carbonate ions in calcium carbonate. Remember that the charges on the ions cancel out in compounds.

When we heat limestone strongly, the calcium carbonate breaks down to form calcium oxide. Carbon dioxide is also produced in this reaction. Breaking down a chemical by heating is called **thermal decomposition**.

We can show the thermal decomposition reaction using the following equations:

Word equation: $$\text{calcium carbonate} \xrightarrow{\text{heat}} \text{calcium oxide} + \text{carbon dioxide}$$

Balanced symbol equation: $$CaCO_3 \rightarrow CaO + CO_2$$

The calcium oxide made is also a very useful substance in the building and farming industries.

links
For information on the formulae of compounds made up of ions, look back at C1 1.4 Forming bonds.

?? Did you know ...?

Chalk is a form of limestone. It was formed millions of years ago from the skeletal remains of tiny sea plants called coccoliths. They were deposited on the seabed between 65 and 130 million years ago. It has been estimated that it took almost 100000 years to lay down each metre of chalk in a cliff face.

Practical

Thermal decomposition

In this experiment you can carry out the reaction that takes place in a lime kiln.

Safety: Make sure the rubber tube is tightly secured to the gas tap and the Bunsen burner before starting the experiment. Do not overstretch the tubing. Do not touch the decomposed carbonate as it is corrosive. Wash your hands if you get any chemicals on them. Wear eye protection.

Place a limestone chip on a tripod and gauze. Using a roaring flame, hold the base of the Bunsen burner and heat a limestone chip strongly from the side. It is best if the tip of the blue cone of the flame heats the limestone directly. You will see signs of a reaction happening on the surface of the limestone.

- What do you see happen as the limestone is heated strongly?

A rotary lime kiln

To make lots of calcium oxide this reaction is done in a furnace called a **lime kiln**. We fill the kiln with crushed limestone and heat it strongly using a supply of hot air. Calcium oxide comes out of the bottom of the kiln. Waste gases, including the carbon dioxide made, leave the kiln at the top.

Calcium oxide is often produced in a **rotary kiln**, where the limestone is heated in a rotating drum. This makes sure that the limestone is thoroughly mixed with the stream of hot air. This helps the calcium carbonate to decompose completely.

Figure 4 Calcium oxide is produced in a rotary lime kiln

links
For more information on the uses of calcium oxide, see C1 2.3 The 'limestone reaction cycle'.

Summary questions

1 Copy and complete using the words below:
   building calcium cement concrete
   Limestone is mostly made of .... carbonate (whose chemical formula is CaCO₃). As well as making blocks of building material, limestone can be used to produce .... and .... that are also used in the .... industry.

2 Produce a poster or PowerPoint presentation to show how limestone is used in building.

3 The stone roof of a building is supported by columns made of limestone. Why might this be unsafe after a fire in the building? Explain the chemical reaction involved in weakening the structure.

Key points

- Limestone is made mainly of calcium carbonate.
- Limestone is widely used in the building industry.
- The calcium carbonate in limestone breaks down when we heat it strongly to make calcium oxide and carbon dioxide. The reaction is called thermal decomposition.

Further teaching suggestions

Word description

- Flash cards of the key words could be created. Hold up the key word, and a student tries to describe it to you, without saying the word.

?? Did you know ...?

Calcium oxide was also spread over plague victims in their mass graves and over executed prisoners, as people thought it helped their bodies decompose quicker. However, it did help to kill microbes.

Answers to in-text questions

a calcium carbonate
b Limestone can be cut into blocks or processed to make materials like cement or concrete.

Summary answers

1 calcium, cement/concrete (either order), building

2 Poster or presentation.

3 The calcium carbonate in the column may have undergone thermal decomposition, making it weaker. The calcium oxide formed is much softer than the original calcium carbonate present in the columns.

C1 2.2

Reactions of carbonates

Learning objectives

Students should learn:

- that metal carbonates will undergo thermal decomposition
- that metal carbonates will react with dilute acids
- how limewater can be used as a test for carbon dioxide as it turns from colourless to cloudy when reacting with the gas
- that a fair and safe test must be used to compare the thermal decompositions of different metal carbonates.

Learning outcomes

Most students should be able to:

- list examples of metal carbonates that react similarly to the calcium carbonate in limestone when they are heated
- write word equations to describe thermal decomposition of a metal carbonate and the reaction of a metal carbonate with acid
- state the test for carbon dioxide
- plan some safety considerations and fair test ideas for the thermal decomposition of metal carbonates.

Some students should also be able to:

- use balanced symbol equations to describe the thermal decomposition of metal carbonates and the reaction of metal carbonates with acid
- explain the test for carbon dioxide using equations.

Support

- For students struggling with chemical equations, molecular model kits can be used. Explain that atoms cannot be created or destroyed, only rearranged to make the products formed.

Extend

- Students should make predictions about other metal carbonates and how they would react. You may wish to ask students to use their observations of the reaction of calcium carbonate with acid to explain how limestone buildings can be affected by rain, which is naturally weakly acidic.

AQA Specification link-up: Chemistry C1.2

- The carbonates of magnesium, copper, zinc, calcium and sodium decompose on heating in a similar way. *[C1.2.1 c)]*
- A solution of calcium hydroxide in water (limewater) reacts with carbon dioxide to produce calcium carbonate. Limewater is used as a test for carbon dioxide. Carbon dioxide turns limewater cloudy. *[C1.2.1 e)]*
- Carbonates react with acids to produce carbon dioxide, a salt and water. Limestone is damaged by acid rain. *[C1.2.1 f)]*

Controlled Assessment: SA4.1 Planning an investigation. *[SA4.1.1 c)]*; SA4.2 Assess and manage risks when carrying out practical work. *[SA4.2.1 a)]*

Lesson structure

Starters

Recap – Ask students to recall:

- A definition for thermal decomposition. [Using heat to break down a substance.]
- The two products when limestone is thermally decomposed. [Calcium oxide and carbon dioxide.]
- Write an equation for the thermal decomposition of limestone in a lime kiln. [Calcium carbonate → carbon dioxide + calcium oxide.] To extend students, you could encourage them to write a symbol equation for this reaction. Support students by reminding them that limestone is a raw material and the reactant is calcium carbonate. *(5 minutes)*

Anagram title – Tell students that today's lesson is about 'creatnois fo braconsate'? [Reactions of carbonates] Encourage students to use their Student Book to define the word carbonates and maybe even give an example detailed as an equation. *(10 minutes)*

Main

- You may wish to tackle the contents of this spread over two lessons, with all students doing both practicals. In this case, the 'Acid plus carbonates' practical can be done and then the planning for the investigation into thermal decomposition, 'Investigating carbonates', could be discussed and started, but carrying out the practical work in the second lesson.
- Alternatively, in one lesson you might do the 'Acid plus carbonates' practical, followed by 'Investigating carbonates' as a planning exercise only. You could perhaps demonstrate the decomposition of a couple of carbonates with student participation.
- At a suitable point, explain why limewater turns cloudy in the test for carbon dioxide.
- You may wish to encourage students to focus on the safety of the investigation. You could give students access to the CLEAPSS students safety sheets and ask them to write a risk assessment before completing the practical work. You may also focus on how to make the investigation a fair test by looking at identifying and classifying the different variables.
- Encourage students to attempt to write a general equation for the reactions in both practicals.

  [metal carbonate → carbon dioxide + metal oxide

  metal carbonate + acid → metal salt + water + carbon dioxide]

Plenaries

Symbol equations – Ask students to complete the following equations (answers in brackets):

calcium carbonate → [calcium oxide + carbon dioxide]

[magnesium carbonate] → magnesium oxide + carbon dioxide

$[CuCO_3] \rightarrow CuO + CO_2$ *(5 minutes)*

Text summary – Ask the students to write down a summary of thermal decomposition and reactions of metal carbonates and acids as a text message. You may wish to give students an outline of a mobile phone to draft their text message answers into. To support students, just concentrate on thermal decomposition. To extend students, you could also ask them to include a symbol equation in their text message. *(10 minutes)*

Practical support

Acid plus carbonates

Equipment and materials required
Boiling tube, bung with delivery tube, spatula, test tube, irritant, limewater, dropping pipette, test tube rack, stand, boss, clamp, eye protection, calcium carbonate chips, 2 mol/dm^3 hydrochloric acid – irritant.

Details
Half-fill the test tube with limewater and place into the rack. Put about one spatula of a metal carbonate to be tested in a boiling tube and clamp in position. Add about 1 cm^3 of dilute acid and quickly fit the bung and delivery tube. Angle the end of the delivery tube into the test tube.

Safety: Wear eye protection. CLEAPSS Hazcard 19B Calcium carbonate; 18 Limewater – irritant; 47A Hydrochloric acid – irritant.

Further teaching suggestions

Honeycomb demonstration
- The thermal decomposition of sodium hydrogencarbonate (bicarbonate) can be illustrated by heating sugar syrup mixture to 150 °C and adding sodium bicarbonate. The carbon dioxide gas released gets trapped in the sugary mixture.

Investigating carbonates

Equipment and materials required
Boiling tube, bung with delivery tube, spatula, test tube, Bunsen burner and safety equipment, eye protection, test tube holder, stand, boss, clamp, samples of metal carbonates (e.g. calcium carbonate, sodium carbonate – irritant, potassium carbonate – irritant, magnesium carbonate, zinc carbonate, copper carbonate – harmful), limewater – irritant. An electric balance and measuring cylinders will be needed if the practical is to be carried out as an investigation into the ease of thermal decomposition.

Details
Put about one spatula of a metal carbonate to be tested in a boiling tube. Clamp into position, and fit the bung and delivery tube. Half-fill the test tube with limewater and place into the rack. Angle the end of the delivery tube into the test tube. Using the Bunsen burner, heat the carbonate and observe the limewater. If the limewater goes cloudy, then carbon dioxide has been produced and thermal decomposition has taken place. Repeat with other carbonates to compare results.

Safety: Wear eye protection throughout the practical and be aware that the boiling tube will still be hot when heating is ceased. Remove end of delivery tube from limewater before heating is stopped to prevent 'such back'. CLEAPSS Hazcard 19B Calcium carbonate; 95A Sodium/potassium carbonate – irritant; 59B Magnesium carbonate; 108B Zinc carbonate; 26 Copper carbonate – harmful; 18 Limewater – irritant. Disposal of waste as per CLEAPSS advice.

C1 2.2 — Reactions of carbonates

Learning objectives
- Do other carbonates behave in the same way as calcium carbonate?
- What happens when dilute acid is added to a carbonate?
- What is the test for carbon dioxide gas?

Buildings and statues made of limestone suffer badly from damage by acid rain. You might have noticed statues where the fine features have been lost. Limestone is mostly calcium carbonate, which reacts with acid. A gas is given off in the reaction.

Testing for carbon dioxide
You can use a simple test to find out if the gas given off is carbon dioxide. Carbon dioxide turns **limewater** solution cloudy. The test works as follows:
- Limewater is a solution of calcium hydroxide. It is alkaline.
- Carbon dioxide is a weakly acidic gas so it reacts with the alkaline limewater.
- In this reaction tiny solid particles of insoluble calcium carbonate are formed as a precipitate.
- The reaction is:

calcium hydroxide + carbon dioxide → calcium carbonate + water
(limewater)   (an insoluble precipitate)

Ca(OH)$_2$ +   CO$_2$ →   CaCO$_3$ +   H$_2$O

- This precipitate of calcium carbonate makes the limewater turn cloudy. That's because light can no longer pass through the solution with tiny bits of white solid suspended in it.

a What is a precipitate?

Carbonates react with acids to give a salt, water and carbon dioxide. For calcium carbonate the reaction with hydrochloric acid is:

calcium carbonate + hydrochloric acid → calcium chloride + water + carbon dioxide

The balanced symbol equation is:

CaCO$_3$ + 2HCl → CaCl$_2$ + H$_2$O + CO$_2$

b Write a word equation for the reaction of magnesium carbonate with hydrochloric acid.

Figure 1 Limestone is attacked and damaged by acids

?? Did you know …?
Sculptures from the Parthenon (a temple), built by the ancient Greeks in Athens, have had to be removed and replaced by copies to avoid any more damage from acid pollution from vehicle exhausts.

Figure 2 The Parthenon in Greece

Practical

Acid plus carbonates
Set up the apparatus as shown.
Try the test with some other carbonates, such as those of magnesium, copper, zinc and sodium.
Record your observations.
- What conclusion can you draw?

(diagram labels: Dilute hydrochloric acid; Metal carbonate; Limewater)

Decomposing carbonates
In C1 2.1 we saw that limestone is made up mainly of calcium carbonate. This decomposes when we heat it. The reaction produces calcium oxide and carbon dioxide. Calcium is an element in Group 2 of the periodic table. As we have already seen, the elements in a group tend to behave in the same way. So, does magnesium carbonate also decompose when you heat it? And what about other carbonates too?

c Why might you expect magnesium carbonate to behave in a similar way to calcium carbonate?

Practical

Investigating carbonates
You can investigate the thermal decomposition of carbonates by heating samples in a Bunsen flame. You will have samples of the carbonates listed below.

Powdered carbonate samples: sodium carbonate, potassium carbonate, magnesium carbonate, zinc carbonate, copper carbonate
- What observations might tell you if a sample decomposes when you heat it?
- How could you test any gas given off?

Plan an investigation to find out how easily different carbonates decompose.
- How will you try to make it a fair test?
- How will you make your investigation safe?

Before you start any practical work, your teacher must check your plan.

Safety: It is important to remove the delivery tube from the limewater before you stop heating the carbonate. If you don't, the cold limewater will be 'sucked back' into the hot boiling tube causing it to smash. You must wear eye protection when doing this practical.

Figure 3 Investigating the thermal decomposition of a solid

Investigations like this show that many metal carbonates decompose when they are heated in a Bunsen flame. They form the metal oxide and carbon dioxide – just as calcium carbonate does. Sodium and potassium carbonate do not decompose at the temperature of the Bunsen flame. They need a higher temperature.

Magnesium carbonate decomposes like this:

magnesium carbonate → magnesium oxide + carbon dioxide

MgCO$_3$ →   MgO   +   CO$_2$

Summary questions

1 Give a general word equation for:
  a the reaction of a carbonate plus an acid
  b the thermal decomposition of a carbonate.

2 Write a word equation for the reaction of sodium carbonate with dilute hydrochloric acid.

3 The formula of zinc carbonate is ZnCO$_3$.
  a Zinc carbonate decomposes when heated, giving zinc oxide and carbon dioxide. Write the balanced equation for this reaction.   [H]
  b Write the balanced symbol equation for the reaction of zinc carbonate with dilute hydrochloric acid.   [H]

Key points
- Carbonates react with dilute acid to form a salt, water and carbon dioxide.
- Limewater turns cloudy in the test for carbon dioxide gas. A precipitate of insoluble calcium carbonate causes the cloudiness.
- Metal carbonates decompose on heating to form the metal oxide and carbon dioxide.

Answers to in-text questions

a An insoluble solid formed by the reaction of two solutions.

b magnesium carbonate + hydrochloric acid
    → magnesium chloride + water + carbon dioxide

c Magnesium and calcium are in the same group (group 2) of the periodic table.

Summary answers

1 **a** metal carbonate + acid → a salt + water + carbon dioxide
  b metal carbonate → metal oxide + carbon dioxide

2 sodium carbonate + hydrochloric acid → sodium chloride + water + carbon dioxide

3 **a** ZnCO$_3$ → ZnO + CO$_2$
  b ZnCO$_3$ + 2HCl → ZnCl$_2$ + H$_2$O + CO$_2$

C1 2.3

The 'limestone reaction cycle'

Learning objectives

Students should learn:

- how calcium oxide can be used to make calcium hydroxide
- the uses of calcium hydroxide
- the reactions in the 'limestone reaction cycle'.

Learning outcomes

Most students should be able to:

- give an example of a use of calcium hydroxide
- describe the reactions of the 'limestone reaction cycle' in word equations
- state the observations at each stage of the 'limestone reaction cycle'.

Some students should also be able to:

- write a balanced symbol equation for each reaction in the 'limestone reaction cycle'
- explain why farmers may choose to use calcium hydroxide on their fields.

Support

- Provide students with diagrams of each stage of the limestone cycle, but in the wrong order. Before students start the practical, investigating the 'limestone reaction cycle', they cut and stick these to create a pictorial method.

Extend

- Ask students to represent each stage of the practical, investigating the 'limestone reaction cycle', using balanced symbol equations. You could extend students further by asking them to generate balanced symbol equations for the neutralisation of waste acidic gases, like sulfur dioxide from the combustion of fossil fuels using calcium hydroxide.

AQA Specification link-up: Chemistry C1.2

- Calcium oxide reacts with water to produce calcium hydroxide, which is an alkali that can be used in the neutralisation of acids. [C1.2.1 d)]
- A solution of calcium hydroxide in water (limewater) reacts with carbon dioxide to produce calcium carbonate. Limewater is used as a test for carbon dioxide. Carbon dioxide turns limewater cloudy. [C1.2.1 e)]

Lesson structure

Starters

Spot the mistake – Write the following sentence on the board and ask the students to spot the deliberate mistake(s):

'Limestone is a metamorphic rock and made of the pure element magnesium carbonate.'

[The mistakes are that limestone is a sedimentary rock. It is made up mainly of calcium carbonate (which is a compound, not an element) but also contains other substances, and so the rock is a mixture of substances, not an element.] (5 minutes)

Chemical formula – Ask students to look at the following formulae and find their chemical name. You may wish to extend students by asking them to count the number and type of atom in each formula. To support students you may wish to give the names of the compounds and they match them to the formulae:

- $CaCO_3$ [calcium carbonate]
- CaO [calcium oxide]
- $Ca(OH)_2$ [calcium hydroxide]
- CO_2 [carbon dioxide] (10 minutes)

Main

- Introduce the idea of a 'limestone reaction cycle'. Draw a brief outline of the cycle on the board. Explain to the students that they are going to complete a number of experiments to follow the cycle.

- Split the class into groups of two or three and ask each group to complete the practical, investigating the 'limestone reaction cycle'. Encourage students to note down any important observations and try to label the type of reaction occurring in each part of the cycle.

- Once the practical has been completed, or using the Student Book for information, a comprehensive flow chart of labelled diagrams to show the limestone reaction cycle could be made. Higher attaining students should include balanced symbol equations for each reaction.

Plenaries

Symbol equations – Ask a student to come to the front and put on eye protection, then blow through a straw into a conical flask containing a liquid (limewater). Ask the students to describe what is happening in terms of an equation. To extend students, they should be encouraged to write a balanced symbol equation. To support lower attaining students, the words of the reactants, products and an arrow could be drawn in separate text boxes in an appropriate computer program. Then using the interactive whiteboard, students could move the words and arrow to create the correct word equation. (5 minutes)

Key concept cards – Create a set of cards (7 cm by 3 cm), each card having a different title (calcium oxide, calcium hydroxide, calcium carbonate). Using the Student Book, students then state the chemical name, formula and how it is made in a symbol or word equation on the appropriate card. They can also be asked to add any more information that they think is important, such as uses of each of these chemicals. This is a revision technique that will help them to discriminate and select key information from text. (10 minutes)

Practical support

Investigating the 'limestone reaction cycle'
Equipment and materials required

Gauze, tripod, Bunsen burner and safety equipment, eye protection, tongs, water, 2 × boiling tube, fluted filter paper, filter funnel, glass rod, test tube rack, calcium carbonate chips, dropping pipette, straw. CLEAPSS Student Safety sheet 32.

Details

Follow the procedure detailed for the thermal decomposition of limestone in C1 2.1 Limestone and its uses.

After heating, the thermally decomposed calcium carbonate holds its heat for a long period of time. Also the calcium products are all basic and should not be touched with hands. Using the tongs,

transfer the cool product to a boiling tube, add a few drops of water very slowly, one drop at a time, and observe. Then add about a third of the boiling tube of water, put a bung in the tube and shake gently. When water is added to the calcium oxide, it will often spit calcium hydroxide, so safety googles must be worn, and if the compound touches the skin it must be washed off immediately.

Filter the mixture, and keep the filtrate (limewater – irritant). Carefully take a straw and submerge it in the limewater and blow gently. The solution should turn cloudy, completing the limestone cycle.

Safety: CLEAPSS Hazcard 18 Limewater – irritant; 18 Calcium oxide – corrosive; 19B Calcium carbonate.

Ensure the rubber tube is tightly secured to the gas tap and the Bunsen burner before starting the experiment. Do not allow students to overstretch the tubing.

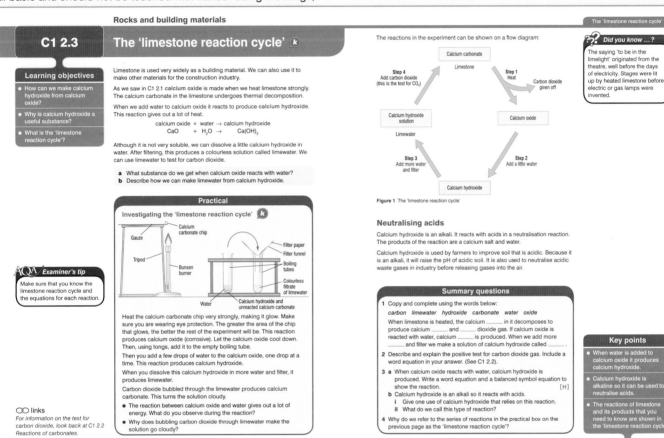

Further teaching suggestions

The limestone industry
- Students could find out how parts of the limestone reaction cycle are carried out in industry, e.g. thermal decomposition of limestone occurs in a lime kiln.

Risk assessment
- You could take a Controlled Assessment focus on the practical by asking students to write a risk assessment for each stage of the 'limestone reaction cycle'.

Soil neutralisation experiment
- You could ask students to plan an experiment where they could test the effectiveness of adding calcium hydroxide to soils.

Timeline
- Students could be asked to make a timeline to show the development of the use of limestone and its products. Students should use the internet to find out key important dates when limestone and its products are first noted to be used, their properties and maybe even a sample of the material could be glued onto the timeline or a picture printed off and added. For each of the different limestone products, students should be encouraged to draw a small table listing its advantages and disadvantages.

Answers to in-text questions

a calcium hydroxide

b Dissolve it in water (and filter off any excess solid calcium hydroxide).

Summary answers

1 carbonate, oxide, carbon, hydroxide, water, limewater

2 The calcium hydroxide in limewater reacts with carbon dioxide to make a fine suspension of calcium carbonate precipitate – which makes the colourless solution turn cloudy.

calcium hydroxide + carbon dioxide → calcium carbonate + water

3 a calcium oxide + water → calcium hydroxide
$$CaO + H_2O \rightarrow Ca(OH)_2$$

b i Raising the pH of acidic soil or to neutralise acidic waste gases in industry.

ii neutralisation

4 Because the sequence of reactions starts with calcium carbonate and ends with calcium carbonate being formed again.

C1 2.4

Cement and concrete

Learning objectives

Students should learn:

- how mortar has been developed over time
- how cement is made
- what is used to make concrete
- how primary data can be improved.

Learning outcomes

Most students should be able to:

- describe how we develop materials to improve their properties
- list some uses of cement and which materials are needed to make it
- describe how concrete is made and list the properties of this material.

Some students should also be able to:

- evaluate data and suggest how their quality can be improved.

??? Did you know ... ?

Mortar reacts with carbon dioxide in the air. Sometimes, when old buildings are demolished, the mortar in some places still has not set. This is because the centre of the mortar was not exposed to carbon dioxide.

Support

- Students may get confused about the relationship between cement, mortar and concrete. You may wish to support students by giving them an outline of a flow chart that they can complete to explain the interaction between these materials.

Extend

- Students could be encouraged to make predictions about the effect of different amounts of raw materials on the properties of cement and mortar.
- Gypsum is added to cement. Ask the students to find out what gypsum is [calcium sulfate, $CaSO_4$] and why it is added [increases the setting time and prevents flash setting]. As the amount of gypsum increases, so does the setting time, allowing you to modify the properties of the material for a specific function.

AQA Specification link-up: Chemistry C1.2

- Limestone is heated with clay to make cement. Cement is mixed with sand to make mortar and with sand and aggregate to make concrete. *[C1.2.1 g)]*
- Evaluate the developments in using limestone, cement and concrete as building materials, and their advantages and disadvantages over other materials. *[C1.2]*

  Controlled Assessment: SA4.1 Planning an investigation. *[SA4.1.1 a) b) c) d) e)]*; SA4.2 Assess and manage risks when carrying out practical work. *[SA4.2.1 a) b)]*; SA4.3 Collect primary and secondary data. *[SA4.3.3 b) c)]*; SA4.5 Analyse and interpret primary and secondary data. *[SA4.5.1 b)]*

Lesson structure

Starters

List – Give small groups of students a sample of cement and concrete. Ask students to list the properties of cement [opaque, hard] and concrete [opaque, hard, can be load bearing i.e. strong]. You could extend students by giving them a specific use of concrete and they have to state which of the properties they have identified makes it suitable for the job [walls in a building because cement is strong]. *(5 minutes)*

Linking pictures – Show students different images of uses of concrete through the ages. Ask them to determine the connection between the pictures [1950s prefab buildings, car parks, screed flooring, and motorway bridges]. Encourage students to think as an individual, and then compare their answers in small groups. Manage the feedback from each group. You may wish to show students pictures of other materials and examples of where they are not suitable for the job or have become redundant as new technology allows us to use concrete instead. *(10 minutes)*

Main

- By doing this they can practise their 'Controlled Assessment' planning skills. Students could be given cement, sand and different sized gravels. They could design an experiment to find out the effect of adding different proportions of each to the mix. Another investigation could be completed by comparing the effect of different gravel sizes in the mix. This can illustrate various aspects of 'Controlled Assessment', e.g. repeatability, accuracy of data collected and validity of investigational design.

- Students should consider improving the repeatability of the data collected. If they repeat a test again and get similar results the data can be described as repeatable. If they can get another person to get similar results, they could describe the results as reproducible. To further improve their results they could take a mean.

- In order to test if their results are reproducible, you could encourage students to look up strength data on the internet. They should then order the concrete data from most to least strong and see if the same pattern is borne out in their results. If their pattern is the same, the results can be described as reproducible.

Plenaries

True or false – Read out these statements and ask if they are true or false:

- Limestone is heated with clay to make cement. [True]
- Mortar is a mix of concrete and clay. [False]
- Concrete is a mixture of sand and aggregate. [True]
- Cement is a compound. [False]
- Concrete is an element. [False] *(5 minutes)*

Predict – Ask students to think about life without limestone building products. Which limestone product would they miss the most and why. You may need to support students by giving them a selection of materials made from limestone products, e.g. glass, cement, mortar, concrete, limestone blocks. To extend students further you could ask them to try and describe how their day would be affected if limestone and its products were not used. *(10 minutes)*

Practical support

Which mixture makes the strongest concrete?

Equipment and materials required

Cement, sand, gravel, spatulas, yoghurt pots, card templates to make concrete moulds, measuring cylinders (plus equipment requested by students to test strength of concrete, e.g. slotted masses, G-clamps), eye protection.

Details

Students make moulds and fill them with various concrete mixes, trying to ensure fair testing. Next lesson, they test the strength of different mixes.

Safety: See CLEAPSS document PS67-09 'Making Concrete' for suggestions and safety advice. Avoid skin contact with cement, it is an irritant. Wear eye protection when making AND testing concrete. Protect floor, feet and bench from falling weights and concrete.

Rocks and building materials

C1 2.4   Cement and concrete

Learning objectives

- How has mortar developed over time?
- How do we make cement?
- What is concrete?
- How can you improve the quality of data collected in an investigation?

Figure 1 Lime mortar is not suitable for building pools as it will not harden when in contact with water

Figure 2 The original lime mortar has flaked away from the surface of the Sphinx in Egypt, and many of the stones are now missing

How Science Works

Development of lime mortar

About 6000 years ago the Egyptians heated limestone strongly in a fire and then combined it with water. This produced a material that hardened with age. They used this material to plaster the pyramids. Nearly 4000 years later, the Romans mixed calcium hydroxide with sand and water to produce **mortar**.

Mortar holds other building materials together – for example, stone blocks or bricks. It works because the lime in the mortar reacts with carbon dioxide in the air, producing calcium carbonate again. This means that the bricks or stone blocks are effectively held together by rock.

$$\text{calcium hydroxide} + \text{carbon dioxide} \rightarrow \text{calcium carbonate} + \text{water}$$
$$Ca(OH)_2 + CO_2 \rightarrow CaCO_3 + H_2O$$

The amount of sand in the mixture is very important. Too little sand and the mortar shrinks as it dries. Too much sand makes it too weak.

Even today, mortar is still used widely as a building material. However, modern mortars, made with cement in place of calcium hydroxide, can be used in a much wider range of ways than lime mortar.

Cement

Although lime mortar holds bricks and stone together very strongly, it does have some disadvantages. For example, lime mortar does not harden very quickly. It will not set at all where water prevents it from reacting with carbon dioxide.

Then people found that heating limestone with clay in a kiln produced cement. Much experimenting led to the invention of Portland cement. This is manufactured this from a mixture of limestone, clay and other minerals. They are heated and then ground up into a fine powder.

This type of cement is still in use today. The mortar used to build a modern house is made by mixing Portland cement and sand. This sets when it is mixed thoroughly with water and left for a few days.

- **a** What does lime mortar need in order to set hard?
- **b** Why will lime mortar not set under water?

Concrete

Sometimes builders add small stones or crushed rocks, called aggregate, to the mixture of water, cement and sand. When this sets, it forms a hard, rock-like building material called concrete.

This material is very strong. It is especially good at resisting forces which tend to squash or crush it. We can make concrete even stronger by pouring the wet mixture around steel rods or bars and then allowing it to set. This makes reinforced concrete, which is also good at resisting forces that tend to pull it apart.

Practical

Which mixture makes the strongest concrete?

Try mixing different proportions of cement, gravel and sand, then adding water, to find out how to make the strongest concrete.
- How can you test the concrete's strength?
- How could you improve the quality of the data you collect?

Summary questions

1 Copy and complete using the words below:
   mortar concrete clay Portland sand bricks
   Cement is made in industry by heating limestone with .... It can be mixed with sand to produce ...., used to hold building materials like .... in place. An even stronger material is made by mixing cement, ... and aggregate to make ....

2 List the different ways in which limestone has been used to build your home or school.

3 Concrete and mortar are commonly used building materials. Evaluate the use of:
   a concrete to make a path rather than using mortar
   b mortar to bind bricks to each other rather than using concrete.

Figure 3 Portland cement was invented nearly 200 years ago. It is still in use all around the world today.

Did you know ...?

The Romans realised that they needed to add something to lime mortar to make it set in wet conditions. They found that adding brick dust or volcanic ash improved its setting. The modified mortar mixture could harden even under water. This method remained in use until the 18th century.

Key points

- Cement is made by heating limestone with clay in a kiln.
- Mortar is made by mixing cement and sand with water.
- Concrete is made by mixing crushed rocks or small stones called aggregate, cement and sand with water.

152   153

Further teaching suggestions

Museum display

- For a more creative approach to this work, students could pretend to work for Portland museum and that they have been asked to design a historical/scientific museum display. Split the students into four groups: one is responsible for the historical development of cement and concrete; the other groups detail the properties, uses and outline the basic production for cement, concrete and mortar. They must design their part of the display including visuals/scripts. If they are to use speech/videos, then storyboards need to be produced. Also they need to produce a list of artefacts that they would like on display. If you have the time, the students could actually construct their 'display' and it could be used in the classroom as an exhibit, although they may need to have images from the internet to represent the artefacts.

Contrasting cement, concrete and mortar

- Using the Student Book and everyday experiences, the students could create a table with three columns labelled cement, concrete and mortar. Each column should include the raw materials to make the product, a use and the properties which make it suitable for that particular use. This encourages students to evaluate which properties make a material fit for each purpose.

Answers to in-text questions

a Carbon dioxide must react with the lime in the mortar to produce calcium carbonate again.

b Because water prevents carbon dioxide getting to the mortar.

Summary answers

1 clay, mortar, bricks, sand, concrete

2 E.g. limestone building blocks, limestone chippings on flat roofs/roads/paths, concrete walls/paths/roads/posts, mortar to bind bricks.

3 a Concrete is strong in compression and can be set in large slabs. Mortar is weaker and would crack under pressure.

   b Mortar is applied as a smooth, thick paste so bricks can be set level in the correct position as slight adjustments are easy to make. However, concrete has small stones in its mixture which would make it difficult to set bricks in line.

C1 2.5

Limestone issues

AQA Specification link-up: Chemistry C1.2

- Limestone, mainly composed of the compound calcium carbonate ($CaCO_3$), is quarried and can be used as a building material. *[C1.2.1 a)]*
- Consider and evaluate the environmental, social and economic effects of exploiting limestone and producing building materials from it. *[C1.2]*
- Evaluate the developments in using limestone, cement and concrete as building materials, and their advantages and disadvantages over other materials. *[C1.2]*

Learning objectives

Students should learn:

- that there are environmental, social and economic effects of quarrying limestone
- that there are advantages and disadvantages of using limestone, cement and concrete as a building material.

Learning outcomes

Most students should be able to:

- list one environmental, social and economic effect of quarrying limestone
- list at least one advantage and one disadvantage of using limestone, cement and concrete as a building material.

Some students should also be able to:

- evaluate the benefits and drawbacks of limestone quarries to the local community
- explain the advantages and disadvantages of using limestone, cement and concrete as building materials.

Lesson structure

Starters

5,4,3,2,1 – Ask students to list five uses for limestone [making cement, making concrete, making mortar, making limewater, making building bricks]; list four names for $CaCO_3$ [limestone, chalk, marble, calcium carbonate]; list three uses of concrete [buildings, bridges, floors]; list two substances added to cement to make concrete [sand and aggregate/small stones/gravel] and list one greenhouse gas involved in the 'limestone reaction cycle' [carbon dioxide]. *(5 minutes)*

Limestone quarry – Show students a picture of a limestone quarry. Ask them to consider if they would like to live near a limestone quarry and give the value as a percentage (0% being not at all and 100% very happy). On one side of the classroom put 0% and the other 100% and ask the students to stand on the line to show how much they would like to live near a limestone quarry. Encourage some students to share their thoughts, and after these students have given their reasons, allow people to change their positions if they would like. To support students, you may wish to have some preprepared statements such as 'Claire is 90% in favour as her Dad is a coalminer and recently lost his job. She thinks that he could have the skills needed to work in the quarry.' Extend students by asking them to classify their reasons as environmental, social or economic. *(10 minutes)*

Main

- Split the class into two halves and ask them to prepare a debate on the motion: 'A new limestone quarry is a good idea in a British National Park.' Ask one half of the class to prepare an argument in favour and the other against. Students could use secondary sources of information such as textbooks and the internet. However, you may wish to give students input by providing them with fictitious people's viewpoints, such as those detailed in the Student Book, and also statistical data, such as unemployment figures and the gross income from a limestone quarry. You could support students by providing a blank table so that they can fill in the pros and cons. After students have been given adequate preparation time, you could chair the debate.

- You could supply students with a fictitious planning application for a local quarry. You could then split the class into groups and provide them with examples of people who have an interest in the planning application. Some examples might be a local unemployed teenager, local GP, member of the Green Party, Greenpeace activist, Cabinet minister, land owner, mining company executive. Ask the students to work in groups to write a biased letter from their fictitious character to the local planning officer. Students should decide if their character would be for or against and what arguments they would put in their letter to persuade the local councillors to arrive at 'the right' decision.

- Students could summarise their thoughts after the debate in a table contrasting the different building materials generated from limestone. Make a table with three headings: limestone, concrete and cement. Ask students to write statements that are advantages in green pen and disadvantages in red pen.

Support

- Students may need some help in differentiating whether statements relate to the economy, the environment or human society. It may be beneficial to provide students with a definition of each and an in-context example, so that they can refer back as necessary.

Extend

- Students should be encouraged to recognise bias and be able to generate bias and balanced arguments themselves.

Plenaries

Statements – Give students statements and ask them to order them as 'for' or 'against' a new limestone quarry and to further group them as social, economic or environmental reasons. To support students, you could give them a table to stick the statements into. Extend students by asking them to generate their own table to sort the statements. *(5 minutes)*

Revisit the limestone quarry – Show students a picture of a limestone quarry. Ask students to reconsider if they would like to live near a limestone quarry and give the value as a percentage (0% being not at all and 100% very happy). On one side of the classroom put 0% and the other 100% and ask the students to stand on the line to show how much they would like to live near a limestone quarry. Ask students to show their hands if they have changed their ideas through the lesson. Encourage some students to share their thoughts. *(10 minutes)*

How Science Works — **Rocks and building materials**

C1 2.5 — Limestone issues

Learning objectives

- What are the environmental, social and economic effects of quarrying limestone?
- What are the advantages and disadvantages of using limestone, cement and concrete as building materials?

Limestone is a very useful raw material, but mining for limestone can affect the local community and environment.

Limestone quarrying

Limestone is quarried from the ground. A quarry forms a huge hole in the ground. The limestone is usually blasted from a quarry by explosives. Then it is taken in giant lorries to be processed. Much of the limestone goes to cement factories which are often found near the quarry.

Figure 1 Limestone is often found in beautiful countryside. Quarrying the limestone scars the landscape.

Explosive charges are used to dislodge limestone from the rock face. This is known as blasting. As well as scarring the landscape the blasting noise scares off wildlife and can disturb local residents. Eventually a huge crater is formed. These can later be filled with water and can be used as a reservoir or for leisure activities. There is also the possibility of use as landfill sites for household rubbish before covering with soil and replanting.

Figure 2 Explosive charges are used to dislodge limestone from the rock face.

Activity

Limestone debate

A large mining company wants to open a new limestone quarry on the edge of a National Park. Look at the views of different people affected by the planning decision to allow the quarry or not.

Take the role of one of the people shown and debate the issues involved. Assign a chairperson to make sure each person gets their say.

- Write your own response to the planning application in a letter to the mining company's managing director after your debate.

'Now we might get that by-pass we've been asking for.'

'This quarry will obviously destroy the habitats of birds and animals. A rare species of toad is found near the proposed site.'

'At last I might be able to get a job around here! I was born here and I really don't want to leave.'

'I'm worried about all the dust that will settle on my crops. They won't grow the same. I also keep sheep on the hills – what about the noise from the blasting?'

'We'll be able to supply limestone for the glass, steel and cement industries in this region now. We predict we'll be quarrying here for 10 years – then we'll landscape the crater before moving on.'

'The lorries carrying limestone will have to go straight through our village. My daughter's primary school is on the main road.'

'I think I'll get a lot more business from the workers at the quarry. I might start selling sandwiches and employ someone to make them freshly each day.'

Developments in limestone, cement and concrete

Bathroom tiles have traditionally been made from ceramics with a glazed finish to make them waterproof. They are very hard wearing. Nowadays more tiles are made from natural stone, such as travertine. These look very attractive with each tile having unique markings. However, travertine tiles are porous and can be easily scratched. They need to be sealed with a waterproof coating.

Cement is used to make mortar and concrete on building sites. Before cement mortar was invented, builders used lime mortar. However, this takes much longer to set fully than cement mortar, especially in wet conditions. The restoration of old buildings still needs lime mortar to repair brickwork. Often the old buildings have shallow, if any, foundations. Their brick walls are much more likely to move than modern buildings. With hard cement mortar this results in cracking along weak points in the walls. However, lime mortar offers more flexibility and will not crack as easily.

Carbon dioxide is a greenhouse gas. The manufacture of cement contributes about 5% of the CO_2 gas produced by humans emitted into the air. About half of this comes from burning fuels used to heat the kilns that decompose limestone. The rest comes from the reaction itself:

$$\text{calcium carbonate} \rightarrow \text{calcium oxide} + \text{carbon dioxide}$$

Using lime mortar would contribute less to carbon dioxide emissions as it absorbs CO_2 as it sets.

Concrete is the world's most widely used building material. Concrete was first reinforced using a wire mesh to strengthen it. Nowadays we can also use:

- glass fibres
- carbon fibres
- steel rods
- poly(propene), nylon, polyesters and Kevlar.

Some of the latest research uses pulp from wood, plants and recycled paper. A little recycled paper can improve concrete's resistance to cracking, impact (making it tougher) and scratching. These reinforcing materials are shredded into small pieces before adding them to the concrete mixture.

It is much cheaper to use reinforced concrete to make a bridge than to make it from iron or steel. However, steel is much stronger (harder to snap) than concrete. Over long spans, suspension bridges can use steel's high-tensile strength in cables between concrete towers. This will support the cheap reinforced concrete sections of bridges on which cars travel. Short span bridges will always be made from reinforced concrete because of its low cost.

Figure 3 Travertine is a form of limestone. Because travertine is made up mainly of calcium carbonate, tiles and worktops can be damaged by acidic solutions.

links

For information on how lime mortar reacts with CO_2 when setting, look back at C1 2.4 Cement and concrete.

Figure 4 The latest high performance concretes give architects new opportunities when designing buildings

Key points

- There are good and bad points about quarrying for limestone. For example, more jobs will be created but there will be a large scar on the landscape.
- Limestone, cement and concrete all have useful properties for use as building materials but the mining and processing of limestone and its products has a major effect on our environment.

Summary questions

1 Give one effect of starting up a new limestone quarry in a National Park in each of the following:
   a an environmental effect
   b a social effect
   c an economic effect.

2 A new material has been developed called ConGlassCrete. It has large pieces of recycled glass embedded into concrete. Its surface is polished smooth which gives a very attractive finish. Give one environmental advantage and one disadvantage of using ConGlassCrete instead of slate as a building material.

154 / 155

Further teaching suggestions

Quarry study

- Students could be asked to study a real-life example of a limestone quarry and its impacts on the community. The Pennines are rich in these quarries. You may need to put together some resources to help them, or you could organise a trip to a quarry if you have one locally and see first hand what the environmental impact of mining is. Alternately the students could design a questionnaire to ask people living locally to a quarry what their opinions are of the quarry, its benefits to the community and any negative impact it has on the community.

Geological mapping

- Students could be given a geological map of the UK and then, using an OHT, they could plot the positions of the current limestone quarries. Students could then suggest where and if any other possible sites for development exist.

Summary answers

1 a Scar on landscape; noise pollution from explosions, crushing; dust pollution; increased traffic.
   b Less unemployment; more useful building materials being produced; improved roads.
   c More money in the area; companies in quarrying and cement industries will benefit.

2 **Advantage:** Uses recycled glass, which would not have to be remelted, using large amounts of energy, to make new objects.
   Disadvantage: Both concrete and slate require the quarrying of rock, which harm the environment but concrete needs large amounts of energy in its manufacture from limestone.

Summary answers

1 a i calcium carbonate → calcium oxide + carbon dioxide

   ii thermal decomposition

   b

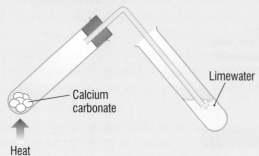

Limewater

Calcium carbonate

Heat

   c calcium oxide + water → calcium hydroxide

2 $CaCO_3 \rightarrow CaO + CO_2$
   $CaO + H_2O \rightarrow Ca(OH)_2$

3 a Limestone is crushed and roasted in a kiln with clay to make cement.

   b i Mix with sand and water.

   ii Mix with sand, aggregate/gravel/small stones/and water.

4 a potassium carbonate + hydrochloric acid
   → potassium chloride + water + carbon dioxide
   $K_2CO_3 + 2HCl \rightarrow 2KCl + H_2O + CO_2$

   b Limewater turns cloudy.

   c The calcium hydroxide in limewater reacts with carbon dioxide to make a calcium carbonate precipitate, which makes the colourless solution turn cloudy.

   calcium hydroxide + carbon dioxide
   → calcium carbonate + water

   d $Ca(OH)_2 + CO_2 \rightarrow CaCO_3 + H_2O$

5 a

Ingredient	gravel	sand	cement	water
Number of buckets	4	3	1	0.5
Percentage	47	35	12	6

   b Vary the composition of the mixtures, keeping dimensions of concrete moulds, volume of mixture placed in the moulds setting temperature, degree of mixing and method of testing, the same.

   Suitable method for testing strength needs to be described, e.g. dropping a weight on a concrete block until it breaks, increasing the height of drop systematically.

6 a The type of metal carbonate.

   b Group 1

   c Group 2

   d Group 2 carbonates decompose on heating in a Bunsen flame while Group 1 carbonates do not.

   e No – because we haven't tested all of the carbonates of Group 1 and 2 metals.

   f copper carbonate → copper oxide + carbon dioxide

   g $MgCO_3 \rightarrow MgO + CO_2$

Summary questions

1 In the process of manufacturing cement, calcium carbonate is broken down by heat.

   a i Write a word equation to show the reaction that happens inside a lime kiln.

   ii What do we call this type of reaction?

   b Draw a diagram to show how you could test for the gas given off in the reaction described in part a.

   c Write a word equation to show the reaction between calcium oxide and water.

2 Write balanced symbol equations for the reactions in Question 1 parts a and c. **[H]**

3 a How is limestone turned into cement?

   b Given cement powder, how would you make:

   i mortar

   ii concrete?

4 Potassium carbonate reacts with dilute hydrochloric acid. The gas given off gives a positive test for carbon dioxide.

   a Write a word equation and a balanced symbol equation to show the reaction between potassium carbonate, K_2CO_3, and dilute hydrochloric acid. **[H]**

   b Describe what you see in a positive test for carbon dioxide.

   c Explain your observations made in part **b**. Include a word equation in your answer.

   d Write a balanced symbol equation for the reaction in part **c**. **[H]**

5 a Here is a set of instructions for making concrete:

   'To make good, strong concrete, thoroughly mix together
   • 4 buckets of gravel
   • 3 buckets of sand
   • 1 bucket of cement
   When you have done this, add half a bucket of water.'

   Design and fill in a table to show the percentage of each substance in the concrete mixture. Give your values to the nearest whole number.

   b Describe an investigation you could use to find out which particular mixture of gravel, sand and cement makes the strongest concrete. What would you vary, what would you keep the same and how would you test the 'strength' of the concrete?

6 In an investigation into the behaviour of carbonate student draws the following conclusions when her samples of carbonates with a Bunsen burner:

Calcium carbonate	✓
Sodium carbonate	✗
Potassium carbonate	✗
Magnesium carbonate	✓
Zinc carbonate	✓
Copper carbonate	✓

(✓ = decomposes, ✗ = does not decompose

   a What was the independent variable in the investigation?

   b To which group in the periodic table do sodium potassium belong?

   c To which group in the periodic table do magne and calcium belong?

   d What do these conclusions suggest about the behaviour of the carbonates of elements in Gro and Group 2?

   e Can you be certain about your answer to questi Give reasons.

   f Write a word equation for the thermal decompo of copper carbonate.

   g Write a balanced symbol equation for the therm decomposition of magnesium carbonate.

Kerboodle resources

Resources available for this chapter on Kerboodle are:

- Chapter map: Rocks and building materials
- Video: Limestone: Building understanding, understanding building (C1 2.1)
- Simulation: Decomposition of carbonates (C1 2.2)
- How Science Works: Competing carbonates (C1 2.2)
- Bump up your grade: Carbonate reactions (C1 2.2)
- Support: Carbonate reactions (C1 2.2)
- Extension: Carbonate reactions (C1 2.2)
- Practical: Reactions of metal carbonates with hydrochloric acid (C1 2.2)
- Practical: The 'limestone reaction cycle' (C1 2.4)
- WebQuest: 'Modern' building materials (C1 2.4)
- Practical: Testing the strength of concrete beams (C1 2.4)
- Interactive activity: Rocks and building materials
- Revision podcast: The 'limestone reaction cycle'
- Test yourself: Rocks and building materials
- On your marks: Limestone
- Examination-style questions: Rocks and building materials
- Answers to examination-style questions: Rocks and building materials

Examination-style questions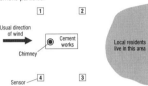

words from the list to complete the sentences.
m carbonate   calcium hydroxide
m oxide   carbon dioxide

tone is mainly made of the compound ....
limestone is heated strongly it decomposes
ucing the gas .... and solid .... When the
reacts with water it produces ....   (4)

n the compounds in the list with the descriptions.
m carbonate   copper carbonate
m carbonate   zinc carbonate

en heated with a Bunsen burner it does not
compose.   (1)
ecomposes when heated to give zinc oxide.   (1)
a blue solid that produces a black solid when
ated.   (1)
an be heated with clay to make cement.   (1)
tone blocks are damaged by acid rain.

words from the list to complete the sentences.
lves   escapes   produces   reacts

m carbonate in the limestone .... with
.... in the rain. With sulfuric acid it ....
m sulfate, carbon dioxide and water. The carbon
de .... into the air. The calcium sulfate
.... in the rainwater.   (4)

dent wanted to make calcium oxide from limestone.
student heated a piece of limestone strongly in a
en burner flame.
mplete the word equation for the reaction that
appened:
cium carbonate → calcium oxide + ...   (1)
student wanted to be sure he had made calcium
e. He crushed the heated limestone and added
r. The mixture got hot. The student cooled the
ure and filtered it. This gave a colourless solution
a white solid that was left in the filter paper.
e student added universal indicator to the
ourless solution and it turned purple.
Name the compound in the solution that causes
the indicator to turn purple.   (1)
Explain how the student's observations show
that he had made some calcium oxide by heating
limestone.   (1)
e student added dilute hydrochloric acid to the
te solid from the filter paper.
e mixture fizzed and produced a gas that turned
ewater cloudy.
What does this tell you about the white solid?   (1)
Was the student successful in changing all of the
limestone into calcium oxide? Explain your answer.
    (1)

d Write balanced equations for the three chemical
   reactions that the student did.   [H] (3)

Residents living near a cement works are concerned
because more children are suffering asthma attacks.
Residents have also noticed that parked cars are
becoming dirty because of smoke particles from the
chimney.

The table shows the possible medical risk from smoke
particles.

Particle size in mm	Medical effect
Larger than 0.4	No medical risks known
0.3 and smaller	Causes asthma attacks
0.2 and smaller	May cause cancer

It is also recommended that to avoid damage to health,
the concentration of any particles should be no higher
than 2 parts per million (ppm).

Scientists were brought in to monitor the emissions
from the cement works' chimney. They positioned four
sensors around the cement works to monitor airborne
smoke particles.

These four sensors only detect particle sizes larger than
0.5 mm and measure the concentration of particles in
ppm. The scientists reported that the particle sensors
showed that the average concentration of particles was
1.8 ppm. The scientists concluded that there was no risk
to health.

a Suggest **two** reasons why the local residents objected
   to the positions of the four sensors.   (2)
b What evidence did the scientists use to conclude that
   there was no risk to health?   (1)
c The local residents were still concerned that there was
   a risk to health. Suggest **three** reasons why.   (3)
   AQA, 2009

157

1 calcium carbonate, carbon dioxide, calcium oxide, calcium
   hydroxide   (4 marks)

2 a sodium carbonate   (1 mark)
   b zinc carbonate   (1 mark)
   c copper carbonate   (1 mark)
   d calcium carbonate   (1 mark)

3 reacts, produces, escapes, dissolves   (4 marks)

4 a carbon dioxide   (1 mark)
   b i calcium hydroxide   (1 mark)
      ii Calcium hydroxide is made when calcium oxide
         reacts with water and this is alkaline/turns UI purple
         OR calcium carbonate/limestone does not react with
         water/is neutral and would give a green colour with
         UI.   (2 marks)
   c i It is or contains calcium carbonate.   (1 mark)
      ii No – because some limestone/calcium carbonate
         remained OR not all of the limestone/calcium
         carbonate decomposed on heating.   (1 mark)
   d $CaCO_3 \rightarrow CaO + CO_2$
      $CaO + H_2O \rightarrow Ca(OH)_2$
      $Ca(OH)_2 + 2HCl \rightarrow CaCl_2 + 2H_2O$ (3 marks)

5 a Any two from: not near where people/residents live, not
      positioned where concentration of particles likely to be
      highest, not positioned downwind, not between cement
      works and where people/residents live.   (2 marks)
   b The average/concentration was 1.8 (ppm) or the
      average concentration was below 2 (ppm).   (1 mark)
   c Any three from: children/people suffering asthma
      attacks, result was an average, readings (at some
      sensors) could have been higher than 2 ppm, sensors
      did not detect particles below 0.5 mm, small particles/
      particles below 0.5 mm/0.4 mm/0.3 mm/0.2 mm could
      (still) cause cancer/asthma. (Ignore global dimmimng,
      cars becoming dirty, position of sensors).   (3 marks)

Examiner's tip

When answering longer questions, students should be
encouraged to check that they have written enough to gain
all the available marks. In doing this, students often repeat
the same point, so should be encouraged to check carefully
what they have written. Students may use bullet points to help
structure their answers to longer questions so that they are sure
they have enough points.

Practical suggestions

Practicals	AQA	k	📖	⚙
Investigation of the limestone cycle: decomposition of $CaCO_3$ to give CaO, reaction with water to give $Ca(OH)_2$, addition of more water and filtering to give limewater and use of limewater to test for CO_2.	✓	✓	✓	
Thermal decomposition of $CaCO_3$ to show limelight.	✓		✓	
Honeycomb demonstration: heat sugar syrup mixture to 150 °C and add sodium bicarbonate.	✓		✓	
Making concrete blocks in moulds, investigation of variation of content and carrying out strength tests.	✓	✓		
Design and carry out an investigation of trends in the thermal decomposition of metal carbonates.	✓		✓	✓
Investigation of the reaction of carbonates with acids.	✓	✓	✓	

C1 3.1

Extracting metals

Learning objectives

Students should learn:

- where metals are obtained from
- examples of how carbon can be used to extract some metals from their ores.

Learning outcomes

Most students should be able to:

- list examples of native metals and metals found in ores
- relate the use of carbon in metal extraction to the reactivity of a metal
- identify a reduction process from a description of a reaction.

Some students should also be able to:

- write a balanced equation to show the reduction of a metal oxide.

 Did you know ... ?

Gold is not used just for jewellery – pure gold is used on the insides of astronauts' helmet sun-visors and in some electrical circuits. A gold compound is also used to treat arthritis sufferers.

Support

- When undertaking the 'reduction by carbon' practical, students should be asked only to reduce a copper ore, as copper is studied later on in the specification. Reducing lots of different ores may just confuse the main focus of the lesson.
- Students could use secondary sources to find out the names of copper ore [malachite], iron ore [haematite] and gold ore [trick question, it is a native metal].

Extend

- Ask students to write a balanced symbol equation for the reduction of copper oxide with carbon. You could further extend students by giving them the formula of other metal oxide compounds and asking them to write the balanced symbol equation for their reduction with carbon. Ensure that the examples are for metals that are below carbon in the reactivity series.

AQA Specification link-up: Chemistry C1.3

- Ores contain enough metal to make it economical to extract the metal. The economics of extraction may change over time. [C1.3.1 a)]
- Ores are mined and may be concentrated before the metal is extracted and purified. [C1.3.1 b)]
- Unreactive metals such as gold are found in the Earth as the metal itself but most metals are found as compounds that require chemical reactions to extract the metal. [C1.3.1 c)]
- Metals that are less reactive than carbon can be extracted from their oxides by reduction with carbon, for example iron oxide is reduced in the blast furnace to make iron. [C1.3.1 d)]

Lesson structure

Starters

Key words – Ask students to look at each definition and to match it to its key word.

1. Removal of oxygen from a compound. [Reduction] 2. A list of elements from the most reactive to the least reactive. [Reactivity series] 3. A rock containing enough metal to make it economic to extract the metal. [Ore] 4. Unreactive metals, found as elements in nature. [Native] *(5 minutes)*

Prediction – Show students samples of ores and ask them to guess the metal that they contain. This should help students see that ores are usually mixtures of compounds and do not share the properties of the metals extracted from them. You may wish to support students by giving them the chemical name of the mineral that the ore contains. To extend students, ask them to give five things that would affect the cost of extracting the mineral from their ores. *(10 minutes)*

Main

- Show students a selection of ores and explain that the metal is locked up in a compound, often an oxide. Ask the students to suggest how the metal could be released [through a chemical reaction, some might mention reduction]. Discuss the need to 'concentrate' the metal compound from the rest of the ore in some cases e.g. copper, aluminium.
- The native metals should also be discussed. Explain that these metals are all relatively unreactive.
- Explain that carbon can be used to 'displace' the metal as long as carbon is more reactive than the metal you wish to extract.
- Ask the students to consult the reactivity series and suggest which metals could be extracted using this technique. [E.g. zinc, iron, copper, lead].
- Students carry out the 'Reduction by carbon' practical, extracting a metal from its oxide (see 'Practical support' for more details).
- You may wish to allow students to compare the reactivity of different metals (see 'Practical support' for more details). Students should be encouraged to write their observations in an appropriate results table and write word equations for all the reactions.

Plenaries

Complete the sentences – Ask the students to complete the following sentences:

- Metal ores are rocks that ... [contain enough metal to make it economic to extract it].
- Gold, platinum and silver are ... [native metals].
- Reduction reactions are used ... [to remove oxygen from a metal oxide].

You could support students by making this a card sort. Supply both halves of the sentences and they could work in pairs to match the six cards to make the three sentences. To extend students, you could ask them to write the formula of each chemical mentioned in their sentences. *(5 minutes)*

Random questions – Create a PowerPoint presentation, with each student's name on a different slide. Set the slide show so that it is continuous. Then start the slide show; the students' names will appear one by one quickly on the screen. Press pause and one slide will hold its position, thus choosing a student. Ask this student to answer a question. Then return to the 'name generator' and press pause again. *(10 minutes)*

Practical support

Reduction by carbon

Equipment and materials required

Bunsen burner and safety equipment, eye protection, test tube/ ignition tube plus test tube holders (alternatively, tripod, crucible, pipe-clay triangle), evaporating dish, spatula, carbon powder, selection of metal oxides (e.g. copper oxide – harmful, magnesium oxide, lead oxide – toxic).

Details

Mix the metal oxide thoroughly with carbon powder as a 1 : 1 ratio. Put the mixture into a test tube (or crucible secured in a pipe-clay triangle) and heat strongly in a blue Bunsen flame. Allow to cool and observe to see metal pieces. The pieces can be washed, and almost 'pan' for the pure metal. Lead oxide should be reduced in a fume cupboard.

The carbon is more reactive than copper (or lead), so it can reduce the metal oxide, leaving the metal element:

copper oxide + carbon → copper + carbon dioxide

$$2CuO + C \rightarrow 2Cu + CO_2$$

Safety: Wear eye protection, ventilate the room well, but use a fume cupboard, if it is available. Hands should be washed after the practical. CLEAPSS Hazcards 47A Hydrochloric acid; 26 Copper oxide – harmful; 56 Lead oxide – toxic. Dispose of waste correctly.

Comparing metal reactivity

Equipment and materials required

Dimple dish, 1 mol/dm³ hydrochloric acid, 2 × dropping pipette, 3 × boiling tube, zinc chips, calcium chips, magnesium chips, copper turnings, spatula, eye protection.

Details

Put a sample of each metal into separate dimples and add a few drops of water to each metal in turn and observe. Add a new piece of each metal into clean dimples and add a few drops of hydrochloric acid to each metal in turn and observe.

Safety: Wear eye protection; ensure all sources of ignition are removed. Dispose of the waste acid and reactive metals correctly. CLEAPSS Hazcards 107 Zinc; 16 Calcium – highly flammable; 59A Magnesium – highly flammable; 26 Copper; 47A Hydrochloric acid – harmful.

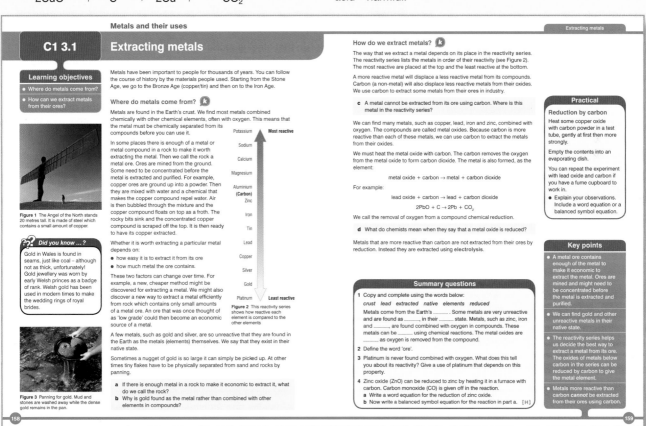

Further teaching suggestions

Revision of the reactivity series

- Students should have studied the reactivity series in KS3. However, this concept underpins much of the work on metal extraction and it could be worth revising this material. For example, give each student an element from the reactivity series printed on a piece of card. On the back of the card is information about that element's reaction with water, acid and oxygen in the air. The task is for the students to line themselves up in order of reactivity using the information given.

Reactivity poster

- If you do not have access to practical equipment, ask students to make a poster detailing the reactivity series. On the poster, they could highlight which metals can be reduced using carbon and include word equations for the metal oxide being reduced. At a later date, this poster could be revisited and the metals that are extracted using eletrolysis could be added.

Answers to in-text questions

a   an ore

b   Because gold is very unreactive.

c   above carbon

d   It has had its oxygen removed, to leave the metal element.

Summary answers

1   crust, elements, native, lead, extracted, reduced

2   A metal ore is a mineral which contains enough of the metal to make it economic to extract the metal.

3   Platinum is very unreactive. It is used in jewellery and in special corrosion-resistant wires.

4   a   zinc oxide + carbon → zinc + carbon monoxide

    b $ZnO + C \rightarrow Zn + CO$

C1 3.2

Iron and steels

Learning objectives

Students should learn:

- that iron is extracted using carbon in a blast furnace
- the properties of cast iron and how this limits its usefulness
- that iron can be alloyed to make it more useful
- the properties and composition of the three main types of steel.

Learning outcomes

Most students should be able to:

- state that iron oxide is reduced to form iron in a blast furnace using carbon
- list the properties of iron produced from the blast furnace
- explain why steels are produced.

Some students should also be able to:

- give examples of different types of steels, and how their properties differ.

Support

- Some students may struggle with the properties of each type of steel. Making a simple table of the composition, properties and uses could help to consolidate these ideas.
- The properties of metals and alloys can be modelled easily by adapting the already familiar KS3 particle model. Give students 22 marbles, polystyrene balls or table tennis balls and sticky-tac. Ask them to make a model of a solid metal. Then give each group a different sized ball to add to their model by replacing one of their atoms, and explain that this is an alloy.

Extend

- To extend students, they could use secondary sources to find out the compositions of different steels and then identify a pattern in their compositions and properties. Students could also be asked to find out about the BOC (Basic Oxygen Steel) process and draw a labelled diagram of the vessel needed to make steel.

AQA Specification link-up: Chemistry C1.3

- Metals that are less reactive than carbon can be extracted from their oxides by reduction with carbon, for example iron oxide is reduced in the blast furnace to make iron. [C1.3.1 d)]
- Iron from the blast furnace contains about 96% iron. The impurities make it brittle and so it has limited uses. [C1.3.2 a)]
- Most iron is converted into steels. Steels are alloys since they are mixtures of iron with carbon. Some steels contain other metals. Alloys can be designed to have properties for specific uses. Low-carbon steels are easily shaped, high-carbon steels are hard, and stainless steels are resistant to corrosion. [C1.3.2 b)]

Lesson structure

Starters

Displaying data – Explain that steel is made of a mixture of iron and carbon. Medium carbon steel is 0.59% carbon. Ask students to display this data in an appropriate scientific form. [A table of % composition and element name.]

Students could be supported by the table being supplied with some of the parts filled in. Students could be extended and asked to explain why they chose this display method [element is a categoric variable and composition is a continuous variable, but there is a big difference between these numbers making it difficult to show this data on a pie chart or bar chart]. *(5 minutes)*

List – Ask students to list as many properties of iron as they can think of, and one use of iron that draws specifically on each property they have listed [e.g. conductor of heat – saucepans; malleable – sculptures]. *(10 minutes)*

Main

- Often the scale of industrial chemistry is difficult to bring into the classroom, but videos or a site visit will help. Students could watch a video on iron production, such as *Industrial Chemistry for Schools and Colleges* (RSC).
- You may wish to show students the model blast furnace demonstration (see 'Practical support' for more details).
- Students need to appreciate that different proportions of constituents are used to make steels with a great variety of properties. Show students a recipe book, then a recipe card such as ones given free in supermarkets. Ask students to create a recipe card for making steel, including variations at the bottom of the card to make different types of steel. You need to follow a recipe to get a repeatable result.
- Ask students to create a 'lonely hearts' column for each type of steel. More artistic students could create the articles and a display could be made.
- You could develop the concept of alloys by testing the suitability of different metal wires in making springs. Students can coil the wires into springs, then test with slotted masses. Their investigations can provide data to plot extension against load graphs.

Plenaries

True or false? – Give each student a red and a green card. If the student thinks a statement is true, they hold up the green card; if they think it is false, they hold up the red card. Ask them these true/false statements:

- Steel is a mixture. [True]
- All steels contain mostly carbon. [False]
- Stainless steels are expensive. [True]
- Stainless steels rust because they contain iron. [False]
- The chemical symbol for steel is St. [False] *(5 minutes)*

List uses – For each type of steel (mild, medium and low carbon), ask the class to give an example of a use and make a note on the board. Split the class into groups and ask each group to come up with a different use for each type of steel and add the second example to their notes. Finally ask students to work as an individual to add a third use for each type of steel. *(10 minutes)*

Practical support

Investigating alloys

Equipment and materials required

Variety of wires (same gauge needed for fair testing), slotted 10 g masses, clamp stand, ruler.

Details

Students choose wires of same gauge to make springs by winding the wire around a pencil. Then they test the wires by measuring extension as successive slotted masses are added.

Model blast furnace

Equipment and materials required

Ignition tube, Bunsen burner and safety equipment, stand, boss and clamp, 0.3 g potassium manganate(VII), 0.15 g carbon powder, 0.15 g iron oxide powder, mineral wool, spatula, paper, magnet, clingfilm, eye protection.

Details

Put the potassium manganate(VII) in the bottom of an ignition tube and add a mineral wool plug. Mix together the carbon and iron oxide on a piece of paper and add on top of the mineral wool into the ignition tube. Add a second mineral wool plug. Hold the ignition tube at the neck in a clamp at an angle in a stand and boss. With the blue Bunsen flame, aim it at the carbon/iron oxide mixture for a couple of minutes and then heat the potassium manganate for a minute. Switch off the Bunsen burner. Allow the ignition tube to cool.

Using a magnet wrapped in cling film, students can take some of the iron oxide/carbon mixture and prove that it is non-magnetic. After the ignition tube has cooled, the reaction mixture can be poured on to paper and shown to be magnetic.

Safety: Wear eye protection. See CLEAPSS document PS67-8 for a detailed explanation. CLEAPSS Hazcard 81 Potassium manganate(VII) – oxidising and harmful; 55A Iron oxide. Dispose of waste safely.

Metals and their uses

C1 3.2 Iron and steels

Learning objectives

- How is iron ore reduced?
- Why is iron from a blast furnace not very useful?
- How is iron changed to make it more useful?
- What are the main types of steel?

Iron ore contains iron combined with oxygen in iron oxide. Iron is less reactive than carbon. So we can extract iron by using carbon to remove oxygen from the iron(III) oxide in the ore. We extract iron in a **blast furnace**.

Some of the iron(III) oxide reacts with carbon. The carbon reduces iron(III) oxide, forming molten iron and carbon dioxide gas. This is one of the reduction reactions which takes place in a blast furnace:

iron(III) oxide + carbon → iron + carbon dioxide

Iron straight from the blast furnace has limited uses. It contains about 96% iron and contains impurities, mainly carbon. This makes it very brittle, although it is very hard and can't be easily compressed. When molten it can be run into moulds and cast into different shapes. This **cast iron** is used to make wood-burning stoves, man-hole covers on roads, and engines.

We can treat the iron from the blast furnace to remove some of the carbon.

Removing all the carbon and other impurities from cast iron gives us pure iron. This is very soft and easily-shaped. However, it is too soft for most uses. If we want to make iron really useful we have to make sure that it contains tiny amounts of other elements. These include carbon and metals, such as nickel and chromium.

We call a metal that is mixed with other elements an **alloy**.

Steel is an alloy of iron. By adding elements in carefully controlled amounts, we can change the properties of the steel.

- **a** Why is iron from a blast furnace very brittle?
- **b** Why is pure iron not very useful?
- **c** How do we control the properties of steel?

Figure 1 The iron which has just come out of a blast furnace contains about 96% iron. The main impurity is carbon.

Steels

Steel is not a single substance. Like all alloys, it is a mixture. There are lots of different types of steel. All of them are alloys of iron with carbon and/or other elements.

Carbon steels

The simplest steels are the carbon **steels**. We make these by removing most of the carbon from cast iron, just leaving small amounts of carbon (from 0.03% to 1.5%). These are the cheapest steels to make. We use them in many products, such as the bodies of cars, knives, machinery, ships, containers and structural steel for buildings.

Often these carbon steels have small amounts of other elements in them as well. High carbon steel, with a relatively high carbon content, is very strong but brittle. On the other hand, low carbon steel is soft and easily shaped. It is not as strong, but is much less likely to shatter on impact with a hard object.

Mild steel is one type of low carbon steel. It contains less than 0.1% carbon. It is very easily pressed into shape. This makes it particularly useful in mass production, such as making car bodies.

Figure 2 Low carbon steel called mild steel is easily pressed into shapes

Alloy steels

Low-alloy steels are more expensive than carbon steels because they contain between 1% and 5% of other metals. Each of these metals produces a steel that is well-suited for a particular use.

Figure 3 The properties of steel alloys make them ideal for use in suspension bridges

Even more expensive are the **high-alloy steels**. These contain a much higher percentage of other metals. The chromium–nickel steels are known as **stainless steels**. We use them to make cooking utensils and cutlery. They are also used to make chemical reaction vessels. That's because they combine hardness and strength with great resistance to corrosion. Unlike most other steels, they do not rust!

Figure 4 The properties of stainless steels make them ideal for making utensils and cutlery

AQA Examiner's tip

Know how the hardness of steels is related to their carbon content.

Summary questions

1 Copy and complete the following sentences using the terms below:

carbon   pure   steel   cast   reduced

Iron(III) oxide is .... (has its oxygen removed) in a blast furnace.

Iron from the blast furnace, poured into moulds and left to solidify is called .... iron.

If all the carbon and other impurities are removed from cast iron we get .... iron.

Iron that has been alloyed with carbon and other elements is called ....

Iron that contains just a small percentage of carbon is called .... steel.

2 How does cast iron differ from pure iron?

3 **a** Make a table to summarise the properties and some uses of low carbon steel, high carbon steel and chromium–nickel steel.

  b Why are surgical instruments made from steel containing chromium and nickel?

Key points

- We extract iron from iron ore by reducing it using carbon in a blast furnace.
- Pure iron is too soft for it to be very useful.
- Carefully controlled quantities of carbon and other elements are added to iron to make alloys of steel with different properties.
- Important examples of steels are:
  - low carbon steels which are easily shaped,
  - high carbon steels which are very hard,
  - stainless steels which are resistant to corrosion.

Further teaching suggestions

Modelling steel

- A different model for iron and steel uses modelling clay. By incorporating different amounts of sand into the modelling clay, its properties can be changed. The modelling clay represents the iron and the sand the carbon. Roll the samples into a sausage shape and then pull them until they break. By comparing the fracture sites you can see the effect of making steel.

Compare and contrast

- Students could be asked to list the properties that both iron and steel share and then list the desirable properties that make steel more useful than iron. Students could also compare and contrast the reduction of iron ore and tungsten ore/zinc ore (which are also reduced using carbon).

Corus Group

- A number of resources are available from the Corus Group website (www.coruseducation.com).

The history of the blast furnace

- Students could research the historical development of the blast furnace.

Answers to in-text questions

a It contains a fairly high percentage of carbon and other impurities.

b It is too soft.

c By adding other elements in carefully controlled amounts.

Summary answers

1 reduced, cast, pure, steel, carbon

2 Cast iron is harder and more brittle than pure iron.

3 **a**

Type of steel	Properties
low carbon	soft, not easily shattered (malleable)
high carbon	very strong but brittle
chromium-nickel (stainless)	hard, strong, corrosion-resistant

b This is stainless steel, which is very resistant to corrosion (any rust on the instruments could harbour harmful microorganisms).

C1 3.3 Aluminium and titanium

Learning objectives

Students should learn:

- that aluminium and titanium are useful metals
- that metals more reactive than carbon are extracted by electrolysis of molten compounds
- that extraction of aluminium and titanium is expensive.

Learning outcomes

Most students should be able to:

- list some useful properties of aluminium and titanium
- state that methods of extraction used for aluminium (as an example of a metal more reactive than carbon) and titanium are expensive
- give examples of uses of aluminium and/or titanium and explain which properties makes them fit for purpose.

Some students should also be able to:

- explain why the extraction of aluminium and titanium is costly.

Support

- Students could be supported by creating a 'cut-and-stick' activity or card sort activity, where the images showing the use, types of metal and property that makes it fit for that purpose are on separate rectangles or cards. Students cut them out and/or sort the information.

Extend

- Students could be extended by being given the symbol equations for each stage of the titanium extraction processes and for aluminium extraction. Students could then balance these equations and be further extended by being encouraged to use state symbols.

AQA Specification link-up: Chemistry C1.3

- Metals that are more reactive than carbon, such as aluminium, are extracted by electrolysis of molten compounds. The use of large amounts of energy in the extraction of these metals makes them expensive. [C1.3.1 e)]
- Aluminium and titanium cannot be extracted from their oxides by reduction with carbon. Current methods of extraction are expensive because
  – there are many stages in the processes
  – large amounts of energy are needed. [C1.3.1 i)]

Lesson structure

Starters

Museum – In five different points around the room put a piece of bauxite, aluminium oxide (sealed in a Petri dish), aluminium metal, titanium metal and rutile. Each sample should be labelled with an information card (chemical's name, formula, hazards, properties, uses). Students should visit each sample and then write two sentences to summarise how the chemicals are related. [Bauxite is an aluminium ore that mainly contains aluminium oxide (Al_2O_3). Rutile is mainly titanium oxide (TiO_2), an ore of titanium.] *(5 minutes)*

Sparkler! – A demonstration to show the reactivity of aluminium: set up a Bunsen burner and sprinkle aluminium powder into the flame. The powder will combust in a twinkling effect to form aluminium oxide. Ask the students to generate a word equation. Students could be supported by being given the names of the chemicals. Extend students by asking them to give a balanced symbol equation for the reaction.
[aluminium + oxygen → aluminium oxide, $4Al + 3O_2 \rightarrow 2Al_2O_3$] *(10 minutes)*

Main

- In this lesson electrolysis is being introduced, although no details are required. Students will be familiar with charged ions from 'C1 3.1 Extracting metals' and should be able to understand that the positive metal ion is attracted to a negatively charged electrode. The use of electrolysis to extract metals is very expensive due to the amount of energy needed for this chemical reaction.

- Some students find it difficult to link specific properties of a material with its uses. Search the internet to find pictures of various items made of aluminium and titanium, e.g. a bike, a hip replacement joint, an aircraft, a saucepan, overhead cables with a pylon, a ring. Ask the students to choose which material it would be made from and give reasons for their choice.

- Explain to students that they are to make a TV commercial encouraging customers to use these metals rather than cheaper metals. Students should work in small teams to produce their one-minute commercial. Encourage students to recognise the bias needed, and to include information about why it is an expensive material.

- Students could be asked to use the Student Book to create two flow charts to explain how titanium and aluminium are extracted from their ores.

Plenaries

'I went to the shops to buy …' – This children's game can be played but the students can only give examples of items made from aluminium or titanium. The teacher could start by saying: 'I went to the shops to buy a titanium aircraft'. The first student then could say: 'I went to the shop to buy a titanium aircraft and some aluminium foil', and so on around the class. To support students, there could be a list of uses of aluminium or titanium on the board. To extend students, they could explain why that metal is chosen, e.g. I went to buy a titanium nuclear reactor, as it is unreactive and resistant to high temperatures. *(5 minutes)*

Questions and answers – Ask students to work in small teams. Complete a question and answer session: if a team gets three questions correct, then they have 'earned the right to leave'; if they are incorrect, then the question goes on to another group. A team who answers incorrectly should be given as many questions as needed to get three correct, therefore more questions than teams need to be written. *(10 minutes)*

Practical support

Sparkler!

Equipment and materials required

Bunsen burner, safety equipment, eye protection, spatula and aluminium powder – highly flammable.

Details

Set the Bunsen burner up with a blue flame over a heatproof mat. Hold the Bunsen at an angle. Half-fill the spatula with aluminium powder, and sprinkle it into the flame. This is a very vigorous reaction.

Safety: Wear eye protection and tie back hair and loose clothing. Keep students well away from the Bunsen burner. CLEAPSS Hazcard 1 Aluminium powder – highly flammable.

Further teaching suggestions

Designing an experiment

- Students could be given samples of different metals, including aluminium and titanium. They could then design a practical to test the chemical and physical properties of the different metals. This would create an opportunity to teach aspects of Controlled Assessment, e.g. designing a fair test.

Did you know ...?

Titanium dioxide is the white material in correction fluid and it is used in white paint.

C1 3.3 Aluminium and titanium

Learning objectives

- Why are aluminium and titanium so useful?
- What method is used to extract metals that are more reactive than carbon?
- Why does it cost so much to extract aluminium and titanium?

Although they are very strong, many metals are also very dense. This means that we cannot use them if we want to make something that has to be both strong and light. Examples are alloys for making an aeroplane or the frame of a racing bicycle.

Where we need metals which are both strong and have a low density, **aluminium** and **titanium** are often chosen. These are also metals which do not corrode.

Properties and uses of aluminium

Aluminium is a silvery, shiny metal. It is surprisingly light for a metal as it has a relatively low density. It is an excellent conductor of energy and electricity. We can also shape it and draw it into wires very easily.

Although aluminium is a relatively reactive metal, it does not corrode easily. This is because the aluminium atoms at its surface react with oxygen in air. They form a thin layer of aluminium oxide. This layer stops any further corrosion taking place.

Aluminium is not a particularly strong metal, but we can use it to form alloys. These alloys are harder, more rigid and stronger than pure aluminium.

Because of these properties, we use aluminium to make a whole range of goods. These include:

- drinks cans
- cooking foil
- saucepans
- high-voltage electricity cables
- aeroplanes and space vehicles
- bicycles.

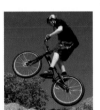

Figure 1 We use aluminium alloys to make bicycles because of their combination of low density and strength

a Why does aluminium resist corrosion?
b How do we make aluminium stronger?

Extracting aluminium

Because aluminium is a reactive metal we cannot use carbon to displace it from its oxide. Instead we extract aluminium using electrolysis. An electric current is passed through molten aluminium oxide at high temperatures to break it down.

First we must mine the aluminium ore. This contains aluminium oxide mixed with impurities. Then the aluminium oxide is separated from the impurities. The oxide must then be melted before electrolysis can take place.

The problem with using electrolysis to extract metals is that it is a very expensive process. That's because we need to use high temperatures to melt the metal compound. Then we also need a great deal of electricity to extract the metal from its molten compound. There are also environmental issues to consider when using so much energy.

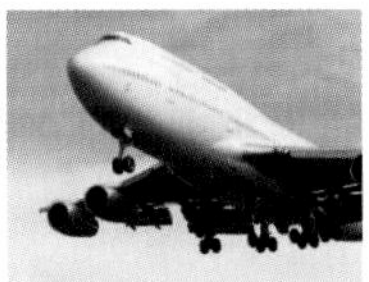

Figure 2 We use aluminium alloys to make aircraft. The alloys are strong yet have a low density so the plane can carry more passengers and cargo.

Properties and uses of titanium

Titanium is a silvery-white metal. It is very strong and very resistant to corrosion. Like aluminium it has an oxide layer on its surface that protects it. Although it is denser than aluminium, it is less dense than most other metals.

Titanium has a very high melting point – about 1660 °C – so we can use it at very high temperatures.

We use titanium for:

- the bodies of high-performance aircraft and racing bikes (because of its combination of strength and relatively low density)
- parts of jet engines (because it keeps its strength even at high temperatures)
- parts of nuclear reactors (where it can stand up to high temperatures and its tough oxide layer means that it resists corrosion)
- replacement hip joints (because of its low density, strength and resistance to corrosion).

c What properties make titanium ideal to use in jet engines and nuclear reactors?

Figure 3 We can use titanium inside the body as well as outside. This is an artificial hip joint, used to replace a natural joint damaged by disease or wear and tear.

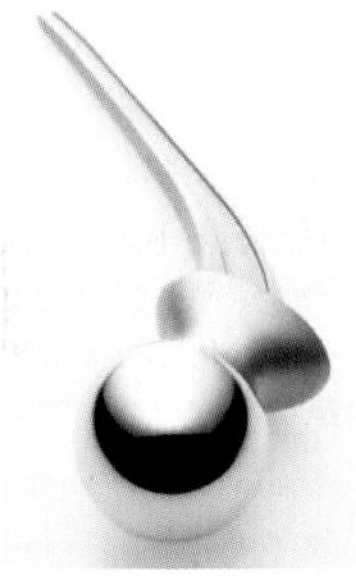

Extracting titanium

Titanium is not particularly reactive, so we could produce it by displacing it from its oxide with carbon. But unfortunately carbon reacts with titanium metal making it very brittle. So we have to use a more reactive metal to displace titanium. We use sodium or magnesium. However, both sodium and magnesium have to be extracted by electrolysis themselves in the first place.

Before displacement of titanium can take place, the titanium ore must be processed. This involves separating the titanium oxide and converting it to a chloride. Then the chloride is distilled to purify it. Only then is it ready for the titanium to be displaced by the sodium or magnesium. Each one of these steps takes time and costs money.

d Why do we need electricity to make:
i aluminium and **ii** titanium?

links
For more information on the environmental impact of extracting metals, see C1 3.6 Metallic issues.

Summary questions

1 Copy and complete using the words below:

corrode energy expensive high low oxide reactive strong

Aluminium and titanium alloys are useful as they are .... and have a .... density. Although aluminium is reactive, it does not .... because its surface is coated with a thin, tough layer of aluminium .... Titanium does not corrode because it is not very .... and also has its oxide layer to protect it. We use large amounts of .... in the extraction of both metals from their ores which makes them .... The large number of steps involved in the extraction of the metals also contributes to their .... cost.

2 Why is titanium used to make artificial hip joints?

3 **a** Explain the different reasons why carbon cannot be used to extract: **i** aluminium, or **ii** titanium.
b Name two processes in the extraction of aluminium that require large amounts of energy.

Key points

- Aluminium and titanium are useful because they resist corrosion.
- Aluminium requires the electrolysis of molten aluminium oxide to extract it as it is too reactive to reduce using carbon.
- Aluminium and titanium are expensive because extracting them from their ores involves many stages and requires large amounts of energy.

Answers to in-text questions

a Because it has a layer of aluminium oxide over its surface that prevents corrosion.
b By alloying it with other elements.
c It is unreactive and very strong at high temperatures.
d **i** Because aluminium extraction requires electrolysis
ii The reactive metals (Mg or Na) used in the extraction of titanium were obtained by electrolysis.

Summary answers

1 strong, low, corrode, oxide, reactive, energy, expensive, high
2 Because of its strength and resistance to corrosion.
3 **a** **i** Carbon is not reactive enough to reduce aluminium oxide/Carbon is less reactive than aluminium so cannot displace it from its compounds.
ii Carbon forms a compound with titanium that makes the metal brittle.
b The melting of aluminium oxide and the electrolysis of aluminium oxide.

C1 3.4

Extracting copper

AQA · Specification link-up: Chemistry C1.3

Learning objectives

Students should learn:

- that copper can be extracted from copper-rich ores by smelting
- that copper can be extracted by different methods from low-grade ores
- that copper can be purified by electrolysis.

Learning outcomes

Most students should be able to:

- describe how to extract copper by smelting.
- explain why low-grade ores are now being exploited
- explain two methods for extracting copper from low-grade ores

Some students should also be able to:

- evaluate the different methods of copper extraction.

- Copper can be extracted from copper-rich ores by heating the ores in a furnace (smelting). The copper can be purified by electrolysis. The supply of copper-rich ores is limited. [C1.3.1 f)]
- New ways of extracting copper from low-grade ores are being researched to limit the environmental impact of traditional mining. Copper can be extracted by phytomining, or by bioleaching. [C1.3.1 g)]
- Copper can be obtained from solutions of copper salts by electrolysis or by displacement using scrap iron. [C1.3.1 h)]

Lesson structure

Starters

Copper photos – Provide students with images of copper being used for different purposes. Ask students to suggest what they all have in common [they are all made of copper]. To extend students, ask them to list what property of copper makes them useful for each purpose [e.g. copper wiring because it is an electrical conductor, copper cooking pans because it is a thermal conductor, copper jewellery because it is shiny]. *(5 minutes)*

Crossword – Use the internet to find a simple program to make a crossword of the key words used in the lesson [copper, extraction, smelting, mining, electrolysis, phytomining, bioleaching]. To support students, you may wish to give them the clues and the key words, so that they just need to match the key word with the clue. *(10 minutes)*

Main

- Explain to students that copper is a very important metal. However, our sources of copper-rich ores are running out. Therefore scientists are developing new ways to extract copper from low-grade ores.

- Students should gain hands-on experience of smelting using the 'extracting copper from malachite' practical (see 'Practical support' for more details). Students often really enjoy this experiment and should be encouraged to detail the reaction in a word equation.

- There are three main methods of copper extraction that students need to be aware of. Split the class into three groups. Each group is going to become the 'experts' on a different part of this spread; smelting, bioleaching and phytomining.

- Each group should produce an A5 set of notes about their topic, and a puzzle to check that the class have understood their work. They could also create a small presentation on the topic, maybe using PowerPoint.

- In the following lesson, each group could deliver their presentation and their handout can be given to the class. The 'experts' are then on hand to help with the activities.

- If you have the time to spare, students could grow brassica plants that have been frequently sprayed with copper compounds, or add copper compounds to the compost. The plants will absorb the copper, which can be extracted from the biomass by electrolysis or displacement. (See C1 3.6 'Practical support' for more details.)

Support

- Students may need support in remembering the three main methods of copper extraction. It may be worth asking students to write a list of key words as a simple explanation of the method in each case.

Extend

- To extend students, they could consider why copper extraction techniques are changing. They should also consider which method they think is best and why.

Plenaries

Summarise – Ask the students to write one sentence to include the following copper extraction methods: smelting, bioleaching and phytomining. Students could be supported by being given part of the sentence and they have to complete it. To extend students, they could be encouraged to explain when and why electrolysis is used to obtain pure copper. *(5 minutes)*

Consequences – Give each student a piece of A5 paper. Ask the students to write down a use of copper at the top of the paper, fold it over and pass it to the right. Then they should write their favourite extraction method and why it is their favourite, fold and pass to the right. Then write a 'boring' fact about copper extraction, fold and pass to the right, and finally a fascinating fact (something new that they have learnt in the lesson) about copper extraction. Ask the student to unfold their current piece of paper and read the comments. Ask a few students to feedback to the class. *(10 minutes)*

Practical support

Extracting copper from malachite

Equipment and materials required

Bunsen burner and safety equipment, eye protection, boiling tube, boiling tube holder, filter funnel, conical flask, spatula, copper carbonate powder (harmful), 1.0 mol/dm³ sulfuric acid (irritant) and filter paper. **For method A:** an iron nail. **For method B:** 2 × carbon electrode, 2 × wire connectors, 2 × crocodile clip, low voltage lab pack, small beaker, copper sulfate solution low voltage (less than 1.0 mol/dm³ would not be harmful).

Details

Fill a boiling tube with two spatulas of copper carbonate and heat on a blue Bunsen flame until the powder has change colour from green to black. Allow the mixture to cool and then add sulfuric acid until the boiling tube is half full. Fold the filter paper and rest in the filter funnel. Put the filter funnel into the neck of the conical flask and filter the mixture. Discard the filter paper and residue. **For method A:** put an iron nail in the solution and observe. **For method B:** set up a series circuit with the lab pack and electrodes. Add some extra copper sulfate solution to the filtrate in a small beaker until it is half full. Submerge the electrodes and turn on the lab pack. Observe as copper is produced at the cathode (negative electrode).

Safety: Wear eye protection, ventilate the room well, especially if method B is followed. CLEAPSS Hazcard 98A Sulfuric acid – irritant, CLEAPSS 26 Copper carbonate – harmful, 27C Copper sulfate – harmful. Hands should be washed after the practical.

Metals and their uses

C1 3.4   Extracting copper

Learning objectives

- How is copper obtained from copper-rich ores?
- What methods can be used to obtain copper from low-grade ores?
- How is copper purified?

Extracting copper from copper-rich ores [k]

We extract most of our copper from copper-rich ores. These are a limited resource and are in danger of running out.

There are two main methods used to remove the copper from the ore.

- In one method we use sulfuric acid to produce copper sulfate solution, before extracting the copper.
- The other process is called **smelting** (roasting). We heat copper ore very strongly in a furnace with air to produce crude copper.

For example, copper can be found in an ore called chalcocite. This contains copper(I) sulfide, Cu_2S. If we heat the copper(I) sulfide in air, it decomposes to give copper metal:

copper(I) sulfide + oxygen → copper + sulfur dioxide

Care has to be taken to avoid letting sulfur dioxide gas into the air. This gas causes acid rain. So chimneys are fitted with basic 'scrubbers' to neutralise the acidic gas.

Then we use the impure copper as the positive electrode in electrolysis cells to make pure copper. About 80% of copper is still produced by smelting.

a What chemical do we use to treat copper ore in order to form copper sulfate?

Smelting and purifying copper ore uses huge amounts of heat and electricity. This costs a lot of money and will have an impact on the environment.

Figure 1 Mining copper ores can leave huge scars on the landscape. This is called open-cast mining. About 90% of copper comes from open-cast mines. Our supplies of copper-rich ores are a limited resource.

links

For information on the charges on metal ions, look back at C1 1.4 Forming bonds.

Figure 2 Extracting copper metal using electricity

Carbon electrodes   Copper sulfate solution

Practical

Extracting copper from malachite

Malachite is a copper ore containing copper carbonate. To extract the copper we first heat the copper carbonate in a boiling tube. Thermal decomposition takes place. Copper oxide is left in the tube.

- Which gas is given off?

We then add dilute sulfuric acid to the copper oxide. Stopper and shake the tube. This makes copper sulfate solution. Filter off any excess black copper oxide in the solution.

To extract the copper metal, either

1. Put an iron nail into the copper sulfate solution
- What happens to the iron nail?

Or

2. Collect some extra copper sulfate solution and place it in a small beaker. Set up the circuit as shown in Figure 2. Turn the power on until you see copper metal collecting.
- Which electrode – the positive or the negative – does the copper form on?

Metal ions are always positively charged. Therefore, in electrolysis they are attracted to the negative electrode. So metals are always deposited at the negative electrode. In industry the electrolysis is carried out in many cells running at once. This method gives the very pure copper needed to make electrical wiring. Electrolysis is also used to purify the impure copper extracted by smelting. In the industrial process, the electrolysis cells use copper electrodes.

The copper can also be extracted from copper sulfate solution in industry by adding scrap iron. Iron is more reactive than copper, so it can displace copper from its solutions:

iron + copper sulfate → iron sulfate + copper

Extracting copper from low-grade copper ores

Instead of extracting copper from our limited copper-rich ores, scientists are developing new ways to get copper from low grade ores. This would be uneconomical using traditional methods. We can now use bacteria (**bioleaching**) and even plants (**phytomining**) to help extract copper.

In phytomining, plants can absorb copper ions from low-grade copper ore as they grow. This could be on slag heaps of previously discarded waste from the processing of copper-rich ores. Then the plants are burned and the metals can be extracted from the ash. The copper ions can be 'leached' (dissolved) from the ash by adding sulfuric acid. This makes a solution of copper sulfate. Then we can use displacement by scrap iron and electrolysis to extract pure copper metal.

In bioleaching, bacteria feed on low-grade metal ores. By a combination of biological and chemical processes, we can get a solution of copper ions (called a 'leachate') from waste copper ore. Once again, we use scrap iron and electrolysis to extract the copper from the leachate.

About 20% of our copper comes from bioleaching. This is likely to increase as sources of copper-rich ores run out.

Bioleaching is a slow process so scientists are researching ways to speed it up. At present it can take years to extract 50% of the metal from a low-grade ore.

Summary questions

1 Copy and complete using the words below:

bacteria smelting electricity phytomining iron low sulfuric

Traditionally, copper can be extracted from some of its ores by heating (............). If copper ore is treated with .... acid, we get a solution of copper sulfate. We can obtain copper metal from this solution either by adding .... metal or by passing .... through the solution. Now new ways are being developed to extract copper using .... (bioleaching) or plants (............). These can extract the copper from ....-grade ores.

2 **a** Explain briefly two traditional ways of extracting copper metal.
   b State an advantage of extracting copper using bacteria rather than traditional methods.
   c Why can copper sometimes be found native (as the element itself)?
   d When copper is purified by electrolysis, which electrode do you think that the pure copper collects at? Why?

3 Write a balanced chemical equation for the extraction of copper:
   a from copper(I) sulfide   [H]
   b from copper sulfate solution using scrap iron   [H]

?? Did you know ...?

Copper metal is so unreactive that some samples of copper exist in nature as the element itself. It is found native. A huge copper boulder was discovered by a diver at the bottom of Lake Superior in North America. It was raised to the surface in 2001. It has a mass of about 15 000 kg.

links

For more information on the environmental impact of extracting metals and phytomining, see C1 3.6 Metallic issues.

Figure 3 In Australia Dr Jason Plumb looks for bacteria that can extract metals from ores. His search takes him to some exciting places – including volcanoes!

Key points

- Most copper is extracted by smelting (roasting) copper-rich ores, although our limited supplies of ores are becoming more scarce.
- Copper can be extracted from copper solutions by electrolysis or by displacement using scrap iron. Electrolysis is also used to purify impure copper, e.g. from smelting.
- Scientists are developing ways to extract copper that use low-grade copper ores. Bacteria are used in bioleaching and plants in phytomining.

Further teaching suggestions

Classify

- Students could be asked to create a table to list the advantages and disadvantages of mining copper. Students could then be extended by classifying each statement as being economic, social or environmental. A copper mine case study can be found at www.mining-technology.com.

I'm most important

- Split the students into four groups and give each group a different key point. The groups could then create a persuasive argument why their key point is the most important and the debate could flow!

Answers to in-text questions

a sulfuric acid

Summary answers

1 smelting, sulfuric, iron, electricity, bacteria, phytomining, low

2 **a** Smelting in which a copper ore is heated to get copper. Adding sulfuric acid to get copper sulfate solution, which is electrolysed or has scrap iron added to it to displace the copper.

   b We can use waste ores, previously dumped because they were too low-grade, reducing open-cast mining and scars on the landscape. Using bacteria will also conserve limited supplies of high-grade ores.

   c Because it is an unreactive metal.

   d It collects at the negative electrode as copper ions are positively charged (as are all metal ions).

3 **a** $Cu_2S + O_2 \rightarrow 2Cu + SO_2$

   b $CuSO_4 + Fe \rightarrow FeSO_4 + Cu$

C1 3.5

Useful metals

Learning objectives

Students should learn:

- what transition metals are and their properties
- why copper is a useful metal
- that alloys are more useful than pure metals.

Learning outcomes

Most students should be able to:

- recognise transition metals and list their properties and some uses
- explain why copper is used in plumbing and for electrical wiring
- define an alloy and give an example.

Some students should also be able to:

- explain why alloys are often more useful than a pure metal.

Support

- Students may need reminding about where the metals are found in the periodic table. Give students a blank periodic table and encourage them to draw a thick black line between the metals and non-metals, colour in the non-metals and add a key. Also share with students that many metals end with -ium, e.g. calcium, magnesium, potassium.

Extend

- Students could be encouraged to find out the composition of different alloys and represent this information in a variety of appropriate formats, e.g. bar charts, tables and pie charts.
- You may wish to extend and build on the information about alloying gold. Encourage students to find out how hallmarks can be used to determine the alloy content of silver metal. Use an internet search engine and look for British hallmarks.

AQA Specification link-up: Chemistry C1.3

- Most metals in everyday use are alloys. Pure copper, gold, iron and aluminium are too soft for many uses and so are mixed with small amounts of similar metals to make them harder for everyday use. [C1.3.2 c)]
- The elements in the central block of the periodic table are known as transition metals. Like other metals they are good conductors of heat and electricity and can be bent or hammered into shape. They are useful as structural materials and for making things that must allow heat or electricity to pass through them easily. [C1.3.3 a)]
- Copper has properties that make it useful for electrical wiring and plumbing. [C1.3.3 b)]
- Low density and resistance to corrosion make aluminium and titanium useful metals. [C1.3.3 c)]

Lesson structure

Starters

Copper poem – Ask students to write an acrostic poem with the first lines beginning with the letters from 'copper'. Students should incorporate the three different extraction techniques into their poem. *(5 minutes)*

Word search – Give students a word search containing a variety of elements from the periodic table (do not include the f-block, as students will not be given this in their GCSE examinations). Ask students to find only the transition metals. To support students, you may wish to create a word search that contains only examples of transition elements that they would be familiar with, such as gold, silver, iron. To extend students, you may wish to give students the symbols of the elements that they need to find. (There is no need to distinguish between the transition metals and d-block elements at GCSE level.) *(10 minutes)*

Main

- Show students some samples of transition metals in sealed Petri dishes. Ask them to use the periodic table to find the symbols of these elements, and where in the periodic table they are found.
- You may wish to extend students by also having some sealed samples of transition metal compounds. Students should conclude that transition metal compounds are coloured, and the same metal ion produces a similar coloured compound, no matter what the negative ion is that it is bonded to.
- Many different alloys exist, but the students need to focus on specific types. Split the class into three groups. Each group is going to become the 'experts' on a different part of this spread:
  - copper and its alloys
  - gold and its alloys
  - aluminium and its alloys.

  Ask the students to write an article for a students' science magazine about one of these topic areas. The article needs to include why the particular metal is an important material and list its properties and uses. Students should then explain why it is often alloyed, give at least one example of an alloy containing that element, its use and why the alloy is more suitable for that job than the pure metal. Students may also wish to produce their articles using a desktop publishing program.
- Then students should get into groups of three and read all of the articles, to gain an overview of the whole topic area. Students should then write a summary paragraph about transition metal alloys.

Plenaries

Key words – Place the key words, copper, alloy, transition metals, gold, aluminium, in a bag. Ask students to volunteer and pick out a key word, which they then need to explain in one sentence to the rest of the class. *(5 minutes)*

AfL (Assessment for Learning) – Give the students an examination question with a fictitious student's answer. Ask the students to work as individuals or in small groups to mark the questions. Then ask students to feed back on each question part saying what mark they would award and why. Support students by giving them an examination question from a Foundation Tier paper. Extend students by giving them a question from a Higher Tier paper. *(10 minutes)*

Further teaching suggestions

Internet research
- Show students some transition metal compounds and their solutions. Encourage them to find some uses [e.g. pottery glazes].

Which metal is best?
- Students could be given some uses of metal alloys, e.g. car bodywork, cooking pan, door handles. Students could suggest which metal alloy would be the most appropriate based on their cost and/or properties [e.g. car bodywork is made of steel as it is easily shaped, is not brittle and is strong].

Top of the class
- A variety of different answers to the same examination question on alloys and their uses could be given to groups of students. They should then order the answers from highest grade to lowest grade. Then give the students the mark scheme and ask them to reflect on their choices.

Metals and their uses

C1 3.5 — Useful metals

Learning objectives
- What are transition metals and why are they so useful?
- Why is copper such a useful metal?
- Why are alloys more useful than pure metals?

Transition metals

In the centre of the periodic table there is a large block of metallic elements. They are called the **transition metals**. Many of them have similar properties. Like all metals, the transition metals are very good conductors of electricity and energy. They are strong but can also be bent or hammered into useful shapes.

Figure 1 The position of the transition metals in the periodic table

a In which part of the periodic table do we find the transition metals?
b Name three properties of these elements.

The properties of the transition metals mean that we can use them in many different ways. You will find them in buildings and in cars, trains and other types of transport. Their strength makes them useful as building materials. We use them in heating systems and for electrical wiring because energy and electricity pass through them easily.

Copper is a very useful transition metal. It can be bent but is still hard enough for plumbers to use as water tanks or pipes. Fortunately, it does not react with water. Copper also conducts electricity and energy very well. So it is ideal where we need:
- pipes that will carry water, or
- wires that will conduct electricity.

Figure 2 Copper is particularly useful because it is such a good conductor of electricity

c What makes copper so useful for a plumber?

Figure 3 Transition metals are used in many different ways because of their useful properties

Copper alloys

Bronze was probably the first alloy made by humans, about 5500 years ago. It is usually made by mixing copper with tin. We use it to make ship's propellers because of its toughness and resistance to corrosion.

We make brass by alloying copper with zinc. Brass is much harder than copper but it is workable. It can be hammered into sheets and pressed into intricate shapes. This property is used to make musical instruments.

d Why are copper alloys more suitable for some uses than pure copper metal?

Aluminium alloys

Aluminium has a low density for a metal. It can be alloyed with a wide range of other elements. There are over 300 alloys of aluminium available. These alloys have very different properties. We can use some to build aircraft while others can be used as armour plating on tanks and other military vehicles.

Gold alloys

As with copper and iron, we can make gold and aluminium harder by adding other elements. We usually alloy gold with copper when we use it in jewellery. Pure gold wears away more easily than its alloy with copper. By varying the proportions of the two metals we also get different shades of 'gold' objects.

Figure 5 Alloying with copper makes gold more hardwearing. This is especially important in wedding rings, which many people wear most of the time.

e What property of aluminium makes it useful for making alloys in the aircraft industry?
f Apart from making gold harder, what else can alloying change?

Figure 4 The Statue of Liberty in New York contains over 80 tonnes of copper

?? Did you know ... ?
The purity of gold is often expressed in 'carats', where 24-carat gold is almost pure gold (99.9%). If you divide the carat number by 24, you get the fraction of gold in your jewellery. So an 18-carat gold ring will contain ¾ (75%) gold.

Summary questions

1 Copy and complete using the words below:

   aluminium brass aircraft bronze soft transition

   The .... metals are found in the central block of the periodic table. Like pure iron, pure copper is too .... to be very useful. We can make copper harder by alloying it with tin to make ...., and with zinc to make ....

   There are over 300 alloys of the low-density metal .... Many of these are used to make .... where strength is also an important property.

2 a Write a list of the properties of a typical transition metal.
  b Why is copper metal used so much in plumbing?

3 Silver and gold are transition metals that conduct electricity even better than copper. Why do we use copper to make electric cables instead of either of these metals?

4 Why can aluminium alloys be used in so many different ways?

Key points
- The transition metals are found in the central block of elements in the periodic table.
- Transition metals have properties that make them useful for building and making things. For example, copper is used in wiring because of its high electrical conductivity.
- Copper, gold and aluminium are all alloyed with other metals to make them harder.

166 / 167

Answers to in-text questions

a In the central block (or between Groups 2 and 3).
b Three of: good conductors of heat/electricity, hard, tough, strong, can be bent/hammered into shapes, have very high melting points (except mercury).
c Used for pipes because it does not react with water and is quite easy to bend.
d They are harder or resistant to corrosion.
e Its low density.
f The colour of 'gold'.

Summary answers

1 transition, soft, bronze, brass, aluminium, aircraft

2 a Good conductors of energy/electricity, hard, tough, strong, can be bent/hammered into shapes, have very high melting points.
  b Copper can be bent but is hard enough to be used to make pipes or tanks. It does not react with water.

3 Silver and gold are much more expensive than copper and less abundant in the Earth's crust.

4 Because there are so many different aluminium alloys, with a wide range of properties.

C1 3.6

Metallic issues

Learning objectives

Students should learn:

- the issues that arise in exploiting metal ores
- the benefits of recycling metals
- that there are advantages and disadvantages of using metals in construction.

Learning outcomes

Most students should be able to:

- list an advantage and a disadvantage of exploiting metal ores
- list reasons for the importance of recycling metals
- state a benefit and a drawback of using metals in construction.

Some students should also be able to:

- explain the benefits, in terms of social, economic and environmental, of exploiting metal ores
- explain the benefits, in terms of social, economic and environmental, of recycling metals.

AQA Specification link-up: Chemistry C1.3

- We should recycle metals because extracting them uses limited resources and is expensive in terms of energy and effects on the environment. [C1.3.1 j)]
- New ways of extracting copper from low-grade ores are being researched to limit the environmental impact of traditional mining. Copper can be extracted by phytomining, or by bioleaching. [C1.3.1 g)]
- Copper can be obtained from solutions of copper salts by electrolysis or by displacement using scrap iron. [C1.3.1 h)]
- Consider and evaluate the social, economic and environmental impacts of exploiting metal ores, of using metals and of recycling metals. [C1.3]
- Evaluate the benefits, drawbacks and risks of using metals as structural materials. [C1.3]

Lesson structure

Starters

Rusting – Show students a rusty nail, or steel bar from reinforced concrete. Make a link to the construction industry. Ask students to list what needs to be present for rusting to happen [water and oxygen]. To extend students, ask them to write a balanced symbol equation for the reaction [$4Fe + 3O_2 \xrightarrow{water} 2Fe_2O_3$]. To support students, you could give them a word equation for rusting [iron + oxygen $\xrightarrow{water}$ hydrated iron oxide] and ask them to use this to help them. Note: rust is actually hydrated iron oxide or $Fe_2O_3 \cdot xH_2O$. *(5 minutes)*

Recycling think, pair square – Ask students to individually consider how they can personally get their waste metal recycled [e.g. can banks at a supermarket]. Then ask students to compare their thoughts with another person and then in small groups. Ask each group to give one new way that they can recycle metals. *(10 minutes)*

Main

- Students could work in small groups to discuss the tasks outlined in the activity 'Mining and processing metal ores – the issues'. The ideas from the group should be distilled to the most important points and two representatives should then feed back the thoughts to the rest of the group.
- Discuss the reasons that we recycle metals. Stress that extracting metals from their ores uses limited resources, uses a lot of energy and affects the environment. Stress the multi-stage process involved in extracting metals.
- Environmental issues, such as the recycling of metals, are a growing concern. Allow students to complete the activity 'Saving energy'.
- Each set of students could create a flow chart to explain the process and highlight the stages that require a lot of energy. Each student could then write a conclusion paragraph to explain how recycling metal could save energy.

Plenary

Thought experiment – Explain to students that they are going to make a prediction about the effect of rusting on steel reinforced concrete [rusting would affect the structure of the material and this affects the ability of the steel to withstand forces, so the structure would not be as strong]. Support students by giving them a writing frame to help make their prediction. Extend students by asking them to consider how the rate of rusting would be affected in a seaside structure compared to an inland structure [salt is a catalyst for rusting and so the seaside structure would rust quicker]. *(5 minutes)*

Support

- Students may find it difficult to generate some of the points to include in the 'Mining and processing metal ores – the issues' activity. Character cards could be made for the students that give a monologue from different characters containing some of the key points. These could be used to launch a discussion.

Extend

- Students could be extended by being asked to find out all of the different methods of protecting iron and steel from rust. Students could be encouraged to make a spider diagram of these methods.

Practical support

Phytomining experiment

Equipment and materials required

Compost, brassica seedlings, plant pot, scissors, string, fume cupboard, Bunsen burner and safety equipment, evaporating basin, eye protection, copper sulfate solution in a spray bottle (0.5 mol/dm³) or copper sulfate powder (harmful), 1.0 mol/dm³ dilute sulfuric acid (irritant), dropping pipette, 250 cm³ conical flask, filter funnel, filter paper, stirring rod. Either magnesium powder (highly flammable) and a spatula or 2 × carbon electrodes, low-voltage power pack, 2 × connecting wire, 2 × crocodile clip, 100 cm³ beaker.

Details

Plant the brassica seedling into a pot. Allow the plants to grow for a month. Spray the leaves of the plant with copper sulfate solution every day. An alternative to spraying is to mix copper sulfate powder into the soil used to pot the plant. Wearing gloves, harvest the leaves, and tie by their stems into a bunch and hang in the fume cupboard to dry. Wearing gloves, crush the plant leaves into an evaporating basin. Set up the Bunsen burner in the fume cupboard and use it to turn the dry leaves to ash. Allow the ash to cool and add enough acid so that the ash is easily covered and stir the mixture until the liquid turns blue. Filter the mixture into the conical flask. Then add a spatula of magnesium powder and stir. Observe as the copper is displaced from the copper sulfate. Alternatively, put the solution into a beaker, and submerge the ends of two carbon electrodes in it. Use the wires and crocodile clips to connect the electrodes in series to the power pack. Turn on the power and observe as copper is collected on the negative electrode.

Safety: Wear eye protection, ventilate room well especially if the brassica is to be sprayed. CLEAPSS Hazcard 98A Sulfuric acid – irritant. CLEAPSS Hazcard 27C Copper sulfate – harmful. Hands should be washed after the practical. Ashing of the brassica should be completed in the fume cupboard.

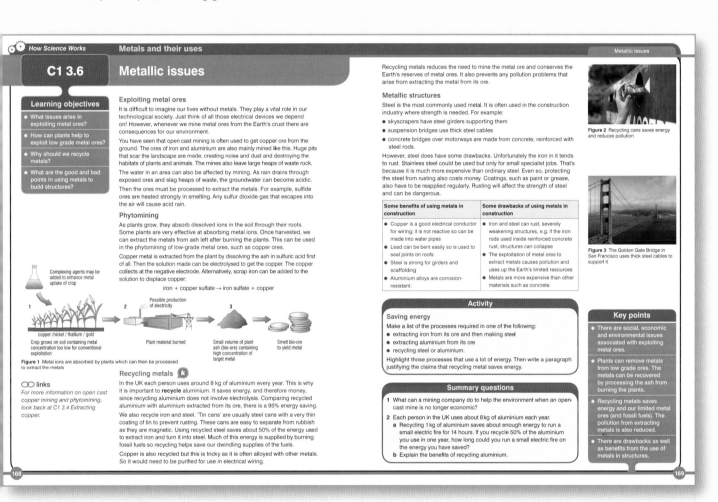

Further teaching suggestions

Charting costs

- Students could create a bar chart to compare the cost of producing 1 kg of titanium and aluminium from their ore with 1 kg of each respective metal from recycled material.

Photo of construction

- Give small groups of students a digital camera and allow them to photograph examples of uses of metals in construction around the school site. These images can then be shared with the rest of the class using a data projector.

Summary answers

1 The huge hole could be used as a landfill site for rubbish, which is then covered in soil and landscaped. Alternatively, it could be filled with water to make a reservoir/leisure activity centre.

2 a About 56 hours.

   b Less energy used in recycling, conserving the Earth's resources of fuels and ores. Less pollution from metal extraction, e.g. from open-cast mining of aluminium ore.

Summary answers

1 a A rock containing enough of a metal to make it economically worthwhile to extract the metal.

b Describes a metal found in the Earth that has not combined with another element.

c The removal of oxygen from a compound.

2 The alloy may be harder, stiffer, and it may be easier to work (shape into different objects).

3 a i bioleaching **ii** phytomining
iii smelting **iv** electrolysis

b bioleaching and phytomining

4 Brassica is grown on the polluted site. The plants are then harvested and burned, collecting the ash. This is processed, e.g smelted, to extract the metals.

5 E.g. extracting copper using bacteria or fungi is likely to use much less energy than conventional extraction techniques. One definite advantage is that it may be useful for extracting copper from ores that would otherwise remain uneconomic. We could also use waste ores, previously dumped because they were low grade, reducing open-cast mining and scars on the landscape.

A disadvantage is the longer length of time it takes to extract the metal. Also, the technology is at present undeveloped, so the true cost of this method of extraction is unknown.

6 a 869 kg **b** 23.9%
c i steel/iron **ii** It is magnetic.

7 a copper or silver

b Hearsay. The hardness increases up to 18 carat and only then decreases.

c Gold alloy (carat) is the independent variable.

d The hardness of the alloy is a continuous variable.

e Suitable graph, which could be a line graph as both variables are continuous. However, as gold is sold in these carats, it might be more suitable to present the data as a bar chart. The axes should be fully labelled and the points plotted correctly. The gold alloy (carat) should be on the x-axis and the maximum hardness on the y-axis.

f As the proportion of gold in the alloy increases, so the hardness increases up to about 18 carat. After this, as the alloy carat increases, the hardness decreases.

Kerboodle resources

Resources available for this chapter on Kerboodle are:
- Chapter map: Metals and their uses
- Animation: Extracting metals (C1 3.1)
- WebQuest: Find an extraction reaction – ore else! (C1 3.1)
- Practical: Extraction of metals (C1 3.1)
- Extension: Extracting zinc (C1 3.1 and C1 3.2)
- Practical: Displacement reactions of metals (C1 3.2)
- Practical: Electrolysis of copper sulfate solution (C1 3.4)
- Bump up your grade: Transition metals are marvellous (C1 3.5)
- Support: Transition metals are marvellous (C1 3.5)
- Viewpoint: Recycling metals: benefits and problems (C1 3.6)
- Interactive activity: Metals and their uses
- Revision podcast: Extracting copper
- Test yourself: Metals and their uses
- On your marks: Metals
- Examination-style questions: Metals and their uses
- Answers to examination-style questions: Metals and their uses

---

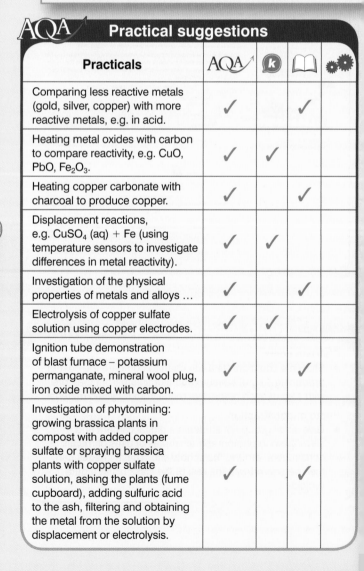

Summary questions

1 Write simple definitions for the following terms:
a metal ore
b native state
c chemical reduction.

2 We can change the properties of metals by alloying them with other elements.

Write down *three* ways that a metal alloy may be different from the pure metal.

3 a What name is given to the method of extracting copper from an ore:
i using bacteria
ii using plants
iii using heat
iv using electricity?

b Which methods in part **a** are being developed to extract copper from low-grade copper ores?

4 Describe how brassicas can be used to decontaminate 'brown-field' sites and recover the polluting metals. [H]

5 Carry out some research to find the advantages and disadvantages of using bioleaching to extract copper metal.

6 By the middle of the decade scrap car dealers are required to recover 95% of all materials used to make a car. The following table shows the metals we find in an average car:

Material	Average mass (kg)	% mass
Ferrous metal (steels)	780	68.3
Light non-ferrous metal (mainly aluminium)	72	6.3
Heavy non-ferrous metal (for example lead)	17	1.5

Other materials used include plastics, rubber and glass.

a What is the average mass of metal in a car?

b What percentage of a car's mass is made up of **non-metallic** materials?

c i What is the main metal found in most cars?
ii Which of this metal's properties allows it to be separated easily from other materials in the scrap from a car?

7 The following was overheard in a jeweller's shop:

"I would like to buy a 24-carat gold ring for my hus…

"Well madam, we would advise that you buy one w… a lower carat gold. It looks much the same but the … gold there is, the softer it is."

Is this actually the case? Let's have a look scientifi… the data.

Pure gold is said to be 24 carats. A carat is a twent… fourth, so $24 \times \frac{1}{24} = 1$ or pure gold. So a 9-carat g… ring will have $\frac{9}{24}$ gold and $\frac{15}{24}$ of another metal, prob… copper or sometimes silver. Most 'gold' sold in sh… therefore an alloy.

How hard the 'gold' is will depend on the amount o… and on the type of metal used to make the alloy.

Here are some data on the alloys and the maximum… hardness of 'gold'.

Gold alloy (carat)	Maximum hardness (
9	170
14	180
18	230
22	90
24	70

a Which metals are used to alloy gold in jewellery?

b The shop assistant said that 'the more gold ther… the less hard it is.' Was this based on science or… hearsay? Explain your answer.

c In this investigation which is the independent va…

d Which type of variable is 'the maximum hardnes… the alloy' – continuous or categoric?

e Plot a graph of the results.

f What is the pattern in the results?

AQA Practical suggestions

Practicals	AQA	k	📖	⚙
Comparing less reactive metals (gold, silver, copper) with more reactive metals, e.g. in acid.	✓		✓	
Heating metal oxides with carbon to compare reactivity, e.g. CuO, PbO, Fe₂O₃.	✓	✓		
Heating copper carbonate with charcoal to produce copper.	✓		✓	
Displacement reactions, e.g. CuSO₄ (aq) + Fe (using temperature sensors to investigate differences in metal reactivity).	✓	✓		
Investigation of the physical properties of metals and alloys …	✓		✓	
Electrolysis of copper sulfate solution using copper electrodes.	✓	✓		
Ignition tube demonstration of blast furnace – potassium permanganate, mineral wool plug, iron oxide mixed with carbon.	✓		✓	
Investigation of phytomining: growing brassica plants in compost with added copper sulfate or spraying brassica plants with copper sulfate solution, ashing the plants (fume cupboard), adding sulfuric acid to the ash, filtering and obtaining the metal from the solution by displacement or electrolysis.	✓		✓	

End of chapter questions

Examination-style questions **k**

...frames are often made from metal tubes. The ...tubes are produced using the steps in this list:

...**g → concentrating → extracting → purifying**
...**g → shaping**

...each of the following statements with the correct
...rom the list.

...metal is produced using chemical reduction. (1)
...metal is mixed with other metals to make it harder
...stronger. (1)
...metal ore is dug from the ground. (1)
...te rock is removed from the metal ore. (1)
...r elements are removed from the metal. (1)
...e correct words from those shown to complete
...sentence.
...d is found in the Earth as .... (1)

...**chloride   gold metal   gold oxide**
... is extracted by reacting iron oxide with .... (1)

...**on   copper   nitrogen**
...inium is extracted from aluminium oxide
...g .... (1)

...**bustion   distillation   electrolysis**
...r metal is used for electric wires. An alloy of copper,
...brass, is used for pins and terminals of electric plugs.
...per metal is relatively soft and flexible. Give
...ther reason why copper is used for electric wires. (1)
...ss is an *alloy*. What is an *alloy*? (1)
...n-cast mining of copper ore makes a very large hole.
...Suggest **one** environmental problem that is caused
...by open-cast mining of copper ore. (1)
...Some copper ores contain copper sulfide, CuS.
...Copper sulfide in heated in air to produce copper
...and sulfur dioxide.
...CuS + O₂ → Cu + SO₂
...gest **one** environmental problem caused by
...ting copper sulfide in air. (1)
... amount of copper-rich ores is estimated to last
... a few more years. New houses need several
...metres of copper wire.
...Explain why the need to use so much copper will
...cause a problem in the future. (1)
...Suggest **two** ways in which society could
...overcome this problem. (2)
                                                    AQA, 2008

...question you will be assessed on using good
...h, organising information clearly and using
...alist terms where appropriate.
...of the iron we use is converted into steels.
...be and explain how the differences in the
...rties of the three main types of steel allow them to
...ed in different ways. (6)

5 Titanium is used in aircraft, ships and hip replacement
joints. Titanium is as strong as steel but 45% lighter, and
is more resistant to acids and alkalis.
Most titanium is produced from its ore, rutile (titanium
oxide), by a batch process that takes up to 17 days.
   Titanium oxide is reacted with chlorine to produce
   titanium chloride →
   Titanium chloride is reacted with magnesium at
   900 °C in a sealed reactor for 3 days →
   The reactor is allowed to cool, then opened and the
   titanium is separated from the magnesium chloride
   by hand.
Titanium reactors produce about 1 tonne of the metal per
day.
Iron blast furnaces produce about 20 000 tonnes of the
metal per hour.
a Give **one** property of titanium that makes it more
   useful than steel for hip replacement joints. (1)
b Suggest **three** reasons why titanium costs more than
   steel. (3)
                                                    AQA, 2008

6 Phytomining uses plants to absorb metal compounds
from the ground. It is often used on land that has been
contaminated by normal mining. It involves these stages:
Sow seeds → grow plants → harvest plants → dry plants
→ burn plants → collect ash
The ash is then treated like a metal ore obtained by
normal mining.
a Suggest **one** environmental advantage of phytomining
   compared with normal mining. (1)
   The table shows information about some metals that
   are absorbed by plants used for phytomining.

Metal	Value of metal in £ per kg	Maximum mass of metal in plants in g per kg	Percentage (%) of metal in normal ore
Gold	25 000	0.10	0.002
Nickel	17	38	2
Copper	4.9	1	.5
Zinc	3.2	4	
Lead	1.5	10	3

b The plants used for gold phytomining give a maximum
   yield of 20 tonnes of plants per hectare. Calculate the
   maximum value of the gold that can be recovered from
   1 hectare. (2)
c One kilogram of plants used for nickel phytomining
   produces 150 g of ash.
   What is the percentage of nickel in the ash? (2)
d Suggest reasons why phytomining has been used to
   produce gold, nickel and copper, but is only rarely
   used to produce zinc and lead. (4)

171

AQA Examination-style answers

1 a extracting   **b** alloying   **c** mining
    d concentrating   **e** purifying   *(5 marks)*

2 a gold metal   **b** carbon   **c** electrolysis
                                                    (3 marks)

3 a good (electrical) conductor (accept low reactivity/
       resistance to corrosion) *(1 mark)*
    b A mixture of metals. *(1 mark)*
    c i Any **one** from: eyesore, destruction of habitats,
         pollution of water, dust pollution, noise, traffic pollution
                                                    (1 mark)
       ii acid rain (accept sulfur dioxide is a pollutant) *(1 mark)*
    d i because we are running out of copper ores or
         because copper ores are limited resources *(1 mark)*
       ii Any **two** from: do not throw away copper/brass or put
         in landfill, reuse/recycle, use low grade copper ores,
         use other metals/materials/plastics in place of copper
                                                    (2 marks)

4 Marks awarded for this answer will be determined by the
Quality of Written Communication (QWC) as well as the
standard of the scientific response.

There is a clear and detailed scientific description of three
main types of steel, a difference in the properties of each,
and how these are related to a different use for each type
of steel. The answer shows almost faultless spelling,
punctuation and grammar. It is coherent and in an organised,
logical sequence. It contains a range of appropriate and
relevant specialist terms used accurately. *(5–6 marks)*

There is a scientific description of two types of steel, and the
difference in their properties related to their uses, or there is
a description of three types of steel with either differences
in properties or uses. There are some errors in spelling,

---

punctuation and grammar. The answer has some structure
and organisation. The use of specialist terms has been
attempted, but not always accurately. *(3–4 marks)*

There is a brief description of at least two types of steel or
two different uses of steels. The spelling, punctuation and
grammar are very weak. The answer is poorly organised with
almost no specialist terms and/or their use demonstrating a
general lack of understanding of their meaning. *(1–2 marks)*

No relevant content. *(0 marks)*

Examples of chemistry points made in the response:

Name or description of main types of steel:
- Low-carbon steels – low percentage, less than 0.1% carbon
- Mild steels – 0.15–0.25% carbon
- High-carbon steels – up to 1.4% carbon
- Stainless steels – 10–20% of other metals, special steels,
  high-alloy steels, nickel-chromium steels or other named
  example
- Low-alloy steels – up to 5% of other metals
- Allow: carbon steels, low-alloy and high-alloy as three types.

Properties:
- Low-carbon steels – softer, more malleable, more easily
  shaped
- Mild steels – stronger, less easily bent
- High-carbon steels – harder, stronger, more brittle, less
  malleable
- Stainless steels – more resistant to corrosion, stronger
- Low-alloy steels – harder, stronger, more resistant to
  corrosion.

Uses:
- Low-carbon steels – wires, rivets, sheet metal
- Mild steels – general engineering purposes, reinforcing
  concrete
- High-carbon steels – tools, e.g. hammers, chisels, cutting
  tools
- Stainless steels – chemical and food industry, kitchens,
  cutlery
- Low-alloy steels – bridges, chains, armour plating, high-
  speed tools.

5 a Any **one** from: less dense/lighter, resistant to acids/alkalis/
       chemicals (accept resits corrosion). *(1 mark)*
    b Any **three** from: takes a long time to process, low
       abundance (of ore), small amount produced, batch
       process or blast furnace is continuous, more stages used,
       more energy used (per tonne of titanium, magnesium/
       chlorine is expensive or produced by electrolysis, labour
       intensive (ignore simple references to cost/usefulness/
       temperature or incorrect process). *(3 marks)*

6 a Any **one** from: No digging, less effect on landscape, can
       remove contamination/pollution/metals from soils. *(1 mark)*
    b £50 000 (working showing 2000 g or 2 kg gold gains 1 mark)
                                                    (2 marks)
    c 25(.3)% (working showing 38/150 gains 1 mark) *(2 marks)*
    d Any **four** from:
       gold: high value of metal (makes it economic), low percentage
       of metal in normal ore
       nickel: high value of metal, high percentage of nickel in ash
       copper: low percentage in normal ore, normal ores running out
       zinc: (relatively) low value of metal, (relatively) high
       percentage in normal ore
       lead: (relatively) low value of metal, low mass of metal
       in plants, kills plants, only (cost effective when) used to
       clean up contaminated sites.
       (Accept any other relevant reasons for specific metals or
       reasons correctly generalised to gold, nickel and copper
       or to zinc and lead). *(4 marks)*

C1 4.1

Fuels from crude oil

Learning objectives

Students should learn:
- what crude oil is
- what an alkane is
- how to represent alkanes.

Learning outcomes

Most students should be able to:
- recognise that crude oil is a mixture and state that it can be separated into fractions by distillation
- define and recognise simple alkanes
- write the correct chemical formula of an alkane represented by a structural formula.
- draw diagrams and write the formulae of simple alkanes when given named examples
- recall and use the formula C_nH_{2n+2} to give the formula of an alkane, when n is given.

Support

- You could support students by giving them a half-finished table detailing alkane names, molecular and displayed formulae. Each row should only have one missing piece of information. For very weak students this task could be a 'cut-and-stick' activity.

Extend

- You could extend students by introducing the idea that alkanes can be branched as well as straight chain molecules. Encourage students to look at different displayed formulae and generate their molecular formula. They should conclude that the branched chain saturated hydrocarbons still conform to the general formula of the alkanes and therefore are classified as alkanes.

AQA Specification link-up: Chemistry C1.4

- Crude oil is a mixture of a very large number of compounds. *[C1.4.1 a)]*
- A mixture consists of two or more elements or compounds not chemically combined together. The chemical properties of each substance in the mixture are unchanged. It is possible to separate the substances in a mixture by physical methods including distillation. *[C1.4.1 b)]*
- Most of the compounds in crude oil consist of molecules made up of hydrogen and carbon atoms only (hydrocarbons). Most of these are saturated hydrocarbons called alkanes, which have the general formula C_nH_{2n+2}. *[C1.4.1 c)]*
- Alkane molecules can be represented in the following forms: C_2H_6. *[C1.4.2 a)]*

Lesson structure

Starters

What is the connection? – Show students a picture related to crude oil, e.g. a drilling rig, petroleum jelly barrier cream, petrol, a road surface or lubrication oil. Ask students to suggest the connection. [All of these products come from crude oil.] *(5 minutes)*

Oil is everywhere – It is essential for students to know that oil affects our everyday lives. Run a quick discussion about all the uses of oil, from fuel to fabrics, plastics and medicines. Ask students how they think the oil price affects all these commodities. Support students by showing them pictures of some of the products of oil to spark discussion. Extend students by giving them data on oil prices and looking to see if it correlates with the retail price index for the same period. *(10 minutes)*

Main

- Explain that crude oil is a mixture of hydrocarbons and ask the students to suggest, from their previous work in Key Stage 3, how mixtures can be separated into their components. Ask them to predict the method used to separate crude oil.

- Show the students the distillation equipment that has been set up and ask them to predict what will happen to the crude oil and why. Develop their ideas of a simple distillation into fractional distillation, using questions and answers. Demonstrate distillation. If this demonstration is done, it is important that it is not used to explain how continuous fractional distillation in a fractionating column works. In a fractionating column, the substances are being continuously evaporated and condensed on trays to achieve the separation.

- The fractions from this simple distillation could then be tested as detailed under 'Practical support' in the next lesson.

- Students often struggle with the idea that molecules are three dimensional. We often represent them in a 2-D format. Give each pair of students a molecular model kit. Then show students which atoms represent H and C, noting the size difference and the number of holes in each type of atom. Give the students the structural formulae of the first three or four alkanes and then set the students the task of making them and writing their molecular formulae. Ask them to list the similarities and differences between these molecules.

Plenaries

Observations – Draw the structural formula of butane on the board. Ask the students to write down as much information as they can about this molecule. To support students, you could give them a selection of key words to choose from. To extend students, encourage them to write the formula of the compound and consider some chemical reactions in which it could be involved, e.g. burning. *(5 minutes)*

Model a molecule – Split the class into groups. Give each group a different hydrocarbon name and some coloured sports vests or bibs. The students must use their bodies to demonstrate a hydrocarbon molecule. Those who represent carbon atoms need to sit down, so that four bonds (holding hands, feet/hands) can be created. *(10 minutes)*

Practical support

Fractional distillation demonstration

Equipment and materials required

A boiling tube with side arm, bung with a thermometer through it, four test tubes (as collecting tubes – ignition tubes can also be used to display small volumes of fractions), two beakers, ice/water mixture, boiling water, mineral wool, 'synthetic' crude oil (for the recipe see CLEAPSS Recipe Card 20 Crude oil or CLEAPSS 45A Hydrocarbons – aliphatic, or it can be purchased already made), Bunsen burner and safety equipment, eye protection, six watch glasses.

Details

Soak the mineral wool in the synthetic crude oil and place in the boiling tube. Fix the bung and ensure that the bulb of the thermometer is adjacent to the side arm. Put a collecting tube into an ice bath and the end of the side arm into the top of it. Gently heat the boiling tube with a Bunsen flame and notice when the temperature reading has stabilised (around 80 °C). When the temperature rises again, quickly change the current collecting tube for a new one. Repeat four times, collecting five fractions and leaving a residue in the boiling tube. During this practical, wear eye protection and complete in a well ventilated room. Each fraction can be collected at about every 50 °C up to about 300 °C. The residues will remain on the mineral wool, making the sixth fraction. The fractions can be ignited. Tip them onto mineral wool on a watch glass. Then ignite the mineral wool, taking great care.

Safety: Tie back hair and loose clothing. CLEAPSS Hazcard 45A Hydrocarbons.

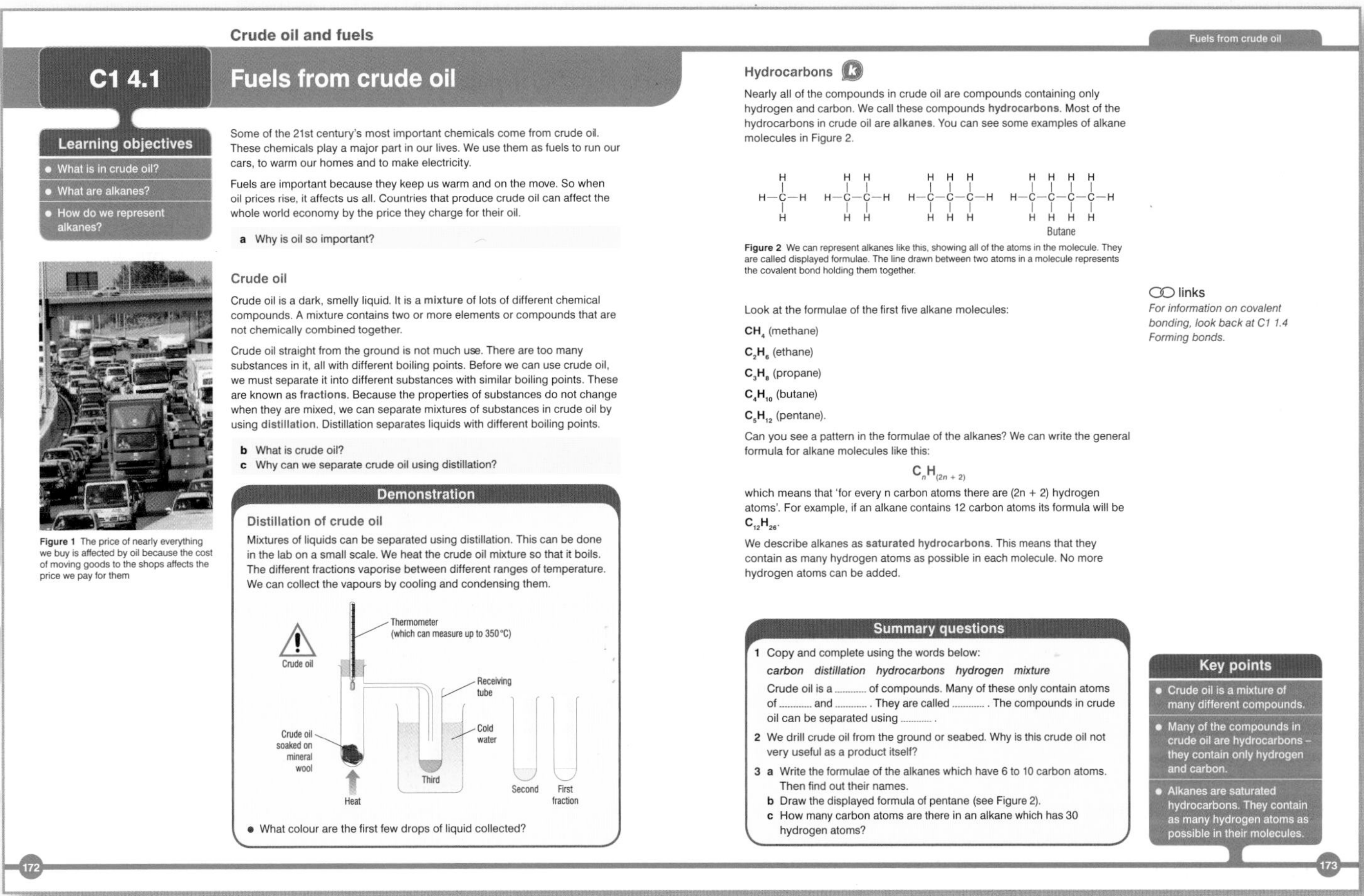

C1 4.1 Fuels from crude oil

Learning objectives

- What is in crude oil?
- What are alkanes?
- How do we represent alkanes?

Some of the 21st century's most important chemicals come from crude oil. These chemicals play a major part in our lives. We use them as fuels to run our cars, to warm our homes and to make electricity.

Fuels are important because they keep us warm and on the move. So when oil prices rise, it affects us all. Countries that produce crude oil can affect the whole world economy by the price they charge for their oil.

a Why is oil so important?

Figure 1 The price of nearly everything we buy is affected by oil because the cost of moving goods to the shops affects the price we pay for them

Crude oil

Crude oil is a dark, smelly liquid. It is a mixture of lots of different chemical compounds. A mixture contains two or more elements or compounds that are not chemically combined together.

Crude oil straight from the ground is not much use. There are too many substances in it, all with different boiling points. Before we can use crude oil, we must separate it into different substances with similar boiling points. These are known as fractions. Because the properties of substances do not change when they are mixed, we can separate mixtures of substances in crude oil by using distillation. Distillation separates liquids with different boiling points.

b What is crude oil?

c Why can we separate crude oil using distillation?

Demonstration

Distillation of crude oil

Mixtures of liquids can be separated using distillation. This can be done in the lab on a small scale. We heat the crude oil mixture so that it boils. The different fractions vaporise between different ranges of temperature. We can collect the vapours by cooling and condensing them.

Thermometer (which can measure up to 350 °C)

Crude oil

Crude oil soaked on mineral wool

Receiving tube

Cold water

Heat

Third   Second   First fraction

- What colour are the first few drops of liquid collected?

Hydrocarbons 🄚

Nearly all of the compounds in crude oil are compounds containing only hydrogen and carbon. We call these compounds **hydrocarbons**. Most of the hydrocarbons in crude oil are alkanes. You can see some examples of alkane molecules in Figure 2.

Butane

Figure 2 We can represent alkanes like this, showing all of the atoms in the molecule. They are called displayed formulae. The line drawn between two atoms in a molecule represents the covalent bond holding them together.

Look at the formulae of the first five alkane molecules:

CH_4 (methane)

C_2H_6 (ethane)

C_3H_8 (propane)

C_4H_{10} (butane)

C_5H_{12} (pentane).

Can you see a pattern in the formulae of the alkanes? We can write the general formula for alkane molecules like this:

$$C_nH_{(2n+2)}$$

which means that 'for every n carbon atoms there are (2n + 2) hydrogen atoms'. For example, if an alkane contains 12 carbon atoms its formula will be $C_{12}H_{26}$.

We describe alkanes as saturated hydrocarbons. This means that they contain as many hydrogen atoms as possible in each molecule. No more hydrogen atoms can be added.

links

For information on covalent bonding, look back at C1 1.4 Forming bonds.

Summary questions

1 Copy and complete using the words below:

   carbon   distillation   hydrocarbons   hydrogen   mixture

   Crude oil is a .... of compounds. Many of these only contain atoms of .... and .... They are called .... The compounds in crude oil can be separated using ....

2 We drill crude oil from the ground or seabed. Why is this crude oil not very useful as a product itself?

3 **a** Write the formulae of the alkanes which have 6 to 10 carbon atoms. Then find out their names.

   b Draw the displayed formula of pentane (see Figure 2).

   c How many carbon atoms are there in an alkane which has 30 hydrogen atoms?

Key points

- Crude oil is a mixture of many different compounds.
- Many of the compounds in crude oil are hydrocarbons – they contain only hydrogen and carbon.
- Alkanes are saturated hydrocarbons. They contain as many hydrogen atoms as possible in their molecules.

Further teaching suggestions

Key words

- Ask the students to try to determine the most important word from the lesson that would help them remember all of the key points. Encourage different students to justify their choice, e.g. **alkanes** as these are saturated hydrocarbons and are contained in crude oil.

Answers to in-text questions

a Oil affects everything we do – heating and lighting our homes, transport and the goods we buy. (Also feedstock for the chemical industry.)

b Crude oil is a mixture of chemical compounds.

c Because the properties of the individual compounds in the mixture remain the same when they are mixed. Distillation relies on the different boiling points of these compounds.

Summary answers

1 mixture, carbon (hydrogen), hydrogen (carbon), hydrocarbons, distillation

2 Because there are too many substances in it.

3 **a** C_6H_{14} (hexane), C_7H_{16} (heptane), C_8H_{18} (octane), C_9H_{20} (nonane), $C_{10}H_{22}$ (decane).

   b

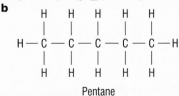

   Pentane

   c Fourteen carbon atoms.

C1 4.2

Fractional distillation

Learning objectives

Students should learn:

- that crude oil is separated into fractions using fractional distillation
- the properties of each fraction and how they relate to the size of the molecules
- which fractions make useful fuels and why.

Learning outcomes

Most students should be able to:

- state that crude oil is separated into fractions by fractional distillation
- list how the properties change from small chain fractions to long chain fractions
- state which fractions are useful fuels.

Some students should also be able to:

- explain the key steps involved in fractional distillation
- relate the trend in properties to molecular size.

Support

- If a teaching assistant is available, split the class in two. The teacher could demonstrate the properties of the different fractions, while the teaching assistant shows the ampoule (sealed glass container) samples of the fractions. Then rotate the groups.
- Students may need some support with remembering the different displayed formulae. You could display these on the board from small to larger. Then draw an arrow from small to large molecules. Ask students to state the trend – the colour darkens, viscosity increases and ease of lighting reduces.

Extend

- Students should be encouraged to understand that there are forces of attraction between the molecules and it is these that have to be overcome and reformed as each molecule slides over others as the liquid is poured. Then encourage students to use this information to explain why larger molecules are more viscous. They could explain this model using a series of cartoons.

AQA Specification link-up: Chemistry C1.4

- The many hydrocarbons in crude oil may be separated into fractions, each of which contains molecules with a similar number of carbon atoms, by evaporating the oil and allowing it to condense at a number of different temperatures. This process is fractional distillation. *[C1.4.2 b)]*
- Some properties of hydrocarbons depend on the size of their molecules. These properties influence how hydrocarbons are used as fuels. *[C1.4.2 c)]*

Lesson structure

Starters

Distil the order – Students could try to put these key words about distillation in order: condense, mixture, separate, boil, heat. [Mixture, heat, boil, condense, separate.] *(5 minutes)*

Fuel list – Ask students to consider what they have used today that relies on a fuel. Ask various students to give their thoughts to the class. For example, transport (petrol, diesel and more recently autogas), heating (gas, oil), cooking (gas, charcoal for barbecues) or lighting (gas, oil). Students could be supported by showing them photographs to act as a stimulus. Extend students by asking them to explain how electricity is related to fuel use. *(10 minutes)*

Main

- To contrast fractional distillation in a school lab with what happens in industry, students could watch a video on the separation of crude oil such as *Industrial Chemistry for Schools and Colleges* (RSC).
- Then the students could be given a drawing of a fractionating column, to which they would add their own notes. To support students, this activity could be adapted into a cut-and-stick exercise, which gives the key points as words and diagrams on a piece of paper and the students assemble a poster.
- Often students do not know what a fraction of crude oil looks like. Ampoules of the different crude oil fractions could be shown to the students (available from BP: www.bpes.com).
- Give the students some string beads. Then ask them to cut or break links to give different lengths to represent the different fractions (each bead represents a carbon atom). Put these onto a demonstration table – one pile for each fraction.
- Show the students samples of different fractions (e.g. light a Bunsen burner or show a camping gas bottle, sample of octane, paraffin, lubricating oil and wax).
- Ask the students to comment on the colour, viscosity and state at room temperature. Then try to ignite some of each fraction and ask the students to note the flame colour and ease of ignition.
- Ask the students to compare the properties with the length of the molecule. This task could be written up in the form of a results table.
- Link here to Controlled Assessment – relationships between variables.

Plenaries

Improvisation – Ask for volunteers to talk about a key word for 30 seconds without 'erms' or pauses. Ask the student to talk about hydrocarbons, fractions or viscosity – without any preparation! The volunteer is given a word and starts talking while the rest of the class listens. If there are any misconceptions, ask the other students to pick them out. Students could be supported by allowing them a few minutes of preparation time and working in small groups. Students could be extended by being asked to use a prop in their talk. *(5 minutes)*

Questions and answers – Give each student either a question or an answer on index cards. Ask the students to find their partners. *(10 minutes)*

Practical support

Comparing fractions (demonstration)

Equipment and materials required

Three samples of different alkanes (flammable) to represent different fractions (choose fractions with very different hydrocarbon chain lengths such as hexane, paraffin and candle wax), eye protection, four watch glasses, evaporting dish, mineral wool, dropping pipette, heatproof mat, matches, molecular model kits.

Details

Pour each alkane onto a separate watch glass, starting with the smallest carbon chain. Ask students to comment on the viscosity,

then the colour. Students should conclude that the longer the hydrocarbon chain, the more viscous the liquid and the darker it is. Then, try lighting a small amount of the alkane soaked into mineral wool, in an evaporating dish. Ask students to comment on the ease of lighting and the colour of the flame. Students should conclude that the flame is 'dirtier' and the hydrocarbons are more difficult to light as the hydrocarbon's length increases. You might wish to have molecular models of each of the fractions to aid students in making the link between hydrocarbon chain length and properties.

Safety: Ensure the stock bottles of alkanes are closed before lighting matches. CLEAPSS Hazcard 45B Paraffin – harmful.

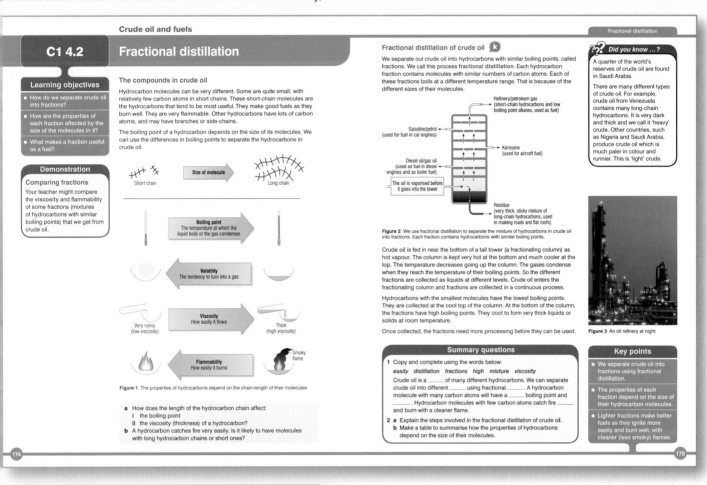

Further teaching suggestions

Red diesel

- Ask students to discover the difference between red diesel and 'normal' diesel. [Brown diesel is used in cars, but red diesel is used in working vehicles, e.g. tractors. The fuel is the same but a dye is added, as red diesel is tax-free.]

Fraction names

- Ask students to find out all the different names used for each fraction, e.g. residue may also be called bitumen.

Alternate fuels

- Students could research alternatives to fossil fuels, e.g. nuclear power, hydrogen fuel cells, renewable resources.

Viscosity demonstration

- Show, by pouring them, that crude oils from different oil fields have different viscosities. Ask the students to suggest why this is so. [Different crude oils have different proportions of each type of hydrocarbon.]

Homologous series

- Students could find out the names and work out the formulae for the first 10 alkanes. Other homologous series could be considered and compared to alkanes, e.g. alkenes.

Answers to in-text questions

a **i** and **ii** Increasing hydrocarbon chain length *increases* both boiling point and viscosity of a hydrocarbon.

b short hydrocarbon chains

Summary answers

1 mixture, fractions, distillation, high, viscosity, easily

2 a Hot vapour enters the fractionating column which is hottest at the bottom. Vapours rise, condensing at different levels as they reach their boiling point temperature.

b Table to summarise properties in Figure 1 in C1 4.2 in Student Book.

175

C1 4.3

Burning fuels

Learning objectives

Students should learn:

- the combustion products formed from the complete combustion of fuels
- the pollutants produced when we burn fuels.

Learning outcomes

Most students should be able to:

- write word equations for the complete combustion of hydrocarbons
- describe differences between incomplete and complete combustion
- list pollutants formed when we burn fuels.

Some students should also be able to:

- complete balanced symbol equations for the complete combustion of simple alkanes
- explain how nitrogen oxides, sulfur dioxide and particulates are produced during the combustion process.

Support

- Balancing symbol equations is not appropriate for some students. Instead, create an activity whereby they need to complete word equations. In the first section, they must always write the word 'oxygen', in the second section of the activity, they must always write the words 'water' and 'carbon dioxide'.

Extend

- You could extend students by asking them to write balanced symbol equations for the incomplete combustion of simple alkanes. For example, they could give one equation for the formation of carbon monoxide and water, and another for carbon plus water.
- You could further extend students by asking them to find out why carbon monoxide is described as toxic. [Carbon monoxide gas binds to the haemoglobin in blood better than oxygen. When incomplete combustion happens, the carbon monoxide is inhaled and slowly reduces the oxygen-carrying ability of the blood, leading to tiredness and ultimately death.]

Specification link-up: Chemistry C1.4

- Most fuels, including coal, contain carbon and/or hydrogen and may also contain some sulfur. The gases released into the atmosphere when a fuel burns may include carbon dioxide, water (vapour), carbon monoxide, sulfur dioxide and oxides of nitrogen. Solid particles (particulates) may also be released. [C1.4.3 a)]
- The combustion of hydrocarbon fuels releases energy. During combustion the carbon and hydrogen in the fuels are oxidised. [C1.4.3 b)]
- Evaluate the impact on the environment of burning hydrocarbon fuels. [C1.4]

Lesson structure

Starter

Triangle – Ask students to recall and draw the combustion (fire) triangle, as studied in Key Stage 3. Students could be supported by being given an outline of the combustion triangle to fill in each side. Students could be extended by being asked to explain how a fire blanket, a CO_2 fire extinguisher and a water fire extinguisher work. (5 minutes)

Main

- Have the demonstration of the combustion products of hydrocarbons (methane) practical already set up. Ask the students to predict the products.
- Students probably have not considered the combustion process that takes place within Bunsen burners in any detail. Encourage the students to experiment with the Bunsen flame to observe the differences between complete and incomplete combustion. See 'Practical support' for more details.
- When hydrocarbons are combusted, they produce chemicals that are pollutants. Split the class into six groups. Give each group one product of combustion to become 'experts' in from the following list: carbon dioxide, water, carbon monoxide, particulates, sulfur dioxide and oxide of nitrogen.
- Students should find out how the products are formed, how they could have a negative impact on the environment and/or human health and how their production can be limited or stopped from entering the atmosphere. Students should use secondary sources such as the internet, newspaper articles and the Student Book to help them.
- Once students have become the 'experts', give each student a summary table. Re-order the students so each team has one expert for each product of combustion. Students should work in their new teams to complete their own summary table.

Plenaries

Equations – Ask students to complete the following equations:

Wax + oxygen → [carbon dioxide] + water

Petrol + [oxygen] → carbon dioxide + [water] + carbon + [carbon monoxide]

You could support students by giving them the missing words that they use to complete the equations. Extend students by asking them to complete balanced equations:

$CH_4 + 2O_2 \rightarrow [CO_2] + [2H_2O]$

$[6]CH_4 + [8]O_2 \rightarrow CO_2 + [12]H_2O + [2]CO + [3]C$ (5 minutes)

Summarise – Split the class into groups and give each team a different topic: combustion; nitrogen oxides; sulfur dioxide; particulates. They could develop a sentence that summarises what they have learned about their topic in the lesson. (10 minutes)

Answers to in-text questions

a carbon dioxide and water (vapour)

b methane + oxygen → carbon dioxide + water

c sulfur

d acid rain

Practical support

Products of combustion

Equipment and materials required

A candle, a small Bunsen burner and safety equipment, eye protection, a glass funnel, a boiling tube, a U-tube, limewater (irritant), ice bath, selection of delivery tubes, a water pump, two bungs with holes in (for the delivery tubes), one bung with two holes in, rubber tubing, matches, three stands, bosses and clamps, beaker, ice.

Details

Place the Bunsen burner or candle onto the heatproof mat, invert the glass funnel and clamp into position about 2 cm above the top of the candle. Using a small piece of rubber tubing, connect an 'n'-shaped delivery tube to the filter funnel. Put the other end through a bung. Mount a U-tube in a large beaker of ice and put in a few pieces of cobalt chloride paper, in one end and fit the bung connected to the funnel. Put a bung and delivery tube in the other end of the U-tube and connect it to a boiling tube of limewater (irritant). The boiling tube bung should have two delivery tubes through it. The final tube should be connected to the water pump. Turn on the water tap for the pump, and light the Bunsen burner. Water should condense and

coiled in the bottom of the U-tube and the limewater should turn cloudy, indicating carbon dioxide is produced.

Safety: Eye protection should be worn. Wash hands after handling cobalt chloride paper. CLEAPSS Hazcard 18 Limewater – irritant.

Investigating combustion

Equipment and materials required

Bunsen burner and safety equipment, boiling tube, boiling tube holder, boiling tube rack, water, stop watch, 10 cm³ measuring cylinder, eye protection.

Details

Add 10 cm³ of tap water to a boiling tube. Hold the boiling tube just above the gas cone and time how long it takes the water to boil. Once boiling, remove the boiling tube from the flame, return the flame to the safety flame and allow the boiling tube to cool in the rack. Visually inspect the outside of the boiling tube and notice how clean it looks. Repeat the experiment with the yellow flame. This time it should take longer for the water to boil and the boiling tube will be covered in a black sooty deposit.

Safety: Eye protection should be worn. Glassware will become hot in the flames. Allow boiling tubes to cool in the rack.

C1 4.3

Burning fuels ⓚ

Learning objectives

- What are the products of combustion when we burn fuels in a good supply of air?
- What pollutants are produced when we burn fuels?

∞ links

For information on useful fractions from crude oil, look back at C1 4.2 Fractional distillation.

Figure 1 On a cold day we can often see the water produced when fossil fuels burn

The lighter fractions from crude oil are very useful as fuels. When hydrocarbons burn in plenty of air they release energy. The reaction produces two new substances – carbon dioxide and water.

For example, when propane burns we can write:

propane + oxygen → carbon dioxide + water

or

$$C_3H_8 + 5O_2 \rightarrow 3CO_2 + 4H_2O$$

The carbon and hydrogen in the fuel are oxidised completely when they burn like this. 'Oxidised' means adding oxygen in a chemical reaction in which oxides are formed.

Practical

Products of combustion

We can test the products given off when a hydrocarbon burns as shown in Figure 2.

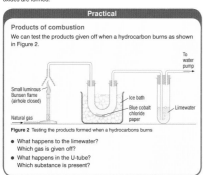

Figure 2 Testing the products formed when a hydrocarbons burns

- What happens to the limewater? Which gas is given off?
- What happens in the U-tube? Which substance is present?

a What are the names of the two substances produced when hydrocarbons burn in plenty of air?

b Methane is the main gas in natural gas. Write a word equation for methane burning in plenty of air.

Pollution from fuels

All fossil fuels – oil, coal and natural gas – produce carbon dioxide and water when they burn in plenty of air. But as well as hydrocarbons, these fuels also contain other substances. Impurities containing sulfur found in fuels cause us major problems.

All fossil fuels contain at least some sulfur. This reacts with oxygen when we burn the fuel. It forms a gas called sulfur dioxide. This gas is poisonous. It is also acidic. This is bad for the environment, as it is a cause of acid rain. Sulfur dioxide can also cause engine corrosion.

c When fuels burn, what element present in the impurities in a fossil fuel may produce sulfur dioxide?

d Which pollution problem does sulfur dioxide gas contribute to?

When we burn fuels in a car engine, even more pollution can be produced.

- When there is not enough oxygen inside an engine, we get **incomplete combustion**. Instead of all the carbon in the fuel turning into carbon dioxide, we also get carbon monoxide gas (CO) formed.

  Carbon monoxide is a poisonous gas. Your red blood cells pick up this gas and carry it around in your blood instead of oxygen. So even quite small amounts of carbon monoxide gas are very bad for you.

- The high temperature inside an engine also allows the nitrogen and oxygen in the air to react together. This reaction makes nitrogen oxides. These are poisonous and can trigger some people's asthma. They also cause acid rain.

- Diesel engines burn hydrocarbons with much bigger molecules than petrol engines. When these big molecules react with oxygen in an engine they do not always burn completely. Tiny solid particles containing carbon and unburnt hydrocarbons are produced. These particulates get carried into the air. Scientists think that they may damage the cells in our lungs and even cause cancer.

Figure 3 A combination of many cars in a small area and the right weather conditions can cause smog to be formed. This is a mixture of SMoke and fOG.

Key points

- When we burn hydrocarbon fuels in plenty of air the carbon and hydrogen in the fuel are completely oxidised. They produce carbon dioxide and water.
- Sulfur impurities in fuels burn to form sulfur dioxide which can cause acid rain.
- Changing the conditions in which we burn hydrocarbon fuels can change the products made.
- In insufficient oxygen, we get poisonous carbon monoxide gas formed. We can also get particulates of carbon (soot) and unburnt hydrocarbons, especially if the fuel is diesel.
- At the high temperatures in engines, nitrogen from the air reacts with oxygen to form nitrogen oxides. These cause breathing problems and can cause acid rain.

Summary questions

1 Copy and complete using the words below:

monoxide carbon nitrogen oxidised particulates sulfur water

When hydrocarbons burn in a good supply of air, ... dioxide and .... are made, as the carbon and hydrogen in the fuel are .... As well as these compounds other substances such as .... dioxide may be made which causes acid rain. Other pollutants that may be formed include .... oxides, carbon .... and ....

2 Explain how **a** sulfur dioxide **b** nitrogen oxides and **c** particulates are produced when fuels burn in vehicles.

3 **a** Natural gas is mainly methane (CH₄). Write a balanced symbol equation for the complete combustion of methane. [H]

b When natural gas burns in a faulty gas heater it can produce carbon monoxide (and water). Write a balanced symbol equation to show this reaction. [H]

Further teaching suggestions

Further research

- Using secondary sources, ask students to find out what fuel and car manufacturing companies are doing to reduce emissions of sulfur dioxide, nitrogen oxides and particulates. Using secondary sources, ask the students to find out why carbon monoxide detectors are important and how they work.

Summary answers

1 carbon, water, oxidised, sulfur, nitrogen, monoxide, particulates

2 **a** When sulfur from impurities in fuel burns it reacts with oxygen to form sulfur dioxide.

b At the high temperatures in the engine, nitrogen gas from the air reacts with oxygen to form nitrogen oxides.

c Incomplete combustion of the fuel can produce small particles of carbon and unburnt hydrocarbons.

3 **a** $CH_4 + 2O_2 \rightarrow CO_2 + 2H_2O$

b $2CH_4 + 3O_2 \rightarrow 2CO + 4H_2O$

C1 4.4

Cleaner fuels

Learning objectives

Students should learn:

- that burning fuels has an environmental impact
- how we can reduce the pollution from burning fuels.

Learning outcomes

Most students should be able to:

- state what causes global warming, global dimming and acid rain
- list some ways of reducing pollutants released when we burn fuels
- explain how acid rain is produced, and how it can be reduced.

Some students should also be able to:

- discuss the relationship between global dimming and global warming
- explain in detail methods of reducing pollutants from fuels.

Answers to in-text questions

a We are burning much more fossil fuel than 100 years ago.

b Four from: particulates, unburnt hydrocarbons, sulfur dioxide, nitrogen oxides, carbon monoxide, carbon dioxide.

Support

- To support students with 'the pyramid' activity, some information could already be printed on the internet, e.g. the start of a diagram, a prose with missing words or just a title. Encourage students to use lots of colour as this aids their learning. They might even want to include a key – e.g. each time they mention the word acid, or an example of an acid, they might write it in red.

Extend

- Often the concepts of global warming, climate change and the greenhouse effect are confused by students. Extend students by asking them to define each of these terms in no more than 50 words each. Then ask students to explain how these terms are related, again in no more than 50 words.

Specification link-up: Chemistry C1.4

- Sulfur dioxide and oxides of nitrogen cause acid rain, carbon dioxide causes global warming, and solid particles cause global dimming. *[C1.4.3 c)]*
- Sulfur can be removed from fuels before they are burned, for example in vehicles. Sulfur dioxide can be removed from the waste gases after combustion, for example in power stations. *[C1.4.3 d)]*
- Evaluate the impact on the environment of burning hydrocarbon fuels. *[C1.4]*
- Consider and evaluate the social, economic and environmental impacts of the uses of fuels. *[C1.4]*

Lesson structure

Starters

Photographs – Show the students an image of a drought area, polar ice caps and flooding. Topical pictures can be found on the web. Ask the students to link the pictures. [Scientists believe these are all effects of global warming.] Then show the students a forest damaged by acid rain, a weathered statue and a weathered building. Again ask the students to link the images. [They are the effects of acid rain.] *(5 minutes)*

Demonstration – Ignite sulfur in oxygen to demonstrate the production of sulfur dioxide in a fume cupboard, wearing eye protection.

Ask the students to write a word equation for the reaction between sulfur and oxygen. Support students by asking them to complete the partly written word equation. Extend students by asking for a balanced symbol equation for the reaction [sulfur + oxygen → sulfur dioxide]. Then ask them how this relates to burning fuels. [Sulfur is found in impurities in fossil fuels; this reaction can occur as the fuel is burned, which leads to the production of acid rain.] *(10 minutes)*

Main

- You may wish to investigate how the concentration of sodium metabisulfite affects the growth of cress seeds. See 'Practical support' for more details. This is a model of the effect of acid rain on plants. You could extend students by encouraging them to design their own experiment.

- During KS3, a number of environmental issues have been considered; but global dimming and its interdependence with global warming have not been studied.

- Split the class into three different groups and assign each a different environmental issue: acid rain, global warming or global dimming. The groups could be given access to different research materials, e.g. the internet and library books. Each member of the group should become an expert on its environmental issue. Then make teams of three. Each team should have one specialist on each issue. Each new group should then answer the questions set out in the objectives.

- Students already have a large body of background knowledge about environmental issues gained from KS3 science, geography and citizenship. Give each student a square-based pyramid net. Each triangular face should contain information about a different environmental issue (as detailed above), using the 'cleaning up our act' section in the Student Book to ensure that the science content is correct. The base should contain information about what can be done to reduce these problems. Once the information has been drawn and written, the students could cut it out and assemble the pyramid.

Plenaries

Crossword – Give the students a crossword to complete in pairs. These can be tailor-made if a puzzle generator is used, e.g. www.discoveryschool.com. *(5 minutes)*

AfL (Assessment for Learning) – Give students an examination question with fictitious answers: a weak, an average and an excellent answer. Students could order them to show which they think is the worst or best answer and why they think this. Then feed back the group's ideas to the class through a question-and-answer session. To support students, use a question from a foundation paper and to extend students use a question from a higher paper. *(10 minutes)*

Practical support

Modelling acid rain

Equipment and materials required

Gas jar of oxygen, sulfur flowers, spatula, deflagrating spoon, Bunsen burner, dropping pipette, water, universal indicator solution, eye protection (chemical splashproof).

Details

Put half a spatula of sulfur in a deflagrating spoon. Heat it in a blue Bunsen flame until it begins to combust (a blue flame is visible). Put it into a gas jar of oxygen. When the reaction is complete, add a little water and universal indicator solution to show the acidic nature of sulfur dioxide.

Safety: Complete in a fume hood, as sulfur dioxide is harmful, wear eye protection and wash hands after use. CLEAPSS Hazcard 69 Oxygen – oxidising; 96A Sulfur; 97 Sulfur dioxide – toxic; 32 Universal indicators – highly flammable and harmful.

Modelling the effect of acid rain

Equipment and materials required

Cotton wool, two Petri dishes, cress seeds, 0.05 mol/dm³ and 0.1 mol/dm³ sodium metabisulfite solutions (prepared and kept in a fume cupboard), distilled water, sticky labels, sunny window sill.

Details

Open the Petri dishes, and put cotton wool in the tops or bottoms to make three open dishes for germinating the seeds. Sprinkle the same number of cress seeds on each piece of cotton wool. Then add water to one Petri dish and different concentrations of sodium metabisulfite to the others. Label your dishes and leave in a sunny position. Ensure that the seeds remain moist using the appropriate water or sodium metabisulfite solution. Monitor the growth rate over a week.

Safety: Complete in a well ventilated room, wear eye protection and wash hands after use. CLEAPSS Hazcard 92 Sodium metabisulfite. Warn asthmatics not to breathe in sulfur dioxide fumes.

Crude oil and fuels

C1 4.4 Cleaner fuels

Learning objectives

- When we burn fuels, what are the consequences for our environment?
- What can we do to reduce the problems?

When we burn fuels, as well as producing carbon dioxide and water, we produce other substances. Many of these harm the environment, and can affect our health.

Pollution from our cars does not stay in one place but spreads through the atmosphere. For a long time the Earth's atmosphere seemed to cope with all this pollution. But the huge increase in our use of fossil fuels in the past 100 years means that pollution is a real concern now.

a Why is there more pollution in the air from fossil fuels now compared with 100 years ago?

What kinds of pollution?

When we burn any fuel containing carbon, it makes carbon dioxide. Carbon dioxide is the main greenhouse gas in the air. It absorbs energy released as radiation from the surface of the Earth. Most scientists think that this is causing **global warming**, which affects temperatures around the world. Look at the increase in our production of carbon dioxide and average global temperature data over recent times:

Figure 1 Cumulative carbon dioxide emissions from burning fossil fuels and the manufacture of cement

Figure 2 Differences from average global temperatures over time. People are worried about changing climates, and melting ice caps that could raise sea levels.

Burning fuels in engines also produces other substances. One group of pollutants is called the particulates. These are tiny solid particles made up of carbon (soot) and unburnt hydrocarbons. Scientists think that these may be especially bad for young children. Particulates may also be bad for the environment too. They travel into the upper atmosphere, reflecting sunlight back into space, causing **global dimming**.

Carbon monoxide is formed when there is not enough oxygen for complete combustion of a fuel. Then the carbon in it is partially oxidised to form carbon monoxide. Carbon monoxide is a serious pollutant because it affects the amount of oxygen that our blood is able to carry. This is particularly serious for people who have problems with their hearts.

Sulfur dioxide and nitrogen oxides from burning fuels damage us and our environment. In Britain, scientists think that the number of people who suffer from asthma has increased because of air pollution. Sulfur dioxide and nitrogen oxides also form acid rain. These gases dissolve in water droplets in the atmosphere and react with oxygen, forming sulfuric and nitric acids. The rain with a low pH can damage plant and animals.

b Name four harmful substances that may be produced when fuels burn.

Cleaning up our act

We can reduce the effects of burning fuels in several ways. For example, we can remove harmful substances from the gases that are produced when we burn fuels. For some time the exhaust systems of cars have been fitted with **catalytic converters**. A catalytic converter greatly reduces the carbon monoxide and nitrogen oxides produced by a car engine. They are expensive, as they contain precious metal catalysts, but once warmed up they are very effective.

The metal catalysts are arranged so that they have a very large surface area. This causes the carbon monoxide and nitrogen oxides in the exhaust gases to react together. They produce carbon dioxide and nitrogen:

carbon monoxide + nitrogen oxides → carbon dioxide + nitrogen

So although catalytic converters reduce the toxic gases given out, they do not help reduce levels of carbon dioxide in the air.

Filters can also remove most particulates from modern diesel engines. The filters need to burn off the trapped solid particles otherwise they get blocked.

In power stations, sulfur dioxide is removed from the waste or 'flue' gases by reacting it with calcium oxide or calcium hydroxide. This is called flue gas desulfurisation. The sulfur impurities can also be removed from a fuel *before* the fuel is burned. This happens in petrol and diesel for cars, as well as in the natural gas and oil used in power stations.

Catalytic converter

Diesel engines can now be fitted with filters to remove solid particulates

Figure 3 Modern cars are fitted with catalytic converters. Filters can also remove most of the particulates from diesel engine exhaust gases.

links

For more information on how we can also use alternative fuels to reduce pollution, see C1 4.5 Alternative fuels.

Key points

- Burning fuels releases substances that spread throughout the atmosphere.
- Sulfur dioxide and nitrogen oxides dissolve in droplets of water in the air and react with oxygen, and then fall as acid rain.
- Carbon dioxide produced from burning fuels is a greenhouse gas. It absorbs energy which is lost from the surface of the Earth by radiation.
- The pollution produced by burning fuels may be reduced by treating the pollutants from combustion. This can remove substances like nitrogen oxides, sulfur dioxide and carbon monoxide.
- Sulfur can also be removed from fuels before we burn them to prevent sulfur dioxide gas being formed.

Summary questions

1 a Why is carbon dioxide called a greenhouse gas?
  b How do you think particulates in the atmosphere might affect the Earth's temperature?
  c Which gases are mainly responsible for acid rain?

2 a Which pollutants from a car does a catalytic converter remove?
  b Why will catalytic converters not help to solve the problem of greenhouse gases in the atmosphere?

3 a Explain how acid rain is formed and how we are reducing the problem.
  b Compare the effects of global warming and global dimming.
  c Particulates in the atmosphere could eventually settle on the polar ice caps. What problem might this make worse?

Summary answers

1 a It absorbs energy from the Earth as it cools down, preventing it escaping to space.
  b They might lower the temperature as they reflect sunlight back into space, so it doesn't get a chance to warm the Earth's surface.
  c Sulfur dioxide and nitrogen oxides.

2 a Carbon monoxide and nitrogen oxides (also unburnt hydrocarbons).
  b Catalytic converters do not remove carbon dioxide from exhaust gases.

3 a Sulfur dioxide and nitrogen oxides react with oxygen and water to form sulfuric and nitric acids, which fall to ground in rain, snow, hail or mist. Reduce by removing sulfur from fuels/removing SO_2 from gases released/removing nitrogen oxides by catalytic converters.
  b Global warming is the increase in average temperature of the Earth (due to an increase in greenhouse gases) whereas global dimming will reduce temperatures (as particulates reduce the energy reaching the Earth's surface from the Sun).
  c As they are darker in colour than the snow, they might absorb more energy from the Sun than the white snow, increasing the risk of polar ice caps melting.

C1 4.5

Alternative fuels

AQA Specification link-up: Chemistry C1.4

- Biofuels, including biodiesel and ethanol, are produced from plant material. There are economic, ethical and environmental issues surrounding their use. [C1.4.3 e)]
- Consider and evaluate the social, economic and environmental impacts of the uses of fuels. [C1.4]
- Evaluate developments in the production and uses of better fuels, for example ethanol and hydrogen. [C1.4]
- Evaluate the benefits, drawbacks and risks of using plant materials to produce fuels. [C1.4]

Learning objectives

Students should learn:

- the definition of a biofuel and some examples
- some of the advantages and disadvantages of biofuels
- that many scientists are interested in developing hydrogen as a fuel.

Learning outcomes

Most students should be able to:

- state a definition of a biofuel
- give an example of a biofuel
- recognise advantages and disadvantages of using biofuels
- explain why scientists are interested in developing hydrogen as a fuel.

Some students should also be able to:

- give a detailed, balanced argument for the use of biofuels, ethanol and hydrogen as fuels.

Support

- Students could be supported by being given the advantages and disadvantages of using biodiesel as simple sentences. These students could then cut and stick the sentences to order them into a table.

Extend

- Students could be extended by asking them to write word equations or even balanced symbol equations for the complete combustion of the different biofuels, e.g. ethanol, biogas (methane).
- Students could be encouraged to find out other forms of biofuel in common use, e.g. biogas from sewage. They could find out where these biofuels are being used and their advantages and disadvantages. Students could compile their findings into a summary table contrasting biodiesel, bioethanol, wood, biomass and biogas.

Lesson structure

Starters

What do you think? – Ask students to find a definition of biofuels and then to consider if they agree with the following statements: 'Biofuel should be the only fuel for cars.' 'Biofuel should be mixed with fuels from crude oil for cars.' 'Biofuels should not be used in cars.' For each statement ask them to express the extent to which they agree as a percentage. *(5 minutes)*

Demonstration – Ignite a small hydrogen balloon to demonstrate a combustion reaction using hydrogen.

Ask the students to write a word equation, support students by asking questions during the demonstration and encourage students to detail the reactants and products. Students could be extended by asking for a balanced symbol equation for the reaction [hydrogen + oxygen → water/$2H_2 + O_2 \rightarrow 2H_2O$]. Ask students to use this observation to explain how hydrogen can be used as a fuel. *(10 minutes)*

Main

- Ask students to use the Student Book to make a table to list the advantages and disadvantages of biodiesel. Students could then supplement this information using secondary sources of information such as the internet to add more information. Each statement should be a summarised bullet point. This will help students construct a balanced argument for the use of biofuels.

- The class could then be split into groups of three. Each member of the group should be given a different task, as detailed in the biodiesel-fuel from plants activity box in the Student Book. Once the students have completed their task, each group should review each team member's work and discuss which biofuel they think is most likely to be used in 20 years' time. Encourage each group to feedback to the class their choice and the reasons why.

- Students could be asked to make 'top-trump' cards for different ways of powering a car. Students should consider biodiesel, bioethanol, hydrogen, petrol/diesel and autogas (methane), listing the advantages and disadvantages of each. They could then give a score out of 100 to give an arbitrary figure for their overall rating. Students could then consider their cards and make a list from best to worst fuel and construct an argument for why they think this.

Plenaries

Biofuel – Explain to students that B100 is 100 per cent biodiesel and B0 would be 100 per cent diesel (made from crude oil). Explain to students that diesel in petrol stations now, by law, must contain a percentage of biodiesel. Ask students to suggest the composition of B6 [6 per cent biodiesel, 94 per cent diesel] and B10 [10 per cent biodiesel, 90 per cent diesel]. You could support students by giving them the diesel content and so students just need to find the biodiesel content. Students could be extended by being asked to suggest why biodiesel mix is being used rather than pure biodiesel. *(5 minutes)*

Reflect: what do you think? – Ask students to consider the same three statements that they examined at the start of the lesson: biofuel should be the only fuel for cars; biofuel should be mixed with fuels from crude oil for cars; biofuels should not be used in cars. Again for each statement ask them to give a percentage of agreement. Then ask students to consider if their views have changed, and why or why not. Ask for a few volunteers to share their thoughts. *(10 minutes)*

Practical support

Demonstrate combustion of hydrogen

Equipment and materials required

Rubber party balloon filled with hydrogen gas, a splint secured on the end of a 1 m ruler with a rubber band, Bunsen burner, eye protection.

Details

Rest the hydrogen balloon on the ceiling away from anything that could combust or be damaged (such as lights or projectors). Put on eye protection and move students a suitable distance away. Light the splint and put it on the stretched part of the rubber balloon.

Safety: Wear eye protection and make sure students are a suitable distance. Do not use a large balloon and be aware that ceiling tiles can be damaged.

Crude oil and fuels

C1 4.5   Alternative fuels

Learning objectives

● What are biofuels?

● What are the advantages and disadvantages of using biodiesel?

● Why are scientists interested in developing hydrogen as a fuel?

Figure 1 This coach runs on biodiesel

Activity

Biodiesel – fuel from plants

In a group of three, each choose a different task:

A Write an article for a local newspaper describing the arguments for using biodiesel instead of other fuels made from crude oil.

B Write a letter to the newspaper pointing out why the article in **A** should not claim that biodiesel makes no overall contribution to global warming.

C Write an article for the newspaper focussing on the drawbacks of using biodiesel.

● Read each other's work and decide whether biodiesel will be a major fuel in 20 years time.

Biofuels

Biofuels are fuels that are made from plant or animal products. For example, biodiesel is made from oils extracted from plants. You can even use old cooking oil as a biofuel. Biogas is generated from animal waste. Biofuels will become more and more important as our supplies of crude oil run out.

a What is biodiesel?

Advantages of biodiesel

There are advantages in using biodiesel as a fuel.

● Biodiesel is much less harmful to animals and plants than diesel we get from crude oil. If it is spilled, it breaks down about five times faster than 'normal' diesel.

● When we burn biodiesel in an engine it burns much more cleanly, reducing the particulates emitted. It also makes very little sulfur dioxide.

● As crude oil supplies run out, its price will increase and biodiesel will become cheaper to use than petrol and diesel.

● Another really big advantage over petrol and diesel is the fact that the crops used to make biodiesel absorb carbon dioxide gas as they grow. So biodiesel is in theory 'CO$_2$ neutral'. That means the amount of carbon dioxide given off when it burns is balanced by the amount absorbed as the plants it is made from grow. Therefore, biodiesel makes little contribution to the greenhouse gases in our atmosphere.

However, we can't claim that biodiesel makes a zero contribution to carbon dioxide emissions. We should really take into account the CO$_2$ released when:
– fertilising and harvesting the crops
– extracting and processing the oil
– transporting the plant material and biodiesel made.

● When we make biodiesel we also produce other useful products. For example, we get a solid waste material that we can feed to cattle as a high-energy food. We also get glycerine which we can use to make soap.

Disadvantages of biodiesel

There are however disadvantages in using biodiesel and other biofuels as a fuel.

● The use of large areas of farmland to produce fuel instead of food could pose problems. If we start to rely on oil-producing crops for our fuel, land once used for food crops will turn to growing biofuel crops.

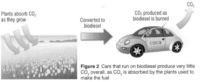

Plants absorb CO$_2$ as they grow → Converted to biodiesel → CO$_2$ produced as biodiesel is burned

Figure 2 Cars that run on biodiesel produce very little CO$_2$ overall, as CO$_2$ is absorbed by the plants used to make the fuel

This could result in famine in poorer countries if the price of staple food crops rises as demand overtakes supply. Forests, which absorb lots of carbon dioxide, might also be cleared to grow the biofuel crops if they get more popular.

● People are also worried about the destruction of habitats of endangered species. For example, orang-utans are under threat of extinction. Large areas of tropical forest where they live are being turned into palm plantations for palm oil used to make biodiesel.

● At low temperatures biodiesel will start to freeze before traditional diesel. It turns into a sludge. At high temperatures in an engine it can turn sticky as its molecules join together and can 'gum up' engines.

Using ethanol as a biofuel

Another biofuel is ethanol. We can make it by fermenting the sugar from sugar beet or sugar cane. In Brazil they can grow lots of sugar cane. They add the ethanol made to petrol, saving money as well as our dwindling supplies of crude oil. As with biodiesel, the ethanol gives off carbon dioxide (a greenhouse gas) when it burns, but the sugar cane absorbs CO$_2$ gas during photosynthesis.

b Why is burning ethanol a better choice of fuel than petrol if we want to reduce carbon dioxide emissions?

⚙ How Science Works

Hydrogen – a fuel for the future

Scientists are very interested in developing hydrogen as a fuel. It burns well with a very clean flame as there is no carbon in the fuel

$$\text{hydrogen} + \text{oxygen} \rightarrow \text{water}$$
$$2H_2 + O_2 \rightarrow 2H_2O$$

As you can see in the equation, water is the only product in the combustion of hydrogen. There are no pollutants made when hydrogen burns and no extra carbon dioxide is added to the air. Not only that, water is potentially a huge natural source of hydrogen. The hydrogen can be obtained from water by electrolysis. But the electricity must be supplied by a renewable energy source if we want to conserve fossil fuels and control carbon dioxide emissions.

However, there are problems to solve before hydrogen becomes a common fuel. When mixed with air and ignited it is explosive. So there are safety concerns in case of leaks, or accidents in vehicles powered by hydrogen. Vehicles normally run on liquid fuels but hydrogen is a gas. Therefore it takes up a much larger volume than liquid fuels. So storage is an issue. We can use high-pressure cylinders but these also have safety problems in crashes.

Summary questions

1 Copy and complete these sentences using the words below:
   carbon dioxide   diesel   plants
   Biodiesel is a fuel made from .... It produces less pollution than .... obtained from crude oil, and absorbs nearly as much .... when the plants that make it grow as it does when it burns.

2 Where does the energy in biodiesel come from?

3 **a** Explain why hydrogen is potentially a pollution-free fuel.
   b Why isn't hydrogen used as an everyday fuel at the moment?

Figure 3 Ethanol can be made from sugar cane

🔗 **links**

For more information on ethanol, see C1 5.5 Ethanol.

Key points

● Biofuels are a renewable source of energy that could be used to replace some fossil fuels.

● Biodiesel can be made from vegetable oils.

● There are advantages, and some disadvantages, in using biodiesel.

● Ethanol is also a biofuel as it can be made from the sugar in plants.

● Hydrogen is a potential fuel for the future.

180   181

Further teaching suggestions

Making biofuels

● You may wish to make biofuels with your students – go to www.sep.org.uk and search under 'What's New' and 'Recycling and sustainability' and 'Biofuels'.

Hydrogen as a fuel

● The University of Birmingham had the first hydrogen fuel station fitted in 2008. The station is used to fuel a fleet of cars used on the campus as part of a research project. Students could study this as a case study and consider the advantages and disadvantages of this fuel in this context. For more information go to www.newscentre. bham.ac.uk and search for hydrogen fuel.

Ethanol as a fuel

● Ethanol-to-fuel cars can be made industrially and use three different methods: hydration of ethene, fermentation with yeast, or using *E. coli*. Ask students to contrast each of these methods and suggest which is best for making ethanol for use as a fuel.

Answers to in-text questions

a The name for any fuel made from vegetable oils.

b Because the plants (e.g. sugar cane) used to make ethanol made from sugars absorbed carbon dioxide from the air as it grew, before releasing it again as ethanol burns (and in the fermentation process).

Summary answers

1 plants, diesel, carbon dioxide

2 From the Sun through photosynthesis.

3 **a** Water is its only product of combustion.

   b It is difficult to store for use as a vehicle fuel; it needs a renewable source of energy to get it from water; it is highly flammable and could be explosive if there is an accident. Hydrogen fuel-cell technology is expensive.

Summary answers

1 a i A compound containing hydrogen and carbon only.
   ii No more hydrogen can bond to its molecules.

b i Propane, C_3H_8.
   ii Atoms of carbon and hydrogen.
   iii (Covalent) bonds

c C_nH_{2n+2}

d $C_{20}H_{42}$

2 a B because it has a lower boiling point. The lower the boiling point, the higher up the fractionating column the compounds condense.

b B because its molecules will be smaller and the smaller the hydrocarbon molecule, the easier it is to ignite. It will burn with a cleaner (less sooty) flame.

c A will be more viscous than B.

3 a Carbon dioxide and water

b Global warming/climate change.

c i Sulfur dioxide
   ii Remove the sulfur impurities from the fossil fuel before it is burned.
   Absorb any sulfur dioxide using a basic substance before it escapes into the atmosphere.
   iii Nitrogen oxides
   iv Catalytic converters

d To remove solid particulates of carbon and unburnt hydrocarbons.

4 a Ethanol

b The same amount of carbon dioxide is absorbed by the plants in photosynthesis as is given off when the biofuel burns.

c No carbon dioxide is given off when hydrogen burns.

d Difficult to store/explosive/expensive technology

e hydrogen + oxygen → water
   $2H_2 + O_2 \rightarrow 2H_2O$

5 a

Fuel	Mass burned (g)		Temperature (°C)			
			Before	After	Before	After
	1	2	1	1	2	2
Ethanol						
Propanol						
Butanol						
Pentanol						

b Variables that need to be controlled include:
   distance from burner to beaker
   volume of water in beaker
   starting temperature of the water
   insulation on beaker
   time left to burn
   size of flame
   draughts
   how the temperature was recorded.

c Stir the water before recording the temperature.
   Use a well-calibrated thermometer.

d The repeats are consistent, so this would suggest that they are precise.

e As a bar graph of the mean temperature rise for each fuel.

Summary questions *k*

1 This question is about the alkane family of compounds.

a The alkanes are all 'saturated hydrocarbons'.
   i What is a hydrocarbon?
   ii What does saturated mean when describing an alkane?

b i Give the name and formula of this alkane:

H–C–C–H (displayed formula with H atoms)

   ii What do the letters represent in this displayed formula?
   iii What do the lines between letters represent?

c What is the general formula of the alkanes (where n = the number of carbon atoms)?

d Give the formula of the alkane with 20 carbon atoms.

2 One alkane, A, has a boiling point of 344 °C and another, B, has a boiling point of 126 °C.

a Which one will be collected nearer the top of a fractionating column in an oil refinery? Explain your choice.

b Which one will be the better fuel? Explain your choice.

c Give another difference you expect between A and B.

3 a Name the two products formed when a hydrocarbon burns in enough oxygen to ensure that complete combustion takes place.

b What problem is associated with the increased levels of carbon dioxide gas in the atmosphere?

c i What gas is given off from fossil fuel power stations that can cause acid rain?
   ii Give **two** ways of stopping this gas getting into the atmosphere from power stations.
   iii Name the other cause of acid rain which comes from car engines.
   iv How do car makers stop the gases in part **iii** entering the air?

d Why are diesel engines now fitted with a filter for their exhaust fumes?

4 a Which one of these fuels could be termed a 'biofuel'?
   Hydrogen   Propane   Ethanol   Petrol   Coal

b Biodiesel is potentially 'CO₂ neutral'. What does this mean?

c Scientists are concerned about the issue of global warming. Why is the use of hydrogen as a fuel one way to tackle the problem?

d State **two** problems with the use of hydrogen as [a fuel?]

e Write a word and a balanced symbol equation for the combustion of hydrogen.

5 This apparatus can be used to compare the energy given out when different fuels are burned.

The burner is weighed before and after to determine the amount of fuel burned. The temperature of the water is taken before and after, to get the temperature rise. The investigation was repeated. From this the amount of energy released by burning a known amount of fuel can be calculated.

a Design a table that could be used to collect the data as you carry out this experiment.

A processed table of results is given below.

Fuel	Mass burned (g)	Temperature (°C)
Ethanol	4.9	48
Propanol	5.1	56
Butanol	5.2	68
Pentanol	5.1	75

b List three variables that need to be controlled.

c Describe how you would take the temperature of the water to get the most accurate measurement possible.

d Do these results show precision? Explain your answer.

e How might you present these results?

AQA Practical suggestions

Practicals	AQA	*k*	📖	⚙
Demonstration of fractional distillation of crude oil using CLEAPPS mixture (take care to avoid confusion with the continuous process in a fractionating column).	✓		✓	
Design an investigation on viscosity, ease of ignition or sootiness of flame of oils or fuels.	✓	✓	✓	
Comparison of the energy content of different fuels, for example by heating a fixed volume of water.	✓			✓
Demonstration of the production of solid particles by incomplete combustion using a Bunsen burner yellow flame or a candle flame to heat a boiling tube of cold water.	✓		✓	
Collecting and testing the products of combustion of candle wax and methane.	✓		✓	
Demonstration of burning sulfur or coal in oxygen and then testing the pH of the gas produced.	✓		✓	
Design an investigation on growing cress from seeds in various concentrations of sodium metabisulfite solution to show how acid rain affects plants.	✓		✓	

Examination-style questions 🄚

table shows some information about the first four
...nes.

...me of alkane	Formula	Boiling point in °C
Methane	CH$_4$	−162
	C$_2$H$_6$	−88
Propane	C$_3$H$_8$	
Butane		0

Name the alkane missing from the table. (1)
What is the formula of butane? (1)
Estimate the boiling point of propane. (1)

...hich one of the following is the formula of the alkane
...ith 6 carbon atoms?

$_8$H$_6$ C$_6$H$_{10}$ C$_6$H$_{14}$ C$_6$H$_{16}$ (1)

...xplain why alkanes are hydrocarbons. (1)

...molecule of methane can be represented as:

H
|
...—C—H
|
H

...raw a molecule of propane in the same way. (2)

...e crude oil was distilled in a fractionating column.
...table shows the boiling ranges of three of the
...ions that were collected.

Fraction	Boiling range in °C
A	60–120
B	160–230
C	240–320

...hich of these fractions is the most flammable? (1)
...hich of these fractions is the most viscous? (1)
...hich of these fractions has the smallest hydrocarbon
...olecules? (1)
...hy do the fractions have boiling ranges and not
...oiling points? (1)

3 Some landfill sites produce a gas that can be collected
and burned as a fuel. The gas is mainly methane.
   a Choose the word from the list to complete the
   sentence.
   condensed   distilled   oxidised
   During the combustion of methane the elements in the
   fuel are .... (1)
   b Write a word equation for the complete combustion of
   methane, CH$_4$. (2)
   c Under what conditions could methane burn to
   produce carbon monoxide? (1)
   d A sample of landfill gas was burned. The waste gases
   contained sulfur dioxide. Explain why. (1)

4 Crude oil is a resource from which fuels can be
separated.
   a The name of the main fuel fractions and one of the
   hydrocarbons in each fraction are shown in the table.

Main fuel fraction	A hydrocarbon in this fraction	Boiling point of hydrocarbon in °C
Gases	Propane, C$_3$H$_8$	−42
Petrol	Octane, C$_8$H$_{18}$	126
Paraffin	Dodecane, C$_{12}$H$_{26}$	216
Diesel	Eicosane, C$_{20}$H$_{42}$	344

Heated
crude oil

   i How does the number of carbon atoms in a
   hydrocarbon affect its boiling point? (1)
   ii Suggest the lowest temperature to which
   crude oil needs to be heated to vaporise all the
   hydrocarbons in the table.
   Temperature = ...°C? (1)
   iii Dodecane boils at 216 °C. At what temperature will
   dodecane gas condense to liquid?
   Temperature = ...°C? (1)
   b *In this question you will be assessed on using good
   English, organising information clearly and using
   specialist terms where appropriate.*
   Describe and explain how the fractions are separated
   in a fractionating column. (6)
   AQA, 2009

Kerboodle resources 🄚

Resources available for this chapter on Kerboodle are:
- Chapter map: Crude oil and fuels
- Bump up your grade: All about alkanes (C1 4.1)
- Support: All about alkanes (C1 4.1)
- Extension: All about alkanes (C1 4.1)
- Animation: Fractional distillation (C1 4.2)
- Practical: Investigating the fractions of crude oil (C1 4.2)
- How Science Works: Burning issues (C1 4.3)
- How Science Works: Governments get hot under the collar about global warming (C1 4.3)
- How Science Works: Haven't the foggiest about which is the smoggiest! (C1 4.4)
- Interactive activity: Crude oil and fuels
- Revision podcast: Fuels and the environment
- Test yourself: Crude oil and fuels
- On your marks: Fractional distillation of crude oil
- Examination-style questions: Crude oil and fuels
- Answers to examination-style questions: Crude oil and fuels

AQA Examiner's tip

Some students confuse distillation with cracking, thinking that
when crude oil is distilled, the molecules are broken down.
Some students find it difficult to relate boiling points to the
temperature gradient in the fractionating column, thinking
that low boiling fractions are collected near the bottom of the
column.

AQA Examination-style answers

1 a   **i** ethane   *(1 mark)*
    ii C$_4$H$_{10}$ *(1 mark)*
    iii any value from −50 to −30 (°C)   *(1 mark)*

b C$_6$H$_{14}$ *(1 mark)*

c contain <u>only</u> carbon and hydrogen   *(1 mark)*

d Correct structure showing 3 C joined with single bonds
and 8 C – H bonds.   *(2 marks)*

2 a A   *(1 mark)*

b C   *(1 mark)*

c A   *(1 mark)*

d They are mixtures or not single compounds/alkanes.
   (1 mark)

3 a oxidised   *(1 mark)*

b methane + oxygen → carbon dioxide + water
reactants, products   *(2 marks)*

c limited supply of air   *(1 mark)*

d (land-fill gas) contains sulfur (compounds)   *(1 mark)*

4 a   **i** The greater the number (of carbon atoms) the higher
its boiling point.   *(1 mark)*
    ii accept numbers in the range 344 to 350 (°C)   *(1 mark)*
    iii 216 (°C)   *(1 mark)*

b There is a clear and detailed scientific description of the
processes that take place during fractional distillation in a
fractionating column, including evaporation, condensation
and collection of fractions at different temperatures. The
answer shows almost faultless spelling, punctuation
and grammar. It is coherent and in an organised, logical
sequence. It contains a range of appropriate or relevant
specialist terms used accurately.   *(5–6 marks)*

There is a scientific description that includes condensation
and collection of fractions at different temperatures. There
are some errors in spelling, punctuation and grammar.
The answer has some structure and organisation. The use
of specialist terms has been attempted, but not always
accurately.   *(3–4 marks)*

There is a brief description of evaporation or
condensation and collection of fractions. The spelling,
punctuation and grammar are very weak. The answer is
poorly organised with almost no specialist terms and/or
their use demonstrating a general lack of understanding
of their meaning.   *(1–2 marks)*

No relevant content.   *(0 marks)*

Examples of chemistry points made in the response:
- crude oil is heated (to above 350 °C)
- crude oil is vaporised
- vapours/gases go into (fractionating) column
- column is hot at bottom, cool at top or correct
  temperature gradient indicated
- substances/vapours condense at their boiling points
- different substances/vapours condense at different
  levels in column
- low boiling points at the top of column or high boiling
  points at the bottom
- collected as liquids
- liquids/fractions contain a mixture of substances
- fractions have substances with a range of boiling
  points
- continuous process.

C1 5.1

Cracking hydrocarbonates

Learning objectives

Students should learn:

- reasons for cracking large hydrocarbon molecules and how it is carried out
- that alkenes contain double bonds and are called unsaturated hydrocarbons.

Learning outcomes

Most students should be able to:

- state a definition of cracking
- list the general conditions needed for cracking, stating that it is a thermal decomposition reaction
- explain why cracking is carried out
- state and use the general formula to work out the formula of an alkene when n is given
- recognise an alkene from a structural or molecular formula
- state and carry out the test for alkenes.

Some students should also be able to:

- balance a symbol equation to represent cracking. [HT only]

Support

- The 'cracking' practical may be too difficult for students with poor manual dexterity. It could be completed as a demonstration instead. Alternatively, if a teaching assistant is available, split the class into two groups. The teaching assistant can then help small groups of students to test for alkenes while you demonstrate cracking to a small group of students.

Extend

- Students could be extended by asking them to draw a table with the name, molecular and structural formula of the first 10 alkenes. You may also wish to show students that from butane onwards, the double bond can be in different positions. You may wish to introduce the term 'isomer'.

 Specification link-up: Chemistry C1.5

- Hydrocarbons can be cracked to produce smaller, more useful molecules. This process involves heating the hydrocarbons to vaporise them. The vapours are either passed over a hot catalyst or mixed with steam and heated to a very high temperature so that thermal decomposition reactions then occur. [C1.5.1 a)]
- The products of cracking include alkanes and unsaturated hydrocarbons called alkenes. Alkenes have the general formula C_nH_{2n}. [C1.5.1 b)]
- Unsaturated hydrocarbon molecules can be represented in the following forms: C_3H_6. [C1.5.1 c)]
- Alkenes react with bromine water, turning it from orange to colourless. [C1.5.1 d)]
- Some of the products of cracking are useful as fuels. [C1.5.1 e)]

Lesson structure

Starters

Recap – Ask students to consider the phrase 'thermal decomposition' (recall limestone work). Ask them to define it and give an example [using heat to break down a substance; heating of calcium carbonate]. *(5 minutes)*

Comparing – On the board, draw the structural formulae of ethane and ethene. Ask the students to list the similarities and differences. [**Similarities:** same number of C atoms/H atoms all have one bond/C atoms all have four bonds/both are hydrocarbons. **Differences:** different number of H atoms/ethane is saturated, ethene is unsaturated/ethane has C—C but ethene has C=C.] Students could be supported by being given a list of questions such as 'how many carbon atoms does each molecule have?' Students could be extended by being asked to explain what is meant by saturated and unsaturated. *(10 minutes)*

Main

- Cracking can be done on a laboratory scale in the classroom. Groups of about three are best as one student can heat the boiling tube and often it takes two students to collect the gas over water.
- Bromine water can be used to test the product and contrast this with the reactant. Ethene is flammable. This can be demonstrated by putting a lighted splint into the test tube and a flame should be seen travelling down the tube (eye protection must be worn). The flame should be smokier than the equivalent alkane (ethane) as there is a higher percentage of carbon.
- Some students can find it difficult to recall the differences between alkanes and alkenes. Encourage them to compare alkanes and alkenes in terms of their structures and how to test them. They could be given a piece of coloured paper to fold in half and make a poster comparing the two families of hydrocarbons.

Plenaries

Chemical formula – Ask the students to use the general formula for an alkene to work out the molecular and displayed formula, if n = 2, 3, 4 [C_2H_4, C_3H_6, C_4H_8]. Students can be supported by being given molecular model kits to help draw the display formula. Students could be extended by asking them to give alternative structures for C_4H_8. [There are two.] *(5 minutes)*

'Alkane or alkene?' practical – Give students a selection of different hydrocarbons labelled with letters and some bromine water. Their task is to identify which liquids are alkenes and which are alkanes. Any alkenes tested should decolourise the bromine water. Alkanes will not. *(10 minutes)*

Answers to in-text questions

a Because we can use it to make smaller, more useful hydrocarbon molecules from larger ones.

b By heating them strongly and passing them over a catalyst or by mixing them with steam and heating to a high temperature.

Practical support

Cracking

Equipment and materials required

Bunsen burner and safety equipment, S-shaped delivery tube (with bung on one end and Bunsen valve on the other), pneumatic trough, boiling tube, mineral wool, three test tubes with bungs, test-tube rack, stand, boss and clamp, a hydrocarbon (medicinal paraffin, petroleum jelly or decane), broken ceramic pot/aluminium oxide powder (catalyst), bromine water.

Details

Soak the mineral wool in paraffin and put at the bottom of the boiling tube. About 2 cm from the bung put in the catalyst (about one spatula full) and clamp in position. Heat the catalyst strongly (with a blue flame) then flash the flame towards the mineral wool, so that the hydrocarbon evaporates and reaches the catalyst. Students should collect the gas over water. The Bunsen valve will help prevent suck back within the apparatus, but tell students to remove the end of the delivery tube from the trough of water by lifting the clamp stand before they finish heating. Eye protection should be worn throughout. The collected gas can be tested with bromine water (as detailed below). The gas is highly flammable and this can be demonstrated by igniting it with a burning splint in the test tube.

Safety: medicinal paraffin, petroleum jelly or decane – flammable; CLEAPSS Hazcard 45 Bromine water – irritant and harmful.

Alkane or alkene?

Equipment and materials required

A selection of hydrocarbons (e.g. hexane, hexene, octane), dropping pipettes, test tubes, bromine water, bungs, test-tube rack, eye protection.

Details

Students should pipette about 1 cm³ of each liquid into separate test tubes, stored in a rack. About the same amount of bromine water should be added to each test tube, and add a bung to each. Shake. Ensure that the students wear eye protection, hold the bung and base of the test tube when they shake it. Bromine vapour may be given off, therefore a well ventilated area is necessary.

Only use weak solutions of bromine water (yellow, not orange) otherwise you are unlikely to see complete discoloration (and there will be less bromine vapour released).

Safety: A selection of hydrocarbons (e.g. hexane, hexene, octane – flammable). CLEAPSS Hazcard 15B; 45 Bromine water – irritant and harmful.

C1 5.1 Cracking hydrocarbons Ⓚ

Learning objectives

- How do we make smaller, more useful molecules from larger, less useful molecules in crude oil?
- What are alkenes and how are they different from alkanes?

Figure 2 In an oil refinery, huge crackers like this are used to break down large hydrocarbon molecules into smaller ones

Some of the heavier fractions that we get by distilling crude oil are not very useful. The hydrocarbons in them are made up of large molecules. They are thick liquids or solids with high boiling points. They are difficult to vaporise and do not burn easily – so they are no good as fuels! Yet the main demand from crude oil is for fuels.

Luckily we can break down large hydrocarbon molecules in a process we call cracking.

The process takes place at an oil refinery in a steel vessel called a cracker.

In the cracker, a heavy fraction produced from crude oil is heated to vaporise the hydrocarbons. The vapour is then either passed over a hot catalyst or mixed with steam and heated to a high temperature. The hydrocarbons are cracked as thermal decomposition reactions take place. The large molecules split apart to form smaller, more useful ones.

a Why is cracking so important?
b How are large hydrocarbon molecules cracked?

Example of cracking Ⓚ

Decane is a medium-sized molecule with ten carbon atoms. When we heat it to 500°C with a catalyst it breaks down. One of the molecules produced is pentane which is used in petrol.

Figure 1 Pentane (C_5H_{12}) can be used as a fuel. This is the displayed formula of pentane.

We also get propene and ethene which we can use to produce other chemicals.

$$C_{10}H_{22} \xrightarrow{800°C + catalyst} C_5H_{12} + C_3H_6 + C_2H_4$$
decane   pentane   propene   ethene

This reaction is an example of thermal decomposition.

Notice how this cracking reaction produces different types of molecules. One of the molecules is pentane. The first part of its name tells us that it has five carbon atoms (pent-). The last part of its name (-ane) shows that it is an alkane. Like all other alkanes, pentane is a saturated hydrocarbon. Its molecules have as much hydrogen as possible in them.

The other molecules in this reaction have names that end slightly differently. They end in -ene. We call this type of molecule an alkene. The different ending tells us that these molecules are unsaturated. They contain a double bond between two of their carbon atoms. Look at Figure 3. You can see that alkenes have one double bond and have the general formula C_nH_{2n}.

Figure 3 A molecule of ethene (C_2H_4) and a molecule of propene (C_3H_6). These are both alkenes – each molecule has a carbon–carbon double bond in it.

Ethene — Double bond
Propene

Practical

Cracking

Medicinal paraffin is a mixture of hydrocarbon molecules. You can crack it by heating it and passing the vapour over hot pieces of broken pot. The broken pot acts as a catalyst.

- Why must you remove the end of the delivery tube from the water before you stop heating?

If you carry out this practical, collect at least two test tubes of gas. Test one by putting a lighted splint in to it. Test the other by shaking it with a few drops of bromine water.

Delivery tube — Gaseous product

Ceramic wool soaked in medicinal paraffin — Heat — Broken pot (catalyst) — Safety valve — Water

A simple experiment like the one above shows that alkenes burn. They also react with bromine water (which is orange). The products of this reaction are colourless. This means that we have a good test to see if a hydrocarbon is unsaturated:

Positive test:

unsaturated hydrocarbon + bromine water → products
(orange-yellow)   (colourless)

Negative test:

saturated hydrocarbon + bromine water → no reaction
(orange)   (orange)

Summary questions

1 Copy and complete using the words below:

alkenes catalyst cracking double heating unsaturated

Large hydrocarbon molecules are broken down by .... them and passing them over a hot .... This is called .... Some of the molecules produced when we do this contain a .... bond. They are called .... hydrocarbons. They are examples of a group of hydrocarbons called the ....

2 Cracking a hydrocarbon makes two new hydrocarbons, A and B. When bromine water is added to A, nothing happens. Bromine water added to B turns from an orange solution to colourless.
a Which hydrocarbon is unsaturated?
b Which hydrocarbon is used as a fuel?
c What type of reaction is cracking an example of?
d Cracking can be carried out by passing large hydrocarbon molecules over a hot catalyst. State another way to crack a hydrocarbon in industry.

3 An alkene molecule with one double bond contains 7 carbon atoms. How many hydrogen atoms does it have? Write down its formula.

4 Decane (with 10 carbon atoms) is cracked into octane (with 8 carbon atoms) and ethene. Write a balanced equation for this reaction. [H]

?? Did you know ...?

Ethene gas makes fruits such as bananas ripen. Bananas are picked and stored as the unripe green fruit. When they are required for display in a shop ethene gas is passed over the stored bananas to start the ripening process.

AQA Examiner's tip

Remember:
alkanes are saturated
alkenes have a double bond = (equals)

Key points

- We can split large hydrocarbon molecules up into smaller molecules by:
  – mixing them with steam and heating them to a high temperature, or
  – by passing the vapours over a hot catalyst.
- Cracking produces saturated hydrocarbons which are used as fuels and unsaturated hydrocarbons (called alkenes).
- Alkenes react with orange bromine water, turning it colourless.

Further teaching suggestions

Cracking equations

- Students could be given the chemical formula of decane, and asked to generate as many balanced equations as possible, to demonstrate all the possible combinations of alkanes and alkenes that could be generated in the cracking reaction. [HT only]

Summary answers

1 heating, catalyst, cracking, double, unsaturated, alkenes

2 a Hydrocarbon B is unsaturated.
  b Hydrocarbon A is used as a fuel.
  c thermal decomposition
  d By mixing them with steam and heating to a high temperature.

3 Fourteen hydrogen atoms. C_7H_{14}

4 $C_{10}H_{22} \rightarrow C_8H_{18} + C_2H_4$

C1 5.2

Making polymers from alkanes

Learning objectives

Students should learn:

- that monomers join together to make polymers
- about some uses of polymers.

Learning outcomes

Most students should be able to:

- state definitions of monomers and polymers
- determine the polymer name, if the monomer name is given
- determine the monomer name, if the polymer name is given
- list some uses of polymer products.

Some students should also be able to:

- draw the structural formula of a polymer, if the monomer is given
- explain polymerisation in terms of bond breaking and making.

Support

- Students often find it difficult to focus on the C=C bond of a monomer to help them write out the polymer structure. You could draw C=C with one line coming off each carbon atom, an arrow and then the displayed structure of a polymer again with C—C, and a line from each C atom. This diagram could then be laminated. Students then use dry wipe pens and erasers to add the groups onto the carbon atoms to draw the displayed formula of one monomer and its polymer. Different examples can be considered quickly by rubbing out and starting again. Students should be able to see that the C=C is the focus and no matter how the monomer is presented, you need to focus on this area.

Extend

- Students could be extended by introducing condensation polymerisation. Students could then make nylon (this is a condensation polymer and is not on the specification). A recipe for this is in *Classic Chemistry Demonstrations* (RSC).

Specification link-up: Chemistry C1.5

- Alkenes can be used to make polymers such as poly(ethene) and poly(propene). In these reactions, many small molecules (monomers) join together to form very large molecules (polymers). For example:

ethene   poly(ethene)

[C1.5.2 a]

- Evaluate the social and economic advantages and disadvantages of using products from crude oil as fuels or as raw materials for plastics and other chemicals. *[C1.5]*

Lesson structure

Starters

What's the connection? – On the board, have a selection of different photographs of plastics being used, e.g. drink bottles, window frames, clothes. Ask the students to suggest how all the images are linked. [They are all polymers.] *(5 minutes)*

List – Ask the students to look around the classroom and write a list of all the things that are made from polymers. Encourage the students to think about more unusual applications, such as elastic in clothes, fillings in teeth and natural polymers such as proteins and DNA. You may wish to support students by having a tray of products that are made from plastic, e.g. rulers, pens or yoghurt pots. You can extend students by asking them to state the property of the plastic that makes it useful for that application. *(10 minutes)*

Main

- You may wish to demonstrate how to make Perspex. See 'Practical support' for more details. The monomer is methyl 2-methylpropenoate and the polymer has the chemical name poly(methylpropenoate). It is better known by its brand name of Perspex. Di(dodecanoyl is used as the initiator – this starts the polymerisation reaction. Show students the displayed formula of the monomer and ask them to try to draw the displayed formula of the polymer.

- Ask students to draw a table with the following column headings: Name of monomer, displayed formula of monomer, molecular formula of monomer, name of polymer and displayed formula of polymer. Students should complete the table using secondary sources of information to help them. You may wish to support students by giving them the information for polyethene, polypropene, polychloroethene and polytetrafluoroethene. Students could then cut out the information to complete their table. Students could be extended by being encouraged to write balanced displayed formula equations for the making of the polymers that they have studied.

- A kinaesthetic approach to polymerisation would use molecular model kits to represent the polymerisation process, as described in the activity box 'Modelling polymerisation' in the Student Book.

- Students could then be encouraged to create their own model of polymerisation by using people as monomers.

Plenaries

Matching – Ask the students to generate the polymer names from these monomer names:
- Ethene → [poly(ethene)]
- Propene → [poly(propene)]
- Styrene → [poly(styrene)]
- Vinyl chloride → [poly(vinyl chloride)]
- Ethene terephthalate → [poly(ethene terephthalate)]

Students can be supported by being given the names of both the monomers and polymers, so they have to match them together. Students could be extended by being given the displayed formula of the monomer and they have to generate the displayed formula of the polymer. *(5 minutes)*

Models – Students act out their polymer models and explain them to the class. *(10 minutes)*

Practical support

Making Perspex

Equipment and materials required

Di(dodecanoyl) peroxide (0.2 g), top pan balance, 25 cm³ plastic syringe, 25 cm³ methyl 2-methylpropenoate, warm water bath, condenser with flat-bottom flask, stand, boss and clamp, chemical-resistant gloves, fume cupboard, eye protection. CLEAPSS Hazcard 29B – oxidising; 43B – highly flammable and irritant.

Details

Ensure that the inhibitor has been removed from the methyl 2-methylpropenoate. Complete this demonstration in a fume cupboard without any sources of ignition. Using the 25 cm³ plastic syringe measure 25 cm³ of methyl 2-methylpropenoate into the flat bottomed flask. Add 0.2 g of di(dodecanoyl) peroxide. Put the flat bottom flask into the warm water bath and fit a condenser in a reflux position. The liquid in the flat-bottom flask become increasingly viscous as the polymerisation occurs.

Safety: CLEAPSS Hazcard 29 Di(dodecanoyl) peroxide – oxidising; 43B Methyl 2-methylpropenoate – highly flammable and irritant. Wear chemical splashproof safety goggles.

Products from oil

Making polymers from alkanes

C1 5.2 Making polymers from alkenes

Learning objectives
● What are monomers and polymers?
● How do we make polymers from alkenes?

The fractional distillation of crude oil and cracking produces a large range of hydrocarbons. These are very important to our way of life. Oil products are all around us. We simply cannot imagine life without them.

Hydrocarbons are our main fuels. We use them in our transport and at home to cook and for heating. We also use them to make electricity in oil-fired power stations.

Then there are the chemicals we make from crude oil. We use them to make things ranging from cosmetics to explosives. But one of the most important ways that we use chemicals from oil is to make plastics.

Plastics

Plastics are made up of huge molecules made from lots of small molecules joined together. We call the small molecules **monomers**. We call the huge molecules they make **polymers**. (*Mono* means 'one' and *poly* means 'many'). We can make many different types of plastic which have very different properties by using different monomers.

a List three ways that we use fuels.
b What are the small molecules that make up a polymer called?

Figure 1 All of these products were manufactured using chemicals made from oil

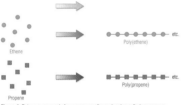
Figure 2 Polymers are made from many smaller molecules called monomers

Ethene (C_2H_4) is the smallest unsaturated hydrocarbon molecule. We can turn it into a polymer known as poly(ethene) or polythene. Poly(ethene) is a really useful plastic. It is easy to shape, strong and transparent (unless we add colouring material to it). 'Plastic' bags, plastic drink bottles, dustbins and clingfilm are all examples of poly(ethene).

Propene (C_3H_6) is another alkene. We can also make polymers with propene as the monomer. The polymer formed is called poly(propene). It forms a very strong, tough plastic. We can use it to make many things, including carpets, milk crates and ropes.

Figure 3 Polymers produced from oil are all around us and are part of our everyday lives

c Is ethene an alkane or an alkene?
d Which polymer can we make from propene monomers?

How do monomers join together?

When alkene molecules join together, the double bond between the carbon atoms in each molecule 'opens up'. It is replaced by single bonds as thousands of molecules join together. The reaction is called polymerisation.

Ethene monomers → Poly(ethene)

We can also write this more simply as:

$$n\ \overset{\displaystyle|}{\underset{\displaystyle|}{C}}=\overset{\displaystyle|}{\underset{\displaystyle|}{C} } \longrightarrow \left(\overset{\displaystyle|}{\underset{\displaystyle|}{C}}-\overset{\displaystyle|}{\underset{\displaystyle|}{C}} \right)_n$$

where n is a large number

Many single ethene monomers → Long chain of poly(ethene)

Activity

Modelling polymerisation

Use a molecular model kit to show how ethene molecules polymerise to form poly(ethene).

Make sure you can see how the equation shown above represents the polymerisation reaction you have modelled.

You should also be able to describe what happens to the bonds in the reaction.

Think up a model to demonstrate the polymerisation of ethene, using people in your class as monomers.

Evaluate the ideas of other groups.

AQA Examiner's tip
The double C=C bond in ethene (an alkene) makes it much more reactive than ethane (an alkane).

Summary questions

1 Copy and complete using the words below:
polymerisation ethene monomers polymers
Plastics are made of large molecules called .... We make these by joining together lots of small, reactive molecules called .... One example of a polymer is poly(ethene), made from .... Poly(ethene) is formed as a result of a .... reaction.

2 Why is ethene the smallest possible unsaturated hydrocarbon molecule?

3 **a** Draw the displayed formula of a propene molecule, showing all its bonds.
b Draw a diagram to show how propene molecules join together to form poly(propene).
c Explain the polymerisation reaction in **b**.

Key points
● Plastics are made of polymers.
● Polymers are large molecules made when monomers (small, reactive molecules) join together. The reaction is called polymerisation.

186 · 187

Answers to in-text questions

a transport, heating, generating electricity
b monomers
c Ethene is an alkene.
d Poly(propene). (Its old name is polypropylene.)

Summary answers

1 polymers, monomers, ethene, polymerisation
2 It has two carbon atoms, the minimum number for a C=C double bond.
3 **a**
$$H-\overset{\overset{\displaystyle H}{|}}{\underset{\underset{\displaystyle H}{|}}{C}}-\overset{\overset{\displaystyle H}{|}}{\underset{\underset{\displaystyle H}{|}}{C}}=\overset{\overset{\displaystyle H}{|}}{C}$$

b
$$\overset{CH_3\ \ \ H}{\underset{H\ \ \ \ H}{C=C}} + \overset{CH_3\ \ \ H}{\underset{H\ \ \ \ H}{C=C}} + \overset{CH_3\ \ \ H}{\underset{H\ \ \ \ H}{C=C}} + etc \longrightarrow \overset{CH_3\ \ H\ \ CH_3\ \ H\ \ CH_3\ \ H}{\underset{H\ \ \ H\ \ \ H\ \ \ H\ \ \ H\ \ \ H}{-C-C-C-C-C-C-}} etc$$

c The double bond 'opens up' in neighbouring propene molecules and forms single bonds, joining molecules together in a chain.

C1 5.3

New and useful polymers

Learning objectives

Students should learn:

- that there are new polymers being developed and being used in innovative ways
- what shape memory polymers are and what they are used for.

Learning outcomes

Most students should be able to:

- give an example of a polymer that is used because of its properties
- give an example of a polymer that has been designed for a specific job.

Some students should also be able to:

- evaluate the suitability of different polymers for particular uses.

AQA Specification link-up: Chemistry C1.5

- Polymers have many useful applications and new uses are being developed, for example: new packaging materials, waterproof coatings for fabrics, dental polymers, wound dressings, hydrogels, smart materials (including shape memory polymers). [C1.5.2 b)]

Controlled Assessment: SA4.1 Planning an investigation. [SA4.1.1 a), [SA4.1.2 c)]

Lesson structure

Starters

Monomer or polymer – Ask the students to link the following statements to the more relevant word – 'monomer' or 'polymer'. The statements could be written down or read out:

- A very long chain hydrocarbon. [polymer] • Contains a double bond. [monomer]
- Reactive molecule. [monomer] • PET. [polymer] • Ethene. [monomer]
- Plastic. [polymer] • Joins together to make a plastic. [monomer]

You could support students by giving them the definitions of a polymer and a monomer on the board. You could extend students by asking them to draw a displayed formula to represent a polymer and monomer at the end of the starter. *(5 minutes)*

Word game – Ask the students to try to make as many words as they can from: 'poly(ethyleneterephthalate)', with double points for any scientific words. *(10 minutes)*

Main

- Plastics are now often developed for a particular purpose. However, new uses for existing plastics are also being found. Set the students the task of designing a new waterproof coat. The students should list the properties of the material that they want the coat to be made out of. They should then complete the 'Evaluating plastics' practical to decide on the best material for the job and why.

- You may wish to encourage students to investigate hydrogels, a type of smart material (see 'Practical support' for more details). Encourage students to suggest how they could make their results more reliable [repeated readings and take an average]. Students could also compare their results with the information that the manufacturers provide and comment on how accurate their results were.

- The two activities above will be useful for teaching aspects of Controlled Assessment – e.g. designing investigations, planning a fair test, and societal influences on decisions made.

- Society is using polymers increasingly, but often they are used for single-use items such as ready-meal packaging. Students could be set the task to choose the best to make a drinks container. In this exercise, they should consider the size of the drinks container, aesthetics, recycling and price. This task could be completed using secondary data from the internet.

- Students need to have some understanding of the vast range in new polymers. Split the class into six groups and give each a topic: 'new packaging materials, waterproof coatings for fabrics, dental polymers, wound dressings, hydrogels, shape memory polymers'. Ask each group to come up with a PowerPoint presentation (no more than 3 minutes long) about their topic. This should include what their material is, its special properties, what it is used for and one fascinating fact. Ask the students to deliver their presentations. Have a stopwatch running, and stop the students when they reach their 3 minutes.

Plenaries

Answers – Ask the students to look back at the objectives in the Student Book and answer the 'questions' that have been posed. *(5 minutes)*

AfL (Assessment for Learning) – Split the class into pairs. Give each pair two short examination questions about new and useful polymers. Allow the students 5 minutes to answer a question each. Then ask the students to swap, and encourage them to mark the other student's work. Allow the two students to sit together 'debriefing' each other about their examination work. Support students using Foundation Tier examination questions and extend students using Higher Tier examination questions. *(10 minutes)*

Support

- Students often forget what a 'smart' material is. Ensure that they understand that it is a material that changes its properties as a stimulus changes. You could show students some plastic examples such as plastic drinks beakers that change colour when heated.

Extend

- Students could be extended by being asked to find out about other 'smart' materials.

- Students could be extended by being asked to find out how 'smart' materials work. The structure of 'smart' materials changes at certain thresholds for a particular stimulus. This means that the properties of the material change due to the arrangement of the particles changing. Students could use simple particle models to explain how a specific example changes.

Practical support

Evaluating plastics

Equipment and materials required

Swatches of different polymer fabrics (untreated nylon, treated nylon, Teflon, wool, cotton, polyester and neoprene), sandpaper, water bath, washing powder, two beakers, hairdryer, stand, boss and clamp, fabric dyes, cobalt chloride paper.

Details

Each fabric can be tested for:

Wearing/durability – Rub the fabric with sandpaper a number of times (set by the students) to see the effect on the wear of the material.

Water permeability – Carefully place on the surface of a water bath and put a piece of cobalt chloride paper onto the fabric. If water seeps through, the paper will turn from blue to pink.

Wind permeability – Set up the fabric stretched out in a stand, boss and clamp. Hold the hairdryer on cold blow at one side, and put your hand on the other, in order to feel the air flow through the fabric.

Dyeing – The coloured dyes could be applied as the instructions to determine how easy it is to change the colour of the fabric.

Wash test – Measure the fabric swatch, then wash it in washing detergent and dry. Remeasure the material to see if it has shrunk.

Safety: Cobalt chloride paper – handle as little as possible. Use freezers. Wash hands after experiment. CLEAPSS Hazcard 25 – harmful.

Investigating hydrogel

Equipment and materials required

Hydrogel (available from garden centres as a water absorbing additive for compost), $100\,cm^3$ measuring cylinder, water, $250\,cm^3$ beaker, top pan balance, dropping pipette, stirring rod.

Details

Measure 1 g of hydrogel into a $250\,cm^3$ beaker. Measure $100\,cm^3$ of tap water into a measuring cylinder. Using the dropping pipette, add water to the hydrogel and mix with the stirring rod. Keep adding water from the dropping pipette until no more water has been absorbed. Record the amount of water that the hydrogel absorbed.

Products from oil

C1 5.3 — New and useful polymers

Learning objectives

- How are we using new polymers?
- What are smart polymers?

Chemists can design new polymers to make materials with special properties to do particular jobs. Medicine is one area where we are beginning to see big benefits from these 'polymers made to order'.

New polymer materials will eventually take over from fillings for teeth which contain mercury. Working with the toxic mercury every day is a potential hazard to dental workers. Other developments include:

- new softer linings for dentures (false teeth)
- new packaging material
- implants that can slowly release drugs into a patient.

a What do we mean by a 'designer polymer'?

Light-sensitive plasters

We all know how uncomfortable pulling a plaster off your skin can be. But for some of us taking off a plaster is really painful. Both very old and very young people have quite fragile skin. But now a group of chemists has made a plaster where the 'stickiness' can be switched off before the plaster is removed. The plaster uses a light-sensitive polymer.

Figure 1 A sticking plaster is often needed when we cut ourselves. Getting hurt isn't much fun – and sometimes taking the plaster off can be painful too.

1 The plaster is put on just like any normal plaster.

2 To remove the plaster, the top layer is peeled away from the lower layer which stays stuck to the skin.

3 Once the lower layer is exposed to the light, the adhesive becomes less sticky, making it easy to peel off your skin.

Figure 2 This plaster uses a light-sensitive polymer

How Science Works

Evaluating plastics

Plan an investigation to compare and evaluate the suitability of different plastics for a particular use.

For example, you might look at treated and untreated fabrics for waterproofing and 'breatheability' (gas permeability) or different types of packaging.

Hydrogels

Hydrogels are polymer chains with a few cross-linking units between chains. This makes a matrix that can trap water. These hydrogels are used as wound dressings. They let the body heal in moist, sterile conditions. This makes them useful for treating burns.

The latest 'soft' contact lenses are also made from hydrogels. To change the properties of hydrogels, scientists can vary the amount of water in their matrix structure.

Shape memory polymers

New polymers can also come to our rescue when we are cut badly enough to need stitches. A new 'shape memory polymer' is being developed by doctors which will make stitches that keep the sides of a cut together. When a shape memory polymer is used to stitch a wound loosely, the temperature of the body makes the thread tighten and close the wound, applying just the right amount of force.

This is an example of a 'smart polymer', i.e. one that changes in response to changes around it. In this case a change in temperature causes the polymer to change its shape. Later, after the wound is healed, the polymer is designed to dissolve and is harmlessly absorbed by the body. So there will be no need to go back to the doctor to have the stitches out.

Figure 3 A shape memory polymer uses the temperature of the body to make the thread tighten and close the wound

New uses for old polymers

The bottles that we buy fizzy drinks in are a good example of using a plastic because of its properties. These bottles are made out of a plastic called PET.

The polymer it is made from is ideal for making drinks bottles. It produces a plastic that is very strong and tough, and which can be made transparent. The bottles made from this plastic are much lighter than glass bottles. This means that they cost less to transport and are easier for us to carry around.

Do you recycle your plastic bottles? The PET from recycled bottles is used to make polyester fibres for clothing, such as fleece jackets, and the filling for duvet covers. School uniforms and football shirts are now also made from recycled drinks bottles.

b Why is PET used to make drinks bottles?

Did you know ...?

PET is an abbreviation for poly(ethene terephthalate). It takes 5 two-litre PET lemonade bottles to make one T-shirt.

links

For more information on recycling, see C1 5.4 Plastic waste.

Key points

- New polymers are being developed all the time. They are designed to have properties that make them specially suited for certain uses.
- Smart polymers may have their properties changed by light, temperature or by other changes in their surroundings.
- We are now recycling more plastics and finding new uses for them.

Summary questions

1 Copy and complete using the words below:

cold hot PET properties shape strong transparent

We choose a polymer for a job because it has certain _____. For example, we make drinks bottles out of a plastic called _____ because it is _____ and _____.

Scientists can also design 'smart' polymers, for example _____ memory polymers. These change their shape when they are _____ or _____.

2 **a** Give one advantage of using a polymer in sticking plasters that is switched off by light making the plaster less sticky.

b Design a leaflet for a doctor to give to a patient, explaining how stitches made from smart polymers work.

Further teaching suggestions

Unusual polymers

- Using secondary sources, students could research into unusual polymers, e.g. surgical glues.

Timeline

- Ask which synthetic polymers have not been around for more than a hundred years. Using secondary sources, students could produce a timeline showing the development of important (e.g. Bakelite) or interesting (e.g. superglue) polymers.

New polymer

- Students should think of a new polymer fit for a particular purpose. Students should list its properties and what specific use it is designed for.

Answers to in-text questions

a Polymers that are designed with ideal properties for a particular job.

b PET bottles are much lighter than glass bottles but are strong, tough (don't smash) and transparent.

Summary answers

1 properties, PET, strong (transparent), transparent (strong), shape, hot (cold), cold (hot)

2 **a** One advantage is needed from; makes the plaster less sticky, reduces pain when the plaster is removed, reduces the likelihood of damaging fragile skin.

b leaflet

C1 5.4

Plastic waste

Learning objectives

Students should learn:

- that problems are caused by the disposal of plastics
- what biodegradeable means
- that biodegradeable plastics can be made.

Learning outcomes

Most students should be able to:

- state a definition of biodegradeable
- give an example of how a plastic can be made biodegradeable
- explain some of the problems arising from plastic disposal.

Some students should also be able to:

- explain how a plastic can be made biodegradeable.

Support

- You can support students by giving them a writing frame to help them construct their leaflet for the 'sorting plastics' activity.

Extend

- You can extend students by asking them to consider why plastics are often not recycled. They could then categorise these reasons as social or economic. [Social – it is time consuming and takes effort to recycle. Economic – it is often cheaper to make new plastic than recycle, limited market for recycled plastic.]

AQA Specification link-up: Chemistry C1.5

- Many polymers are not biodegradable, so they are not broken down by microbes and this can lead to problems with waste disposal. *[C1.5.2 c)]*
- Plastic bags are being made from polymers and cornstarch so that they break down more easily. Biodegradable plastics made from cornstarch have been developed. *[C1.5.2 d)]*
- Evaluate the social, economic and environmental impacts of the uses, disposal and recycling of polymers. *[C1.5]*

  Controlled Assessment: SA4.4 Select and process primary and secondary data. *[SA4.4.2 b)]*

Lesson structure

Starters

Plastic recycling – Ask students to make a list of all the ways that they can recycle plastics [recycling collection at home, plastic recycle banks e.g. at supermarkets]. *(5 minutes)*

Interpreting data – The average household bin contains 35 per cent organic waste, 30 per cent paper, 12 per cent construction materials, 9 per cent plastics, 6 per cent metal, 3 per cent glass and 5 per cent other. Ask students to display this information in a bar chart. Students could be supported by being given the labelled axes and scale. Extend students by asking them to display this information in a pie chart. *(10 minutes)*

Main

- Many plastics only degrade through physical weathering, and this process can take hundreds of years. Ask students to consider why plastics are used and the downsides of their disposal. Students could create a table listing the advantages and disadvantages of the use of common plastics.

- You could ask students to complete the activity 'sorting plastics'. Students should write a leaflet for householders to persuade them to recycle more plastic waste. You may wish to show students some examples of leaflets and adverts to help galvanise their thoughts.

- There is a wide range of different plastics, all with very different properties and uses. Some consumer goods and packaging will be made out of more than one type of plastic. Explain to students that plastics must be sorted before they can be recycled. Ask students to find out the recycling codes for plastics. They could then make an A4 or A5 label that could be put up on a recycling bin to help householders separate plastics before they are recycled.

- Plastics are being developed and modified so that they are biodegradable. Allow students to make cornstarch and test its properties. See 'Practical support' for more details.

Plenaries

Reduce, reuse, recycle – Ask students to make suggestions about their own lives that would reduce the plastic waste that they generate. Ask volunteers to share their thoughts with the whole class and manage the discussions. *(5 minutes)*

Classify – Give the students a selection of household plastic refuse and ask them to sort them into the different types of plastic (using the universal plastic identification symbol). Time the students and the first group to finish could be given a prize. Encourage students to reflect why it is expensive to recycle plastic [the plastic needs to be collected, then sorted, often manually, often before recycling can begin]. Students could be supported by being given waste plastic that is of only one type, and limiting the types of plastic to three. Students could be extended by being given things with more than one plastic, e.g. a plastic fizzy drink bottle is made from a different plastic from its cap. *(10 minutes)*

Practical support

Investigating cornstarch

Equipment and materials required

One tablespoon of cornflour, 15 cm³ water, three drops of cooking oil, dropping pipette, microwave oven, 100 cm³ glass beaker, stirring rod, table spoon, food colouring (optional).

Details

In the glass beaker mix the cornflour, water, cooking oil and food colouring until an opaque paste is formed. Use a microwave to heat the mixture in the beaker until it becomes yellow gel-like material, almost transparent (takes up to 30 seconds). Remove the beaker and allow the mixture to cool. Once the mixture is cool, it can be moulded into a shape or pushed into a mould, e.g. an ice cube tray. Allow the material to fully cool and solidify (this may take up to 24 hours). The plastic's properties can then be tested, which could include dropping it in water and watching it dissolve.

Students can alter the ratios of cornflour, oil and water and experiment to determine how the properties are different.

Safety: Take care with hot materials.

Testing the properties of cornstarch

Equipment and materials required

Samples of cornflour plastic, Bunsen burner and safety equipment, tongs, water bath, mounted needle, hand lens, eye protection.

Details

Students should first look at the plastic, using the hand lens to observe the different textures. Then, using the mounted needle, they need to try to scratch the plastic to find out how hard it is and gently pull at the plastic to consider its flexibility. In a fume cupboard only, take a small piece of the plastic and hold in the Bunsen flame, using tongs, in order to find out if it is flammable and whether it is a thermosoftening or a thermosetting plastic.

Safety: Take care with burning plastics.

C1 5.4   Plastic waste

Learning objectives

- What are the problems caused by disposing of plastics?
- What does biodegradable mean?
- How can polymers be made biodegradable?

One of the problems with plastics is what to do with them when we've finished with them. Too much ends up as rubbish in our streets. Even the beaches in the remotest parts of the world can be polluted with plastic waste. Wildlife can get trapped in the waste or eat the plastics and die.

Not only that, just think of all the plastic packaging that goes in the bin after shopping. Most of it ends up as rubbish in landfill tips. Other rubbish in the tips rots away quite quickly. Microorganisms in the soil break it down. Many waste plastics last for hundreds of years before they are broken down completely. So they take up valuable space in our landfill sites. What was a useful property during the working life of the plastic (its lack of reactivity) becomes a disadvantage in a landfill site.

a   Why are waste plastics proving to be a problem for us?

Figure 1 Finding space to dump and bury our waste is becoming a big problem

Biodegradable plastics

Scientists are working to solve the problems of plastic waste. We are now making more plastics that do not rot away in the soil when we dump them. These plastics are called **biodegradable**. They can be broken down by microorganisms.

Scientists have found different ways to speed up the decomposition. One way uses granules of cornstarch built into the plastic. The microorganisms in soil feed on the starch. This breaks the plastic up into small pieces more quickly.

Other types of plastic have been developed that are made from plant products. A plastic called PLA, poly(lactic acid), can be made from cornstarch. The plastic is totally biodegradable. It is used in food packaging. However, it cannot be put in a microwave which limits its use in ready-meal packaging.

We can also make plastic carrier bags using PLA. In carrier bags the PLA is mixed with a traditional plastic. This makes sure the bag is strong enough but will still biodegrade a lot more quickly.

Using plastics such as PLA also helps preserve our supplies of crude oil. Remember that crude oil is the raw material for many traditional plastics, such as poly(ethene).

Figure 2 The breakdown of a biodegradable plastic. PLA can be designed to break down in a few months.

Disadvantages of biodegradable plastics

However, the use of a food crop like corn to make plastics can raise the same issues as biofuels. Farmers who sell their crops to turn into fuel and plastics could cause higher food prices. The lack of basic food supplies could result in starvation in developing countries. Another problem is the destruction of tropical forests to create more farmland. This will destroy the habitats of wildlife and could affect global warming.

Other plastics used for bags will break down in light. However, they will not decompose when buried in a landfill site. Probably the best solution is to reuse the same plastic carrier bags over and over again.

⊙⊙ links

For information on the issues of using biofuels, look back at C1 4.5 Alternative fuels.

Practical

Investigating cornstarch

Cornstarch can be fermented to make the starting material for PLA. However, cornstarch itself also has some interesting properties. You can make your own plastic material directly from cornstarch.

- How do varying the proportions of cornstarch and water affect the product?

Recycling plastics 🄺

Some plastics can be recycled. Once sorted into different types they can be melted down and made into new products. This can save energy and resources.

However, recycling plastics does tend to be more difficult than recycling paper, glass or metals. The plastic waste takes up a lot of space so is awkward to transport. Sorting out plastics into their different types adds another tricky step to the process. The energy savings are less than we get with other recycled materials. It would help recyclers if they could collect the plastics already sorted. You might have seen recycling symbols on some plastic products.

PET   HD PE   PVC   LD PE   PP   PS   Others
(polyethene (high density
terephthalate) poly(ethene))

Figure 3 These symbols could help people sort out their plastic waste to help the recycling process

b   How does recycling plastic waste help conserve our supplies of crude oil?

Figure 4 Recycling is becoming part of everyday life in the UK

Activity

Sorting plastics

a Imagine you are the head of your council's waste collection department. You have to write a leaflet for householders persuading them to recycle more of their plastic waste. They will be provided with extra bins to sort the plastics out before they are collected, once every two weeks.

b Write a letter back to the council from an unhappy person who is not willing to do any more recycling than they do already.

c Take a class vote on which action, **a** or **b**, you would support.

Summary questions

1 What do we mean by a biodegradable plastic?

2 a Why are plastics whose raw materials are plants becoming more popular?

   b PLA is a biodegradable plastic. What is its monomer?

3 Non-biodegradable plastics such as poly(ethene) can be made to decompose more quickly by mixing with additives. These enable the polymer chain to be broken down by reacting with oxygen. Why might this be a waste of money if the plastic is buried and compressed under other waste in a landfill site?

Key points

- Non-biodegradable plastics cause unsightly rubbish, can harm wildlife and take up space in landfill sites.

- Biodegradable plastics are decomposed by the action of microorganisms in soil. Making plastics with starch granules in their structure help the microorganisms break down a plastic.

- We can make biodegradable plastics from plant material such as cornstarch.

Further teaching suggestions

Biodegradable plastics

- Ask students to find some examples of biodegradable plastics in use today, e.g. refuse sacks, nappy sacks, supermarket carrier bags, washing bags used by the NHS.

The Science Enhancement Programme

- Innovative practicals looking at recycling of plastics can be found at www.sep.org.uk. Search for 'recycling' and 'sustainability' under 'What's New'.

Local council research

- Ask students to find out how plastics are sorted and recycled by their local council. Sorting is often by hand but eddy currents, density and radiation can also be used.

Answers to in-text questions

a Plastic waste forms unsightly rubbish, which can harm wildlife. It also takes up valuable space in landfill sites.

b The raw material for making most polymers is crude oil which is a non-renewable resource. Recycling plastics means we do not have to use crude oil to make new plastics.

Summary answers

1 A plastic that is broken down by microorganisms in the soil.

2 a Because they do not rely on crude oil (which is a non-renewable resource) as a raw material and they are more biodegradable.

   b lactic acid

3 There will be very little oxygen available to react with the polymer chains, so they will not be broken down.

C1 5.5

Ethanol

Learning objectives

Students should learn:

- that there are two main methods for making ethanol
- that there are advantages and disadvantages of each method for making ethanol.

Learning outcomes

Most students should be able to:

- describe in outline the two methods of making ethanol
- state an advantage and disadvantage of each method for making ethanol
- write the word equation and conditions for the production of ethanol from ethene
- write the word equation and conditions for the production of ethanol by fermentation.

Some students should also be able to:

- evaluate the advantages and disadvantages of using ethanol as a fuel
- write the symbol equation for the reaction of ethene with steam and for the fermentation of sugar. [HT only]

Answers to in-text questions

a carbon dioxide

b enzymes

c Crude oil (in the cracking of its heavy fractions).

Support

- You could support students by giving them a half-finished flow chart for each method for making ethanol industrially. Then you could give them key diagrams and statements that they cut out and add to the flow chart to finish it.

Extend

- You could extend students by asking them to find out about how genetically modified *E. coli* can be used to make ethanol.

AQA Specification link-up: Chemistry C1.5

- Ethanol can be produced by hydration of ethene with steam in the presence of a catalyst. [C1.5.3 a)]
- Ethanol can also be produced by fermentation with yeast, using renewable resources. This can be represented by: sugar → carbon dioxide + ethanol. [C1.5.3 b)]
- Evaluate the advantages and disadvantages of making ethanol from renewable and non-renewable sources. [C1.5]

Lesson structure

Starters

What is the connection? – Show students a picture of bread, beer, a packet of dried yeast and a microscope image of a yeast cell and ask the students to state the connection [they all contain/are pictures of yeast]. *(5 minutes)*

Sorting – Get pictures of different fuels for cars at least A4 in size (oil, biodiesel, diesel, gas, petrol, alcohol and hydrogen). Laminate the pictures, and put sticky-tac on the back. Draw a table with two columns (renewable, non-renewable). Ask two students to explain what the two words in the table mean. Then ask seven students, in turn, to move one image into the renewable or non-renewable column. They should take the image and stick it in the appropriate column. You could support the students by giving them the definitions of renewable and non-renewable. You could extend the students by asking them to consider if electricity for powering a car is renewable or non-renewable. [If it is generated by renewable resources such as solar, it would be renewable, however it is often generated from fossil fuel power stations and is therefore non-renewable.] *(10 minutes)*

Main

- Ethanol can be made from non-renewable sources by reacting ethene and steam in a reaction called hydration. However, ethanol can also be made by fermentation. Discuss the advantages and disadvantages of each method for making ethanol.

- You may wish students to use fermentation to make their own ethanol (see 'Practical support'). You can leave the experiments set up until next lesson, then collect enough of the fermented mixture to fractionally distil. Allow students to smell the distilled ethanol. Show the students that the ethanol can be ignited on a watch glass.

- There is always development in car designs and their engines. Cars were run using petrol for many years; it has been relatively recently that other fuels have started to be investigated and used in the UK, e.g. autogas power.

- People are often slow to change, especially when innovations are based on unproven technology. So car companies will have to make some persuasive advertisements to encourage people to change their cars to run on ethanol.

- Organise students into their preferred learning styles (auditory, kinaesthetic, visual). Ask the visual group to design a billboard poster, the kinaesthetic group to make an advert for TV and the auditory group to make a radio advert. All of the marketing material should aim to persuade drivers to convert to ethanol. Students could be played TV adverts about fuel/engine developments as stimulus material for producing their own marketing material.

Plenaries

Objective answer – Ask the students to answer the objective 'questions'. You could support students by giving them a selection of answers for each question. Each answer should be correct, but some should be more scientific than others (using key terms, word equations etc.). Students should choose one of the answers to copy down and give the reason for their choice. You could extend students by asking them to write an exam-style mark scheme for these questions. Students should consider the number of marks they would award, why, alternative acceptable answers and answers that would not be good enough to be awarded a mark. *(5 minutes)*

AfL (Assessment for Learning) – Each group displays/acts out their marketing material. Question the students about any misconceptions in the adverts. Then ask students to vote for the most persuasive advert; then that group could be given a prize. *(10 minutes)*

Practical support

Fermentation

Equipment and materials required

You will need 1 g yeast, 5 g sugar, a 100 cm³ measuring cylinder, water bath set at 40 °C, 100 cm³ conical flask, cotton wool, a stirring rod, bung and delivery tube, test tube, limewater.

Details

Measure 50 cm³ of warm water into the conical flask and add the sugar and stir until dissolved. Add the yeast and stir to mix. Put the cotton wool into the neck of the conical flask and leave in the water bath to ferment. Alternatively, using a bung with a delivery tube in the centre, the evolved gas could be tested. This can be achieved by half filling a test tube with limewater, then placed in a test tube rack on the outside of the water bath. Put the delivery tube into the limewater so evolved gas blows through. The distillate in the practical can be poured onto a watch glass and ignited to demonstrate its use as a fuel.

Fractional distillation of fermented ethanol mixture

Equipment and materials required

Fermented ethanol mixture, filter paper, filter funnel, round-bottom flask, heating mantle, claisen adaptor, condenser, access to cold water tap and sink, 2 × collecting flasks, watch glass, stand, boss and clamp, thermometer.

Details

Collect all of the students' fermented mixtures and filter into a round-bottom flask. Place the round-bottom flask in a heating mantle and fractionally distil. The boiling point of ethanol is 78 °C.

Safety: Ethanol is flammable, keep away from naked flames.

CLEAPSS Hazcard 40A Ethanol – highly flammable and harmful. Do not taste.

Products from oil

Ethanol

C1 5.5   Ethanol

Learning objectives

- What are the two methods used to make ethanol?
- What are the advantages and disadvantages of these two methods?

Ethanol is a member of the group of organic compounds called the alcohols. Its formula is C_2H_6O but it is more often written as C_2H_5OH. This shows the –OH group that all alcohols have in their molecules.

Making ethanol by fermentation

Ethanol is the alcohol found in alcoholic drinks. Ethanol for drinks is made by the fermentation of sugar from plants. Enzymes in yeast break down the sugar into ethanol and carbon dioxide gas:

$$\text{sugar} \xrightarrow{\text{yeast}} \text{ethanol} + \text{carbon dioxide}$$
(glucose)

$$C_6H_{12}O_6 \longrightarrow 2C_2H_5OH + 2CO_2$$

a Which gas is given off when sugar is fermented?

b Yeast is a living thing. It is a type of fungus. What type of molecules in yeast enable it to ferment sugar?

Figure 1 Some people brew their own alcoholic drinks. The fermentation stage is often carried out by leaving the fermenting mixture in a warm place. The enzymes in yeast work best in warm conditions.

?? Did you know … ?

The yeast in a fermenting mixture cannot survive in concentrations of ethanol beyond about 15%. Alcoholic spirits, such as whisky or vodka, need to be distilled to increase the ethanol content to about 40% of their volume. Ethanol in high concentrations is toxic, which is why ethanol in the lab should never be drunk!

Practical

Fermentation

In this experiment you can ferment sugar solution with yeast and test the gas given off.

Glucose solution and yeast — Limewater

If you leave your apparatus till next lesson, your teacher can collect some fermented mixtures together and distil it to collect the ethanol formed. We use fractional distillation for the best separation as water and ethanol have similar boiling points. Ethanol boils at 78 °C. The ethanol collected will ignite and burn with a 'clean' blue flame.

○ links

For information on using ethanol as a fuel, look back at C1 4.5 Alternative fuels.

Ethanol is also used as a solvent. Methylated spirit is mainly ethanol. Decorators can use it to clean brushes after using an oil-based paint. It is also used to make perfume. We have already seen how ethanol can be used as a fuel. It can be mixed with petrol or just used by itself to run cars.

Making ethanol from ethene (hydration)

Ethanol for industrial use as a fuel or solvent can be made from ethene gas instead of by fermentation. Remember that ethene is made when oil companies crack hydrocarbons to make fuels. Ethene is the main by-product made in cracking. Ethene gas can react with steam to make ethanol.

$$\text{ethene} + \text{steam} \xrightarrow{\text{catalyst}} \text{ethanol}$$
$$C_2H_4 + H_2O \longrightarrow C_2H_5OH$$

This reaction is called hydration.

c Where do we get the ethene from to make industrial ethanol?

The reaction requires energy to heat the gases and to generate a high pressure. The reaction is reversible so ethanol can break down back into ethene and steam. So unreacted ethene and steam need to be recycled over the catalyst.

This process is continuous. It also produces no waste products. Both of these are advantages when making products in industry. When ethanol is made industrially by fermentation, the process is carried out in large vats which have to be left. This is called a batch process, which takes a lot longer than a continuous process. Carbon dioxide, a greenhouse gas, is also given off in fermentation.

However, using ethene to make ethanol relies on crude oil which is a non-renewable resource. Therefore making ethanol as a biofuel, by fermenting sugars from plant material (a renewable resource), will become ever more important. The sugars are from crops such as sugar cane or sugar beet. Any cereal crop can also be used as the raw material. These need their starch to be broken down to sugars before fermentation takes place. However as we have seen before there are issues that need to be addressed when using crops for large-scale industrial processes.

○ links

For information on cracking, look back at C1 5.1 Cracking hydrocarbons.

Figure 2 Industrial fermentation is a slow batch process. The ethanol must be distilled off from the fermented mixture. This requires energy even though the fermentation process itself is energy efficient.

○ links

For information on the issues of using crops for large scale industrial processes, look back at C1 4.5 Alternative fuels.

Summary questions

1 Copy and complete using the words below:

catalyst sugar yeast steam

Ethanol can be made by two processes, ethene reacting with ...., under pressure in the presence of a ...., or the fermentation of .... using enzymes in ....

2 Write a word equation to show the production of ethanol from:
   a ethene
   b glucose.

3 Why is a continuous process better than a batch process for making a product in industry?

4 How can people claim that the fermentation of plant materials does not contribute to the increase in carbon dioxide in the air?

Key points

- Ethanol can be made from ethene reacting with steam in the presence of a catalyst. This is called hydration.
- Ethanol is also made by fermenting sugar (glucose) using enzymes in yeast. Carbon dioxide is also made in this reaction.
- Using ethene to make ethanol needs non-renewable crude oil as its raw material whereas fermentation uses renewable plant material.

Further teaching suggestions

Magazine article

- Ask students to write a feature article in a car magazine about the developments in using ethanol as a fuel for cars.

Top Trumps

- You could ask students to make 'Top Trump'-style cards contrasting the production of ethanol by fermentation and by hydration of ethene. Students should evaluate the two methods and suggest which they think is better and why. Encourage students to try to classify their reasoning as social, environmental or economical.

Summary answers

1 steam, catalyst, sugar, yeast

2 **a** ethene + steam $\xrightarrow{\text{catalyst}}$ ethanol

   b glucose $\xrightarrow{\text{yeast}}$ ethanol + carbon dioxide

3 The process never has to be stopped, unlike a batch process, to separate off the product and re-stock the reactants. This makes a continuous process more efficient.

4 Although fermentation gives off carbon dioxide, the gas is also taken in when the sugar was made by the plant when it made the sugar originally (during photosynthesis).

Summary answers

1 a A compound that contains only hydrogen and carbon.

  b The use of heat and a catalyst to break down a longer chained hydrocarbon to form a shorter chain alkane and alkenes.

  c A method used to separate mixtures of liquids with different boiling points.

  d A molecule with only single bonds that contains only carbon and hydrogen atoms.

  e A molecule with at least one $C=C$ bond that contains only carbon and hydrogen atoms.

  f Small, reactive molecules that react together to make a polymer.

  g Very large molecules made from many repeating units/monomers.

  h A polymer that can be broken down by microorganisms in the soil.

  i The reaction in which glucose/sugar is turned into ethanol plus carbon dioxide by the action of enzymes in yeast.

2 a C_3H_6

  b 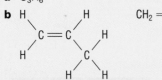 $CH_2 = CH - CH_3$

  c Unsaturated, as it is an alkene and contains $C=C$ (its molecules do not contain maximum number of hydrogen atoms).

  d Put bromine water into each tube. Shake well. The tube that decolourises contains the unsaturated hydrocarbon, which is propene. The tube with propane will not change the colour of the bromine water – it will remain yellow/orange.

  e i polymerisation
    ii The polymer product is a solid at room temperature whereas the propene is a gas.
    iii $nC_2H_4 \rightarrow -(CH_2 - CH_2)_n-$

3 a Because it is not biodegradable it takes many, many years to break down, persisting as rubbish and taking up space in landfill sites.

  b They can build starch into the structure of a plastic so bacteria can feed on the starch and break the plastic into smaller pieces, which break down more quickly. Or they can use the starch to make biodegradable plastics which bacteria can use as food.

4 a
    ethene + steam $\xrightarrow{\text{catalyst}}$ ethanol
    $C_2H_4 \; + \; H_2O \rightarrow C_2H_5OH$

  b
    glucose $\xrightarrow{\text{yeast}}$ ethanol + carbon dioxide
    $C_6H_{12}O_6 \rightarrow 2C_2H_5OH + \quad 2CO_2$

5

Ethanol from ethene		Ethanol from fermenting plant sugars	
Advantage	Disadvantage	Advantage	Disadvantage
Continuous process	Uses up crude oil (non-renewable)	Uses plants (renewable) as its raw material	Batch process

6 Water molecules from sweat can pass through the tiny pores in the material so the wearer does not feel clammy – it is described as 'breatheable' because water vapour passes out into the air (as it does when we breathe out).

Products from oil: C1 5.1–C1 5.5

Summary questions ⓚ

1 Write simple definitions for the following words:
  a hydrocarbon
  b cracking
  c distillation
  d saturated hydrocarbon
  e unsaturated hydrocarbon
  f monomer
  g polymer
  h biodegradable polymer
  i fermentation.

2 Propene is a hydrocarbon molecule containing three carbon atoms and six hydrogen atoms.
  a What is the chemical formula of propene?
  b Draw the display formula of propene, showing all its bonds.
  c Is propene a saturated molecule or an unsaturated molecule? Explain your answer.
  d You are given two unlabelled test tubes. One test tube contains propane gas, while the other test tube contains propene gas. Explain how you could test which tube contains which gas, stating clearly the results obtained in each case.
  e Propene molecules will react together to form long chains.
    i What do we call this type of reaction?
    ii Compare the properties of the reactants to those of the product.
    iii A molecule of ethene is a similar to a molecule of propene. Give an equation to show the reaction of ethene to make poly(ethene).

3 a Why does the disposal of much of our plastic waste cause problems?
  b How can chemists help to solve the issues in part a using a plant material such as starch from corn?

4 a Write a word equation and a balanced symbol equation for the reaction between ethene and steam. [H]
  b Write a word and balanced symbol equation for the fermentation of glucose. [H]

5 Draw a table showing the advantages and disadvantages of making ethanol from ethene or from sugar obtained from plant material.

6 Chemists have developed special waterproof ma_ made from polymers. The polymer materials have pores that are 2000 times smaller than a drop of However, the tiny pores are 700 times larger than molecule. Explain why these materials are descri_ 'breathable'.

7 Non-biodegradable plastic has been used for man_ years for growing melons. The plants are put into_ in the plastic and their shoots grow up above the_ The melons are protected from the soil by the pla_ grow with very few marks on them. Biodegradab_ has been tested – to reduce the amount of non-r_ waste plastic.

In this investigation two large plots were used to_ melons. One using biodegradable plastic, the oth_ using normal plastic. The results were as follows_

Plastic used	Total yield (kg/hectare)	Average of me produce_
Non-biodegradable	4829	2._
Biodegradable	3560	2._

a This was a field investigation. Describe how th_ experimenter would have chosen the two plots_
b What conclusion can you draw from this inves_
c How could the reliability of these results be tes_
d How would you view these results if you were_ they were funded by the manufacturer of the t_ non-biodegradable plastic?

---

7 a The plots should have been chosen to minimise any differences in relation to, for example, soil conditions or weather conditions. Any changes in these conditions should be similar in all plots.

  b The total yield is much less with the biodegradable plastic. The average melon weight is also less with the biodegradable plastic.

  c To test the reliability of these results, the investigation should be repeated by other scientists. An investigation could be carried out in more controlled conditions, e.g. in a glasshouse. Increase the sample size investigated. Repeat the investigation on another soil type.

  d With scepticism, because they have an interest in selling their plastic and could be using selected results. They might not be telling the whole truth.

Kerboodle resources ⓚ

Resources available for this chapter on Kerboodle are:
● Chapter map: Products from oil
● Animation: Cracking crude oil (C1 5.1)
● Bump up your grade: Cracking up – alkenes (C1 5.1)
● Support: Cracking up – alkenes (C1 5.1)
● Extension: Cracking up – alkenes (C1 5.1)
● Viewpoint: In the bag (C1 5.4)
● Practical: Making a biodegradable plastic (C1 5.4)
● Interactive activity: Products from crude oil
● Revision podcast: Biodegradable polymers
● Test yourself: Products from crude oil
● On your marks: Using polymers
● Examination-style questions: Products from oil
● Answers to examination-style questions: Products from oil

A Examination-style questions (k)

ge alkanes from crude oil are broken down to give
ller molecules.

ge alkane (e.g. $C_{15}H_{26}$) → vaporised and passed
hot catalyst → smaller alkane (e.g. C_6H_{12}) + alkene
. C_2H_4)

ose the correct word from the list to complete each
tence.

his process is called ....

racking   distillation   fermentation   (1)

he reaction is an example of thermal ....

ecomposition   evaporation   polymerisation   (1)

he smaller alkane can be used as a ....

lastic   monomer   fuel   (1)

he alkene will turn bromine water ....

lue   colourless   orange   (1)

he general formula for an alkene is ....

$_nH_{2n-2}$ C_nH_{2n} C_nH_{2n+2} (1)

ene is used to mke the plastic poly(ethene).

omplete the equation to show the formation of
oly(ethene).   (3)

      H   H
      | |
      C=C   ⟶
      | |
      H   H

n the equation, what does the letter n represent?   (1)

What name is used for the small molecules that join to
nake a polymer?   (1)

lame the polymer that is made from butene.   (1)

Which one of the following could be used in a similar
ray to make a polymer?

$_3H_6$ C_3H_8 C_4H_{10} (1)

anol can be used as a fuel for cars. Pure ethanol
0%) can be used in specially adapted car engines.
ol with up to 10% ethanol can be used in ordinary car
ines. To mix with petrol the ethanol must not contain
water.

anol can be made from plants or from crude oil.
       fermentation   distillation   dehydration
nts → sugars → 15% ethanol → 96% ethanol → 100%
                   in water   ethanol
       distillation   cracking   catalyst + steam
de oil → fractions → ethene   →   100% ethanol

uggest one environmental advantage of making
thanol fuel from plants rather than from crude oil. (1)

b Suggest one economic disadvantage of producing
ethanol fuel from plants rather than from crude oil. (1)

c Suggest one environmental disadvantage of
producing ethanol fuel from plants.   (1)

d 10% ethanol in petrol can be used in ordinary car
engines. Suggest one other advantage of using 10%
ethanol in petrol as a fuel rather than pure ethanol. (1)

4 Scientists develop new polymers and modify existing
polymers.

a Polylactic acid (PLA) is a bioplastic that is
biodegradable. It can be used to make sandwich
containers, plastic cups and plastic cutlery. PLA is
made from cornstarch. In the USA large amounts
of maize are grown and used to make cornstarch,
which has many uses. To make PLA the cornstarch is
fermented with microbes to make lactic acid, which is
then polymerised.

The structure of PLA is

(structure diagram showing $-[O-CH-\overset{CH_3}{\underset{}{\overset{|}{C}}}\overset{O}{\overset{||}{}}-]_n-$)

i Give one way in which the structure of PLA is
different from the structure of poly(ethene).   (1)

ii Give one way in which the structure of PLA is
similar to the structure of poly(ethene).   (1)

iii Suggest what is meant by bioplastic.   (1)

iv Suggest two reasons why PLA was developed. (2)

b In this question you will be assessed on using good
English, organising information clearly and using
specialist terms where appropriate.

Copper was considered to be the most suitable
material to use for hot water pipes. PEX is now used
as an alternative material for hot water pipes. PEX is
made from poly(ethene).

Copper is extracted from its ore by a series of processes.
1 The low-grade ore is powdered and concentrated.
2 Smelting is carried out in an oxygen flash
furnace. This furnace is heated to 1100°C using a
hydrocarbon fuel. The copper ore is blown into the
furnace with air, producing impure, molten copper.
3 Oxygen is blown into the impure, molten copper
to remove any sulfur. The copper is cast into
rectangular slabs.
4 The final purification of copper is done by
electrolysis.

Suggest the possible environmental advantages of
using PEX instead of copper for hot water pipes. (6)
AQA, 2009

Practicals	AQA	(k)	📖	⚙️
Demonstration of the cracking of liquid paraffin using broken pottery as the catalyst.	✓		✓	
Testing for unsaturation in the alkenes using bromine water.	✓		✓	
Making a polymer from cornstarch.	✓	✓	✓	
Demonstration of making Perspex.	✓		✓	
Molecular modelling of polymers.	✓		✓	
Design an investigation of a property of different plastics, e.g. strength, flexibility, biodegradability.	✓		✓	
Investigate the amount of water that can be absorbed by a hydrogel (e.g. those used as additives to garden composts).	✓		✓	
Testing coated fabrics for water penetration.	✓			

AQA Examination-style answers

1 a	cracking	(1 mark)
b	decomposition	(1 mark)
c	fuel	(1 mark)
d	colourless	(1 mark)
e	C_nH_{2n}	(1 mark)

2 a single C—C, with 2H— attached to each C (1), brackets
around this with – through brackets on both sides (1)
subscript n outside right bracket (1)   (3 marks)

b a large number   (1 mark)

c monomers   (1 mark)

d poly(butene)   (1 mark)

e C_3H_6 (1 mark)

3 a One environmental advantage from: renewable (source),
carbon neutral, resources conserved.   (1 mark)

b One economic disadvantage from: more labour intensive,
takes long(er) time, more steps/processing (to make pure
ethanol).   (1 mark)

c Land/crops used (that could be used for food) or
deforestation.   (1 mark)

d Can use existing supply/storage system (petrol stations/
tanks) or does not need new/different/special system.
                         (1 mark)

4 a i Contains oxygen (atoms), has a double bond, is not a
hydrocarbon, different monomer/repeating unit.
                         (1 mark)

ii Made from monomers, has a repeating unit.   (1 mark)

iii Plastic made from biological/plant/biomass resources
or made using microbes.   (1 mark)

iv Two from: To replace poly(ethene) or other (non-
biodegradable) plastics, it is biodegradable, it
uses renewable source material, cornstarch readily
available, cornstarch cheap, (accept economic
reasons such as to keep farmers in jobs, use up
surplus corn).   (2 marks)

b There is a clear, balanced and detailed scientific
description of the environmental advantages of using PEX
instead of copper for hot water pipes. The answer shows
almost faultless spelling, punctuation and grammar. It
is coherent and in an organised, logical sequence. It
contains a range of appropriate or relevant specialist
terms used accurately.   (5–6 marks)

There is a scientific description that includes some of the
environmental advantages of using PEX. There are some
errors in spelling, punctuation and grammar. The answer
has some structure and organization. The use of specialist
terms has been attempted, but not always accurately.
                        (3–4 marks)

There is a brief description of at least one advantage of
using PEX. The spelling, punctuation and grammar are
very weak. The answer is poorly organised with almost no
specialist terms and/or their use demonstrating a general
lack of understanding of their meaning.   (1–2 marks)

No relevant content.   (0 marks)

Examples of chemistry points made in the response:
• Less (hydrocarbon) fuel used
• Less energy used
• Less/no electricity used (allow no electrolysis)
• Carbon/carbon dioxide emissions reduced or less
global warming
• Less/no pollution by sulfur dioxide/acid rain
• Conserve copper resources
• Reduces the amount of solid waste rock or less waste
(allow copper ores are low-grade)
• Reduces the need to dig large hole/pits/mines.

C1 6.1

Extracting vegetable oil

Learning objectives

Students should learn:

- that oils can be extracted from plants
- that vegetable oils are important foods
- what unsaturated oils are and how we can test for them.

Learning outcomes

Most students should be able to:

- describe how oils can be extracted from plants
- recognise an unsaturated oil
- describe why plant oils are important in foods
- state the test for a compound containing a carbon–carbon double bond.

Some students should also be able to:

- detail a method for extracting and testing unsaturated oils.

Answers to in-text questions

a   Pressing and (steam) distillation.
b   The orange bromine water will be decolourised (turn colourless).

Support

- Some students may struggle to remember the test for saturation and to interpret the results correctly. You could give students two diagrams of two test tubes with an arrow between them. Ask them to use colours and labels to represent the test for saturation. Students can look back at their diagrams to help them interpret the results of their practical.

- Ask the students to imagine that they work for a marketing company. They should make a poster to encourage students to think about science in their everyday lives (such as the RSC posters 'scientists don't always wear white coats'). Their poster should include all the key points in this chapter and should be added to as each topic is covered.

Extend

- You could stretch students by giving them some displayed formula of different fats that we eat. Ask students to classify them as saturated, unsaturated, monounsaturated and polyunsaturated and explain why.

AQA Specification link-up: Chemistry C1.6

- Some fruits, seeds and nuts are rich in oils that can be extracted. The plant material is crushed and the oil removed by pressing or in some cases by distillation. Water and other impurities are removed. [C1.6.1 a)]
- Vegetable oils are important foods and fuels as they provide a lot of energy. They also provide us with nutrients. [C1.6.1 b)]
- Vegetable oils that are unsaturated contain double carbon–carbon bonds. These can be detected by reacting with bromine water. [C1.6.3 a)]

Lesson structure

Starters

List – Ask students to make a list of oily foods. Then ask them to consider where the oil comes from, e.g. crisps – sunflower seeds, chocolate spread – nuts, olive oil – seeds. *(5 minutes)*

Sentences – Ask students to finish the sentence: 'Plants get their energy ...' Encourage students to try to finish it four times, each sentence becoming progressively more scientific, e.g.

1   Plants get their energy from the Sun.
2   Plants get their energy from sugar, that is made by using sunlight.
3   Plants get their energy using photosynthesis to make the sugar glucose.
4   Plants get their energy according to the following equation:

$$\text{carbon dioxide} + \text{water} \rightarrow \text{sugar (glucose)} + \text{oxygen}$$

You may wish to support students by giving the four sentences and asking them to order the statements from the most to the least scientific. To extend students, you could ask them to write a balanced symbol equation for photosynthesis. You may wish to give students the formula of glucose [$C_6H_{12}O_6$] to aid them. Ensure that the Student Book is closed to do this extension of the starter. *(10 minutes)*

Main

- Some plants quickly release oil when they are crushed, e.g. nuts and seeds. Other oils are more difficult to extract and steam distillation needs to be used. This can be seen by crushing nuts and looking at the grease stain produced, see 'Practical support' for more detail.

- Students can complete steam distillation on a micro-scale or crush plant material to extract oil (be aware of nut allergies and eye protection must be worn) using mortar and pestle. (See if you get a translucent stain on filter paper.)

- Students should undertake the 'Testing for unsaturation' practical to reinforce the test for a saturated or unsaturated compound.

- Fats are an important part of the human diet. In the media, we often hear terms such as 'saturated, unsaturated, and polyunsaturated fats'. Students often do not realise that these terms have a scientific meaning. Ask them to consider these words and define them [saturated – no double bonds, unsaturated – contains double bonds, polyunsaturated – contains many double bonds]. They can then classify different fats as saturated or unsaturated using bromine water, see 'Practical support' for more detail.

Plenaries

Questions and answers – Ask a student to pick a number from 1 to the number of students in the class. Look at which number this corresponds to in the register. Then ask the student to generate a question about the topic studied and choose a person to answer it. The question maker then decides if the answer is correct. If misconceptions are highlighted, then you should take over the question and answer in order to correct them. *(5 minutes)*

Flow chart – Ask the students to make a flow chart to demonstrate two different ways of extracting plant oils. You may wish to support students by asking them to work in small groups and giving the stages in one flow chart as a card sort. Students then just sort the cards to put the stages in the correct order. The students in each group should then compare their flow chart with another group to review both methods. To extend students, you could ask them to evaluate the two methods and comment on which is likely to be the most expensive to operate [distillation, as this still needs to be heated and therefore uses more energy]. *(10 minutes)*

Practical support

Oils from nuts

Equipment and materials required
Paper towel, nuts (e.g. walnuts).

Details
Put a nut on a paper towel and fold it over, so that the nut is wrapped in the towel. Push onto the nut with the palm of your hand so that the nut is crushed. Remove the nut and observe the fat stains on the paper towel.

Safety: Be aware of nut allergies. Large seeds are an alternative (broad beans).

Extracting plant oil by distillation

Equipment and materials required
Orange, grater, antibumping granules, methylated spirits, silicone oil, microscale distillation apparatus (see 'Student Book').

Details
Grate the zest from part of an orange and place it in a small vial in the apparatus shown – one-quarter full. Mix with water to half fill the vial and add a few antibumping granules. Heat gently, to avoid the mixture boiling over. Collect a few drops of the 'orange oil' emulsion in a small well. Note its smell and cloudy appearance. (The apparatus is available from Edulab, Karoo Close, Bexwell, Norfolk PE38 9GA.) This process can be used to extract oils from other plant materials including lemon zest and lavender flowers.

Safety: Follow instructions for equipment. CLEAPSS Hazcard 40A Methylated spirit – highly flammable and harmful.

Testing for unsaturation

Equipment and materials required
A selection of fats (e.g. butter, margarine, dripping, lard, olive oil, vegetable oil), dropping pipettes, test tubes, bromine water, bungs, test-tube rack, water bath, ethanol, eye protection.

Details
Students should pipette about 1 cm³ of each liquid into separate test tubes, stored in a rack. If a solid fat is to be tested, e.g. dripping, then it needs to be dissolved in ethanol. About the same amount of bromine water should be added to each test tube, and each bunged and shaken. Ensure that the students wear eye protection and hold the bung and base of the test tube when they shake it. Bromine vapour may be given off (so use pale yellow bromine water); therefore a well-ventilated area is necessary and students should wash their hands after the practical. Asthmatics may experience problems with any bromine vapour present.

Safety: CLEAPSS Hazcard 15B Bromine water. It is only harmful at concentration used. CLEAPSS Hazcard 40A Ethanol – highly flammable and harmful. No naked flames.

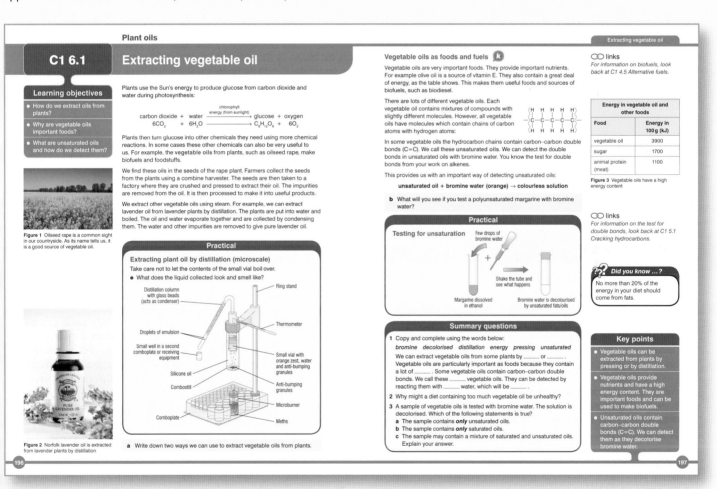

Further teaching suggestions

Making perfume
- Students could extract oils from petals in order to make their own 'perfume'. Students can extract oil from fruits such as olives see www.sep.org.uk.

Summary answers

1 pressing (distillation), distillation (pressing), energy, unsaturated, bromine, decolorised

2 Because vegetable oils contain a lot of energy, which becomes stored as fat in the body if it is not used up.

3 Answer **c** – we can be certain that the sample contains unsaturated oils because it decolorises bromine water but we cannot be certain whether or not it contains saturated oils because these have no effect on bromine water.

C1 6.2 Cooking with vegetable oils

Learning objectives

Students should learn:

- reasons why people cook with vegetable oils
- what 'to harden' vegetable oils means [HT only]
- how to turn vegetable oils into spreads [HT only]

Learning outcomes

Most students should be able to:

- list advantages and a disadvantages of using vegetable oils for cooking.

Some students should also be able to:

- define the term 'harden' [HT only]
- explain why and how oils are turned into spreads by the addition of hydrogen to give hydrogenated oils with melting points above room temperature. [HT only]

Support

- Students could be supported during the debate by reducing the number of characters involved. Students could work in small teams to prepare just one member for an active role in the debate. They could also be provided with some statements and views that the person knows/holds and the students could use this as an input considering if they are advantages/ disadvantages and whether they are facts or opinions.

Extend

- Students could be extended by being shown the displayed formula of a polyunsaturated fat and using arrow – pushing show how the hydrogen attaches across the double bond. Refer back to 'C1 1.4 Forming bonds' to remind students of the importance of electrons in bonding. This might help students visualise the process, although they do not need to know the mechanism.

Specification link-up: Chemistry C1.6

- Vegetable oils have higher boiling points than water and so can be used to cook foods at higher temperatures than by boiling. This produces quicker cooking and different flavours but increases the energy that the food releases when it is eaten. [C1.6.1 c)]
- Vegetable oils that are unsaturated can be hardened by reacting them with hydrogen in the presence of a nickel catalyst at about 60 °C. Hydrogen adds to the carbon–carbon double bonds. The hydrogenated oils have higher melting points so they are solids at room temperature, making them useful as spreads and in cakes and pastries. [C1.6.3 b)] [HT only]

Controlled Assessment: SA4.1 Planning an investigation. [SA4.1.1 b)]

Lesson structure

Starters

Stand-by – Put the key words: 'saturated' and 'unsaturated' onto two large pieces of paper and pin them at opposite sides of the room. Read out different examples of chemicals. Students should decide whether they are saturated or unsaturated and stand by the appropriate sign, for instance alkenes [unsaturated], alkanes [saturated], ethene [unsaturated], propane [saturated], octane [saturated]. *(5 minutes)*

Thermometer – Draw a thermometer on the board. Draw two lines to divide it approximately into thirds. Ask the students to label the states of matter, label the state change points and give the changes that occur to the organisation of particles at each state change. You could support students by using a familiar substance – water – to illustrate how the state of the substance relates to the melting point and boiling point. You could extend students by giving them the melting point and freezing point of different saturated and unsaturated fats and asking them to suggest the state at a particular temperature. *(10 minutes)*

Main

- When foods are cooked at different temperatures they have different flavours, appearances, smells and nutritional content. Students could compare potatoes that have been prepared in different ways. Encourage the students to design their own results table to record their observations. Support students by allowing them to copy a previously prepared one.
- Students taking the higher paper need to know the processes involved in creating a spread from an oil and the reasons why this is done. Split students into small groups and ask them to imagine that they are going to produce a short feature, as part of a TV programme about how food is manufactured. Give students ideas. For example, interview a chemical engineer at the oil plant. Students could then make a storyboard to show what would happen in each scene and the information that would be given. **[HT only]**
- Students could investigate the degree of saturation in a variety of oils using bromine water. 'How Science Works' concepts of fair testing and measurement can be practised. Some might try a colorimeter or a light sensor and data logger to get quantitative data on how much bromine remains after reaction with the oils. A little ethanol will help the oil and aqueous layers to mix for the test.

Plenaries

Objectives – Ask students to answer the questions posed by the objectives. You could support the students by encouraging them to work in small groups to craft their answers. You could extend them by asking them to illustrate their answers with examples. *(5 minutes)*

Question loop – Small pieces of paper are given to each student. They write a question and its answer. They then separate the question from the answer and all the papers are collected and shuffled. Each student is then given a question and an answer. The first student reads the question. The student with the correct answer reads their answer, then his or her own question and so on. *(10 minutes)*

Practical support

Investigating cooking
Equipment and materials required

Raw potato cores, boiled potato cores, fried potato cores, mounted needle, magnifying glass, cooker, chip pan, cooking oil, saucepan, water, stopwatch, knife.

Details

Ask the students to study the appearance of the three different samples, using the magnifying glass. They should note the colour and smell. Then, using a mounted needle, they can scratch the surface and comment on the textures.

Students should carefully cook the potato cores in cooking oil (this may be completed as a demonstration because boiling oil can be dangerous) and boiling water. They should time how long it takes for each. They could repeat the test three times to gain an average, or pool the class results in order. The subjectivity of 'the time to cook' can be discussed. Once the potatoes have been cooked, they could

be tasted (but not in the laboratory), and students could comment on their different taste and texture in the mouth due to the cooking conditions. Alternatively, the potato cores can be cooked in oil and in water for equal lengths of time, allowed to cool and then tested.

Safety: Know how to extinguish a fat fire. If tasting, move to food technology room.

Comparing oils for degree of unsaturation
Equipment and materials required

Bromine water, variety of plant oils, ethanol, test tubes, bungs, dropping pipettes (possibly colorimeter, light sensor, data logging equipment), eye protection.

Details

Mix the oil and bromine water. Stopper and shake. Judge amount of decolourisation.

Safety: CLEAPSS Hazcard 15B Bromine water – irritant and harmful; 40A Ethanol – highly flammable and harmful. No naked flames.

Plant oils

Cooking with vegetable oils

C1 6.2 — Cooking with vegetable oils

Learning objectives

- What are the advantages and disadvantages of cooking with vegetable oils?
- What does it mean when we 'harden' vegetable oils? [H]
- How do we turn vegetable oils into spreads? [H]

When we cook food we heat it to a temperature where chemical reactions cause permanent changes to happen to the food. Cooking food in vegetable oil gives very different results to cooking food in water. This is because the boiling points of vegetable oils are much higher than the boiling point of water. Therefore, vegetable oils can be used at a much higher temperature than boiling water.

What's the difference?

So the chemical reactions that take place in the food are very different in oil and in water. When we cook using vegetable oil:

- the food cooks more quickly
- very often the outside of the food turns a different colour, and becomes crispier
- the inside of the food should be softer if you don't cook it for too long.

a How does the boiling point of a vegetable oil compare to the boiling point of water?

Cooking food in oil also means that the food absorbs some of the oil. As you know, vegetable oils contain a lot of energy. This can make the energy content of fried food much higher than that of the same food cooked by boiling it in water. This is one reason why regularly eating too much fried food is unhealthy.

Figure 1 An electric fryer like this one enables vegetable oil to be heated safely to a high temperature

Figure 2 Boiled potatoes and fried potatoes are very different. One thing that probably makes chips so tasty is the contrast of crispy outside and soft inside, together with the different smell and taste produced by cooking at a higher temperature. The different colour may be important too as golden chips look more appetising than a pale boiled potato.

Practical

Investigating cooking

Compare the texture and appearance of potato pieces after equal cooking times in water and oil.

You might also compare the cooking times for boiling, frying and oven-baking chips.

If possible carry out some taste tests in hygienic conditions.

AQA Examiner's tip

No chemical bonds are broken when vegetable oils melt or boil – these are physical changes.

b How is food cooked in oil different to food cooked in water?

Hardening unsaturated vegetable oils [k]

Unsaturated vegetable oils are usually liquids at room temperature.

The boiling and melting points of these oils can be increased by adding hydrogen to the molecules. The reaction replaces some or all of the carbon–carbon double bonds with carbon–carbon single bonds.

With this higher melting point, the liquid oil becomes a solid at room temperature. We call changing a vegetable oil like this hardening it. We harden a vegetable oil by reacting it with hydrogen gas (H_2). To make the reaction happen, we must use a nickel catalyst, and carry it out at about 60 °C.

$$-C=C- \xrightarrow[60°C]{Nickel} -C-C-$$

Figure 3 The hydrogen adds to the carbon–carbon double bonds in a vegetable oil when it is hardened and this can be used to make margarine

c What do we call it when we add hydrogen to a vegetable oil?

Oils that we have treated like this are sometimes called hydrogenated oils. They are solids at room temperature. This means that they can be made into spreads to be put on bread. We can also use them to make cakes, biscuits and pastry.

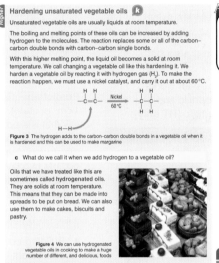

Figure 4 We can use hydrogenated vegetable oils in cooking to make a huge number of different, and delicious, foods

AQA Examiner's tip

When oils are hardened with hydrogen, a chemical change takes place, producing hydrogenated oils (which have a higher melting point than the original oil). These are used in margarines.

Summary questions

1 Copy and complete using the words below:
water energy higher tastes
The boiling points of vegetable oils are .... than the boiling point of water. This means that food cooked in oil .... different to food boiled in .... It also contains more ....

2 Copy and complete using the words below:
hydrogen hydrogenated hardening melting nickel
The .... points of oils may also be raised by adding .... to their molecules. We call this .... the oil. The reaction takes place at 60 °C in the presence of a .... catalyst. The reaction produces a .... oil. [H]

3 a Why are hydrogenated vegetable oils more useful than oils that have not been hydrogenated? [H]
   b Explain how we harden vegetable oils. [H]

Key points

- Vegetable oils are useful in cooking because of their high boiling points. However, this increases the energy content of foods compared with cooking in boiling water.
- Vegetable oils are hardened by reacting them with hydrogen to increase their melting points. This makes them solids at room temperature which are suitable for spreading. [H]
- The hardening reaction takes place at 60 °C with a nickel catalyst. The hydrogen adds onto C = C bonds in the vegetable oil molecules. [H]

198 / 199

Further teaching suggestions

Comparing nutritional information

- Give students the nutritional information for different potato products. Ask them to draw a graph to compare their fat/calorie contents.

Displaying data

- Ask students to find out the boiling points of different fats used in cooking and to show this information in an appropriate diagram, e.g. a bar chart. You can extend students by plotting a line graph comparing molecular mass to the boiling point and determining the trend.

Flow chart

- Students could summarise the hydrogenation of fats in a flow chart format. Give students outline of the flow chart with prose, and the students could then draw a picture for each stage below the text.

Answers to in-text questions

a The boiling point of vegetable oils is much higher.

b Food cooked in oil cooks more quickly. The outside often turns a different colour and becomes crisper. The food absorbs some of the oil, which increases its energy content.

c hardening

Summary answers

1 higher, tastes, water, energy

2 melting, hydrogen, hardening, nickel, hydrogenated

3 a They have a higher melting point and can be used to make spreadable solids at room temperature.
   b Heat the oil and hydrogen at 60 °C with a nickel catalyst.

C1 6.3

Everyday emulsions

Learning objectives

Students should learn:

- what emulsions are and how they are made
- that emulsions made from vegetable oils have many uses
- that emulsifiers keep the oil and water mixed together in an emulsion
- how an emulsifier works. [HT only]

Learning outcomes

Most students should be able to:

- describe what an emulsion is
- give an example of an emulsion
- describe what an emulsifier is.

Some students should also be able to:

- explain how an emulsifier works in terms of its hydrophilic and hydrophobic properties. [HT only]

Support

- Some students would probably benefit from being reminded of the parts of the microscope before using the equipment to look at everyday emulsions. Provide these students with a diagram of a microscope and ask them to label the key parts. You could turn this into a kinaesthetic activity by giving each pair of students a microscope and reading out the parts while the students point to them.

Extend

- You could extend students by telling them that emulsions are part of a group of mixtures called 'colloids'. These students could then be encouraged to define and give examples of other colloids, e.g. sol, gel, foam.
- Give students a diagram of an emulsifier and ask them to annotate it using the key words 'hydrophilic' and 'hydrophobic'. Students should then use this diagram to explain how an emulsifier works.

AQA Specification link-up: Chemistry C1.6

- Oils do not dissolve in water. They can be used to produce emulsions. Emulsions are thicker than oil or water and have many uses that depend on their special properties. They provide better texture, coating ability and appearance, for example in salad dressings, ice creams, cosmetics and paints. *[C1.6.2 a)]*
- Emulsifiers have hydrophilic and hydrophobic properties. *[C1.6.2 b)]* **[HT only]**

  Controlled Assessment: SA4.3 Collect primary and secondary data. *[SA4.3.2 a) b) c)]*

Lesson structure

Starters

Order – Split the students into groups of six. Give each group a set of cards. Each card should be labelled with one of the following: 'whole milk', 'Jersey milk', 'skimmed milk', 'semi-skimmed milk', 'whole goat milk' and 'semi-skimmed goat milk'. On the back of each card, have the nutritional information for that type of milk. Ask the students to line up in order of the most to the least fat content. [The order should be: Jersey milk, whole milk, whole goat milk, semi-skimmed milk, semi-skimmed goat milk.] Introduce the idea that milk is an emulsion. *(5 minutes)*

Prediction – Give each student a bung and a test tube with water and oil in it (about 1 cm³ of each). Ask the students how you could make the oil and water mix. Some might say that it is possible to shake it. Encourage the class to make a prediction as to what will happen. Then let the students shake their tubes and allow them time to observe. Ask the students what has happened [the oil and water mix at first but eventually separate out into two layers again]. Ask the students to think of a way of keeping oil and water mixed. Encourage them to think about doing the washing up or clothes washing, i.e. what happens to the fat from plates or on clothes? *(10 minutes)*

Main

- Building on the Starter, 'Prediction', allow students to test the effects of using different emulsifiers to find out which is the most effective. Ask the class to reach a consensus about what the control variables, independent variable and dependant variables are and how they will record their results.
- Students come into contact with many emulsions in everyday life. One of the most common is milk, which is fat suspended in water. Ask the students what type of fat is in milk [animal fat and therefore saturated]. Students could make wet slides of different types of milk to see the different emulsions using a microscope. Students could record their results in the form of a diagram, but they should also work out the magnification on the microscope (eye lens × object lens).
- Students could make another common emulsion – mayonnaise. If you can spare a lesson, a room swap can be completed into a food technology room, the students could take the mayonnaise home. Ask the students to try to identify the emulsifier in this mixture [egg yolk].
- Then students doing the Higher Tier paper can use the key words hydrophobic, hydrophilic, emulsifier and emulsion, to explain how mayonnaise is made. **[HT only]**

Plenaries

List – Ask students to list as many emulsions as they can. [For example, salad dressing, mayonnaise, salad cream, milk, ice cream, paint.] Students could be supported by being shown a selection of photographs, all of which are emulsions. Students could be extended by being asked to explain why emulsion paint is both an emulsion and a suspension. [It is a suspension of a solid (pigment) and liquid (resin). The resin is an emulsion of resin in water.] *(5 minutes)*

Label the emulsifier – Give the students a diagram of an emulsifier with its head in water and its tail in oil. Ask students to label the diagram fully using the terms 'hydrophobic' and 'hydrophilic' to explain how an emulsifier works. *(10 minutes)* **[HT only]**

Practical support

Making and testing emulsions
Equipment and materials required

Boiling tube, bung, boiling tube rack, cooking oil, water, selection of liquid detergents with a dropping pipette, selection of detergents and a spatula, eye protection.

Details

Add about a quarter of a boiling tube of cooking oil and water until the boiling tube is half full. Add some detergent and put in the bung. Shake and observe. Repeat for all the different detergents.

Safety: Detergents are irritants and may be corrosive. Wear eye protection and wash hands when the practical is completed.

Making mayonnaise
Equipment and materials required

Eggs, salt, vegetable oil, vinegar, mustard powder, pepper, cooking bowl, hand whisk or fork and teaspoon.

Details

Here is a recipe for mayonnaise. Beat the eggs with a pinch of salt. Add the oil, one or two teaspoons at a time, while continuing to beat the mixture. After some of the oil has been added, add one or two teaspoons of vinegar. Continue to add oil slowly and beat the mixture. Add mustard and pepper to taste.

Safety: If tasting, move to food technology room. Be aware of food allergies and salmonella due to raw egg.

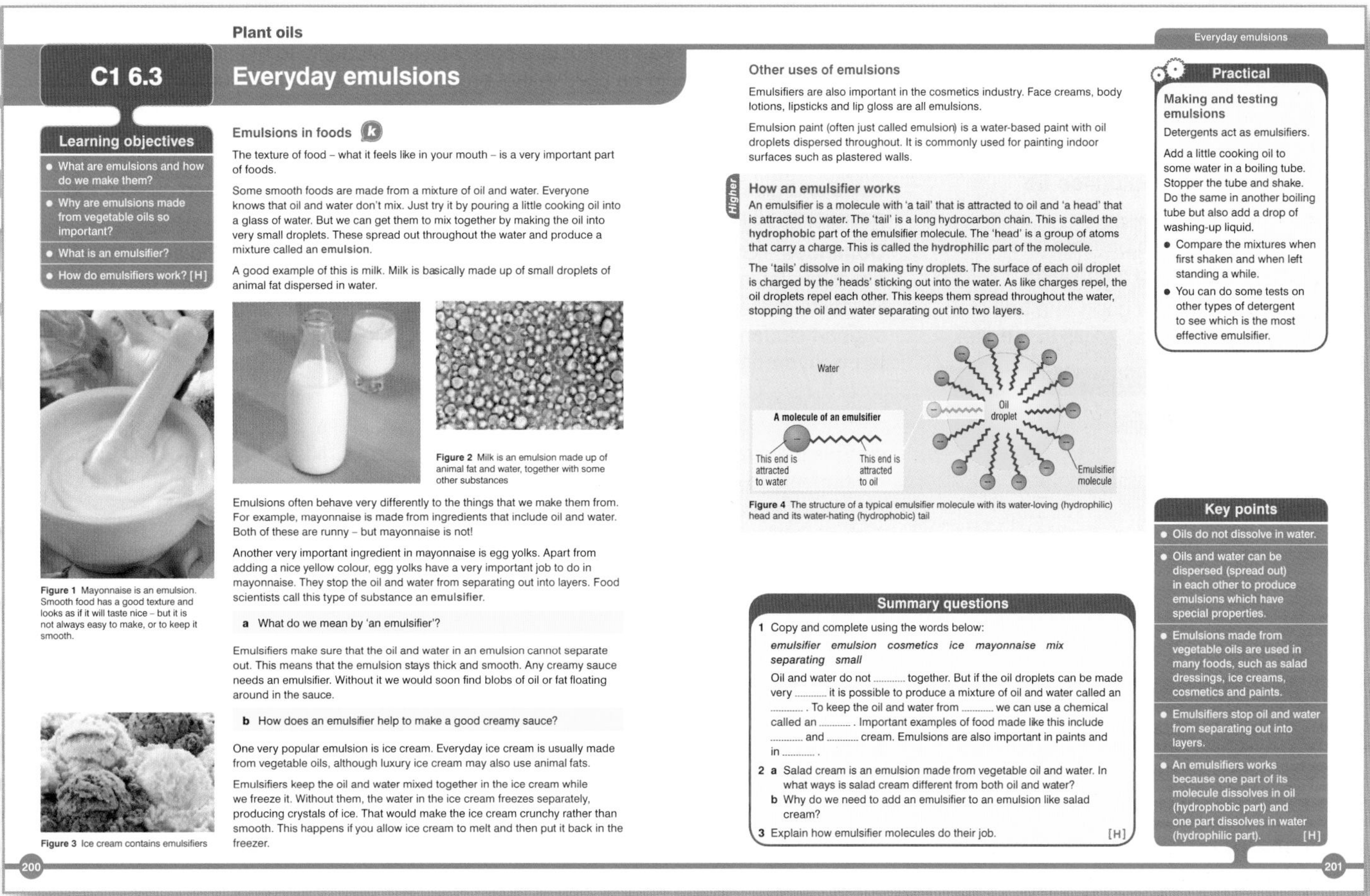

Plant oils

C1 6.3   Everyday emulsions

Everyday emulsions

Learning objectives

- What are emulsions and how do we make them?
- Why are emulsions made from vegetable oils so important?
- What is an emulsifier?
- How do emulsifiers work? [H]

Emulsions in foods

The texture of food – what it feels like in your mouth – is a very important part of foods.

Some smooth foods are made from a mixture of oil and water. Everyone knows that oil and water don't mix. Just try it by pouring a little cooking oil into a glass of water. But we can get them to mix together by making the oil into very small droplets. These spread out throughout the water and produce a mixture called an emulsion.

A good example of this is milk. Milk is basically made up of small droplets of animal fat dispersed in water.

Figure 1 Mayonnaise is an emulsion. Smooth food has a good texture and looks as if it will taste nice – but it is not always easy to make, or to keep it smooth.

Figure 2 Milk is an emulsion made up of animal fat and water, together with some other substances

Emulsions often behave very differently to the things that we make them from. For example, mayonnaise is made from ingredients that include oil and water. Both of these are runny – but mayonnaise is not!

Another very important ingredient in mayonnaise is egg yolks. Apart from adding a nice yellow colour, egg yolks have a very important job to do in mayonnaise. They stop the oil and water from separating out into layers. Food scientists call this type of substance an emulsifier.

a What do we mean by 'an emulsifier'?

Emulsifiers make sure that the oil and water in an emulsion cannot separate out. This means that the emulsion stays thick and smooth. Any creamy sauce needs an emulsifier. Without it we would soon find blobs of oil or fat floating around in the sauce.

b How does an emulsifier help to make a good creamy sauce?

One very popular emulsion is ice cream. Everyday ice cream is usually made from vegetable oils, although luxury ice cream may also use animal fats.

Emulsifiers keep the oil and water mixed together in the ice cream while we freeze it. Without them, the water in the ice cream freezes separately, producing crystals of ice. That would make the ice cream crunchy rather than smooth. This happens if you allow ice cream to melt and then put it back in the freezer.

Figure 3 Ice cream contains emulsifiers

Other uses of emulsions

Emulsifiers are also important in the cosmetics industry. Face creams, body lotions, lipsticks and lip gloss are all emulsions.

Emulsion paint (often just called emulsion) is a water-based paint with oil droplets dispersed throughout. It is commonly used for painting indoor surfaces such as plastered walls.

How an emulsifier works (Higher)

An emulsifier is a molecule with 'a tail' that is attracted to oil and 'a head' that is attracted to water. The 'tail' is a long hydrocarbon chain. This is called the hydrophobic part of the emulsifier molecule. The 'head' is a group of atoms that carry a charge. This is called the hydrophilic part of the molecule.

The 'tails' dissolve in oil making tiny droplets. The surface of each oil droplet is charged by the 'heads' sticking out into the water. As like charges repel, the oil droplets repel each other. This keeps them spread throughout the water, stopping the oil and water separating out into two layers.

Figure 4 The structure of a typical emulsifier molecule with its water-loving (hydrophilic) head and its water-hating (hydrophobic) tail

Summary questions

1 Copy and complete using the words below:

emulsifier emulsion cosmetics ice mayonnaise mix separating small

Oil and water do not .... together. But if the oil droplets can be made very .... it is possible to produce a mixture of oil and water called an .... To keep the oil and water from .... we can use a chemical called an .... Important examples of food made like this include .... and .... cream. Emulsions are also important in paints and in ....

2 a Salad cream is an emulsion made from vegetable oil and water. In what ways is salad cream different from both oil and water?
  b Why do we need to add an emulsifier to an emulsion like salad cream?

3 Explain how emulsifier molecules do their job. [H]

Practical

Making and testing emulsions

Detergents act as emulsifiers.

Add a little cooking oil to some water in a boiling tube. Stopper the tube and shake. Do the same in another boiling tube but also add a drop of washing-up liquid.

- Compare the mixtures when first shaken and when left standing a while.
- You can do some tests on other types of detergent to see which is the most effective emulsifier.

Key points

- Oils do not dissolve in water.
- Oils and water can be dispersed (spread out) in each other to produce emulsions which have special properties.
- Emulsions made from vegetable oils are used in many foods, such as salad dressings, ice creams, cosmetics and paints.
- Emulsifiers stop oil and water from separating out into layers.
- An emulsifiers works because one part of its molecule dissolves in oil (hydrophobic part) and one part dissolves in water (hydrophilic part). [H]

Further teaching suggestions

Milk taste test

- The different types of milk could be purchased and the students could taste them in a food technology room or outside the laboratory to see what difference fat makes to the milk (be aware of lactose-intolerant students).

Ice cream is an emulsion too!

- If there is access to an ice-cream machine, then this emulsion could also be made.

Flexicam

- If microscopes are limited, then by connecting a flexicam to the head of the microscope the image of the different milk emulsions could then be projected or shown on a TV screen.

Answers to in-text questions

a A substance that stops oil and water separating out into layers.

b It keeps the sauce thick and smooth.

Summary answers

1 mix, small, emulsion, separating, emulsifier, mayonnaise, ice, cosmetics

2 **a** Salad cream is thick (viscous) and is not transparent.
  b To prevent the oil and water in the emulsion from separating out into layers.

3 The 'tails' of the emulsifier molecules dissolve into the oil, leaving 'heads' of the molecules lining the surface of the oil droplet. These droplets then repel each other and remain spread throughout the water.

C1 6.4

Food issues

AQA
Specification link-up: Chemistry C1.6
- Evaluate the effects of using vegetable oils in foods and the impacts on diet and health. [C1.6]
- Evaluate the use, benefits, drawbacks and risks of emulsifiers in foods. [C1.6]

Learning objectives

Students should learn:

- the benefits and drawbacks of using emulsifiers
- the advantages and disadvantages of using vegetable oils in our diet.

Learning outcomes

Most students should be able to:

- state one benefit and one drawback of using emulsifiers
- state one benefit and one drawback of eating vegetable oils.

Some students should also be able to:

- explain in detail the benefits and drawbacks of using emulsifiers
- explain in detail the good and bad points about vegetable oils in our diet.

Lesson structure

Starters

Food packaging – Give each student a piece of food packaging with an emulsifier on the ingredients label, for example custard pots. Ask the students to highlight the emulsifier and explain why it would be used in that product. You may wish to support students by giving them a selection of cards with common emulsifiers – e.g. egg yolk, lectins and E400 – and detail why they would be used in specific examples of food that match with the packaging that has been given out. You could extend students by asking them to name and give the E number (if applicable) for all the emulsifiers detailed on their food packaging. *(5 minutes)*

Dominoes – Give the students a card sort with the key words: 'food additive, emulsifier, emulsion, fat, and vegetable oil' written on it. Each card should also have a definition. Students should work in pairs to match the ends up, as in a domino game. You could support students by giving them a glossary. You could extend students by including the terms 'hydrophilic' and 'hydrophobic'. *(10 minutes)*

Main

- Split the class into two groups and give each group a different task. Ask half of the students to design and make a leaflet to be put in supermarkets to explain what emulsifiers are and why you might want to add them to your cooking.
- The remaining students should design a leaflet to be put in a pharmacy. The leaflet should explain why vegetable oils are an important part of our diet, but also the negative effects of eating too much of them.
- Pair students with the two different styles of leaflet (emulsifiers and vegetable oils). Ask each student to read his or her partner's work, then to decide if emulsifiers and vegetable fats are on balance a good or bad addition to our diet. This could be extended into a debate.
- Vegetable oils are a useful part of our diet as they provide energy and nutrients. Allow students to choose which activity from the 'Food for thought' feature they would like to complete about the advantages and disadvantages of eating vegetable oils.

Support

- Students may need some help in forming arguments. You could supply facts about additives or consumption of vegetable fats and encourage them to sort the statements into pros and cons. This will help them to order their thoughts and to construct an argument. You may wish to provide the students with a writing frame to help them structure their article, poster or script.

Plenaries

AfL (Assessment for Learning) – Put the students leaflets, posters, scripts or articles around the room. Ask each student to 'visit' three pieces of work and use the school marking policy to assess the work. Ensure that each student also writes a constructive comment. Ask the 'owners' of the work to review what has been written and write a comment of their own. You could support students by giving them a 'level ladder' to help focus their assessment and some statements that they might want to include in their comment. You could stretch students by asking them to take their work home and action the comments and any more ideas they have to improve their work further. *(10 minutes)*

Reflection – Ask the students to think about one thing that they have learned today and one thing that they have revised. These could be facts or skills. Ask a selection of students to share their thoughts with the rest of the class. *(5 minutes)*

Extend

- Students could be extended by being asked to complete the 'food for thought' activity three times. They could write an argument for the use of vegetable fats, a case against their use and a balanced piece. In this way, students will consider how some facts are stressed for persuasive purposes.

Further teaching suggestions

Food scares

- In recent years, there have been a number of food scares involving fats in our diet, e.g. trans fats made during the hardening of unsaturated fats. Students could look into these using the internet (e.g. search newspaper websites for 'food scare') and newspaper clippings kept in the school library. They could look at the economic and social effect of scares such as this and the impact on the British food industry.

Natural/unnatural

- Ask students to make a table to list some common examples of natural emulsifiers, for example egg yolk and synthetic emulsifiers, e.g. polyoxyethylene(8) stearate. Then ask students to consider the advantages and disadvantages of natural and synthetic emulsifiers. Some will be common for both. For example, an advantage of both is that they keep emulsions stable. Others will be particular to one class of emulsifiers. For instance, a disadvantage of synthetic emulsifiers is that people do not want to eat 'unnatural' chemicals.

How Science Works **Plant oils**

C1 6.4 Food issues

Learning objectives

- What are the benefits and drawbacks of using emulsifiers in our food?
- What are the good and bad points about vegetable oils in our food?

Figure 1 Modern foods contain a variety of additives to improve their taste, texture or appearance, and to give them a longer shelf-life

links

For information on how an emulsifier works, look back at C1 6.3 Everyday emulsions.

Emulsifying additives

For hundreds of years we have added substances like salt or vinegar to food to help keep it longer. As our knowledge of chemistry has increased we have used other substances too, to make food look or taste better.

We call a substance that is added to food to preserve it or to improve its taste, texture or appearance a food additive. Additives that have been approved for use in Europe are given E numbers. These can be used to identify them.

a What is a food additive?

Each group of additives is given a range of E numbers. These tell us what kind of additive it is. Emulsifiers are usually given E numbers in the range 400 to 500, along with stabilisers and thickeners.

E number	Additive	What the additive does	Example
E4 _ _	emulsifiers, stabilisers and thickeners	Help to improve the texture of the food – what it feels like in your mouth. Many foods contain these additives, for example, jam and the soya proteins used in veggie burgers.	E440 – pectin

Emulsifiers stop oil and water separating out into two layers. This means that emulsifiers make it less obvious that foods are rich in oil or fat. Chocolate is a good example. The cocoa butter, which has a high energy content, is usually mixed in well, often with the help of emulsifiers. However, have you ever left a bar of chocolate past its sell-by date? Then you can see a white haze on the surface of the chocolate. This is the fatty butter starting to separate out. Then most people will throw the bar away.

So emulsifiers make oil and fat more edible in foods. They can make a mixture that is creamier and thicker in texture than either oil or water. This makes it easier and more tempting for us to eat too much fatty food.

a  b

Figure 2 Which is more appetising – mayonnaise with emulsifier (**a**) or mayonnaise without emulsifier (**b**)?

Vegetable oils in our diet

Everyone knows the benefits of a healthy diet. But do you know the benefits of ensuring that you eat vegetable oils as part of your diet?

Scientists have found that eating vegetable oils instead of animal fats can do wonders for the health of your heart. The saturated fats you find in things like butter and cheese can make the blood vessels of your heart become clogged up.

However, the unsaturated fats in vegetable oils (like olive oil and corn oil) are very good for you. They are a source of nutrients such as vitamin E. They also help to keep your arteries clear and reduce the chance of you having heart disease. The levels of a special fat called cholesterol in your blood give doctors an idea about your risk of heart disease. People who eat vegetable oils rather than animal fats tend to have a much lower level of 'bad' cholesterol in their blood.

b Name a vitamin that we get from olive oil.

The fats used to cook chips and other fast foods often contain certain fats that are not good for us. Scientists are concerned that eating these fats might have caused an increase in heart disease.

Changes in food labelling are very important. But many products, including fast foods, often contain high levels of potentially harmful fats from the oil they were cooked in. Yet these are exempt from labelling regulations and may be advertised as 'cholesterol-free' and 'cooked in vegetable oil'.

Figure 3 Butter contains saturated fats which raise health concerns

Figure 4 Chips have a high energy content and may contain potentially harmful fats from cooking oil

Activity

Food for thought

1 Write an article for a family lifestyle magazine about 'Feeding your family'. Include in this article reasons for including vegetable oils in a balanced diet and their effect on people's health.
2 Design a poster with the title 'Vegetable oils – good or bad'?
3 Write the script for a two-minute slot on local radio about the benefits and drawbacks of using emulsifiers in foods.

Summary questions

1 Draw a table to summarise the advantages and disadvantages of vegetable oils in our diet.
2 **a** Give a list of five foods that can contain emulsifiers as additives.
  b Why could it be said that emulsifiers have played a role in increasing childhood obesity rates?

Key points

- Vegetable oils are high in energy and provide nutrients. They are unsaturated and believed to be better for your health than saturated animal fats and hydrogenated vegetable oils.
- Emulsifiers improve the texture of foods enabling water and oil to mix. This makes fatty foods more palatable and tempting to eat.

Answers to in-text questions

a A substance that is added to food to make it keep longer or to improve its taste or appearance.

b vitamin E

Summary answers

1

Advantages of vegetable oils	Disadvantages of vegetable oils
Contain nutrients such as vitamin E. Have a high energy value to provide plenty of energy for exercise. Higher in unsaturated fats which protect against heart disease.	Have a high energy value which can turn to fat if you do not do enough exercise. Hydrogenated vegetable oils contain trans-fat, which has been associated with heart disease.

2 **a** For example, ice cream, chocolate, mayonnaise, salad cream, yoghurt.

  b Emulsifiers enable oil and fats to be mixed in watery solutions without separating out to give an oily layer on top or blobs of fat. They can make foods creamier and thicker in texture which result in them being more tempting to eat.

Summary answers

1 a Substances produced by plants containing long hydrocarbon chains.

b Oils containing one or more C=C bonds.

c Oils containing as much hydrogen as possible in which there are no C=C bonds.

d A mixture of liquids that do not dissolve into each other.

e A substance that enables liquids that do not dissolve into each other to remain mixed without separating out into layers.

2 a Bromine water (which is yellow/orange) reacts with C=C bonds when the vegetable oil is unsaturated. When partial hydrogenation takes place, there are still some C=C bonds left but not as many, so it takes longer to decolourise the bromine water. Once it has been completely hardened, the oil is saturated; there are no C=C bonds, so no reaction occurs.

b Hardening plant oils increases their melting point, making them into a more solid/waxy smooth paste, which is spreadable.

c Heat the plant oil and hydrogen to 60 °C with a nickel catalyst.

3 The same-sized potato will cook quicker in boiling oil than in boiling water. Very often the outside of the food turns a different colour when cooked at the higher temperature of the boiling oil, and becomes crispier. Inside the crispy coating, the potato is soft and 'fluffy'. A boiled potato is paler in colour. Cooking food in oil also means that the food absorbs some of the oil. This makes the energy content of food cooked in oil much higher than that of the same food cooked by boiling it in water.

4 a The ice cream emulsion has separated, so that there are parts of the mixture which contain pure water instead of water with droplets of fat in it. When the mixture is refrozen the water freezes and forms ice that is 'crunchy' when compared to the frozen emulsion.

b To prevent the emulsion from separating out/keep it mixed.

c egg yolk

5

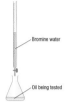

Water

Oil droplet

A molecule of an emulsifier

This end is attracted to water

This end is attracted to oil

Emulsifier molecule

6 a In its use in making biodiesel fuel.

b In its use as a method to cook foods: some of the oil is absorbed by food during cooking.

7 a So that the results could be compared. The instructions acted as a control. Bromine water is also hazardous.

b Controls that should have been included in the instructions:
  • The amount of oil used
  • How the bromine water was added
  • What to look for as an end point.

c There are no anomalies. The variation in results is to be expected.

Summary questions

1 Write simple definitions for the following words:
  a vegetable oils
  b unsaturated oils
  c saturated oils
  d emulsion
  e emulsifier.

2 a A vegetable oil removes the colour from bromine water.

It takes longer to decolourise the bromine water when the vegetable oil is partially hydrogenated.

When the vegetable oil has been completely hardened it does not react with bromine water.

Explain these observations.

b Explain why plant oils need to be hardened and the effect this has on the melting point of the oil. [H]

c Give the conditions for the reaction between a plant oil and hydrogen. [H]

3 Compare the cooking of a potato in boiling water and in vegetable oil.

4 a Some ice cream is left standing out on a table during a meal on a hot day. It is then put back in the freezer again. When it is taken out of the freezer a few days later, people complain that the ice cream tastes 'crunchy'. Why is this?

b A recipe for making ice cream says: 'Stir the ice cream from time to time while it is freezing'. Why must you stir ice cream when freezing homemade ice cream?

c Look at this list of ingredients for making ice cream:
  8 large egg yolks
  $\frac{3}{4}$ cup of sugar
  $2\frac{1}{2}$ cups of whipping cream
  $1\frac{1}{2}$ cups cold milk
  1 vanilla pod

Which ingredient acts as an emulsifier in the mixture?

5 Draw a diagram of the structure of a typical emulsifier. [H]

6 State a use of vegetable oils where their high energy content is:
  a an advantage.
  b a disadvantage.

7 A teacher decided that her class should do a sur of different cooking oils to find out the degree of unsaturated oils present in them. She chose five oils and divided them among her students. This a each oil to be done twice, by two different groups were given strict instructions as to how to do the t

Bromine water was added to each oil from a bure volume added before the mixture in the conical fl no longer colourless was noted.

Bromine water

Oil being tested

The results are in this table.

Type of oil	Amount of bromine water a (cm³)	
	Group 1	Grou
Ollio	24.2	23.9
Soleo	17.8	18.0
Spreo	7.9	8.
Torneo	13.0	12.9
Margeo	17.9	17.4

a Why was it important that the teacher gave stri instructions to all of the groups on how to carry tests?

b List some control variables that should have be included in the instructions.

c Are there any anomalous results? How did you decide?

d What evidence is there in the results that indica they are reproducible?

e How might the accuracy be checked?

f How would you present these results on a grap Explain your answer.

---

d The repeats are very close to each other and they have been done by two different groups.

e Accuracy could be further increased or checked by obtaining data from the manufacturers or doing a third titration.

f Results are best presented as a bar graph of mean volume of bromine water added for each oil type. This is done as the independent variable (type of oil) is categoric.

Kerboodle resources

Resources available for this chapter on Kerboodle are:
  ● Chapter map: Plant oils
  ● How Science Works: Plant oils – food for thought (C1 6.1)
  ● Support: Boiled or fried (C1 6.2)
  ● Extension: Making margarine (C1 6.2)
  ● Bump up your grade: Making oil and water mix (C1 6.3)
  ● How Science Works: It's no yolk when you're a compulsive emulsive (C1 6.3)
  ● Practical: Making mayonnaise (C1 6.3)
  ● Interactive activity: Plant oils
  ● Revision podcast: Vegetable fat and our diet
  ● Test yourself: Plant oils
  ● On your marks: Cooking with oil
  ● Examination-style questions: Plant oils
  ● Answers to examination-style questions: Plant oils

Examination-style questions 🄺

able oils can be extracted from parts of plants that ch in oils.

se the correct word from the list to complete each nce.

nflower oil is extracted from sunflower ....

ves petals seeds (1)

extract olive oil the olives are crushed and ....

led evaporated pressed (1)

e oil may contain small pieces of solid plant material t can be removed by ....

ndensing distilling filtering (1)

ne oil contains water it can be removed by leaving it stand because oil and water ....

aporate mix separate (1)

nder oil can be extracted from lavender plants by ation.

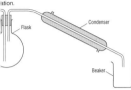

e following steps into the correct order, 1 to 6:

der plants are harvested → 1 → 2 → 3 → 4 → 5 → 6
ender oil is collected.

vender oil and steam are condensed

vender oil separates from water

eam is passed into the flask

vender plants are put into the flask

vender oil and water are collected

vender oil and water evaporate (3)

3 Potatoes cooked in boiling water take about 20 minutes to cook. Potato chips can be cooked in less than 10 minutes by deep frying in hot oil. This is one reason why fast food outlets cook chips rather than potatoes.

  a Explain why chips cook faster in hot oil than in boiling water. (2)

  b Suggest another advantage for fast food outlets to cook chips. (1)

  c Suggest a disadvantage for fast food outlets cooking chips. (1)

  d Suggest an advantage for consumers who eat chips rather than boiled potatoes. (1)

  e Suggest a disadvantage for consumers who eat chips rather than boiled potatoes. (1)

4 a A vegetable oil was shaken with water in flask 1 and with water and an emulsifier in flask 2. The diagrams show the results after leaving the mixtures to stand for 5 minutes.

  a i Give a reason for the result in Flask 1. (1)
     ii Explain the result in Flask 2. (2)

  b Give an example of a product that contains an emulsifier and give **two** ways in which its properties are better than those of the liquids from which it is made. (3)

  c Explain how an emulsifier works. Your answer should include a diagram of a simple model of an emulsifier molecule. [H] (3)

AQA, 2007

205

1 **a** seeds (1 mark)

  b pressed (1 mark)

  c filtering (1 mark)

  d separate (1 mark)

2 In order D→C→F→A→E→B   all correct (3 marks)

Four in correct sequence = 2 marks, three in correct sequence = 1 mark

3 **a** Oil is at higher temperature than (boiling) water, because oil has higher boiling point than water. (2 marks)

  b Any advantage, e.g. people will buy more, people prepared to pay more (than for boiled potatoes) people prefer the taste (to boiled potatoes), easier to handle or wrap. (1 mark)

  c Any disadvantage, e.g. waste oil for disposal (cannot go down drains), dangers of hot oil (including flammability), cost of oil (compared to water). (1 mark)

  d Any advantage for consumer, e.g. easier to handle (can use fingers), stay hot longer, (allow taste better), if unsaturated/vegetable oils – positive impact on health or positive impact on diet e.g. provide more nutrients, provide more energy. (1 mark)

  e Any disadvantage for consumer, e.g. negative impact on diet – more energy/calories/joules/fat/fattening, negative impact on health (if saturated oils/fats), greasy/grease on fingers/clothes. (1 mark)

4 **a** **i** Water and oil do not mix or are immiscible or do not dissolve into each other. (1 mark)

     ii Any two from: forms an emulsion, does not separate, emulsifier keeps oil and water together/mixed, emulsifier stops them separating, (accept description of how an emulsifier works). (2 marks)

  b Named example of product that is an emulsion, e.g. ice cream, salad dressing, cosmetics, paint. Any two improved properties, e.g. better coating ability, appearance, texture. (3 marks)

  c Diagram of emulsifier molecule showing head and tail or two distinct parts.

    Hydrophilic/water–attracting head and hydrophobic/oil attracting tail.

    forms small globules of oil with heads on outside attracted to water or converse for water globules or diagram (3 marks)

AQA Practical suggestions

Practicals	AQA	🄺	📖	⚙
Pressing nuts (e.g. walnuts) between paper towels and studying the grease marks.	✓		✓	
Steam distillation of lavender oil, orange oil, lemon oil, olive oil, rapeseed oil or vegetable oil.	✓		✓	
Simple calorimetery investigations using small spirit burners or bottle tops to measure the energy released from various oils (weigh before and after, and measure the temperature change for a known mass of water).	✓			✓
Making emulsions, e.g. oil/water, oil/vinegar.	✓	✓	✓	
Design and carry out an investigation into the effect of emulsifiers on the stability of emulsions.	✓			✓
Using bromine water to test fats and oils for unsaturation, e.g. testing sunflower oil against butter (using colourimeter to measure level of unsaturation).	✓		✓	

AQA Examiner's tip

Foundation Tier students should know what emulsifiers do and Higher Tier students should be able to give a simple explanation in terms of hydrophobic and hydrophilic parts of molecules. Information about intermolecular forces is in Unit 2 and so only a simple explanation is expected in Unit 1. Students are not expected to know the formulae of fats and oils or emulsifiers. Explore the problems of unsaturation, hydrogenation and hardening of oils. Many students find these terms and ideas difficult.

AQA Examiner's tip

Students are expected to be familiar with methods of extracting oils. They should have seen oils extracted in the laboratory and in video clips of home-based and commercial extractions. They should understand the sequence of steam distillation but are not expected to have been taught the theory of the process other than that the oils evaporate with the steam to produce a mixture that separates when condensed.

AQA Examiner's tip

Many students are given the idea that chips are bad for you. They are an important food. Ask students to write about or discuss the positive as well as the negative aspects of foods cooked in fats and oils, when answering questions about foods cooked in fat or oil.

C1 7.1

Structure of the Earth

Learning objectives

Students should learn:
- the basic structure of the Earth
- the relative size of each layer of the Earth's structure
- where minerals and other resources are found in the Earth's structure.

Learning outcomes

Most students should be able to:
- label the basic structure of the Earth
- describe the relative size of each layer of the Earth's structure
- state where minerals and other resources are found in the Earth's structure.

Some students should also be able to:
- describe how we discovered the Earth's structure.

Support

- You could support students by giving them a diagram of the Earth's structure and labels. They could then complete a 'cut-and-stick' activity to ensure that all the relevant information is correctly positioned.

Extend

- You could extend students by asking them to compare the structure of the Earth with the structure of other planets in our solar system. They could be encouraged to find out if other planets also have layers and if their compositions are similar or different.

AQA Specification link-up: Chemistry C1.7

- The Earth consists of a core, mantle and crust and is surrounded by the atmosphere. [C1.7.1 a]
- Recognise that the Earth's crust, the atmosphere and the oceans are the only source of minerals and other resources that humans need. [C1.7]

Lesson structure
Starters

Citizenship – Write on the board: 'How was the Earth made?' Encourage the students to list as many ideas as they can – scientific, religious and cultural. Then hold a quick discussion about all of these ideas. Explain that scientists have come up with a number of theories using the evidence they have observed although no one can be absolutely certain if any of them are correct. *(5 minutes)*

Brainstorm – Ask the students to think about geography and rocks in science. Ask them to complete a brainstorm about the structure of the Earth in the back of their books. Support students by providing them with a framework for their brainstorm. Extend students by asking them to consider the composition of the atmosphere. Ask one student to be a scribe and write on the board. They could pick students from the class to add ideas to the whole-class brainstorm. *(10 minutes)*

Main

- It is important that the students recognise a diagram of the Earth and that they can label its structure. Ask them to use secondary sources, e.g. the internet (search for 'Earth structure' at www.bbc.co.uk) and the Student Book, to make a poster about the Earth's structure.
- To ensure that students include the relevant information, state that their poster must include at least one diagram, one measurement and the key terms 'core', 'mantle', 'crust' and 'atmosphere'.
- For kinaesthetic and artistic students, a 3-D model of the Earth and its structure could be made, although this may take a couple of lessons to be completed fully.
- The students could use papier mâché to make the model of the Earth. Some students may be allergic to wallpaper paste – cellulose paste can be purchased that does not contain a fungicide. The shell should be cut in half and then decorated to show the Earth and its layers. Small pieces of coloured paper or card could be used to add information about the layers and then stuck to the model. String or thread can then be attached, so the model can be suspended, e.g. from the ceiling.

Plenaries

Label – Give the students a laminated diagram of the Earth's structure. Supply a paper towel and a washable pen. Ask the students to label as much as they can remember on their diagram. Then show them a fully labelled image (which should include a section of the Earth, depth, properties and materials) via a projector or a photocopied sheet. Ask the students to count how many of their labels were correct. *(5 minutes)*

Answers and questions – Give the students answers that are key to this topic. They should put up their hand with a question that matches the answer. Some answers could be 'Earth', 'crust', 'mantle', 'core', 'iron', 'nickel', 'atmosphere'. You could support students by asking them to work in small groups to come up with questions. You could extend them by asking them to produce a 'Foundation Tier' and a 'Higher Tier' question, both of which should have the same answer. Students should think about the choice of language in the questions. You may wish to produce more expansive answers, which would allow students to write questions that use a higher level of Bloom's taxonomy, e.g. questions involving evaluation or explanation. *(10 minutes)*

Further teaching suggestions

Interactive labelling
- An image of the Earth can be placed into interactive whiteboard software and labelled. The labels can be covered with boxes and used as a class quiz exercise.

How old is the Earth?
- Ask students to use secondary sources and find out how old scientists believe the Earth to be [about 4 600 000 000 years old]. You could extend students further by asking them to find out what evidence is used to support this idea.

Our changing planet

C1 7.1   Structure of the Earth

Learning objectives
- What is the structure of the Earth?
- What are the relative sizes of each layer of the Earth's structure?
- In which parts of the Earth's structure are our minerals and other resources found?

How big do you think the Earth is? The deepest mines go down to about 3500 m, while geologists have drilled down to more than 12 000 m in Russia. Although these figures seem large, they are tiny compared with the diameter of the Earth. The Earth's diameter is about 12 800 km. That's more than one thousand times the deepest hole ever drilled!

What's inside? 🅚

The Earth is made up of layers that formed many millions of years ago, early in the history of our planet. Heavy materials sank towards the centre of the Earth while lighter material floated on top. This produced a structure consisting of a dense core, surrounded by the mantle. Outside the mantle there is a thin outer layer called the crust.

Above the Earth's crust we have a thin layer of gases called the **atmosphere**.

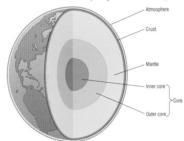

Atmosphere
Crust
Mantle
Inner core
Outer core } Core

Figure 1 The structure of the Earth

The Earth's crust is a very thin layer compared to the diameter of the Earth. Its thickness can vary from as thin as 5 km under the oceans to 70 km under the continents.

Underneath the crust is the mantle. This layer is much, much thicker than the crust. It is nearly 3000 km thick. The mantle behaves like a solid, but it can flow in parts very slowly.

Finally, inside the mantle lies the Earth's core. This is about half the radius of the Earth. It is made of a mixture of the magnetic metals, nickel and iron. The core is actually two layers. The outer core is a liquid, while the inner core is solid.

a What is the solid outer layer of the Earth called?
b What is the next layer down of the Earth called?

Atmosphere	Crust	Mantle	Core
About 80% of the air in our atmosphere lies within 10 km of the surface. (Most of the rest is within 100 km but it is hard to judge exactly where our atmosphere ends and space begins).	The average thickness of the crust is about 6 km under the oceans; about 35 km under continental areas.	Starts underneath crust and continues to about 3000 km below Earth's surface. Behaves like a solid, but is able to flow very slowly.	Radius of about 3500 km. Made of nickel and iron. Outer core is liquid, inner core is solid.

All the minerals and other resources that we depend on in our lives come from the thin crust of the Earth, its oceans and atmosphere. We get all the natural materials we use plus the raw materials for synthetic and processed materials from these sources. There is a limited supply of resources available to us so we should take care to conserve them for future generations.

Figure 2 All the resources that we depend on come from the thin crust of the Earth, its oceans and atmosphere

⚙ How Science Works

Developing scientific ideas from evidence

How do we know the structure inside the Earth if nobody has ever seen it?

Scientists use evidence from earthquakes. Following an earthquake, seismic waves travel through the Earth. The waves are affected by different layers in the Earth's structure. By observing how seismic waves travel, scientists have built up our picture of the inside of the Earth.

Also, by making careful measurements, physicists have been able to measure the mass of the Earth, and to calculate its density. The density of the Earth as a whole is much greater than the density of the rocks found in the crust. This suggests that the centre of the Earth must be made from a different material to the crust. This material must have a much greater density than the material in the crust.

⁇ Did you know …?

The temperature at the centre of the Earth is between 5000°C and 7000°C.

Summary questions

1 Copy and complete using the words below:
core crust mantle slowly solid thin atmosphere

The structure of the Earth consists of three layers – the .... in the centre, then the .... and the outer layer of ...., with the .... above the surface. The outer layer of the Earth is very .... compared to the Earth's diameter. The layer below this is .... but can flow in parts very ....

2 Why do some people think that the mantle is best described as a 'very thick syrupy liquid'?

3 Why should we do our best to conserve the Earth's resources?

Key points
- The Earth consists of a series of layers. Starting from the surface we have the crust, the mantle then the core in the centre. A thin layer of gases called the atmosphere surrounds the Earth.
- The Earth's limited resources come from its crust, the oceans and the atmosphere.

⁇ Did you know …?

It is not possible to measure the temperature of the centre of the Earth directly. The scientifically accepted temperature of up to 7000°C, is based on models of the Earth and experimentation.

Answers to in-text questions
a crust
b mantle

Summary answers

1 core, mantle, crust, atmosphere, thin, solid, slowly

2 It can flow but only very slowly.

3 Because all the raw materials we need come from the crust, oceans and atmosphere and many of them, such as mineral deposits, are non-renewable – once we have used them up they will not be replaced.

C1 7.2

The restless Earth

Learning objectives

Students should learn:

- what tectonic plates are
- why tectonic plates move
- that earthquakes and volcanic eruptions are difficult to predict.

Learning outcomes

Most students should be able to:

- state that the outer layer (crust and the upper part of the mantle) of the Earth is made up of tectonic plates
- state why the tectonic plates move
- list what happens at plate boundaries
- explain why Wegener's ideas on continental drift were not generally accepted in his time
- explain why earthquakes and volcanic activity are difficult to predict.

Some students should also be able to:

- explain in detail how convection currents cause tectonic plates to move.

Support

- To support students you may wish to provide a writing frame and a few websites for students to use for their research into plate boundaries.

Extend

- You could extend students by asking them to think about other convection currents that occur naturally on Earth [winds, ocean currents]. They could apply the same models to show convection currents in mantle to these new situations.

AQA Specification link-up: Chemistry C1.7

- The Earth's crust and the upper part of the mantle are cracked into a number of large pieces (tectonic plates). [C1.7.1 b)]
- Convection currents within the Earth's mantle driven by heat released by natural radioactive processes cause the plates to move at relative speeds of a few centimetres per year. [C1.7.1 c)]
- The movements can be sudden and disastrous. Earthquakes and/or volcanic eruptions occur at the boundaries between tectonic plates. [C1.7.1 d)]
- Explain why Wegener's theory of crustal movement (continental drift) was not generally accepted for many years. [C1.7]
- Explain why scientists cannot accurately predict when earthquakes and volcanic eruptions will occur. [C1.7]

Lesson structure

Starters

Pictionary – Ask for five volunteers. They are each given a key word (crust, atmosphere, mantle, core, Earth). They should draw a picture: no noise, symbols, numbers or text are allowed; the image should explain their key word to the class. The first student in the remainder of the class to guess the word could win a prize. *(5 minutes)*

Card sort – Give the students cards with different theories about how the features on the Earth's surface were created. Start with religious viewpoints, e.g. Creationism, James Dwight Dana (The Contracting Earth), Clarence Dutton (Isostacy), Geological Society of America (Mighty Creeping Movements), Alfred Wegener (plate tectonics/continental drift) and finish with Alexander du Toit (supporter of Wegener). Ask the students to sort them into date order, and guess the dates. You could support students by giving them the century or decade the idea was published. You could extend students by asking them to think about whether scientists definitely now know how features have been created. *(10 minutes)*

Main

- The tectonic plates move on convection currents. Convection currents should have been studied in KS3. However, students may benefit from seeing the convection current demonstration.
- This can be completed as a demonstration or a class practical. Pieces from a polystyrene tile can be floated in larger beakers to model the tectonic plate movement. Discuss the limitations of this model.
- Students could be encouraged to draw a diagram of the experiment and label it (e.g. beaker, potassium manganate(VII), convection current, Bunsen burner) in blue. Then ask students to relate this to the Earth, and label these in red (e.g. mantle, magma, heat spot, tectonic plates).
- Students need to know what happens at plate boundaries and the effects of natural disasters. Show some images of plate boundaries and the destruction caused. Split the class into three groups: one group researches volcanoes, another earthquakes and the third looks at prediction and prevention of damage/loss of life.
- Each group should be supplied with video footage of natural disasters caused by earthquakes and volcanoes, for example http://video.nationalgeographic.com. Search under 'Natural Disasters'. Students then use this information, coupled with textbooks, to write a revision page for an imaginary textbook. The pages could be collected and selected ones photocopied and given to each student to add to their notes.
- Students should appreciate how theories were developed and others disproved. Ask students to imagine that they are Wegener and that they are going to attend an international conference for scientists. They are to have a 'slot' to explain his new theory and explain why previous theories were incorrect. Students should prepare a presentation that is about 3 minutes long.

Plenary

Lava lamps – Set up a lava lamp (this needs to be done at least 30 minutes before the end of the lesson). Ask the students to look at the lava lamp and relate it to the lesson. You should extend students by encouraging them to link the movement in the lava lamp with that which occurs in the mantle of the Earth. You could support students by explaining the link to plate tectonics using separate sentences and asking them to put them in order, working in pairs. *(5 minutes)*

Practical support

Convection currents

Equipment and materials required

Potassium manganate(VII) crystals (oxidising agent and harmful), tweezers, large glass beaker, cold water, Bunsen burner and safety equipment, tripod and gauze, eye protection.

Details

Fill the beaker about 75 per cent with cold water and put onto a tripod. With a set of tweezers, add one potassium manganate(VII) crystal to the bottom of the beaker. Put the Bunsen burner under the beaker at the point where the crystal is and heat on the blue flame. The convection current should become visible.

Safety: CLEAPSS Hazcard 81 Potassium manganate(VII) – oxidising and harmful. Handle carefully, as crystals will stain hands and clothing.

Our changing planet

C1 7.2 The restless Earth

Learning objectives

● What are tectonic plates?
● Why do the plates move?
● Why is it difficult for scientists to predict when earthquakes and volcanic eruptions will occur?

The continents are moving

The map of the world hasn't always looked the way it does today. Look at the map shown in Figure 2. Find the western coastline of Africa and the eastern coastline of South America. Can you see how the edges of the two continents look like they could slot together?

The fossils and rock structures that we find when we look in Africa and South America are also similar. Fossils show that the same reptiles and plants once lived on both continents. Also, the layers of rock in the two continents have been built up in the same sequence.

Scientists now believe that they can explain these facts. They think that the two continents were once joined together as one land mass.

a What evidence is there that Africa and South America were once joined to each other?

Tectonic plates

Of course, the continents moved apart very, very slowly. In fact, they are still moving today, at the rate of a few centimetres each year. They move because the Earth's crust and uppermost part of the mantle is cracked into a number of huge pieces. We call these **tectonic plates**.

Deep within the Earth, radioactive atoms decay, producing vast amounts of energy. This heats up molten minerals in the mantle which expand. They become less dense and rise towards the surface. Cooler material sinks to take their place. Forces created by these **convection currents** move the tectonic plates slowly over the surface of the Earth.

Where the boundaries (edges) of the plates meet, huge stresses build up. These forces make the plates buckle and deform, and mountains may be formed. The plates may also suddenly slip past each other. These sudden movements cause earthquakes.

However, it is difficult for scientists to know exactly where and when the plates will suddenly slip like this.

b What causes an earthquake to occur?

Figure 1 *Mesosaurus* was a reptile that existed million years ago. Its fossils have been found in Africa and in South America.

Key
× Earthquake zones
+ Volcanoes
— Plate boundaries

Figure 2 The distribution of volcanoes and earthquakes around the world largely follows the boundaries of the Earth's tectonic plates

How Science Works

Trying to predict the unpredictable!

Earthquakes and volcanic eruptions can be devastating. But making accurate predictions of when they will take place is difficult. Markers placed across a plate boundary or across the crater of a volcano can be monitored for movement. Scientists also monitor the angles of the slopes on volcanoes. The sides of some volcanoes start to bulge outwards before an eruption. Any abnormal readings can be used as a warning sign.

It has also been found that rocks heat up before earthquakes as a result of extreme compression. So satellites with infrared cameras can monitor the Earth's surface for unexpected rises in temperature. Our ability to predict these natural events, and evacuate people at risk, will improve as advances are made by scientists.

Figure 3 Earthquakes can be devastating to people living close by

How Science Works

Wegener's revolutionary theory

In the past, scientists thought that features like mountain ranges were caused by the crust shrinking as the early molten Earth cooled down. They thought of it rather like the skin on the surface of a bowl of custard. It tends to shrink, then wrinkle, as the custard cools down.

The idea that huge land masses once existed before the continents we know today, was put forward in the late 19th century by the geologist Edward Suess. He thought that a huge southern continent had sunk. He suggested that this left behind a land bridge (since vanished) between Africa and South America.

The idea of continental drift was put forward first by Alfred Wegener in 1915. However, his fellow scientists found Wegener's ideas hard to accept. This was mainly because he could not explain *how* the continents had moved. So they stuck with their existing ideas.

His theory was finally shown to be right almost 50 years later. Scientists found that the sea floor is spreading apart in some places, where molten rock is spewing out between two continents. This led to a new theory, called plate tectonics.

Summary questions

1 Copy and complete using the words below:
   convection earthquakes mantle tectonic volcanoes
   The surface of the Earth is split up into a series of .... plates. These move across the Earth's surface due to .... currents in the .... Where the plates meet and rub against each other, we get .... and ....

2 **a** Explain how tectonic plates move.
   b Why are earthquakes and volcanic eruptions difficult to predict?

3 Imagine that you are a scientist who has just heard Wegener's ideas for the first time. Write a letter to another scientist explaining what Wegener has said and why you have chosen to reject his ideas.

Did you know …?

With the latest GPS (global positioning satellite) technology we can detect movement of tectonic plates down to 1 mm per year.

AQA Examiner's tip

The Earth's tectonic plates are made up of the crust and the upper part of the mantle (not just the crust).

Key points

● The Earth's crust and upper mantle is cracked into a number of massive pieces (tectonic plates) which are constantly moving slowly.

● The motion of the tectonic plates is caused by convection currents in the mantle, due to radioactive decay.

● Earthquakes and volcanoes happen where tectonic plates meet. It is difficult to know when the plates may slip past each other. This makes it difficult to predict accurately when and where earthquakes will happen.

Further teaching suggestions

Role play

● Ask the students to think of questions or arguments that Wegener might have faced from the scientific community. A volunteer or group of volunteers could pretend to be Wegener, then other students could pose their questions/ arguments for Wegener and his team to answer.

Seismologist

● Students could research the job of a seismologist and find out what their 'tools of the trade' are.

Guest speaker

● You may wish to contact your school's geography department and see if there is a geologist who could come into the science classroom as a 'guest' speaker. Allow students to prepare questions and then invite the students to ask the expert.

Did you know …?

The earliest evidence for plate tectonics was discovered in 2002 by US/Chinese scientists. They found rocks near the Great Wall of China that show that plates were moving 2.5 billion years ago – this is about 500 million years earlier than scientists first thought.

Answers to in-text questions

a The similar shapes of their coastlines, similar rock types, similar fossils.

b Tectonic plates suddenly slipping past one another after stress builds up at their boundaries. These sudden movements cause earthquakes.

Summary answers

1 tectonic, convection, mantle, volcanoes (earthquakes), earthquakes (volcanoes)

2 **a** Convection currents, caused by energy from natural radioactive processes, form in the mantle beneath the tectonic plates.
   b Although we know where plate boundaries lie, we cannot tell exactly when and where the forces building up will cause the sudden movement that produces an earthquake or when the magma building up in a volcano will cause an explosive eruption.

3 Letter. [Mark based on ideas from description of Wegener's ideas in the spread.]

C1 7.3 — The Earth's atmosphere in the past

Learning objectives

Students should learn:

- what the Earth's atmosphere was like in the past
- how the mixture of gases in the Earth's atmosphere was produced
- how oxygen was released into the Earth's atmosphere.

Learning outcomes

Most students should be able to:

- name the gases that probably made up the Earth's early atmosphere
- list the major events that formed today's atmosphere
- state how oxygen entered the Earth's atmosphere.

Some students should also be able to:

- explain a theory how the Earth and its atmosphere were formed.

Support

- You could support students by supplying them with images and text to explain the five stages of development of the Earth's atmosphere. They could then cut and stick them into the appropriate cartoon strip boxes.

Extend

- You could extend students by asking them to discover some examples of other theories and ideas used to explain how the atmosphere developed. For example, some scientists disagree about the composition of the gases in the early atmosphere, thinking that there was a greater mix than in the currently scientifically accepted theory. Encourage students to consider what evidence has been collected to support the current main scientifically-accepted theory. Students could think about how this theory could still be refined or what evidence would need to be collected for the theory to be disproved.

Specification link-up: Chemistry C1.7

- During the first billion years of the Earth's existence, there was intense volcanic activity. This activity released the gases that formed the early atmosphere and water vapour that condensed to form the oceans. [C1.7.2 b)]
- There are several theories about how the atmosphere was formed. One theory suggests that during this period the Earth's atmosphere was mainly carbon dioxide and there would have been little or no oxygen gas (like the atmospheres of Mars and Venus today). There may also have been water vapour and small proportions of methane and ammonia. [C1.7.2 c)]
- Plants and algae produced the oxygen that is now in the atmosphere. [C1.7.2 f)]
- Explain and evaluate theories of the changes that have occurred and are occurring in the Earth's atmosphere. [C1.7]

Lesson structure

Starters

Chemical equations – Ask students to copy out the word equation for photosynthesis. Then set them the task of completing the symbol equation. Ask students to explain why this equation is so important. [This chemical reaction is believed to be responsible for putting oxygen into the Earth's atmosphere.] (5 minutes)

Grouping gases – Ask students to list as many gases as they can think of. Then put three titles on the board: 'element', 'compound' and 'mixture'. Encourage each student to go to the board and add a gas from their list under the correct column heading. Look at the board and, if there are any incorrect answers, tell the class how many mistakes there are. Then ask the students to see if they can pick out the errors. You could support students by giving them cards with the name of a gas and a simple particle model of the gas, rather then generating their own list. You could extend them by asking them to write the chemical formula of each gas rather than its name. (10 minutes)

Main

- Give students a cartoon strip with five frames, with space to draw a picture and write notes. Encourage students to use a textbook to detail five stages in the development of the atmosphere. They should draw an image and write text to explain the atmosphere's composition and how it compares to other planets in our solar system.
- Separate the class into groups. Ask the groups to imagine that they are astronauts who have landed on Earth in the different stages of atmospheric development. Ask them to design a sketch or role-play to describe the surroundings. The activity could include a predictive stage in which students consider the atmosphere in 500 years' time.
- Not all students need be involved in the acting side but all students should collect research about the development. This activity could encourage students to manage their own time and group dynamics.
- Alternatively, you could give each student a role, e.g. chair person or resource manager, and encourage the students to stick to their roles, allowing them to experience a different role in a group compared to their preferred choice.
- Groups of students could act out their sketch. The rest of the class comments on misconceptions in the sketch and then votes on the best. A prize could be awarded.

Plenaries

Ordering – Ask the students, in small groups, to arrange a series of key events in the creation of the atmosphere in chronological order. Support them by allowing them access to the Student Book to revise for one minute before they start the task. Extend students by asking them to try to remember the formula of the gases in the atmosphere during the key events. (5 minutes)

Pass it on – Give each group of three students a piece of paper with the same question printed on: 'Where does oxygen come from?' On the piece of paper, the first student starts the answer and is timed for 30 seconds. Then ask the students to pass the paper to their left (even if they are mid-sentence) and give the next student one minute, then pass the paper again and give the final student one-and-a-half minutes. Each student should read the answer so far, change anything that they feel is incorrect and add further information if they think they can. Then pick a few groups to read their papers. (10 minutes)

Further teaching suggestions

Graph work
- Students could display the composition of the Earth's atmosphere at different stages in the form of charts and graphs.

Venus
- Students could contrast the Earth's atmospheric development with that of Venus. Some scientists believe that it has had a runaway greenhouse effect that has caused its current atmosphere.

Pyramid summery
- Give students a pyramid. They should put the main idea at the top (Earth's atmosphere) and draw a line underneath it. Then they write the main points and draw a line. This continues until all the information has been summarised from C1 7.3 in the Student Book.

Our changing planet

C1 7.3

The Earth's atmosphere in the past

Learning objectives
- What was the Earth's atmosphere like in the past?
- How were the gases in the Earth's atmosphere produced?
- How was oxygen produced?

Scientists think that the Earth was formed about 4.5 billion years ago. To begin with it was a molten ball of rock and minerals. For its first billion years it was a very violent place. The Earth's surface was covered with volcanoes belching fire and gases into the atmosphere.

Did you know ...?

Comets could also have brought water to the Earth. As icy comets rained down on the surface of the Earth, they melted, adding to its water supplies. Even today many thousands of tonnes of water fall onto the surface of the Earth from space every year.

Figure 1 Volcanoes moved chemicals from inside the Earth to the surface and the newly forming atmosphere

The Earth's early atmosphere

There are several theories about the Earth's early atmosphere. One suggests that volcanoes released carbon dioxide, water vapour and nitrogen gas and these gases formed the early atmosphere.

The water vapour in the atmosphere condensed as the Earth gradually cooled down, and fell as rain. Water collected in hollows in the crust as the rock solidified and the first oceans were formed.

As the Earth began to stabilise, the atmosphere was probably mainly carbon dioxide. There could also have been some water vapour, and traces of methane and ammonia. There would have been very little or no oxygen at that time. Some scientists believe nitrogen was another gas present at this time.

This is very like the atmospheres which we know exist today on the planets Mars and Venus.

Figure 2 The surface of one of Jupiter's moons, Io, with its active volcanoes releasing gases into its sparse atmosphere. This gives us a reasonable glimpse of what our own Earth was like billions of years ago.

a What was the main gas in the Earth's early atmosphere?
b How much oxygen was there in the Earth's early atmosphere?

After the initial violent years of the history of the Earth, the atmosphere remained quite stable. That is until life first appeared on Earth.

Oxygen in the atmosphere

There are many theories as to how life was formed on Earth billions of years ago. Scientists think that life on Earth began about 3.4 billion years ago. That is when simple organisms similar to bacteria appeared. These could make food for themselves, using the breakdown of other chemicals as a source of energy.

Later, bacteria and other simple organisms, such as algæ, evolved. They could use the energy from the Sun to make their own food by photosynthesis. This produced oxygen gas as a waste product.

By two billion years ago the levels of oxygen were rising steadily as algae and bacteria thrived in the seas. More and more plants evolved. All of them were photosynthesising, removing carbon dioxide and making oxygen.

$$carbon\ dioxide + water \xrightarrow{\text{(energy from sunlight)}} sugar + oxygen$$

As plants evolved, they successfully colonised most of the surface of the Earth. So the atmosphere became richer and richer in oxygen. This made it possible for animals to evolve. These animals could not make their own food and needed oxygen to respire.

On the other hand, many of the earliest living microorganisms could not tolerate a high oxygen concentration (because they had evolved without it). They largely died out, as there were fewer places where they could live.

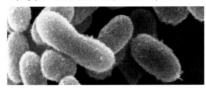

Figure 4 Not only do bacteria such as these not need oxygen – they die if they are exposed to it, but they can survive and breed in rotting tissue and other places where there is no oxygen

Figure 3 Some of the first photosynthesising bacteria probably lived in colonies like these stromatolites. They grew in water and released oxygen into the early atmosphere.

Did you know ...?

Scientists have reconstructed what they think the atmosphere must have been like millions of years ago based on evidence from gas bubbles trapped in ancient rocks. They also use data gathered from the atmospheres of other planets and their moons in the solar system.

Summary questions

1 Copy and complete using the words below:
dioxide methane oxygen volcanoes water
The Earth's early atmosphere probably consisted mainly of the gas carbon .... There could also have been .... vapour and nitrogen, plus small amounts of .... and ammonia. These gases were released by .... as they erupted. Plants removed carbon dioxide from the atmosphere and produced .... gas.

2 Describe how the Earth's early atmosphere was probably formed?

3 Why do scientists believe there was no life on Earth for 1.1 billion years?

4 Draw a chart that explains the early development of the Earth's atmosphere.

Key points
- The Earth's early atmosphere was formed by volcanic activity.
- It probably consisted mainly of carbon dioxide. There may also have been water vapour together with traces of methane and ammonia.
- As plants spread over the Earth, the levels of oxygen in the atmosphere increased.

210

211

Did you know ...?

Ice cores can be drilled out from polar ice caps. The bubbles of trapped gas are laid down year by year, then released by melting the ice. This gas is tested to find out the composition of the past atmosphere many thousands of years before records could first be made.

Answers to in-text questions

a carbon dioxide

b very little or none

Summary answers

1 dioxide, water, methane, volcanoes, oxygen

2 From gases emitted by volcanoes.

3 The temperature was too high.

4 Student chart showing development from early volcanic atmosphere to the first plant-produced oxygen and the removal of carbon dioxide during photosynthesis.

C1 7.4

Life on Earth

Learning objectives

Students should learn:

- the reasons why there are many theories for how life began on Earth
- how ammonia, hydrocarbons and lightening could have been the source of life on Earth. [HT only]

Learning outcomes

Most students should be able to:

- explain why there are so many theories to how life started on Earth

Some students should also be able to:

- explain how ammonia, hydrocarbons and lightening could have started life on Earth. [HT only]
- evaluate the theories about how life started on Earth. [HT only]

Support

- You could support students by giving them short bulleted printouts of the main points about the different theories about how life on Earth began. They could then order them and stick them onto their timeline. Other information, such as diagrams, could be supplied, which students could also transpose onto their work.

- Students often struggle to understand how a primordial soup became a life form. Scientists are also trying to find out how this occurred and they are trying to start life from a mixture of chemicals. Theories range from lightening striking the primordial soup to dormant life forms from a meteorite starting life when they hit the surface of the early Earth. It is worth stressing to students that no one currently knows the answer. The idea of a missing part of the theory can be demonstrated by mixing a ground up vitamin tablet with protein powder and water. This has all of the chemicals needed for life but the mixture does not come into life.

Extend

- Students could be extended by being asked to suggest how scientists could try to find out if life existed elsewhere in the universe (SETI, study of meteorite, space probes).

Specification link-up: Chemistry C1.7

- There are many theories as to how life was formed billions of years ago. *[C1.7.2 d)]*
- One theory as to how life was formed involves the interaction between hydrocarbons, ammonia and lightning. *[C1.7.2 e)]* **[HT only]**
- Describe why we do not know how life was first formed. *[C1.7]* **[HT only]**

Lesson structure

Starters

Life in the universe – Ask the students to decide if they think that there is life elsewhere in the universe. Ask them to give and justify a rating out of 100, where 100 is definitely life elsewhere and 0 that there is only life on Earth. *(5 minutes)*

Have a think! – Ask students to consider how they think life could have started on Earth. Ask for volunteers to share their thoughts. Manage the class discussion. You could support students by providing them with some cards showing some theories/religious ideas. They can choose which they think is most likely. You can extend students by asking them to group the suggestions as ideas [e.g. religious views, which are not backed up by scientific evidence] and theories [ideas backed up by scientific evidence]. *(10 minutes)*

Main

- Students often have their own thoughts about how life started on Earth. However, they have rarely considered that ideas for how life has started have changed over time. Discuss with students why ideas change in science. This may be due to technological developments, research being completed and information being circulated.

- The Miller–Urey experiment was a radical experiment and its results have been re-analysed many years later. Encourage students to work in small groups to write a two-minute radio news report to explain the importance of the experiment. You may wish to record the report using a suitable piece of computer software. The best recording could be used as a podcast on the school's virtual learning platform as a revision tool. **[HT only]**

- Ask students to make a timeline, showing some of the different theories and ideas about how life started on the Earth. Their timelines should briefly outline the theory and they should bullet point any evidence used to support it or persuade people to accept it. They could also list any reasons/evidence that could be used to argue that the theory or idea is not correct. Encourage students to include the Miller–Urey experiment and the Murchison meteorite.

- You could encourage students to write an advert to try to persuade people that the generally accepted theory for how life started on Earth is correct. Students could work in their preferred learning styles and could make a billboard poster, if they are visual learners, a radio advert if they are auditory learners and they could be filmed doing a TV advert if they are kinaesthetic learners. Ask students to share their adverts with the class. They could assess each other's work. **[HT only]**

Plenaries

Life in the universe part two – Ask the students to reconsider and decide if they think that there is life elsewhere in the universe after studying this lesson. Again ask students to give a rating and reflect on their new score and original score. If it has changed, why? *(5 minutes)*

Summarise Miller–Urey – Ask the students to imagine that they are trying to advertise the Miller–Urey theory for how life began on Earth. They should try and construct an advertising strap line. Students could be supported by the whole class working together to generate the strap line. Students could be extended by being told key words that they must include. The best strap line could be given a prize. *(10 minutes)* **[HT only]**

Further teaching suggestions

Planning to create life
- Students could write the plan for the Miller–Urey experiment, detailing the aim, equipment, method and safety. **[HT only]**

Revision guide
- Students could write a page for a revision guide to try to explain how life could have started on Earth. Their page should be aimed at KS4 students, should be no larger than A4 and contain questions or activities to check that people understand the information. You could then choose the best one, photocopy it and use it as a class homework or starter.

Murchison
- Students could write a newspaper article for the day when the results from the Murchison meteorite were discovered. Students could use an appropriate desk top publishing package to write up their article. Quotations could be added, using internet search engines, from people who worked on the analysis and interpretation of results, e.g. Michael Engel, Bartholomew Nagy and Philippe Schmitt-Kopplin. **[HT only]**

C1 7.4 Life on Earth

Learning objectives
- Why are there many theories about how life began on Earth?
- Why does one theory involve hydrocarbons, ammonia and lightning? **[H]**

Most theories of how our atmosphere developed include the arrival of living things on Earth. The oxygen in our atmosphere today is explained by photosynthesis in plants. The plants probably evolved from simple organisms like plankton and algae in the ancient oceans.

But where did the molecules that make up the cells of even the simplest living things come from? And how were they formed? Any theories to answer these questions are bound to be tentative. They will be based on assumptions. The best theories will be the ones that explain most of the widely-accepted evidence.

∞ links
For information on theories about the Earth's early atmosphere, look back at C1 7.3 The Earth's atmosphere in the past.

Miller–Urey experiment

We know the type of molecules that make up living things. To make these we need compounds called amino acids. These amino acids make proteins.

Most amino acids contain the elements carbon, hydrogen, nitrogen and oxygen. So one way forward is to try to re-create the conditions in the early atmosphere in an experiment. Could amino acids have been made in those conditions? That is the question the scientists Miller and Urey tried to answer in 1952. Figure 1 shows a diagram of their apparatus.

They used a mixture of water (H_2O), ammonia (NH_3), methane (CH_4) and hydrogen (H_2) to model the early atmosphere. Under normal conditions, these gases do not react together. However, Miller and Urey used a high voltage to produce a spark to provide the energy needed for a reaction. This simulated lightning in a storm. The experiment ran for a week then they analysed the mixture formed. It looked like a brown soup. In it they found 11 different amino acids.

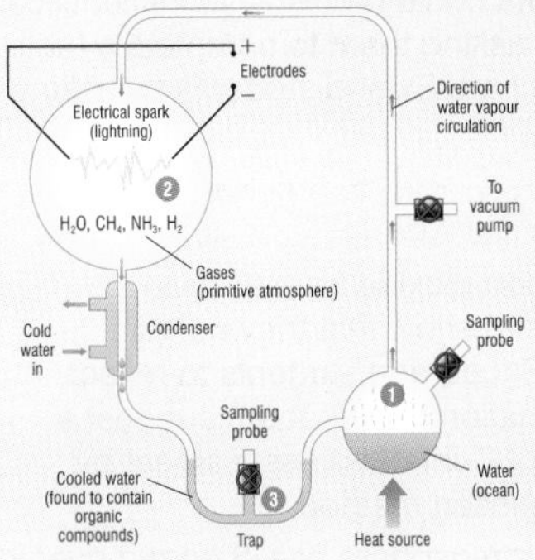

a Which elements make up most amino acids?

This experiment provided evidence that it was possible to make the molecules of life from gases that may have been in our early atmosphere. Miller and Urey published their findings in 1953. They froze some of the mixtures formed in their experiments and stored it. In 2008 other scientists analysed it using modern techniques. They found 22 amino acids, as well as other molecules important for life.

Theories of the composition of the early atmosphere have changed since the 1950s. For example many people think the atmosphere was mainly carbon dioxide and nitrogen before the first life on Earth. However when they carry out similar experiments to Miller and Urey, they still get similar biological molecules made.

Figure 1 The classic Miller–Urey experiment

[Diagram labels: Electrodes; Electrical spark (lightning); Direction of water vapour circulation; To vacuum pump; H_2O, CH_4, NH_3, H_2; Gases (primitive atmosphere); Cold water in; Condenser; Sampling probe; Sampling probe; Cooled water (found to contain organic compounds); Trap; Heat source; Water (ocean)]

There are opponents of the theory that biological material can be made from non-biological material. They argue that the Miller–Urey experiment only works in the absence of oxygen. They believe that oxygen would have been present before the generally accepted time for its appearance. This would make any conclusions based on Miller–Urey or similar experimental results invalid.

Other theories

Another theory is based on analysis of meteors that crash to Earth from space. In 1969 a meteorite fell from the sky above Australia. Known as the Murchison meteorite, its mass was over 100 kg. However, more interesting were the range of organic molecules found in it.

The latest studies of fragments of the meteorite have identified about 70 different amino acids. This shows that the molecules capable of starting life on Earth might have arrived from outer space.

b Why were scientists interested in the Murchison meteorite?

Another source of biological molecules could have been deep under the oceans. Next to volcanic vents on the seabed we get both the conditions and chemicals needed.

But just because the 'building blocks' of life might have been on Earth, it does not explain the really difficult step. How do they go on to form life?

The organic molecules, from whatever source, could have formed a 'primordial soup'. All the molecules needed to start life could have been in the seas. Then they would have had to react together to somehow make the first primitive cells. Protein molecules capable of replicating themselves might have been involved at this stage.

Others think that simple living organisms could have arrived on Earth in meteorites or comets. Their evolution had started elsewhere. This 'extraterrestrial seeding' from outer space supports the theory of life in other parts of the universe. Of course, nobody knows for sure but the search for evidence goes on.

Figure 2 Part of the Murchison meteorite, which is rich in organic molecules – the molecules of life

Figure 3 Volcanic vents under the sea might have helped form a 'primordial soup' of organic molecules

Summary questions

1 Look at Figure 1.
  a Explain what Miller and Urey did in their experiment.
  b Which one of these statements best describes the outcome of their experiment:
    A It showed how life can be formed from simple molecules.
    B It showed how carbon dioxide and methane are essential parts of a living cell.
    C It showed that biological molecules can be made from substances that could have been in the early atmosphere.
    D It showed that the Earth's early atmosphere must have been made up of only carbon dioxide, ammonia, water vapour and methane. **[H]**

2 a What do we mean by a 'primordial soup'?
  b What role might a 'primordial soup' have played in developing life on Earth? **[H]**

Key points
- One theory states that the compounds needed for life on Earth came from reactions involving hydrocarbons, such as methane, and ammonia. The energy required for the reaction could have been provided by lightning. **[H]**
- All the theories about how life started on Earth are unproven. We can't be sure about the events that resulted in the first life-forms on Earth. **[H]**

Answers to in-text questions

a carbon, hydrogen, nitrogen and oxygen

b Because it contains organic molecules which support the theory that the molecules of life might have arrived from outer space.

Summary answers

1 **a** They reacted a mixture of water, ammonia, methane and hydrogen to model the early atmosphere. To produce the energy needed for reactions to take place they used a high voltage. They kept the experiment going for a week, then analysed the mixture of new compounds formed.

  b C – It showed that biological molecules can be made from substance that could have been in the early atmosphere.

2 **a** The mixture of organic compounds brewing in prehistoric seas.

  b The organic molecules could have reacted together to make biological molecules, such as self-replicating proteins, that could have gone on to make the first cells.

C1 7.5

Gases in the atmosphere

Learning objectives

Students should learn:

- the sinks for the majority of the carbon dioxide from the early atmosphere
- the main gases in the current atmosphere
- the percentage composition of the current atmosphere
- how the gases in the air can be separated. [HT only]

Learning outcomes

Most students should be able to:

- list the main gases in the atmosphere and the approximate proportions of gases in the atmosphere
- explain how carbon dioxide was removed from the Earth's atmosphere.

Some students should also be able to:

- explain how air can be separated by fractional distillation [HT only]
- state some uses of the products of the fractional distillation of air. [HT only]

Support

- You could support students by providing them with discrete sentences, which they could use to generate the story about the changing Earth's atmosphere. Flow chart boxes could be provided and information given for students to cut and stick directly onto the diagram.

Extend

- You could extend students by asking them to find out what scientists predict will happen to the composition of the Earth's atmosphere. It is important that the students list their sources. In the next lesson the information can be compared and students can consider whether bias has crept into the evidence gathered.

AQA

Specification link-up: Chemistry C1.7

- For 200 million years, the proportions of different gases in the atmosphere have been much the same as they are today: about four-fifths (80%) nitrogen, about one-fifth (20% oxygen, small proportions of various other gases, including carbon dioxide, water vapour and noble gases. *[C1.7.2 a)]*
- Most of the carbon from the carbon dioxide in the air gradually became locked up in sedimentary rocks as carbonates and fossil fuels. *[C1.7.2 g)]*
- Air is a mixture of gases with different boiling points and can be fractionally distilled to provide a source of raw materials used in a variety of industrial process. *[C1.7.2 j)]* **[HT only]**
- Explain and evaluate theories of the changes that have occurred and are occurring in the Earth's atmosphere. *[C1.7]*

  Controlled Assessment: SA4.2 Assess and manage risks when carrying out practical work. *[SA4.2.1 a) b)]*

Lesson structure

Starters

Reflection – Give the students an A4 sheet of paper and ask them to make three columns. The first should be headed with 'what I already know', then 'what I want to know' and finally 'what I know now'. Ask the students to consider the title of the topic and complete the first two columns with bullet points of information. *(5 minutes)*

Pie chart – Ask the students to estimate the percentage of each gas in the current atmosphere. This should bring out any misconceptions that oxygen is the predominant gas in the atmosphere. Then give the actual percentages so they can see how close they were. Encourage students to consider the way these data could be displayed scientifically (table, bar chart or pie chart). Support students by only asking them to complete a table of gas percentages, then represent these data in a bar chart. Extend students by asking them to present the data using a pie chart. *(10 minutes)*

Main

- After a brief explanation about the movement of carbon dioxide from the early atmosphere into rocks, students could test seashells to show that they contain carbonates. See 'Practical support' for more detail. Encourage students to reflect on the work completed in C1.2 and to use this information to help them suggest a method. You could extend students' understanding of Controlled Assessment by asking them to write a full risk assessment for their chosen method.
- The percentage composition of gases in the Earth's atmosphere has changed over time but has remained relatively constant in the last 200 million years. Ask students to imagine that they are Earth and to write a creative story about how its 'clothes' (its atmosphere) has changed and why.
- The class could be split into three groups. Students in the first write the beginning of the story, another group writes the middle and the final group writes the end. In order to complete this last suggestion, a link sentence from each section needs to be provided to the groups so they know where/how to start and/or finish their part of the story.
- Ask Higher Tier students to make a flow chart to explain how air can be separated. On their flow chart they should include details of the uses for each of the gases. The RSC Industrial Chemistry series has a short video of this process, which you could play to the students before they complete this task. You should link the fractional distillation of air to the process used to separate crude oil (C1 4.2). **[HT only]**

Plenaries

Guess what? – Ask the students to break off into pairs. Give each pair a pack of cards with separate key words per card, e.g. oxygen, nitrogen, air, gas, carbon dioxide, photosynthesis, argon, fractional distillation. The students should take it in turns to pick a card and look at the key term. They should explain it to their partner without using the key word and the other student should guess the word. You could support students by giving them the explanation to read out and then work together to match it up to the key word. You could extend them by asking them to mime the key word rather than describe it. *(5 minutes)*

Reflection part two – Ask the students to return to their A4 table. Ask them to add information to the last column, 'what I now know', that isn't included in the middle column. They should also correct any misconceptions from the middle column and ask for help if they have not found out some information that they wanted. *(10 minutes)*

Practical support

Investigating sea shells
Equipment and materials required
Sea shells (e.g. cockle, oyster), pestle and mortar, spatula, hydrochloric acid (2 mol/dm³) – irritant, 2 × dropping pipettes, boiling tube, bung with a hole in the centre fitted with a delivery tube, test tube, test-tube rack, limewater – irritant, eye protection.

Details
Students can plot their own investigation to see which type of shell contains the highest percentage of carbonate mineral. The same mass of crushed shell could be added to excess dilute hydrochloric acid. Any remaining sediment can be filtered off, washed and left to dry, then reweighed. You can show that the gas liberated is carbon dioxide using limewater. Check the students' plans, including risk assessment, before allowing any practical work to commence.

Safety: CLEAPSS Hazcard 47A Hydrochloric acid – corrosive. CLEAPSS Hazcard 18 Limewater – irritant.

Our changing planet

C1 7.5 — Gases in the atmosphere

Learning objectives
- What happened to most of the carbon dioxide in the early atmosphere?
- What are the main gases in the atmosphere today and what are their relative proportions?
- How can the gases in the air be separated? [H]

Figure 1 There is clear fossil evidence in carbonate rocks of the organisms which lived millions of years ago

Practical
Shelly carbonates

Carry out a test to see if crushed samples of shells contain carbonates. Think of the reaction that all carbonates undergo with dilute acid. How will you test any gas given off?
- Record your findings.

We think that the early atmosphere of the Earth contained a great deal of carbon dioxide. Yet the Earth's atmosphere today only has around 0.04% of this gas. So where has it all gone? The answer is mostly into living organisms and into materials formed from living organisms.

Carbon 'locked into' rock
Carbon dioxide is taken up by plants during photosynthesis. The carbon can end up in new plant material. Then animals eat the plants and the carbon is transferred to the animal tissues, including bones, teeth and shells.

Over millions of years the dead bodies of huge numbers of these living organisms built up at the bottom of vast oceans. Eventually they formed sedimentary carbonate rocks like limestone (containing mainly calcium carbonate).

Some of these living things were crushed by movements of the Earth and heated within the crust. They formed the fossil fuels coal, crude oil and natural gas. In this way much of the carbon from carbon dioxide in the ancient atmosphere became locked up within the Earth's crust.

a Where has most of the carbon dioxide in the Earth's early atmosphere gone?

Carbon dioxide also dissolved in the oceans. It reacted and made insoluble carbonate compounds. These fell to the seabed and helped to form more carbonate rocks.

Ammonia and methane
At the same time, the ammonia and methane, from the Earth's early atmosphere, reacted with the oxygen formed by the plants.

$$CH_4 + 2O_2 \rightarrow CO_2 + 2H_2O$$
$$4NH_3 + 3O_2 \rightarrow 2N_2 + 6H_2O$$

This got rid of methane and ammonia. The nitrogen (N_2) levels in the atmosphere built up as this is a very unreactive gas.

The atmosphere today
By 200 million years ago the proportions of gases in the Earth's atmosphere had stabilised. These were much the same as they are today. Look at the percentage of gases in the atmosphere today in the pie chart in Figure 2.

- Nitrogen 78%
- Oxygen 21%
- Argon 0.9%
- Carbon dioxide 0.04%
- Trace amounts of other gases

Figure 2 The relative proportions of nitrogen, oxygen and other gases in the Earth's atmosphere

b What gas did plants produce that changed the Earth's atmosphere?

Higher — Separating the gases in air
In industry the gases are separated by the fractional distillation of liquid air. Fractional distillation is a process in which liquids with different boiling points are separated. So first we have to get air cold enough for it to condense into a liquid. It has to be cooled to a temperature below −200°C.

In industry they do this by compressing the air to about 150 times atmospheric pressure. This actually warms the air up. So it is cooled down to normal temperatures by passing the air over pipes carrying cold water.

But the main cooling takes place when the pressure is released. As this happens, the air is allowed to expand rapidly. This is similar to what happens in an aerosol can when pressure is released as the aerosol is sprayed. The temperature drops far enough for even the gases in air to condense to liquids. The carbon dioxide and water can be removed from the mixture as they are solids at this low temperature.

Here are the boiling points of the main substances left in the liquid air mixture: Nitrogen = −196°C, Argon = −186°C, Oxygen = −183°C.

The liquid is then allowed to warm up and at −196°C nitrogen boils off first. It is collected from the top of a tall fractionating column.

Liquid nitrogen is used to cool things down to very low temperatures. At these temperatures most things solidify. It is used to store sperm in hospitals to help in fertility treatment. Nitrogen gas is very unreactive so we use it in sealed food packaging to stop food going off. It is also used on oil tankers when the oil is pumped ashore to reduce the risk of explosion. In industry, nitrogen gas is used to make ammonia which we convert into fertilisers.

The oxygen separated off is used to help people breathe, often at the scene of an accident or in hospital. It is also used to help things react. Examples include high temperature welding and in the steel-making process.

Figure 4 Biological samples are preserved in liquid nitrogen until they are needed

links
For information on the fractionating column used to separate crude oil into fractions, look back at C1 4.2 Fractional distillation.

Gaseous nitrogen out
−190°C
Liquefied air in at −200°C
−185°C
Liquid oxygen out

Figure 3 Fractional distillation of liquid air

AQA Examiner's tip
In a fractionating column the individual gases can be separated because of their different boiling points.

Summary questions
1 Copy and complete the table showing the proportion of gases in the Earth's atmosphere today.

nitrogen	oxygen	argon	carbon dioxide	other gases
%	%	%	%	%

2 **a** Which technique is used to separate the main gases in liquid air? [H]
  b How can water and carbon dioxide be removed from the air before the gases enter the fractionating column. [H]
  c Look at the boiling points of nitrogen, argon and oxygen above:
    i Which gas boils off after nitrogen?
    ii Why is it difficult to obtain 100% pure oxygen? [H]

Key points
- The main gases in the Earth's atmosphere are oxygen and nitrogen.
- About four-fifths (80%) of the atmosphere is nitrogen, and about one-fifth (20%) is oxygen.
- The main gases in the air can be separated by fractional distillation. These gases are used in industry as useful raw materials. [H]

Further teaching suggestions

Summary mnemonic
- Students taking the Higher Tier paper could be asked to summarise fractional distillation of air into a list of words, which represent the different parts of the process. They could then create a mnemonic to help them remember the order of the stages more easily (cool the air), compress, condense, boil, collect). **[HT only]**

Key questions
- Ask students to generate questions for which each key point in the Student Book is the answer. Then cut out each question and give them to another student. Their task is to match the question with the key point. The pairs of students then feed back to each other about where their sorting was correct and about how the question was phrased.

Spider diagram
- Students taking the Higher Tier paper could make a spider diagram detailing how air is separated and the uses of each of the products. **[HT only]**

Links
- Give students a sheet of A4 paper and ask them to fold it in half. On one side they should draw a labelled diagram of fractional distillation of crude oil and a bullet point explanation as to how crude oil is separated. On the second side they should do the same but for fractional distillation of air. Hopefully students will then see that the explanation is the same but the chemical names and boiling points are different. **[HT only]**

Answers to in-text questions
a into carbonate rocks
b oxygen

Summary answers
1

nitrogen	oxygen	argon	carbon dioxide	other gases
78%	21%	0.9%	0.04%	trace

2 **a** fractional distillation
  b They solidify out by cooling the air.
  c **i** argon
    ii Because the boiling points of argon and oxygen are very close together.

C1 7.6

Carbon dioxide in the atmosphere

Learning objectives

Students should learn:

- that carbon dioxide moves in and out of the atmosphere
- that the amount of carbon dioxide is increasing in the atmosphere.

Learning outcomes

Most students should be able to:

- describe how carbon dioxide moves into and out of the atmosphere
- state that burning fossil fuels has increased the amount of carbon dioxide in the atmosphere and describe why this could cause problems.

Some students should also be able to:

- explain why there is a general trend that the amount of carbon dioxide in the air is increasing and evaluate the possible consequences.

Support

- You could support students by supplying key words on the board to help them follow what happens to carbon dioxide in the natural course of events. Alternatively, the exercise could be turned into a 'cut-and-stick' activity.
- Show students some posters from environmental charities such as Greenpeace and the WWF. Ask students to design a similar poster to explain how burning fossil fuels could affect marine environments.

Extend

- You could extend students by asking them to suggest or research some ways in which the amount of carbon dioxide in the atmosphere could be reduced [e.g. carbon capture schemes].

AQA Specification link-up: Chemistry C1.7

- The oceans also act as a reservoir for carbon dioxide but increased amounts of carbon dioxide absorbed by the oceans has an impact on the marine environment. [C1.7.2 h)]
- Nowadays the release of carbon dioxide by burning fossil fuels increases the level of carbon dioxide in the atmosphere. [C1.7.2 i)]
- Explain and evaluate the effects of human activities on the atmosphere. [C1.7]

Lesson structure

Starters

Demonstration – If solid carbon dioxide can be obtained, e.g. from a spare black carbon dioxide fire extinguisher, put it into water and dry ice will be created. Be careful not to handle the solid for too long or burns will be caused. Tweezers should be used to manipulate it. Students can then put their hands briefly into the water (as long as they do not touch the solid) and it will feel really cold. Ask the students to suggest what is happening. [The solid carbon dioxide is boiling in the water.] (5 minutes)

Describe – Supply carbon dioxide gas in a gas jar to each table. Ask the students to describe its physical appearance [colourless, transparent gas]. You could support students by giving them a list of words on the board [colourless, coloured, transparent, opaque, gas, liquid, solid] and they would have to choose from the list. You could extend students by asking them to explain the laboratory test for carbon dioxide (links to C1 2.2). Ask students to discuss their ideas in small groups and then manage whole-class feedback. (10 minutes)

Main

- The carbon cycle is a network of different reactions, which remove carbon from, or add it into, the atmosphere. However, in C1 students are only required to understand that carbon dioxide sinks include the oceans and sedimentary rocks and fossil fuels. Students need to know that burning fossil fuels releases carbon dioxide and that heating the oceans reduces the amount of carbon dioxide that they can absorb. They should also be aware that when carbon dioxide is absorbed, the pH of the oceans is reduced.

- Carbon dioxide is produced as a product of respiration. You may wish to measure the amount of carbon dioxide in air and contrast this to exhaled air. See 'Practical support' for more detail.

- To demonstrate the effect on the pH of water when carbon dioxide is dissolved, blow carbon dioxide through a mixture of water and universal indicator. See 'Practical support' for more detail. Ask students to suggest what affect this may have on ecosystems [it changes the species that can live in an area].

- Give students a graph that shows the percentage of carbon dioxide in the atmosphere over the last 300 years. Ask students to state the trend [carbon dioxide levels were stable until about 1850, then the levels increased, and the rate of increase is accelerating]. Students should then be encouraged to explain the trend, thinking about the use of fossil fuels.

Plenaries

Agree? – Ask for a volunteer to stand in the centre of the classroom. The volunteer should make a statement about the content of the lesson (it could be correct or deliberately incorrect), e.g. 'carbon can be found in rocks'. The rest of the class decides how much they agree with this statement. The more they agree, the closer they should stand to the person who spoke. Then ask a few students why they are positioned as they are and feedback whether the statement is correct. Ask all the students to sit down and for another volunteer to repeat the idea. (5 minutes)

Key reminders – Ask students to copy out the key points onto a flash card. On the other side, draw an image that will help them remember/represent the key point. Students could be supported by being supplied with the diagrams, which they should match to the key point. Students can be extended by representing the first key point with balanced symbol equations showing the hydrolysis of carbon dioxide and photosynthesis. (10 minutes)

Practical support

Measuring carbon dioxide

Equipment and materials required
Carbon dioxide probe, data logger, lung volume bags.

Details
Use the carbon dioxide probe attached to a data logger to record the concentration of carbon dioxide in the air. Exhale into a lung volume bag and then put the probe into the bag and measure the concentration of carbon dioxide in exhaled air.

Acidification of water

Equipment and materials required
Carbon dioxide cylinder with regulator, rubber tube, 250 cm³ beaker, universal indicator solution, distilled water.

Details
Half-fill the beaker with distilled water. Put a few drops of universal indictor into the water. Connect the rubber tube to the carbon dioxide cylinder and put the open end into the water. Turn the gas on, so that the flow rate is about one bubble per second. Observe the colour change of the universal indicator as the water becomes acidified.

Safety: CLEAPSS Hazcard 32 Universal indicator – highly flammable and harmful.

Our changing planet

C1 7.6 — Carbon dioxide in the atmosphere

Learning objectives
- How does carbon move in and out of the atmosphere?
- Why has the amount of carbon dioxide in the atmosphere increased recently?

Over the past 200 million years the levels of carbon dioxide in the atmosphere have not changed much. This is due to the natural cycle of carbon in which carbon moves between the oceans, rocks and the atmosphere.

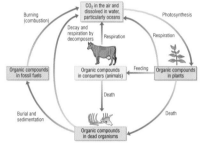

Figure 1 The level of carbon dioxide in the atmosphere has remained steady for the last 200 million years as a result of this natural cycle. However, over the past 200 years the carbon dioxide levels have risen as people started to burn more and more fossil fuels.

Left to itself, this cycle is self-regulating. The oceans act as massive reservoirs of carbon dioxide. They absorb excess CO_2 when it is produced and release it when it is in short supply. Plants also remove carbon dioxide from the atmosphere. We often call plants and oceans carbon dioxide 'sinks'.

a What has kept carbon levels roughly stable over the past 200 million years?

The changing balance
Over the recent past we have greatly increased the amount of carbon dioxide released into the atmosphere . We burn fossil fuels to make electricity, heat our homes and run our cars. This has enormously increased the amount of carbon dioxide we produce.

There is no doubt that the levels of carbon dioxide in the atmosphere are increasing.

We can record annual changes in the levels of carbon dioxide which are due to seasonal differences in the plants. The variations within each year show how important plants are for removing CO_2 from the atmosphere. But the overall trend over the recent past has been ever upwards.

The balance between the carbon dioxide produced and the carbon dioxide absorbed by 'CO_2 sinks' is very important.

How Science Works

Increasing levels of carbon dioxide

Look at the data collected by scientists monitoring the proportion of carbon dioxide in the atmosphere at one location:

- Why is the line not a smooth curve?
- Explain the overall trend shown by the data.

links
For information about the effect humans have had on the levels of carbon dioxide in the atmosphere, look back at C1 4.4 Cleaner fuels.

Think about what happens when we burn fossil fuels. Carbon has been locked up for hundreds of millions of years in the fossil fuels. It is released as carbon dioxide into the atmosphere when used as fuel. For example:

$$propane + oxygen \rightarrow carbon\ dioxide + water$$
$$C_3H_8 + 5O_2 \rightarrow 3CO_2 + 4H_2O$$

As carbon dioxide levels in the atmosphere go up, the reactions of carbon dioxide in sea water also increase. The reactions make *insoluble* carbonates (mainly calcium carbonate). These are deposited as sediment on the bottom of the ocean. They also produce *soluble* hydrogencarbonates, mainly of calcium and magnesium. These compounds simply remain dissolved in the sea water.

In this way the seas and oceans act as a buffer, absorbing excess carbon dioxide but releasing it if necessary. However there are now signs that the seas cannot cope with all the additional carbon dioxide that we are currently producing. For example, coral reefs are dying in the more acidic conditions caused by excess dissolved carbon dioxide.

How Science Works

Thinking of solutions but at what cost?

Most of the electricity that we use in the UK is made by burning fossil fuels. This releases carbon dioxide into the atmosphere. Scientists have come up with a number of solutions. One solution would be to pump carbon dioxide produced in fossil fuel power stations deep underground to be absorbed into porous rocks. This is called 'carbon capture and storage'. It is estimated that this would increase the cost of producing electricity by about 10%.

- Give an advantage and a disadvantage of reducing carbon dioxide emissions using 'carbon capture and storage'.

Summary questions

1 Match up the parts of sentences:

a	Carbon dioxide levels in the Earth's atmosphere ...	A	... carbon locked up long ago is released as carbon dioxide.
b	Plants and oceans are known as ...	B	... were kept steady by the natural recycling of carbon dioxide in the environment.
c	When we burn fossil fuels ...	C	... the reactions of carbon dioxide in sea water increase.
d	As carbon dioxide levels rise ...	D	... carbon dioxide sinks

2 Draw a labelled diagram to illustrate how boiling an electric kettle may increase the amount of carbon dioxide in the Earth's atmosphere.

3 Why has the amount of carbon dioxide in the Earth's atmosphere risen so much in the recent past?

Figure 2 Most of the electricity that we use in the UK is made by burning fossil fuels

?? Did you know ...?
Some scientists predict that global warming may mean that the Earth's average temperature could rise by as much as 5.8°C by the year 2100!

People are worried about changing climates (including increasingly common extreme weather events) and rising sea levels as a result of melting ice caps and expansion of the warmer oceans. Low-lying land then might disappear beneath the sea.

Key points
- Carbon moves into and out of the atmosphere due to plants, animals, the oceans and rocks.
- The amount of carbon dioxide in the Earth's atmosphere has risen in the recent past largely due to the amount of fossil fuels we now burn.

Further teaching suggestions

Investigating carbon dioxide
- All animals breathe out carbon dioxide gas, and students often talk about it, but rarely can they explain the physical and chemical properties of the gas. They could complete a series of experiments and note their observations. They could then summarise the properties of this chemical (see 'Practical support' for more details).

Model
- Ask students to make a model of a molecule of CO_2 using a molecular model kit. Describe the bonds holding the black carbon and red oxygen atoms together. You could support students by giving them the formula of carbon dioxide and the colour and number of each type of atom. You could extend students by asking them to classify the bonding in this molecule (it is covalent) (links to C1 1.4).

Answers to in-text questions
a The natural recycling of carbon dioxide between oceans, rocks and the atmosphere.

Summary answers

1 **a** B
  b D
  c A
  d C

2 Diagram to show how an electric kettle may use energy produced by burning fossil fuels. It should include drilling, mining for fossil fuels, transport of the fossil fuels, a power station producing electricity and a kettle heating the water.

3 Mainly due to our increased burning of fossil fuels to satisfy our energy requirements in the industrial world.

Summary answers

1 a Middle layer of the Earth, made of molten rock about 3000 km thick and lying about 100 km under the surface.

b Innermost layer of the Earth made of iron and nickel.

c The relatively thin layer of gases above the Earth's surface.

d Part of the Earth's crust made of solid rock that moves and causes continental drift, earthquakes, volcanoes and mountains.

2 a The shapes of coastlines of west Africa and South America seemed like two pieces in a jig-saw. The similarity of fossils and rock types in west Africa and South America. The single land mass moved apart because the tectonic plates that make up the Earth's outer layer moved at a relative speed of a few centimetres per year. This happens because of convection currents set up in the mantle due to heat given off from radioactive atoms.

b Wegener could not adequately explain how tectonic plates could possibly move at that time (and he was not a geologist).

3 a The amount of oxygen, methane and ammonia decreased, nitrogen increased.

b Reaction of oxygen with ammonia and methane.

c i methane + oxygen → carbon dioxide + water

ii ammonia + oxygen → nitrogen + water

d Because there has been a dramatic increase in our burning fossil fuels since then, resulting in ever-increasing amounts of carbon dioxide being released.

4 a They showed that it is possible to make the organic molecules, such as amino acids, on which living things are based, from the simple molecules that could have been present in the Earth's early atmosphere.

b Although they showed that the molecules of life could be made under certain conditions, they did not show how these molecules combined to make living cells.

5 Mark poster based on facts about Earth's early atmosphere, how this has changed, the atmosphere today and how it continues to change.

6 a The graph should have the axes correctly and fully labelled. The points should be accurately plotted. The date should be on the x-axis and the CO_2 concentration on the y-axis.

b The line of best fit should be a curve.

c There should be a slow increase in the concentration of CO_2 at the start of the data, followed by more rapid increases in more recent years. Some might spot the anomalies around 1945. This might prompt a debate about the causes, which could prove very interesting. Remember these probably represent global figures and they might conclude that they would like more detailed data between 1935 and 1955 to try to sort out what might have happened. This is given in Table 1.

d That the concentration of carbon dioxide in the atmosphere has increased.

That it has increased at a faster rate in more recent years. Caution here about taking conclusions too far and resist the conclusion that this alone is evidence for the greenhouse effect or global warming.

e Yes – they are two totally different ways of deriving the data. Students might want to know of any overlap between the two sets of data and the correlation between the two. The data is given in Table 2.

Our changing planet: C1 7.1–C1 7.6

Summary questions

1 Write simple definitions for the following words describing the structure of the Earth:

a mantle

b core

c atmosphere

d tectonic plate.

2 Wegener suggested that all the Earth's continents were once joined in a single land mass.

a Describe the evidence for this idea, and explain how the single land mass separated into the continents we see today.

b Why were other scientists slow to accept Wegener's ideas?

3 The pie charts show the atmosphere of a planet shortly after it was formed (A) and then millions of years later (B).

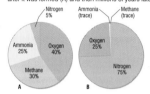

a How did the atmosphere of the planet change?

b What might have caused the change in part **a**?

c Copy and complete the word equations showing the chemical reactions that may have taken place in the atmosphere.

i methane + ... → carbon dioxide + ...

ii ammonia + ... → nitrogen + ...

d Why have levels of carbon dioxide in the Earth's atmosphere increased so dramatically over the past 200 years?

4 a Describe how the Miller–Urey experiment advanced our understanding of how life might have first formed on Earth. [H]

b Why didn't their experiment prove how life began on Earth? [H]

5 The Earth and its atmosphere are constantly cha... Design a poster to show this. It should be suitable displaying in a classroom with children aged 10–... years. Use diagrams and words to describe and c ideas and to communicate them clearly to the ch...

6 Core samples have been taken of the ice from Antarctica. The deeper the sample the longer it h... been there. It is possible to date the ice and to ta... samples from it. The air was trapped when the ice formed. It is possible therefore to test samples of that have been trapped in the ice for many thousa... years.

This table shows some of these results. The more... results are from actual air samples taken from a P... island.

Year	CO_2 concentration (ppm)	Sourc...
2005	379	Pacific isl...
1995	360	Pacific isl...
1985	345	Pacific isl...
1975	331	Pacific isl...
1965	320	Antarcti...
1955	313	Antarcti...
1945	310	Antarcti...
1935	309	Antarcti...
1925	305	Antarcti...
1915	301	Antarcti...
1905	297	Antarcti...
1895	294	Antarcti...
1890	294	Antarcti...

a If you have access to a spreadsheet, enter the and produce a line graph.

b Draw a line of best fit.

c What pattern can you detect?

d What conclusion can you make?

e Should the fact that the data came from two di... sources affect your conclusion? Explain why.

Table 1

Year	'35	'36	'37	'38	'39	'40
CO_2 conc. (ppm)	309.4	309.8	310.0	310.2	310.3	310.4
Year	'41	'42	'43	'44	'45	'46
CO_2 conc. (ppm)	310.4	310.3	310.2	310.1	310.1	310.1
Year	'47	'48	'49	'50	'51	'52
CO_2 conc. (ppm)	310.2	310.3	310.5	310.7	311.1	311.5
Year	'53	'54	'55			
CO_2 conc. (ppm)	311.9	312,4	313.0			

Table 2

Year	'78	'77	'76	'75	'74
Pacific island CO_2 conc. (ppm)	335.5	333.9	332.1	331.1	330.2
Antarctica CO_2 conc. (ppm)	333.7	332.6	331.5	330.3	329.2
Year	'73	'72	'71	'70	'69
Pacific island CO_2 conc. (ppm)	329.7	327.5	326.3	325.7	324.6
Antarctica CO_2 conc. (ppm)	328.0	326.9	325.8	324.8	323.8

Examination-style questions

atch a word from the list with each of the labels A, B,
and D on the diagram of the Earth.

mosphere   core   crust   mantle

(4)

om which parts of the Earth do we get all of our raw
aterials?

 atmosphere, core and crust
 atmosphere, crust and oceans
 atmosphere, core and mantle
 core, mantle and oceans   (1)

out one hundred years ago there was a scientist
lled Alfred Wegener. He found evidence that the
ntinents, such as South America and Africa, had
ce been joined and then drifted apart.

Africa

South America

Key
■ Sedimentary rocks
   containing fossils

the diagram to suggest **two** pieces of evidence that
d be used to show that the continents had once
joined.   (2)

out fifty years ago, new evidence convinced
ientists that the Earth's crust is made up of tectonic
ates that are moving very slowly.

ve **two** pieces of evidence that have helped to
nvince these scientists that the tectonic plates are
oving.   (2)

escribe as fully as you can what causes the Earth's
ctonic plates to move.   (3)
                                        AQA, 2009

the Earth's atmosphere the percentage of carbon
oxide has remained at about 0.03% for many
ousands of years. The graph shows the percentage
carbon dioxide in the Earth's atmosphere over the
st 50 years.

Graph: Carbon dioxide (%) vs Year (1960–2010), y-axis 0.031–0.040

i   What was the percentage of carbon dioxide in the
    Earth's atmosphere in 1965? .... %   (1)
ii What change has happened to the percentage of
    carbon dioxide in the Earth's atmosphere over the
    last 50 years?   (1)
iii Suggest **one** reason for this change.   (1)
iv Why does this change worry some people?   (1)

There are different theories about the Earth's early
atmosphere.

b Some scientists believe the Earth's early atmosphere
   was mainly carbon dioxide and water vapour. What do
   the scientists believe produced these gases?   (1)

c In 1953 some scientists believed the Earth's early
   atmosphere was mainly water vapour, methane,
   ammonia and hydrogen. In the Miller–Urey experiment,
   electricity was passed through a mixture of these gases
   and produced amino acids, the building blocks for
   proteins and life. Give two reasons why the experiment
   does not prove that life began in this way.   [H] (2)

d Most scientists agree that there was very little oxygen
   in the Earth's early atmosphere. Explain how the
   oxygen that is now in the atmosphere was produced.
                                                 [H] (3)

4 The elements oxygen, nitrogen and argon can be
   separated from the air. Carbon dioxide and water vapour
   are removed from air, which is then cooled to –200°C. The
   liquid obtained is a mixture of oxygen, nitrogen and argon.
   The table shows the boiling points of these elements.

Element	Boiling point in °C
argon	–183
nitrogen	–196
oxygen	–186

Explain how these elements can be separated by
fractional distillation of the liquid.   [H] (3)

219

Examination-style answers

1 **a** A core, B mantle, C crust, D atmosphere.   *(4 marks)*
   b B – atmosphere, crust and oceans   *(1 mark)*

2 **a** Any **two** from: the shapes of the continents fit together,
        the same type of rocks have been found, the same fossils
        have been found, accept rocks match, fossils match,
        magma rising through a gap under the Atlantic. *(2 marks)*
   b Any **two** from: earthquakes, volcanoes, idea of distance
        between America and Europe/Africa is increasing,
        oceanic ridges, formation of mountain ranges, formation
        of islands, nmagnetic stripes, tsunamis.   *(2 marks)*
   c Any **three** from: (natural) radioactivity produces heat,
        (causes) convection currents, in the mantle, mantle able
        to move or (behaves) like a liquid, create forces (to move
        plates).   *(3 marks)*

3 **a** i   0.0317 (%)   *(1 mark)*
          ii increased   *(1 mark)*
          iii burning fossil fuels or deforestation   *(1 mark)*
          iv Global warming or greenhouse gas, accept causes
              floods or sea level rise or climate change or extreme
              weather.   *(1 mark)*
   b volcanoes or volcanic activity   *(1 mark)*
   c Any **two** from: cannot be sure what was in the
        atmosphere, only produced building blocks or amino
        acids are only one step towards living things, evidence is
        in dispute or only theory or not conclusive.   *(2 marks)*
   d Because plants evolved or increased or colonised the
        Earth, plants photosynthesise, which uses carbon dioxide
        or removes carbon dioxide from the atmosphere. *(3 marks)*

4 EITHER any **three** from: Liquid into fractionating column,
     nitrogen collected at top and oxygen collected at the bottom,
     argon collected from in between or part way up column,
     nitrogen has lowest boiling point, nitrogen collected as gas,
     oxygen has highest boiling point, oxygen collected as liquid,
     OR any **three** from: nitrogen has lowest boiling point so
     nitrogen boils first or is collected as gas, argon has next
     lowest boiling point or boils next, oxygen has highest boiling
     point so boils last or remains as liquid.   *(3 marks)*

Examiner's tip

Students find fractional distillation difficult, and even more so
with negative numbers, so Question 5 gives an opportunity to
check understanding of these topics.

Kerboodle resources

Resources available for this chapter on Kerboodle are:
- Chapter map: Our changing planet
- Support: Where does it come from? (C1 7.1)
- Bump up your grade: How did the atmosphere get to be like
  this? (C1 7.3)
- Practical: How did plants alter the Earth's atmosphere?
  (C1 7.3)
- Maths skills: Composition of the atmosphere (C1 7.5)
- How Science Works: Analysis that is truly atmospheric
  (C1 7.5)
- WebQuest: Capturing carbon (C1 7.6)
- Extension: What's the link? (C1 7.6)
- Interactive activity: Our changing planet
- Revision podcast: The development of the Earth's atmosphere
- Test yourself: Our changing planet
- On your marks: The early atmosphere
- Examination-style questions: Our changing planet
- Answers to examination-style questions: Our changing planet

Practical suggestions

Practicals	AQA	k	📖	⚙
Investigating the composition of air by passing air over heated copper using gas syringes and measuring the percentage of oxygen. Then burning magnesium in the nitrogen to form Mg_3N_2. Add water to produce ammonia (nitrogen must have come from the air).	✓			✓
Collecting gas produced by aquatic plants and testing for oxygen (using dissolved oxygen sensor).	✓	✓		
Measuring the amount of carbon dioxide in inhaled and exhaled air (using carbon dioxide sensor).	✓		✓	
Testing the products of combustion of fuels to show that carbon dioxide is produced.	✓		✓	
Design an investigation to compare the amount of carbon dioxide released by reacting crushed shells (e.g. cockle, oyster) with dilute hydrochloric acid.	✓		✓	

AQA Examination-style answers

1 a correctly labelled: electron, nucleus *(2 marks)*

   b **i** oxygen, accept O_2, ignore air *(1 mark)*

     ii Any one from: (water) does not pollute, (only) water is produced, no carbon dioxide (is produced), no sulfur dioxide (is produced), no nitrogen oxides (are produced), no carbon or no particles (are produced), accept no harmful gas(es), no greenhouse gas(es), no acid rain. *(1 mark)*

2 a **i** 8 *(1 mark)*

     ii 8 *(1 mark)*

   b 2,8,7 *(1 mark)*

   c Because it has 7 electrons in highest energy level/outer shell, or (has structure) 2,7 or same number of outer electrons or same number (of electrons) in highest energy level/outer shell, ignore just "same number of electrons". *(1 mark)*

   d Both have 8 electrons in highest energy level/outer shell or 8 outer electrons, accept both have the same number of electrons in highest energy level/outer shell, ignore "both have the same structure" their electronic structures/arrangements are very stable. *(2 marks)*

3 a **i** 2 *(1 mark)*

     ii 3 *(1 mark)*

     iii 5 *(1 mark)*

   b **i** zinc oxide *(1 mark)*

     ii carbon dioxide *(1 mark)*

4 a Limestone is heated or thermally decomposed (to make calcium oxide), (calcium oxide is reacted with) water (to make calcium hydroxide). *(2 marks)*

   b Calcium hydroxide reacts with acids, because it is an alkali. *(2 marks)*

   c Limestone is/contains (mainly) calcium carbonate, carbonate(s) react with acids. *(2 marks)*

   d Calcium hydroxide/alkali is caustic/corrosive or damages skin/eyes or calcium carbonate/limestone is not caustic/corrosive or does not damage skin do not accept vague statements e.g. limestone is safer to handle. *(1 mark)*

   e Any sensible suggestion, e.g. calcium hydroxide is made by heating limestone, two reactions needed (to make it), (crushed) limestone needs less energy (to make it) or only needs to be crushed. *(1 mark)*

   f $CaCO_3 \rightarrow CaO + CO_2$
     $CaO + H_2O \rightarrow Ca(OH)_2$ *(2 marks)*

   g $Ca(OH)_2 + 2HCl \rightarrow CaCl_2 + 2H_2O$ reactants and products balancing *(2 marks)*

   h $CaCO_3 + 2HCl \rightarrow CaCl_2 + CO_2 + H_2O$ reactants and products balancing *(2 marks)*

5 a Less dense or lighter (more) resistant to corrosion. *(2 marks)*

   b There is a clear, logical and detailed scientific explanation of why titanium costs more than steel. The answer shows almost faultless spelling, punctuation and grammar. It is coherent and in an organised, logical sequence. It contains a range of appropriate and relevant specialist terms used accurately. *(5–6 marks)*

   There is a scientific explanation of why titanium costs more than steel. There are some errors in spelling, punctuation and grammar. The answer has some structure and organization. The use of specialist terms has been attempted, but not always accurately. *(3–4 marks)*

   There is a brief explanation of why titanium costs more than steel that includes at least one correct comparison of the

Examination-style questions

1 a The diagram shows the parts of a hydrogen atom. Use words from the list to label the diagram.
electron group nucleus symbol (2)

   b Hydrogen can be used as a *clean fuel* for cars.
     i When hydrogen burns in air, it reacts with another element. Complete the word equation for this reaction. (1)
     hydrogen + ... → water
     ii Suggest **one** reason why hydrogen is called a *clean fuel*. (1)
                  AQA, 2008

2 Use a periodic table to help you to answer this question. Oxygen is in Group 6 of the periodic table.

   a **i** How many protons are in an atom of oxygen? (1)
     ii How many electrons are in an atom of oxygen? (1)

   b Chlorine is in Group 7 of the periodic table. Complete the electronic structure of chlorine: 2, ... (1)

   c Fluorine is also in Group 7. Explain why in terms of electronic structure. (1)

   d Neon and argon are in Group 0 of the periodic table. They are very unreactive elements. What does this tell you about their electronic structures? (2)

3 When calcium carbonate is heated it decomposes. The equation for this reaction is: $CaCO_3 \rightarrow CaO + CO_2$

   a Use numbers from the list to complete the sentences.
     2 3 4 5 6
     i The number of products in the equation is .... (1)
     ii The formula $CaCO_3$ shows that calcium carbonate was made from .... different elements. (1)
     iii The equation is balanced because there are .... atoms on both sides. (1)

   b Other metal carbonates decompose in a similar way.
     i Name the solid produced when zinc carbonate decomposes. (1)
     ii Name the gas produced when copper carbonate decomposes. (1)

4 Farmers can use calcium hydroxide to neutralise soils that are too acidic. Limestone is mainly calcium carbonate, $CaCO_3$. Limestone is used to make calcium hydroxide, $Ca(OH)_2$.

   a What are the two reactions used to make calcium hydroxide from limestone? (2)
   b Explain why calcium hydroxide neutralises soils that are too acidic. (2)
   c Farmers can also use powdered limestone to neutralise soils that are too acidic. Explain why. (2)
   d Suggest one reason why it may be safer for farmers to use powdered limestone instead of calcium hydroxide. (1)
   e Suggest one reason why powdered limestone costs less than calcium hydroxide. (1)
   f Write balanced equations for the reactions in 4(a) [H] (2)
   g The formula of calcium chloride is $CaCl_2$. Write a balanced equation for the reaction of calcium hydroxide with hydrochloric acid, HCl. [H] (2)
   h Write a balanced equation for the reaction of calcium carbonate with hydrochloric acid. [H] (2)

220

AQA Examiner
When you are asked complete a word eq for a reaction, read t information in the qu carefully and you sh find the names of the reactants and produ

AQA Examiner
The AQA data sheet you will have in the e has a periodic table.

AQA Examiner
Remember that each symbol represents o atom of an element that small (subscript) numbers in a formul multiply only the ato follow.

AQA Examiner
Attempt all parts of a question. If you com part you cannot answ not be put off readin next parts.

processes or costs involved. The spelling, punctuation and grammar are very weak. The answer is poorly organised with almost no specialist terms and/or their use demonstrating a general lack of understanding of their meaning. *(1–2 marks)*

No relevant content. *(0 marks)*

Examples of chemistry points made in the response:

- Number of steps: Steel production involves fewer reactions/steps or simpler reactions/steps.
- Time and yield: titanium takes longer, smaller amounts (per day)
- Process: Iron production (allow steel or part of steel production) is continuous, titanium is batch process
- Cost of reagents: chlorine, magnesium (have to be produced by electrolysis) more expensive than carbon/coke (from coal) and/or air and/or oxygen (from air). (ignore cost of metal ores)
- Energy costs: more energy needed to produce titanium, cost of electricity (for electrolysis or electric furnace), titanium needs to be melted again
- Labour costs: Less labour needed for making iron/steel.

6 a pressed *(1 mark)*

   b (oil) does not mix (with water) *(1 mark)*

   c Any **two** from: does not damage/decompose the oil, does not change its flavour, does not damage nutrients, does not use (fossil) fuel/energy for heating. *(2 marks)*

   d (olive oil/it) burns (in air) produces energy *(2 marks)*

...anium is as strong as steel but is much more expensive. It is used to make jet engines ... aircraft and to make replacement hip joints for people.

Give two properties that make titanium better than steel for making jet engines and replacement hip joints. (2)

In this question you will be assessed on using good English, organising information clearly and using specialist terms where appropriate.

Titanium is made in batches of about 10 tonnes that takes up to 15 days. The main steps to make titanium are:

* Titanium oxide is reacted with chlorine to produce titanium chloride.
* Titanium chloride is reacted with magnesium at 900 °C in a sealed reactor for three days to give a mixture of titanium and magnesium chloride.
* The reactor is cooled for 7 days, and then the mixture is removed.
* The magnesium chloride is removed from the mixture by distillation at very low pressure.
* The titanium is melted in an electric furnace and poured into moulds.

Steel is produced at about 8000 tonnes per day. The main steps to make steel are:

* Iron oxide is reacted with carbon (coke) in a blast furnace that runs continuously.
* The molten impure iron flows to the bottom of the furnace and is removed every four hours.
* Oxygen is blown into the molten iron for about 20 minutes to produce steel.
* The steel is poured into moulds.

Explain why titanium costs more than steel. (6)

AQA, 2008

...ives are the fruits of the olive tree. Olive oil is extracted from olives.

Use a word from the list to complete the sentence.

condensed   evaporated   pressed

In the first step to extract the oil the olives are crushed and .... (1)

This gives a mixture of liquids and solids that is left to settle.

— Olive oil
— Water
— Solids

Why does the olive oil separate from the water? (1)

The olive oil is removed from the water and filtered to remove any small pieces of solids.

Suggest **two** reasons why separating olive oil by this method is better than separating it by distilling. (2)

Olive oil can be used as a fuel. Explain why. (2)

Food can be cooked in olive oil. Give one advantage and one disadvantage of cooking food in olive oil. (2)

Olive oil can be used with vinegar to make salad dressings. Name the type of substance that is added to salad dressings to stop them from separating. (1)

AQA *Examiner's tip*

You may be given information about familiar or unfamiliar applications of chemistry. The information you are given should help you to answer the questions. Q5(b) requires you to organise information clearly. Think about the points in the information and decide which ones make titanium more expensive than steel. Underline or circle the points you are going to use on the question paper. Add brief notes, perhaps numbers for the order that you will use. Think about how you are going to write your answer. Rehearse it in your head before you write your answer.

AQA *Examiner's tip*

Always be aware of the number of marks for a question. If it is two marks, you need to make two points in your answer. Sometimes this is obvious, as in Q6(c), but in Q6(d) you need to make sure you have not given just a single simple statement.

221

Bump up your grades

Questions that examine quality of written communication should be clearly and logically written using correct scientific terms. You should encourage your students to plan their answers before writing, using space on the question paper for notes. If information is given in the question relevant points should be used in the student's answers.

Bump up your grades

Encourage your students to always check the marks allocated to a question. They show how many points or steps are expected in the answer. Two-mark questions either require two distinct points or one point with some amplification, so a simple statement is not usually sufficient to gain both marks. Encourage students to read their answers when they have finished writing them and check the number of points against the number of marks.

e One advantage from: different/better flavour, different/better texture e.g. crisper, provides more energy, (mono)unsaturated so healthier (than saturated fats).

One disadvantage from: provides more energy/calories/joules, costs more (than alternatives), greasy or stains clothes/fabrics. *(2 marks)*

f Emulsifier, allow a named type of emulsifier such as egg yolk. *(1 mark)*

P1 1.1

Infrared radiation

Learning objectives

Students should learn:

- that infrared radiation is the transfer of energy by electromagnetic waves
- that all objects emit and absorb infrared radiation
- that the amount of infrared radiation emitted in a given time increases with the temperature of the object.

Learning outcomes

Most students should be able to:

- describe infrared radiation as electromagnetic waves
- state that there is radiation, similar to light but invisible; that it is emitted by all objects
- explain that the hotter an object is, the more infrared radiation it emits in a given time.

Support

- Concentrate on sharing the key ideas, the transfer of energy by radiation (point out the similarities to light) and look for correct drawings of rays of 'energy'. Link this to a change in temperature when this energy is emitted (cooling) or absorbed (heating).

Extend

- Students could explore infrared satellite imagery. This is used in weather forecasting and analysis of land use. Students could investigate how infrared satellites are used to monitor the weather and to analyse how land is used in different countries. They could find out how different types of vegetation or habitation show up in infrared imagery or even other parts of the electromagnetic spectrum. There are many excellent images available to explore on the internet: students could start with the various 'landsat' or weather forecasting websites.

AQA Specification link-up: Physics P1.1

- All objects emit and absorb infrared radiation. *[P1.1.1 a)]*
- The hotter an object is the more infrared radiation it radiates in a given time. *[P1.1.1 b)]*

  Controlled Assessment: SA4.1 Planning an investigation. *[SA4.1.1 a) b) c) d)]* and *[SA4.1.2 c)]*

Lesson structure

Starters

Seeing at night – To support students, you could search the internet for infrared images, show them and ask students to identify the objects. Can students identify the hotter parts of the objects from the colder ones? Many pictures come with scales to help. *(5 minutes)*

Hand warming – Ask students to draw a diagram explaining why holding your hands *in front* of a fire warms them up. Students should use a ray diagram to show the radiation leaving the fire and being absorbed by the hands. *(10 minutes)*

Main

- Why is it that being in sunlight makes you feel warm while the shade can feel cool? Start the main part of the lesson by discussing this idea; try to draw out the scientific language, absorb and transmit.
- Discuss infrared images and how all objects are giving off invisible infrared radiation due to the energy in them. Link the temperature of the object to the amount of energy emitted in a given time.
- Demonstrating the rise in temperature mentioned in the text requires a bright white light source. A sensitive thermometer or sensor should also be used.
- Discuss the meaning of the words 'radiate' (to spread out from a source) and 'radiation' (the energy that is spread) to make sure students have a full understanding.
- Emphasise that there is empty space (a vacuum) between the Earth and the Sun and that infrared radiation passes through this vacuum easily, otherwise we would receive no energy from the Sun. Check that students can understand or draw a ray diagram showing this information.
- You could use a diagram to show how all of the energy is focused in a solar oven, pointing out that the rays travel in straight lines – just like visible light. A concave mirror could be used to focus rays on a blackened thermometer bulb to show the effect. As a simple alternative, use a magnifying glass to ignite a piece of paper to show how high temperatures can be reached by bringing rays together.
- A discussion of the greenhouse effect is best presented using a diagram to point out what you mean by wavelength. Show two waves and discuss the energy the waves carry; the shorter the wavelength, the more energy the wave carries. Another two diagrams could be used to link the greenhouse effect with a real greenhouse. To support students, you could provide incomplete diagrams of the greenhouse effect for them to annotate with important information.
- Students could plan the investigation 'A huddle test' to practise 'How Science Works' skills (see Student Book).

Plenaries

- **Temperature order** – Show a list of objects or materials (e.g. the Sun's surface, boiling water, etc.) and ask students to put them in temperature order. You could provide students with some cards showing the actual temperatures to match up with the objects after they have been placed in order. For example, solid carbon dioxide: $-78\,°C$, melting ice: $0\,°C$, boiling ethanol: $78\,°C$, boiling water: $100\,°C$, melting iron $1538\,°C$, surface of sun $6000\,°C$. *(5 minutes)*
- **By stealth** – If you have a passive infrared detector in your room, you could test its sensitivity. It responds to changes in energy and, if you move slowly enough, it will not trigger. Some students could have a competition to see how far they can travel (very slowly) without being detected. *(10 minutes)*

Practical support

Detecting infrared radiation

You may prefer to do this as a demonstration if you don't want to coat a lot of thermometers with paint.

Equipment and materials required

For each group: bright white light source (power supply and ray box), sensitive thermometer (to 0.5 °C) with bulb painted matt black, clean prism.

Details

Shine the light through the prism and produce the spectrum. (This could be projected on the wall if you are just demonstrating.) Position the thermometer just beyond the red part of the spectrum and the temperature reading will rise.

Demonstrating a solar oven

Small solar ovens are available and could be used to boil small quantities of water. As an alternative, an old parabolic car headlight could be used. If a match is mounted at the focus of the parabola (this takes some practice) and the headlight is pointed towards a bright light source (such as the Sun or another headlight), the match will ignite.

Energy transfer by heating

P1 1.1   Infrared radiation

Learning objectives

- What is infrared radiation?
- Do all objects give off infrared radiation?
- How does infrared radiation depend on the temperature of an object?

Figure 1 Keeping watch in darkness

links
For more information on infrared heaters, see P1 1.9 Heating and insulating buildings.

Did you know …?
A passive infrared (PIR) detector in a burglar alarm circuit will 'trigger' the alarm if someone moves in front of the detector. The detector contains sensors that detect infrared radiation from different directions.

links
For more information on electromagnetic waves, see P1 6.1 The electromagnetic spectrum.

Seeing in the dark

We can use special cameras to 'see' animals and people in the dark. These cameras detect **infrared radiation**. Every object gives out (**emits**) infrared radiation.

The hotter an object is, the more infrared radiation it emits in a given time.

Look at the photo in Figure 1. The rhinos are hotter than the ground.

a Why is the ground darker than the rhinos?
b Which part of each rhino is coldest?

Practical

Detecting infrared radiation

You can use a thermometer with a blackened bulb to detect infrared radiation. Figure 2 shows how to do this.

- The glass prism splits a narrow beam of white light into the colours of the spectrum.
- The thermometer reading rises when it is placed just beyond the red part of the spectrum. Some of the infrared radiation in the beam goes there. Our eyes cannot detect it but the thermometer can.
- Infrared radiation is beyond the red part of the visible spectrum.

What would happen to the thermometer reading if the thermometer were moved away from the screen?

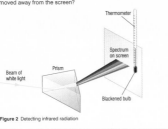

Figure 2 Detecting infrared radiation

The electromagnetic spectrum

Radio waves, microwaves, infrared radiation and **visible light** are parts of the electromagnetic spectrum. So too are ultraviolet rays and X-rays. Electromagnetic waves are electric and magnetic waves that travel through space.

Energy from the Sun

The Sun emits all types of electromagnetic radiation. Fortunately for us, the Earth's atmosphere blocks most of the radiation that would harm us. But it doesn't block infrared radiation from the Sun.

Figure 3 shows a solar furnace. This uses a giant reflector that focuses sunlight.

The temperature at the focus can reach thousands of degrees. That's almost as hot as the surface of the Sun, which is 5500 °C.

The greenhouse effect

The Earth's atmosphere acts like a greenhouse made of glass. In a greenhouse:

- short wavelength infrared radiation (and light) from the Sun can pass through the glass to warm the objects inside the greenhouse
- infrared radiation from these warm objects is trapped inside by the glass because the objects emit infrared radiation of longer wavelengths that can't pass through the glass.

So the greenhouse stays warm.

Gases in the atmosphere, such as water vapour, methane and carbon dioxide, trap infrared radiation from the Earth. This makes the Earth warmer than it would be if it had no atmosphere.

But the Earth is becoming too warm. If the polar ice caps melt, it will cause sea levels to rise. Reducing our use of fossil fuels will help to reduce the production of 'greenhouse gases'.

Figure 3 A solar furnace in the Eastern Pyrenees, France

How Science Works

A huddle test
Design an investigation to model the effect of penguins huddling together. You could use beakers of hot water to represent the penguins.

Figure 4 Penguins keeping warm

Summary questions

1 Copy and complete **a** and **b** using the words below. Each word can be used more than once.

temperature   radiation   waves

a Infrared .... is energy transfer by electromagnetic ....
b The higher the .... of an object is, the more .... it emits each second.

2 a Copy and complete the table to show if the object emits infrared radiation or light or both.

Object	Infrared	Light
A hot iron		
A light bulb		
A TV screen		
The Sun		

b How can you tell if an electric iron is hot without touching it?

3 Explain why penguins huddle together to keep warm.

Key points

- Infrared radiation is energy transfer by electromagnetic waves.
- All objects emit infrared radiation.
- The hotter an object is, the more infrared radiation it emits in a given time.

Further teaching suggestions

A coffee conundrum
Equipment and materials required

Two identical cups, coffee powder, milk, kettle and data loggers. No tasting in laboratory.

- A cup of coffee is left for 10 minutes to cool down. Would the coffee be cooler if the milk was poured in immediately after it was made, after 5 minutes, or immediately before drinking it? Extend students by asking them to plan and carry out an experiment that would test their theories. Analysis of the results of an experiment like this will allow discussion about the rate of energy transfer and lead to the conclusion that the rate of energy transfer is proportional to the temperature difference between an object and the surroundings.

Temperature measurement

- There are a number of methods of measuring temperature, so students could be assigned the task of investigating one or another. You could assign different students different techniques such as: thermal imaging, infrared, thermocouples, thermistors, resistance temperature detectors, bimetallic strips, Galilean thermometers. Some of these are more complex than others, so select which to assign to individual students allowing for clear differentiation by task.

Answers to in-text questions

a The ground is cooler than the body surface of each rhino.
b The feet are the coldest parts of each rhino.

Summary answers

1 a radiation, waves
   b temperature, radiation

2 a

Object	Infrared	Light
A hot iron	✓	✗
A light bulb	✓	✓
A TV screen	✗	✓
The Sun	✓	✓

   b Put your hand near it and see if it gets warm due to radiation from the iron.

3 They lose less heat through radiation when they huddle together because they radiate energy to each other.

P1 1.2

Surfaces and radiation

Energy transfer by heating

Learning objectives

Students should learn:

- that matt black surfaces are the best emitters and best absorbers of infrared radiation
- that shiny surfaces are the worst emitters, worst absorbers and best reflectors of infrared radiation.

Learning outcomes

Most students should be able to:

- describe which surfaces are the best emitters of infrared radiation
- describe which surfaces are the best absorbers and reflectors of infrared radiation.

Some students should also be able to:

- explain how the choice of a surface colour can affect the rate of temperature change of an object.

Answers to in-text questions

a Sand makes the ice surface dark and matt so it absorbs radiation from the Sun better. The sand grains become warm and melt the ice.

b A dark matt surface absorbs more radiation from the Sun.

Support

- As in the last lesson, look for the clear idea of energy being transferred leading to heating and cooling. You could provide support worksheets for either of the practical tasks, so that students can focus on collecting evidence.

Extend

- Students could analyse the shape of cooling curves to determine that the rate of cooling depends on the temperature difference between objects. They should be able to link this to the change in gradient of the cooling graphs; the graphs are flatter towards the end of the experiments. Students will return to this idea later.

Specification link-up: Physics P1.1

- Dark, matt surfaces are good absorbers and good emitters of infrared radiation. *[P1.1.1 c)]*
- Light, shiny surfaces are poor absorbers and poor emitters of infrared radiation. *[P1.1.1 d)]*
- Light, shiny surfaces are good reflectors of infrared radiation. *[P1.1.1 e)]*

  Controlled Assessment: SA4.1 Planning an investigation. *[SA4.1.2 a) b) c)]*

Lesson structure

Starters

Definitions – Show students the key words for this spread (absorb, reflect, emit). Ask students to match up descriptions of these processes and diagrams showing them taking place. Check that these diagrams are using the idea of rays demonstrating the transfer of energy. *(5 minutes)*

Out in the sun – Discuss with students how it feels to go out in a black T-shirt on a sunny day. Encourage the use of key scientific language such as absorb, reflect and emit. *(10 minutes)*

Main

- Most students will understand that the inside of a black car feels very hot on a sunny day, so start with these ideas about heating. Focus on energy entering the object and that this is the cause of an increase in temperature.
- Watch out for misunderstanding of the word 'absorb'; many students have the impression that it means that the surface somehow 'sucks in' the energy from its surroundings.
- This topic presents an early opportunity for developing the students' practical skills. You could introduce some of the concepts covered in 'How Science Works' in this lesson, e.g. the nature of different types of variable, how to present results and evaluating the design of investigations. You could also use the first practical as an open-ended planning exercise.
- If time is available, you can try both practical activities with the students. If time is short, then half the students could do one of the practical tasks while the other half does the second. They could share results and ideas at the end.
- After the first practical, check that students actually achieved the results you expected; the difference in temperature can be small and it is not unusual to reach the wrong conclusion. Discuss how to improve the practical to make it fairer or more accurate.
- The second practical may also be performed as a demonstration if equipment or time is limited. Check understanding of both the absorption and emission practicals and, in particular, the correct use of key words.
- A Leslie's cube is ideal to demonstrate that two surfaces at the same temperature can emit different amounts of infrared radiation. An infrared sensor could be used to detect levels of infrared radiation from the cube. The difference is easily felt by placing the back of the hand a few centimetres from the surfaces, but take care that students do not actually touch the surface. Ask a teaching assistant to manage the queue waiting to test out the Leslie's cube while you move on.

Plenaries

Choosing the right colour – Give students a series of simple scenarios, such as 'What colour cup should you use to keep orange juice cold on a hot day?' and ask them to give reasons. Make sure that the reasons are based on the ideas of absorption and emission. *(5 minutes)*

Without words – Ask students to draw illustrations showing why black surfaces are better emitters and absorbers, without using any words on the diagrams. *(10 minutes)*

Practical support

⚙ Testing radiation from different surfaces

Equipment and materials required

Kettles or another way of heating water. For each group: drinks cans (or two beakers or boiling tubes) one painted silver and the other matt black, two thermometers (to 0.5 °C), aluminium foil (if beakers are used), stop clock and a measuring cylinder.

Details

The students should add the same volume of hot water to each of the cans and record the temperature every 30 seconds for 5 to 10 minutes. Higher starting temperatures give greater temperature drops in reasonable times, but students will need to be extra careful with hot water. If you use beakers or boiling tubes then you should add foil lids to reduce evaporation.

⚙ Absorption tests

Equipment and materials required

Two metal plates (one should have a matt black surface and the other be left shiny and metallic), wax, two small coins and a radiant heater.

Details

Fix the coins onto the plates in advance as shown in the diagram. Place the radiant heater in the middle of the plates and turn on. While the plates are heating you should explain what is happening in terms of absorption and reflection of the energy.

Further teaching suggestions

Leslie's cube

- The Leslie's cube was devised by Sir John Leslie to demonstrate the importance of surface colour on the radiation of energy. By using data-logging equipment, the experiment could be expanded to show that the dull black surface always radiates more energy than the silver one and that the amount of energy radiated depends on the temperature of the water in the cube.

Equipment and materials required

- Leslie's cube, data-logging equipment (including two infrared sensors and a temperature probe), kettle.

Details

- Set up the cube with two infrared sensors, one 5 cm from the matt black surface and another 5 cm from the silver one. Place a temperature probe into the container and add boiling water. (Take care!) Record the cooling of the container and the amount of energy radiated from the surfaces over a period of up to half an hour. Students could then analyse the results and reach conclusions about the relationships. If only one infrared probe is available, students could describe the relationship between the temperature and the amount of energy radiated by each surface separately; to save time record some data in advance for comparison.

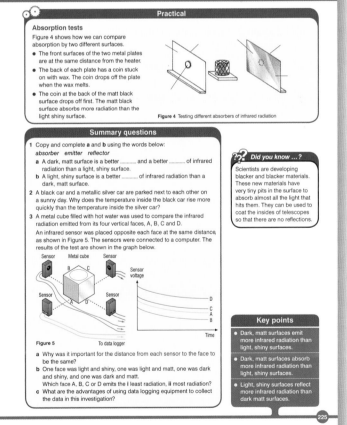

Summary answers

1 a absorber, emitter (absorber and emitter in any order)

b reflector

2 The black surface absorbs more infrared radiation from the Sun than the silver surface.

3 a To make the test fair. The temperature recorded will differ at different distances from the cube.

b i D **ii** B

c Greater accuracy, collects multiple sets of data at whatever time intervals you choose.

P1 1.3

States of matter

Learning objectives

Students should learn:

- that solids, liquids and gases have different properties
- that the arrangement of particles in solids, liquids and gases gives rise to their properties, including density and whether they are able to flow.

Learning outcomes

Most students should be able to:

- describe the physical characteristics of solids, liquids and gases
- describe the arrangement and movement of particles in solids, liquids and gases.

AQA Specification link-up: Physics P1.1

- The use of kinetic theory to explain the different states of matter. *[P1.1.2 a)]*
- The particles of solids, liquids and gases have different amounts of energy. *[P1.1.2 b)]*

Lesson structure

Starters

State the facts – Support students by providing a diagram on which they have to label the five changes of state from solid to liquid to gas. Students should describe whether energy is taken into the substances or given out during these changes. A few students might be aware of sublimation [gas to solid directly]. *(5 minutes)*

Property match – Before they use the Student Book, give students some cards describing the properties of solids, liquids and gases. Ask students to match these with other cards describing some example properties including density, fluidity and compressibility. Extend students by challenging them to give explanations of these properties in terms of particle arrangement. *(10 minutes)*

Main

- Students will have looked at the three states of matter during KS3 and the majority of them should remember the basics. Some may need to be reminded about the idea of matter being composed of particles. The 'Modelling states of matter' demonstration is a simple way of doing this.

- The term 'particles' is used throughout the unit but, depending on the ability of students, you might want to talk about atoms and molecules (or ions) as *examples* of these particles.

- Demonstrate the changes of state of dry ice if you have some (see 'Further teaching suggestions').

- Density is tackled later in the course but you could push some students to calculate the density of materials or at least understand what the term means scientifically: the amount of mass in a 'unit' volume. Show a table of some example densities pointing out some materials with exceptionally high or low density (osmium 22.6 g/cm^3 and helium 0.000 18 g/cm^3).

- Show students some mercury if you have a container holding a few cubic centimetres, to demonstrate that some liquids can be very dense compared with some solids.

- Some students may ask about materials such as expanded polystyrene. This contains a lot of air, which reduces the density. Show some unexpanded polystyrene as a contrast.

- Animations about changes of state are fairly essential at this point in the lesson. Use them to show the behaviour of the particles as a change of state happens. Be careful to use an animation that shows that the particles in a solid are vibrating even when the temperature reaches 0 °C. Some simulations can allow the particles to reach absolute zero (−273 °C) and you could extend students by discussing this idea.

- Demonstrate the reverse change of state as well to show the particles slowing as they lose energy.

Support

- It can be quite time-consuming to draw diagrams of particles, so you may wish to produce a worksheet for students to add their own notes. Be aware that particle diagrams of gases and liquids are often too similarly drawn. For liquids, the particles should be touching with no patterns but gas particles should be very separate.

Extend

- You could go into more detail about the extra phase changes (sublimation) and the fourth state of matter: plasma. What is plasma and why is it different from a basic gas?

Plenaries

Particle behaviour – Students could act out the states of matter. Ask them to behave like particles in a solid [close together and just shaking], liquid [close together and milling around] and gas [zipping about far apart]. Think carefully about the layout of the room if you want to try this. *(5 minutes)*

Particle diagrams – Ask students to make large particle diagrams. Provide them with a lot of small circles to use as the particles (from a hole punch) and let them create a diagram representing the three states and the transition between them. Select the best diagram and display it. You could use this large diagram in future discussions about conduction, convection and evaporation. *(10 minutes)*

Practical support

Changing state

Equipment and materials required

For each group: Bunsen burner, tripod, heatproof mat, gauze, beaker (250 cm³), icy cold spoon or something similar. Optional: ice.

Details

Students could simply heat the water or start from a block of ice if you have a little more time. They need to observe the changes of state and think about the idea of energy being provided to cause the changes. Students should perform a simple risk assessment of the practical before starting. Make sure the glassware is borosilicate and heat carefully at the start if using ice.

Modelling states of matter

This could be a simple demonstration or you might prefer the students to take part, if you have time and enough marbles.

Equipment and materials required

A plastic tray, marbles, ping-pong balls or other small balls.

Details

Place a few balls in the tray and allow them to roll around. This is similar to a gas; the particles can move freely and are generally far apart. Almost fill the bottom layer of the tray; the particles can still move a bit but there are few gaps between them. This situation is similar to a liquid. Finally, fill the tray so that the particles cannot move; they are closely packed together in a manner similar to the particles in a solid. Extend students by discussing the reasons why this is not a good model. [The model is 2-D and there are no representations of the forces between the particles.]

Energy transfer by heating

States of matter

P1 1.3 — States of matter

Learning objectives

- How are solids, liquids and gases different?
- How are the particles in a solid, liquid and a gas arranged?
- Why is a gas much less dense than a solid or a liquid?

Everything around us is made of matter in one of three states – solid, liquid or gas. The table below summarises the main differences between the three **states of matter**.

	Flow	Shape	Volume	Density
Solid	no	fixed	fixed	much higher than a gas
Liquid	yes	fits container shape	fixed	much higher than a gas
Gas	yes	fills container	can be changed	low compared with a solid or liquid

a   We can't see it and yet we can fill objects like balloons with it. What is it?
b   When an ice cube melts, what happens to its shape?

Change of state 🅚

A substance can change from one state to another, as shown in Figure 2. We can make these changes by heating or cooling the substance. For example,

- when water in a kettle boils, the water turns to steam. Steam, also called water vapour, is water in its gaseous state
- when solid carbon dioxide or 'dry ice' warms up, the solid turns into gas directly
- when steam touches a cold surface, the steam condenses and turns to water.

Figure 1 Spot the three states of matter

Figure 2 Change of state

c   What change of state occurs when hailstones form?

Practical

Changing state

1 Heat some water in a beaker using a Bunsen burner, as shown in Figure 3. Notice that:
- steam or 'vapour' leaves the water surface before the water boils
- when the water boils, bubbles of vapour form inside the water and rise to the surface to release steam.
2 Switch the Bunsen burner off and hold a cold beaker or cold metal object above the boiling water. Observe condensation of steam from the boiling water on the cold object. Take care with boiling water.

Figure 3 Changing state

The kinetic theory of matter

Solids, liquids and gases consist of particles. Figure 4 shows the arrangement of the particles in a solid, a liquid and a gas. When the temperature of the substance is increased, the particles move faster.

- The particles in a solid are held next to each other in fixed positions. They vibrate about their fixed positions so the solid keeps its own shape.
- The particles in a liquid are in contact with each other. They move about at random. So a liquid doesn't have its own shape and it can flow.
- The particles in a gas move about at random much faster. They are, on average, much further apart from each other than in a liquid. So the density of a gas is much less than that of a solid or liquid.
- The particles in solids, liquids and gases have different amounts of energy. In general, the particles in a gas have more energy than those in a liquid, which have more energy than those in a solid.

Did you know ...?

Random means unpredictable. Lottery numbers are chosen at random.

Figure 4 The arrangement of particles in a a solid, b a liquid and c a gas

Summary questions

1 Copy and complete **a** to **d** using the words below. Each word can be used more than once.

   gas   liquid   solid

   a A .... has a fixed shape and volume.
   b A .... has a fixed volume but no shape.
   c A .... and a .... can flow.
   d A .... does not have a fixed volume.

2 State the scientific word for each of the following changes.
   a A mist appears on the inside of a window in a bus full of people.
   b Steam is produced from the surface of the water in a pan when the water is heated before it boils.
   c Ice cubes taken from a freezer thaw out.
   d Water put into a freezer gradually turns to ice.

3 Describe the changes that take place in the movement and arrangement of the particles in an ice cube when the ice melts.

Key points

- Flow, shape, volume and density are the properties used to describe each state of matter.
- The particles in a solid are held next to each other in fixed positions.
- The particles in a liquid move about at random and are in contact with each other.
- The particles in a gas move about randomly and are much further apart than particles in a solid or liquid.

Further teaching suggestions

Dry ice

- It may be possible to find a local source of solid carbon dioxide for teacher demonstrations. This can be shown to sublime. You could demonstrate that the mass is reducing by placing a piece on a balance with tongs and noting the decrease in mass over a period of time.

Distillation

- You could show the changes of state from ice to liquid, water to gas and back to liquid water using a distillation apparatus. Start with crushed ice in the round bottomed flask and show the stages, explaining the changes of energy required.

Answers to in-text questions

a Gas.
b It loses its shape.
c Water changes from a liquid to a solid.

Summary answers

1 a solid
   b liquid
   c liquid, gas (liquid and gas in any order)
   d gas

2 a condensation
   b evaporation/vaporisation
   c melting
   d freezing

3 The particles start to move about each other at random and are no longer in fixed positions.

Conduction

Learning objectives

Students should learn:

- that conduction is a process of energy transfer by heating
- that metals are good conductors because they have free electrons that carry energy
- that non-metal solids are generally poor conductors because they rely on atomic vibrations to carry energy.

Learning outcomes

Most students should be able to:

- state that metals are good conductors of energy
- list some poor conductors or insulators.

Some students should also be able to:

- explain why metals are good conductors of energy in terms of electron behaviour.

Answers to in-text questions

a Plastic and wood are poor conductors, so the handle doesn't get hot.

b The material the rods are made from is the independent variable. The dependent variable is the time taken for the wax to melt.

c Felt.

d The starting temperature.

Support

- Compare the student results across groups. You could then provide a graph of the average results (do this 'live' with a spreadsheet if possible) and this will let the students concentrate on explaining the results and evaluating them.

Extend

- The insulation experiment could be expanded to investigate the effectiveness of different thicknesses of materials, e.g. are two layers of felt twice as good as one?

AQA Specification link-up: Physics P1.1

- The transfer of energy by conduction ... involves particles, and how this transfer takes place. *[P1.1.3 a)]*
- The rate at which an object transfers energy by heating depends on:
  - surface area and volume
  - the material from which the object is made
  - the nature of the surface with which the object is in contact. *[P1.1.3 c)]*

Lesson structure

Starters

The wooden spoon – Ask students for an explanation of why it is all right to leave a wooden spoon in a pan of soup when heating it, but not a metal spoon. If possible, ask them to draw diagrams of what they think the particles are doing inside the objects. You may want to provide some students with a diagram showing the basic particles in the structure. *(5 minutes)*

A heatproof mat – Is a heatproof mat *really* heatproof? Extend students by asking them to design a reliable experiment to find out just how heat-resistant the material is. You could revisit this idea later in the chapter when discussing U-values. Good ideas should include some system of recording the time for energy to pass through the mat and heat/melt something on the other side. Extend students by asking them to consider how to measure the temperature changes precisely. *(10 minutes)*

Main

- Carry out the 'testing rods' activity. Adding drawing pins attached to the end of the rods with petroleum jelly, so that they fall off when the jelly melts, gives a touch of drama and helps timing. Discuss the accuracy of timings, precision and validity ('How Science Works').

- If you tried the heat-proof mat starter, you could show how slowly the mat conducts, by heating a cube of ice with a Bunsen burner through a mat sitting on a tripod.

- The 'conduction/insulation' practical is a fairly simple concept but is quite fiddly to do successfully. Give students adequate time to set it up carefully and then get readings (5–10 minutes of cooling is required to notice a difference).

- Students should be encouraged to make accurate readings during the experiment and this would be an excellent time to introduce data logging as an alternative to watching a thermometer for a long time. After the practical, students should be able to tell you which material was the best conductor and which was the worst. This practical work gives another opportunity to cover aspects of 'How Science Works', e.g. the reliability of data collected, the nature of variables and experimental design.

- The poor conductivity of air can be shown by holding an ice cube (in tongs) alongside a Bunsen flame, where it melts only slowly, and then a few centimetres above the top of the flame.

- The concept of free electrons will be unfamiliar to many students. A visual approach with animation is ideal for introducing this concept. An analogy, such as students staying in their place (representing ions in a metal) and throwing objects to each other (representing electrons carrying energy), could be used with the right kind of group. After explaining this, students should be able to tell you what the electrons do to move energy from one end of a rod to the other.

- Conduction by lattice vibration again requires clear diagrams to picture this idea. An ionic lattice model (e.g. sodium chloride) can help a lot here. Describe how poor this method of energy transfer is compared with the free electron method. This should reinforce the key point about good and poor conductors.

Plenaries

A model for conduction – Extend students by asking them to describe a physical analogy for lattice vibration, to give them a visual idea of what is going on. [They could come up with holding each other at arm's length and passing a shake along a line.] *(5 minutes)*

An electron story – To reinforce the correct use of scientific language including vibration, energy, transfer, diffuse, conductor, support students by asking them to describe their 'experience' as an electron in a metal rod being heated at one end. This use of imagination is often very helpful in cementing abstract ideas. *(10 minutes)*

Practical support

Testing sheets of material as insulators

Equipment and materials required

Kettles or another way of heating water. For each group: two containers (beakers or metal cans), two thermometers (graduated in 0.5 °C), sample materials (cotton wool, felt, paper, foam, etc.), two elastic bands, stop clock and a 100 cm³ measuring cylinder.

Details

It can be difficult to control this experiment because the materials are different thicknesses, and if the materials become wet, a lot of energy is lost through the process of evaporation. Make sure that students take care in lagging the containers and that the containers are on an insulated base, otherwise much of the energy is conducted into the bench. When carrying out practicals using cans of water, it is essential to use covers because heat loss by energy transfer evaporation is significant and will affect the results. The experiment works best with hotter water, but this increases the hazards.

Safety: Take care as some objects remain hot for a considerable time.

Conducting rods

Equipment and materials required

As a demonstration: set of metal rods with wax/petroleum jelly on one end (aluminium, copper, steel, brass and possibly glass), drawing pins, Bunsen burner, tripod, heatproof mat, eye protection.

Details

A specialised conduction demonstration apparatus works better than simple rods. Some metal strips have liquid crystal strips mounted on them and can be placed in hot water; this gives a much more visual demonstration and students can see the temperature gradient through the metals.

Aluminium's melting point is lower than the temperature of a blue Bunsen flame, so be careful not to melt the aluminium rod. A glass rod can be heated strongly until the glass is red hot and yet the other end is still cool, demonstrating just how poor a conductor it is.

Safety: Take care as some objects remain hot for a considerable time.

Energy transfer by heating

Conduction

P1 1.4 Conduction

Learning objectives

- What materials make the best conductors?
- What materials make the best insulators?
- Why are metals good conductors?
- Why are non-metals poor conductors?

When you have a barbecue, you need to know which materials are good conductors and which are good insulators. If you can't remember, you are likely to burn your fingers!

Testing rods of different materials as conductors

The rods need to be the same width and length for a fair test. Each rod is coated with a thin layer of wax near one end. The uncoated ends are then heated together.

Look at Figure 2. The wax melts fastest on the rod that conducts best.

Figure 1 At a barbecue – the steel cooking utensils have wooden or plastic handles

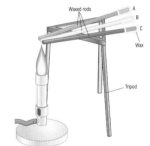

Waxed rods A B C Wax

Tripod

Figure 2 Comparing conductors

- Metals conduct energy better than non-metals.
- Copper is a better conductor than steel.
- Wood conducts better than glass.

a Why do steel pans have handles made of plastic or wood?
b Name the independent and the dependent variables investigated in Figure 2.

links
For more information on independent and dependent variables, look back at H3 Starting an investigation.

Practical

Testing sheets of materials as insulators

Use different materials to insulate identical cans (or beakers) of hot water. The volume of water and its temperature at the start should be the same.

Use a thermometer to measure the water temperature after a fixed time. The results should tell you which insulator was best.

The table below gives the results of comparing two different materials using the method explained in the practical.

Material	Starting temperature (°C)	Temperature after 300 s (°C)
paper	40	32
felt	40	36

c Which material, felt or paper, was the best insulator?
d Which variable shown in the table was controlled to make this a fair test?

Conduction in metals

Metals contain lots of free electrons. These electrons move about at random inside the metal and hold the positive metal ions together. They collide with each other and with the positive ions. (Ions are charged particles.)

⊕ Ion
○ Electron
◯ Atom

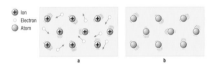

a b

Figure 4 Energy transfer in **a** a metal, **b** a non-metal

When a metal rod is heated at one end, the free electrons at the hot end gain kinetic energy and move faster.

- These electrons diffuse (i.e. spread out) and collide with other free electrons and ions in the cooler parts of the metal.
- As a result, they transfer kinetic energy to these electrons and ions.

So energy is transferred from the hot end of the rod to the colder end.

In a non-metallic solid, all the electrons are held in the atoms. Energy transfer only takes place because the atoms vibrate and shake each other. This is much less effective than energy transfer by free electrons. This is why metals are much better conductors than non-metals.

Summary questions

1 Copy and complete **a** to **c** using the words below:
fibreglass plastic steel wood
a A material called .... is used to insulate a house loft.
b The handle of a frying pan is made of .... or ....
c A radiator in a central heating system is made from ....

2 **a** Choose a material you would use to line a pair of winter boots. Explain your choice of material.
b How could you carry out a test on three different lining materials?

3 Explain why metals are good conductors of energy.

Figure 3 Insulating a loft. The air trapped between fibres make fibreglass a good insulator.

?? Did you know ... ?

Materials like wool and fibreglass are good insulators. This is because they contain air trapped between the fibres. Trapped air is a good insulator. We use materials like fibreglass for loft insulation and for lagging water pipes.

links
For more information about ions, see C1 1.4 Forming bonds.

Key points

- Metals are the best conductors of energy.
- Materials such as wool and fibreglass are the best insulators.
- Conduction of energy in a metal is due mainly to free electrons transferring energy inside the metal.
- Non-metals are poor conductors because they do not contain free electrons.

Further teaching suggestions

Feeling colder

- Why do blocks of cold metal feel colder than blocks of cold wood? Give students some blocks straight from the freezer and ask them to explain the difference. [The answer lies in the rate that energy can leave your hand and enter the material; the faster this happens, the colder the block will feel.]

Home insulation

- List the materials used for insulation in your own home and where they are found. Why are these materials chosen? Which materials are designed to be good conductors and where are these found?

Summary answers

1 **a** fibreglass
  b wood, plastic (wood and plastic in any order)
  c steel

2 **a** Felt or synthetic fur could be used, because they are good insulators.
  b Student's plan. Look for design of a fair test.

3 The free electrons that gain kinetic energy diffuse through the metal quickly, passing on energy to other electrons and ions in the metal.

P1 1.5

Convection

Learning objectives

Students should learn:

- that convection currents are the movement of particles in fluids
- how convection currents carry energy in fluids
- how expansion and changes in density cause convection currents.

Learning outcomes

Most students should be able to:

- give examples of where convection currents occur
- describe the process of convection in terms of particle movement in liquids and gases, and explain why convection cannot happen in solids.

Some students should also be able to:

- give a detailed description of convection in terms of particle movement, expansion and density changes.

Support

- Students could use worksheets with the processes in a convection current mixed up. They could cut these up and stick them in their books in the correct sequence.

Extend

- Students should describe the change in the particle behaviour during convection in detail. They should make links between increased temperature and the increase in the kinetic energy of the particles causing the spacing to increase slightly. This should include the speeding up of particles in a gas as the gas is heated.

AQA Specification link-up: Physics P1.1

- The transfer of energy by … convection … involves particles, and how this transfer takes place. *[P1.1.3 a)]*
- The rate at which an object transfers energy by heating depends on:
  - surface area and volume
  - the material from which the object is made
  - the nature of the surface with which the object is in contact. *[P1.1.3 c)]*

Lesson structure

Starters

Heat haze – Search an internet image bank for photographs or a video clip of heat haze above a road and ask students to describe what they think is happening. Link this back to the black road absorbing a lot of infrared radiation and becoming very hot. You may be able to demonstrate the effect by heating a metal sheet above a Bunsen burner if the lighting conditions are right in your laboratory. Try it out first to avoid disappointment. *(5 minutes)*

Density demonstration – Demonstrate the expansion of a material when heated (mercury in a thermometer, a ball and chain, etc.) and ask students to explain what is happening in terms of particle behaviour. This should link in closely with the previous lessons. Make sure that students do not think that the particles themselves are expanding! Support students by asking them to draw clear diagrams showing the difference and check that the 'spaces' between the particles are changing but not the particles themselves. *(10 minutes)*

Main

- Emphasise the fact that a **fluid** is a substance where the *particles* can move past each other, so both gases and liquids are fluid. Because gases have completely separated particles, these can flow faster than liquids.
- Demonstrating the chimney effect with the apparatus shown in the Student Book is very helpful. Brown corrugated card produces a lot of fine smoke when it is stubbed out, and the students can see the flow of smoke down the first chimney and up the second. Point out to students that using a fire with a chimney is the cause of some draughts in houses.
- If you have convection heaters, you could demonstrate (or let students have a go at making) spirals of paper hung on string. These move due to the current above the heater. Don't leave big ones up because they could set off motion-sensitive alarms in the middle of the night!
- Convection currents in water can be shown using a small potassium permanganate crystal placed carefully in the bottom of a large beaker, and heating gently using a Bunsen burner directly beneath it; the larger the beaker, the better the effect. A glass convection loop is better than a beaker if available. See 'Practical support'.
- Students need to go through the stages that cause a convection current with emphasis on the use of the correct words at each stage. They could label a diagram or draw a flow chart.
- Make sure that they are using the terms 'expand' and 'contract' correctly before the plenary. A common misconception is that expansion is caused by the particles themselves expanding. This should be addressed directly when explaining convection.

Plenaries

Convection loops – Test understanding of convection, conduction and radiation with a question loop game. Possible questions could include: what happens when a gas is heated? [it expands]; what happens to the particles in the gas as it heats up? [they move further apart]; what happens to the density? [it decreases]; why does the gas rise upwards? [because it is less dense] and so on until the complete convection cycle is covered. *(5 minutes)*

The sea by night – Extend students by asking them to apply the knowledge gained here in similar situations using the ideas from this lesson; students could draw a diagram and give an explanation about why there is a breeze from the land to the sea in the evening at the coast. The diagram should include energy being transferred from the sea causing warming of the air above it. They should then use convection currents to explain the movement of the air. *(10 minutes)*

Practical support

Chimney effect

The chimney-effect apparatus is fairly standard, but could be improvised if necessary. Use smouldering cardboard or matches to produce smoke. The container must have a glass or Perspex front, so that air cannot enter from this route.

Demonstrating convection in liquids

The potassium manganate (VII) can be placed at the bottom of the beaker by the following method so that it does not dissolve as it falls.

Equipment and materials required

Large (100 cm³) beaker or glass convection loop, Bunsen burner, tripod, gauze, mat, tweezers, glass tube and small crystal of potassium manganate(VII).

Details

Fill the beaker with water. Place your thumb over the end of a glass tube and push it into the beaker so that it touches the bottom and doesn't let any water in. Take your thumb off and, hopefully, the tube will remain empty. Finally drop the crystal down the tube using forceps and remove the tube. Then you should get a perfectly placed crystal.

With a glass convection loop, the crystal should be placed at the top and the tube heated at the bottom. Don't try to get it in the bottom corner.

Safety: CLEAPSS Hazcard 81 Potassium manganate(VII) – harmful and oxidising. Its crystals will stain hands and clothing. Handle crystals with tweezers.

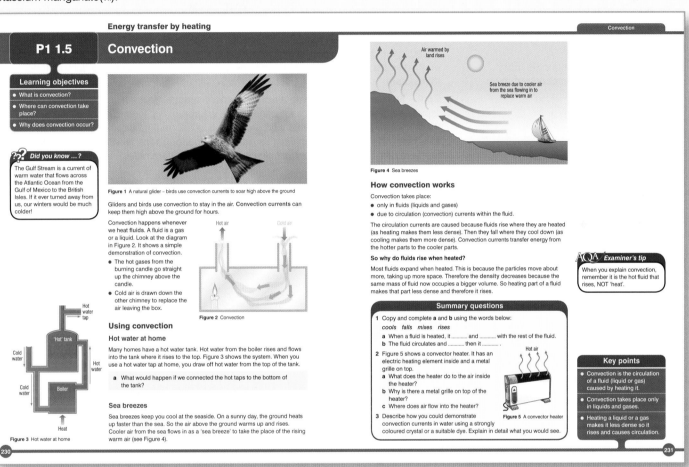

Figure 1 A natural glider – birds use convection currents to soar high above the ground

Figure 2 Convection

Figure 3 Hot water at home

Figure 4 Sea breezes

Figure 5 A convector heater

Further teaching suggestions

Convection in a boiling tube

- Demonstrate conduction and convection in water. Hold a small ice cube at the bottom of a boiling tube with a bit of metal gauze and three-quarters fill the tube with water. Heat the water in the middle of the tube with a Bunsen burner; the water at the top will boil while the ice remains frozen. Ask students to explain this in terms of conduction and convection.

Galilean thermometer

- The Galilean thermometer relies on changes of density in liquids and solids to show temperature. Demonstrate one and ask students to explain how it works.

Convection and climates

- Convection currents are very important in the oceans and dramatically affect the weather of the British Isles. Compare London's winter to Moscow's. Students could research the effect of the Gulf Stream and what the weather would be like without it. As an alternative, they could find out about El Niño.

Answers to in-text questions

a The water from the taps would be cold.

Summary answers

1 a rises, mixes   b cools, falls

2 a It heats it and makes it rise.
  b The hot air passes through the grille into the room.
  c Cold air flows into the heater at the bottom.

3 Drop the crystal into a beaker of water through a tube. Heat gently under one corner. The colour rises above point of heating and travels across the top and falls at opposite side of beaker (where density of cooler water is greater). The colour then travels across the bottom of the beaker to replace lower density warmer water that rises above the Bunsen flame.

P1 1.6

Evaporation and condensation

Learning objectives

Students should learn:

- that evaporation is the change of state from a liquid into a gas and condensation is the change of state from a gas into a liquid
- that the rate of evaporation is increased by increasing:
  - the temperature of the liquid
  - the surface area of the liquid
  - the flow of gas above the liquid's surface.
- that during evaporation, the most energetic particles escape reducing the average kinetic energy of the remaining particles and so reducing the temperature.

Learning outcomes

Most students should be able to:

- state the factors that increase the rate of evaporation
- describe the processes of evaporation and the process of condensation in terms of particle behaviour.

Some students should also be able to:

- explain in detail how evaporation has a cooling effect on a liquid.

Support

- Put marks on the watch glasses (or Petri dishes) so that students put in the correct amount of liquid. These marks correspond to selected surface areas, so that the students can avoid doing the calculations. You could then provide a simple table for them to fill in that will allow the plotting of a graph. Alternatively, a qualitative result could be expected.

Extend

- Students could look at the role of evaporation in cooling of humans. Let them find out about why humans sweat and how this helps us cool down. They could also look at the effect of cooling by radiation and why blood is moved to the surface layers. What do furry animals do to cool?

Specification link-up: Physics P1.1

- The transfer of energy by … evaporation and condensation involves particles, and how this transfer takes place. *[P1.1.3 a)]*
- The factors that affect the rate of evaporation and condensation. *[P1.1.3 b)]*

Lesson structure

Starters

Cool demonstration – If you have some alcohol-based hand cleaning gel you could ask a student coat their hands and then use a cool air blower (or just get them to blow) to cause the gel to evaporate. This can have a significant cooling effect on the skin. You might also be able to obtain a cooling spray from the PE department to demonstrate. *(5 minutes)*

Spill – Spill some ethanol onto a non-absorbent surface. Students should watch while it rapidly evaporates. Ask them what they think is happening. Extend students by asking them to draw particle diagrams explaining what is happening. Open the bottle again and ask them why it is not evaporating as quickly even though the ethanol is at the same temperature. [There is a much smaller surface area.] *(10 minutes)*

Main

- An important concept the students need to grasp is that a liquid will evaporate even when it is well below its boiling point. The liquid does not need to be 'hot' to evaporate because some of the particles will have significantly more energy than others. Students will be aware of evaporation but most will not connect it with energy transfer or the particle model.

- Ensure that students are aware that temperature is related to the average kinetic energy of the particles. The higher the temperature, the greater the average kinetic energy the particles have. There will still be some slower particles when the temperature increases but there will be more 'fast' particles.

- Studenst may have difficulty in understanding the cooling effect of evaporation, so take some time describing how the particles with the most energy escape first. This means that the average (mean) energy of the particles decreases, and this means that the temperature falls.

- It is always worth showing the cooling effect of evaporation as detailed in the Student Book. This can be simply achieved by using the 'cool demonstration' starter or simply dipping your finger in ethanol and blowing on it. The ethanol will evaporate quickly and have a significant cooling effect on the surface of your finger. A more detailed example is discussed in 'Practical support'.

- If you have time then the 'Investigating evaporation' practical is well worth trying out (see 'Practical support'). It is simple but can give good results for analysis. It allows students to develop mathematical skills such as calculating surface area, finding change in mass and plotting of graphs with fairly awkward numbers (small masses and areas).

Plenaries

Tropical sweats – Search out some relative humidity figures for different countries. Show students that some places have more water in the air than others and ask them to explain what this will feel like. They should be able to link this with the experiment from earlier and the movement of air. *(5 minutes)*

Evaporation analysis – Provide data for the evaporation of different liquids. Students plot this on the same set of axes and notice that some liquids evaporate more quickly than others for the same temperature and surface area. Can they explain this? Extend students by asking them to develop ideas about the 'size' (mass) of the molecules involved; once this is achieved give them some data about the mass of the particles for them to confirm their ideas. *(10 minutes)*

Practical support

Demonstrating cooling by evaporation

This demonstration shows the cooling effect of evaporation. Enough energy is removed by evaporation, so that water freezes.

Equipment and materials required

Fume cupboard, a small (100 cm³) glass beaker, block of wood, cold water, ethoxyethane (ether) – extremely flammable/harmful.

Details

The experiment must be carried out in a working fume cupboard to make sure that there is a good air flow to cause rapid evaporation and to remove the ether fumes. Wet the wooden block and base of the beaker so that there is a thin 'puddle' between them. Half fill the beaker with ether and rest it on the block inside the fume cupboard. The ether should evaporate and, in doing so, cool the water so much that it freezes. This is a good opportunity to discuss why a good flow of air is required. The water will take a few minutes to freeze, so come back to it later in the lesson.

Safety: CLEAPSS Hazcard 42 Ethoxyethane (ether) – extremely flammable and harmful. Wear eye protection. Make sure there are no naked flames in the same room.

Investigating evaporation

Students could investigate the rate of evaporation using ethanol and watch glasses.

Equipment and materials required

Each group will require a range of watch glasses, ethanol – highly flammable/harmful, stop clock, top-pan balance, ruler.

Details

Students pour some ethanol onto a small watch glass and measure the diameter. They then measure the mass and allow the ethanol to evaporate for a set time (two minutes should be enough if a precise balance is used). They measure the mass again after the time has expired and calculate the mass loss by evaporation. During the two minutes they should calculate the surface area of the ethanol.

Repeat with other surface areas (using the different watch glasses to help). Once the results are collected, students could compare the amount of evaporation that has taken place with the surface area to determine a pattern.

Safety: CLEAPSS Hazcard 40A Ethanol – extremely flammable and harmful. Make sure there are no naked flames in the same room.

Textbook page P1 1.6 Evaporation and condensation

Further teaching suggestions

Investigative skills

- Students could plot a graph of the results of the 'Investigating evaporation' practical and reach a conclusion about the results. This could include sharing of results to verify reliability.

Answers to in-text questions

a The molecules in the condensed water can escape into the air and then escape from the room through the window.

b There are lots of water molecules in the air on a damp day and many of them can condense on the clothing.

Summary answers

1 a evaporates
  b condenses
  c evaporates, cools

2 The air in the room becomes damp as everyone breathes out water vapour. The water vapour condenses on the inside of the windows.

3 a Water evaporates faster from the wet clothes on a hot day than on a cold day because they are warmer.
  b Evaporation of water from the wet clothes on a windy day makes the clothes cooler which makes the wearer colder than someone wearing dry clothes.

P1 1.7

Energy transfer by design

Learning objectives

Students should learn:

- the factors that affect the rate of energy transfer
- ways of controlling the flow of energy
- how we can reduce or increase the rate of energy transfer in a variety of situations
- how to plan an investigation into energy transfer.

Learning outcomes

Most students should be able to:

- investigate factors that affect the rate of energy transfer.

Some students should also be able to:

- explain in detail how the design of a vacuum flask reduces the rate of energy transfer.

Answers to in-text questions

a To increase the rate of energy transfer by radiation.

b It increases.

c The plastic case, the screw cap lid, the plastic support spring, the sponge pads. The rate at which energy was transferred away from the glass container would increase.

Support

- Work on gaining quantitative results in the practical task. Students should be given containers that are clearly large, medium and small and this will produce a simple pattern.

Extend

- Extend students by asking them to calculate the ratio of surface area to volume for the containers. This will involve measuring the diameter and height of any beaker and then performing the calculations for surface area and volume.

AQA   Specification link-up: Physics P1.1

- The rate at which an object transfers energy by heating depends on:
  - surface area and volume
  - the material from which the object is made
  - the nature of the surface with which the object is in contact. *[P1.1.3 c)]*
- The bigger the temperature difference between an object and its surroundings, the faster the rate at which energy is transferred by heating. *[P1.1.3 d)]*
- Evaluate the design of everyday appliances that transfer energy by heating … *[P1.1]*

Controlled Assessment: SA4.1 Planning an investigation. *[SA4.1.1 a) b) c)]*

Lesson structure

Starters

Keeping warm – How could you keep a cup of tea warm? Students should come up with some ideas. They should be able to think of ways of reducing the rate of conduction [change the material of the cup], convection and evaporation [a lid] and radiation [have a white or silver cup]. You might have a travel mug available to show that this had already been designed to keep drinks warm. Extend students by asking them to evaluate each other's designs and move on to consider the cost or practicality of the measures. *(5 minutes)*

Cooling down – How can a substance be cooled quickly? This is the opposite of the above task. Can students design a really good way of cooling by using their knowledge from the last few lessons? *(10 minutes)*

Main

- With students watching, fill a glass beaker and a vacuum flask with the same volume of boiling water at the start of the lesson for later use.
- If a radiator from a small refrigerator is available, this makes an excellent prop to discuss how to design an object to transfer energy quickly. Emphasise the way the surface area is maximised to allow air to flow and transfer energy.
- Discuss how a cup of tea can be cooled by blowing over it, and describe how the energy escapes the tea.
- Students could investigate the difference in cooling for objects with a large surface area and those with a small surface area, as described in 'Practical support'. You could leave this experiment running while you move on to the vacuum flask demonstration. Other students could look at different initial temperatures. All investigative aspects of 'How Science Works' could be covered here.
- Some students will struggle in understanding that the larger beaker has a smaller surface area to volume ratio. Cubic containers may help the students, if some are available.
- Show some vacuum flasks in various states of construction (without the silvering) and explain their features. It is important to emphasise that there is no air between the glass walls. Show students the point where the air has been removed before sealing.
- Show students the difference in temperature of the water in the cup and in the flask to illustrate how good the flask is at keeping water hot. Check that students can describe what each feature of the flask does to prevent energy transfer. Reinforce to students that vacuum flasks also keep cold things cold.

Plenaries

Warming up the lab – Support students by asking them to list or design improvements to reduce the rate of transfer from the laboratory. This will allow you to evaluate their understanding of radiation, conduction, convection and evaporation. They can prioritise these improvements. This links in nicely with the next lesson. *(5 minutes)*

Explorer pack – Students could list and explain the purpose of the clothing they would need to take on a range of scenarios during their exploration of the world. They will be visiting Antarctica, the Sahara, the Amazonian jungle and climbing Mount Everest. Not a bad day out. *(10 minutes)*

Practical support

Investigating the rate of energy transfer

Equipment and materials required

Large (500 cm³) and small (250 cm³) glass beakers, data loggers, temperature sensors, thermometers, Bunsen burners, heatproof mats and tripods, gauzes, aluminium foil for lids, eye protection.

Details

Fill the beakers with hot water and then boil the water with the Bunsen burners to make sure that both beakers start at the same temperature. Turn off the Bunsen burners, carefully remove hot beakers and stand on heatproof mat. Add a foil lid and thermometer and monitor the cooling for 10 minutes. The smaller beaker should cool substantially more than the larger one. These ideas can lead to a more complete investigation of the relationship between surface area and cooling.

Students could then investigate if the temperature difference between the water and its surroundings affects its rate of cooling.

Safety: Wear eye protection. Take care with boiling water.

Demonstrating the effectiveness of a vacuum flask

Equipment and materials required

Vacuum flask, kettle, similarly-sized beaker with lid, two thermometers.

Details

Fill the flask and beaker with the same volume of boiling water. Put the lid on the flask and allow the containers to cool for as long as possible during the lesson. The flask will keep the water very hot, usually above 80 °C, while the water in the beaker will be quite cool. For an even greater difference leave the beaker on a conductive surface.

Safety: Take care with boiling water. Do not drop thermometer into the glass vacuum flask.

P1 1.7 — Energy transfer by design

Learning objectives

- What design factors affect the rate at which a hot object transfers energy?
- What can we do to control the rate of energy transfer to or from an object?

Figure 1 A car radiator

Figure 2 Motorcycle engine fins

Did you know ...?

Some electronic components get warm when they are working, but if they become too hot they stop working. Such components are often fixed to a metal plate to keep them cool. The metal plate increases the effective surface area of the component. We call the metal plate a **heat sink**.

Figure 3 A heat sink in a computer

How Science Works

Cooling by design

Lots of things can go wrong if we don't control energy transfer. For example, a car engine that overheats can go up in flames.

- The cooling system of a car engine transfers energy from the engine to a radiator. The radiator is shaped so it has a large surface area. This increases the rate of energy transfer through convection in the air and through radiation.
- A motorcycle engine is shaped with **fins** on its outside surface. The fins increase the surface area of the engine in contact with air so the engine transfers energy to its surroundings faster than if it had no fins.
- Most cars also have a cooling fan that switches on when the engine is too hot. This increases the flow of air over the surface of the radiator.

a Why do car radiators have a large surface area?
b What happens to the rate of energy transfer when the cooling fan switches on?

The vacuum flask

If you are outdoors in cold weather, a hot drink from a vacuum flask keeps you warm. In the summer the same vacuum flask keeps your drinks cold.

In Figure 4, the liquid you drink is in the double-walled glass container.

- The vacuum between the two walls of the container cuts out energy transfer by conduction and convection between the walls.
- Glass is a poor conductor so there is little energy transfer by conduction through the glass.
- The glass surfaces are silvery to reduce radiation from the outer wall.
- The spring supporting the double-walled container is made of plastic which is a good insulator.
- The plastic cap stops cooling by evaporation as it stops vapour loss from the flask. In addition, energy transfer by conduction is cut down because the cap is made from plastic.

Figure 4 A vacuum flask

- Plastic cap
- Double-walled glass (or plastic) container
- Plastic protective cover
- Hot or cold liquid
- Sponge pad (for protection)
- Inside surfaces silvered to stop radiation
- Vacuum prevents conduction and convection
- Plastic spring for support

So why does the liquid in the flask eventually cool down?

The above features cut down but do not totally stop the transfer of energy from the liquid. Energy transfer occurs at a very low rate due to radiation from the silvery glass surface and conduction through the cap, spring and glass walls. The liquid transfers energy slowly to its surroundings so it eventually cools.

c List the other parts of the flask that are good insulators. What would happen if they weren't good insulators?

Factors affecting the rate of energy transfer

The bigger the temperature difference between an object and its surroundings, the faster the rate at which energy is transferred. In addition, the above examples show that the rate at which an object transfers energy depends on its design. The design factors that matter are:

- the materials the object is in contact with
- the object's shape
- the object's surface area.

In addition, the object's mass and the material it is made from are important. That is because they affect how quickly its temperature changes (and therefore the rate of transfer of energy to or from it) when it loses or gains energy.

How Science Works

Foxy survivors

A desert fox has much larger ears than an arctic fox. Blood flowing through the ears transfers energy from inside the body to the surface of the ears. Big ears have a much larger surface area than little ears so they transfer energy to the surroundings more quickly than little ears.

- A desert fox has big ears so it keeps cool by transferring energy quickly to its surroundings.
- An arctic fox has little ears so it transfers energy more slowly to its surroundings. This helps keep it warm.

Summary questions

1 Hot water is pumped through a radiator like the one in Figure 6.
Copy and complete **a** to **c** using the words below:

conduction   radiation   convection

a Energy transfer through the walls of the radiator is due to ....
b Hot air in contact with the radiator causes energy transfer to the room by ....
c Energy transfer to the room takes place directly due to ....

Figure 6 A central heating radiator

2 An electronic component in a computer is attached to a heat sink.
a i Explain why the heat sink is necessary.
ii Why is a metal plate used as the heat sink?
b Plan a test to show that double glazing is more effective at preventing energy transfer than single glazing.

3 Describe, in detail, how the design of a vacuum flask reduces the rate of energy transfer.

links

For more information on factors affecting energy transfer, see P1 1.8 Specific heat capacity.

Practical

Investigating the rate of energy transfer

You can plan an investigation using different beakers and hot water to find out what affects the rate of cooling.

- Write a question that you could investigate.
- Identify the independent, dependent and control variables in your investigation.

Figure 5 Fox ears a A desert fox b An arctic fox

Key points

- The rate of energy transferred to or from an object depends on:
  - the shape, size and type of material of the object
  - the materials the object is in contact with
  - the temperature difference between the object and its surroundings.

Further teaching suggestions

- Use temperature sensors and data logging software to capture more detail and save time plotting the graphs in the experiments.

Heat sinks

- Computer components become exceptionally hot and this energy needs to be removed. The microprocessor will have a cooling system and the case will be designed to allow energy to be dispersed by convection. You could open up the case of a PC and explain how the cooling systems work in terms of conduction, convection and radiation.

Safety: Ensure the PC cannot be plugged into the mains. (Don't allow any access to a mains lead.)

Vacuum flask

- Sir James Dewar invented the vacuum flask (or Dewar jar). Students could research the history of this and his other important chemical discoveries.

Keeping warm

- Many small animals huddle together to keep warm, famously penguins do this en masse. Can students give a scientific explanation of this behaviour? This is based on the surface area to volume ideas.

Summary answers

1 a conduction
  b convection
  c radiation

2 a i To prevent the component overheating.
    ii Metal is a good conductor. The heat sink is plate-shaped to increase its surface area, so it transfers energy to the surrounding air as effectively as possible.
  b Plan must have a fair system that compares a single plate of glass to a pair of plates, ideally with a sealed air gap between.

3 Student's explanation to include the role played by the plastic cap, double-walled plastic container, silvered inside surfaces, vacuum layer.

P1 1.8

Specific heat capacity

AQA   Specification link-up: Physics P1.1

- The specific heat capacity of a substance is the amount of energy required to change the temperature of one kilogram of the substance by one degree Celsius.
  $E = m \times c \times \theta$ [P1.1.4 d)]
- Evaluate different materials according to their specific heat capacities. [P1.1]

  Controlled Assessment: SA4.3 Collect primary and secondary data. [SA4.3.1 a)]

Learning objectives

Students should learn:

- that the greater the mass of an object, the more energy is required to raise its temperature
- the material that an object is made of affects the amount of energy required to raise its temperature and each material has a specific heat capacity
- storage heaters rely on substances to store and transfer energy.

Learning outcomes

Most students should be able to:

- state that more energy is required to raise the temperature of objects with a greater mass
- explain that different materials of the same mass require different amounts of energy to raise their temperatures by the same amount.

Some students should also be able to:

- calculate the energy required to raise a known mass of material by a known temperature.

Lesson structure

Starters

Hot metal – Heat a smallish block of metal until it is clearly **very** hot using a Bunsen burner, gauze and tripod. Use tongs to drop it (carefully) into a litre of water and show the increase in temperature; a temperature sensor is easier to see than a thermometer. Why doesn't the water boil when the block was clearly far above 100 °C? Return to this question after the lesson. *(5 minutes)*

Boiling up – Demonstrate the heating of two different masses of water until they boil. You can do this in a kettle or with traditional heating apparatus. Ask students to come up with their own explanation as to why the smaller mass boils first. This demonstrates clearly that the mass of the material is significant.

Main

- You could start the lesson with the boiling demonstration. If you have a data logging apparatus then it is very helpful to record the temperate rise and show that the smaller mass of water has a more rapid rise in temperature.
- This topic contains some of the first mathematics that students will encounter in this part of the course and it is important to take students slowly through the process.
- Go through each of the factors that affect the temperature rise of an object as outlined in the Student Book. If you take each one in turn then students will gain a good understanding. They will easily understand that the more energy you provide, the more the temperature will rise. Then they will find it fairly obvious that the greater the mass of the object the less the temperate will rise. [This is because the energy is shared out between more particles.] Finally, the substance the material is made of is important; you could link this to the way the particles are held together.
- Now you can tackle the idea of specific heat capacity; this can confuse even able students, so describe it carefully. Basically, the specific heat capacity is the amount of energy needed to increase the temperate of 1 kg of a material by 1 °C. Give a few simple examples: it takes 4000 J to make the temperature of 1 kg of water rise by 1 °C. It takes 8000 J to make it rise by 2 °C.
- Discuss the amount of energy required to raise the temperature of 2 kg of water and 0.5 kg and so on. You could then discuss other materials; use aluminium as you will have a sample prop on hand.
- Students should perform a range of calculations based on the equation provided. The more they do, the simpler the idea becomes. You coud also use this as a planning exercise.

Plenaries

Hot water – It takes a lot of energy to heat a small mass of water. Why is water used in central heating systems? Students could come up with a range of reasons why it is chosen. [It is non-toxic, it is cheap, it can flow easily, it can carry a large amount of energy in a small volume.] *(5 minutes)*

Crossword – Students should complete a crossword based on the previous lessons of this chapter. This should form a summary of their learning about energy transfer. Provide differentiated clues to different groups of students: simple questions to support some students and somewhat more difficult ones to extend others. *(10 minutes)*

Answers to in-text questions

a 840 000 J

b The room would heat up quickly then become much cooler.

Support

- Support students with plenty of help with the calculation through this lesson. Provide a worksheet with plenty of examples showing how they are preformed. Make sure the questions do not require any rearrangement of the equation.

Extend

- Students could be extended by looking into why water has such a large specific heat capacity. They may find out about hydrogen bonding between molecules. Ask the student with the best explanation to report to the rest of the class.
- Students may be extended in the 'Hot metal' starter by thinking about the number of particles in the materials and even the energy of each particle.

Practical support

⚙ Investigating heating
Equipment and materials required
Per group: low voltage power supply, aluminium heating block, heating element, thermometer, stop clock and beaker (size depends on the mass of the metal block).

Details
Aluminium blocks specifically designed for this experiment should be available; they have one large hole for the heating element to be placed in the top and another for the thermometer. Emphasise that it is important that the thermometer makes good contact with the metal to record an accurate temperature rise.

Students heat the block for a set time; five minutes is enough. They record the temperate each minute to see if the rise is consistent.

They then repeat the process with a beaker of water that has the same mass, so the beaker has to be able to hold sufficient volume. They should compare the two temperature rises and notice that the aluminium's temperature rise is greater.

⚙ Measuring the specific heat capacity of a metal
Equipment and materials required
Per group: low voltage power supply, aluminium heating block, heating element, thermometer, joulemeter, connecting leads and stop clock.

Details
In this experiment students need to heat the aluminium block again, but this time they need to know how much energy has been provided to perform the calculation. In their plan they should list their measurements in the correct order.

When students attempt to measure the specific heat capacity of aluminium, it is likely that their value will not match the stated one. They could discuss the reasons that their values are different; this is mainly due to energy transferred to the environment.

Safety: Wear eye protection. Warn students that items will stay hot for a long time after heating.

Energy transfer by heating

P1 1.8 — Specific heat capacity ⓚ

Learning objectives
- How does the mass of a substance affect how quickly its temperature changes when it is heated?
- What else affects how quickly the temperature of a substance changes when it is heated?
- How do storage heaters work?

Joulemeter

To power unit

Heater — Thermometer

Aluminium block

Insulation

Figure 1 Heating an aluminium block

A car in strong sunlight can become very hot. A concrete block of equal mass would not become as hot. Metal heats up more easily than concrete. Investigations show that when a substance is heated, its temperature rise depends on:
- the amount of energy supplied to it
- the mass of the substance
- what the substance is.

Practical
Investigating heating

Figure 1 shows how we can use a low voltage electric heater to heat an aluminium block.

Energy is measured in units called joules (J).

Use the energy meter (or joulemeter) to measure the energy supplied to the block. Use the thermometer to measure its temperature rise.

Replace the block with an equal mass of water in a suitable container. Measure the temperature rise of the water when the same amount of energy is supplied to it by the heater.

Your results should show that aluminium heats up more than water.

The following results were obtained using two different amounts of water. They show that:
- 1600 J was used to heat 0.1 kg of water by 4 °C
- 3200 J was used to heat 0.2 kg of water by 4 °C.

Using these results we can say that:
- 16 000 J of energy would have been needed to heat 1.0 kg of water by 4 °C
- 4000 J of energy is needed to heat 1.0 kg of water by 1 °C.
More accurate measurements would give 4200 J per kg per °C for water. This is its **specific heat capacity.**

The specific heat capacity of a substance is the energy needed or energy transferred to 1 kg of the substance to raise its temperature by 1 °C.

The unit of specific heat capacity is the joule per kilogram per °C.

For a known change of temperature of a known mass of a substance:

$$E = m \times c \times \theta$$

Where:

E is the energy transferred in joules, J; m is the mass in kilograms, kg; c is the specific heat capacity, J/kg °C; θ is the temperature change in degrees Celsius, °C

To find the specific heat capacity you need to rearrange the above equation:

$$c = \frac{E}{m \times \theta}$$

a How much energy is needed to heat 5.0 kg of water from 20 °C to 60 °C?

??? Did you know ... ?
Coastal towns are usually cooler in summer and warmer in winter than towns far inland. This is because water has a very high specific heat capacity. Energy from the Sun (or lack of energy) affects the temperature of the sea much less than the land.

Practical
Measuring the specific heat capacity of a metal

Use the arrangement shown in Figure 1 to heat a metal block of known mass. Here are some measurements using an aluminium block of mass 1.0 kg.

Starting temperature	= 14 °C
Final temperature	= 22 °C
Energy supplied	= 7200 J

To find the specific heat capacity of aluminium, the measurements above give:

E = energy transferred = energy supplied = 7200 J
θ = temperature change = 22 °C − 14 °C = 8 °C

Inserting these values into the rearranged equation gives:

$$c = \frac{E}{m \times \theta} = \frac{7200\,J}{1.0\,kg \times 8\,°C} = 900\,J/kg\,°C$$

The table below shows the values for some other substances.

Substance	water	oil	aluminium	iron	copper	lead	concrete
Specific heat capacity (joules per kg per °C)	4200	2100	900	390	490	130	850

Storage heaters

A storage heater uses electricity at night (off-peak) to heat special bricks or concrete blocks in the heater. Energy transfer from the bricks keeps the room warm. The bricks have a high specific heat capacity so they store lots of energy. They warm up slowly when the heater element is on and cool down slowly when it is off.

Electricity consumed at off-peak times is sometimes charged for at a cheaper rate, so storage heaters are designed to be cost effective.

b How would the temperature of the room change if the bricks cooled quickly?

Figure 2 A storage heater

Summary questions

1 A small bucket of water and a large bucket of water are left in strong sunlight. Which one warms up faster? Give a reason for your answer.

2 Use the information in the table above to answer this question.
   a Explain why a mass of lead heats up more quickly than an equal mass of aluminium.
   b Calculate the energy needed
      i to raise the temperature of 0.20 kg of aluminium from 15 °C to 40 °C.
      ii to raise the temperature of 0.40 kg of water from 15 °C to 40 °C.

3 State two ways in which a storage heater differs from a radiant heater.

Key points
- The greater the mass of an object, the more slowly its temperature increases when it is heated.
- The rate of temperature change of a substance when it is heated depends on:
  – the energy supplied to it
  – its mass
  – its specific heat capacity.
- Storage heaters use off-peak electricity to store energy in special bricks.

Further teaching suggestions

Data logging
- Use temperature sensors and data-logging software to capture more detail and save time plotting the graphs in the experiments.

More calculations
- Students could complete more example questions and calculations until they have perfected the technique.

Summary answers

1 The small bucket warms up faster because the mass of water in it is much less than in the large bucket.

2 a Lead has a lower specific heat capacity than aluminium. Less energy is needed by lead for a given temperature rise.
  b i 4500 J ii 42 000 J

3 A storage heater contains bricks or concrete that are heated by the heater element. A radiant heater does not contain bricks or concrete.

  A storage heater transfers energy to the surroundings gradually. A radiant heater transfers heat instantly.

P1 1.9

Heating and insulating buildings

Learning objectives

Students should learn:

- there are various methods to reduce energy transfer from a house
- how the insulating properties can be measured using U-values
- that solar heating has no fuel costs (expect for pumping systems) but can have high initial costs.

Learning outcomes

Most students should be able to:

- list methods of saving energy in a house and give a brief evaluation of the techniques
- find the payback time of various energy saving measures
- state the general relationship between U-values and insulation properties.

Some students should also be able to:

- explain energy transfers using U-values for materials.

Answers to in-text questions

a The insulation prevents the movement of air, cutting down convection currents.

b 'Staywarm' is twice as good an insulator.

Support

- Use this final energy lesson to link back to all of the previous ideas. You might like to make a giant house diagram and ask students to add the key ideas to it. Select the best explanations of how the energy-saving measures work and add them to the master diagram.

Extend

- Students could find information on modern building design that reduces energy costs. They could find out about the physical design of the structure allowing increased air flow for cooling, or even some of the newer smart materials that can change colour at different temperatures. Why would a brick that changes from white to black when it warms up be useful? How could glass that becomes 'mirrored' in bright sunlight be used?

AQA Specification link-up: Physics P1.1

- U-values measure how effective a material is as an insulator. *[P1.1.4 a)]*
- The lower the U-value, the better the material is as an insulator. *[P1.1.4 b)]*
- Solar panels may contain water that is heated by radiation from the Sun. This water may then be used to heat buildings or provide domestic hot water. *[P1.1.4 c)]*
- Compare ways in which energy is transferred in and out of objects by heating and ways in which the rates of these transfers can be varied. *[P1.1]*
- Evaluate the design of everyday appliances that transfer energy by heating, including economic considerations. *[P1.1]*
- Evaluate the effectiveness of different types of material used for insulation, including U-values and economic factors including payback time. *[P1.1]*

Lesson structure

Starters

Is it worth it? – Swapping over your mobile phone to a new one will cost you £200 but you will be able to enter a new contract for £10 less each month on a two-year contract. Should you swap your phone? What other factors you would have to consider? [Talk time, number of texts, internet access]. *(5 minutes)*

Hot house – Support students by providing a large diagram of a house showing the various locations that heat can be transferred. They could draw on (or label) energy-saving measures. Later in the lesson they could prioritise these improvements. You can differentiate by making the house as simple or complicated as you want. *(10 minutes)*

Main

- This lesson is focused on applying students' knowledge of energy transfer to a real situation: keeping a house warm. You could also look at energy-saving measures in other locations such as your school building or an office block.
- Excluding draughts is often the most cost-effective method of reducing energy costs but the reduced airflow can make some places a bit stuffy.
- The concept of payback time is straightforward when enough examples are understood. Go through each possibility in turn and lead students through the calculation. You can find some costs and savings on a range of energy-saving tips websites. The smaller changes have shorter payback times, as they are relatively cheap. However, once this is achieved, the annual savings are small.
- Show some expanded polystyrene or similar foam when talking about insulation of walls. Although this is not the same as the foam injected, it shows the same idea of preventing the movement of air. New-build houses use this type of foam with aluminium foil on both sides. You can easily obtain this from DIY shops.
- Glass is a reasonable insulator (try passing heat along a glass rod) but windows are thin and have large surface areas, making them worse insulators than thick walls. Make this point to show that the area of a surface is clearly important as to how much energy passes through; this links to some previous experiments.
- The U-value is quite a complex idea because it depends on surface area and a rate of energy transfer. It is appropriate for most students to know that the smaller the value, the better the material is at providing insulation.
- The model house could be used to investigate the effectiveness of materials more fully. There are a range of problems with the model that you could discuss or let students identify. For example, there is only one room and the materials are not brick. You could use this as an open-ended planning exercise.
- If you have time you could demonstrate a solar heating panel, as described in 'Practical support'. It could alternatively be demonstrated later in the course.

Plenary

Energy neutral house – Students can use their knowledge of energy transfer to design an energy neutral house. They can use all of the measures here and may include some of the upcoming ideas on electricity generation. Use their work to help you decide exactly which concepts to focus on in the next chapter. *(10 minutes)*

Practical support

Demonstrating solar heating

It is possible to show solar heating using sunlight or a bright lamp.

Equipment and materials required

Cold water tank and warmed water tank, two temperature sensors attached to a data logger, a pipe clamp, and a large metal plate sprayed matt black with a long thin tube mounted on it in a series of 's' shapes. The tube should also be black but you could leave some gaps, so that students can see the water pass through it.

Details

The cold water tank could be a plastic beaker with a hole drilled in its side near the base, so that a thin rubber tube can be attached. Clamp the tube at the top before starting. Connect the cold reservoir (tank) high up, so that the water pressure will force water down through the long tube. Turn on the lamp to start heating the metal plate and then release a slow trickle of water. The water at the bottom should be warmer than that at the top.

Tips: Turn the lamp on a little in advance to allow the board to heat up a bit. You could also use ice cold water for the top reservoir; this causes the water to heat up due to the room temperature as it flows down the tube – it is cheating but works well.

Safety: Take care if using mains lamps – keep away from water.

Constructing a model house

Students could investigate the effect of insulation using a model house.

Equipment and materials required

Each group will need: A cardboard box to insulate (large enough to contain the heater or lamp (protected e.g. an inspection lamp)), a mains-powered filament lamp or low-voltage heating element, insulating materials (polystyrene, wool, shredded paper, etc.), data loggers or thermometers.

Details

The lamp or heating element is used to provide energy to the inside of the house and make it warmer than the surroundings. The box represents the house and the walls (or roof) can be insulated with one material at a time. Students need to measure the internal temperature of the box, compare it with the external temperature and use this data to evaluate the effectiveness of the insulating material. They will have to turn the heater on and wait a set time to be able to detect energy passing through the walls.

Safety: The lamp or heating element will become hot and should not be in direct contact with combustible material.

Energy transfer by heating

P1 1.9 — Heating and insulating buildings

Learning objectives
- How can we reduce the rate of energy transfer from our homes?
- What are U-values?
- Is solar heating free?

Did you know ...?
A duvet is a bed cover filled with 'down' or soft feathers or some other suitable thermal insulator such as wool. Because the filling material traps air, a duvet on a bed cuts down the transfer of energy from the sleeper. The 'tog' rating of a duvet tells you how effective it is as an insulator. The higher its tog rating is, the more effective it is as an insulator.

How Science Works

Reducing the rate of energy transfers at home

Home heating bills can be expensive. Figure 1 shows how we can reduce the rate of energy transfer at home and reduce our home heating bills.

Figure 1 Saving money

- **Loft insulation** such as fibreglass reduces the rate of energy transfer through the roof. Fibreglass is a good insulator. The air between the fibres also helps to reduce the rate of energy transfer by conduction.
- **Cavity wall insulation** reduces energy loss through the outer walls of the house. The 'cavity' of an outer wall is the space between the two layers of brick that make up the wall. The insulation is pumped into the cavity. It is a better insulator than the air it replaces. It traps the air in small pockets, reducing convection currents.
- **Aluminium foil** between a radiator panel and the wall reflects radiation away from the wall.
- **Double-glazed windows** have two glass panes with dry air or a vacuum between the panes. Dry air is a good insulator so it reduces the rate of energy transfer by conduction. A vacuum cuts out energy transfer by convection as well.

  a Why is cavity wall insulation better than air in the cavity between the walls of a house?

U-values

We can compare different insulating materials if we know their U-values. This is the energy per second that passes through one square metre of material when the temperature difference across it is 1°C.

The lower the U-value, the more effective the material is as an insulator.

For example, replacing a single-glazed window with a double-glazed window that has a U-value four times smaller would make the energy loss through the window four times smaller.

b The U-value of 'MoneySaver' loft insulation is twice that of 'Staywarm'. Which type is more effective as an insulator?

U-value of the material = energy/s passing per m² for 1°C temperature difference

Figure 2 U-values

Solar heating panels

Heating water at home using electricity or gas can be expensive. A solar heating panel uses solar energy to heat water. The panel is usually fitted on a roof that faces south, making the most of the Sun's energy. Figure 3 shows the design of one type of solar heating panel.

The panel is a flat box containing liquid-filled copper pipes on a matt black metal plate. The pipes are connected to a heat exchanger in a water storage tank in the house.

A transparent cover on the top of the panel allows solar radiation through to heat the metal plate. Insulating material under the plate stops energy being transferred through the back of the panel.

On a sunny day, the metal plate and the copper pipes in the box become hot. Liquid pumped through the pipes is heated when it passes through the panel. The liquid may be water or a solution containing antifreeze. The hot liquid passes through the heat exchanger and transfers energy to the water in the storage tank.

Figure 3 A solar heating panel

How Science Works

Payback time

Solar heating panels save money because no fuel is needed to heat the water. But they are expensive to buy and install.

Suppose you pay £2000 to buy and install a solar panel and you save £100 each year on your fuel bills. After 20 years you would have saved £2000. In other words, the payback time for the solar panel is 20 years. This is the time taken to recover the up-front costs from the savings on fuel bills.

links

For more information on payback times, see P1 3.4 Cost effectiveness matters.

Summary questions

1 Copy and complete **a** to **c** using the words below. Each word can be used more than once.

   conduction   convection   radiation

   a Cavity wall insulation reduces the rate of energy transfer due to ....
   b Aluminium foil behind a radiator reduces the rate of energy transfer due to ....
   c Closing the curtains in winter reduces the rate of energy transfer due to .... and ....

2 Some double-glazed windows have a plastic frame and a vacuum between the panes.
   a Why is a plastic frame better than a metal frame?
   b Why is a vacuum between the panes better than air?

3 A manufacturer of loft insulation claimed that each roll of loft insulation would save £10 per year on fuel bills. A householder bought 6 rolls of the loft insulation at £15 per roll and paid £90 to have the insulation fitted in her loft.
   a How much did it cost to buy and install the loft insulation?
   b What would be the saving each year on fuel bills?
   c Calculate the payback time.

Key points
- Energy transfer from our homes can be reduced by fitting:
  - loft insulation
  - cavity wall insulation
  - double glazing
  - draught proofing
  - aluminium foil behind radiators.
- U-values tell us how much energy per second passes through different materials.
- Solar heating panels do not use fuel to heat water but they are expensive to buy and install.

Further teaching suggestions

Energy efficiency
- Energy efficiency is also a key concern in industry. You can find information about measures that can be taken on numerous business websites.

Energy neutral house
- The energy neutral house task makes a good homework task. Students could be asked to go a lot further and conduct some independent research for their designs.

Summary answers

1 **a** conduction **b** radiation **c** convection and radiation (convection and radiation in any order)

2 **a** Plastic is a poor conductor. Metal is a good conductor. Energy transfer through a metal frame would therefore be greater than through a plastic frame.
   b Energy transfer due to conduction and convection takes place in the space between the panes if the space is filled with air but not if there is a vacuum there.

3 **a** £180   **b** £60   **c** 3 years.

Summary answers

1 a A matt surface absorbs infrared radiation more easily than a smooth shiny surface does.

b A smooth shiny surface is better because it would not get as hot in sunlight.

c It absorbs infrared radiation better and the water gets hotter than with any other surface.

d A matt black surface is a better emitter of infrared radiation than any other surface.

2 a electrons, collide

b atoms, vibrate

3 a By conduction through the plate.

b The larger the surface area, the greater the rate of energy transfer due to radiation and convection from the plate. This stops the metal plate and the component becoming too hot.

4 a convection

b radiation

c conduction

d radiation

5 a Gloves are made of insulating material. The inside of the gloves becomes warm due to infrared radiation and convection from the hand. The glove material is a good insulator and the inside stays warm because it does not conduct energy from the inside.

b Your ears are warmer than the air around them, so energy will be transferred from your ears to the air. Infrared radiation from your ears would be stopped by covering them.

6 a The metal casing conducts energy from the bearings of the motor to the outside of the case.

b The warm water in the radiator rises to the top due to convection. The inside of the radiator at the top becomes warm and so conduction takes place from the inside to the outside of the radiator at the top.

c Infrared radiation from the grill is absorbed by the bread, making the bread hot and toasting its surface.

7 a i The water heated at the bottom rose to the top causing convection in the tube and melting the ice cube at the top.

ii The water was warmed at the top and stayed there as it is less dense than cold water. Conduction through the water eventually made the water at the bottom warm, and then the ice cube melted.

b 2. Energy transfer in water is mainly due to convection.

AQA Examiner's tip

For their exam, students will need to understand four mechanisms for energy transfer involving particles: conduction, convection, evaporation and condensation. For instance, condensation will heat a surface on to which a vapour condenses. Students must understand what is happening to the particles in all of these processes.

AQA Practical suggestions

Practicals	AQA	k	📖	⚙
Passing white light through a prism and detecting the infrared radiation with a thermometer.	✓		✓	

240

Summary questions ⓚ

1 a Why does a matt surface in sunshine get hotter than a shiny surface?

b What type of surface is better for a flat roof – a matt dark surface or a smooth shiny surface? Explain your answer.

c A solar heating panel is used to heat water. Why is the top surface of the metal plate inside the panel painted matt black?

d Why is a car radiator painted matt black?

2 Copy and complete **a** and **b** using the words below:

collide electrons atoms vibrate

a Energy transfer in a metal is due to particles called .... moving about freely inside the metal. They transfer energy when they .... with each other.

b Energy transfer in a non-metallic solid is due to particles called .... inside the non-metal. They transfer energy because they ....

3 A heat sink is a metal plate or clip fixed to an electronic component to stop it overheating.

Figure 1 A heat sink

a When the component becomes hot, how does energy transfer from where it is in contact with the plate to the rest of the plate?

b Why does the plate have a large surface area?

4 Copy and complete **a** to **d** using the words below. Each word can be used more than once.

conduction convection radiation

a .... cannot happen in a solid or through a vacuum.

b Energy transfer from the Sun is due to ....

c When a metal rod is heated at one end, energy transfer due to .... takes place in the rod.

d .... is energy transfer by electromagnetic waves.

5 a In winter, why do gloves keep your hands warm outdoors?

b Why do your ears get cold outdoors in winter if are not covered?

6 Energy transfer takes place in each of the following examples. In each case, state where the energy t occurs and if the energy transfer is due to condu convection or radiation.

a The metal case of an electric motor becomes w due to friction when the motor is in use.

b A central heating radiator warms up first at the when hot water is pumped through it.

c A slice of bread is toasted under a red-hot elec

7 A glass tube containing water with a small ice cu floating at the top was heated at its lower end. Th taken for the ice cube to melt was measured. The was repeated with a similar ice cube weighted do the bottom of the tube of water. The water in this was heated near the top of the tube. The time tak the ice cube to melt was much longer than in the test.

Weighted lump of ice

Boiling water

Figure 2 Energy transfer in water

a Energy transfer in the tube is due to conduction convection or both.

i Why was convection the main cause of ene transfer to the ice cube in the first test?

ii Why was conduction the only cause of ene transfer in the second test?

b Which of the following conclusions about these is true?

1 Energy transfer due to conduction does no place in water.

2 Energy transfer in water is mainly due to convection.

3 Energy transfer in water is mainly due to conduction.

240

Practicals	AQA	k	📖	⚙
Demonstration using balls in a tray to show the behaviour of particles in substances in different states.	✓		✓	
Measuring the cooling effect produced by evaporation; putting wet cotton wool over the bulb of a thermometer or temperature probe.	✓	✓	✓	✓
Plan and carry out an investigation into factors that affect the rate of cooling of a can of water, e.g. shape, volume, and colour of can.	✓		✓	
Using Leslie's cube to demonstrate the effect on radiation of altering the nature of the surface.	✓		✓	
Plan and carry out an investigation using immersion heaters in a metal block to measure specific heat capacity.	✓	✓	✓	
Investigating thermal conduction using rods of different materials.	✓		✓	
Plan and carry out an investigation by constructing a model house, using sensors and data logger to measure temperatures with and without various types of insulation.	✓		✓	

Examination-style questions

ection takes place in fluids.

words from the list to complete each sentence. Each
can be used once, more than once or not at all.

acts expands rises sinks transfers

a fluid is heated it ...., becomes less dense,
.... The warm fluid is replaced by cooler, denser,
The resulting convection current .... energy
ghout the fluid. (3)

e are three states of matter: solid, liquid and gas.
plete each sentence.

solid has
xed shape and a fixed volume.
xed shape but not a fixed volume.
xed volume but not a fixed shape.
ther a fixed shape nor a fixed volume. (1)

liquid has
xed shape and a fixed volume.
xed shape but not a fixed volume.
xed volume but not a fixed shape.
ther a fixed shape nor a fixed volume. (1)

gas has
xed shape and a fixed volume.
xed shape but not a fixed volume.
xed volume but not a fixed shape.
ither a fixed shape nor a fixed volume. (1)

uids are
lids or liquids.
lids or gases.
uids or gases. (1)

e particles in a solid
ove about at random in contact with each other.
ove about at random away from each other.
rate about fixed positions. (1)

experiment a block of copper is heated from 25 °C
°C.

ve the name of the process by which energy is
ansferred through the copper block. (1)

e the mass of the block is 1.3 kg.
alculate the energy needed to increase the
mperature of the copper from 25 °C to 45 °C.
ecific heat capacity of copper = 380 J/kg °C.
ow clearly how you work out your answer. (3)

4 The diagram shows some
water being heated with
a solar cooker.

The curved mirror reflects the sunlight that falls on it.
The sunlight can be focused on to the cooking pot. The
energy from the sunlight is absorbed by the pot, heating
up the water inside.

a Suggest **one** reason why a matt black pot has been
used. (2)

b When the water has been heated, equal amounts of
the water are poured into two metal pans. The pans
are identical except one has a matt black surface and
the other has a shiny metal surface.
Which pan will keep the water warm for the longer
time? Explain your answer. (2)

5 The continuous movement of water from the oceans to
the air and land and back to the oceans is called the
water cycle.

a The Sun heats the surface of the oceans, which
causes water to evaporate.
How does the rate of evaporation depend on
i the wind speed (1)
ii the temperature (1)
iii the humidity? (1)

b Explain how evaporation causes a cooling effect. (3)

6 Double-glazed windows are used to reduce the rate of
energy transfer from buildings. The diagrams show
cross-sections of single-glazed and double-glazed
windows.

Single-glazed
window
Double-glazed
window

Give two reasons why a double-glazed window reduces
conduction more effectively than a single-glazed
window. (2)

7 In this question you will be assessed on using good
English, organising information clearly and using
specialist terms where appropriate.
Compare the similarities and differences between the
process of conduction in metals and non-metals. (6)

241

Kerboodle resources (k)

Resources available for this chapter on Kerboodle are:

● Chapter map: Energy transfer by heating
● Interactive activity: States of matter and energy transfer
(P1 1.3)
● Support: What a state! (P1 1.3)
● How Science Works: Does melting ice expand? (P1 1.3)
● Bump up your grade: Toil, sweat and tears (P1 1.6)
● Practical: Investigating the chill factor (P1 1.6)
● Maths skills: Specific heat capacity (P1 1.8)
● Practical: Measuring specific heat capacity (P1 1.8)
● WebQuest: Solar cells (P1 1.9)
● WebQuest: Home insulation (P1 1.9)
● How Science Works: Solar cells (P1 1.9)
● Extension: Energy in buildings (P1 1.9)
● Revision podcast: Energy transfer by heating
● Test yourself: Energy transfer by heating
● On your marks: Energy transfer by heating
● Examination-style questions: Energy transfer by heating
● Answers to examination-style questions: Energy transfer by
heating

AQA Examination-style answers

1 When a fluid is heated it **expands**, becomes less dense, and
rises. The warm fluid is replaced by cooler, denser, fluid. The
resulting convection current **transfers** energy throughout the
fluid. (3 marks)

---

2 a A solid has **a fixed shape and a fixed volume**. (1 mark)

b A liquid has **a fixed volume but not a fixed shape**. (1 mark)

c A gas has **neither a fixed shape nor a fixed volume**. (1 mark)

d Fluids are **liquids or gases**. (1 mark)

e The particles in a solid **vibrate about fixed positions**. (1 mark)

3 a conduction (1 mark)

b $E = m \times c \times \theta$
$E = 1.3\,\text{kg} \times 380\,\text{J/kg}\,°\text{C} \times 20\,°\text{C}$
$E = 9880\,\text{J}$ (3 marks)

4 a A matt black surface is a very good absorber of infrared
compared to light, shiny surfaces. (2 marks)

b Shiny metal. Shiny surfaces are poor emitters of infrared.
Matt black surfaces are good emitters of infrared. (2 marks)

5 a i The higher the wind speed, the greater the rate of
evaporation. (1 mark)

ii The higher the temperature, the greater the rate of
evaporation. (1 mark)

iii The higher the humidity, the slower the rate of
evaporation. (1 mark)

b The most energetic molecules leave the surface
of the liquid, so the average kinetic energy of the
remaining molecules is less.
The temperature depends on the average kinetic
energy, so it is reduced. (3 marks)

6 There is more glass and glass is a good insulator.
The air between the glass is a good insulator. (2 marks)

7 Marks awarded for this answer will be determined by the
Quality of Written Communication (QWC) as well as the
standard of the scientific response.

There is a clear, balanced and detailed description of the
similarities and differences in conduction in metals and
non-metals. The answer shows almost faultless spelling,
punctuation and grammar. It is coherent and in an organised,
logical sequence. It contains a range of appropriate or
relevant specialist terms used accurately. (5–6 marks)

There is a description of a range of similarities and
differences in conduction in metals and non-metals. There
are some errors in spelling, punctuation and grammar.
The answer has some structure and organisation. The use
of specialist terms has been attempted, but not always
accurately. (3–4 marks)

There is a brief description of at least one similarity or
difference, which has little clarity and detail. The spelling,
punctuation and grammar are very weak. The answer is
poorly organised with almost no specialist terms and/or their
use demonstrating a general lack of understanding of their
meaning. (1–2 marks)

No relevant content. (0 marks)

Examples of physics points made in the response:
Similarities:
• involve particles
• atoms vibrate causing neighbouring atoms to vibrate, so
energy is passed along.
Differences:
• metals have free electrons
• these collide with other free electrons and ions
• passing energy along
• this process much more effective, so metals better
conductors.

P1 2.1

Forms of energy

Learning objectives

Students should learn:

- the words commonly used to describe energy in a range of situations
- how energy is transferred in common situations
- that gravitational potential energy and kinetic energy are often transferred, as when objects fall.

Learning outcomes

Most students should be able to:

- state what form of energy is stored in fuels, hot objects and stretched objects
- draw simple energy–transfer diagrams showing changes in energy.

Some students should also be able to:

- describe, in detail, energy transfers involving gravitational, kinetic and energy by heating.

Answers to in-text questions

a Electrical energy.
b It is transferred as light and energy to the surroundings by heating.

Support

- Spend some extra time developing the ideas of energy transfer diagrams; these are a simple way to describe all of the changes students will encounter. Try a few where there is one change followed by another. You can expand on these in future lessons by using Sankey diagrams to show the conservation of energy in a visual way.

Extend

- Extend students by asking them to find out about the question:

  Are sound and energy transferred to heating the surroundings just forms of kinetic energy?

  Encourage students to research and explain the links, then decide if we really need to use the terms 'sound' and 'energy transferred to heating'.

AQA
Specification link-up: Physics P1.2

- Energy can be transferred usefully, stored, or dissipated, but cannot be created or destroyed. *[P1.2.1 a)]*

Lesson structure
Starters

Off like a rocket – Show students a video of a firework rocket (search for 'fireworks' at an internet video hosting site). Ask them to draw an energy transfer diagram of what they see happening. Check through their diagrams and show them a good example. [chemical → kinetic + thermal + light + sound + gravitational potential]. *(5 minutes)*

What is energy? – Ask students to express their ideas about what the word 'energy' means. They could produce a mind map to show their prior knowledge. Support students by providing a partially completed map for them to add additional details to. Extend students by providing some more challenging concepts [conservation, efficiency, measurement] that students need to define in their maps. Keep the maps safe; at the end of this chapter, students should redraw their map with the additional information they have learned. *(10 minutes)*

Main

- Fuels are a familiar form of chemical energy and sample fuels should be made available for students to look at in the first part of the lesson. This can lead to a discussion about what you can do with fuels and this leads readily on to the forms of energy you can get from them once burned.

- Most students will already be aware of many of the words used to describe energy. Ask them to write out a complete list of these words with an example showing each one. The key ones required are: 'light, sound, electrical, kinetic, chemical, gravitational potential, elastic strain energy, nuclear'. You should strongly encourage the use of these words and try to make students avoid using any other words in their transfer diagrams. Make sure that all students have constant access to a list like this so that you can enforce the use of correct terms, even if you have to provide a printed one.

- Some students tend to think of 'potential' as a form of energy all on its own and not just a way of describing stored energy, for example, elastic strain energy and chemical energy are both potential energy. This misconception should be addressed at this point.

- Dropping something large to ensure it makes a loud noise shows the energy transfer from gravitational potential to sound and heat. It is hard to demonstrate the transfer of energy to the surroundings, without dropping an object over and over again.

- Energy transfer diagrams (or Sankey diagrams) are very common and students should draw a number of them. It is important that they label these only with the correct terms as listed above.

- After discussing the forms of energy, allow students to explore simple energy transfers in an energy circus as described in 'Practical support'. If you have a teaching assistant, they could supervise some stations in the energy circus. Make sure that students have described the correct energy transfer for each of the devices at the end of the task.

- It is always worth demonstrating the heating effect of a current in a wire. Use a thin constantan or Nichrome wire, and let it ignite a piece of paper on a heat-proof mat. Do not forget to discuss the energy changes in the burning paper.

Plenaries

What's the transfer? – Ask students to describe simple energy transfers going on around the room, e.g. the ticking of a clock, the growth of a plant or the ringing of the bell marking the end of the lesson. They should also look at more complicated ones where the energy may be transferred in one way and then another. *(5 minutes)*

Energy links – Ask students to draw a large circle with all the forms of energy listed around the outside. They must then link the forms of energy together with an arrow, labelled with a device that can transfer the first form to the second form. For example, they could draw an arrow from the word 'electrical' to the word 'kinetic' and have it labelled 'motor', while an arrow going the other way would say 'generator'. *(10 minutes)*

Practical support

Energy transfers

When an object starts to fall freely, it gains kinetic energy, because it speeds up as it falls. So its gravitational potential energy changes to kinetic energy as it falls.

Look at Figure 3 in the Student Book – it shows a box that hits the floor with a thud. All of its kinetic energy is transferred to the surroundings at the point of impact. The proportion of kinetic energy transferred to sound is much smaller than that transferred by heating.

● Draw an energy flow diagram to show the changes in Figure 3.

Demonstrating energy transfers

Throughout this unit, students will see a range of energy transfers. You should challenge them to describe the transfers in each of them using only the recognised terms, avoiding common misconceptions

such as 'steam energy'. Using many small demonstrations reminds students continually that all transfers can be described fairly simply.

Energy circus

Students could carry out a range of simple experiments and describe the energy transfers involved. Some suggested objects/transfers are:

A yo-yo   A dynamo
A portable radio   An MP3 player
Dropping a steel ball bearing on to a wooden block
Burning a candle or fuel burner.

A remote-control car: what energy is reaching the car? [Radio waves reach the car but the energy for movement comes from the chemical energy in the batteries inside the car.]

Safety: Warn students to take care with mains electricity and not to have wet hands. Take care with burning fuels.

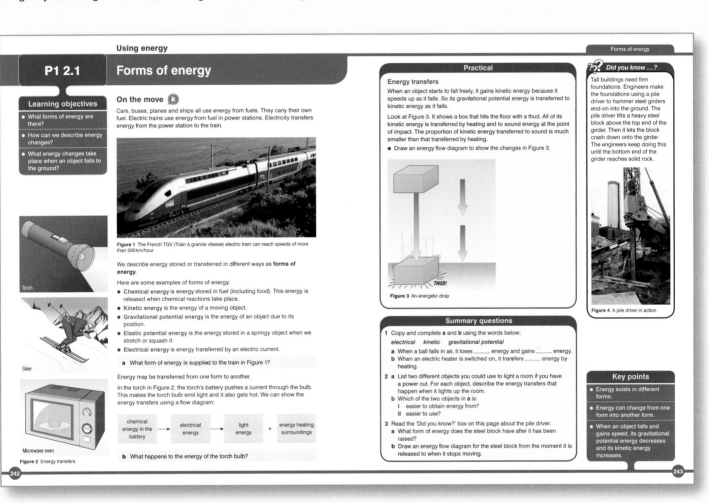

Further teaching suggestions

A pile driver
● You could demonstrate something similar to a pile driver by dropping an iron block onto a nail that has already been partly knocked into a block of wood. Keep students clear and use a safety screen just in case you happen to hit the nail at the wrong angle and knock it out of the wood. Make sure the nail is not so long that it will go all of the way through the block and into the desk!

Energy transfers in the home
● Students should make a list of the energy transfers that take place in devices at home. They should be able to find a wide range of these.

Summary answers

1 a gravitational potential, kinetic
   b electrical

2 a For example: a candle and a torch.
      A candle transfers chemical energy to light and heat. A torch transfers chemical to electrical and then light and heat.
   b i A torch is usually more convenient.
      ii This is a matter of opinion.

3 a gravitational potential energy
   b The diagram should include these transfers:
      gravitational potential energy → kinetic energy of the falling block → sound energy (realised during impact) + kinetic energy of the girder and the block → heat energy in the surroundings and the ground.

P1 2.2

Conservation of energy

AQA **Specification link-up: Physics P1.2**

- Energy can be transferred usefully, stored, or dissipated, but cannot be created or destroyed. *[P1.2.1 a)]*
- When energy is transferred only part of it may be usefully transferred, the rest is 'wasted'. *[P1.2.1 b)]*

Controlled Assessment: SA4.3 Collect primary and secondary data. *[SA4.3.3 b) e)]*

Learning objectives

Students should learn:

- that energy is conserved in all energy transfers.

Learning outcomes

Most students should be able to:

- state that energy cannot be created or destroyed
- describe energy transfers between gravitational, kinetic and elastic strain energy.

Some students should also be able to:

- describe, in detail, energy transfers involving gravitational, kinetic and elastic strain energy, taking into account transfer by heating.

Answers to in-text questions

a i Kinetic energy is transferred by heating the brakes and the surroundings.

  ii Kinetic energy transfers to gravitational potential energy as it climbs the hill. The gravitational potential energy transfers back to kinetic energy as it descends. Energy transfers by heating to the surroundings due to air resistance and friction throughout.

b It is transferred to kinetic energy and the air resistance heating the surroundings.

c

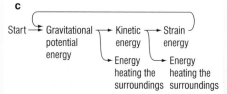

Support

- Students often confuse potential energies and they also resort to using the term 'movement energy', which is not acceptable at GCSE level. Rigorously enforce the correct terms.

Extend

- You may be able to find designs for perpetual motion machines on the internet along with descriptions of how these may work. Extend students by encouraging them to discover the flaws in the designs; some designs are very clever indeed.

Lesson structure

Starters

Where does it all go? – Support students with a simple starter to refresh their ideas: light a candle and ask them to describe what happens to the chemical energy stored in the wax [chemical energy → by heating + light energy]. You could also ask the about the changes in the match. *(5 minutes)*

A plane journey – Ask students to draw a cartoon of an aeroplane journey describing the changes in gravitational, kinetic and chemical energy. The aeroplane lands back at the same place it took off; ask them where the energy in the fuel has gone. To save some time, you could provide a small comic strip for them to add annotations. Use the ideas that they produce here later in the lesson to discuss the idea that energy cannot 'go away'; it is all accounted for. *(10 minutes)*

Main

- The topic opens with a look at the transfer of gravitational potential energy to kinetic and back again. This is a common theme in examinations and time should be taken discussing the aspect with plenty of examples.
- Point out that energy is wasted during each transfer, so a roller coaster can never get as high as it first starts out. This means that the highest point on the track is at the start of the first drop.
- The law of conservation of energy is a **very** important one and must be emphasised very strongly. Try to account for the 'missing' energy in any energy transfer from now on. This is generally energy lost to the surroundings as heat; this is true for both the pendulum and the bungee experiments.
- The 'Practical support' activities may take a bit of time to set up and are fiddly. Students should be thinking about how to improve the accuracy of the measurements (related to 'How Science Works') but it is unlikely they will think of using the shadow idea on their own. You could give hints about this.
- Use a webcam to record the pendulum swinging or you could record a video clip of the pendulum shadow in advance and show it during the lesson. If you project this on a whiteboard, you can mark the heights of the swings as they happen.
- Watch and discuss a video of a bungee jump. Find one at an internet video-hosting site.
- Check that students can explain what is causing the apparent loss of energy in these systems; frictional forces transferring energy by heating. You could demonstrate that the loss is caused by air resistance by attaching a piece of stiff card to the bob and increasing its drag. This rapidly reduces the swing. You could also demonstrate the bungee example using a mass on a spring or, more excitingly, with a toy on a length of fishing elastic.

Plenaries

Measuring the energy in food – Ask students, as a class or in groups, to discuss some of the issues around designing an experiment to measure the energy in a food sample. Students should aim to minimise energy loss to the surroundings. This can be quite a difficult task, so provide a checklist of energy losses that need to be accounted for – for example, waste gases are hot and the energy in them needs to be measured. *(5 minutes)*

Evaluate and improve – Students could be extended by evaluating the results of their experiments ('How Science Works'). They should design improvements to the experiment. This might include the use of ICT or some system that enables them to measure the heights accurately and consistently. Groups could compare results and decide who had the best technique. *(10 minutes)*

Practical support

Investigating energy changes

Pendulum swinging

Equipment and materials required

For each group: retort stand, string with bob (or 50 g mass tied to end), graph paper and some reusable adhesive to mount it, torch, stop clock.

Details

Students could release the pendulum from a fixed height and let it swing for 30 seconds (or just a set number of swings). They then compare the initial height of the swing with the height after this time period. One way to measure the height of a pendulum swing is to shine a bright light on it and measure the position of the shadow.

Position the light so that the shadow falls on a piece of graph paper when the bob is swinging. Students mark where the shadow falls after a number of swings and then look at the pattern in height against time.

Bungee jumping

Equipment and materials required

For each group: retort stand, elastic with mass (or toy tied to end), graph paper and some reusable adhesive to mount it, torch.

Details

A similar shadow technique to the above activity could be used to measure the height of the bounces or video logging technology could be employed if you have it. You could video an experiment in advance so that you can discuss the details with the whole class.

Using energy

P1 2.2 Conservation of energy

Learning objectives
- What do we mean by 'conservation of energy'?
- Why is conservation of energy a very important idea?

AQA Examiner's tip

Never use the term 'movement energy' in the exam; you will only gain marks for using 'kinetic energy'.

At the funfair

Funfairs are very exciting places because lots of energy transfers happen quickly. A roller coaster gains gravitational potential energy when it climbs. This energy is then transferred as the roller coaster races downwards.

As it descends:

its gravitational potential energy → kinetic energy + sound + energy transfer by heating due to air resistance and friction

The energy transferred by heating is 'wasted' energy, which you will learn more about in P1 2.3.

a When a roller coaster gets to the bottom of a descent, what energy transfers happen if:
  i we apply the brakes to stop it
  ii it goes up and over a second 'hill'?

Figure 1 On a roller coaster – having fun with energy transfers!

Practical

Investigating energy changes

Pendulum swinging

When energy changes happen, does the total amount of energy stay the same? We can investigate this question with a simple pendulum.

Figure 2 shows a pendulum bob swinging from side to side.

As it moves towards the middle, its gravitational potential energy is transferred to kinetic energy.

As it moves away from the middle, its kinetic energy transfers back to gravitational potential energy. If the air resistance on the bob is very small, you should find that the bob reaches the same height on each side.

- What does this tell you about the energy of the bob when it goes from one side at maximum height to the other side at maximum height?
- Why is it difficult to mark the exact height the pendulum bob rises to? How could you make your judgement more accurate?

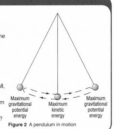

Maximum gravitational potential energy   Maximum kinetic energy   Maximum gravitational potential energy

Figure 2 A pendulum in motion

Conservation of energy

Scientists have done lots of tests to find out if the total energy after a transfer is the same as the energy before the transfer. All the tests so far show it is the same.

This important result is known as the conservation of energy.

It tells us that **energy cannot be created or destroyed**.

Bungee jumping

What energy transfers happen to a bungee jumper after jumping off the platform?

- When the rope is slack, some of the gravitational potential energy of the bungee jumper is transferred to kinetic energy as the jumper falls.
- Once the slack in the rope has been used up, the rope slows the bungee jumper's fall. Most of the gravitational potential energy and kinetic energy of the jumper is transferred into elastic strain energy.
- After reaching the bottom, the rope pulls the jumper back up. As the jumper rises, most of the elastic strain energy of the rope is transferred back to gravitational potential energy and kinetic energy of the jumper.

The bungee jumper doesn't return to the same height as at the start. This is because some of the initial gravitational potential energy has been transferred to its surroundings by heating as the rope stretched then shortened again.

b What happens to the gravitational potential energy lost by the bungee jumper?
c Draw a flow diagram to show the energy changes.

Practical

Bungee jumping

You can try out the ideas about bungee jumping using the experiment shown in Figure 4.

Figure 3 Bungee jumping

Figure 4 Testing a bungee jump

∞ links
For more information on variables, look back at H2 Fundamental ideas about how science works.

Summary questions

1 Copy and complete using the words below:
electrical   gravitational potential   kinetic
A person going up in a lift gains .... energy. The lift is driven by electric motors. Some of the .... energy supplied to the motors is wasted instead of being transferred to .... energy.

2 **a** A ball dropped onto a trampoline returns to almost the same height after it bounces. Describe the energy transfer of the ball from the point of release to the top of its bounce.
  b What can you say about the energy of the ball at the point of release compared with at the top of its bounce?
  c You could use the test in **a** above to see which of three trampolines was the bounciest.
    i Name the independent variable in this test.
    ii Is this variable categoric or continuous?

3 One exciting fairground ride acts like a giant catapult. The capsule, in which you are strapped, is fired high into the sky by the rubber bands of the catapult. Explain the energy transfers taking place in the ride.

Key points
- Energy cannot be created or destroyed.
- Conservation of energy applies to all energy changes.

Further teaching suggestions

Slow down
- Sometimes we want to get rid of kinetic energy quickly. Students could find out how we slow down planes on landing, or drag racers, and make a booklet or short presentation. This would be good for homework.

ICT link-up
- Use video capture equipment to record the pendulum or 'bungee' for analysis. Some software can calculate speed and displacement.

Measuring the energy in food
- Ask students to design the experiment for homework.

Summary answers

1 gravitational potential, electrical, kinetic

2 **a** **On descent:** Gravitational potential energy → kinetic energy + energy heating the surroundings due to air resistance.
    On impact: Kinetic energy → elastic energy of trampoline + energy heating the surroundings due to impact + sound.
    On ascent: Elastic energy of trampoline → kinetic energy → gravitational potential energy + energy heating the surroundings due to air resistance.
  b The ball has less energy at the top of its bounce than at the point of release.
  c **i** Type of trampoline
    ii Categoric

3 Elastic energy of the rubber straps is transferred to kinetic energy of the capsule. This kinetic energy is transferred to gravitational potential energy as the capsule rises to the top of its flight etc. as with the bungee jumper in the Student Book.

P1 2.3

Useful energy

Learning objectives

Students should learn:

- that energy is wasted heating the surroundings in energy transfers
- that this 'wasted' energy spreads out and is no longer of use.

Learning outcomes

Most students should be able to:

- identify useful and wasted energy in transfers
- describe how friction is the cause of much wasted energy
- understand that energy that escapes to the surroundings by heating is not available for other energy transfers and so is useless.

Answers to in-text questions

a   It is gained by the surroundings by heating.

b   It is transferred to the surroundings by heating due to friction between its moving parts and in the brakes, and by air resistance.

c   The hot water mixes with the cold water. Its energy spreads out and cannot be used again.

Support

- Students can struggle with the idea that energy spreads out and becomes 'useless'. Spend some time discussing the idea that the energy transferred to the surroundings by heating cannot be made to collect together in one place to make it useful again; this would actually take more energy to do than it's worth.

Extend

- What really causes frictional forces? Very smooth surfaces often produce larger frictional effects than rougher ones. Extend students by asking them to come up with a detailed explanation of what is going on. They will need to research how our idea of friction has developed over hundreds of years.

AQA   Specification link-up: Physics P1.2

- When energy is transferred only part of it may be usefully transferred, the rest is 'wasted'. *[P1.2.1 b]*
- Wasted energy is eventually transferred to the surroundings, which become warmer. The wasted energy becomes increasingly spread out and so becomes less useful. *[P1.2.1 c]*
- Describe the energy transfers and the main energy wastages that occur with a range of appliances. *[P1.2]*
  Controlled Assessment: SA4.3 Collect primary and secondary data. *[SA4.3.3 b) c) e)]*

Lesson structure

Starters

Useful or useless? – Show energy transfer diagrams and ask students to identify the useful energy outputs and the useless ones in each case. This will support students and refresh the language of energy transfer. *(5 minutes)*

Overheating – Extend students by asking them to explain why humans become hot when they work hard. How is this excess heat removed from the body? Why do we need to eat less in hot weather? Links can be made to biological processes. This can lead to a discussion about where the energy in our food actually ends up. *(10 minutes)*

Main

- In this unit, avoid the use of the term 'lost' for energy if possible; it implies that the energy disappears. The energy spreads out into the surroundings and becomes useless or 'wasted'.
- A video clip of a car performing an emergency stop (search a video-hosting website) is an excellent way of helping students understand that the kinetic energy of a car has to go somewhere when it stops. A dramatic one with burning rubber works best.
- Frictional effects are best explained using simple diagrams or animations; you should be able to find a range of these. The surfaces rub or catch on each other and this rubbing causes heating. You could show the roughness of 'smooth' surfaces with micrographs or even electron micrographs.
- Rubbing two metal blocks across each other will show frictional heating. Adding oil should make the movement smoother. Check students understand that friction causes heating, because of the forces between the surfaces of objects that rub together.
- Students need to be encouraged to describe exactly where there is friction in a device. They should know about air resistance, drag in water, friction of surfaces in contact and around a pivot.
- If time allows, students could reinforce 'How Science Works' concepts of accuracy and precision by investigating friction themselves. (See 'Practical support'). Stress the progression evident in the concepts needed to tackle an investigation that students will be familiar with. To save time, you could just demonstrate the practical technique described and show what we mean by accuracy and precision.

Plenaries

Sticky problems – Ask students to draw up a table of the ways friction can be reduced and give examples of exactly where this happens. You could provide a table of suggested places and ask students to complete it to explain how the friction could be reduced. *(5 minutes)*

What's wrong? – Support students by asking them to correct some sentences describing energy and friction. This can be used to challenge some misconceptions. Examples can include: 'When a car stops at traffic lights, the speed energy is destroyed by the brakes and is lost.' [Kinetic energy is actually transferred by heating in the tyres and brakes.], 'Rubbing your hands together makes them warmer.' *(10 minutes)*

Practical support

Investigating friction

Many students will have investigated friction before, but you may wish to look in more detail here. The focus should be on improving the technique, focusing on the concepts of accuracy and precision in the specification. (This relates to 'How Science Works'.)

Equipment and materials required

For each group: string, pulley, clamp, 10 × 50 g masses, 1 kg mass (with hoop), three different surfaces to test (desk surface, carpet tiles, rubber mat).

Details

Students place the 1 kg mass on the surfaces and attach it to a mass holder hanging over the desk via the pulley. They then find out what mass is required to start the 1 kg sliding across the surface. To improve the accuracy of the measurements, encourage students to add smaller masses when they get near to the sliding point of the mass, so several runs will be required. Students may find out that their mats or carpet tiles start to move before the mass, so they will need some tape or reusable adhesive to hold it in place. How does this work?

Safety: Protect floor from falling weights and keep feet clear.

Investigating bouncy balls

There are a range of factors that affect how a ball bounces on a surface. In this investigation students could consider the factors and relate the bounce height to energy lessons.

Equipment and materials required

For each group: ping-pong ball, tennis ball, rubber 'bouncy' ball (and others), metre rule, range of surfaces to drop the ball on to.

Details

Students could drop the ping-pong balls from a range of heights on to a solid surface and measure the bounce height. This will be less than the drop height and students could relate this to energy losses using the impact. It can be difficult to measure the bounce height, so students should come up with ideas to do this such as repeating the drops and positioning their heads correctly. They could then move on to exploring what happens with different types of ball before looking at the effect of different surfaces.

This investigation gives ample opportunity for developing planning, recording and analysis skills. You might like to limit the factors that each group investigates and have the groups report back to the class. For example, one group only investigates drop height while another investigates surface. You may also want some students to use video equipment to accurately record the bounces and share the results with the rest of the class.

Safety: Students need to be well-behaved and keep close control of the balls.

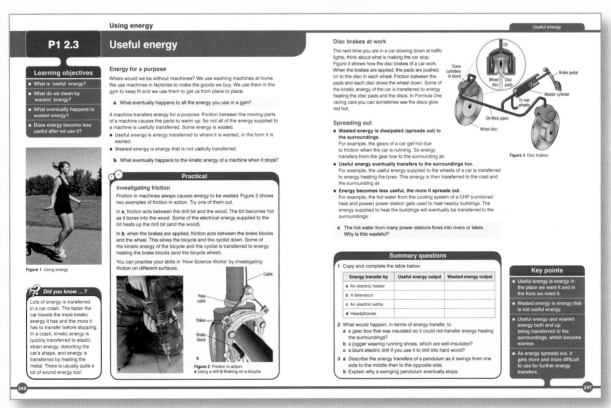

Summary answers

1

	Useful energy output	Wasted energy output
a	energy of the element	energy of the case
b	light energy, sound energy	energy transferred to surroundings as heat
c	energy of the water	energy of steam and of the kettle itself
d	sound energy	energy in the wire

2 a It would heat up. The lubricating oil and the gears would get too hot.

b His feet would get too hot and sweaty.

c The drill would heat up and smoke if it burns the wood.

3 a As the pendulum swings towards the middle, its gravitational potential energy decreases and its kinetic energy increases. As it moves from the middle to the highest position on the opposite side, its kinetic energy transfers back to gravitational potential energy. Air resistance acting causes some of its kinetic energy to be transferred to the surrounding as heat.

b Air resistance causes friction as the pendulum swings. This produces heat and so the pendulum transfers energy to the surroundings and stops.

P1 2.4

Energy and efficiency

Learning objectives

Students should learn:

- that efficiency is a measurement of how effective a device is at transferring energy
- how to measure the efficiency of a motor
- how to calculate the efficiency of a range of devices
- how we can reduce energy consumption.

Learning outcomes

Most students should be able to:

- describe what is meant by the efficiency of a device
- calculate the efficiency of a device.

Some students should also be able to:

- perform calculations including the rearrangement of the efficiency equation. [HT only]

Support

- You might want to use calculation templates to help students learn how to organise their calculations. These are sheets that show the layout of the calculation; students simply put the values from the question into the right places and then perform the calculation. Check the answers to each one until students are confident that they can perform the calculations. For additional support, you could provide an experiment template and results table for the practical task. This could also include a set of appropriately labelled graph axes.

Extend

- Students could try a more complex rearrangement of the equation. For example, they could work out how much electrical energy would be required to do 500 J of work if a motor is only 40% efficient [1250 J]. They could also try multi-stage transfers, where the first stage is 50% efficient and the second stage is 25% efficient; they should find out that the whole process would then only be 12.5% efficient.

AQA Specification link-up: Physics P1.2

- To calculate the efficiency of a device using:

$$\text{efficiency} = \frac{\text{useful energy out}}{\text{total energy in}} \ (\times \ 100\%)$$

$$\text{efficiency} = \frac{\text{useful power out}}{\text{total power in}} \ (\times \ 100\%) \qquad [P1.2.1 \ d)]$$

- Describe the energy transfers and the main energy wastages that occur with a range of appliances. *[P1.2]*
- Interpret and draw a Sankey diagram. *[P1.2]*

  Controlled Assessment: SA4.5 Analyse and interpret primary and secondary data. *[SA4.5.3 a)]*

Lesson structure

Starters

Staying on – Ask students to explain why some electrical devices of the same type (e.g. two models of phones or even two torches) last longer than others even though they use the same batteries. Students could be extended by linking this to the efficiency of the device. They should also describe the subtle differences in what the devices do. For example, one phone may have many more functions than another. *(5 minutes)*

Efficiency – What is 'efficiency' and why do we want it? What are the advantages of an efficient device? Form students into groups and ask them to read some energy company literature. Challenge them to agree on a simple description of what efficiency is and why it is important. The groups should share their descriptions. *(10 minutes)*

Main

- Students need to lay out the calculations clearly and show all of the stages of their working; emphasise that they will find it difficult to remember the correct technique and score full marks on a science examination without doing this. Students should also be aware that equations will not be given in questions for this specification. Students will have to pick the equation from an equation sheet.

- The calculations are not particularly challenging, but many students become confused about percentage or fractional efficiency, so tackle first one and then the other. Ensure that all students can complete the basic calculations; lots of practice is needed.

- More mathematically-able students need to perform rearrangement. Even fairly able students of science can struggle with this skill, so it is well worth discussing how this type of calculation is taught in the mathematics department, so that you can be consistent with them.

- It may be difficult to investigate the efficiency of the winch without a lot of equipment. A demonstration may be more effective. Students could still record the results of your demonstration and analyse them. They should find that the motor becomes less efficient, as the weight increases. This introduces concepts of 'How Science Works' involving presentation of data and relationships between variables.

- You may like to discuss how the efficiency of an elevator could be measured. Should the weight of the elevator itself be counted? This could lead to a discussion of why it is not efficient (or cost effective) to drive a large car with only one person in it.

- It is important to explain that sometimes we actually want to transfer electricity by heating and this is an efficient process.

Plenaries

Car efficiency – Give students advertisements for cars and ask them to arrange them in order of energy efficiency, using the fuel consumption figures in the small print. Extend students, by asking them to investigate further and look at the questions of passenger numbers. Is a bus more energy-efficient than a car? *(5 minutes)*

Energy efficiency poster – Students could draw a poster encouraging people to be more energy-efficient in their home. The poster has to include information about why efficiency is important and some suitable suggestions as to what to do. Extend students by asking them to select suitable success or marking criteria for the poster themselves. *(10 minutes)*

Practical support

Investigating efficiency

This investigation can be used to develop and assess students' investigative skills, in particular those related to measurement.

Equipment and materials required

For each group: joulemeter, variable low voltage power supply, connecting leads, small electric winch (motor), 5 × 100 g masses (each weighing 0.1 N), metre rule, clamps to secure the winches to benches, cardboard box or piece of carpet to protect the floor.

Details

Students will lift a range of masses to a fixed height. A full metre is a good height – if the motor were 100% efficient it would require 0.1 J

for each mass. In reality, it will be much less efficient than this. If the winches are quite powerful, you may need to use larger weights to notice the reduction in efficiency.

Safety: Protect the floor and keep feet clear from falling weights. Stop motor before masses reach the pulley.

Electrical heating efficiency

Demonstrate a kettle heating water (a transparent kettle is great). The students could identify energy losses here as sound. Explain that these losses are very small and electrical heating is very efficient. You could mention that the generation of electricity is not very efficient though.

Safety: Take care when using mains electricity and keep hands dry.

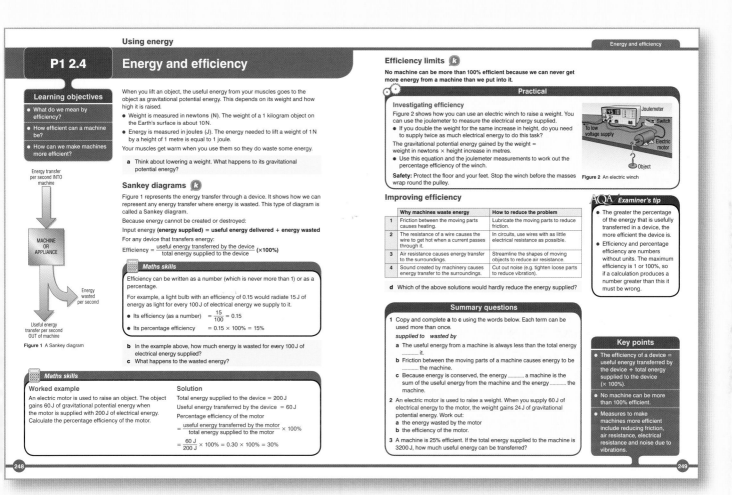

Further teaching suggestions

Car efficiency

- Students could research into car efficiency. A large amount of information is available about the performance of a car; students could find this and produce a graph showing which is the most fuel efficient. Several groups could look into different classes of car to find the 'best in class' and share their findings.

Calculations

- Provide a worksheet with additional calculations. You could provide data from the lifting experiment for students to analyse, if they did not try the task during the lesson.

  The student poster (energy efficiency poster plenary) could also be tacked as a homework task; use the time in the lesson to decide on the success criteria for the work.

Answers to in-text questions

a You use your muscles, so the gravitational potential energy is transferred in them by heating.

b 85 J

c It is transferred by heating the lamp holder and the surroundings.

d Solution 4

Summary answers

1 a supplied to

   b wasted by

   c supplied to, wasted by

2 a 36 J

   b 0.40 (or 40%)

3 800 J

Summary answers

1 1 B   2 C   3 A

2 electrical, light, useful, wasted

3 a 0.15 (or 15%)

  b 8500 J

  c

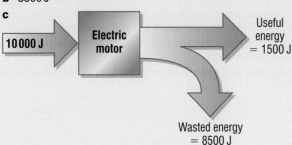

4 a 4.0 J

  b 4.0 J

  c 1.0 J

  d Some of the energy lost was transferred directly to the surroundings as sound and some was eventually transferred to the surroundings by heating.

5 a 1200 J

  b 300 J

  c

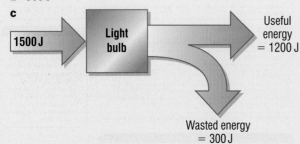

6 a i She loses gravitational potential energy and gains kinetic energy. Some energy may be wasted due to air resistance.

    ii She loses some more gravitational potential energy and all her kinetic energy. The energy she loses is mostly transferred into the rope as elastic strain energy. Some of her energy may be wasted due to air resistance.

  b 12 000 J

7 a i 1500 J   **ii** 10 500 J   **iii** 12.5%

  b Apply oil to the bearings of the motor to reduce friction.

Summary questions ⓚ

1 The devices listed below transfer energy in different ways.

  1 Car engine   2 Electric bell   3 Electric light bulb

  The next list gives the useful form of energy the devices are designed to produce.

  Match words A, B and C with the devices numbered 1 to 3.

  A Light   B Kinetic energy   C Sound

2 Copy and complete using the words below:

  useful wasted light electrical

  When a light bulb is switched on, ... energy is transferred into .... energy and energy that heats the surroundings. The energy that radiates from the light bulb is .... energy. The rest of the energy supplied to the light bulb is .... energy.

3 You can use an electric motor to raise a load. In a test, you supply the motor with 10 000 J of electrical energy and the load gains 1500 J of gravitational potential energy.

  a Calculate its efficiency.

  b How much energy is wasted?

  c Copy and complete the Sankey diagram below for the motor.

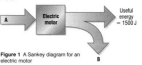

Figure 1 A Sankey diagram for an electric motor

4 A ball gains 4.0 J of gravitational potential energy when it is raised to a height of 2.0 m above the ground. When it is released, it falls to the ground and rebounds to a height of 1.5 m.

  a How much kinetic energy did it have just before it hit the ground? Assume air resistance is negligible.

  b How much gravitational potential energy did it transfer when it fell to the ground?

  c The ball gained 3.0 J of gravitational potential energy when it moved from the ground to the top of the rebound. How much energy did it transfer in the impact at the ground?

  d What happened to the energy it transferred on impact?

5 A low energy light bulb has an efficiency of 80%. U[...] an energy meter, a student found the light bulb us[...] 1500 J of electrical energy in 100 seconds.

  a How much useful energy did the light bulb trans[...] this time?

  b How much energy was wasted by the light bulb[...]

  c Draw a Sankey diagram for the light bulb.

6 A bungee jumper jumps from a platform and trans[...] 12 000 J of gravitational potential energy before th[...] attached to her becomes taut and starts to stretch[...] then transfers a further 24 000 J of gravitational po[...] energy before she stops falling and begins to rise.

  a Describe the energy changes:

    i after she jumps before the rope starts to stre[...]

    ii after the rope starts to stretch until she stops[...] falling.

  b What is the maximum kinetic energy she has du[...] her descent?

7 On a building site, an electric winch and a pulley w[...] used to lift bricks from the ground.

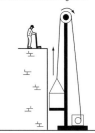

Figure 2 An electric winch and pulley

The winch transferred 12 000 J of electrical energy[...] raise a load through a height of 3.0 m. The load ga[...] 1500 J of gravitational potential energy when it wa[...] raised.

  a i How much useful energy was transferred by[...] motor ?

    ii Calculate the energy wasted.

    iii Calculate the percentage efficiency of the sy[...]

  b How could the efficiency of the winch be improv[...]

250

Kerboodle resources ⓚ

Resources available for this chapter on Kerboodle are:

- Chapter map: Using energy
- Support: Where does it all go? (P1 2.1)
- Interactive activity: Energy transfers and conservation (P1 2.2)
- How Science Works: Falling cupcakes (P1 2.2)
- Practical: Investigating a model bungee jump (P1 2.2)
- Bump up your grade: Using a Sankey diagram (P1 2.4)
- Extension: Using energy conservation (P1 2.4)
- Practical: Investigating the efficiency of an electric motor (P1 2.4)
- Revision podcast: Useful energy
- Test yourself: The efficient use of energy
- On your marks: Using energy
- Examination-style questions: Using energy
- Answers to examination-style questions: Using energy

AQA Examiner's tip

Students often do not fully understand the law of energy conservation. Drawing Sankey diagrams to scale helps them understand this concept and this is required in some exam questions.

AQA Examiner's tip

Energy can be transferred usefully, stored or dissipated. Energy is dissipated, for example, when energy is 'wasted' due to friction. This energy is transferred to the surroundings, which become warmer. The student must realise that the wasted energy has not been *destroyed*, and the total energy remains the same throughout.

Examination-style questions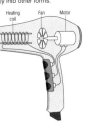

...vision transfers electrical energy.

...words from the list to complete each sentence. Each ...can be used once, more than once or not at all.

...rical   light   sound   warmer

...vision is designed to transfer .... energy into
...and .... energy. Some energy is transferred to
...urroundings, which become .... (3)

...dryer contains an electrical heater and a fan driven
... electric motor. The hairdryer transfers electrical
...y into other forms.

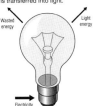

Heating coil   Fan   Motor

...art from energy by heating, name **two** of the other
...ms of energy. (2)

...t all of the energy supplied to the fan is usefully
...nsferred. Name **one** form of energy that is wasted
... the fan. (1)

...nich of the following statements about the energy
...sted by the fan is true?

... It eventually becomes very concentrated.
... It eventually makes the surroundings warmer.
... It is eventually completely destroyed.
... It is eventually transferred into electrical energy. (1)

...e fan in another hairdryer transfers useful energy at
... same rate but wastes more of the energy supplied
...it. What does this tell you about the efficiency of this
...irdryer? (1)

...ot water system water is heated by burning gas in
...ler. The hot water is then stored in a tank. For every
... of energy released from the gas, 100 J of energy is
...rbed by the water in the boiler.

...lculate the percentage efficiency of the boiler.
...rite down the equation you use. Show clearly how
...u work out your answer. (4)

b The energy released from the gas but **not** absorbed
by the boiler is 'wasted'. Explain why this energy is of
little use for further energy transfers. (1)

c The tank in the hot water system is surrounded by a
layer of insulation. Explain the effect of the insulation
on the efficiency of the hot water system. (3)

4 A chairlift carries skiers to the top of a mountain. The
chairlift is powered by an electric motor.

a What type of energy have the skiers gained when they
reach the top of the mountain? (1)

b The energy required to lift two skiers to the top of the
mountain is 240 000 J.
The electric motor has an efficiency of 40%.
Calculate the energy wasted in the motor.
Write down the equation you use. Show clearly how
you work out your answer and give the unit. [H] (4)

c Explain why some energy is wasted in the motor. (2)

5 A light bulb transfers electrical energy into useful light
energy and wasted energy to the surroundings. For
every 100 J of energy supplied to the bulb, 5 J of energy
is transferred into light.

Wasted energy → Light energy

Electricity

Draw and label a Sankey diagram for the light bulb. (3)

6 *In this question you will be assessed on using good
English, organising information clearly and using
specialist terms where appropriate.*

Explain why an electric heater is the only appliance that
can possibly be 100% efficient. (6)

---

3 a Efficiency

$$= \frac{\text{useful energy transferred by the device}}{\text{total energy supplied to the device}} \ (\times\ 100\%)$$

Efficiency $= \dfrac{100\,J}{111\,J} \times 100\%$

Efficiency $= 0.90 \times 100\%$

Efficiency $= 90\%$ *(4 marks)*

b The energy becomes too spread out to use. *(1 mark)*

c The insulation reduces the rate at which energy is lost
from the tank to the surroundings.
The water in the tank will stay hotter for longer.
This increases the efficiency of the hot water system.
(3 marks)

4 a Gravitational potential energy. *(1 mark)*

b Efficiency

$$= \frac{\text{useful energy transferred by the device}}{\text{total energy supplied to the device}} \ (\times\ 100\%)$$

total energy supplied $= \dfrac{240\ 000\,J}{0.4}$

total energy supplied $= 600\ 000\,J$

energy wasted $= 600\ 000\,J - 240\ 000\,J$

energy wasted $= 360\ 000\,J$ *(4 marks)*

c Friction between the moving parts of the motor
causes some energy to be transferred by heating.
(Or the current flowing in the motor has a heating effect.)
(2 marks)

5 Electrical energy

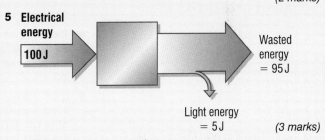

100 J

Wasted energy = 95 J

Light energy = 5 J *(3 marks)*

6 There is a clear, balanced and detailed description of why
an electric heater is the only appliance that can possibly be
100% efficient. The answer shows almost faultless spelling,
punctuation and grammar. It is coherent and in an organised,
logical sequence. It contains a range of appropriate or
relevant specialist terms used accurately. *(5–6 marks)*

There is a partial description of why an electric heater is the
only appliance that can possibly be 100% efficient. There
are some errors in spelling, punctuation and grammar.
The answer has some structure and organisation. The use
of specialist terms has been attempted, but not always
accurately. *(3–4 marks)*

There is a brief description of why an electric heater is the
only appliance that can possibly be 100% efficient, which has
little clarity and detail. The spelling, punctuation and grammar
are very weak. The answer is poorly organised with almost
no specialist terms and/or their use demonstrating a general
lack of understanding of their meaning. *(1–2 marks)*

No relevant content. *(0 marks)*

Examples of physics points made in the response:

- all electrical appliances convert some energy by heating
- in most appliances some energy is wasted
- energy is usually wasted by heating
- the useful energy transfer in the heater is by heating
- an appliance is 100% efficient only if all the energy transfer
is useful
- the heater can be 100% efficient if no energy is wasted as
light.

AQA Practical suggestions

Practicals	AQA	(k)	📖	⚙
An energy 'circus' to demonstrate various energy transfers.		✓		✓

AQA Examination-style answers

1 A television is designed to transfer **electrical** energy into
light and **sound** energy. Some energy is transferred to the
surroundings, which become **warmer**. *(3 marks)*

2 a Kinetic energy, sound. *(2 marks)*

b Sound. *(1 mark)*

c **B** It eventually makes the surroundings warmer. *(1 mark)*

d It is less efficient. *(1 mark)*

P1 3.1

Electrical appliances

Learning objectives

Students should learn:

- that electrical appliances are very useful
- about a range of energy transfers that happen in electrical appliances.

Learning outcomes

Most students should be able to:

- describe the energy transfers in a range of electrical appliances
- choose a particular appliance for a particular purpose based on the energy transfer required.

Support

- Ensure students are using the 'official' lists of energy forms. For example, try to encourage the use of 'kinetic energy' instead of movement.

Extend

- Students could be extended by finding out who first discovered how electricity could be used to produce movement. How and where was this first demonstrated? Was its importance realised? This is an important moment in practical science. [Faraday demonstrated a primitive motor but worked with other scientists who were upset that they were not credited.]

AQA / Specification link-up: Physics P1.3

- Examples of energy transfers that everyday electrical appliances are designed to bring about. [P1.3.1 a)]
- Compare the advantages and disadvantages of using different electrical appliances for a particular application. [P1.3]
- Consider the implications of instances when electricity is not available. [P1.3]

Lesson structure

Starters

Electricity everywhere – Support students by asking them to list all of the electrical appliances that they use during the day. Include mains-powered and battery-operated. They could then describe how their lives would be more difficult if these appliances did not exist. This should bring home to them how important the discovery of electricity was. *(5 minutes)*

Using energy – Challenge students to design an experiment to compare how much energy is stored in different batteries. Their ideas could include measuring how long a bulb could stay lit for or even how long a toy operates for (as used in many adverts). You could then discuss measuring the energy with a joulemeter as you may have in previous practical tasks. *(10 minutes)*

Main

- The core part of this topic is a discussion of why electricity is so useful in our society. Students will appreciate that electricity can be transferred easily into other forms of energy, so spend some time mentioning and showing the key appliances that do the job.

- Show a wire heating when a current passes through it and ask students what this effect is used in. Use a heatproof mat and turn up the current until the wire becomes white hot (for a moment). Students need to be out of touching distance. Ask: 'What is this effect used in [electrical heating elements] and how do we make sure that the wire does not melt?'

- Show an electric motor operating, pointing out the magnets, and ask how this effect is used. Also ask: 'What is the effect of increasing the current and providing more energy to the motor?' This will be covered in detail if students go on to study GCSE Physics.

- Demonstrate a simple electromagnet and again see if students realise how this effect can be used in loudspeakers (have one handy with a signal generator). With each of the demonstrations, ask students to consider how energy is being wasted to the surroundings.

- Once students are aware of the range of possible energy transfers, they should discuss how to choose a particular appliance for a job. Include a discussion of the clockwork radio – see the 'How Science Works' box in the Student Book.

Plenaries

Making connections – Ask students to complete the paragraph 'Electrical energy is a very convenient form of energy because ...' including these words: 'energy', 'transfer' and 'current'. [For example, 'It is very easy to transfer electrical energy into other forms such as light and movement. The energy can be carried over long distances by the electric current, so we can get the energy to where we need it easily.'] *(5 minutes)*

Electrical energy table – To support students, give them a cut-up table similar to the one in the Student Book and ask them to assemble it to show the useful and wasted energy from more electrical appliances. You could use mobile phone, projector, vacuum cleaner and electric fan. For some students, you could add challenging appliances such as a computer. [The useful energy might only be the light emitted by the monitor and the sound from any speakers.] *(10 minutes)*

Practical support

Energy transfers

This is a simple survey. You could provide students with a supporting worksheet if you think that they will need one.

Demonstrating heating effect of electrical current

You will need a low-voltage power supply (variable), connecting wires, resistance wire, heatproof mat. Make sure that the paper is a small piece so that the fire cannot spread beyond the mat. The plastic insulation of the leads should be kept away from the flames too.

Demonstrating a motor

Ideally, you should use a motor where students can see the moving parts. This way, you can describe the effect the current is having and point out important features, such as the way wires are connected by brushes, so the motor is free to turn without them becoming tangled.

Demonstrating a loudspeaker

The loudspeaker should be a large one, and you should demonstrate that all it is doing is moving in and out by showing some low-frequency vibrations. Connect to a signal generator if required.

Electrical energy

P1 3.1
Electrical appliances

Learning objectives

- Why are electrical appliances so useful?
- What do we use most everyday electrical appliances for?
- How do we choose an electrical appliance for a particular job?

Everyday electrical appliances

We use electrical appliances every day. They transfer electrical energy into useful energy at the flick of a switch. Some of the electrical energy we supply to them is wasted.

Figure 1 Electrical appliances – how many can you see in this photo?

Practical

Energy transfers

Carry out a survey of electrical appliances you find at school or at home.

Record the useful and wasted energy transfers of each appliance.

?? Did you know ...?

Unlike high voltage electrical injuries, people do not get many burns when they are struck by lightning. Damage is usually to the nervous system. The brain is frequently damaged as the skull is the most likely place to be struck. Lightning that strikes near the head can enter the body through the eyes, ears and mouth and flow internally through the body.

Table 1

Appliance	Useful energy	Energy wasted
Light bulb	Light from the glowing filament.	Energy transfer from the filament heating surroundings.
Electric heater	Energy heating the surroundings.	Light from the glowing element.
Electric toaster	Energy heating bread.	Energy heating the toaster case and the air around it.
Electric kettle	Energy heating water.	Energy heating the kettle itself.
Hairdryer	Kinetic energy of the air driven by the fan. Energy heating air flowing past the heater filament.	Sound of fan motor (energy heating the motor heats the air going past it, so is not wasted). Energy heating the hairdryer itself.
Electric motor	Kinetic energy of object driven by the motor. Potential energy of objects lifted by the motor.	Energy heating the motor and sound energy of the motor.
Computer disc drive	Energy stored in magnetic dots on the disc.	Energy heating the motor that drives the disc.

a What energy transfers happen in an electric toothbrush?

How Science Works

Clockwork radio

People without electricity supplies can now listen to radio programmes – thanks to the British inventor Trevor Baylis. In the early 1990s, he invented and patented the clockwork radio. When you turn a handle on the radio, you wind up a clockwork spring in the radio. When the spring unwinds, it turns a small electric generator in the radio. It doesn't need batteries or mains electricity. So people in remote areas where there is no mains electricity can listen to their radios without having to walk miles for a replacement battery. But they do have to wind up the spring every time it runs out of energy.

Figure 2 Clockwork radios are now mass-produced and sold all over the world

Choosing an electrical appliance

We use electrical appliances for many purposes. Each appliance is designed for a particular purpose and it should waste as little energy as possible. Suppose you were a rock musician at a concert. You would need appliances that transfer sound energy into electrical energy and then back into sound energy. But you wouldn't want them to produce lots of energy heating the appliance itself and its surroundings. See if you can spot some of these appliances in Figure 3.

b What electrical appliance transfers:
 i sound energy into electrical energy?
 ii electrical energy into sound energy?
c What other electrical appliance would you need at a concert?

Figure 3 On stage

Summary questions

1 Copy and complete using the words below:
 electrical light heating
 When a battery is connected to a light bulb, ... energy is transferred from the battery to the light bulb. The filament of the light bulb becomes hot and so energy transfers to its surroundings by .... and as .... energy.

2 Match each electrical appliance in the list below with the energy transfer A or B it is designed to bring about.
 1 Electric drill
 2 Food mixer
 3 Electric bell
 Energy transfer A Electrical energy → sound energy
 B Electrical energy → kinetic energy

3 a Why does a clockwork radio need to be wound up before it can be used?
 b What energy transfers take place in a clockwork radio when it is wound up then switched on?
 c Give an advantage and a disadvantage of a clockwork radio compared with a battery-operated radio.

Key points

- Electrical appliances can transfer electrical energy into useful energy at the flick of a switch.
- Uses of everyday electrical appliances include heating, lighting, making objects move (using an electric motor) and creating sound and visual images.
- An electrical appliance is designed for a particular purpose and should waste as little energy as possible.

252

253

?? Did you know ...?

Electricity and life have been linked ever since scientists noticed that a battery could be used to make dead frogs' legs twitch as if they were alive. Some people thought that electricity might even be used to bring the dead back to life, and this was the idea that inspired the 17-year-old Mary Shelley to write her novel *Frankenstein*. Even today, scientists are accused of trying to produce 'Frankenstein foods' with genetic engineering.

Further teaching suggestions

Applications

- Students could find out where all the electrical effects demonstrated today are used in industry or around the school.

Extended writing

- The 'Electricity everywhere' Starter could be used as the topic of a longer story that students could write, if not used during the lesson. This could be used as homework.

Answers to in-text questions

a Electrical energy transfers to kinetic energy of the brush, heating due to friction between the moving parts and resistance, and sound.

b i A microphone. ii A loudspeaker.

c An amplifier.

Summary answers

1 electrical, heating, light

2 1 B, 2 B, 3 A

3 a Energy needs to be stored in its spring so that the spring will turn a generator to provide the electricity supply to the radio.

 b Elastic energy in the spring is transferred into kinetic energy of the generator which is transferred into electrical energy + sound + heating due to friction between the moving parts of the generator.

 c E.g. advantage – clockwork radio saves the cost of replacing batteries; disadvantage – needs winding up regularly whereas with batteries you can switch on and listen immediately, as long as the batteries are working.

P1 3.2

Electrical power

AQA Specification link-up: Physics P1.3

- The amount of energy an appliance transfers depends on how long the appliance is switched on and its power. *[P1.3.1 b)]*

Learning objectives

Students should learn:

- that the power rating of an appliance is a measure of how much energy it transfers each second
- how to calculate the power of an appliance
- how to calculate the efficiency of an electrical appliance.

Learning outcomes

Most students should be able to:

- state that the watt is the unit of power
- calculate the power output of appliances using the equation: $P = \dfrac{E}{t}$
- calculate the efficiency of an electrical appliance from power or energy data.

Some students should also be able to:

- perform calculations involving the rearrangement of the equation. **[HT only]**

Lesson structure

Starters

Big numbers – Give students a set of units with SI prefixes and ask them to place the units in order of size. These could be mm, cm, m, km and another set containing mg, g, and kg. You could then add in larger units such as mega (M) and giga (G). Students may not have encountered these before. *(5 minutes)*

Match up – Ask students to sort a range of electrical appliances into order of energy use (power rating). You could do this with real objects or with cards to represent them. The objects could be set up on a long bench and students should add post-it notes for their ranking. Discuss these rankings after everybody has had a go. To extend the task, you could ask students to guess the power ratings (in watts). They could then add post-it notes indicating the useful energy transfers and wasted energy on each. *(10 minutes)*

Main

- Begin with a discussion of power and the clear scientific definition as 'the amount of energy transferred each second'. You could show some appliances and say which has the higher power rating; students should soon get to grips with the idea.
- Recap energy use by electrical appliances using the Practical support 'Measuring energy use'. The unit 'watt' is exactly the same as 'a joule per second' and this is a common concept tested in examinations. Some students seem to struggle with the term 'per' and you might explain this as meaning 'each'. You could also use this practical as an open-ended planning exercise.
- Emphasise that the prefix 'kilo' just means 'one thousand'. Check that students understand numbers like 2.4 kW and 0.5 kW, as some have difficulty; if they are struggling it is sometimes best to say the 'kilo' means 'multiply the number by one thousand'. Similarly, some students will need the prefix 'mega' explained to them carefully.
- Provide plenty of example calculations as students need to develop a clear layout for their calculations. Adhere to a rigorous method, and check that students are reaching the correct answers with their method.
- Extend students by encouraging them to rearrange the equation. As before, to ensure consistency, check with the mathematics department how this rearrangement is usually tackled.
- The efficiency of weightlifters is not very good. Although the weightlifter may be producing a useful power output of 600 W, they may actually be using chemical energy at 1000 W. This is more than an electrical fire – so it is no wonder that they get hot!
- The efficiency calculation links back to the previous chapter. This time you are using power statistics but the techniques should be exactly the same as you used last time to ensure consistency.

Plenaries

Matching the power – Give students a set of pictures of household electrical appliances and a set of power ratings. Ask them to match the ratings with the appliances. [Examples could include: kettle 2 kW, washing machine 0.5 kW, desktop computer 200 W, dishwasher 1.5 kW, electric clock 1 W, iron 1 kW, CD player 30 W, blender 300 W]. *(5 minutes)*

Calculation loop – This is similar to most loop games, but students have to match calculation questions with numerical answers to match. There should be a set of calculations and only one card with the correct answer. Students work out the correct answer and then ask the question on their card. Repeat until all of the questions are answered. This should ensure plenty of practice at the calculations from the lesson. Prepare a slideshow of the calculations, so that you can show the right approach at the end of each question. *(10 minutes)*

Support

- You may need to provide a layout template for the calculations for some students to support and develop their skills. This template may contain partly completed equations.

Extend

- The power output of our Sun, a typical star, is much greater than the power needed for everybody on the Earth. How could we harness this power to meet our energy demands for the next billion years? Students could look into exotic solutions, such as space mirrors, ring worlds and Dyson spheres. The outcome could be a dramatic presentation of the far future.

Practical support

Measuring energy use

You could demonstrate the energy use of electrical appliances using a joulemeter, if you have not already done so in previous practical work. Connect up appliances to a low-voltage power supply and measure the energy using the joulemeter. Demonstrate a range of bulbs so students can link the energy use to the brightness. Then move on to motors, showing larger motors requiring more energy. You could even show the low power heating elements again.

P1 3.2 — Electrical power

Learning objectives

- What do we mean by power?
- How can we calculate the power of an appliance?
- How can we calculate the efficiency of an appliance in terms of power?

Figure 1 A lift motor

When you use a lift to go up, a powerful electric motor pulls you and the lift upwards. The lift motor transfers energy from electrical energy to gravitational potential energy when the lift goes up at a steady speed. We also get electrical energy transferred to wasted energy heating the motor and the surroundings, and sound energy.

- The energy we supply per second to the motor is the power supplied to it.
- The more powerful the lift motor is, the faster it moves a particular load.

In general, we can say that:

the more powerful an appliance, the faster the rate at which it transfers energy.

We measure the power of an appliance in watts (W) or kilowatts (kW).

1 watt is a rate of transfer of energy of 1 joule per second (J/s).

1 kilowatt is equal to 1000 watts (i.e. 1000 joules per second or 1 kJ/s).

You can calculate power using:

$$P = \frac{E}{t}$$

Where:

P is the power in watts, W

E is the energy transferred to the appliance in joules, J

t is the time taken for the energy to be transferred in seconds, s.

Maths skills

Worked example

A motor transfers 10 000 J of energy in 25 s. What is its power?

Solution

$$P = \frac{E}{t}$$

$$P = \frac{10\,000\ \text{J}}{25\ \text{s}} = 400\ \text{W}$$

a What is the power of a lift motor that transfers 50 000 J of energy from the electricity supply in 10 s?

Power ratings

Here are some typical values of power ratings for different energy transfers:

Appliance	Power rating
A torch	1 W
An electric light bulb	100 W
An electric cooker	10 000 W = 10 kW (where 1 kW = 1000 watts)
A railway engine	1 000 000 W = 1 megawatt (MW) = 1 million watts
A Saturn V rocket	100 MW
A very large power station	10 000 MW
World demand for power	10 000 000 MW
A star like the Sun	100 000 000 000 000 000 000 MW

Figure 2 Rocket power

b How many 100 W electric light bulbs would use the same amount of power as a 10 kW electric cooker?

Muscle power

How powerful is a weightlifter?

A 30 kg dumbbell has a weight of 300 N. Raising it by 1 m would give it 300 J of gravitational potential energy. A weightlifter could lift it in about 0.5 seconds. The rate of energy transfer would be 600 J/s (= 300 J ÷ 0.5 s). So the weightlifter's power output would be about 600 W in total!

c An inventor has designed an exercise machine that can also generate 100 W of electrical power. Do you think people would buy this machine in case of a power cut?

Efficiency and power

For any appliance

- its useful power out (or output power) is the useful energy **per second** transferred by it.
- its total power in (or input power) is the energy **per second** supplied to it.

In P1 2.4 Energy and efficiency, we saw that the efficiency of an appliance

$$= \frac{\text{useful energy transferred by the device}}{\text{total energy supplied to it}} \; (\times\ 100\%)$$

Because power = energy **per second** transferred or supplied, we can write the efficiency equation as:

$$\text{Efficiency} = \frac{\text{useful power out}}{\text{total power in}} \; (\times\ 100\%)$$

For example, suppose the useful power out of an electric motor is 20 W and the total power in is 80 W, the percentage efficiency of the motor is:

$$\frac{\text{useful power out}}{\text{total power in}} \times 100\% = \frac{20\ \text{W}}{80\ \text{W}} \times 100\% = 25\%$$

Figure 3 Muscle power

Summary questions

1 **a** Which is more powerful?
   i A torch bulb or a mains filament bulb.
   ii A 3 kW electric kettle or a 10 000 W electric cooker.
   b There are about 20 million occupied homes in England. If a 3 kW electric kettle was switched on in 1 in 10 homes at the same time, how much power would need to be supplied?

2 The total power supplied to a lift motor is 5000 W. In a test, it transfers 12 000 J of electrical energy to gravitational potential energy in 20 seconds.
   a How much electrical energy is supplied to the motor in 20 s?
   b What is its efficiency in the test?

3 A machine has an input power rating of 100 kW. If the useful energy transferred by the machine in 50 seconds is 1500 kJ, calculate
   a its output power in kilowatts
   b its percentage efficiency.

Key points

- Power is rate of transfer of energy.
- $P = \frac{E}{t}$
- Efficiency = $\frac{\text{useful power out}}{\text{total power in}} \; (\times\ 100\%)$

Further teaching suggestions

Measuring energy output of a battery

- The energy output of a battery can be measured using data logging techniques. Connect up two simple circuits containing a battery and a light bulb with a current sensor. In one circuit, use normal batteries and in the other, use long-life batteries. Use the data logging software to record how the current changes over a long period of time, and present the graphs to students during the next lesson for discussion. Do the long-life batteries last up to four times as long?

Equipment and materials required

Batteries (two types), light bulbs and holders, connecting leads, battery holders, current sensors, data loggers.

Horsepower

- Further calculations may be useful. Students could look into the origin of the term 'horsepower' and find out how many watts are equivalent to one horsepower. This could be done as a piece of homework.

Answers to in-text questions

a 5000 W (5 kW)

b 100 light bulbs

c Probably not, as 100 W would keep one or two light bulbs on, but only when you pedal.

Summary answers

1 **a** **i** A mains filament bulb.
   ii A 10 000 W electric cooker.
   b 6 million kilowatts.

2 **a** 100 000 J
   b 0.12 (or 12%)

3 **a** 30 kW
   b 30%

P1 3.3

Using electrical energy

Learning objectives

Students should learn:

- how to calculate the energy transferred by mains-supplied electrical appliances
- how to calculate the cost of operating electrical appliances.

Learning outcomes

Most students should be able to:

- calculate the amount of energy used by a mains appliance (in kW h)
- calculate the cost of the electricity used.

Some students should also be able to:

- carry out rearrangement of the appropriate equations. [HT only]

Support

- As in previous lessons, provide students with a layout template for calculations to help them with the work presented here.

Extend

- Extend students by asking them to calculate the energy use from a 100 W bulb left running for a year, in joules. They could then compare low energy bulbs that sometimes cost more to buy but are much cheaper to run each year. This may lead on to the idea of 'payback time'.

AQA

Specification link-up: Physics P1.3

- To calculate the amount of energy transferred from the mains using: $E = P \times t$ [P1.3.1 c)]
- To calculate the cost of mains electricity given the cost per kilowatt-hour. [P1.3.1 d)]

Lesson structure

Starters

Paying for electricity – Students should list the reasons that electricity should be paid for, e.g. the cost of materials, the workforce and the meter readers. Students could be extended by considering how these production costs could be reduced. They should realise that different productions techniques will have different costs associated with them. *(5 minutes)*

True cost – Show students a few electricity bills from different companies, so that they understand that different companies use different rates. They should get an appreciation of the complexity including different rates at different times of the day, standing charges, VAT and so on. They should check that the bills are correct. *(10 minutes)*

Main

- This is another quite mathematical concept with important calculations. You might like to start with some basic cost calculations of simple things like food to make sure students can complete them.
- The most common difficulty is the name of the units. Students really need to understand that a 'kilowatt-hour' is a measure of an amount of energy, so spend some time going through this.
- Students should be reminded that the amount of energy an appliance uses is linked to the power it uses and time the appliance is activated for.
- Make sure that students can work out how many kilowatt-hours have been used when given two different meter readings. It is a simple subtraction, but some students just choose one of the two meter readings and think that this is the number of units used.
- Some students struggle when talking about immaterial things like 'kilowatt-hours', and you may need to give analogies like 'how many gobstoppers could you buy for £2 if they cost 12p each' and so on.
- Students now have two methods of calculating energy use: kilowatt-hours and joules. Students need not translate between the two.
- Extend students by asking them to work out how many kilowatt-hours could be bought with a set amount of money. How long can they keep a TV running for if they have £1?

Plenaries

Big bill – Show students a copy of the school electricity bill and ask them to think of ways they could reduce it. They should gain an appreciation of running all of the equipment they use every day. They could also try out the calculations to see if they come up with the same answer as the electricity company. *(5 minutes)*

Choosing the best supplier – Extend students by giving them copies of two pricing structures: one with a standing charge, and one without a standing charge but with a higher price per kilowatt-hour. Ask students to find out which company each of three different families should use. (For example: Ultra-Elec has a standing charge of 20 pence per day and a cost of 10 pence per kW h. Top-Power has no standing charge but cost of 12 pence per kW h. If the Bauer family use 300 kW h in a period of 90 days, which company is cheaper for them to use?) You will return to this idea in the next lesson. *(10 minutes)*

Practical support

The cost of electricity

Students could check the weekly usage of electricity from their own electricity meters and note it in a diary over a few months. They need to ensure that this is safe, so get them to check with their parents and then record the reading every week at a fixed time. The data would have to be collected over a fairly long period (several months) and then students could analyse their usage patterns. As an example, they could plot a graph showing their weekly use against the weekly temperature (either recorded or from records from the internet) to see if there is a correlation between the two, and discuss questions such as 'Do we use more electricity when it is colder?'

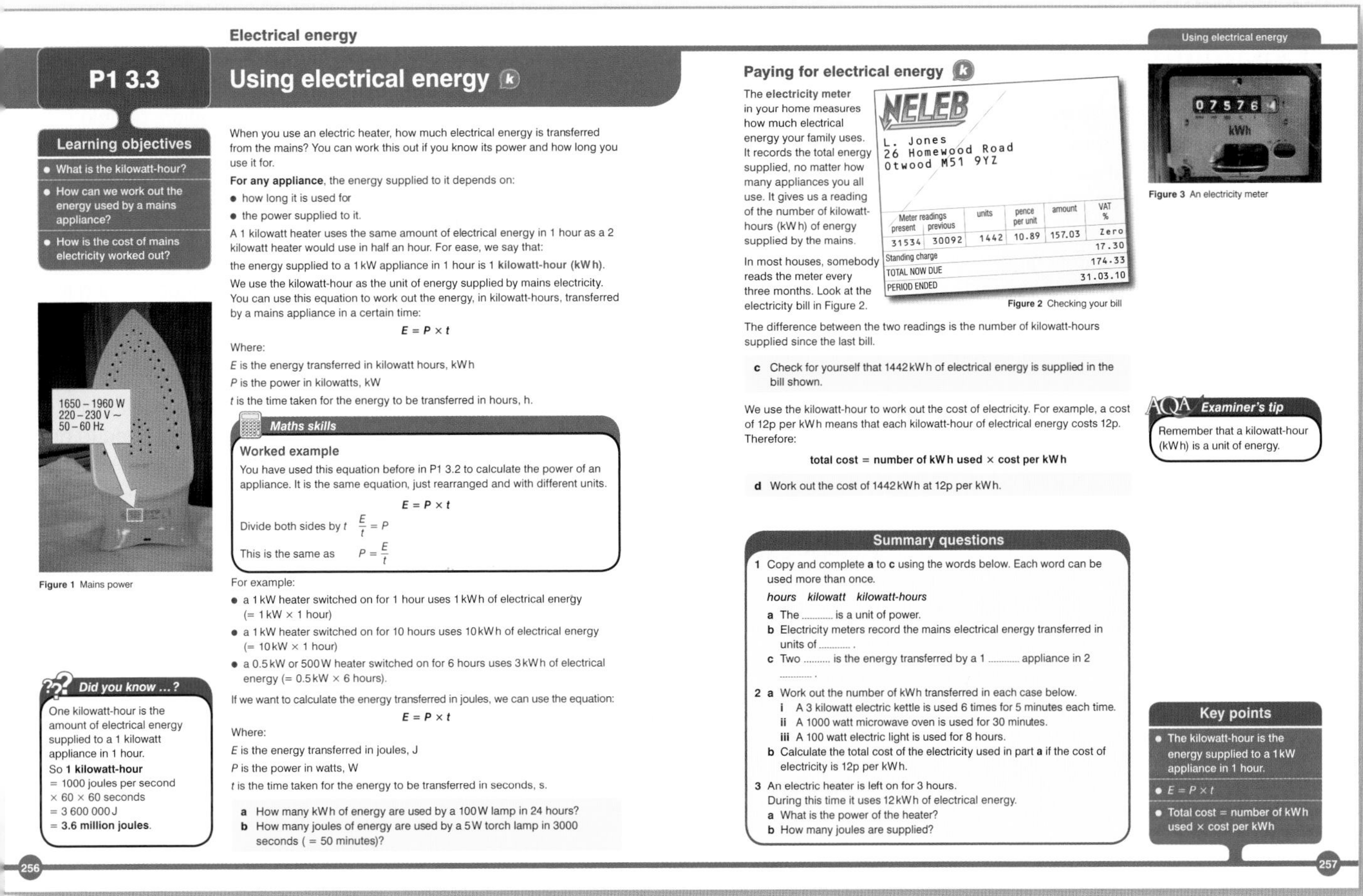

Electrical energy

P1 3.3   Using electrical energy 🄺

Learning objectives

- What is the kilowatt-hour?
- How can we work out the energy used by a mains appliance?
- How is the cost of mains electricity worked out?

1650 – 1960 W
220 – 230 V ~
50 – 60 Hz

Figure 1 Mains power

??? Did you know …?

One kilowatt-hour is the amount of electrical energy supplied to a 1 kilowatt appliance in 1 hour.
So **1 kilowatt-hour**
= 1000 joules per second
  × 60 × 60 seconds
= 3 600 000 J
= **3.6 million joules**.

When you use an electric heater, how much electrical energy is transferred from the mains? You can work this out if you know its power and how long you use it for.

For any appliance, the energy supplied to it depends on:

- how long it is used for
- the power supplied to it.

A 1 kilowatt heater uses the same amount of electrical energy in 1 hour as a 2 kilowatt heater would use in half an hour. For ease, we say that:

the energy supplied to a 1 kW appliance in 1 hour is 1 kilowatt-hour (kW h).

We use the kilowatt-hour as the unit of energy supplied by mains electricity. You can use this equation to work out the energy, in kilowatt-hours, transferred by a mains appliance in a certain time:

$$E = P \times t$$

Where:

E is the energy transferred in kilowatt hours, kW h

P is the power in kilowatts, kW

t is the time taken for the energy to be transferred in hours, h.

▦ Maths skills

Worked example

You have used this equation before in P1 3.2 to calculate the power of an appliance. It is the same equation, just rearranged and with different units.

$$E = P \times t$$

Divide both sides by t $\dfrac{E}{t} = P$

This is the same as $P = \dfrac{E}{t}$

For example:

- a 1 kW heater switched on for 1 hour uses 1 kW h of electrical energy (= 1 kW × 1 hour)
- a 1 kW heater switched on for 10 hours uses 10 kW h of electrical energy (= 10 kW × 1 hour)
- a 0.5 kW or 500 W heater switched on for 6 hours uses 3 kW h of electrical energy (= 0.5 kW × 6 hours).

If we want to calculate the energy transferred in joules, we can use the equation:

$$E = P \times t$$

Where:

E is the energy transferred in joules, J

P is the power in watts, W

t is the time taken for the energy to be transferred in seconds, s.

a How many kWh of energy are used by a 100W lamp in 24 hours?

b How many joules of energy are used by a 5W torch lamp in 3000 seconds (= 50 minutes)?

Paying for electrical energy 🄺

The electricity meter in your home measures how much electrical energy your family uses. It records the total energy supplied, no matter how many appliances you all use. It gives us a reading of the number of kilowatt-hours (kW h) of energy supplied by the mains.

In most houses, somebody reads the meter every three months. Look at the electricity bill in Figure 2.

NELEB

L. Jones
26 Homewood Road
Otwood M51 9YZ

Meter readings		units	pence per unit	amount	VAT %
present	previous				
31534	30092	1442	10.89	157.03	Zero
					17.30
Standing charge				174.33	
TOTAL NOW DUE					
PERIOD ENDED				31.03.10	

Figure 2 Checking your bill

The difference between the two readings is the number of kilowatt-hours supplied since the last bill.

c Check for yourself that 1442 kWh of electrical energy is supplied in the bill shown.

We use the kilowatt-hour to work out the cost of electricity. For example, a cost of 12p per kW h means that each kilowatt-hour of electrical energy costs 12p. Therefore:

total cost = number of kWh used × cost per kWh

d Work out the cost of 1442 kWh at 12p per kWh.

07576 4

kWh

Figure 3 An electricity meter

AQA Examiner's tip

Remember that a kilowatt-hour (kW h) is a unit of energy.

Summary questions

1 Copy and complete **a** to **c** using the words below. Each word can be used more than once.

  hours kilowatt kilowatt-hours

  a The .... is a unit of power.

  b Electricity meters record the mains electrical energy transferred in units of ....

  c Two .... is the energy transferred by a 1 .... appliance in 2 ....

2 **a** Work out the number of kWh transferred in each case below.

    i A 3 kilowatt electric kettle is used 6 times for 5 minutes each time.

    ii A 1000 watt microwave oven is used for 30 minutes.

    iii A 100 watt electric light is used for 8 hours.

  b Calculate the total cost of the electricity used in part **a** if the cost of electricity is 12p per kWh.

3 An electric heater is left on for 3 hours. During this time it uses 12 kWh of electrical energy.

  a What is the power of the heater?

  b How many joules are supplied?

Key points

- The kilowatt-hour is the energy supplied to a 1kW appliance in 1 hour.
- $E = P \times t$
- Total cost = number of kWh used × cost per kWh

256   257

Further teaching suggestions

ICT link-up

- This is a great opportunity for students to use a simple spreadsheet to calculate the cost of the electricity used. They could then very easily find out what would happen to the price if the cost per kW h increased or decreased by altering just one number. You could design the sheet or ask students confident with ICT to make one of their own.

??? Did you know …?

In standby mode, a large TV operates at 10 W. If it is left on standby for 12 hours, it will use 0.12 kW h. That means it costs 0.84p per night or £3 per year.

Around the world, machines in standby mode consume 4 TW h of energy in standby mode each year. (£280 million at UK prices.)

Answers to in-text questions

a 2.4 kW h

b 15 000 J

c Students to check answer.

d £173.04

Summary answers

1 **a** kilowatt

  b kilowatt-hours

  c kilowatt-hours, kilowatt, hours

2 **a** **i** 1.5 kW h

    ii 0.5 kW h

    iii 0.8 kW h

  b 33.6p

3 **a** 4 kW

  b 43.2 million joules (4000 × 3 × 60 × 60)

P1 3.4

Cost effectiveness matters

Learning objectives

Students should learn:

- that a cost-effective appliance is efficient and provides good value for money
- that the cost effectiveness can be compared by looking at the efficiency of the appliance and the original (capital) cost.

Learning outcomes

Most students should be able to:

- compare appliances or techniques to find out which is most cost effective based on running costs and capital costs
- take into account other cost factors such as environmental impact in their assessments.

AQA Specification link-up: Physics P1.2

- Compare the efficiency and cost effectiveness of methods used to reduce 'energy consumption'. [P1.2]

Lesson structure

Starters

Cosy home – Before students look at the Student Book, support students by giving them a diagram of a house and ask them to think of all the ways that energy is being wasted. They should suggest ways that the house could be made more energy efficient. They should be able to come up with all of the ways mentioned in this spread and possibly more. [For example, draught excluders, cavity wall insulation, loft insulation, double glazing, carpeted floors.] *(5 minutes)*

Value pack – Show students some cornflake packets (or similar) of different sizes along with the price. They then have to work out a fair comparison of value (e.g. cost per 100 g). Then show them a supermarket brand in different-sized packages and ask them to find the best value. They could discuss if the supermarket brand is exactly the same as the better-known brand. This could link into the central idea of cost effectiveness during the lesson. *(10 minutes)*

Main

- Begin this lesson by clearly defining the terms you are going to use. Capital cost is the original cost of purchasing. Running costs are more difficult, as you may need to go back and review the previous calculations. Interest costs are usually not considered by most students', but you will have to introduce them here. The environmental costs are harder to work out in monetary value; you could deal with them as a discussion later.

- There are four sections to the lesson, each looking in detail at a particular example:

- The first activity focuses on the idea of payback time in a house. You could expand on this by incorporating other measures. For example, fitting draught excluders may cost £10 and save £20 each year. This gives a very short payback time. Double glazing costs £4000 and saves only £200 each year, giving a payback time of 20 years (although it reduces noise levels too).

- For the shop-around task, you could use the plenary from the previous lesson if it was not attempted, or you could make up a few more scenarios. Tailor these to the ability of the students; add standing charges if you want to make the task more demanding.

- The low energy light bulb task is one about which most students should have some prior knowledge. You could point out the lighting systems in your school that are most likely low energy fluorescent tubes and explain the reasons the school uses them. You should look at the cost of LED lighting; this is changing quickly and the costs may have fallen a great deal each year.

- The final activity is a straightforward choice; students need to consider what makes a 'good' heater in this scenario.

Plenaries

Truthful advertising – Ask students to come up with some ideas for an advertisement poster for a hybrid car pointing out the advantages in terms of fuel efficiency and environmental impact. They could do this by brainstorming as a class or by individually sketching their ideas. *(5 minutes)*

I'll waste if I want to! – Do you have the right to waste energy? The government have restricted the sale of filament light bulbs but shouldn't people with enough money be able to use whatever amount of energy they want to? Similarly, cars with larger engines are more heavily road-taxed even though the petrol itself is taxed anyway. Is it fair to tax people who want to use more fuel, even more money? Students could discuss issues such as larger families needing bigger cars, car-sharing, and family cars that may carry six people at weekends but only one during the week. Extend students by asking them to discuss this concept in some depth or to write a letter of complaint to the government. They will need to use persuasive argument and include scientific facts. *(10 minutes)*

Support

- There are a few mathematical concepts here, so check students' calculations carefully and provide extra assistance where necessary.

Extend

- There is plenty of scope here to discuss improvements in energy efficiency in detail. Students could research emerging technology like hydrogen fuel cells for cars.

Further teaching suggestions

Different rates: Are they fair?

- Most electricity companies charge more per unit for pre-pay meters. This means that the poorest people actually pay more for each unit. You could have a discussion about whether this is a fair practice. Be careful to respect the privacy or feelings of some students who may be using these meters.

Truthful advertising

- Students could complete their advertisement poster as homework. They could make the the poster more honest by incorporating all of the disadvantages of the technology: cost, range, speed.

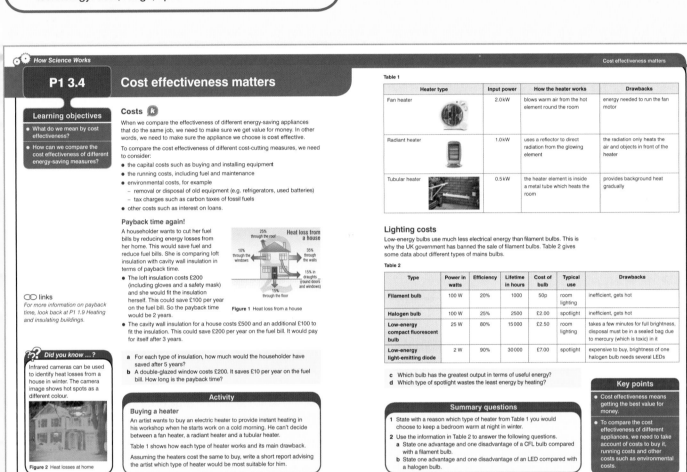

Answers to in-text questions

a Loft insulation £300; cavity wall insulation £400

b 20 years

c The halogen bulb.

d The LED.

Summary answers

1 The tubular heater, as the room would be too hot with either of the other two heaters on throughout the night.

2 a The CFL bulb uses much less electrical energy than the filament bulb. However, it contains mercury and needs to be disposed of carefully.

b The LED uses less electrical energy. However, you need several LEDs for the same brightness as a halogen bulb and they are much more expensive than a single halogen bulb.

Summary answers

1 **a** **i** A TV or visual display unit (VDU).
   ii An electric motor.
   b **i** sound, wasted
   ii kinetic, sound

2 **a** joule, kilowatt-hour
   b C, B, A, D

3 **a** **i** The higher one.
   ii 243 kW h
   iii £29.16
   b **i** 10 kW h
   ii 5 hours

4 **a** 500 kW h
   b £60
   c £12

5 **a** The heater
   b A 4.0 kW h   B 1.0 kW h   C 1.5 kW h
   c 78p

6 **a** **i** 0.12 kW h
   ii 432 000 J
   b Electrical energy to sound and light and energy transfer by heating.
   c Some energy is always wasted when a battery is used or recharged. Less energy would be used overall by using the computer with the charging unit connected to it, because the battery would not be used.

7 **a** 3.6 kW h
   b 43.2p

Summary questions 🄚

1 **a** Name an appliance that transfers electrical energy into:
   i light and sound energy
   ii kinetic energy.
   b Complete the sentences below.
   i In an electric bell, electrical energy is transferred into useful energy in the form of .... energy, and .... energy.
   ii In a dentist's drill, electrical energy is transferred into useful energy in the form of .... energy and sometimes as .... energy.

2 **a** Which two words in the list below are units that can be used to measure energy?
   joule kilowatt kilowatt-hour watt
   b Rank the electrical appliances below in terms of energy used from highest to lowest.
   A a 0.5 kW heater used for 4 hours
   B a 100 W lamp left on for 24 hours
   C a 3 kW electric kettle used 6 times for 10 minutes each time
   D a 750 W microwave oven used for 10 minutes.

3 **a** The readings of an electricity meter at the start and the end of a month are shown below.

0	9	3	7	2

0	9	6	1	5

   i Which is the reading at the end of the month?
   ii How many kilowatt-hours of electricity were used during the month?
   iii How much would this electricity cost at 12p per kWh?
   b A pay meter in a holiday home supplies electricity at a cost of 12p per kWh.
   i How many kWh would be supplied for £1.20?
   ii How long could a 2kW heater be used for after £1.20 is put in the meter slot? [H]

4 An escalator in a shopping centre is powered by a 50 kW electric motor. The escalator is in use for a total time of 10 hours every day.
   a How much electrical energy in kWh is supplied to the motor each day?
   b The electricity supplied to the motor costs 12p per kWh. What is the daily cost of the electricity supplied to the motor?
   c How much would be saved each day if the motor was replaced by a more efficient 40 kW motor?

5 The data below show the electrical appliances use[d in a] house in one evening.
   A a 1.0 kW heater for 4 hours
   B a 0.5 kW television for 2 hours
   C a 3 kW electric kettle three times for 10 minutes [each] time.
   a Which appliance uses most energy?
   b How many kWh of electrical energy is used by [each] appliance?
   c Each kWh costs 12p. How much did it cost to u[se the] three appliances?

6 The battery of a laptop computer is capable of sup[plying] 60 watts to the computer circuits for 2 hours befor[e it] needs to be recharged.
   a Calculate the electrical energy the battery can s[upply] in two hours in:
   i kilowatt-hours
   ii joules.
   b Describe the energy transfers that take place w[hen the] computer is being used.
   c A mains charging unit can be connected to the computer when in use to keep its battery fully charged. Would the computer use less energy [with] the charging unit connected than without it connected?

7 A student has an HD television at home that uses [...] watts of electrical power when it is switched on. H[e] monitors its usage for a week and finds it is switch[ed on] for 30 hours.

Figure 1 An HD TV in use

   a How many kilowatt-hours of electrical energy a[re] supplied to it in this time?
   b Calculate the cost of this electrical energy at 12[p per] kilowatt-hour.

Examiner's tip

Students often do not grasp the fact that joules and kilowatt-hours are alternative units for energy. The presence of the 'W' in kW h often persuades the student that it is a unit of power. Kilowatt-hours are used by energy companies because a kW h is a fairly typical amount of energy used when a fairly typical appliance is left on for 1 hour. The numbers are easy to work with and understand. They sometimes even drop the kW h and call it a 'unit'. The irony is, that in GCSE Physics, having this alternative unit and then calling it a 'unit' causes more confusion than it prevents!

Examiner's tip

To keep things simple in calculating kW h, students can be encouraged to express the number of hours as a fraction, e.g. 15 minutes can be written as 15/60 hours.

Examiner's tip

Students need to understand that the same equation for power (power = energy × time) is being used. However, no rearrangement of the equation will be asked for when dealing with the cost of electricity.

Kerboodle resources 🄚

Resources available for this chapter on Kerboodle are:
- Chapter map: Electrical energy
- Maths skills: Electrical energy (P1 3.3)
- Support: Power to the kitchen (P1 3.3)
- Bump up your grade: Read a meter (P1 3.3)
- Interactive activity: Electrical energy calculations (P1 3.4)
- Extension: The best rates (P1 3.4)
- Revision podcast: Electricity costs
- Test yourself: Electrical energy
- On your marks: Electrical energy
- Examination-style questions: Electrical energy
- Answers to examination-style questions: Electrical energy

Examination-style questions

[pictures] show six different household appliances.

heater Vacuum cleaner Washing machine

[i]ron Kettle Blender

[Nam]e the **four** appliances in which electrical energy is [us]fully transferred into kinetic energy. (4)

[An ele]ctric motor is used to lift a load. The useful power [out]put of the motor is 30 W. The total input power to the [moto]r is 75 W.

[Calc]ulate the efficiency of the motor.

[Writ]e down the equation you use. Show clearly how you [work] out your answer. (3)

[Whic]h **two** of the following units are units of energy?

[J]
[kW]h

(1)

[This] diagram shows the readings on a household [elect]ricity meter at the beginning and end of one week.

| 2 | 3 | 4 | 0 | | 5 | 2 | 5 | 5 | 5 |

[Be]ginning of the week   End of the week

[a Ho]w many kWh of electricity were used during the [we]ek? (1)

[b I]n one day 35 kWh of electricity were used. The total [co]st of this electricity was £5.25.

[W]rite down the electricity cost per kWh.

[W]rite down the equation you use. Show clearly how [y]ou work out your answer and give the unit. [H] (3)

[c D]uring the week a 2.4 kW kettle was used for 2 hours. [Ca]lculate how much energy was transferred by the [ke]ttle.

[W]rite down the equation you use. Show clearly how [y]ou work out your answer and give the unit. (3)

5 A student uses some hair straighteners.

a The hair straighteners have a power of 90 W.
What is meant by *a power of 90 W*? (2)

b Calculate how many kilowatt-hours of electricity are used when the straighteners are used for 15 minutes.
Write down the equation you use. Show clearly how you work out your answer and give the unit. (3)

c The electricity supplier is charging 14p per kWh.
Calculate how much it will cost to use the straighteners for 15 minutes a day for one year.
Write down the equation you use. Show clearly how you work out your answer and give the unit. (2)

6 Filament bulbs are being replaced by compact fluorescent bulbs.

A compact fluorescent bulb costs £12, a filament bulb costs 50p.

A 25 W compact fluorescent bulb gives out as much light as a 100 W filament bulb.

A filament bulb lasts for about 1000 hours; a compact fluorescent bulb lasts for about 8000 hours, although this time is significantly shorter if the bulb is turned on and off very frequently.

A compact fluorescent bulb contains a small amount of poisonous mercury vapour.

a Explain how a 25 W compact fluorescent bulb provides the same amount of light as a 100 W filament bulb but use less electricity. (2)

b *In this question you will be assessed on using good English, organising information clearly and using specialist terms where appropriate.*

Compare the advantages and disadvantages of buying compact fluorescent bulbs rather than filament bulbs. (6)

261

End of chapter answers

AQA Examination-style answers

1 Fan heater
Washing machine
Blender
Vacuum cleaner (4 marks)

2 Efficiency $= \dfrac{\text{useful power out}}{\text{total power in}} \times 100\%$

Efficiency $= \dfrac{30\,\text{W}}{75\,\text{W}} \times 100\%$

Efficiency $= 40\%$ (3 marks)

3 a (J) and **c** (kWh) – both required (1 mark)

4 a 215 (1 mark)

b Total cost = number of kWh used × cost per kWh
cost per kWh = total cost/number of kWh used
cost per kWh = 525p/35
cost per kWh = 15p (3 marks)

c $E = P \times t$
$E = 2.4\,\text{kW} \times 2\,\text{h}$
$E = 4.8\,\text{kWh}$ (3 marks)

5 a 90 joules of energy are transferred each second (2 marks)

b $E = P \times t$
$E = 0.09\,\text{kW} \times 0.25\,\text{h}$
$E = 0.0225\,\text{kWh}$ (3 marks)

c cost = number of kWh used × cost per kWh
cost per day = 0.0225 kWh × 14p = 0.315p
cost for the year = 0.315p × 365 = 115p or £1.15 (2 marks)

6 a Compact fluorescent bulb is more efficient than the filament bulb.

A bigger proportion of the energy supplied to the compact fluorescent bulb is transferred to light and less wasted to the surroundings by heating. (2 marks)

b There is a clear, balanced and detailed description of the advantages and disadvantages of buying compact fluorescent bulbs rather than filament bulbs. The answer shows almost faultless spelling, punctuation and grammar. It is coherent and in an organised, logical sequence. It contains a range of appropriate or relevant specialist terms used accurately. (5–6 marks)

There is a description of a range of the advantages and disadvantages of buying compact fluorescent bulbs rather than filament bulbs. There are some errors in spelling, punctuation and grammar. The answer has some structure and organisation. The use of specialist terms has been attempted, but not always accurately. (3–4 marks)

There is a brief description of at least two advantages and disadvantages of buying compact fluorescent bulbs rather than filament bulbs, which has little clarity and detail. The spelling, punctuation and grammar are very weak. The answer is poorly organised with almost no specialist terms and/or their use demonstrating a general lack of understanding of their meaning. (1–2 marks)

No relevant content. (0 marks)

Examples of physics points made in the response:

Advantages of compact fluorescent bulbs:
• more efficient/4 times more efficient
• cheaper to use
• last longer/lasts 8 times as long
• better for the environment.

Disadvantages of compact fluorescent bulbs:
• more expensive to buy/cost 24 times as much to buy
• disposal a problem because of mercury vapour
• shortened lifespan if turned on and off very frequently.

AQA Practical suggestions

Practicals	AQA	k	📖	⚙
Candidates reading the electricity meter at home on a daily or weekly basis. They could then look for trends in usage and try to explain these, e.g. in terms of weather conditions.		✓		✓
Plan and carry out an investigation using an electrical joulemeter to measure the energy transferred by low voltage bulbs of different powers, low voltage motors and low voltage immersion heaters.		✓		✓

261

P1 4.1 Fuel for electricity

Learning objectives

Students should learn:

- how a fossil fuel-based power station operates
- the differences between using fossil fuels and nuclear fuels in electricity generation
- that other fuels (e.g. biofuel) can also be used to generate electricity.

Learning outcomes

Most students should be able to:

- draw a flow chart showing the stages of electricity generation in a power station
- describe the similarities and differences between different power stations.

Some students should also be able to:

- evaluate in detail the advantages and disadvantages of nuclear power in comparison with fossil fuels.

Answers to in-text questions

a It is condensed to water and goes back to the boiler.

b It is carried away by the hot water from the cooling tower, escaping into the air.

Support

- Students could be provided with a diagram of a power station and complete the labelling of the important components. This will allow them to concentrate on how the parts behave.

Extend

- Students can find out a lot more about the internal working of a power station by visiting appropriate websites. They should be able to find some statistics about fuel use, employment, pollution and sustainability.

AQA Specification link-up: Physics P1.4

- In some power stations an energy source is used to heat water. The steam produced drives a turbine that is coupled to an electrical generator. Energy sources include:
  - the fossil fuels (coal, oil and gas) which are burned to heat water or air
  - uranium and plutonium, when energy from nuclear fission is used to heat water
  - biofuels that can be burned to heat water. [P1.4.1 a)]
- Evaluate different methods of generating electricity. [P1.4]

Lesson structure

Starters

Fossil fuels – Get the students to describe how coal, oil and natural gas have formed. Support students by giving them pictures of some of the stages and ask them to put them into order. They can annotate these diagrams. Have some samples to show the students. *(5 minutes)*

Burning? – What is burning? The students should draw a spider diagram or mind map covering what they know about combustion of fuels. They can do this while watching a birthday candle burn; they have to stop when the candle is finished; choose a candle that will last for a few minutes. Support students by providing some example fuels for them to describe and expect then to produce a clear, and general, word equation. Extend students by expecting them to give an example symbol equation. *(10 minutes)*

Main

- Start by demonstrating the combustion of some fuel. This could be a simple Bunsen flame or a spirit burner. Discuss energy being released during oxidation of carbon linking back to the first starter if possible. You could demonstrate that water is being produced too with a cold sheet of glass or metal. You could extend this demonstration by putting a conical flask of water above the flame and letting it boil. Add a bung with a delivery tube to show steam generation; this is a vital process in power stations.

- Link these ideas to electricity generation; an animation of the processes involved in a power station gets the stages across clearly. Emphasise the difference in scale and the high pressure and temperature of the steam in a power station in comparison with your earlier demonstration. The students need to be able to state what each part of the power station does, so it is best to go through them thoroughly and check understanding at each stage.

- Demonstrate a turbine using the apparatus above or as outlined in 'Practical support'. You could use a biofuel to heat the water at this stage to introduce the concept. Show wood but use a spirit burner with ethanol in it as it burns cleanly and is easy to control.

- The carbon neutrality of biofuel is an important issue. Point out that the growing plant takes in the same amount of carbon as it released during burning. However, you can bring in the idea of energy being wasted during farming, processing and transporting the crop/biofuel to show that even biofuels have a carbon cost.

- When discussing the amount of energy produced by a kilogram of fuel, use a kilogram of coal to give a visual clue. There is enough energy in a kilogram of coal to keep a bright (100 W) light bulb running for 1000 hours; that is over 41 days. There is enough energy released by 1 kg of uranium to keep the same bulb running for 10 million hours. That's over a thousand years.

Plenaries

Anagrams – Ask students to decipher anagrams of important key words from this spread. These could be ['lace run: nuclear, be foul I: biofuel, I lo: oil, cola: coal, aural tangs: natural gas, a ruin um: uranium, clue sun: nucleus.] You can add some more about energy resources too and see if the students can figure them out [bend ruin wit: wind turbine, hamlet ogre: geothermal]. Obviously you can differentiate, extending or supporting, by using single words or more complex phrases. *(5 minutes)*

Lightning (brain) storm – Some people suggest harnessing the electricity from lightning strikes for power. The students could brainstorm the advantages and disadvantages of this idea. They should come up with the ideas that the energy would be 'free' but unreliable. They could then go on to research how much energy is actually provided by a lightning strike as part of a homework task. [~500 MJ] *(10 minutes)*

Practical support

Turbines

It is possible to buy turbine-demonstrating apparatus, but even if you haven't got any then the general principle is simple enough to show.

Equipment and materials required

Metal can with bung and glass delivery tube to let out steam, paper turbine or one of those fairground windmills on a stick, Bunsen, tripod and heatproof mat, a piece of metal, conical flask, spirit burner, ethanol.

Details

Half-fill the can with water and put the bung and glass delivery tube in. Heat on a medium flame to get a decent flow of steam and then place the windmill in the flow and watch it turn. It is important to point out that the steam is invisible and can cause severe burns.

Tips: Keep the glass delivery tube short so that energy is not wasted and boil the water in a kettle beforehand to save a bit of time. You might get a faster flow of steam if you taper the end of the glass delivery tube, but sometimes this just causes the steam to condense, so it is best to experiment beforehand to get the results you want.

Safety: Take care with hot water and steam. Wear eye protection. CLEAPSS Hazcard XOA Ethanol – highly flammable/harmful.

Generating electricity

P1 4.1 — Fuel for electricity

Learning objectives

- How is electricity generated in a power station?
- Which fossil fuels do we burn in power stations?
- How do we use nuclear fuels in power stations?
- What other fuels can be used to generate electricity?

Inside a power station

Figure 1 Inside a fossil fuel power station

Figure 2 Inside a gas-fired power station

Almost all the electricity you use is generated in power stations.

- In **coal-** or **oil-fired power stations**, and in most **gas-fired power stations**, the burning fuel heats water in a boiler. This produces steam. The steam drives a **turbine** that turns an electricity **generator**. Coal, oil and gas are fossil fuels, which are fuels obtained from long-dead biological material.

a What happens to the steam after it has been used?
b What happens to the energy of the steam after it has been used?

- In some gas-fired power stations, we burn natural gas directly in a gas turbine engine. This heats the air drawn into the engine. It produces a powerful jet of hot gases and air that drives the turbine. A gas-fired turbine can be switched on very quickly.

Practical

Turbines

See how we can use water to drive round the blades of a turbine.

- Why is steam better than water?

Figure 3 Using biofuel to generate electricity

Biofuels

We can get methane gas from cows or animal manure and from sewage works, decaying rubbish and other sources. It can be used in small-scale gas-fired power stations. Methane is an example of a **biofuel**.

A biofuel is any fuel obtained from living or recently living organisms such as animal waste or woodchip. Other biofuels include ethanol (from fermented sugar cane), straw, nutshells and woodchip.

A biofuel is:

- **renewable** because its biological source continues to exist and never dies out as a species
- **carbon-neutral** because, in theory, the carbon it takes in from the atmosphere as carbon dioxide can 'balance' the amount released when it is burned.

Nuclear power

Figure 4 shows you that every atom contains a positively charged nucleus surrounded by electrons. The atomic nucleus is composed of two types of particles: neutrons and protons. Atoms of the same element can have different numbers of neutrons in the nucleus.

How is electricity obtained from a nuclear power station?

The fuel in a nuclear power station is uranium (or plutonium). The uranium fuel is in sealed cans in the core of the reactor. The nucleus of a uranium atom is unstable and can split in two. Energy is released when this happens. We call this process nuclear fission. Because there are lots of uranium atoms in the core, it becomes very hot.

The energy of the core is transferred by a fluid (called the 'coolant') that is pumped through the core.

- The coolant is very hot when it leaves the core. It flows through a pipe to a 'heat exchanger', then back to the reactor core.
- The energy of the coolant is used to turn water into steam in the heat exchanger. The steam drives turbines that turn electricity generators.

Figure 4 The structure of the atom

How Science Works

Comparing nuclear power and fossil fuel power

Fuel	Nuclear power station	Fossil fuel power station
Fuel	Uranium or plutonium	Coal, oil or gas
Energy released per kg of fuel	1 000 000 kWh (= about 10 000 × energy released per kg of fossil fuel)	100 kWh
Waste	Radioactive waste that needs to be stored for many years	Non-radioactive waste
Greenhouse gases	No – because uranium releases energy without burning	Yes – because fossil fuels produce gases such as carbon dioxide when they burn

Summary questions

1 Copy and complete a to c using the words below:
coal   gas   oil   uranium
 a The fuel that is not a fossil fuel is ....
 b Power stations that use .... as the fuel can be switched on very quickly.
 c Greenhouse gases are produced in a power station that uses coal, gas or .... as fuel.

2 a State one advantage and one disadvantage of:
  i an oil-fired power station compared with a nuclear power station
  ii a gas-fired power station compared with a coal-fired power station.
 b Look at the table above.
  How many kilograms of fossil fuel would give the same amount of energy as 1 kilogram of uranium fuel?

3 a Explain why ethanol is described as a biofuel.
 b Ethanol is also described as carbon-neutral. What is a carbon-neutral fuel?

Key points

- Electricity generators in power stations are driven by turbines.
- Coal, oil and natural gas are burned in fossil fuel power stations.
- Uranium or plutonium are used as the fuel in a nuclear power station. Much more energy is released per kg from uranium or plutonium than from fossil fuel.
- Biofuels are renewable sources of energy. Biofuels such as methane and ethanol can be used to generate electricity.

Further teaching suggestions

ICT link-up

- Many of the energy generating companies have websites with information about power stations. Students can explore these to get a better idea of what is going on.

Is nuclear power the future?

- Many countries are developing nuclear programmes to generate electricity, but is this the way forward? There are clear advantages and disadvantages of nuclear power and fossil fuels, so the students could produce a booklet allowing people to vote on which of the two methods should be developed further in the UK. The booklet should contain all of the facts from both sides of the argument and a detachable voting slip. This activity could be set as homework, giving the students clear guidelines on how much time to spend on this task.

Summary answers

1 a uranium
 b gas
 c oil

2 a i E.g. advantage of oil-fired power station: no radioactive waste; disadvantage: produces greenhouse gases.
  ii E.g. advantage of gas-fired power station: can be started quicker; disadvantage: gas supplies will run out before coal supplies.
 b 10 000 kg

3 a A biofuel is any fuel from a biological source. Ethanol can be obtained from sugar cane.
 b Burning the ethanol from a sugar plant puts carbon dioxide into the atmosphere. The growth of a sugar cane plant takes the same amount of carbon dioxide from the atmosphere. Thus ethanol is described as carbon-neutral. Any fuel that, in theory, can 'balance' its intake and output of carbon dioxide is described as a carbon-neutral fuel.

P1 4.2

Energy from wind and water

AQA

Specification link-up: Physics P1.4

- Water and wind can be used to drive turbines directly. *[P1.4.1 b)]*
- Evaluate different methods of generating electricity. *[P1.4]*

Learning objectives

Students should learn:

- how wind turbines can be used to generate electricity
- how water can be used to generate electricity in a variety of ways
- the advantages and disadvantages of the above methods of electricity generation.

Learning outcomes

Most students should be able to:

- describe how wind turbines generate electricity
- describe the different ways in which the flow of water can generate electricity
- list some advantages and disadvantages of these methods of electricity generation.

Some students should also be able to:

- evaluate in detail the advantages and disadvantages of these methods of electricity generation.

Support

- Try to use models for all of the explanations, so that the students can see them in action. You can use a ripple tank to show the idea of wave generators, emphasising the changes in energy taking place.

Extend

- Provide the students with some data about the power output of different-sized wind turbines in different wind conditions. Can they find any patterns? There should be a relationship between the area the blades sweep out and the power output. There should also be a relationship between the wind speed and power output. These patterns can be found by plotting graphs of the data and analysing the shape.

Lesson structure

Starters

Wind and convection currents – Support students by giving them a set of cards describing how wind is caused and ask them to put them in the correct order. This links back to their previous studies. Cards can include: sunlight warms the ground, energy is radiated and warms up the air near the ground, the air expands and rises, when the hot air rises cooler air is drawn into the gap, the movement of this cooler air is the wind. Students can be extended by asking them to explain the causes of the flow of air themselves in terms of expansion and density changes. *(5 minutes)*

Water cycle recap – To support students, ask them to draw a diagram explaining the water cycle. You may need to provide a basic diagram showing an ocean, land, mountains and a river for the students to annotate. The students should use scientific language including evaporation, condensation and precipitation. Link this cycle to hydroelectricity later. *(10 minutes)*

Main

- You may want to show the students the ideas behind a turbine and generator. It can be difficult to light up a bulb with wind power. Try using a large desk fan, as the source of wind, and a large bladed demonstration wind turbine connected to a low voltage lamp. You could try an LED if you can't get enough energy to light the bulb. Obviously, this is a very inefficient way of lighting a bulb, so you can revise energy transfer and efficiency here. You might want to get some students to design or carry out an investigation into the efficiency of wind power with a set-up similar to this.

- A video clip of a wind farm in operation gives a good idea of the scale of these structures and may also highlight the noise issue. Search for 'wind farm' at an internet video-hosting site. If you want to impress the noise problem on the students, play a sample in a continuous loop while they try to work through some of the summary questions. If you have an exercise cycle with a dynamo, you can illustrate that turning the wheel more quickly produces more electrical energy.

- There are several alternative designs for wave-powered generators; you could ask the students how they think they work. As usual, discuss changes in energy.

- The idea behind a hydroelectric scheme can be shown simply by letting water flow down a pipe from a raised reservoir. This can be directed onto a paddle wheel, causing it to spin. You may need to show students accelerated video clips of a tide coming in or out, as they may not have seen the effect before. If you have access to the internet, you may be able to find a webcam showing a real-time image of a major estuary. Is the tide in or out? Search the internet for 'webcam estuary'.

- Compare and contrast advantages/disadvantages of the energy sources covered in this lesson as a class discussion.

Plenaries

Designing a tidal barrier – You could extend students by asking them to design a tidal barrier that generates electricity, allows traffic to cross the river, and lets boats through when necessary. This could be made into quite a complicated task or left at a simple level, depending whether students require more support. Students could discuss their ideas as a group, and complete the task as homework. *(5 minutes)*

Wind farm advertisement – Design a poster to persuade a local community to allow a wind farm in the vicinity. Other students could design an 'anti' poster. The poster could include information about new jobs, noise, reliability, cheaper or more expensive electricity. You might like to extend students to set their own marking criteria for the task such as what data is required and how many images can be used. They can then evaluate each other's work. For extra support, you can provide some of the information in the form of brochures or resident interviews. *(10 minutes)*

Practical support

Demonstrating a water turbine

There are a range of water turbine kits that can be attached to a tap and simple generator. It can be hard to get a big enough power output from one, so test a few bulbs connected to the generator first to see what it is capable of. Be careful to test the fittings as high water pressure can spray everywhere.

Pumped storage

It is difficult to demonstrate this with improvised equipment, but with the correct kit, it should be possible. You may wish to demonstrate it as two separate phases: pumping water uphill and then generating electricity as the water flows back.

Equipment and materials required

A 12 V electric water pump, rubber tubing and two reservoirs (buckets). Water turbine and generator, connecting leads, low voltage bulb and holder.

Details

Fill the lower reservoir with water and place one end of the tubing in it. Place the other in a second reservoir on a desk. You should be able to pump water to this height; if the second bucket is placed higher up you can also show the difficulty of pumping water 'uphill'. To drive a turbine is more difficult; you will need a specialised water turbine and generator connected to a lamp or similar. You will also need an upper reservoir with a hole to let water flow out and downhill to the generator.

Generating electricity

Energy from wind and water

P1 4.2 — Energy from wind and water

Learning objectives

- What does a wind turbine consist of?
- How do we use waves to generate electricity?
- What type of power station uses water running downhill to generate electricity?
- How can we use the tides to generate electricity?

Strong winds can cause lots of damage on a very stormy day. Even when the wind is much weaker, it can still turn a wind turbine. Energy from the wind and other natural sources such as waves and tides is called renewable energy. That's because such natural sources of energy can never be used up.

In addition, no fuel is needed to produce electricity from these natural sources so they are carbon-free to run.

Wind power

A wind turbine is an electricity generator at the top of a narrow tower. The force of the wind drives the turbine's blades around. This turns a generator. The power generated increases as the wind speed increases.

a What happens if the wind stops blowing?

Wave power

A wave generator uses the waves to make a floating generator move up and down. This motion turns the generator so it generates electricity. A cable between the generator and the shore delivers electricity to the grid system.

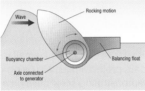
Figure 2 Energy from waves

Figure 1 A wind farm – why do some people oppose these developments?

Wave generators need to withstand storms and they don't produce a constant supply of electricity. Also, lots of cables (and buildings) are needed along the coast to connect the wave generators to the electricity grid. This can spoil areas of coastline. Tidal flow patterns might also change, affecting the habitats of marine life and birds.

b What could happen if the waves get too high?

How Science Works

When electricity demand is low, we can use electricity from wind turbines, wave generators and other electricity generators to pump water uphill into a reservoir. When demand is high, we can let the water run downhill through a hydroelectric generator.

Hydroelectric power

We can generate hydroelectricity when rainwater collected in a reservoir (or water in a pumped storage scheme) flows downhill. The flowing water drives turbines that turn electricity generators at the foot of the hill.

c Where does the energy for hydroelectricity come from?

Tidal power

A tidal power station traps water from each high tide behind a barrage. We can then release the high tide into the sea through turbines. The turbines drive generators in the barrage.

One of the most promising sites in Britain is the Severn estuary. This is because the estuary rapidly becomes narrower as you move up-river away from the open sea. So it funnels the incoming tide and makes it higher.

d Why is tidal power more reliable than wind power?

Figure 3 A hydroelectric scheme

Summary questions

1 Copy and complete **a** to **d** using the words below:
hydroelectric tidal wave wind
a .... power does not need water.
b .... power does not need energy from the Sun.
c .... power is obtained from water running downhill.
d .... power is obtained from water moving up and down.

2 **a** Use the table below for this question. The output of each source is given in millions of watts (MW).
   i How many wind turbines would give the same total power output as a tidal power station?
   ii How many kilometres of wave generators would give the same total output as a hydroelectric power station?
   b Use the words below to fill in the location column in the table.
   coastline estuaries hilly or coastal areas mountain areas

Figure 4 A tidal power station

	Output	Location	Total cost in £ per MW
Hydroelectric power station	500 MW per station		50
Tidal power station	2000 MW per station		300
Wave power generators	20 MW per kilometre of coastline		100
Wind turbines	2 MW per wind turbine		90

3 The last column of the table above shows an estimate of the total cost per MW of generating electricity using different renewable energy sources. The total cost for each includes its running costs and the capital costs to set it up.
   a The capital cost per MW of a tidal power station is much higher than that of a hydroelectric power station. Give one reason for this difference.
   b **i** Which energy resource has the lowest total cost per MW?
      ii Give two reasons why this resource might be unsuitable in many areas.

Key points

- A wind turbine is an electricity generator on top of a tall tower.
- Waves generate electricity by turning a floating generator.
- Hydroelectricity generators are turned by water running downhill.
- A tidal power station traps each high tide and uses it to turn generators.

264 / 265

Further teaching suggestions

Pumped storage
- You can demonstrate this concept if you have the correct equipment; see 'Practical support'.

Tidal barrages
- Why not build a tidal barrage across the Severn or the Mersey? These rivers are ideal for generating lots of electrical energy, but what are the problems involved? Get the students to debate the issue. This can be done in class or the research can be completed at home before the discussion.

Answers to in-text questions

a No electricity is generated.
b The wave would flow over the top of the generator reducing it's efficiency significantly.
c From the gravitational potential energy of water in the reservoirs.
d The tides are very predictable whereas the wind isn't.

Summary answers

1 **a** wind
  b tidal
  c hydroelectric
  d wave

2 **a** **i** 1000
    ii 25 km
  b From top to bottom: mountain areas, estuaries, coastline, hilly or coastal areas.

3 **a** The area of the trapped water needs to be much greater in a tidal power station than in a hydroelectric station, as the water drops much less. So the barrage needs to be much longer in a tidal power station.
  b **i** The hydroelectric power station.
      ii Hydroelectricity is only suitable in mountainous areas where there is plenty of rainfall. Many areas do not have enough rainfall or do not have mountains.

P1 4.3

Power from the Sun and the Earth

Learning objectives

Students should learn:

- how solar cells can be used to generate electricity at high cost and in relatively small amounts
- how geothermal energy can be used to generate electricity in a variety of ways
- the advantages and disadvantages of the above methods of electricity generation.

Learning outcomes

Most students should be able to:

- describe how a solar cell can be used to produce electricity
- describe the different ways in which geothermal energy can generate electricity
- list some advantages and disadvantages of these methods of electricity generation.

Some students should also be able to:

- evaluate in detail the advantages and disadvantages of these methods of electricity generation.

Support

- Geothermal energy is the most difficult concept and the most difficult to demonstrate. Use video clips of hot springs or even volcanoes to show that the inside of the Earth is very hot.

Extend

- Ask students to find out about the source of the Earth's internal heat. They will have to find some facts about radioactive decay and its role in providing this energy over billions of years.

AQA Specification link-up: Physics P1.4

- Electricity can be produced directly from the Sun's radiation. *[P1.4.1 c)]*
- In some volcanic areas hot water and steam rise to the surface. The steam can be tapped and used to drive turbines. This is known as geothermal energy. *[P1.4.1 d)]*
- Evaluate different methods of generating electricity. *[P1.4]*

Lesson structure

Starters

Old Faithful – Show a video clip of 'Old Faithful' (search for 'Old Faithful' at an internet video-hosting site). Ask students if they have ever seen a geyser and if they know what causes them. Try to get them to explain where the heat comes from; they may assume that there are chemical reactions whereas the truth is that the energy is due to radioactive decay. *(5 minutes)*

To the centre of the Earth – The students should draw a simple diagram showing the structure and properties of the layers of the Earth (crust, mantle and core). You can provide the basic diagram for support. Extend the students by asking for a more detailed description of the properties of the layers such as the idea of density. They should be aware that the core has a molten layer and that the centre of the Earth is very hot. *(10 minutes)*

Main

- Demonstrate a solar cell being used to turn a small fan; you may need a bright bulb to do this. If you have a data projector and are using this during the lesson, it is also a great light source for demonstrating solar cells on a dreary day. You can even show that some solar cells work better in different coloured light; just use coloured backgrounds to blank slides. You can show how inefficient the cells are by using a very bright light shining on a panel that is lighting up a small bulb.

- If students are not investigating how the amount of light falling on the cell affects the output, they can simply show this idea by moving the cell further from the bulb; the small bulb should grow visibly dimmer. Students can develop concepts of 'How Science Works' by considering how to gather quantitative data when investigating solar cells.

- Small solar-powered garden lights are available from garden centres quite cheaply. Charge one of these up during the day and then cover the light sensor during the lesson, to show that it has been charged by collecting energy from the Sun. Link this to the idea that solar panels are far more useful when coupled with a battery, as they can then provide the energy when needed (in the dark in this case). However adding a battery to the system will increase the expense even more. Show some images of solar cells used on satellites and discuss why they are an ideal solution for electricity generation in space. Here the solar panels are the cheapest solution.

- Demonstrating geothermal energy is not easy, so use video clips and diagrams to get the ideas across. The focus should be on understanding that the energy comes from hot rocks. You may mention that the source of the heat is radioactivity, explain that this will be covered later in the course or extend students by asking them to find out more about this source of heat.

Plenaries

Solar car – Search the internet for 'solar car video' to show the students a video clip of a solar car in action; you might be able to find a toy one too. Ask them to list the advantages and disadvantages of the design. They can discuss whether solar-powered transport is a possibility in the future. You can tell them that solar-powered planes have also been developed but these can only transport one person at a time so far. *(5 minutes)*

Keep cool – Ask the students to come up with a design for a device that keeps you cooler, the brighter the Sun is. They could produce an advertisement explaining how it works. A solar-powered fan is a typical design but colour-changing clothing is a possibility with smart materials (white on the side that faces the Sun, but black on the opposite side). You could extend the students by asking them to build a prototype of a design if it is feasible or support some by providing example smart materials or components. *(10 minutes)*

Practical support

Solar cells

A solar cell can be demonstrated with a low-power electric motor.

Equipment and materials required

Solar cell, motor and bulb. Rechargeable solar garden lamp.

Details

A low-power motor will be required; complete kits containing a matched solar panel and motor are available. The students should be able to discover that the motor will turn faster the closer the bulb is to the cell. They might like to compare the speed of the motor in bright sunlight to that produced by a bulb. Covering part of the solar panel will reduce the energy output too.

Generating electricity

P1 4.3   Power from the Sun and the Earth

Learning objectives

- What are solar cells and how do we use them?
- What is the difference between a panel of solar cells and a solar heating panel?
- What is geothermal energy?
- How can we use geothermal energy to generate electricity?

Solar radiation transfers energy to you from the Sun. That can sometimes be more energy than you want if you get sunburnt. But we can use the Sun's energy to generate electricity using **solar cells**. We can also use the Sun's energy to heat water directly in solar heating panels.

a Which generates electricity – a solar cell or a solar heating panel?

Practical

Solar cells

Use a solar cell panel to drive a small electric motor.

- See what happens if you gradually cover the solar cells with a card.

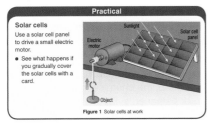

Figure 1 Solar cells at work

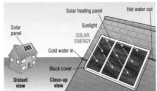

Figure 2 A solar-powered vehicle. Think of some advantages and disadvantages of this car.

links

For more information on solar heating panels, look back at P1 1.9 Heating and insulating buildings.

Figure 3 Solar water heating

Solar cells at present convert less than 10% of the solar energy they absorb into electrical energy. We can connect them together to make solar cell panels.

- They are useful where we only need small amounts of electricity (e.g. in watches and calculators) or in remote places (e.g. on small islands in the middle of an ocean).
- They are very expensive to buy even though they cost nothing to run.
- We need lots of them – and plenty of sunshine – to generate enough power to be useful.

A **solar heating panel** heats water that flows through it. Even on a cloudy day in Britain, a solar heating panel on a house roof can supply plenty of hot water.

b If the water stopped flowing through a solar heating panel, what would happen?

A solar power tower uses thousands of flat mirrors to reflect sunlight on to a large water tank at the top of a tower. The mirrors on the ground surround the base of the tower.

- The water in the tank is turned to steam by the heating effect of the solar radiation directed at the water tank.
- The steam is piped down to ground level where it turns electricity generators.
- The mirrors are controlled by a computer so they track the Sun.

A solar power tower in a hot dry climate can generate more than 20 MW of electrical power.

c The solar furnace shown in Figure 3 in P1 1.1 uses 63 flat tracking mirrors to reflect solar radiation on to the giant reflector. Why does the solar power tower in Figure 4 opposite collect much more solar radiation than this solar furnace?

Geothermal energy

Geothermal energy comes from energy released by radioactive substances, deep within the Earth.

- The energy released by these radioactive substances heats the surrounding rock.
- As a result, energy is transferred by heating towards the Earth's surface.

We can build **geothermal power stations** in volcanic areas or where there are hot rocks deep below the surface. Water gets pumped down to these rocks to produce steam. Then the steam produced drives electricity turbines at ground level.

In some areas, we can heat buildings using geothermal energy directly. Heat flow from underground is called ground heat. It can be used to heat water in long lengths of underground pipes. The hot water is then pumped round the building. Ground heat is used as under-floor heating in some large 'eco-buildings'.

d Why do geothermal power stations not need energy from the Sun?

Summary questions

1 Copy and complete **a** to **c** using the words below:
geothermal   solar   radiation   radioactivity
 a A suitable energy resource for a calculator is .... energy.
 b .... inside the Earth releases .... energy.
 c .... from the Sun generates electricity in a solar cell.

2 A satellite in space uses a solar cell panel for electricity. The panel generates 300 W of electrical power and has an area of 10 m².
 a Each cell generates 0.2 W. How many cells are in the panel?
 b The satellite carries batteries that are charged by electricity from the solar cell panels. Why are batteries carried as well as solar cell panels?

3 A certain geothermal power station has a power output of 200 000 W.
 a How many kilowatt-hours of electrical energy does the power station generate in 24 hours?
 b State one advantage and one disadvantage of a geothermal power station compared with a wind turbine.

Power from the Sun and the Earth

Figure 4 A solar power tower

AQA Examiner's tip

Make sure you know the difference between a solar cell panel (in which sunlight is used to make electricity) and a solar heating panel (in which sunlight is used to heat water).

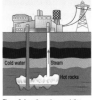

Figure 5 A geothermal power station

Key points

- Solar cells are flat solid cells that convert solar energy directly into electricity.
- Solar heating panels use the Sun's energy to heat water directly.
- Geothermal energy comes from the energy released by radioactive substances deep inside the Earth.
- Water pumped into hot rocks underground produces steam to drive turbines that generate electricity.

Further teaching suggestions

Investigating solar panels

- The students could investigate the energy output of solar panels. This provides an important opportunity to develop or assess investigative skills; the students should be encouraged to form their own detailed plans. There are two main variants:
  - Investigating how the energy output is related to the area of the panel.
  - Investigating how the energy output is related to the distance of the light source from the panel. These students can measure the output voltage (pd) from the panel instead of the actual energy output.

  Equipment required for each group: solar panel, bright bulb, sensitive ammeter and voltmeter, leads, metre rule or tape measure, black card to cover parts of panel.

Power plants

- As a research project, the students can find out where the best places to site geothermal power plants and solar power plants are. They should be reminded that the plants should not be too far from civilisation.

Answers to in-text questions

a A solar cell.

b The water in the panel would continue to heat up and possibly increase the pressure in the system damaging it.

c The power tower has many more flat mirrors tracking the Sun than the solar furnace has.

d The energy is from radioactive substances inside the Earth.

Summary answers

1 a solar
  b radioactivity, geothermal
  c radiation

2 a 1500
  b To supply electricity when the solar panels are in darkness.

3 a 4800 kW h
  b Geothermal energy does not depend on the weather like the wind; geothermal energy is not available in many areas.

P1 4.4

Energy and the environment

Learning objectives

Students should learn:

- about how burning fossil fuels affects the environment
- that there are severe potential hazards associated with the use of nuclear power and the disposal of nuclear waste.

Learning outcomes

Most students should be able to:

- describe how burning fossil fuels affects the environment
- describe the ways in which using renewable energy resources affect the environment.

Some students should also be able to:

- explain the issues relating to nuclear power and renewable energy sources.

Specification link-up: Physics P1.4

- Small-scale production of electricity may be useful in some areas and for some uses, e.g. hydroelectricity in remote areas and solar cells for roadside signs. *[P1.4.1 e)]*
- Using different energy resources has different effects on the environment. These effects include:
  - the release of substances into the atmosphere
  - the production of waste materials
  - noise and visual pollution
  - the destruction of wildlife habitats. *[P1.4.1 f)]*
- Evaluate different methods of generating electricity. *[P1.4]*
- Evaluate ways of matching supply with demand, either by increasing supply or decreasing demand. *[P1.4]*

Lesson structure

Starters

Renewable or not? – Give the students a list of energy resources and ask them to place them in either pile. You can use these non-renewable ones: coal, oil, natural gas, uranium and these renewable ones: tidal, solar, geothermal, wind, wave, biofuel. *(5 minutes)*

Acid rain – Ask students to explain what acid rain is and what causes it. Extend students by expecting them to explain some of the chemical reactions that lead to the formation of the acid; these could be word or balanced symbol equations. Students can be supported by recapping what an acid is and demonstrate that rainwater is slightly acidic using universal indicator and some freshly collected (or made up) rainwater. *(10 minutes)*

Main

- This topic lends itself well to debate and students will wish to put their ideas forward.
- In the context of the lesson the term 'reliable' should be used to mean a resource that produces electricity in a predictable and fairly constant way.
- Many students rule nuclear power out as a possible source of energy almost immediately without considering its benefits. You may need to point out these benefits to the students to make sure that they put a bit of thought into the issue. Remind the students that most nuclear power stations operate safely and some countries have many nuclear power stations. You can also mention that there have been a large number of deaths due to coal-mining and that, if global warming estimates are correct, the number of deaths caused by burning fossil fuels would far outweigh those caused by nuclear power.
- Check again that the students do not think that nuclear fuel is renewable. This is a common error because students are aware that the fuel is not burned but is reprocessed, and some of them assume that this is the same as recycling.
- A tidal barrage is reliable, in that it will always be able to produce electricity in a well-understood pattern but the output varies from day to day. The damage to wildlife in the estuary, or to a habitat in flooded valleys, is the main environmental concern and is frequently tested in examinations. This is also true for hydroelectricity and the flooding of valleys. Wind, wave and solar are less reliable and we could not guarantee a constant or predictable amount of electricity from them.
- The disadvantages of the renewable sources of energy should lead the students to the idea that it is unwise to rely on a single type of energy resource. We will need to rely on a combination of the resources in future and this is likely to include large-scale power plants (fossil fuel or nuclear) alongside smaller-scale, more local, renewable operations.

Support

- To develop mathematical skills, you might like to find the most recent data of energy resources used in the UK (or even the world) and have the students produce a pie chart or other form of graph.

Extend

- What is the real cost of building and decommissioning nuclear power stations? Ask the students to find out if any nuclear power stations have actually been fully dismantled and how much this has cost. Where has the waste from this decommissioning process been stored and for how long will it be kept? What happens in countries that have nuclear power stations but are unable to afford to decommission them?

Plenaries

What's the problem? – Support students by showing cards (or photographs) of environmental problems and ask the students to write down an energy resource that causes this problem. Students can be extended by asking them to offer solutions to the problems and evaluate the impact of the solutions themselves. *(5 minutes)*

Energy resource crossword – Let the students complete a crossword of all of the key words from this chapter so far. You can provide differentiated clues to the students enabling suitable support or extension. *(10 minutes)*

Further teaching suggestions

Chernobyl disaster
- The students may like to research the details of the Chernobyl disaster. A lot of material is available on the internet from a simple search, but they will have to be careful to find information at the correct level for them to understand.

A field trip
- It may be possible to arrange a field trip to visit a nearby fossil fuel power station or a nuclear one. This may be run in conjunction with another department, such as geography.

If students go on such a trip make sure that they produce a suitable report: a few digital cameras or a video camera would help with this.

Safety: Follow local guidelines for out-of-school activities.

Saving energy at home
- Ask the students to work out how much money they could save each year if they replaced all of the light bulbs in their house with energy-saving ones. They need to find the power rating of the bulbs to do this.

Energy and the environment

P1 4.4 Energy and the environment

Learning objectives
- What do fossil fuels do to our environment?
- Why are people concerned about nuclear power?
- How do renewable energy resources affect our environment?

Can we get energy without creating any problems? Look at the pie chart in Figure 1.

It shows the energy sources we use at present to generate electricity. What effect does each one have on our environment?

How Science Works

When a popular TV programme ends, lots of people decide to put the kettle on. The national demand for electricity leaps as a result. Engineers meet these surges in demand by switching gas turbine engines on in gas-fired power stations.

Fossil fuel problems
- When we burn coal, oil or gas, greenhouse gases such as carbon dioxide are released. We think that these gases cause global warming. We get some of our electricity from oil-fired power stations. We use much more oil to produce fuels for transport.
- Burning fossil fuels can also produce sulfur dioxide. This gas causes acid rain. We can remove the sulfur from a fuel before burning it to stop acid rain. For example, natural gas has its sulfur impurities removed before we use it.
- Fossil fuels are non-renewable. Sooner or later, we will have used up the Earth's reserves of fossil fuels. We will then have to find alternative sources of energy. But how soon? Oil and gas reserves could be used up within the next 50 years. Coal reserves will last much longer.
- Carbon capture and storage (CCS) could be used to stop carbon dioxide emissions into the atmosphere from fossil fuel power stations. Old oil and gas fields could be used for storage.

a Burning fossil fuels in power stations pollutes our atmosphere. Which gas contributes towards:
  i global warming?
  ii acid rain?

Figure 1 Energy sources for electricity

Other fuels 5% and renewables
Oil 1%
Hydro 1%
Nuclear 16%
Gas 46%
Coal 31%

links
For more information on pollution from fuels, see C1 4.3 Burning fuels, and C1 4.4 Cleaner fuels.

GAS   OIL   COAL
Increasing greenhouse gas emissions →

Figure 2 Greenhouse gases from fossil fuels

Nuclear v. renewable
We need to cut back on our use of fossil fuels to stop global warming. Should we rely on nuclear power or on renewable energy in the future?

Nuclear power
Advantages
- No greenhouse gases (unlike fossil fuel).
- Much more energy from each kilogram of uranium (or plutonium) fuel than from fossil fuel.

Did you know ... ?
The Gobi Desert is one of the most remote regions on Earth. Many areas do not have mains electricity. Yet people who live there can watch TV programmes – just as you can. All they need is a solar panel and satellite TV.

Disadvantages
- Used fuel rods contain radioactive waste, which has to be stored safely for centuries.
- Nuclear reactors are safe in normal operation. However, an explosion at one could release radioactive material over a wide area. This would affect these areas for many years.

b Why is nuclear fuel non-renewable?

Renewable energy sources and the environment
Advantages
- They will never run out.
- They do not produce greenhouse gases or acid rain.
- They do not create radioactive waste products.
- They can be used where connection to the National Grid is uneconomic. For example, solar cells can be used for road signs and hydroelectricity can be used in remote areas.

Disadvantages
- Wind turbines create a whining noise that can upset people nearby and some people consider them unsightly.
- Tidal barrages affect river estuaries and the habitats of creatures and plants there.
- Hydroelectric schemes need large reservoirs of water, which can affect nearby plant and animal life. Habitats are often flooded to create dams.
- Solar cells would need to cover large areas to generate large amounts of power.

c Do wind turbines affect plant and animal life?

Summary questions

1 Copy and complete **a** to **c** using the words below:
  acid rain fossil fuels greenhouse gas plant and animal life radioactive waste
  a Most of Britain's electricity is produced by power stations that burn ....
  b A gas-fired power station does not produce .... or much ....
  c A tidal power station does not produce .... as a nuclear power station does but it does affect .... locally.

2 Match each energy source with a problem it causes.

Energy source	Problem
i Coal	A Noise
ii Hydroelectricity	B Acid rain
iii Uranium	C Radioactive waste
iv Wind power	D Takes up land

3 **a** List three possible renewable energy resources that could be used to generate electricity for people on a remote flat island in a hot climate.
  b List three types of power stations that do not release greenhouse gases into the atmosphere.

Did you know ... ?

In 1986, some nuclear reactors at Chernobyl in Ukraine overheated and exploded. Radioactive substances were thrown high into the atmosphere. Chernobyl and the surrounding towns were evacuated. Radioactive material from Chernobyl was also deposited on parts of Britain.

Figure 3 Chernobyl, the site of the world's most serious accident at a nuclear power station

Figure 4 The effects of acid rain

Key points
- Fossil fuels produce increased levels of greenhouse gases which could cause global warming.
- Nuclear fuels produce radioactive waste.
- Renewable energy resources can affect plant and animal life.

Did you know ... ?

After the Chernobyl disaster, some radioactive caesium fell onto UK farmland and contaminated the grassland. Over 4 million sheep feeding off this grass became contaminated and dangerous for human consumption, so their slaughter was banned. Were the sheep lucky or unlucky? The final UK bans probably won't be lifted until 2026; that's 40 years after the accident.

Summary answers

1 **a** fossil fuels
  b acid rain, greenhouse gas
  c radioactive waste, plant and animal life

2 **i** B
  ii D
  iii C
  iv A

3 **a** solar cell panels, wave generators, wind turbines
  b nuclear, hydroelectric, tidal

Answers to in-text questions

a i Carbon dioxide.
  ii Sulfur dioxide.

b It turns into radioactive waste when it is used.

c They affect birds and can upset humans.

P1 4.5

The National Grid

AQA Specification link-up: Physics P1.4

- Electricity is distributed from power stations to consumers along the National Grid. *[P1.4.2 a)]*
- The uses of step-up and step-down transformers in the National Grid. *[P1.4.2 c)]*
- For a given power increasing the voltage reduces the current required and this reduces the energy losses in the cables. *[P1.4.2 b)]*

Learning objectives

Students should learn:

- how the National Grid is used to distribute electricity around the country
- why transformers are used to increase and decrease the voltage of alternating current.

Learning outcomes

Most students should be able to:

- explain the advantages of providing electricity via a National Grid
- describe the role of pylons, cables and transformers in the National Grid
- explain why electricity is transferred at very high voltage.

Lesson structure

Starters

Danger of death 1 – Show the students a picture of the 'Danger of death' icon used on transformer sub-stations. Ask them what they think the danger is and what the icon is showing. You could also check the students' knowledge of other hazard symbols here or even introduce the different categories. The icons are readily available from CLEAPSS. *(5 minutes)*

Choosing wisely – Give the students samples of a range of materials and a list of their properties. Ask them to choose which materials would be suitable for particular jobs and to explain why. Extend students by asking for clear descriptions of the properties of the materials themselves, not just particular objects. Jobs could include conducting electricity [copper], electrical insulation [plastic], making jewellery [gold], cutting [hardened steel] and so on. You may support students by asking them to link materials directly to properties using a worksheet or card-matching. Use the properties of aluminium (light, corrosion-resistant, good conductor) to explain why it can be used in power cables later in the lesson. *(10 minutes)*

Main

- Discussing the National Grid would be best with props. It may be possible to find a ceramic insulator or even a short length of pylon cable. Local electrical engineering companies may have off-cuts or broken parts. The thicker the cable you can find, the better.

- If you don't have a ceramic insulator, then you can discuss how the high voltage leads are insulated from the pylons by showing some pottery and describing that it is a particularly good insulator. You could extend students by linking to the idea that there are no free electrons and so conduction cannot occur.

- If a sample of aluminium cable is not available, then use sample blocks of aluminium and steel to compare the density of the two materials. The students will easily see the advantage of using aluminium. It also helps if the steel is a bit on the rusty side, so that you can show the aluminium is also easier to maintain.

- It is possible to demonstrate the saving in energy at higher voltages. See 'Practical support'; make sure you try it out in advance as it can be fiddly to get just right.

- The calculation is straightforward. Students may be confused about why you would bother to raise the voltage and lower the current if the power you get is the same anyway. You could extend students by introducing the equation mentioned in the Support and extension box.

Support

- You could revisit the idea of electrical conduction by using a circuit to test materials to see if they conduct. A simple circuit in which a test component is used to bridge a gap and light a bulb is sufficient. You can then let the students test long pieces of thin wire to show that these do not conduct as well. This brings home the idea that energy is lost when current travels through long thin wires.

Extend

- Resistance and power. The electrical power transferred by a wire is given by $P = I^2R$. This comes from combining the two key electrical equations $P = VI$ and $V = IR$, where P is power, I is current, V is voltage and R is the resistance of the wire. This power, and hence energy wasted in the wire, is dependent on the square of the current, so a small increase in current will dramatically increase the power of the wire. This is why the current is kept as small as possible and the voltage is kept very high.

Plenaries

Electrical flow – Support students by giving them a set of cards describing the passage of electricity from the generator to the light bulb, and ask them to sort the cards into order. You could use: 'The generator produces a voltage', 'The voltage causes a current in wires in the power station', 'A step-up transformer is used to increase the voltage and decrease the current', 'The electrical energy is transmitted through the National Grid system', 'A step-down transformer is used to reduce the voltage to 230 V and increase the current', 'The electrical energy is transmitted through the wires in a house to a plug socket'. Extend students by asking them to come up with a detailed description of their own. *(5 minutes)*

Danger of death 2 – Can the students produce an improved design for the hazard symbol? They should use the standard hazard symbol colours [yellow and black] and shape [triangle] but can change the design in any other way. You could discuss why safety symbols must have a standard appearance and colour scheme. *(10 minutes)*

Demonstration support

Modelling the National Grid

To demonstrate that high voltages are more efficient at transferring electrical energy, the following method can be used. It is fiddly to get just right, so make sure that you have tested it first.

Equipment and materials needed

Two matched transformers with a step-up or step-down ratio of about five (e.g. 100 turns input and 500 turns output). Two 2 m lengths of thin wire with high resistivity (nichrome or constantan work well), a 1.25 V lamp and a low voltage (1–1.5 V) ac power supply.

Details

Connect the power supply directly to the bulb through the long wires. The bulb should light dimly at best. This is because most of the energy is being wasted in heating the wires. Don't leave this set-up on for long, or the wires could overheat.

Next, connect the wires to the step-up transformer at the power supply end and the step-down transformer at the bulb end. The voltage in the wires will increase by a factor of five and the current will be reduced by a similar amount. This will lead to a twenty-fifth of the heating effect and energy wastage, so the lamp should be much brighter.

To make the demonstration more like the National Grid, you could suspend the wires on retort stands.

Generating electricity

P1 4.5 The National Grid Ⓚ

Learning objectives

- What is the National Grid?
- What do the transformers do in the National Grid?
- Why do we use high voltages in the National Grid?

Your electricity supply at home reaches you through the **National Grid**. This is a network of cables that distributes electricity from power stations to homes and other buildings. The network also contains transformers. Step-up transformers are used at power stations. Step-down transformers are used at substations near homes.

The National Grid's voltage is 132 000 V or more. This is because transmitting electricity at a high voltage reduces power loss, making the system more efficient.

Power stations produce electricity at a voltage of 25 000 V.

- We use step-up transformers to step this voltage up to the grid voltage.
- We use step-down transformers at local substations to step the grid voltage down to 230 V for use in homes and offices.

Figure 1 The National Grid

Figure 2 Electricity pylons carry the high voltage cables of the National Grid

Demonstration

Modelling the National Grid

Watch a demonstration of the effect of a transformer using this apparatus.

Figure 3 A model power line

AQA Examiner's tip

Remember that step-up transformers are used at power stations and step-down transformers are used at sub-stations near homes.

Did you know ...?

The National Grid was set up in 1926. The UK government decided electricity would be supplied to homes at 240 V. This was lowered to 230 V in 1994.

Power and the grid voltage

The electrical power supplied to any appliance depends on the appliance's current and its voltage. To supply a certain amount of power, we can lower the current if we raise the voltage. This is what a step-up transformer does in the grid system.

A step-up transformer raises the voltage, so less current is needed to transfer the same amount of power. A lower current passes through the grid cables. So energy losses due to the heating effect of the current are reduced to almost zero. But we need to lower the voltage at the end of the grid cables before we can use mains electricity at home.

a What difference would it make if we didn't step-up the grid voltage?

How Science Works

Underground or overhead?

Lots of people object to electricity pylons. They say they spoil the landscape or they affect their health. Electric currents produce electric and magnetic fields that might affect people.

Why don't we bury all cables underground?

Underground cables would be much more expensive, much more difficult to repair, and difficult to bury where they cross canals, rivers and roads.

What's more, overhead cables are high above the ground. Underground cables could affect people more because the cables wouldn't be very deep.

b Suggest two reasons why underground cables are more difficult to repair than overhead ones.

Summary questions

1 Copy and complete **a** and **b** using the words below:
higher down lower up

 a Power stations are connected to the National Grid using step-............ transformers. This type of transformer makes the voltage ....
 b Homes are connected to the National Grid using step-............ transformers. This type of transformer makes the voltage ....

2 **a** Why is electrical energy transferred through the National Grid at a much higher voltage than the voltage generated in a power station?
 b Why are transformers needed to connect local substations to the National Grid?

3 A step-up transformer connects a power station to the cables of the National Grid.
 a What does the transformer do to
  i the voltage
  ii the current?
 b Why are step-down transformers used between the end of the grid cables and the mains cables that supply mains electricity to our homes?

AQA Examiner's tip

You need to remember that:
- step-up transformers raise the voltage and lower the current
- step-down transformers lower the voltage and raise the current.

Did you know ...?

The insulators used on electricity pylons need to be very effective or else the electricity would short-circuit to the ground. In winter, ice on the cables can cause them to snap. Teams of electrical engineers are always on standby to deal with sudden emergencies.

Figure 4 Engineers at work on the Grid. They certainly need a head for heights!

Key points

- The National Grid is a network of cables and transformers that distributes electricity to our homes from distant power stations and renewable energy generators.
- Step-up transformers are used to step up power station voltages to the grid voltage. Step-down transformers are used to step the grid voltage down for use in our homes.
- A high grid voltage reduces energy loss and makes the system more efficient.

Further teaching suggestions

Do pylons affect our health?

- Some groups believe that the electromagnetic fields produced by electrical cables seriously affect our health. The students can try to find out if there is any evidence supporting this position. It is important that the students understand the nature and quality of the evidence presented to them, so they can judge the validity of any conclusions drawn (this relates to 'How Science Works' Analysing secondary data). This can lead to a discussion about the nature of anecdotal evidence.

Underground/overhead

- There are a number of reasons for choosing which method and there is plenty of information available about how the decisions are made. The students could be given a scenario (or several) and choose which method to use to transfer electricity. The National Grid has its own website which is a good place to start the research.

Hazards

- If the students did not redesign the 'danger of death' symbol, they could do this on a larger scale at home. They could produce a booklet warning of the hazards of messing with electricity pylons.

Answers to in-text questions

a Electrical energy would be wasted in the cables. Less electrical power would be supplied to the consumers.

b Faults would be harder to find. The ground would need to be dug up to make the repair.

Summary answers

1 **a** up, higher
 b down, lower

2 **a** To reduce the energy wasted in transmitting the electricity.
 b To reduce the voltage to a safer level for cables inside towns and cities.

3 **a** **i** It increases the voltage.
  ii It reduces the current.
 b Mains devices operate at 230 V. The grid voltage needs to be stepped down by transformers from 132 000 V to 230 V for safe use in our homes.

P1 4.6

Big energy issues

Specification link-up: Physics P1.4

- Evaluate different methods of generating electricity. *[P1.4]*
- Evaluate ways of matching supply with demand, either by increasing supply or decreasing demand. *[P1.4]*
- Compare the advantages and disadvantages of overhead power lines and underground cables. *[P1.4]*
- Small-scale production of electricity may be useful in some areas and for some uses, e.g. hydroelectricity in remote areas and solar cells for roadside signs. *[P1.4.1 e)]*

Learning objectives

Students should learn:

- how we utilise our electricity supplies to meet our demands
- that there are a range of factors that need to be considered when deciding on how to meet future energy needs.

Learning outcomes

Most students should be able to:

- describe the advantages and disadvantages of producing electricity by different techniques
- evaluate the possible resources and come to a conclusion about which are viable options for generation of electricity in the future.

Support

- Some students find it very difficult to discuss ideas or debate as they lack the confidence to express scientific ideas. You can provide prompt sheets that describe the role each person is playing in the discussion. These should contain relevant facts and figures that can help the student take an active role in the discussion. For example, you could provide a sheet describing the advantages and disadvantages of wind farms along with the current level of energy produced by this resource.

Extend

- The students can expand the issues here onto a global scale. They should consider the increasing demand from developing countries and discuss the effect that this demand would have on limited resources and prices.

Lesson structure

Starters

Not the right room for an argument – In this lesson the students are going to discuss energy issues. This could become a chaotic argument without proper ground rules. Extend the students by getting them to work on a set of rules that will let the discussion progress effectively. Rules need to include things like who can speak and when, who is recording discussions or decisions, if roles are going to be assigned or students are free to take on any position they want. Support students by defining these ground rules yourself. *(5 minutes)*

Getting the facts straight – Before the debate the students prepare fact sheets summarising the information about the different energy resources they have studied. You could support students by providing sheets with tables on for the students to complete, or extend students by asking them to design their own fact sheets. *(10 minutes)*

Main

- Start the lesson by recapping the possible energy resources. You will need to give extra information about start-up times (fairly simple) and the concept of 'base load' (a bit harder). You can show a graph showing electricity demand through a typical day and point out that there is always a demand so many power stations are fully active all of the time to cover this. Nuclear power stations are left running all of the time. Extra stations are turned on to meet times of increased demand.

- The rest of this lesson is centred about a debate about how to meet future energy needs. The debate is relevant because the students present will probably not have access to 'unlimited' fossil fuel supplies as the last few generations have. This could be as a result of shortages or commitments to reduce carbon emissions by the government. The result of this is an energy gap that needs to be filled by new resources.

- Before starting any debate, set the ground rules. You could do this with the starter activity or you could show a set of your own. Explain the purpose of the debate and the outcomes that are needed (a set of proposals) so the students know that they have to reach conclusions. Give timings and establish roles within the groups if they are needed. You can chair or you can split the class into smaller groups so that more students will take an active part.

- Success criteria could include:
  - Everybody has had their say and taken part.
  - We have used scientific facts to reach our conclusions.
  - We have discussed the costs of our suggestions and are willing to accept them.
  - We have produced two suggestions to go forward to the class.

- At the end of the discussion, the students will need to have produced a clear set of proposals about what to do. You need at least four suggestions to vote on really. If you are not certain that the groups will give suitable suggestions, you can prepare a few of your own as back up. You can then use these in the 'democracy in action' plenary to end the lesson and reach consensus.

Plenaries

Democracy in action – The students vote on a range of proposals for energy production. You can make this an anonymous vote with ballot papers giving various options. The results can be declared immediately by a nominated returning officer or you can deliver them next lesson. If you have several classes, you can keep a running total and declare this at an opportune point. *(5 minutes)*

You work for me – The students can write a letter to their MP outlining the decision they have reached. They need to explain what they have decided to do and ask the MP to act on the decision. This should be a formal letter if possible; you can even post the letters or deliver them by hand the next time your MP comes to visit the school. Students can be extended by giving them clear success criteria about the content of the letter, including how many facts and figures are required. You may like to support students with the start of the letter leading up to the point where the scientific facts are introduced. *(10 minutes)*

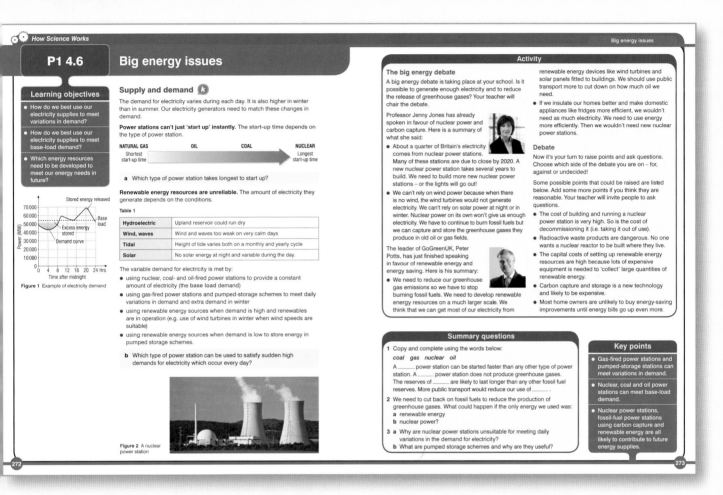

P1 4.6 | Big energy issues

Learning objectives

- How do we best use our electricity supplies to meet variations in demand?
- How do we best use our electricity supplies to meet base-load demand?
- Which energy resources need to be developed to meet our energy needs in future?

Figure 1 Example of electricity demand

Supply and demand

The demand for electricity varies during each day. It is also higher in winter than in summer. Our electricity generators need to match these changes in demand.

Power stations can't just 'start up' instantly. The start-up time depends on the type of power station.

NATURAL GAS — OIL — COAL — NUCLEAR
Shortest start-up time → Longest start-up time

a Which type of power station takes longest to start up?

Renewable energy resources are unreliable. The amount of electricity they generate depends on the conditions.

Table 1

Hydroelectric	Upland reservoir could run dry
Wind, waves	Wind and waves too weak on very calm days
Tidal	Height of tide varies both on a monthly and yearly cycle
Solar	No solar energy at night and variable during the day.

The variable demand for electricity is met by:

- using nuclear, coal- and oil-fired power stations to provide a constant amount of electricity (the base load demand)
- using gas-fired power stations and pumped-storage schemes to meet daily variations in demand and extra demand in winter
- using renewable energy sources when demand is high and renewables are in operation (e.g. use of wind turbines in winter when wind speeds are suitable)
- using renewable energy sources when demand is low to store energy in pumped storage schemes.

b Which type of power station can be used to satisfy sudden high demands for electricity which occur every day?

Figure 2 A nuclear power station

Activity

The big energy debate

A big energy debate is taking place at your school. Is it possible to generate enough electricity and to reduce the release of greenhouse gases? Your teacher will chair the debate.

Professor Jenny Jones has already spoken in favour of nuclear power and carbon capture. Here is a summary of what she said:

- About a quarter of Britain's electricity comes from nuclear power stations. Many of these stations are due to close by 2020. A new nuclear power station takes several years to build. We need to build more new nuclear power stations – or the lights will go out!
- We can't rely on wind power because when there is no wind, the wind turbines would not generate electricity. We can't rely on solar power at night or in winter. Nuclear power on its own won't give us enough electricity. We have to continue to burn fossil fuels but we can capture and store the greenhouse gases they produce in old oil or gas fields.

The leader of GoGreenUK, Peter Potts, has just finished speaking in favour of renewable energy and energy saving. Here is his summary:

- We need to reduce our greenhouse gas emissions so we have to stop burning fossil fuels. We need to develop renewable energy resources on a much larger scale. We think that we can get most of our electricity from

renewable energy devices like wind turbines and solar panels fitted to buildings. We should use public transport more to cut down on how much oil we need.

- If we insulate our homes better and make domestic appliances like fridges more efficient, we wouldn't need as much electricity. We need to use energy more efficiently. Then we wouldn't need new nuclear power stations.

Debate

Now it's your turn to raise points and ask questions. Choose which side of the debate you are on – for, against or undecided!

Some possible points that could be raised are listed below. Add some more points if you think they are reasonable. Your teacher will invite people to ask questions.

- The cost of building and running a nuclear power station is very high. So is the cost of decommissioning it (i.e. taking it out of use).
- Radioactive waste products are dangerous. No one wants a nuclear reactor to be built where they live.
- The capital costs of setting up renewable energy resources are high because lots of expensive equipment is needed to 'collect' large quantities of renewable energy.
- Carbon capture and storage is a new technology and likely to be expensive.
- Most home owners are unlikely to buy energy-saving improvements until energy bills go up even more.

Summary questions

1 Copy and complete using the words below:

coal gas nuclear oil

A .... power station can be started faster than any other type of power station. A .... power station does not produce greenhouse gases. The reserves of .... are likely to last longer than any other fossil fuel reserves. More public transport would reduce our use of ....

2 We need to cut back on fossil fuels to reduce the production of greenhouse gases. What could happen if the only energy we used was:
 a renewable energy
 b nuclear power?

3 a Why are nuclear power stations unsuitable for meeting daily variations in the demand for electricity?
 b What are pumped storage schemes and why are they useful?

Key points

- Gas-fired power stations and pumped-storage stations can meet variations in demand.
- Nuclear, coal and oil power stations can meet base-load demand.
- Nuclear power stations, fossil-fuel power stations using carbon capture and renewable energy are all likely to contribute to future energy supplies.

Further teaching suggestions

Cut back

- Demand for electricity is increasing, as more electrical devices are produced. One way to preserve resources is to cut back on waste and to stop using some things altogether. As an alternative to the main discussion, students can look at where they would cutback on a personal and then national level. They should be able to find lots of suggestions from environmental campaign groups.

Answers to in-text questions

a Nuclear power stations.

b Hydroelectric power stations.

Summary answers

1 gas, nuclear, coal, oil

2 a Our energy sources may not be reliable (available when we need them). For example, we may not have enough energy during the summer months if we only relied on wind power.

 b Our electricity supplies would be reliable but people would be concerned about the storage of radioactive waste.

3 a Nuclear power stations have a very long start-up time and could not be started or stopped quickly to match daily variations in demand.

 b A pumped storage scheme is a hydroelectric scheme with electricity generators that can be reversed to act as pumps. When demand is low, surplus electricity from the National Grid is used to pump water uphill in an upland reservoir. When demand is high, the water flow is reversed, so it runs downhill and the generators generate electricity.

Summary answers

1 a coal, oil and natural gas

  b coal and oil

  c coal, oil, natural gas and wood

  d uranium

  e uranuium

2 a i tidal

   ii hydroelectric

   iii wave

   iv wind

  b i wind

   ii hydroelectricity

   iii waves

3 a i geothermal

   ii hydroelectric

   iii coal-fired

   iv nuclear

  b i renewable

   ii non-fossil

4 a 1 Wind energy

   2 Hydroelectricity

   3 Solar energy

  b i Hydroelectricity

   ii Solar energy

5 a cheaper, cheaper

  b longer

  c more expensive

  d shorter

6 a i To change the voltage from the power station generator to a suitably high grid voltage and reducing the grid voltage to a suitable mains voltage for our homes.

   ii A step-up transformer.

  b i The grid voltage is much higher.

   ii The current supplied to the grid is much smaller.

   iii Power is wasted in the cables due to the heating effect of the current. The less the current, the less the power that is wasted.

Generating electricity: P1 4.1–P1 4.6

Summary questions

1 Answer **a** to **e** using the list of fuels below:

coal   natural gas   oil   uranium   wood

  a Which fuels from the list are fossil fuels?

  b Which fuels from the list cause acid rain?

  c Which fuels release chemical energy when they are used?

  d Which fuel releases the most energy per kilogram?

  e Which fuel produces radioactive waste?

2 a Copy and complete **i** to **iv** using the words below:

hydroelectric   tidal   wave   wind

   i .... power stations trap sea water.

   ii .... power stations trap rain water.

   iii .... generators must be located along the coastline.

   iv .... turbines can be located on hills or offshore.

  b Which renewable energy resource transfers:

   i the kinetic energy of moving air to electrical energy

   ii the gravitational potential energy of water running downhill into electrical energy

   iii the kinetic energy of water moving up and down to electrical energy?

3 a Copy and complete **i** to **iv** using the words below:

coal-fired   geothermal   hydroelectric   nuclear

   i A .... power station does not produce greenhouse gases and uses energy which is from inside the Earth.

   ii A .... power station uses running water and does not produce greenhouse gases.

   iii A .... power station releases greenhouse gases.

   iv A .... power station does not release greenhouse gases but does produce waste products that need to be stored for many years.

  b Wood can be used as a fuel. State whether it is

   i renewable or non-renewable

   ii a fossil fuel or a non-fossil fuel.

4 a Figure 1 shows a landscape showing three diff[...] renewable energy resources, numbered 1 to 3. [...] each type of energy resource with one of the la[...] below.

Figure 1 Renewable energy

Hydroelectricity   Solar energy   Wind energy

  b Which of the three resources shown is not likel[...] produce as much energy as the others if the a[...]

   i hot, dry and windy

   ii wet and windy?

5 Copy and complete **a** to **d** using the words below. [...] word or phrase can be used more than once.

cheaper   more expensive   longer   shorter

  a Wind turbines are .... to build than nuclear p[...] stations and .... to run.

  b Nuclear power stations take .... to decomm[...] than fossil fuel power stations.

  c Solar cells are .... to install than solar heati[...] panels.

  d A gas-fired power station has a .... start-up [...] compared to a nuclear power station.

6 a i What are transformers used for in the Natio[...] Grid?

   ii What type of transformer is connected betw[...] generators in the power station and the cabl[...] the grid system?

  b i What can you say about the voltage of the c[...] the grid system compared with the voltages [...] power station generator and at the mains ca[...] into the home?

   ii What can you say about the current through [...] grid cables compared with the current from [...] power station generator?

   iii What is the reason for making the grid voltag[...] different from the generator voltage?

AQA Examiner's tip

Many students have some background knowledge of the issues surrounding electricity generation. However, make sure they are able to evaluate the different methods particularly with regard to building costs, decommissioning, reliability and start-up time. All data will be given.

AQA Examiner's tip

Also be aware of methods of storing and distributing electricity by suggesting when pumped storage systems could be used and comparing underground and overhead power cables.

AQA Examiner's tip

Students need to understand the similarities and differences in how electricity is generated from different resources and their different effects on the environment.

Kerboodle resources

Resources available for this chapter on Kerboodle are:

- Chapter map: Generating electricity
- Interactive activity: How are fuels used to produce electricity? (P1 4.1)
- WebQuest: Biofuels (P1 4.1)
- Viewpoint: Is nuclear power the answer to the world's energy crisis? (P1 4.4)
- How Science Works: Wind turbines (P1 4.2)
- Revision podcast: Energy and the environment (P1 4.4)
- Animation: The National Grid (P1 4.5)
- Extension: Power lines (P1 4.5)
- Bump up your grade: The big issue (P1 4.6)
- Test yourself: Methods we use to generate electricity
- On your marks: Methods we use to generate electricity
- Teacher notes: Generating electricity
- Examination-style questions: Generating electricity
- Answers to examination-style questions: Generating electricity

A Examination-style questions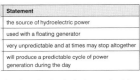

...ctricity may be generated in a coal-fired power
...ion.

...y and complete the following sentences using words
...n the list below. Each word can be used once, more
...n once or not at all.

...ctricity fuel generator steam turbine
...er wood

... coal-fired power station, ... is burned to heat
..... . This produces .... at high pressure which
...kes a .... spin round. This then drives a .... that
...duces ....   (6)

...ous power sources can be used to generate
...ctricity.

...ch the power sources in the list with the statements
... 4 in the table.
...alling water
...des
...aves
...ind

Statement
the source of hydroelectric power
used with a floating generator
very unpredictable and at times may stop altogether
will produce a predictable cycle of power generation during the day

(4)

...olar cell panel and a solar heating panel work in
...erent ways.

...ich statement below is correct?

...A solar cell produces light when it is supplied with
...electricity.

...A solar cell generates electricity when it is supplied
...with light.

...A solar heating panel produces heat when it is
...supplied with electricity.

...A solar heating panel produces electricity when it is
...supplied with heat.   (1)

...s-fired power stations have a shorter start-up time than
...er power stations. Give one reason why is it important
...have power stations with a short start-up time.   (2)

...ring the night, when demand for electricity is low, a
...d farm may be generating a large amount of power.
...plain how, by using another type of power station, this
...ver could be stored and used when it is needed.   (3)

6 Explain why step-up transformers are used in the
National Grid.   (2)

7 Palm oil can be used to make a biofuel called biodiesel.
Biodiesel can be used instead of the normal type of
diesel obtained by refining crude oil.

a Suggest **two** advantages of using biodiesel rather
than normal diesel.   (2)

b Suggest **two** disadvantages of using biodiesel rather
than normal diesel.   (2)

8 The pie chart shows the main sources of energy used in
power stations in a country last year.

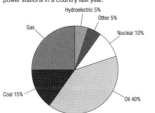

a What fraction of the energy used in power stations
was obtained from gas?   (2)

b Name **one** source of energy shown that is a fossil fuel.
                                                                            (1)

c Name **one** source of energy shown that is renewable.
                                                                            (1)

d Name **one** source of energy that could be included in
the label 'other'.   (1)

e Name **one** source of energy that does not cause
carbon dioxide to be released when it is used.   (1)

9 *In this question you will be assessed on using good
English, organising information clearly and using
specialist terms where appropriate.*

Power stations that burn fossil fuels produce waste
gases that can cause pollution.

Describe the effect that these gases could have on the
environment and what could be done to reduce the
amount of these gases emitted by power stations.   (6)

275

AQA Examination-style answers

1 In a coal-fired power station, **fuel** is burned to heat **water**.
This produces **steam** at high pressure, which makes a
turbine spin round. This then drives a **generator** that
produces **electricity**.   *(6 marks)*

2 A falling water   1
   B tides   4
   C waves   2
   D wind   3   *(4 marks)*

3 B A solar cell generates electricity when it is supplied with
   light.   *(1 mark)*

4 To increase power quickly to meet changing demand or to
prevent power cuts.   *(1 mark)*

5 Pumped storage; electric pumps pump water into a high
reservoir and this is later released through a turbine.
                                                                      (3 marks)

6 To increase the voltage on the cables and reduce power
losses.   *(2 marks)*

7 a Any **two** from the following:
      conserves crude oil reserves;
      is a renewable resource;
      is carbon neutral   *(2 marks)*

   b Any **two** from the following:
      may lead to deforestation;
      reduces land available for growing food;
      may lead to soil erosion   *(2 marks)*

8 a All other sources account for 75%;
      gas is 25% or $\frac{25}{100}$ or 0.25   *(2 marks)*

   b Gas/coal/oil   *(1 mark)*

   c Hydroelectric   *(1 mark)*

   d Any sensible answer, e.g. wood burning.   *(1 mark)*

   e Nuclear or hydroelectric   *(1 mark)*

9 There is a clear, balanced and detailed description of the
effect that gases could have on the environment and what
could be done to reduce the gas emitted. The answer shows
almost faultless spelling, punctuation and grammar. It is
coherent and in an organised, logical sequence. It contains
a range of appropriate or relevant specialist terms used
accurately.   *(5–6 marks)*

There is a description of at least 2 effects that gases could
have on the environment and at least one example of what
could be done to reduce the gas emitted. There are some
errors in spelling, punctuation and grammar. The answer has
some structure and organisation. The use of specialist terms
has been attempted, but not always accurately.   *(3–4 marks)*

There is a brief description of at least one effect that gases
could have on the environment or one example of what could
be done to reduce the gas emitted. The answer has little
clarity and detail. The spelling, punctuation and grammar
are very weak. The answer is poorly organised with almost
no specialist terms and/or their use demonstrating a general
lack of understanding of their meaning.   *(1–2 marks)*

No relevant content.   *(0 marks)*

Examples of physics points made in the response:
- carbon dioxide/greenhouse gas
- can contribute to global warming
- carbon dioxide may be removed by CCS
- sulfur dioxide (named)
- dissolves in rain water
- to form acid rain
- which can destroy vegetation/cause leaf loss in trees, etc.
- sulfur may be removed from fuels before burning.

AQA Practical suggestions

Practicals	AQA	(k)	📖	⚙
Investigating the effect of changing different variables on the output of solar cells, e.g. distance from the light source, the use of different-coloured filters and the area of the solar cells.	✓		✓	
Planning and carrying out an investigation into the effect of changing different variables on the output of model wind turbines, e.g. the number or pitch of the blades, the wind velocity.	✓	✓		✓
Demonstrating a model water turbine linked to a generator.	✓		✓	
Modelling the National Grid.	✓		✓	

P1 5.1

The nature of waves

Learning objectives

Students should learn:

- that waves transfer energy from one point to another without the transfer of matter
- that waves are categorised as mechanical or electromagnetic
- that electromagnetic waves are transverse and mechanical waves may be transverse or longitudinal.

Learning outcomes

Most students should be able to:

- give examples of mechanical and electromagnetic waves
- give examples of longitudinal waves and transverse waves and describe the differences between them.

Some students should also be able to:

- explain the motion of particles in longitudinal and transverse mechanical waves.

AQA Specification link-up: Physics P1.5

- Waves transfer energy. *[P1.5.1 a)]*
- Waves may be either transverse or longitudinal. *[P1.5.1 b)]*
- Electromagnetic waves are transverse, sound waves are longitudinal and mechanical waves may be either transverse or longitudinal. *[P1.5.1 c)]*
- All types of electromagnetic waves travel at the same speed through a vacuum (space). *[P1.5.1 d)]*
- Longitudinal waves show areas of compression and rarefaction. *[P1.5.1 f)]*

Lesson structure

Starters

Aftershock value – There is a great deal of footage of tsunami and recent earthquakes. You can use some of this to demonstrate the power of an 'uncontrolled' wave. Point out the regular vibration in earthquakes; shaking buildings and so on. *(5 minutes)*

Wave – Start with a simple task to support the students in revisiting their basic wave knowledge; ask the student to list as many types of wave as possible. Check through a few lists with the class and then ask the students to explain what a wave actually does. Use some of the examples to get them to realise that waves move energy but not material. When doing this, watch out for things like waves at the beach; these are moving water and are more complicated than the simple waves covered in this unit. Students can be extended by describing why these waves are not simple, by comparing them with the definition in the Student Book. *(10 minutes)*

Main

- During the lesson you should show off as many types of wave as you can; you will be revisiting some kinds during this chapter and the next, but it is a good idea to show the variety. Show water waves with video clips or a ripple tank, show sound waves with an obviously vibrating loudspeaker, use the rope to show transverse and the slinky to show longitudinal waves (and also transverse – See 'Practical support'). You can even show light and explain that it is transferring energy without material and you will demonstrate that it is a wave in a later lesson (using diffraction).

- Mechanical waves are fairly easy for the students to grasp; make sure they note the wave shape in transverse waves and emphasise that the particles in the material may be vibrating but they are returning back to their starting positions. You can use the ribbon or a sticky label to mark points on the wave.

- It's difficult to see the wave's shape in longitudinal waves; you can just watch the motion back and forth. A simulation of wave motion is very helpful indeed. There is a good range available for free that can be found on the internet. These can show the motion of an individual particle in the wave which is very helpful in demonstrating that the particle doesn't end up going anywhere; it just vibrates back and forth around a fixed point.

- The key phrases about longitudinal and transverse waves are obviously important; repeat them several times when describing the waves and check that all of the students can restate them.

Support

- The students struggle with the terms longitudinal and transverse; you will need to repeat these terms and demonstrate the motion many times in this lesson and a few of the future lessons too. Keep showing that parallel means in the same direction the wave is moving and perpendicular means at right angles to the direction.

Extend

- The particles in a longitudinal and transverse wave appear to be doing very different things, but their behaviour is actually very similar. If you have simulations, let the students observe the behaviour of a single particle over a period of time. They should be able to see that the particles are both actually moving in the same way; they are following a repeating sinusoidal pattern around a fixed point. It is this simple motion that defines the wave.

Plenaries

The same but different – The students can conclude the lesson by creating a summary of the two types of wave (mechanical and electromagnetic) and the two types of wave motion (longitudinal and transverse). These should emphasise the similarities and differences in the waves. If you have a wave wall then select the best work and add it immediately. *(5 minutes)*

Mexican brain wave – Put the students into three or four rows all seated. Select one student to be the questioner in each row and give them a set of questions and answers about waves. The student asks the first person in the row a question; if they get the answer right then all of the people that have answered correctly stand up, wave, sit down and the questioner moves on. If they don't answer correctly, the second question is asked. The first row that waves all the way to the end is the winner. You could also do this in one big circle with smaller classes. You can differentiate by giving different sets of questions to each group of students. *(10 minutes)*

Practical support

Observing mechanical waves

Equipment and materials required

A slinky spring and piece of ribbon (or some sticky tape).

Details

To demonstrate longitudinal waves, stretch the spring out slightly and then move one end of the slinky in and out while keeping the other end still. The emphasis should be on the vibrations of the particles without them actually progressing. Sticking a bit of ribbon on a point on the spring can show this more effectively.

Transverse waves can be produced by moving the spring from side to side, showing the particles vibrating at right angles to the direction of propagation of the wave.

● Answer: The ribbon vibrates (moves) back and forth but ends up in the same place once the wave has passed.

Waves

P1 5.1 The nature of waves Ⓚ

Learning objectives

● What can we use waves for?

● What are transverse waves?

● What are longitudinal waves?

● Which types of waves are transverse and which are longitudinal?

Figure 1 Big waves

links
For more information on electromagnetic waves, see P1 6.1 The electromagnetic spectrum.

AQA Examiner's tip
You are **not** required to recall the value of the speed of electromagnetic waves through a vacuum. If you need it to answer a question, it will be provided for you.

We use waves to transfer information and we can use them to transfer energy. We can use information transferred by waves in communications, for example when you use a mobile phone or listen to the radio.

There are different types of waves. These include:

● sound waves, water waves, waves on springs and ropes and seismic waves produced by earthquakes. These are examples of mechanical waves, which are vibrations that travel through a medium (substance).

● light waves, radio waves and microwaves. These are examples of electromagnetic waves which can all travel through a vacuum at the same speed of 300 000 kilometres per second. No medium is needed.

Practical

Observing mechanical waves

Figure 2 shows how we can make waves on a rope by moving one end up and down.

Figure 2 Transverse waves

Tie a ribbon to the middle of the rope. Move one end of the rope up and down. You will see that the waves move along the rope but the ribbon doesn't move along the rope – it just moves up and down. This type of wave is known as a **transverse wave**. We say the ribbon vibrates or oscillates. This means it moves repeatedly between two positions. When the ribbon is at the top of a wave, we say it is at the **peak** (or crest) of the wave.

Repeat the test with the slinky. You should observe the same effects if you move one end of the slinky up and down.

However, if you push and pull the end of the slinky as shown in Figure 3, you will see a different type of wave, known as a **longitudinal wave**. Notice that there are areas of **compression** (coils squashed together) and areas of **rarefaction** (coils spread further apart) moving along the slinky.

Direction of travel

Hand moved backwards and forwards along the line of the slinky

Compression   Compression   Compression

Figure 3 Making longitudinal waves on a slinky

● How does the ribbon move when you send **longitudinal** waves along the slinky?

Transverse waves Ⓚ

Imagine we send waves along a rope which has a white spot painted on it. The spot would be seen to move up and down without moving along the rope. In other words, the spot would vibrate perpendicular (at right angles) to the direction which the waves are moving. The waves on a rope are called transverse waves because the vibrations are up and down or from side to side. All electromagnetic waves are transverse waves.

The vibrations of a transverse wave are perpendicular to the direction in which the waves transfer energy.

a State one type of wave that is mechanical and transverse.

Longitudinal waves

The slinky spring in Figure 3 is useful to demonstrate how sound waves travel. When one end of the slinky is pushed in and out repeatedly, vibrations travel along the spring. The vibrations are parallel to the direction in which the waves transfer energy along the spring. Waves that travel in this way are called longitudinal waves.

Sound waves are longitudinal waves. When an object vibrates in air, it makes the air around it vibrate as it pushes and pulls on the air. The vibrations (compressions and rarefactions) which travel through the air are sound waves. The vibrations are along the direction in which the wave travels.

The vibrations of a longitudinal wave are parallel to the direction in which the waves are travelling.

Therefore mechanical waves can be transverse or longitudinal.

b When a sound wave passes through air, what happens to the air particles at a compression?

Summary questions

1 Copy and complete a to d using the words below:

longitudinal parallel perpendicular transverse

a Sound waves are .... waves.

b Light waves are .... waves.

c Transverse waves vibrate .... to the direction of energy transfer of the waves.

d Longitudinal waves vibrate .... to the direction of energy transfer of the waves.

2 A long rope with a knot tied in the middle lies straight along a smooth floor. A student picks up one end of the rope. This sends waves along the rope.

a Are the waves on the rope transverse or longitudinal waves?

b What can you say about:

i the direction of energy transfer along the rope?

ii the movement of the knot?

3 Describe how to use a slinky spring to demonstrate to a friend the difference between longitudinal waves and transverse waves.

links
For more information on sound, see P1 5.5 Wave properties: diffraction, and P1 5.6 Sound.

AQA Examiner's tip
Make sure that you understand the difference between transverse waves and longitudinal waves.

Did you know ... ?
When we pluck a guitar string, it vibrates because we send transverse waves along the string. The vibrating string sends sound waves into the surrounding air. The sound waves are longitudinal.

Key points

● We use waves to transfer energy and transfer information.

● Transverse waves vibrate at right angles to the direction of energy transfer of the waves. All electromagnetic waves are transverse waves.

● Longitudinal waves vibrate parallel to the direction of energy transfer of the waves. A sound wave is an example of a longitudinal wave.

● Mechanical waves, which need a medium (substance) to travel through, may be transverse or longitudinal waves.

Further teaching suggestions

Slow-motion waves

● You can show the motion of waves more clearly if you use video clips. If you have video logging equipment, you can record your own clips to show. Alternatively look for some slow motion clips of vibrations using the internet; here you should be able to see the vibrations of a guitar string, detailed motion of water waves and so on.

Wave wall

● If you have space, create a 'wave wall'. Add large diagrams to this throughout this chapter starting with ones that show the difference between transverse and longitudinal waves. Keep the text large and use the minimum number of words, so most of the students can review it when needed.

Answers to in-text questions

a Waves on a rope or on a string.

b The particles become closer together.

Summary answers

1 a longitudinal

   b transverse

   c perpendicular

   d parallel

2 a transverse

   b i Along the rope away from the student.

      ii The knot moves repeatedly up and down along a line that is perpendicular to the direction of energy transfer along the rope (which is along original line of the rope).

3 Hold the slinky at one end and ask the friend to hold the other end. Move away from each other to stretch the slinky. To demonstrate a longitudinal wave, push your end of the slinky towards and away from your friend repeatedly to send compression waves along the slinky. To demonstrate a transverse wave, move the end of the slinky repeatedly from one side to the other side or up and down. This will send waves along the slinky that are always at right angles to the line of the undisturbed slinky.

P1 5.2

Measuring waves

Learning objectives

Students should learn:

- that waves can be described by their wavelength, frequency, amplitude and speed
- the relationship between the wave speed, frequency and wavelength.

Learning outcomes

Most students should be able to:

- label a diagram of a wave to show the wavelength and amplitude
- calculate the wave speed when given the frequency and speed.

Some students should also be able to:

- apply the wave speed equation in a range of situations including rearrangement of the equation. **[HT only]**

Answers to in-text questions

a amplitude: 9 mm; wavelength: 34 mm

Support

- The students can have calculation templates for the first few wave calculations. For the practical task, you can provide the student with a couple of methods that they can use or ask them to come up with a plan on their own.

Extend

- The students investigate the relationship between the depth of water and the wave speed as described in the 'Practical support' feature.

AQA ## Specification link-up: Physics P1.5

- The terms frequency, wavelength and amplitude. *[P1.5.1 i)]*
- All waves obey the wave equation: $v = f \times \lambda$ *[P1.5.1 j)]*

Lesson structure

Starters

Speed up – Ask the students to perform some simple speed calculations to remind them of this work from KS3. Make sure that they are using the correct units for speed, distance and time. Extend students by asking them to rearrange the equation and given more challenging data to use. You might need to support students by going through the stages of the calculations and units in more detail. *(5 minutes)*

Light on knowledge – The students need to list the properties of light and any other facts that they know about it. They should be able to come up with a range of facts from KS3, possibly including these: [it's very fast, travels in straight lines, white light can be split into colours, it can be reflected and refracted, filters can be used to allow only certain colours through]. *(10 minutes)*

Main

- Start with a study of a wave's shape, point out the crests and troughs clearly. It is very common for students to mark the amplitude incorrectly. Students often label amplitude as the full 'height' of the wave from peak to trough, as mentioned in the Examiner's tip. Watch out for this and emphasise its correction when it occurs.

- Demonstrate what frequency is with a signal generator and big loudspeaker, a ripple tank or animation. Simply put, frequency is just the 'number of waves each second'. Show the wide range of possible frequencies if you use a signal generator; you can test the range of student hearing.

- Sketching waves can be surprisingly difficult for some students, especially if you want to keep the wavelength consistent. Squared paper is a good idea as this allows some consistency. You can also ask students to make measurements of waves by looking at the squares.

- The students can try to verify the relationship between frequency and wavelength with the 'skipping rope' practical or you can get one group to demonstrate to the class.

- Ripple tanks can be fiddly to set up so that the waves can be seen clearly. The exact set-up will depend on the model that you have but it's always wise to test everything out before the lesson to make sure it is capable of showing wave motion clearly.

- Performing the second practical task in one way or another is a really good way of reinforcing wave movement. You could just provide the equipment and ask the students to come up with a plan to measure the speed; this is a fairly straightforward task. To extend them more, they could look into the relationship between wavelength and frequency, or even the water depth and speed of the wave. This can be linked back to the tsunami of the previous lesson; is it important to know the speed of the wave? Does the wave get faster or slower when it approaches the coast?

- The wave speed calculation is a simple multiplication. You should try to encourage the students to convert lengths to metres and times to seconds so that you can have a speed consistently measured in m/s. Plenty of practice is recommended. Extend students by asking them to calculate the frequency or wavelength when given the other two values.

- Don't forget to add some of the best examples of calculations to the wave wall and refer back to them now and again to drive the calculation home.

Plenaries

Wave taboo – Split the students into groups and give them some cards with key words written on (transverse, longitudinal, reflect, speed, etc.) and a list of words they can't use in describing the key word. How many can the group get in a set time limit? An example card could be [reflect: can't use bounce, rebound, ponder]. *(5 minutes)*

Kinaesthetic maths challenge – Provide the students with cards labelled wavelength, wave speed, frequency, times and equals. Each card has a number on it too. The students must form themselves into living equations by standing in groups of five making a correct equation. Extend students by providing more difficult numbers and questions that require rearrangements. An example set could be ['wave speed (30 m/s)', '=' 'wavelength (1.5 m)' '×', 'frequency (20 Hz)']. To support students, you can use coloured cards to make it easier to match them up. *(10 minutes)*

Practical support

Frequency and wavelength

Equipment and materials required
A skipping rope for each group (longish), stop clock, meter ruler.

Details
The students stretch the rope out but not too taut. One student oscillates the rope up and down smoothly while the others observe the wavelength of the wave formed. As the frequency of the oscillation increases, they should see that the wavelength decreases. The students can measure the frequency with a stop clock and the wavelength with the meter ruler.

Making straight (plane) waves

This can be performed as a demonstration if there is not enough equipment or you can use simple trays and have the students make their own waves.

Equipment and materials required
Ripple tank, stop watch, ruler and a tray, signal generator, loudspeaker, connecting leads.

Details
The experiment is as described in the Student Book. If you don't have a wave tank, then the students can make do with waterproof trays. Most laboratories have lots of these. The students can fill the tray to about 1 cm depth; moving the ruler at one end should send a wave along the tray and this can be measured. Alternatively, a sharp tap on the outside of the tray can send a good quality wave pulse. Students can be extended by using this technique to see if altering the depth of the water increases or decreases the wave speed. The changes to depth should only be by 1 mm at a time between 1 and 2 cm.

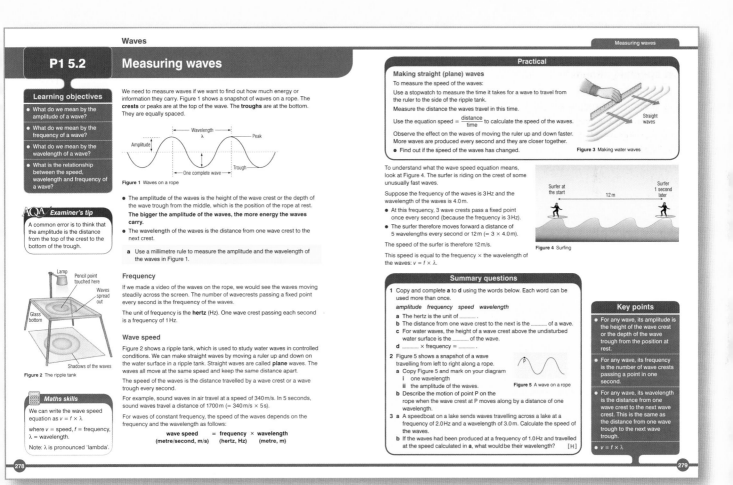

Waves

P1 5.2   Measuring waves

Learning objectives
- What do we mean by the amplitude of a wave?
- What do we mean by the frequency of a wave?
- What do we mean by the wavelength of a wave?
- What is the relationship between the speed, wavelength and frequency of a wave?

We need to measure waves if we want to find out how much energy or information they carry. Figure 1 shows a snapshot of waves on a rope. The **crests** or peaks are at the top of the wave. The **troughs** are at the bottom. They are equally spaced.

Figure 1 Waves on a rope

- The amplitude of the waves is the height of the wave crest or the depth of the wave trough from the middle, which is the position of the rope at rest. **The bigger the amplitude of the waves, the more energy the waves carry.**
- The wavelength of the waves is the distance from one wave crest to the next crest.

a Use a millimetre rule to measure the amplitude and the wavelength of the waves in Figure 1.

Examiner's tip
A common error is to think that the amplitude is the distance from the top of the crest to the bottom of the trough.

Frequency
If we made a video of the waves on the rope, we would see the waves moving steadily across the screen. The number of wavecrests passing a fixed point every second is the frequency of the waves.

The unit of frequency is the **hertz** (Hz). One wave crest passing each second is a frequency of 1 Hz.

Wave speed
Figure 2 shows a ripple tank, which is used to study water waves in controlled conditions. We can make straight waves by moving a ruler up and down on the water surface in a ripple tank. Straight waves are called **plane** waves. The waves all move at the same speed and keep the same distance apart.

Figure 2 The ripple tank

The speed of the waves is the distance travelled by a wave crest or a wave trough every second.

For example, sound waves in air travel at a speed of 340 m/s. In 5 seconds, sound waves travel a distance of 1700 m (= 340 m/s × 5 s).

For waves of constant frequency, the speed of the waves depends on the frequency and the wavelength as follows:

Maths skills
We can write the wave speed equation as $v = f \times \lambda$
where v = speed, f = frequency, λ = wavelength.
Note: λ is pronounced 'lambda'.

$$\text{wave speed} = \text{frequency} \times \text{wavelength}$$
$$\text{(metre/second, m/s)} \quad \text{(hertz, Hz)} \quad \text{(metre, m)}$$

Practical

Making straight (plane) waves
To measure the speed of the waves:
Use a stopwatch to measure the time it takes for a wave to travel from the ruler to the side of the ripple tank.
Measure the distance the waves travel in this time.
Use the equation speed = $\dfrac{\text{distance}}{\text{time}}$ to calculate the speed of the waves.
Observe the effect on the waves of moving the ruler up and down faster. More waves are produced every second and they are closer together.
- Find out if the speed of the waves has changed.

Figure 3 Making water waves

To understand what the wave speed equation means, look at Figure 4. The surfer is riding on the crest of some unusually fast waves.

Suppose the frequency of the waves is 3 Hz and the wavelength of the waves is 4.0 m.
- At this frequency, 3 wave crests pass a fixed point once every second (because the frequency is 3 Hz).
- The surfer therefore moves forward a distance of 5 wavelengths every second or 12 m (= 3 × 4.0 m).

The speed of the surfer is therefore 12 m/s.

This speed is equal to the frequency × the wavelength of the waves: $v = f \times \lambda$.

Figure 4 Surfing

Summary questions

1 Copy and complete **a** to **d** using the words below. Each word can be used more than once.
amplitude   frequency   speed   wavelength
a The hertz is the unit of ....
b The distance from one wave crest to the next is the .... of a wave.
c For water waves, the height of a wave crest above the undisturbed water surface is the .... of the wave.
d .... × frequency = ...

2 Figure 5 shows a snapshot of a wave travelling from left to right along a rope.
a Copy Figure 5 and mark on your diagram
 i one wavelength
 ii the amplitude of the waves.
b Describe the motion of point P on the rope when the wave crest at P moves along by a distance of one wavelength.

Figure 5 A wave on a rope

3 a A speedboat on a lake sends waves travelling across a lake at a frequency of 2.0 Hz and a wavelength of 3.0 m. Calculate the speed of the waves.
b If the waves had been produced at a frequency of 1.0 Hz and travelled at the speed calculated in **a**, what would be their wavelength?   [H]

Key points
- For any wave, its amplitude is the height of the wave crest or the depth of the wave trough from the position at rest.
- For any wave, its frequency is the number of wave crests passing a point in one second.
- For any wave, its wavelength is the distance from one wave crest to the next wave crest. This is the same as the distance from one wave trough to the next wave trough.
- $v = f \times \lambda$

Further teaching suggestions

Drawing and labelling waves
- Wavelength is a reasonably simple concept, but many mistakes are made drawing and labelling waves in examinations. Point out that the wavelength can also be measured from trough to trough, or in fact any point in a wave to the next point that is doing exactly the same thing. Watch out for students who draw the wavelength incorrectly; this is usually from the point where the wave crosses zero displacement to the next zero, i.e. half a wavelength. A similar problem arises when labelling the amplitude on wave diagrams. This must be from the peak to the zero displacement position, i.e. half of the 'height' of the wave, not the full 'height' as many students draw.

Summary answers

1 a frequency
  b wavelength
  c amplitude
  d wavelength, speed

2 a i The wavelength should be from one wave crest to the next.
     ii The amplitude should be from a wave crest directly down to the mid-point between the wave crest and the wave trough.
  b As the wave moves across, P moves down to the bottom of the wave then back to the top as the next wave crest arrives.

3 a 6.0 m/s
  b 6.0 m

P1 5.3

Wave properties: reflection

Learning objectives

Students should learn:

- what the normal is in a ray diagram
- that the angle of incidence is the angle between the normal and the incident ray of light
- that the angle of reflection is the angle between the reflected ray and the normal
- that the angle of incidence and the angle of reflection are equal for plane mirrors.

Learning outcomes

Most students should be able to:

- draw a diagram showing reflection by a plane mirror which shows the angle of incidence, the angle of reflection and the normal
- explain that the image in a mirror is virtual; it cannot be projected onto a screen.

Some students should also be able to:

- draw a diagram to show the formation of the image of a point object in a plane mirror.

Answers to in-text questions

a **i** 20°
   ii 40°
b virtual

Support

- Use a worksheet with the mirror position and incident rays marked on. This can also have a normal and protractor printed on if necessary. Make sure students are familiar with angular measurements by asking them to take some measurements of known angles first. Place extra emphasis on the terms **incident ray** and **reflected ray** and make sure the students are measuring the angles to the normal line; it is common for students to be measuring the angle to the surface of the mirror by mistake.

Extend

- There are two laws of reflection. The students should find out what the other law is and explain what it means. This states that the reflected ray is in the same plane as the incident plane.

AQA Specification link-up: Physics P1.5

- Waves can be reflected ... [P1.5.1 g)]
- The normal is a construction line perpendicular to the reflecting surface at the point of incidence. [P1.5.2 a)]
- The angle of incidence is equal to the angle of reflection. [P1.5.2 b)]
- The image produced in a plane mirror is virtual, upright and laterally inverted. [P1.5.2 c)]

Controlled Assessment: SA4.5 Analyse and interpret primary and secondary data. [SA4.5.2 a) b) c) d)]

Lesson structure

Starters

Virtually real – Ask: 'What does the word 'virtual' mean?' The students should give several examples of its use. What about the word 'real'? Many will have heard of virtual reality; point out that the terms have a specific meaning in optics. *(5 minutes)*

Ray diagram – Ask the students to draw a ray diagram showing how they can see a non-luminous object, such as the writing in their books. Make sure that the students are using a ruler to draw rays of light and that the rays are reflecting cleanly from the surface. Be fussy about gaps in the rays; this is a common error and leads to lost marks in examinations. Extend students by asking them to critique each other's work and advise each other how to correct the work to make it the highest possible standard. To support students you can start to form a set of rules about how to draw ray diagrams and add it to a prominent list displayed on the wall for the next series of lessons. *(10 minutes)*

Main

- The students need to be aware of the difference between diffuse reflection, where no image is formed, and normal reflection. The difference is obvious when showing them a mirror and a sheet of paper. When discussing the position of the image in the mirror, use the 'image distance' activity in 'Further teaching suggestions'.

- The normal is a very important part of ray diagrams and the students must draw it on all such diagrams. Return to the ray diagram the students drew in the starter (or get them to draw a diagram now). Introduce the idea of the normal and make sure the students adapt their diagrams.

- All angles are measured from the normal, so make sure that the students are not measuring them from the surface of the mirror to the incident or reflected ray. Many students remember the law of reflection, but the experiment allows them to become familiar with the equipment that they may not have used for several years. Check that they are forming and directing the rays correctly and that they are drawing a normal to aim the rays at.

- Getting across the ideas of real and virtual images can be tricky; a real image is formed when the light rays really pass a point but a virtual image is formed when the light rays seem to have come from a point; they never actually meet at the point.

- Demonstrate lateral inversion using some mirror writing and have the students read it 'through' a mirror.

- If you have time available, the construction of periscopes is a good activity for some groups requiring more support.

Plenaries

Pepper's ghost – Show students this simple but classic optical illusion and ask them to come up with an explanation of how it works. This leads to the idea of partial reflection; an effect they often see when looking through glass. The students should be challenged to draw ray diagrams explaining the effect. *(5 minutes)*

Mirror maze – Support students in checking their understanding of the law of reflection by asking them to add mirrors to a simple maze diagram so that a light ray can pass through it to the centre. They can do this by simply drawing the mirror positions on to a worksheet or you could demonstrate a solution using a laser. You can extend students by asking them to design a similar maze that may be solved using a set of five mirrors with precise positioning. *(10 minutes)*

Practical support

A reflection test

The students may have carried out similar experiments during KS3, but it is worthwhile to get them used to the equipment again. The experiment is best carried out in a darkened lab, but full blackout is not required.

Equipment and materials required

Power supply, ray box, single slit, ray box stops, plane mirror, ruler, protractor and a sheet of A3 paper.

Details

The students set up the ray box so that it produces a single ray. The mirror is fixed to the back of the paper using a holder or sticky-tac, so that the ray can be reflected by it. Then the students shine rays at the centre of the mirror from a range of angles and measure the angles of incidence and reflection. This is best done by marking the path of each ray at two points with a cross and then joining these with a ruler. The lines should be drawn to the back of the mirror where reflection takes place. You might find that the experiment works best if the mirror is tilted downwards very slightly.

Waves

P1 5.3 — Wave properties: reflection (k)

Learning objectives

- What is the normal in a diagram showing light rays?
- What is an angle of incidence?
- What can we say about the reflection of a light ray at a plane mirror?
- How is an image formed by a plane mirror?

If you visit a Hall of Mirrors at a funfair, you will see some strange images of yourself. A tall, thin image or a short, broad image of yourself means you are looking into a mirror that is curved. If you want to see a normal image of yourself, look in a **plane mirror**. Such a mirror is perfectly flat. You see an exact mirror **image** of yourself.

Figure 1 A good image

Investigating the reflection of waves using a ripple tank

Light consists of waves. Figure 2 shows how we can investigate the reflection of waves using a ripple tank. The investigations show that when plane (straight) waves reflect from a flat reflector, the reflected waves are at the same angle to the reflector as the incident waves.

a Wavefronts parallel to the reflector

b Wavefronts at a non-zero angle to the reflector

Figure 2 Reflection of plane waves

The law of reflection (k)

We use light rays to show us the direction light waves are moving in. Figure 3 shows how we can investigate the reflection of a light ray from a ray box using a plane mirror.

$i = r$

Figure 3 The law of reflection

- The perpendicular line to the mirror is called the normal.
- The angle of incidence is the angle between the incident ray and the normal.
- The angle of reflection is the angle between the reflected ray and the normal.

Measurements show that for any light ray reflected by a plane mirror:

the angle of incidence = the angle of reflection

a If the angle of reflection of a light ray from a plane mirror is 20° what is:
  i the angle of incidence?
  ii the angle between the incident ray and the reflected ray?

Practical

A reflection test

Use a ray box and a plane mirror as shown in Figure 3 to test the law of reflection for different angles of incidence.

Image formation by a plane mirror

Figure 4 shows how an image is formed by a plane mirror. This ray diagram shows the path of two light rays from a point object that reflect off the mirror. The image and the object in Figure 4 are at equal distances from the mirror.

Figure 4 Image formation by a plane mirror

Real and virtual images

The image formed by a plane mirror is virtual, upright (the same way up as the object) and laterally inverted (back to front but not upside down). A virtual image can't be projected on to a screen like the movie images that you see at a cinema. An image on a screen is described as a real image because it is formed by focusing light rays on to the screen.

b When you use a mirror, is the image real or virtual?

Summary questions

1 Copy and complete **a** to **c** using the words below. Each word can be used once, more than once, or not at all.

   equal to   greater than   less than

   a The angle of incidence of a light ray at a plane mirror is always .... 90 degrees.
   b The angle between the normal and the mirror is always .... 90 degrees.
   c The angle of incidence of a light ray at a plane mirror is always .... the angle of reflection of the light ray.

2 A point object O is placed in front of a plane mirror, as shown.

   Figure 6

   a Complete the path of the two rays shown from O after they have reflected off the mirror.
   b i Use the reflected rays to locate the image of O.
      ii Show that the image and the object are the same distance from the mirror.

3 Two plane mirrors are placed perpendicular to each other. Draw a ray diagram to show the path of a light ray at an angle of incidence of 60° that reflects off both mirrors.

Did you know ... ?

Ambulances and police cars often carry a 'mirror image' sign at the front. This is so a driver in a vehicle in front looking at their rear-view mirror can read the sign as it gets 'laterally inverted' (back to front but not upside down).

Figure 5 A mirror sign on an ambulance

Key points

- The normal at a point on a mirror is a line drawn perpendicular to the mirror.
- For a light ray reflected by a plane mirror:
  1 The angle of incidence is the angle between the incident ray and the normal.
  2 The angle of reflection is the angle between the reflected ray and the normal.
- The law of reflection states that:
  the angle of incidence = the angle of reflection.

Further teaching suggestions

Image distance

- A quick way to show that the image lies the same distance behind the mirror as the object is in front of it, is to place a 30 cm ruler pointing out from just beneath your nose. Place the plane mirror at the 30 cm point and look at your reflection. You can clearly see that the mirror is 30 cm away and that your reflected image appears 30 cm further away than that.

Mirror writing

- The students can try to write a message backwards without the help of a mirror. Check the results. Add some backwards writing to your 'Wave wall' started in P1 5.1.

Did you know ... ?

One of the first movies to shock people was the moving image of a train coming towards the camera. The film *Arrival of a Train*, by the Lumière brothers, is just a 50 s clip of a train arriving at a station. You should be able to find a copy of this clip by searching for 'trainarrival.mov' on the internet. Somehow it's not as frightening as it used to be. There are plenty of other early clips around to show how cinema has developed.

Summary answers

1 **a** less than
  b equal to
  c equal to

2 **a, b i ii**

   Object O   Image

   Mirror

3

   60°

P1 5.4

Wave properties: refraction

Learning objectives

Students should learn:

- that refraction is the changing of direction of a wave at an interface between different materials
- that refraction occurs because light changes speed when it moves from one medium to another
- that a prism disperses white light into a spectrum because each frequency is refracted by a different amount.

Learning outcomes

Most students should be able to:

- draw diagrams showing how light is refracted when entering and leaving a transparent substance.

Some students should also be able to:

- explain why refraction takes place
- draw a diagram showing the refraction of light by a prism and explain the process that causes this effect.

Answers to in-text questions

a yes

Support

- As with the reflection experiments, you may want to use worksheets that have the position of the glass block and incident rays marked on to save some time.

Extend

- The speed that light travels in a material and how much refraction takes place at its surface are determined by something called the 'refractive index' of the material. Can the students find out why diamond separates out light into different colours so well?

AQA Specification link-up: Physics P1.5

- Waves can be refracted... *[P1.5.1 g)]*
- Waves undergo a change of direction when they are refracted at an interface. *[P1.5.1 h)]*

Lesson structure

Starters

It's just a broken pencil – Place a pencil in a beaker of water. Can the students come up with an explanation of why the pencil looks broken? This is quite difficult; make sure that the students see the effect clearly (have a big photograph on the interactive whiteboard if needed). The explanations may include rays of light bending. *(5 minutes)*

See through – Support students' understanding of transmission and absorption by giving them definitions of three words: 'transparent', 'opaque', and 'translucent'. They can then sort an example set of materials into these three groups. Include some awkward materials that are just about transparent and some coloured filters, so that the students will have to come up with explanations like: 'The red filter is transparent to red light but it is opaque to other colours'. Students can be extended by not giving them the categories but asking them to come up with criteria and examples of their own. *(10 minutes)*

Main

- Make sure that, when the students are using the term 'bending' when talking about refraction, they are not thinking that the light is 'following a curved path'. Most of the refraction here is a clear and sudden change of direction, so you might want to restrict your use of the word as far as possible.

- During the initial investigation, watch out for the students marking out and then drawing the rays correctly. They should notice that the ray leaves the block parallel to the direction it entered. The students may also notice some total internal reflection and you might like to remind them of the uses of this phenomenon.

- If possible, demonstrate the changing of wave speed with a ripple tank or use a simulation. You can't beat seeing the waves speeding up and slowing down. The reason for the change in speed is difficult to explain, but most students just accept it. There are several analogies about why the change in speed causes a change in direction; a column of soldiers marching from a road into mud, a four-wheel drive vehicle doing the same. Use whichever one the students are comfortable with.

- Refraction from a prism can be shown as a demonstration, or you might like the class to have a go. You can get an excellent spectrum using your data projector as a white light source. This 'spreading' of the different colours is called dispersion and it occurs because the different frequencies of light all travel at different speeds in the glass, so refract at slightly different angles.

- Getting a good recombination of a spectrum into white light is almost impossible, but it is worth trying to give the idea of recombining, so that you can tell the story of Newton and his work on light.

Plenaries

Reflect or refract – Students to make a big diagram for the wave wall to show the difference between these two words, so that nobody gets it wrong again. The best diagram goes up on the wall for future reference. You can have the students come up with clear criteria for what 'best' means in a diagram of this sort. *(5 minutes)*

The magic penny – Place a penny at the bottom of an opaque cup so that you just about can't see it. Pour water into the cup and it reappears. The students should explain why, using a diagram. To support students, you can provide a partial diagram of the scenario and ask them to complete it. This should be a ray diagram showing the reflection of light off the coin, travelling in straight lines and refraction at the surface. Students should also draw a normal line at the refraction point. Students can be extended by asking them to consider why a swimming pool looks shallower than it actually is, a ray diagram of this scenario should also be drawn. *(10 minutes)*

Practical support

Investigating refraction of light

The students may have performed a similar experiment during KS3, but here the emphasis should be placed on taking measurements from the normal.

Equipment and materials required

For each group: low voltage power supply, ray box, single slit, ray box stops, rectangular glass block, ruler, protractor and a sheet of A3 paper.

Details

The glass block should be placed in the centre of the A3 sheet of paper. It's a good idea to draw around it in case it gets knocked. The students can shine rays into the block from a range of angles aiming for a fixed point on the front surface. They should draw small crosses to mark the path and then measure the angles of incidence and refraction. The angles must be measured from the normal. As in P1 5.3, this provides an opportunity to discuss the accuracy of measurements and errors involved in the experiment. Examine the protractors to show that measurement to the nearest degree may not always be possible, have several students measure the same angle and see if they come up with the same measurement. ('How Science Works'.)

Investigating refraction by a prism

This can be run as a simple demonstration or you can let the students have a quick go.

Equipment and materials required

For each group: low voltage power supply, ray box, single slit, ray box stops, prism.

Details

Simply shine the ray through the prism and rotate the prism until a spectrum is produced. Newton was able to recombine the dispersed rays back into a ray of white light with a second prism, but this takes a great deal of skill. Use a data projector as a source of light if a larger spectrum is needed.

Refraction of water waves

Equipment and materials required

Ripple tank with wave generator, thin glass block.

Details

Set up the ripple tank with enough water in it to cover the glass block. It should be strongly illuminated from below so that the shadow of waves can be seen on the ceiling (or the board if you have a mirror). Show the students the behaviour of simple waves and then place the glass block in to show that wave speed changes above the block. Rotating the block will show that the wave direction is different when the block is at an angle. This show the waves are being refracted.

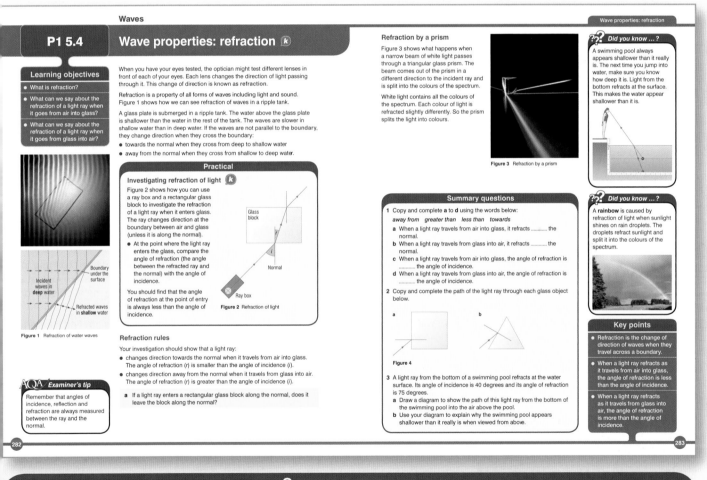

Summary answers

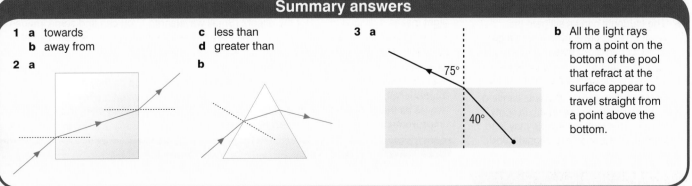

1 a towards
   b away from

   c less than
   d greater than

2 a

   b

3 a 75°   40°

   b All the light rays from a point on the bottom of the pool that refract at the surface appear to travel straight from a point above the bottom.

P1 5.5

Wave properties: diffraction

Learning objectives

Students should learn:

- that diffraction is the spreading effect of waves produced when they pass through a gap or past an obstacle
- that the diffraction effect is greatest when the waves are of a similar size to the gaps.

Learning outcomes

Most students should be able to:

- draw a diagram showing how waves diffract when they pass through gaps
- list and describe the factors that affect the amount of diffraction that takes place
- give examples of diffraction of mechanical and electromagnetic waves.

Answers to in-text questions

a The light waves are transverse and the ultrasonic sound waves are longitudinal.

b radiowaves

Support

- The students can make thought balloons. They blow up a balloon (can be any shape) and make notes on it about reflection, refraction and diffraction using permanent pen. This can be put on the wall or deflated for ease of transport.

Extend

- The students can investigate the relationship between wavelength and diffraction in more detail. This is really only possible with a real ripple tank where the frequency can be adjusted.
- What's waving? The students can find out about what is oscillating in light waves. This high-level topic may lead them to find out about magnetic and electric fields.

AQA Specification link-up: Physics P1.5

- Waves can be … diffracted. *[P1.5.1 g]*

Lesson structure

Starters

Safe harbour – Show some video footage of water waves passing through a harbour entrance. Ask students to sketch a diagram of what is happening to the waves. Look for the different designs they come up with and chose one that shows the wave peaks clearly. This is the kind of diagram you will be asking students to use, so show the best one to the whole class and add it to the 'Wave wall' started in P1 5.1 The nature of waves. *(5 minutes)*

Ray or wave – Show the students a traditional diagram showing a light ray, then ask them to show the rays coming from a light bulb. Show them the ripples caused by a pebble being dropped into water. Discuss the fact that this is wave motion. How can these two different ways of representing light be brought together? Support students by showing them that the rays are straight paths that connect the wave fronts by showing diagrams or simulations of this motion. Students can be extended by considering what happens to the waves and the idea of rays once they pass through gaps or even reflect. They may consider the wave front explanation of reflection (using a simulation) at a simple level so that they can compare models of light behaviour. *(10 minutes)*

Main

- Start the lesson with a basic demonstration of the effect of diffraction; use both water and light. Make sure you show the shape of the spreading pattern and the fact that the extent of this spreading can be changed by adjusting the gap. You can look at the effect of changing the wavelength of the wave on the diffraction pattern if you want to extend the students.

- Simulations of diffraction are easy to find and make this topic far easier to understand. Use them to show the waves spreading as they pass through the gaps. You should be able to adjust the size of the gaps to see the effect. Most simulations also let you alter the wavelength or frequency too. You can return to the simulation at key points in the lesson to reinforce the learning.

- There are plenty of diagrams and video clips of ultrasound scans that you can use to discuss the use of ultrasound. Go beyond the usual foetal scans and have a look at a heart beating; you could even show some industrial uses; checking metal objects for cracks is a suitable example.

- You can then demonstrate the test with microwaves. Some students still find it hard to appreciate that there are actually waves being transmitted and received. Start with a large gap between the metal plates; show how far they spread with the detector and then decrease the gap size and repeat. You should find the waves spread in nearly all directions when the gap size reaches 3 cm.

- The explanation of TV reception can confuse students; they have probably not realised how houses in hilly areas have poor reception unless they actually live in such an area. You can discuss the use of satellite or cable TV in these areas to overcome the problem.

Plenaries

Does light diffract? – Why don't we notice light diffract around objects? What property of light makes it difficult to detect the effect? [Small wavelength.] You can find some images showing light diffracting around very small objects to show the students. A laser can also be used as mentioned in the 'Practical support'. *(5 minutes)*

Breaking the waves – A new harbour is being designed to keep boats safer. The students can design the features that would cause waves to be broken up as they enter the harbour. You could support students by showing some designs that are used to break waves as they reach a beach. Students could be extended by asking them to suggest improvements to existing designs. *(10 minutes)*

Practical support

Investigating diffraction

This may have to be a demonstration unless you have a large stock of equipment. You can also use simulations as described in the main lesson plan.

Equipment and materials required

For each group: ripple tank (or large tray), metal or glass blocks.

Details

The students can use a full ripple tank set-up; this will have a suitable source of waves produced by a vibrating motor. If this is unavailable, they can improvise by producing water waves as described in the previous lesson. It is difficult to get consistent waves though.

They should notice that changing the gap size changes the amount of diffraction that takes place. When the gap size reaches the wavelength, the diffraction should be very large.

Diffraction of laser light

Diffraction is one of the fundamental processes that shows light behaving like a wave, so it is important to try to demonstrate this effect to the students.

Equipment and materials required

A laser (LED lasers are fine), a narrow slit for the laser light to pass through.

Details

Most laser kits come with an adjustable narrow slit. Pass the beam through the slit and adjust it so show that the narrow beam spreads. By adjusting the slit, the beam spreads more or less. Explain that this is showing that light is spreading just like water waves and this can only be explained if light is behaving like a wave.

Safety: Do not look directly at a laser light beam – see CLEAPSS P5 5.2 or Handbook 12.12.

Tests using microwaves

Microwaves are good examples of electromagnetic waves that can be seen to noticeably diffract around simple objects.

Equipment and materials required

Microwave transmitter, receiver and metal plates. One of the plates should have a gap of 1 cm to allow diffraction of the microwaves.

Details

Demonstrate that the receiver can detect a microwave signal from the transmitter. You can then allow the waves to pass through the gap and move the detector in a semicircular arc detector to show that the microwaves have diffracted.

You should also demonstrate that the microwaves diffract when they pass the **edge** of the metal plate and so a signal can be detected behind the plate. Point the transmitter at the edge of the plate and move the detector in an arc again; the signal should be detectable behind the plate.

● Answer: The microwaves from the transmitter are reflected by the metal plates.

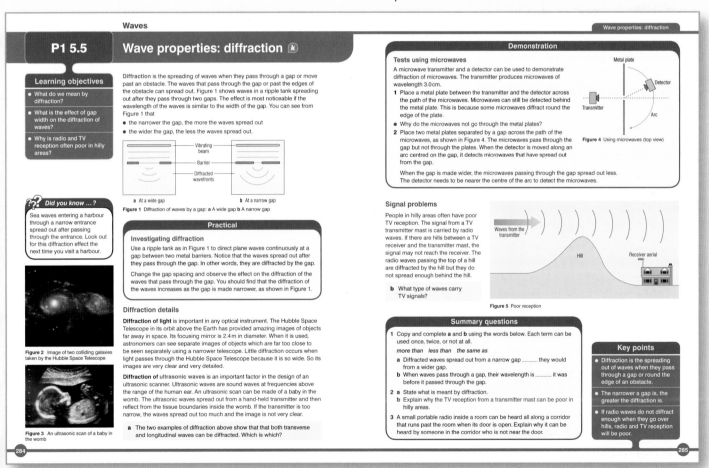

P1 5.5   Wave properties: diffraction Ⓚ

Learning objectives

● What do we mean by diffraction?

● What is the effect of gap width on the diffraction of waves?

● Why is radio and TV reception often poor in hilly areas?

Diffraction is the spreading of waves when they pass through a gap or move past an obstacle. The waves that pass through the gap or past the edges of the obstacle can spread out. Figure 1 shows waves in a ripple tank spreading out after they pass through two gaps. The effect is most noticeable if the wavelength of the waves is similar to the width of the gap. You can see from Figure 1 that

● the narrower the gap, the more the waves spread out

● the wider the gap, the less the waves spread out.

a At a wide gap   **b** At a narrow gap

Figure 1 Diffraction of waves by a gap: **a** A wide gap **b** A narrow gap

Did you know ...?

Sea waves entering a harbour through a narrow entrance spread out after passing through the entrance. Look out for this diffraction effect the next time you visit a harbour.

Figure 2 Image of two colliding galaxies taken by the Hubble Space Telescope

Figure 3 An ultrasonic scan of a baby in the womb

Practical

Investigating diffraction

Use a ripple tank as in Figure 1 to direct plane waves continuously at a gap between two metal barriers. Notice that the waves spread out after they pass through the gap. In other words, they are diffracted by the gap.

Change the gap spacing and observe the effect on the diffraction of the waves that pass through the gap. You should find that the diffraction of the waves increases as the gap is made narrower, as shown in Figure 1.

Diffraction details

Diffraction of light is important in any optical instrument. The Hubble Space Telescope in its orbit above the Earth has provided amazing images of objects far away in space. Its focusing mirror is 2.4 m in diameter. When it is used, astronomers can see separate images of objects which are far too close to be seen separately using a narrower telescope. Little diffraction occurs when light passes through the Hubble Space Telescope because it is so wide. So its images are very clear and very detailed.

Diffraction of ultrasonic waves is an important factor in the design of an ultrasonic scanner. Ultrasonic waves are sound waves at frequencies above the range of the human ear. An ultrasonic scan can be made of a baby in the womb. The ultrasonic waves spread out from a hand-held transmitter and then reflect from the tissue boundaries inside the womb. If the transmitter is too narrow, the waves spread out too much and the image is not very clear.

a The two examples of diffraction above show that that both transverse and longitudinal waves can be diffracted. Which is which?

Demonstration

Tests using microwaves

A microwave transmitter and a detector can be used to demonstrate diffraction of microwaves. The transmitter produces microwaves of wavelength 3.0 cm.

1 Place a metal plate between the transmitter and the detector across the path of the microwaves. Notice that some microwaves diffract round the edge of the plate.

● Why do the microwaves not go through the metal plates?

2 Place two metal plates separated by a gap across the path of the microwaves, as shown in Figure 4. The microwaves pass through the gap but not through the plates. When the detector is moved along an arc centred on the gap, it detects microwaves that have spread out from the gap.

When the gap is made wider, the microwaves passing through the gap spread out less. The detector needs to be nearer the centre of the arc to detect the microwaves.

Figure 4 Using microwaves (top view)

Signal problems

People in hilly areas often have poor TV reception. The signal from a TV transmitter mast is carried by radio waves. If there are hills between a TV receiver and the transmitter mast, the signal may not reach the receiver. The radio waves passing the top of a hill are diffracted by the hill but they do not spread enough behind the hill.

b What type of waves carry TV signals?

Figure 5 Poor reception

Summary questions

1 Copy and complete **a** and **b** using the words below. Each term can be used once, twice, or not at all.

more than   less than   the same as

a Diffracted waves spread out from a narrow gap .... they would from a wider gap.

b When waves pass through a gap, their wavelength is .... it was before it passed through the gap.

2 a State what is meant by diffraction.

b Explain why the TV reception from a transmitter mast can be poor in hilly areas.

3 A small portable radio inside a room can be heard all along a corridor that runs past the room when its door is open. Explain why it can be heard by someone in the corridor who is not near the door.

Key points

● Diffraction is the spreading out of waves when they pass through a gap or round the edge of an obstacle.

● The narrower a gap is, the greater the diffraction is.

● If radio waves do not diffract enough when they go over hills, radio and TV reception will be poor.

Summary answers

1 a more than   **b** the same as

2 a Diffraction is the spreading out of waves when they pass through a gap or round an obstacle.

b Where TV reception is poor, radio waves carrying the TV signal from the transmitter mast do not diffract enough when they travel over hills. TV receivers which are much below the diffracted waves will not receive a strong enough signal to give a good TV picture.

3 The sound waves from the portable radio diffract when they pass through the open door and some of the waves travel along the corridor.

P1 5.6

Sound

AQA

Specification link-up: Physics P1.5

- Sound waves are longitudinal waves and cause vibrations in a medium, which are detected as sound. *[P1.5.3 a)]*
- Echoes are reflections of sounds. *[P1.5.3 c)]*

Learning objectives

Students should learn:

- that the human ear can detect a range of frequencies from 20 to 20 000 Hz
- that sound is a mechanical wave that requires a medium to travel through and so cannot pass through a vacuum (space)
- about the difference between a sound wave and a light wave.

Learning outcomes

Most students should be able to:

- state the range of hearing for a typical human
- describe the properties of a sound wave, including its longitudinal nature
- describe the behaviour of a sound wave, including reflection and refraction.

Some students should also be able to:

- explain why mechanical vibrations produce sound waves.

Lesson structure

Starters

Sound facts – Give the students a set of 'facts' about sound and let them use traffic light cards to indicate if they agree (green), don't know (amber) or disagree (red). Facts can include these correct ones: sound needs particles to travel; the speed of sound in air is 300 m/s, and sound travels faster in more dense materials. You can also use these incorrect ones: we hear sounds when particles travel from a source to our ears; sound travels as fast as light; we can hear all sound waves. The facts provided can be differentiated to allow extra support or extension. *(5 minutes)*

Good vibrations – How do different instruments produce sound waves? The students should describe what is going on for five different ways of producing a sound. Try to demonstrate a drum, guitar, flute or recorder, loudspeaker and singing. This should show that vibrations are needed to produce sound waves. *(10 minutes)*

Main

- The contents of this lesson are mostly revision for the students, so you can spend a bit of time clearing up any misconceptions. The initial practical/demonstration should remind the students of the basics of sound, and allow you to describe the operation of a signal generator and loudspeaker in more detail. If possible, use a bell jar to show that particles are required for sound waves to travel. Use a safety screen in case glass implodes.

- Remind the students of the nature of mechanical longitudinal waves using a slinky. They will have to be able to describe what is happening to the particles in air. Students should know that sound can be reflected and this is simply called an 'echo'. Go through this again when you use the slinky.

- The behaviour of particles in air is actually more complex than the students might think. The particles actually *are* moving around from place to place quite rapidly but in a random way. A sound wave is a vibration superimposed on top of this random motion. Some simulations will show this, but others will show the particles vibrating around fixed positions for simplicity. You can discuss the limitations of the models.

- It can be worth discussing sound-absorbing materials and the lengths sound recording studios will go to in order to prevent reflections.

- You can investigate the reflection of sound waves in more detail using 'Investigating sound waves' from the 'Practical support', if you feel it is appropriate.

- Refraction of sound is very hard to show, but the students should be aware that things like distant traffic sounds are louder at night. This is due to the sound waves being refracted in the atmosphere similar to light waves in a mirage.

- In the next lesson, the students will need some musical instruments, so ask them to bring some in if they can play them.

Support

- The students may need extra support with the oscilloscopes. Squared paper helps students a lot with sketching accurate waveforms.

Extend

- Ask: 'Is there any relationship between the physical size of an animal's ear and the range of frequencies it can detect?' The students will need to find information from reference books or, more likely, the internet.

Plenaries

Oscilloscope guide – Can the students write their own guide to using an oscilloscope so that they can always find the trace? This will help them learn the names of the controls and allow them to write in a scientific way. The guide can have some example traces drawn, for example a trace where the waves' peaks are too close together to see clearly, and measures to fix the problems (reduce the time base). *(5 minutes)*

Let's hear it then – The students need to design a simple experiment that will show that sound travels faster in solid materials than it does in air. This could be a basic plan or a more detailed one. Students can be supported by providing some suggested equipment and recording techniques. Extend students by asking them carry out the tests along these lines: Place the microphones a measured distance apart separated by the material, and connected to a timing system. Make a sound that triggers the first microphone and then the second. Use the speed equation to measure the speed from the distance and time. They can then evaluate the success of the experiment or perhaps consider a link between density and the speed of sound. *(10 minutes)*

Practical support

Investigating sound waves

This makes a better demonstration than a student practical, but if you have lots of equipment it can be useful to get the students used to it for the next topic.

Equipment and materials required

Signal generator and loudspeaker. Connecting leads, paper discs.

Details

At the start of the investigation, you will need to show the students how to operate the signal generator and how it should be connected to the loudspeaker. Some generators have several outputs, so make sure that the students are using the right one if they are having a go. To see the vibrations of the loudspeaker clearly, they can drop some paper discs from a hole punch on to it – these will bounce around. To test the hearing limits of the students, it is better to get them to raise their hands at the start and put them down when they can no longer hear the noise. Some students can still hear the high frequency sounds when you secretly turn the power off; truly amazing!

Waves

Sound

P1 5.6 | Sound

Learning objectives

- What range of frequencies can be detected by the human ear?
- What are sound waves?
- What are echoes?

Figure 1 Making sound waves

??? Did you know …?

When you blow a round whistle, you force a small ball inside the whistle to go round and round inside. Each time it goes round, its movement draws air in then pushes it out. Sound waves are produced as a result.

Investigating sound waves 🇰

Sound waves are easy to produce. Your vocal cords vibrate and produce sound waves every time you speak. Any object vibrating in air makes the layers of air near the object vibrate. These layers make the layers of air further away vibrate. The vibrating object pushes and pulls repeatedly on the air. This sends out the vibrations of the air in waves of compressions and rarefactions. When the waves reach your ears, they make your eardrums vibrate in and out so you hear sound as a result.

The vibrations travelling through the air are sound waves. The waves are longitudinal because the air particles vibrate along the direction in which the waves transfer energy.

Practical

Investigating sound waves

You can use a loudspeaker to produce sound waves by passing alternating current through it. Figure 2 shows how to do this using a signal generator. This is an alternating current supply unit with a variable frequency dial.

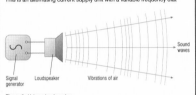
Figure 2 Using a loudspeaker

- If you observe the loudspeaker closely, you can see it vibrating. It produces sound waves as it pushes the surrounding air backwards and forwards.
- If you alter the frequency dial of the signal generator, you can change the frequency of the sound waves.

Find out the lowest and the highest frequency you can hear. Young people can usually hear sound frequencies from about 20 Hz to about 20 000 Hz. Older people in general can't hear frequencies at the higher end of this range.

a Which animal produces sound waves at a higher frequency, an elephant or a mouse?

Sound waves cannot travel through a vacuum. You can test this by listening to an electric bell in a bell jar. As the air is pumped out of the bell jar, the ringing sound fades away.

b What would you notice if the air is let back into the bell jar?

Reflection of sound

Have you ever created an echo? An echo is an example of reflection of sound. Echoes can be heard in a large hall or gallery which has bare, smooth walls.

- If the walls are covered in soft fabric, the fabric will absorb sound instead of reflecting it. No echoes will be heard.
- If the wall surface is uneven (not smooth), echoes will not be heard because the reflected sound is 'broken up' and scattered.

c What happens to the energy of the sound waves when they are absorbed by a fabric?

Refraction of sound

Sound travels through air at a speed of about 340 m/s. The warmer the air is, the greater the speed of sound. At night you can hear sound a long way from its source. This is because sound waves refract back to the ground instead of travelling away from the ground. Refraction takes place at the boundaries between layers of air at different temperatures. In the daytime, sound refracts upwards, not downwards, because the air near the ground is warmer than air higher up.

Figure 3 A sound test

Figure 4 Refraction of sound

Summary questions

1 Copy and complete **a** and **b** using the words below:
   absorbed   reflected   scattered
   a An echo is heard when sound is .... from a bare, smooth wall.
   b Sound waves are .... by a rough wall and .... by soft fabric.

2 **a** What is the highest frequency of sound the human ear can hear?
   b Why does a round whistle produce sound at a constant frequency when you blow steadily into it?

3 **a** A boat is at sea in a mist. The captain wants to know if the boat is near any cliffs so he sounds the horn and listens for an echo. Why would hearing an echo tell him he is near the cliffs?
   b Explain why someone in a large cavern can sometimes hear more than one echo of a sound.

Key points

- The frequency range of the normal human ear is from about 20 Hz to about 20 000 Hz.
- Sound waves are vibrations that travel through a medium (substance). They cannot travel through a vacuum (as in space).
- Echoes are due to sound waves reflected from a smooth, hard surface.

286

287

Further teaching suggestions

Particle behaviour

- Yet again, there are some fine simulations of the behaviour of sound waves showing particle behaviour. These are very handy when discussing what is happening to these invisible particles.

Answers to in-text questions

a A mouse.

b The ringing sound can be heard again.

c The sound energy is transferred by heating and the fabric warms up.

Summary answers

1 **a** reflected
  b scattered, absorbed

2 **a** About 20 000 Hz.
  b When the whistle is blown, a small ball in the whistle goes round the inside of the whistle at high speed and makes the air inside vibrate. This makes the air outside the whistle vibrate and creates sound waves in the air outside the whistle.

3 **a** Cliffs nearby would reflect the sound waves from the horn as their surfaces are hard and smooth.
  b Sound waves reflecting from the wall of the cavern would then reflect elsewhere on the cavern wall. Someone in the cavern would hear echoes due to these different reflections.

P1 5.7

Musical sounds

Learning objectives

Students should learn:

- that the pitch of a sound increases as the frequency increases
- that the loudness of the sound increases as the amplitude increases.

Learning outcomes

Most students should be able to:

- describe the properties of a sound wave in terms of frequency and amplitude.

Some students should also be able to:

- explain how sound is produced by different types of musical instruments and compare the sounds they produce, including pitch and loudness.

Answers to in-text questions

a An ambulance, a police vehicle, a fire engine, an ice cream van.

b The waves are not as tall.

c The waves would be smaller in height and stretched out more.

Support

- Focus on the use of the oscilloscope to trace waves. You may have to recap how to adjust the control so that the waveform is clear. Make sure the students understand that making changes to the oscilloscope only affects how the wave is displayed so that it is easier to see; it is not changing the original wave.

Extend

- Ask: 'What happens when two notes are played together?' The students should look at the waveform generated when two tuning forks are used at the same time. The effect can also be generated by putting two loudspeakers playing at slightly different frequencies next to each other. This beat phenomenon is very important in music.

AQA — Specification link-up: Physics P1.5

- The pitch of a sound is determined by its frequency and loudness by its amplitude. [P1.5.3 b)]

Lesson structure

Starters

It's music to my ears – Play some short extracts of music, from classical to punk and ask the students to list the instruments they can hear. Ask: 'Which music is the best?' Get the students to discuss what 'musical' is. Play some example of white noise and other sounds too. *(5 minutes)*

The intro round – Using a personal music player (through headphones on low volume so the rest of the class cannot hear it), a student listens to the introductions of some songs and has to reproduce them using only their vocal skills. Simple tunes can be used to support students or you can make the task more challenging by having students work together in groups. You can select a variety of modern tunes and slip in a few sounds that are fairly impossible for humans to make. *(10 minutes)*

Main

- The analysis of sound waves is made much easier if you have a digital oscilloscope that allows capture of waveforms. These can be used to store data about the waveform directly into a computer system and so the waves can be projected for all the class to see. If you have a system like this then, with a bit of practice, you can get it to find frequency and amplitude quite easily.

- The investigation is quite extensive and it may be difficult for all of the students to have a go. At the end of it, make sure that the students have all reached the correct conclusions.

- If you want the students to sketch out some of the waveforms, then give them some squared paper to help them out as you have done in previous lessons. Make sure that the students are using the appropriate words clearly (amplitude, loudness, frequency, pitch) correctly when describing the waves.

- After consolidating the students' findings, show some additional musical instruments to show how complex waveforms can quickly become.

- Voice recognition systems are improving all of the time, but you may want to show the limitations of the current technology. The operating system of your computer, or some of your applications, will probably have voice recognition built in, so give it a try and see how it does. Try to confuse it with sentences like: 'Which witches wear our weather predicting watches?'

- Resonance is an important phenomena; showing the structure of instruments will show how they are designed to resonate at certain key frequencies. You should be able to use a signal generator and loudspeaker to make an acoustic guitar resonate. Play about with the frequency until the guitar starts humming. The sound box is now resonating. You could also use a violin.

Plenaries

Perfect pitch – Which of the students can produce the purest note according to the oscilloscope? Connect a microphone directly to the 'scope and the students can try to see who is best able to produce a sine wave. Try whistling compared to singing. *(5 minutes)*

Compare traces – The students must compare three oscilloscope traces in terms of frequency, amplitude and quality of the note. They describe the differences and explain how they will sound different when produced by a musical instrument. Extend students by asking them to use real instruments to provide traces on the oscilloscope and then provide a detailed description of the traces. Students can be supported by providing relatively simple traces marked out on a grid showing amplitude and time period. Provide the formula to convert time period to frequency so that it is easier to determine the frequency. *(10 minutes)*

Practical support

Investigating different sounds

You may well not have enough equipment to let the students carry this out as a full class practical, but it is worth considering letting them use it in small groups one at a time, so that they can appreciate the techniques involved.

Equipment and materials required

For each group: signal generator, loudspeaker, microphone, oscilloscope, tuning forks and some musical instruments.

Details

The main problems you may have are the background noise in the classroom and lack of experience with the oscilloscope. A teaching assistant or helpful technician may help with the latter, but the background noise will always distort the waveforms from instruments in a class practical; you may want to show what the waves should look like with a demonstration at the end of the practical. Most signal generators have two outputs, so you can connect one to the loudspeaker and one to the cathode ray oscilloscope (CRO). This removes the background noise completely. Make sure that you mark the cm/s dial so that the students know which one to adjust. They should not need to alter any other settings to display the wave. Musically-inclined students should be able to use a range of instruments and compare the waveform with the pure wave of the tuning forks.

Musical instruments

Equipment and materials required

As above.

Details

The students will have to use a microphone and oscilloscope to capture the waveform. It can be very difficult for them to adjust the oscilloscope to the correct settings to see the wave clearly. If you have a digital oscilloscope, you can have some pre-recorded waveforms to display in case the students can't record them clearly.

P1 5.7 Musical sounds Ⓚ

Learning objectives

- What determines the pitch of a note?
- What happens to the loudness of a note as the amplitude increases?
- How are sound waves created by musical instruments?

Figure 1 Making music

What type of music do you like? Whatever your taste in music is, when you listen to it you usually hear sounds produced by specially-designed instruments. Even your voice is produced by a biological organ that has the job of producing sound.

- Musical notes are easy to listen to because they are rhythmic. The sound waves change smoothly and the wave pattern repeats itself regularly.
- Noise consists of sound waves that vary in frequency without any pattern.

a Name four different vehicles that produce sound through a loudspeaker or a siren.

Practical

Investigating different sounds

Use a microphone connected to an oscilloscope to display the waveforms of different sounds.

Figure 2 Investigating different sound waves

Figure 3 Tuning fork waves

1 Test a tuning fork to see the waveform of a sound of constant frequency.
2 Compare the pure waveform of a tuning fork with the sound you produce when you talk or sing or whistle. You may be able to produce a pure waveform when you whistle or sing but not when you talk.
3 Use a signal generator connected to a loudspeaker to produce sound waves. The waveform on the oscilloscope screen should be a pure waveform.

b What can you say about the waveform of a sound when you make the sound quieter?

Your investigations should show you that:

- **increasing the loudness** of a sound increases the **amplitude** of the waves. So the waves on the screen become taller.
- **increasing the frequency of a sound** (the number of waves per second) increases its pitch. This makes more waves appear on the screen.

Figure 4 shows the waveforms for different sounds from the loudspeaker.

c How would the waveform in Figure 4a change if the loudness and the pitch are both reduced?

a Loud and high-pitched
b Loud and low-pitched
c Quiet and high-pitched (higher pitch than a)
Figure 4 Investigating sounds

Musical instruments

When you play a musical instrument, you create sound waves by making the instrument and the air inside it vibrate. Each new cycle of vibrations makes the vibrations stronger at certain frequencies. We say the instrument resonates at these frequencies. Because the instrument and the air inside it vibrate strongly at these frequencies when it is played, we hear recognisable notes of sound from the instrument.

- A wind instrument such as a flute is designed so that the air inside resonates when it is played. You can make the air in an empty bottle resonate by blowing across the top gently.
- A string instrument such as a guitar produces sound when the strings vibrate. The vibrating strings make the surfaces of the instrument vibrate and produce sound waves in the air. In an acoustic guitar, the air inside the hollow body of the guitar (the sound box) vibrates too.
- A percussion instrument such as a drum vibrates and produces sound when it is struck.

Summary questions

1 Copy and complete **a** to **c** using the words below:
   amplitude   frequency   vibrations
   a When a drum is struck, sound waves are created by the .... of the drumskin.
   b The loudness of a sound is increased by increasing the .... of the sound waves.
   c The pitch of a sound is increased by increasing the .... of the sound waves.

2 A microphone and an oscilloscope are used to investigate sound from a loudspeaker connected to a signal generator. What change would you expect to see on the oscilloscope screen if the sound is:
   a made louder at the same frequency
   b made lower in frequency at the same loudness?

3 **a** How does the note produced by a guitar string change if the string is
      i shortened **ii** tightened?
   b Compare the sound produced by a violin with the sound produced by a drum.

AQA Examiner's tip

Be sure you know the meaning of the words **frequency** and **amplitude**.

Practical

Musical instruments

Investigate the waveform produced by a musical instrument, such as a flute.

You should find its waveform changes smoothly, like the one in Figure 5 – but only if you can play it correctly. The waveform is a mixture of frequencies rather than a single frequency waveform like Figure 3.

Figure 5 Flute wave pattern

Key points

- The pitch of a note increases if the frequency of the sound waves increases.
- The loudness of a note increases if the amplitude of the sound waves increases.
- Vibrations created in an instrument when it is played produce sound waves.

Further teaching suggestions

Scientific instruments

- Why not make some pan pipes with test tubes? Just fill a set up with differing amounts of water and give them a play.

Pop idle

- Does listening to music make you work better or put you off? Can the students come up with an experiment? This can be quite a demanding task. They could look at the effect of noise on concentration; try working when listening to annoying background noises. They can look at the differences that ambient music has in comparison with some heavy metal.

Summary answers

1 **a** vibrations
   b amplitude
   c frequency

2 **a** The waves would be taller but would have the same spacing.
   b The waves would be more stretched out but would have the same height.

3 **a** **i** The note has a higher pitch (frequency).
      ii The note has a higher pitch (frequency).
   b The sound of a violin (played correctly) lasts as long as the violin bow is in contact with a string. The sound of a drum dies away after the drum skin has been struck. A drum note is less rhythmical than a violin note.

Summary answers

1 a They are the same.

b

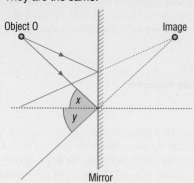

Object O   Image

x
y

Mirror

c They are the same.

2 a i

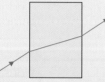

ii The light ray bends towards the normal, where it enters the block and bends away from the normal where it leaves the block. Its direction on leaving the block is the same as before it entered the block.

b i refraction
ii diffraction
iii reflection

3 a light, radio (light and radio in any order)
b sound
c sound

4 a 3.0 m/s

b speed = frequency × wavelength

3.0 m/s = frequency × 1.5 m

frequency = $\frac{3.0}{1.5}$ = 2.0 Hz.

5 a The sound waves spread out as they travel away from the loudspeaker, so the sound becomes fainter and the amplitude becomes smaller.

b i The waves on the screen become taller.
ii The waves on the screen become more stretched out across the screen, so fewer waves appear on the screen.

6 a reflected, smooth
b rough, scattered
c soft, absorbed

7 a Approximately 20 000 Hertz.

b Keep the frequency and the loudness of the sound from the loudspeaker the same throughout. Keep the loudspeaker, the board or cushion and the sound meter in the same positions throughout.

With the board in position, measure the sound meter reading.

Replace the board with the cushion and measure the sound meter reading again.

If the reading for the board is higher than the reading for the cushion, the board reflects more sound than the cushion.

AQA Examiner's tip

Students may be required to draw ray diagrams in their exams. Most students throw away marks because they don't think straight lines, accuracy and direction arrows are at all important!

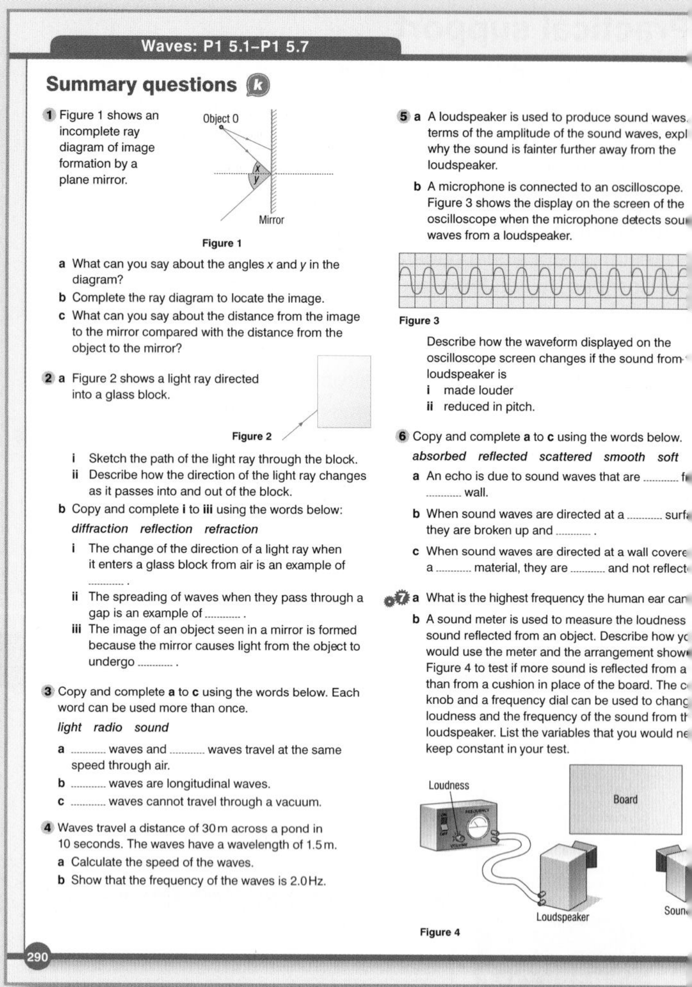

Summary questions 🄺

1 Figure 1 shows an incomplete ray diagram of image formation by a plane mirror.

Object O

Mirror

Figure 1

a What can you say about the angles x and y in the diagram?
b Complete the ray diagram to locate the image.
c What can you say about the distance from the image to the mirror compared with the distance from the object to the mirror?

2 a Figure 2 shows a light ray directed into a glass block.

Figure 2

i Sketch the path of the light ray through the block.
ii Describe how the direction of the light ray changes as it passes into and out of the block.
b Copy and complete **i** to **iii** using the words below:

diffraction   reflection   refraction

i The change of the direction of a light ray when it enters a glass block from air is an example of ....
ii The spreading of waves when they pass through a gap is an example of ....
iii The image of an object seen in a mirror is formed because the mirror causes light from the object to undergo ....

3 Copy and complete **a** to **c** using the words below. Each word can be used more than once.

light   radio   sound

a .... waves and .... waves travel at the same speed through air.
b .... waves are longitudinal waves.
c .... waves cannot travel through a vacuum.

4 Waves travel a distance of 30 m across a pond in 10 seconds. The waves have a wavelength of 1.5 m.
a Calculate the speed of the waves.
b Show that the frequency of the waves is 2.0 Hz.

5 a A loudspeaker is used to produce sound waves. terms of the amplitude of the sound waves, expl why the sound is fainter further away from the loudspeaker.

b A microphone is connected to an oscilloscope. Figure 3 shows the display on the screen of the oscilloscope when the microphone detects sou waves from a loudspeaker.

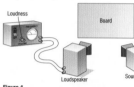

Figure 3

Describe how the waveform displayed on the oscilloscope screen changes if the sound from loudspeaker is
i made louder
ii reduced in pitch.

6 Copy and complete **a** to **c** using the words below.

absorbed   reflected   scattered   smooth   soft

a An echo is due to sound waves that are .... f .... wall.
b When sound waves are directed at a .... surfa they are broken up and ....
c When sound waves are directed at a wall covere a .... material, they are .... and not reflect

7 a What is the highest frequency the human ear can
b A sound meter is used to measure the loudness sound reflected from an object. Describe how yo would use the meter and the arrangement show Figure 4 to test if more sound is reflected from a than from a cushion in place of the board. The c knob and a frequency dial can be used to chang loudness and the frequency of the sound from th loudspeaker. List the variables that you would ne keep constant in your test.

Loudness

Board

Loudspeaker   Soun

Figure 4

Kerboodle resources 🄺

Resources available for this chapter on Kerboodle are:

- Chapter map: Waves
- Animation: Waves (P1 5.1)
- Interactive activity: The properties of transverse and longitudinal waves (P1 5.1)
- Support: Waves – knowing the words is half the battle (P1 5.1)
- Practical: Investigating the reflection of light (P1 5.3)
- Simulation: Refraction (P1 5.4)
- Practical: Investigating refraction (P1 5.4)
- Bump up your grade: Wave diagrams (P1 5.5)
- How Science Works: Measuring sound (P1 5.6)
- Extension: Waves (P1 5.7)
- Revision podcast: Wave properties
- Test yourself: Waves
- On your marks: Waves
- Examination-style questions: Waves
- Answers to examination-style questions: Waves

AQA Examiner's tip

Diffraction is often poorly understood at GCSE level. Diffraction effects are only significant when the gap/obstacle is of the same order of magnitude as the wavelength. Students should understand that this means the diffraction effect is not considered significant if the gap is more than 10 times the wavelength or the wavelength is more than 10 times the size of the gap.

Examination-style questions

Draw labelled diagrams to explain what is meant by
- a transverse wave (2)
- a longitudinal wave. (2)

Match the words in the list with the descriptions **1** to **4** in the table.

amplitude
frequency
wave speed
wavelength

Description
The distance travelled by a wave crest every second.
The distance from one crest to the next.
The height of the wave crest from the rest position.
The number of crests passing a fixed point every second. (4)

Which of the following is a correct description of the image in a plane mirror?

- It is a virtual image
- It can be focused on to a screen
- It is on the surface of the mirror
- It is upside down (1)

When a ray of light passes from air into glass it usually changes direction.

- What is the name given to this effect? (1)
- Which diagram correctly shows what happens to a ray of light as it passes through a glass block?

(1)

5 The diagram represents some water waves passing through a narrow gap.

Give the name of the effect being shown by the waves. When is it most significant? (2)

6 Give one similarity and one difference between a sound wave and a light wave. (2)

7 A sound wave in air has a frequency of 256 Hz. The wavelength of the wave is 1.3 m.
Calculate the speed of sound in air. Write down the equation you use. Show clearly how you work out your answer and give the unit. (2)

8 a Give **one** example of each of the following from everyday life.
   i reflection of light (1)
   ii reflection of sound (1)
   iii refraction of light (1)
   iv diffraction of sound (1)
  b We do not normally see diffraction of light in everyday life.
   Suggest a reason for this. (2)

9 Electromagnetic waves travel at a speed of 300 000 000 m/s.
BBC Radio 4 is transmitted using a wavelength of 1500 metres.
Calculate the frequency of these waves.
Write down the equation you use. Show clearly how you work out your answer and give the unit. [H] (3)

10 In this question you will be assessed on using good English, organising information clearly and using specialist terms where appropriate.
The diagram shows an oscilloscope trace of the sound wave produced by a musical instrument.

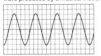

Explain, in detail, how the wave form would change if the instrument produced a sound which was louder and at a higher pitch. (6)

291

Practicals	AQA	k	📖	⚙
Reflecting light off a plane mirror at different angles.	✓	✓	✓	
Using a class set of skipping ropes to investigate frequency and wavelength.	✓		✓	
Demonstrating transverse and longitudinal waves with a slinky spring.	✓		✓	
Carrying out refraction investigations using a glass block.	✓	✓	✓	
Carrying out investigations using ripple tanks, including the relationship between depth of water and speed of wave.	✓		✓	

AQA Examiner's tip

There are a lot of terms that need to be defined and understood. It is important for students to practice correctly identifying and sketching situations involving reflection, refraction and diffraction. These terms often get students in a muddle.

AQA Examination-style answers

1 a Diagram must show direction of wave travel.
Diagram must show direction of vibration perpendicular to direction of wave travel. *(2 marks)*

b Diagram must show direction of wave travel.
Diagram must show direction of vibration parallel to direction of wave travel. *(2 marks)*

2 A amplitude   3
  B frequency   4
  C wave speed   1
  D wavelength   2   *(4 marks)*

3 A It is a virtual image.   *(1 mark)*

4 a refraction   *(1 mark)*
  b Diagram B   *(1 mark)*

5 Diffraction, when the gap is of the same order of magnitude as the wavelength. *(2 marks)*

6 **Similarity**: They can both be reflected, refracted, diffracted.
Difference: Light waves are much faster/sound waves are much slower OR light waves are transverse/sound waves are longitudinal. *(2 marks)*

7 $v = f \times \lambda$ so $256 \times 1.3 = 333$ m/s *(2 marks)*

8 a i Any example using a mirror/water or a shiny smooth surface. *(1 mark)*
    ii Any example of an echo. *(1 mark)*
    iii Any example using a lens, e.g. spectacles, cameras. *(1 mark)*
    iv Any example of hearing a sound around a corner. *(1 mark)*

  b The wavelength of light is very small, so diffraction only occurs when light passes through a very narrow gap.
  OR
  The wavelength of light is very small, so the diffraction effect is very small. *(2 marks)*

9 Wave speed = frequency × wavelength
$$\text{Frequency} = \frac{\text{speed}}{\text{wavelength}}$$
$$\text{Frequency} = \frac{300\,000\,000 \text{ m/s}}{1500 \text{ m}}$$
Frequency = 200 000 Hz *(3 marks)*

10 There is a clear, balanced and detailed description of how the wave form would change including increased amplitude and frequency. The answer shows almost faultless spelling, punctuation and grammar. It is coherent and in an organised, logical sequence. It contains a range of appropriate or relevant specialist terms used accurately. *(5–6 marks)*

There is a description of at least one of the ways in which the wave form would change. There are some errors in spelling, punctuation and grammar. The answer has some structure and organisation. The use of specialist terms has been attempted, but not always accurately. *(3–4 marks)*

There is a brief description of at least one way in which the wave form would change, which has little clarity and detail. The spelling, punctuation and grammar are very weak. The answer is poorly organised with almost no specialist terms and/or their use demonstrating a general lack of understanding of their meaning. *(1–2 marks)*

No relevant content. *(0 marks)*

Examples of physics points made in the response:
- louder sound means larger amplitude
- so height of crests increases
- depth of troughs increases
- speed is constant
- higher pitch means higher frequency
- so wavelength becomes smaller
- crests are closer together.

P1 6.1

The electromagnetic spectrum

Learning objectives

Students should learn:

- the names of the regions of the electromagnetic spectrum
- that all electromagnetic waves travel at the same speed through a vacuum
- how to calculate the wavelength or frequency of an electromagnetic wave. **[HT only]**

Learning outcomes

Most students should be able to:

- state the parts of the electromagnetic spectrum in order of wavelength
- state that all electromagnetic waves travel at the same speed through a vacuum.

Some students should also be able to:

- rearrange and use the wave speed equation. **[HT only]**

Support

- For extra support, you can give the students a large diagram of the electromagnetic spectrum to annotate over the next few lessons. They can add uses in communications and dangers to it as they go. You should also provide templates to help the students perform the calculations.

Extend

- Extend students by asking them to find out about electromagnetic waves in other media; they have been told that electromagnetic waves all travel at the same speed in a vacuum, but is this true of other media? They can find out about how the speed depends on the wavelength and how this leads to dispersion in prisms and lenses.

$\mathcal{AQA}$ **Specification link-up: Physics P1.5**

- All types of electromagnetic waves travel at the same speed through a vacuum (space). *[P1.5.1 d)]*
- Electromagnetic waves form a continuous spectrum. *[P1.5.1 e)]*
- All waves obey the wave equation: $v = f \times \lambda$ *[P1.5.1 j)]*

Lesson structure

Starters

The visible spectrum – Students should be familiar with the visible spectrum already. Let them use this knowledge to outline their understanding by asking them to show how light is reflected, transmitted or refracted. Move on to see if they can explain reflection from coloured surfaces; this includes reflection and absorption. This can be accompanied by a demonstration. *(5 minutes)*

Calculating speed – Can the students remember how to calculate the speed of something? Ask them to write down the equation and answer a couple of simple speed questions. This will lead into the wave equation later in the lesson. Start with some easy questions to support those that find calculations difficult. You can use some 'difficult' numbers and calculations needing rearrangement to extend others. For example, what is the speed of light if it takes 1.3 s to travel from the Earth to the Moon, a distance of 390 000 km [300 000 km/s^{-1} or 300 000 000 m/s]. *(10 minutes)*

Main

- Throughout these next few topics, it will be useful to have a large diagram of the electromagnetic spectrum on the wall so that you can refer to it regularly. You could put up a giant poster and have the students add notes to it throughout the chapter. Photograph this at the end and give copies to everybody.

- The students will have studied the electromagnetic spectrum at KS3, but many will be unfamiliar with the word 'electromagnetic'. You might like to simply explain that these waves are caused by changes in electric and magnetic fields. These are similar to the fields around a bar magnet, which they should remember. The most important thing, however, is that the students understand that no matter (material) is transferred from place to place.

- It is important to get across the idea that the electromagnetic waves travel best through empty space: a vacuum. When doing this, they all travel at the same speed (which is the maximum speed at which anything can travel). Also emphasise that the spectrum is continuous: there are ranges of each of the regions. This idea can be shown by discussing the range of different wavelengths of red, pointing out that there is not just one 'red'.

- The main difficulty in any calculations will be the rather difficult numbers that electromagnetic waves present. You may find that some calculators cannot cope with them. Standard eight-digit calculators cannot display 300 000 000; so you may have to remind students of how to cancel out some of the zeros. With students that are more mathematically able, you may wish to use numbers in standard form, e.g. 3.00×10^8 m/s.

- You can then move through the spectrum pointing out the behaviour of waves when they interact with materials or cross boundaries. The focus is on the group of waves used in communications (visible, IR, microwave and radio) but you can mention that other waves behave in a similar manner.

Plenary

RMIVUXG? – The students may know an acronym to give the order of electromagnetic waves within the spectrum (ROYGBIV). Can they think up a method of remembering the regions of the electromagnetic spectrum? They need to use this to remember the order of the spectrum and so cannot change the order of the letters. An example could be 'Really Massive Iguanas Viciously Upset Xenophobic Gorillas'. As you can see the VUX part can be a bit of a problem. *(5 minutes)*

Further teaching suggestions

The wave equation
- The students can reinforce their understanding of the wave equation by trying some further calculations. This work could be set as homework.

Electromagnetic waves

P1 6.1   The electromagnetic spectrum ⓚ

Learning objectives
- What are the parts of the electromagnetic spectrum?
- How can we calculate the frequency or wavelength of electromagnetic waves?

We all use waves from different parts of the **electromagnetic spectrum**. Figure 1 shows the spectrum and some of its uses.

Electromagnetic waves are electric and magnetic disturbances that transfer energy from one place to another.

Electromagnetic waves do not transfer matter. The energy they transfer depends on the **wavelength** of the waves. This is why waves of different wavelengths have different effects. Figure 1 shows some of the uses of each part of the electromagnetic spectrum.

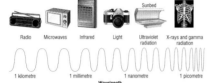

Radio   Microwaves   Infrared   Light   Ultraviolet radiation   X-rays and gamma radiation

1 kilometre   1 millimetre   1 nanometre   1 picometre

Wavelength
(1 nanometre = 0.000 001 millimetres, 1 picometre = 0.001 nanometres)

Figure 1 The spectrum is continuous. The frequencies and wavelengths at the boundaries are approximate as the different parts of the spectrum are not precisely defined.

Waves from different parts of the electromagnetic spectrum have different wavelengths.
- Long-wave radio waves have wavelengths as long as 10 km.
- X-rays and gamma rays have wavelengths as short as a millionth of a millionth of a millimetre (= 0.000 000 000 001 mm).

a Where in the electromagnetic spectrum would you find waves of wavelength 10 millimetres?

The speed of electromagnetic waves

All electromagnetic waves travel at a speed of 300 million m/s through space or in a vacuum. This is the distance the waves travel each second.

We can link the speed of the waves to their frequency and wavelength using the wave speed equation:

$$v = f \times \lambda$$

Where:
v = wave speed in metres per second, m/s
f = frequency in hertz, Hz
λ = wavelength in metres, m

b Work out the wavelength of electromagnetic waves of frequency 200 million Hz.
c Work out the frequency of electromagnetic waves of wavelength 1500 m.

AQA *Examiner's tip*

The spectrum of visible light covers just a very tiny part of the electromagnetic spectrum. The wavelength decreases from radio waves to gamma rays.

◯◯ **links**
For more information on the wave speed equation, look back at P1 5.2 Measuring waves.

Maths skills

Higher

We can work out the wavelength if we know the frequency and the wave speed. To do this, we rearrange the equation into:

$$\lambda = \frac{v}{f}$$

We can work out the frequency if we know the wavelength and the wave speed. To do this, we rearrange the equation into:

$$f = \frac{v}{\lambda}$$

Where:
v = speed in metres per second, m/s
f = frequency in hertz, Hz
λ = wavelength in metres, m.

Worked example
A mobile phone gives out electromagnetic waves of frequency 900 million Hz. Calculate the wavelength of these waves. The speed of electromagnetic waves in air = 300 million m/s.

Solution
wavelength λ (in metres) = $\dfrac{\text{wave speed } v \text{ (in m/s)}}{\text{frequency } f \text{ (in Hz)}}$ =

$$\frac{300\,000\,000\,\text{m/s}}{900\,000\,000\,\text{Hz}} = 0.33\,\text{m}$$

Energy and frequency
The wave speed equation shows us that the shorter the wavelength of the waves, the higher their frequency is. The energy of the waves increases as the frequency increases. The energy and frequency of the waves therefore increases from radio waves to gamma rays as the wavelength decreases.

Summary questions

1 Copy and complete **a** to **c** using the words below:
  greater than   smaller than   the same as
  a The wavelength of light waves is .... the wavelength of radio waves.
  b The speed of radio waves in a vacuum is .... the speed of gamma rays.
  c The frequency of X-rays is .... the frequency of infrared radiation.

2 Fill in the missing parts of the electromagnetic spectrum in the list below.
  radio ...a... infrared visible ...b... X-rays ...c...

3 Electromagnetic waves travel through space at a speed of 300 million metres per second. Calculate:
  a the wavelength of radio waves of frequency 600 million Hz
  b the frequency of microwaves of wavelength 0.30 m.

4 A distant star explodes and emits light and gamma rays simultaneously. Explain why the gamma rays and the light waves reach the Earth at the same time.

Key points
- The electromagnetic spectrum (in order of decreasing wavelength, increasing frequency and energy) is:
  - radio waves
  - microwaves
  - infrared radiation
  - light
  - ultraviolet radiation
  - gamma radiation and X-rays.
- The wave speed equation is used to calculate the frequency or wavelength of electromagnetic waves.

Answers to in-text questions

a microwaves
b 1.5 m
c 200 000 Hz

Summary answers

1 **a** smaller than
  b the same as
  c greater than

2 **a** microwaves
  b ultraviolet radiation
  c gamma rays

3 **a** 0.5 m
  b 1000 million Hz

4 They are emitted at the same time. They travel the same distance at the same speed, so they arrive at the Earth together at a later time.

P1 6.2

Light, infrared, microwaves and radio waves

AQA

Specification link-up: Physics P1.5

- Radio waves, microwaves, infrared and visible light can be used for communication. *[P1.5.1 k)]*
- Compare the use of different types of waves for communication. *[P1.5]*

Learning objectives

Students should learn that:

- the ways in which infrared, microwaves and radio waves are used in communication systems.

Learning outcomes

Most students should be able to:

- state the uses of infrared, microwaves and radio waves in communication.

Some students should also be able to:

- explain how infrared, microwaves and radio waves are used in communication.

Lesson structure

Starters

Radio 'gaga' – Give the students a set of mixed-up sentences about radio waves and ask them to sort the words into the right order to produce correct sentences. Examples could include: atmosphere are used through waves television radio the transmit to signals [Radio waves are used to transmit television signals through the atmosphere; microwaves can be used for communicating with satellites]. *(5 minutes)*

Colour filters – Shine a bright white light through a series of filters and ask the students to explain what is happening with a diagram. Extend students by asking them to consider the use of multiple filters. Support students by reminding them that white light is composed of bands of colours and give and example of the effect of a filter before asking them to try some of their own. Ask the students if they think that there will be a similar effect for the non-visible parts of the spectrum. This leads into the absorption of electromagnetic energy as it passes through materials, so you can show the effect again to enhance that point later. *(10 minutes)*

Main

- Using a data projector at the beginning of this lesson is very handy. You can use it as a bright light source to show dispersion through a prism producing a very bright spectrum. If the projector is ceiling mounted, then mount the prism on a stick. A bit of fiddling should produce a clear spectrum somewhere in the room.

- You can show a film camera and a digital camera. If you have any old ones that can be taken apart, you can show the places where the film of CCD would sit and let the students look through the lens system.

- The students should already be familiar with the heating effect of IR from 'P1 1.1 Energy transfer by heating', but it is worth showing an IR heater again as reinforcement. Demonstrating an infrared remote control should be fairly simple but the students may not be aware that the infrared can be reflected, so try turning some equipment, like the data projector, on or off by reflecting the signal off the whiteboard.

- If you have a microwave oven available, you can use it to demonstrate the heating effect by cooking something. The cooking can be very uneven and you might want to discuss why this is with some students. You could also discuss shielding. The front door should contain a metal mesh used to absorb microwaves so that none leak out. These would be dangerous to people, as they would cause heating of the water in tissues. Simple microwave detectors are available.

- It is worth demonstrating a radio, especially one with a dial to adjust the frequency received. It is even better if you have a very old radio with the wavelength and frequency on the dial; so that you can discuss the connection between the two.

Support

- Provide a plan for the testing of infrared radiation. After completing this task, the students can make their own plan to test the range of the signal from a remote or even if the infrared rays follow the same laws of reflection as visible light.

Extend

- If you carry out the microwave experiment (and the transmitter is a polarised one, as it usually is) you may like to challenge the students to find an explanation for polarisation. Point the transmitter and receiver directly at each other and switch on to show the maximum signal. Position a metal diffraction grille (a set of vertical wires) between the transmitter and receiver and rotate it. The signal should vary from maximum to zero just by rotating the plate.

Plenaries

EM wave summary – The students should produce a summary about all of the areas of the electromagnetic spectrum they have studied so far. This can be in the form a table, brief summary phrases or a mind map. *(5 minutes)*

What's the frequency? – Give the students the frequency of some local radio stations and ask them to work out the wavelengths (and vice versa). This recaps the calculations from earlier. Some stations are listed here for the Orkney Islands, you can add more: Radio 1 98.9 MHz [3.03 m], Radio 2 89.3 MHz [3.36 m], Radio 3 91.5 MHz [3.28 m]. Students should be extended by tackling rearrangement of the necessary equation or supported by the use of calculation templates. *(10 minutes)*

Practical support

Testing infrared radiation

Infrared signals are able to pass through several paper sheets as long as the batteries on the remote are in good order.

Equipment and materials required

Infrared remote control and device. A TV is fine, as is a data projector.

Details

Simply place layers of paper over the transmitter one at a time to find out how many layers are needed to block the signal. You should find that larger transmitters, such as those for TVs, can send a signal through at least three sheets. Low-power transmitters, such as those operated by a button cell, struggle to get a signal through two sheets.

Demonstrating microwaves

If you have low-power microwave equipment, you may like to look at the laws of reflection for microwave radiation.

Equipment and materials required

Low-power microwave transmitter and receiver, aluminium screen, large protractor, A3 paper and ruler.

Details

Position the aluminium screen towards the back of the paper and mark its position. Draw a normal to the screen to measure angles from. Now position the transmitter so that it is off the normal and pointing to the centre of the screen. Move the receiver in an arc, always pointing to the centre of the screen, until a maximum reflected signal is found. Compare the angle of incidence and reflection for a few points to show that the law of reflection is obeyed. During the experiment, discuss why aluminium is used as opposed to paper.

You may also like to investigate the penetrating power of the microwaves by seeing if they pass through various thicknesses of paper or card. Does making the paper wet make a difference? Why? (You can choose from a range of 'How Science Works' to develop in this investigation, e.g. collecting primary data.)

The polished metal surface reflects the microwaves. The direction of the reflected waves is at the same angle to the metal plate as the direction of incident waves.

Electromagnetic waves
Light, infrared, microwaves and radio waves

P1 6.2
Light, infrared, microwaves and radio waves

Learning objectives

- What is white light?
- What do we use infrared radiation, microwaves and radio waves for?
- What are the hazards of these types of electromagnetic radiation?

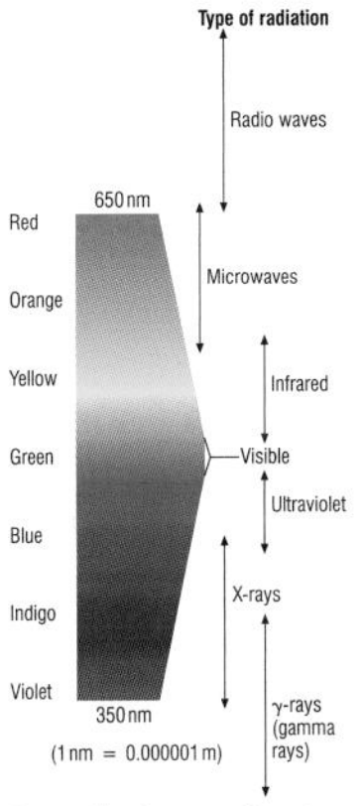

Figure 1 The electromagnetic spectrum with an expanded view of the visible range

Type of radiation

Radio waves

Microwaves

Red 650 nm
Orange
Yellow — Infrared
Green — Visible
Blue — Ultraviolet
Indigo — X-rays
Violet 350 nm — γ-rays (gamma rays)
(1 nm = 0.000001 m)

○○ links
For more information on infrared radiation, look back at P1 1.1 Infrared radiation.

Light and colour

Light from ordinary lamps and from the Sun is called white light. This is because it has all the colours of the visible spectrum in it. The wavelength increases across the spectrum as you go from violet to red.

You see the colours of the spectrum when you look at a rainbow. You can also see them if you use a glass prism to split a beam of white light.

Photographers need to know how shades and colours of light affect the photographs they take.

1 **In a film camera**, the light is focused by the camera lens on to a light-sensitive film. The film then needs to be developed to see the image of the objects that were photographed.
2 **In a digital camera**, the light is focused by the lens on to a sensor. This consists of thousands of tiny light-sensitive cells called **pixels**. Each pixel gives a dot of the image. The image can be seen on a small screen at the back of the camera. When a photograph is taken, the image is stored electronically on a memory card.

a Why is a 10 million pixel camera better than a 2 million pixel camera?

Infrared radiation

All objects emit infrared radiation.

- The hotter an object is, the more infrared radiation it emits.
- Infrared radiation is absorbed by the skin. It damages or kills skin cells because it heats up the cells.

b Where does infrared radiation lie in the electromagnetic spectrum?

Infrared devices

- **Optical fibres** in communications systems use infrared radiation instead of light. This is because infrared radiation is absorbed less than light in the glass fibres.
- **Remote control handsets** for TV and video equipment transmit signals carried by infrared radiation. When you press a button on the handset, it sends out a sequence of infrared pulses.
- **Infrared scanners** are used in medicine to detect 'hot spots' on the body surface. These hot areas can mean the underlying tissue is unhealthy.
- You can use **infrared cameras** to see people and animals in darkness.

c Does infrared radiation pass through a thin sheet of paper?

Microwaves

Microwaves lie between radio waves and infrared radiation in the electromagnetic spectrum. They are called '**micro**waves' because they are shorter in wavelength than radio waves.

We use microwaves for communications, e.g. **satellite TV**, because they can pass through the atmosphere and reach satellites above the Earth. We also use them to beam signals from one place to another. That's because microwaves don't spread out as much as radio waves. Microwaves (as well as radio waves) are used to carry **mobile phone** signals.

Radio waves

Radio wave frequencies range from about 300 000 Hz to 3000 million Hz (where microwave frequencies start). Radio waves are longer in wavelength and lower in frequency than microwaves.

As explained in P1 6.3, we use radio waves to carry **radio, TV and mobile phone** signals.

We can also use radio waves instead of cables to connect a computer to other devices such as a printer or a 'mouse'. For example, Bluetooth-enabled devices can communicate with each other over a range of about 10 metres. No cables are needed – just a Bluetooth radio in each device and the necessary software. Such wireless connections work at frequencies of about 2400 million hertz, and they operate at low power.

Bluetooth was set up by the electronics manufacturers. They realised the need to agree on the radio frequencies to be used for common software.

d If wireless-enabled devices operated at higher power, how would their range be affected?

Summary questions

1 Copy and complete **a** and **b** using the words below:
infrared radiation   visible light   microwaves   radio waves
a In a TV set, the aerial detects .... and the screen emits ....
b A satellite TV receiver detects ...., which pass through the atmosphere, unlike ...., which have a shorter wavelength.

2 Mobile phones use electromagnetic waves in a wavelength range that includes short-wave radio waves and microwaves.
a What would be the effect on mobile phone users if remote control handsets operated in this range as well?
b Why do our emergency services use radio waves in a wavelength range that no else is allowed to use?

3 The four devices listed below each emit a different type of electromagnetic radiation. State the type of radiation each one emits.
a A TV transmitter mast.
b A TV satellite.
c A TV remote handset.
d A TV receiver.

Practical

Testing infrared radiation
Can infrared radiation pass through paper? Use a remote handset to find out.

Demonstration

Demonstrating microwaves
Look at the demonstration.
- What does this show?

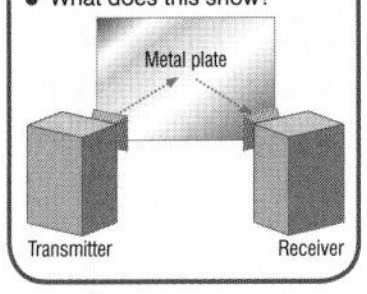

Metal plate

Transmitter   Receiver

Key points

- White light contains all the colours of the visible spectrum.
- Infrared radiation is used for carrying signals from remote handsets and inside optical fibres.
  We use microwaves to carry satellite TV programmes and mobile phone calls.
  Radio waves are used for radio and TV broadcasting, radio communications and mobile phone calls.
- Different types of electromagnetic radiation are hazardous in different ways. Microwaves and radio waves can cause internal heating. Infrared radiation can cause skin burns.

Answers to in-text questions

a The image has more fine detail.

b Between microwaves and light.

c Yes.

d The range would be increased.

Summary answers

1 **a** radio waves, visible light
  b microwaves, infrared radiation

2 **a** A remote handset used when pointed at a mobile phone user would disrupt the mobile phone's reception if it operated at the same wavelength.
  b So that there will be no interference with their communications systems.

3 **a** radio waves
  b microwaves
  c infrared radiation
  d visible light

P1 6.3

Communications

AQA Specification link-up: Physics P1.5

- Radio waves, microwaves, infrared and visible light can be used for communication. [P1.5.1 k)]
- Evaluate the possible risks involving the use of mobile phones. [P1.5]

Learning objectives

Students should learn:

- that microwaves and short-wave radio waves are used in mobile phone networks
- how the atmosphere affects the range that different waves can travel
- that there are risks and benefits associated with the use of mobile phones
- how optical fibres can be used to carry waves.

Learning outcomes

Most students should be able to:

- state that satellite TV signals are carried by microwaves
- evaluate the risks of using mobile phones
- draw a diagram to show how light or infrared waves travel along an optical fibre.

Some students should also be able to:

- explain why microwaves can be used for satellite communications but not terrestrial TV signals
- explain how optical fibres can be used to carry waves, allowing them to be contained and travel around bends due to total internal reflection.

Support

- The experiment to discover total internal reflection is a very good one for students to carry out. You can provide a sheet for it that has the incident rays, normal and the location for the glass block already printed on it. This makes the experiment considerably more reliable.

Extend

- What is the fastest way of sending a signal to the opposite side of the Earth? Sending a signal via a satellite or sending the signal through optical fibres? The students can find out about this and the way optical fibre networks are at the core of the internet.

Lesson structure

Starters

Mb fns – How does mobile phone texting work? Ask the students to explain how a text message gets from one phone to another phone in the same room. Can they write their answers in txt? You should extend students by insisting that they draw a flow chart of the process and include key words that you provide. Support some students by providing the stages and asking them to place them into a flow chart. *(5 minutes)*

Get the message across – The students must think up as many ways as possible to communicate with each other and pass on a simple message, like 'I am hungry' or 'I am thirsty'. [Speech, mime, semaphore, passing a note, Morse code, texting, using a social networking site and so on]. Which methods are best in which situations? *(10 minutes)*

Main

- You can get a complete breakdown of the radio frequency spectrum from Ofcom (www.ofcom.org.uk/radiocomms/isu/ukfat). This is a comprehensive document so you might just want to select a bit of it but it shows the importance of allocating particular parts of the spectrum for particular uses. You could discuss with the students what would happen if there was a 'free for all'.

- The debate about the safely of mobile phones seems to have receded. No reliable evidence of damage has been found. However, there are still occasional campaigns about wireless computer networks in schools and the placement of transmitter masts. The intensity of the radiation from the mast could be much higher than that from a phone if the students were nearby and, as some masts are placed on schools, parents groups are worried about this. Is there a mast in your school?

- Many students will not be aware that the atmosphere has many layers; you may wish to take a bit of time and show them a diagram of its structure from the Earth's surface to space. Emphasise how thin it is; only 100 km or so. Using a globe to explain how the waves can reach places below the horizon is very helpful.

- If you are talking about satellite TV, you may wish to briefly mention the geostationary position of the satellites and the distances involved. With a typical globe (diameter 30 cm) the satellite would be nearly 1 m above the surface. This is part of the reason that satellite transmissions for communications show a 'time lag'. The microwaves are partly absorbed by the atmosphere but most of the distance is empty space.

- Demonstrate or allow the students to discover total internal reflection and then the optical fibre, see 'Practical support'. If you have a model optical fibre (a large curvy block designed to show multiple total internal reflections), you can show how the ray is contained within the glass; no energy leaves the glass. Optical fibres are used in endoscopes in medicine and also by spies and the military for seeing through walls or around corners. You may be able to find video clips of their use.

Plenaries

Round the bend – Give the students a diagram of an optical fibre with a reasonably contorted path and ask them to draw the path of a ray that is shown entering the fibre. It is possible to extend students by providing them with a more convoluted fibre and insist on proper construction of the reflection (normal included and accurate angles.) You can also support students by providing a diagram where some of the reflection points are already marked with normals, making the diagram easier to complete accurately. *(5 minutes)*

Sorry for the inconvenience – The students should design a leaflet from a TV or satellite TV company explaining why the television signal has been poor recently. It should explain how the TV signal is transmitted to the house and what kinds of things can affect the signal (rain, snow, sunspots). *(10 minutes)*

Practical support

Demonstrating an optical fibre
Optical fibres are easy to demonstrate in a laboratory, even in fairly bright conditions.

Equipment and materials required
A length of optical fibre (anywhere between 2–10 m) a bright light source (preferably one that can be switched on and off quickly).

Details
Bend the fibre around several objects (perhaps the whole room). Don't bend it too much though, or the glass might crack; anything smaller than a 10 cm radius is dodgy. Allow one student to observe the distant end while you flash a torch into the near end. Even with the thinnest of fibres, the transmitted light should be obvious. The students can pass the fibre end along while the light is flashing.

Total internal reflection
The students may well be aware of this effect, but if they are not then it is simple to discover.

Equipment and materials required
For each group: ray box, power supply, single slit, blanking plates, rectangular glass or Perspex block (or semicircular), protractor, ruler, pencil and A3 paper.

Details
The students position the block on the paper and draw around it to mark its position, in case it moves. They shine a ray of light at the front surface of the block at a small angle to the normal and mark the direction the ray enters and leaves the block. This is best done by marking the path of the ray with two small crosses, and then joining them with a straight line with the ruler. They then increase the angle and repeat the process. They should find that at a certain point, the ray is reflected by the surface of the block; it is totally internally reflected.

Electromagnetic waves

P1 6.3 Communications 🔘

Learning objectives
- Why do we use radio waves of different frequencies for different purposes?
- Which waves do we use for satellite TV?
- How can we evaluate whether or not mobile phones are safe to use?
- What are optical fibres?

Figure 1 Sending microwave signals to a satellite

Did you know ...?
Satellite TV signals are carried by microwaves. We can detect the signals on the ground because they pass straight through a layer of ionised gas in the upper atmosphere. This layer reflects lower-frequency radio waves.

Figure 2 A mobile phone mast

Radio communications
Radio waves are emitted from an aerial when we apply an alternating voltage to the aerial. The frequency of the radio waves produced is the same as the frequency of the alternating voltage.

When the radio waves pass across a receiver aerial, they cause a tiny alternating voltage in the aerial. The frequency of the alternating voltage is the same as the frequency of the radio waves received. The aerial is connected to a loudspeaker. The alternating voltage from the aerial is used to make the loudspeaker send out sound waves.

The radio and microwave spectrum is divided into bands of different wavelength ranges. This is because the shorter the wavelength of the waves:
- the more information they can carry
- the shorter their range (due to increasing absorption by the atmosphere)
- the less they spread out (because they diffract less).

Radio wavelengths
Microwaves and radio waves of different wavelengths are used for different communications purposes. Examples are given below.
- **Microwaves** are used for satellite phone and TV links and satellite TV broadcasting. This is because microwaves can travel between satellites in space and the ground. Also, they spread out less than radio waves do so the signal doesn't weaken as much.
- **Radio waves of wavelengths less than about 1 metre** are used for TV broadcasting from TV masts because they can carry more information than longer radio waves.
- **Radio waves of wavelengths from about 1 metre up to about 100 m** are used by local radio stations (and for the emergency services) because their range is limited to the area round the transmitter.
- **Radio waves of wavelengths greater than 100 m** are used by national and international radio stations because they have a much longer range than shorter wavelength radio waves.

  a Why do microwaves spread out less than radio waves do?

Mobile phone radiation 🔘
A mobile phone sends a radio signal from your phone. The signal is picked up by a local mobile phone mast and is sent through the phone network to the other phone. The 'return' signal goes through the phone network back to the mobile phone mast near you and then on to you. The signals to and from your local mast are carried by radio waves of different frequencies.

The radio waves to and from a mobile phone have a wavelength of about 30 cm. Radio waves at this wavelength are not quite in the microwave range but they do have a similar heating effect to microwaves. So they are usually referred to as microwaves.

  b Why should signals to and from a mobile phone be at different frequencies?

How Science Works
Is mobile phone radiation dangerous?
The radiation is much weaker than the microwave radiation in an oven. But when you use a mobile phone, it is very close to your brain. Some scientists think the radiation might affect the brain. As children have thinner skulls than adults, their brains might be more affected by mobile phone radiation. A UK government report published in May 2000 recommended that the use of mobile phones by children should be limited.

Mobile phone hazards
Here are some findings by different groups of scientists:
The short-term memory of volunteers using a mobile phone was found to be unaffected by whether the phone was on or off.
The brains of rats exposed to microwaves were found to respond less to electrical impulses than the brains of unexposed rats.
Mice exposed to microwaves by some scientists developed more cancers than unexposed mice. Other scientists were unable to confirm this effect.
A survey of mobile phone users in Norway and Sweden found they experienced headaches and fatigue. No control group of people who did not use a mobile phone was surveyed.
- What conclusions do you draw from the evidence above?
- Suggest how researchers could improve the validity of any conclusions we can draw.

Optical fibre communications
Optical fibres are very thin glass fibres. We use them to transmit signals carried by light or infrared radiation. The light rays can't escape from the fibre. When they reach the surface of the fibre, they are reflected back into the fibre.
In comparison with radio waves and microwaves:
- optical fibres can carry much more information – this is because light has a much smaller wavelength than radio waves so can carry more pulses of waves
- optical fibres are more secure because the signals stay in the fibre.

  c Why are signals in an optical fibre more secure than radio signals?

Demonstration
Demonstrating an optical fibre
Observe light shone into an optical fibre. You should see the reflection of light inside an optical fibre. This is known as total internal reflection.

Figure 3 Optical fibres

Key points
- Radio waves of different frequencies are used for different purposes because the wavelength (and therefore frequency) of waves affects:
  – how far they can go
  – how much they spread
  – how much information they can carry.
- Microwaves are used for satellite TV signals.
- Further research is needed to evaluate whether or not mobile phones are safe to use.
- Optical fibres are very thin transparent fibres that are used to transmit signals by light and infrared radiation.

Summary questions
1 Copy and complete **a** to **c** using the words below. Each term can be used more than once.
   infrared radiation   microwaves   radio waves
   a Mobile phone signals are carried by ....
   b Optical fibre signals are carried by ....
   c A beam of .... can travel from the ground to a satellite but a beam of .... cannot if its frequency is below 30 MHz.
2 a Why could children be more affected by mobile phone radiation than adults?
   b Why can light waves carry more information than radio waves?
3 Explain why microwaves are used for satellite TV and radio waves for terrestrial TV.

Further teaching suggestions

A guest speaker
- One of your network technicians, or IT teachers, could present a brief talk about the school network, discussing all of the components (bridges, routers, modems, etc.) and what they do. They can put particular emphasis on the wireless part of the network.

Answers to in-text questions
a They spread out less because their wavelength is less.
b If the mast-to-phone signal reflected back to the mast, it would disrupt the signal from the phone.
c Radio waves spread out and can be detected by any radio receiver. Signals in an optical fibre stay in the fibre until they reach the receiver at the end of the fibre.

Summary answers
1 a radio waves
  b infrared radiation
  c microwaves, radio waves
2 a Children have thinner skulls than adults and mobile phone radiation could pass through their skulls more easily than through adult skulls.
  b The light has a much shorter wavelength so can carry more pulses than radio waves.
3 The distance satellite TV signals travel is much greater than the distance terrestrial signals travel. The signals spread out and weaken more the further they travel. Microwaves spread out less than radio waves, so they don't weaken as much as radio waves do.

P1 6.4

The expanding universe

Learning objectives

Students should learn:

- that the universe is a vast collection of billions of galaxies each containing billions of stars
- that the velocity of distant galaxies can be measured by analysis of the red-shift of light from those galaxies
- that the evidence gained from red-shift analysis shows that the universe is expanding.

Learning outcomes

Most students should be able to:

- state that the universe contains a vast number of galaxies and stars
- describe why the light from distant galaxies is shifted in wavelength
- explain that red-shift evidence shows that the universe is expanding.

AQA Specification link-up: Physics P1.5

- If a wave source is moving relative to an observer, there will be a change in the observed wavelength and frequency. This is known as the Doppler effect. [P1.5.4 a)]
- There is an observed increase in the wavelength of light from most distant galaxies. The further away the galaxies are, the faster they are moving, and the bigger the observed increase in wavelength. This effect is called 'red-shift'. [P1.5.4 b)]

Lesson structure

Starters

How many stars? – Give the class estimates on the number of stars in a galaxy and the number of galaxies. Ask them to work out how many stars they could have each if they shared them out among the class. This should give a quick impression of just how large the universe is. There are estimated to be 100 billion stars in a galaxy like ours and 125 billion galaxies, so that should give around 417 billion stars each for a class of 30 students. *(5 minutes)*

Stars and planets – Make the students define the properties of stars and planets. To support them, you can give them sets of cards describing the properties and behaviours of stars and planets, and ask them to sort them into two piles, one corresponding to stars and one to planets. You can extend students by asking them to work out the properties themselves and then make cards to sort (you can use these with other groups later). *(10 minutes)*

Main

- You might like to ask the students why there are no photographs of the complete Milky Way galaxy; they should realise that we could never get a probe to sufficient distance. If you want to show a model galaxy, try using a blank CD with a small bulge of plasticine in the centre. You can draw the spiral arms on the label. It's about the right proportions (according to NASA). We are on the western spiral arm about 1 cm from the rim. You can then show the separation of galaxies. Our neighbour Andromeda would be about 1 m away on this scale; other galaxies would most likely be outside your room.

- A Doppler effect for sound can be demonstrated with a tube (or hose) with a funnel in the end. Blow through the tube while spinning it and the students should hear changes in the pitch (or wavelength) of the note as the funnel end approaches or recedes from them. The students may be familiar with the effect when hearing sirens on cars passing by. It is useful to show the students several simple examples of absorption spectra to show what these lines would look like. They can then show the effect of shifting the lines to the red part of the spectrum.

- Hubble's two conclusions are very important and lead to the conclusion that the universe is expanding. The students really need to be able to state these conclusions and link them to the supporting evidence; they are a common concept on examination papers.

- The idea of an expanding universe that has no centre is a bit strange. The closest simple analogy is the surface of an expanding balloon. It is worth showing this. Blow up a balloon with galaxies drawn on its surface and they all move further apart from one another and none of them are in the middle. The universe is a bit like this.

Support

- The numbers involved in this topic are well out of the range that most students can grasp. Present as much of this visually as you can; students don't need to know the numbers just the order of sizes.

Extend

- Students can be extended by asking them to look at emission spectra. If you have a set of gas emission spectrum tubes, you can demonstrate the emission spectra of different hot gases. With a suitable diffraction grating and spectroscope, you can clearly see the distinct lines produced by different elements. If you don't have a spectroscope, you can still show the different colours from different elements.

Plenaries

True or false – Give the students a set of 'facts' about galaxies and the universe, and ask them to say if they are true or false. You might have some 'unknown' ones too. *(5 minutes)*

Space is big – Give the students a list of distances and ask them to put them in order (e.g. your school to France, your school to New York, the Earth to the Moon, the Earth to the Sun, the Earth to Pluto, the Sun to the nearby star Alpha Centauri, the Sun to the centre of the Milky Way (or galaxy), the Milky Way to Andromeda, the Milky Way to the edge of the observable universe). Students can be asked to match up distance cards given in kilometres. Extend students by asking them to convert the numbers into standard form and discuss why this is generally used for large numbers. Students can be supported by making this task a card sort activity; matching up the distances with the descriptions. *(10 minutes)*

Practical support

Doppler and sound

Demonstrate Doppler shift in sound. This can look a bit silly, but it works.

Equipment and materials required

A 1.5 m length of hosepipe (narrower tubes do not work as well) with a large funnel securely attached to one end.

Details

Simply swing the funnel end of the hosepipe around your head (in a lasso style) while blowing into the other end. The pitch (and frequency and wavelength of the sound) changes as it swings towards and away from the students. When it is moving away, the wavelength is increased so the sound is lower pitched and vice versa.

P1 6.4   The expanding universe

Learning objectives

- What do we mean by red-shift of a light source?
- How does red-shift depend on speed?
- How do we know the distant galaxies are moving away from us?
- Why do we think the universe is expanding?

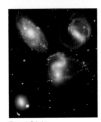

Figure 1 Galaxies

The Doppler effect

The Doppler effect is the change in the observed wavelength (and frequency) of waves due to the motion of the source of the waves. Christian Doppler discovered the effect in 1842 using sound waves. He demonstrated it by using an open railway carriage filled with trumpeters. The spectators had to listen to the pitch of the trumpets as they sped past. Another example, explained below, is the red-shift of the light from a distant galaxy moving away from us.

Red-shift

We live on the third rock out from a middle-aged star on the outskirts of a big galaxy we call the Milky Way. The galaxy contains about 100000 million stars. Its size is about 100000 light years across. This means that light takes 100000 years to travel across it. But it's just one of billions of galaxies in the universe. The furthest galaxies are about 13000 million light years away!

   a Why do stars appear as points of light?

We can find out lots of things about stars and galaxies by studying the light from them. We can use a prism to split the light into a spectrum. The wavelength of light increases across the spectrum from blue to red. We can tell from its spectrum if a star or galaxy is moving towards us or away from us. This is because:

- the light waves are stretched out if the star or galaxy is moving away from us. The wavelength of the waves is increased. We call this a red-shift because the spectrum of light is shifted towards the red part of the spectrum.
- the light waves are squashed together if the star or galaxy is moving towards us. The wavelength of the waves is reduced. We call this a blue-shift because the spectrum of light is shifted towards the blue part of the spectrum.

The dark spectral lines shown in Figure 2 are caused by absorption of light by certain atoms such as hydrogen that make up a star or galaxy. The position of these lines tells us if there is a shift and if so, whether it is a red-shift or a blue-shift.

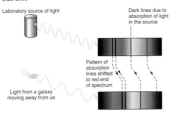

Laboratory source of light

Dark lines due to absorption of light in the source

Pattern of absorption lines shifted to red end of spectrum

Light from a galaxy moving away from us

Figure 2 Red-shift

The bigger the shift, the more the waves are squashed together or stretched out. So the faster the star or galaxy must be moving towards or away from us. In other words:

the faster a star or galaxy is moving (relative to us), the bigger the shift is.

   b What do you think happens to the wavelength of the light from a star that is moving towards us?

Expanding universe

In 1929, Edwin Hubble discovered that:
1 the light from distant galaxies was red-shifted
2 the further a galaxy is from us, the bigger its red-shift is.

He concluded that:
- the distant galaxies are moving away from us (i.e. receding)
- the greater the distance a galaxy is from us, the greater the speed is at which it is moving away from us (its speed of recession).

Why should the distant galaxies be moving away from us? We have no special place in the universe, so all the distant galaxies must be moving away from each other. In other words, **the whole universe is expanding**.

   c Galaxy X is 2000 million light years away. Galaxy Y is 4000 million light years away. Which galaxy, X or Y, has the bigger red-shift?

Summary questions

1 Copy and complete **a** to **d** using the words below:
   approaching expanding orbiting receding
   a The Earth is .... the Sun.
   b The universe is ....
   c The distant galaxies are ....
   d A blue-shift in the light from a star would tell us it is ....

2 **a** Put these objects in order of increasing size:
     Andromeda galaxy Earth Sun universe
   b Copy and complete **i** and **ii** using the words below:
     galaxy star red-shift planet
     i The Earth is a .... in orbit round a .... called the Sun.
     ii There is a .... in the light from a distant ....

3 Galaxy X has a larger red-shift than galaxy Y.
   a Which galaxy, X or Y, is
     i nearer to us
     ii moving away faster?
   b The light from the Andromeda galaxy is not red-shifted. What does this tell you about Andromeda?

Did you know ...?

You can hear the Doppler effect when an ambulance with its siren on goes speeding past.

- As it approaches, the sound waves it sends out are squashed up so their frequency is higher (and the wavelength shorter) than if the siren was stationary. So you hear a higher pitch.
- As it travels away from you, the sound waves it sends out are stretched out so their frequency is lower (and the wavelength longer) than if the siren was stationary. So you hear a lower pitch.

Key points

- The red-shift of a distant galaxy is the shift to longer wavelengths of the light from it because the galaxy is moving away from us.
- The faster a distant galaxy is moving away from us, the greater its red-shift is.
- All the distant galaxies show a red-shift. The further away a distant galaxy is from us, the greater its red-shift is.
- The distant galaxies are all moving away from us because the universe is expanding.

Further teaching suggestions

ICT link-up

- Why do scientists need more and more powerful computers? Simulations of galaxies smashing together may look nice, but it takes a lot of computing power to work out when a billion stars meet another billion stars. Many of the simulations online have been carried out by 'supercomputers' thousands of times more powerful than a simple PC.

Matching spectra

- Can the students discover what elements are present in real stellar spectra? Give the students a card showing the absorption spectrum of the Sun and a set of spectra for different elements, some of which are present in the Sun. Ask the students to work out which ones match. Make sure the cards are printed to the same scale though.

Andromeda ascendant

- The Andromeda galaxy is one of our nearest galactic neighbours and it is getting nearer all the time. It's moving towards us at about half a million kilometres per hour and may eventually collide in three to four billion years' time. The students could look into the possible outcomes of this collision, and collisions on this scale generally. There are numerous excellent computer simulations, and Hubble Space Telescope images of real collisions, available on the internet.

Answers to in-text questions

a Because they are so far away.

b It is blue-shifted because its wavelength is reduced.

c Galaxy Y.

Summary answers

1 **a** orbiting
   b expanding
   c receding
   d approaching

2 **a** Earth, Sun, Andromeda galaxy, universe.
   b **i** planet, star
     ii red-shift, galaxy

3 **a** **i** Y
     ii X
   b It is not moving away from us. It is much nearer to us than the galaxies with red-shifts.

P1 6.5

The Big Bang

Specification link-up: Physics P1.5

- How the observed red-shift provides evidence that the universe is expanding and supports the 'Big Bang' theory (that the universe began from a very small initial 'point'). *[P1.5.4 c)]*
- Cosmic microwave background radiation (CMBR) is a form of electromagnetic radiation filling the universe. It comes from radiation that was present shortly after the beginning of the universe. *[P1.5.4 d)]*
- The 'Big Bang' theory is currently the only theory that can explain the existence of CMBR. *[P1.5.4 e)]*
- Consider the limitations of the model that scientists use to explain how the universe began and why the universe continues to expand. *[P1.5]*

Learning objectives

Students should learn:

- that the universe is thought to have begun in an awesome event called the Big Bang
- that the expansion of the universe supports the Big Bang theory
- that the cosmic microwave background radiation is a primary piece of evidence supporting this theory.

Learning outcomes

Most students should be able to:

- state that the Big Bang generated the universe
- describe the evidence for the expansion of the universe and how it supports the Big Bang theory
- state the evidence for this conclusion.

Some students should also be able to:

- describe limitations in the Big Bang theory.

Support

- As in the last lesson, the concepts can be difficult to grasp without careful explanations. The key idea to put across is that the universe was very different early on and there is strong evidence that there was a beginning. Don't worry if the students think that this was just a big explosion but make sure that they do not think that the Earth was formed in this explosion.

Extend

- Students can be extended by asking: Just how small is 'small'? These students may wish to look into the concept of singularities: objects of zero volume and infinite density; it is from one of these that the universe is thought to have originated. The ideas are closely linked to black holes, which the students will study if they take GCSE Physics; you may wish to leave this until then and link the two ideas together.

Lesson structure

Starters

Heat death – Remind students that all energy transfers lead to energy being transferred by heating. Ask them to describe what will happen when all of the energy the universe started with is 'wasted'. This is quite a high-level concept and can lead to quite a detailed discussion about the eventual fate of the universe. You might want to back this idea up with a short video clip outlining the possibilities. *(5 minutes)*

Your history – Give the students a list of historical events reaching back through human history, and then to the formation of the Earth. Ask them to put the events in order. You can support students by giving some example dates to match up with the events. You can then add other events such as the formation of the solar system, start of life on Earth and the start of the universe to this. Extend the students by giving the correct times of the events and get the students to lay out the card separated by a correctly scaled distance (they may try 1 cm representing 1000 years). This will be impossible but they will understand the idea that the universe is very old compared to civilisation. *(10 minutes)*

Main

- This lesson is all about big ideas and how scientists have to provide evidence for them. (It is ideal for teaching aspects of 'How Science Works' issues.)
- Many students may ask what was before the Big Bang. The best approach is to talk about the meaning of 'before'. As scientists believe that time only started with the Big Bang there was no time before it, so it is meaningless to ask questions about what happened.
- Students may also be a bit confused by the term 'explosion'. The Big Bang is better described as a sudden expansion and the production of a lot of energy. As the universe continues to expand, this energy gets more and more dissipated and so the universe cools down.
- The main thrust of the lesson is to explain to the students that an idea like the Big Bang needs to have *evidence* before it is accepted by scientists. It is not enough to come up with the best sounding explanations. This links to the 'Fundamental ideas' section of 'How Science Works'. Those that did not accept the theory were right to question it, until they were given evidence of the *cosmic microwave background radiation*. They should then accept the new model, or come up with an alternative explanation that takes the new evidence into account.
- Changes to ideas like this are important to science; the students need to know that scientists will analyse new ideas and accept them if they explain the evidence better than the old ideas. This process ensures that scientific knowledge develops and becomes a better description of the universe. You should also point out that recent discoveries, such as the possible speeding up of the expansion, will also have to be explained by scientists over the coming years; we do not have a complete description of the universe and may never have.
- Conditions in the very early universe were **very** different than they are now. The temperatures were so high that atoms could not exist, and even protons and neutrons could not form.
- The end of the universe is still open to debate but it is a long way off, and students should not worry too much about it. We have a few billion years to go before a 'Big Crunch' or a 'Big Yawn'.

Plenaries

The Lords of Time – If time travel were possible, we could go back and get conclusive evidence about the early universe, formation of the solar system and so on. The students can speculate about the advantages and dangers of using this apparently impossible technology for scientific research. Extend the students by suggesting some of the potential hazards and seeing if they can come up with some practical rules to avoid them. You may want to support some students by making up some rules of your own (no visiting your own family) and discussing why you think they would be needed by the Time Agency. *(5 minutes)*

Sceptic – Understanding the Big Bang is very difficult and the course can only cover the simplest ideas. Can the students summarise the evidence about the expanding universe and cosmic background microwave information in order to explain it to a reasonably intelligent but sceptical person? *(10 minutes)*

Electromagnetic waves

P1 6.5 — The Big Bang ⓚ

Learning objectives

- What is the Big Bang theory of the universe?
- Why is the universe expanding?
- What is cosmic microwave background radiation?
- What evidence is there that the universe was created in a Big Bang?

The universe is expanding, but what is making it expand? The Big Bang theory was put forward to explain the expansion. This states that:

- the universe is expanding after exploding suddenly in a Big Bang from a very small initial point
- space, time and matter were created in the Big Bang.

Many scientists disagreed with the Big Bang theory. They put forward an alternative theory, the Steady State theory. The scientists said that the galaxies are being pushed apart. They thought that this is caused by matter entering the universe through 'white holes' (the opposite of black holes).

Which theory is weirder – everything starting from a Big Bang or matter leaking into the universe from outside? Until 1965, most people supported the Steady State theory.

Figure 1 The Big Bang

?? Did you know ...?

You can use an analogue TV to detect background microwave radiation very easily – just disconnect your TV aerial. The radiation causes lots of fuzzy spots on the screen.

Figure 2 A microwave image of the universe from, the Cosmic Background Explorer satellite

How Science Works

Evidence for the Big Bang

Scientists had two conflicting theories about the evolution of the universe: it was in a Steady State or it began at some point in the past with a Big Bang. Both theories could explain why the galaxies are moving apart, so scientists needed to find some way of selecting which theory was correct. They worked out that if the universe began in a Big Bang then there should have been high-energy electromagnetic radiation produced. This radiation would have 'stretched' as the universe expanded and become lower-energy radiation. Experiments were devised to look for this trace energy as extra evidence for the Big Bang model.

It was in 1965 that scientists first detected microwaves coming from every direction in space. The existence of this cosmic microwave background radiation can only be explained by the Big Bang theory.

The cosmic microwave background radiation is not as perfectly evenly spread as scientists thought it should be. Their model of the early universe needs to be developed further by gathering evidence and producing theories to explain this 'unevenness' in the early universe.

a How do scientists decide between two conflicting theories?

Cosmic microwave background radiation

- It was created as high-energy gamma radiation just after the Big Bang.
- It has been travelling through space since then.
- As the universe has expanded, it stretched out to longer and longer wavelengths and is now microwave radiation.
- It has been mapped out using microwave detectors on the ground and on satellites.

b What will happen to cosmic microwave background radiation as the universe expands?

How Science Works

The future of the universe

Will the universe expand forever? Or will the force of gravity between the distant galaxies stop them from moving away from each other? The answer to this question depends on their total mass and how much space they take up – in other words, the density of the universe.

- If the density of the universe is less than a certain amount, it will expand forever. The stars will die out and so will everything else as the universe heads for a Big Yawn!
- If the density of the universe is more than a certain amount, it will stop expanding and go into reverse. Everything will head for a Big Crunch!

Recent observations by astronomers suggest that the distant galaxies are accelerating away from each other. These observations have been checked and confirmed by other astronomers. So astronomers have concluded that the expansion of the universe is accelerating. It could be we're in for a Big Ride followed by a Big Yawn.

The discovery that the distant galaxies are accelerating is puzzling astronomers. Scientists think some unknown source of energy, now called 'dark energy', must be causing this accelerating motion. The only known force on the distant galaxies, the force of gravity, can't be used to explain 'dark energy' as it is an attractive force and so acts against their outward motion away from each other.

c What could you say about the future of the universe if the galaxies were slowing down?
d i An object released above the ground accelerates as it falls. What makes it accelerate?
  ii Why are scientists puzzled by the observation that the distant galaxies are accelerating?

Figure 3 The future of the universe?

Summary questions

1 Copy and complete a to d using the words below:
   created   detected   expanded   stretched
   a The universe was .... in an explosion called the Big Bang.
   b The universe .... suddenly in and after the Big Bang.
   c Microwave radiation from space can be .... from all directions.
   d Radiation created just after the Big Bang has been .... by the expansion of the universe and is now microwave radiation.

2 Put the following events A–D in the correct time sequence:
   A The distant galaxies were created.
   B Cosmic microwave background radiation was first detected.
   C The Big Bang happened.
   D The expansion of the universe began.

3 a Why do astronomers think that the expansion of the universe is accelerating?
   b What would have been the effect on the expansion of the universe if its density had been greater than a certain value?

Key points

- The universe started with the Big Bang, a massive explosion from a very small point.
- The universe has been expanding ever since the Big Bang.
- Cosmic microwave background radiation (CMBR) is electromagnetic radiation created just after the Big Bang.
- CMBR can only be explained by the Big Bang theory.

Further teaching suggestions

ICT link-up

- There are several websites explaining the Big Bang and theories about possible ends to the universe. Some are a bit technical, but students may wish to find out more from them. Search at www.nasa.gov or www.bbc.co.uk.

Improving evidence

- Ever since the discovery of the cosmic microwave background radiation, scientists have been trying to find improved ways of measuring it, so that they can find out the structure of the early universe. The students can find out how satellites, including the COBE mentioned in the Student Book, have been used to map the radiations and find variations in it. There are several satellites that have been used, or are due for launch in the coming years, all with dedicated websites.

Answers to in-text questions

a They weigh up the evidence they have and design experiments to collect more evidence until a clear decision can be made.
b It will be stretched even more to longer wavelengths.
c The expansion might reverse or it might just gradually stop.
d i The force of the Earth's gravity on the object causes it to accelerate.
  ii The force of gravity on the distant galaxies from the rest of the universe could not make them accelerate.

Summary answers

1 a created   c detected
  b expanded   d stretched

2 CDAB

3 a The distant galaxies are accelerating away from each other.
  b The universe would stop expanding and go into reverse, ending in a Big Crunch.

Summary answers

1 a D, A, B, C.

  b i $v = f \times \lambda$

  ii 300 million m/s

2 A: light   B: X-rays   C: microwaves   D: radio

3 a microwave, radio waves

  b mobile phone, TV (mobile phone and TV in any order)

4 a Radio waves.

  b Light and infrared radiation.

  c i Mobile phone radiation can penetrate the skull. Too much radiation may affect the brain. The tests are to ensure they do not cause too much radiation to be absorbed by the head.

  ii Phone A is safer, because less radiation is absorbed from A than from B.

5 a an increase

  b a red-shift

  c away from us

  d It would be shifted to smaller wavelengths.

6 a i Galaxy A.

  ii Galaxy C is further away than galaxy A.

  b i It is expanding.

  ii We are not in any special place.

7 a i X, because it appears smaller than Y, as seen from the Earth.

  ii X, because it is further away than Y, so it is moving faster and has a larger red-shift than Y.

  b i Z is moving away faster than X is because Z has a larger red-shift.

  ii Z is further away than X because we know it is moving faster than X and the greater the speed of a galaxy is, the further away it must be.

Summary questions 🄺

1 a Place the four different types of electromagnetic waves listed below in order of increasing wavelength.
  A Infrared waves
  B Microwaves
  C Radio waves
  D Gamma rays

  b The radio waves from a local radio station have a wavelength of 3.3 metres in air and a frequency of 91 million Hz.
  i Write down the equation that links frequency, wavelength and wave speed.
  ii Calculate the speed of the radio waves in air.

2 In P1 6.1 you will find the typical wavelengths of electromagnetic waves. Give the type of electromagnetic wave for each of the wavelengths given.
  A 0.0005 mm
  B 1 millionth of 1 millionth of 1 mm
  C 10 cm
  D 1000 m

3 Copy and complete **a** and **b** using the words below:
  microwave   mobile phone   radio waves   TV

  a A .... beam can travel from a ground transmitter to a satellite, but a beam of .... cannot if its frequency is below 30 MHz.

  b .... signals and .... signals always come from a local transmitter.

4 Mobile phones send and receive signals using electromagnetic waves near or in the microwave part of the electromagnetic spectrum.

  a Name the part of the electromagnetic spectrum which has longer wavelengths than microwaves have.

  b Which two parts of the electromagnetic spectrum may be used to send information along optical fibres?

  c New mobile phones are tested for radiation safety and given an SAR value before being sold. The SAR is a measure of the energy per second absorbed by the head while the phone is in use. For use in the UK, SAR values must be less than 2.0 W/kg. SAR values for two different mobile phones are given below.
  Phone A   0.2 W/kg
  Phone B   1.0 W/kg
  i What is the main reason why mobile phones are tested for radiation safety?
  ii Which phone, A or B, is safer? Give a reason for your answer.

5 Light from a distant galaxy has a change of wavele due to the motion of the galaxy.

  a Is this change of wavelength an increase or a decrease?

  b What is the name for this change of wavelength

  c Which way is the galaxy moving?

  d What would happen to the light it gives out if it w moving in the opposite direction?

6 a Galaxy A is further from us than galaxy B.
  i Which galaxy, A or B, produces light with a g red-shift?
  ii Galaxy C gives a bigger red-shift than galaxy What can we say about the distance to galax compared with galaxy A?

  b All the distant galaxies are moving away from ea other.
  i What does this tell us about the universe?
  ii What does it tell us about our place in the universe?

7 The diagram shows two galaxies X and Y, which have the same diameter.

  a i Which galaxy, X or Y, is further from Earth? Give a reason for your answer.
  ii Which galaxy, X or Y, produces the larger red-shift?

  b A third galaxy Z seen from Earth appears to be the same size as X but it has a larger red-shift than X.
  i What can you say about the speed at which Z is moving away from us compared with the speed at which X is movi away?
  ii What can you deduce about the distance to compared with the distance to X? Give a rea your answer.